Birding

in Venezuela

Birding in Venezuela
Mary Lou Goodwin

Robin Restall, Illustrator
Clemencia Rodner, Editor
Pamela Pierce, Juanita Tyzska,
& Chris Sharpe, Advisors

Sociedad Conservacionista
AUDUBON de Venezuela
Lynx Edicions

5th. Edition, 2003

Lynx Edicions

Cover: Yellow-knobbed Curassow by Robin Restall

5th edition completely revised and updated 2003

© **Lynx Edicions** - Montseny, 8, 08193 Bellaterra, Barcelona (Spain)

Printed by S.A. de Litografía, Barcelona (Spain)
Depósito Legal: B-21125-2003
ISBN: 84-87334-48-2

Acknowledgments

The very first thing I wish to do in this 5th Edition is express my sincere appreciation to all the birders who have sent me trip reports after visiting Venezuela (especially Dick Ryan, who never fails to send a wonderful account). Their bird lists were very helpful, but even more appreciated were their criticisms and complaints, which generated many of the changes and corrections herein. Please keep it up.

Next, I cannot thank our Venezuelan guides enough –Maria Rosa Cuesta, Gustavo Rodriguez, Chris Sharpe and Rodney Fuentes– Much of the previous success of this book is due to the generosity of these friends, who always collaborate with me completely, never hesitating to call when they find new birding areas and happily giving me their bird lists for those new discoveries.

To Miguel Lentino, who has acted, with great patience and affection, as "Family Ornithologist" to all of us, all these years. To Robin Restall, my talented and gentlemanly illustrator, who is a long-standing friend. And, last but not least, to Clemencia Rodner, my obnoxious editor and adopted daughter. I also wish to express my thanks to my lovely Gringa friend and wonderful traveling companion, now part of the team of advisors and reviewer, Pamela Pierce [1], even if she doesn't know didley about birds and calls everything a buzzard, but she is far less severe in her criticisms than those two fundamentalists, Clemencia and Juanita. I have been most fortunate in having not one but three collaborators, birding companions and reviewers for this edition. Aside from Clemencia and Pamela, Juanita Tyzska has given invaluable help with her stern criticisms of my English. And then there is Chris Sharpe, our English ornithologist, who has tried to correct any and all scientific errors. Finally Alberto Blanco was great in helping me with the maps.

---

[1] Pamela´s Comment: MLG should really consider changing the title of The Book to 'Birding and Driving in Venezuela'. Another option is: 'Driving and Birding in Venezuela'. (Maybe we could have 2 different covers to target 2 different audiences.) There are several reasons for this:

1. It would reach a much wider audience - and sell more books!
2. It could introduce birding to drivers, and driving to birders.
3. There are NO, none, zero, zip, books on driving in Venezuela. And the book is a driver's godsend. Really. Example: When Dan and I were at El Cedral, the Brit Twitchers/Twitters were amazed that we DROVE there from Caracas. They said - and I quote: "How on earth did you ever find this place?" We said - THIS BOOK! Think about it.

I also want to express my deep appreciation to all my Venezuelan friends who over the years have given me many hours of pleasure and countless laughs. I have always maintained that if the Venezuelans could bottle their sense of humor, they would not need petroleum.

... I wish to dedicate this 5th edition of
Birding in Venezuela
to my Venezuelans,
with love.

Mary Lou Goodwin
Junko, June 2001

Table of Contents

Section I. To Begin With...A Bird's Eye View 15
 I - 1. How to Use this Book 16
 I - 2. The Birding Experience in Venezuela 20
 I - 3. A Birding Calendar 23
 I - 4. A National Parks Manual 25
         The Natural Monuments 27
 I - 5. Dos and Don'ts 29
         On Health 29
         On Personal Safety 31
         On Clothes 33
         On Arriving in Venezuela 33
         On Taxis and Buses 34
         On Car Rentals 36
         On Driving 37
         On Asking for Directions 37
         On Accidents 38
         On National Guards 38
         On Hotels and Hotel Reservations 39
         Using ATMs in Venezuela 40
         On Sleeping in Hammocks 40
         On Requesting the Help of the Venezuelan Audubon 41
         On Phone Calls 42
         On Credit Card Fraud 42
         On Easter and Carnival (and maybe Christmas) 43
         Summing It All Up 43
         Last Cautions 43

Section II. Central Venezuela: The Coastal Range 45
 II - 1. Caracas & its Outskirts 46
          General Directions 46
              Flying into the Caracas Airport 46
              On getting to Caracas from the Airport 46
              On getting out of Caracas 46
              Hotels in Caracas 47
              Birding in and around Caracas 49
              Turgua 50
              The Universidad Simón Bolívar 52
              The "Litoral" - Vargas State 52
              The Junquito-Carayaca Road 55
              Macarao National Park 57
              Bird Guides living in Caracas 59
 II - 2. State of Miranda 60
          Introduction 60
          Guatopo National Park 60
 II - 3. State of Aragua 63
          Introduction 63

Getting to Maracay and Henri Pittier N.P. 63
Henri Pittier National Park (rancho grande) 66
The Northern Side 70
The Choroní Road 72
Chuao & Cepe 74
On Staying in Maracay 74
On Eating in Maracay 75
Colonia Tovar 76
How to Get There 76
Where to Stay 77
Where to Bird 77
To Colonia Tovar via La Victoria 78
To Maracay, from Colonia Tovar, via La Victoria 79
El Limón 79
Puerto Cruz / Puerto Maya 82
Parque Nacional Maracao 83
II - 4.   **State of Carabobo** 85
Introduction 85
Casa María 85
Palmichal 86
The Canoabo Dam 89
The Marshes of San Pablo 90
The Road to the Capita River 91

Section III. Northwestern Venezuela 93

III - 1.   **State of Falcón** 94
Introduction 94
On Getting to Falcon 94
Eastern Falcón 95
Where to Stay 95
In Tucacas 97
Near Parque Nacional Morrocoy 97
In Sanare 98
Chichiriviche 98
Where to Bird 100
The Road to Rio Agualinda 100
Isla de Pájaros 101
The Cerro Chichiriviche 101
Buena Vista 102
Cuare Wildlife Refuge 102
The Dams of Játira and Tacarigua 103
San Juan de los Cayos 104
The Tucurere River Marshes 104
The Highway Sanare to Coro 105
Hato La Corianera 105
Cerro La Misión 106
Campeche Marsh 107
Riecito 107
The Tacarigua Marsh 107
Sauca Lagoon 107

Coro 108
The Paraguaná Peninsula 108
The Road to Acurigua: a short outing from Coro 111
The Sierra de San Luis 111
Sierra de San Luis National Park 112
    Cerro Galicia 113
    El Haiton 113
    La Uria 114
    The Spanish Trail 115
III - 2. State of Zulia 116
    Introduction 116
    Caño Concha and the Marshes of Juan Manuel 116
    Going to Puerto Concha from the State of Mérida 119
Section IV. The Andes 121
IV - 1. State of Lara 123
    Introduction 123
    Yacambú National Park 123
        On Getting There 123
        On Where to Stay 124
        The Park 124
    The Crafts of Tintorero and Guadalupe 126
    Xerophitic Birding in Lara 127
        Vermilion Cardinal 127
    Pavia 127
IV - 2. State of Trujillo 130
    Introduction 130
    On Getting To Trujillo 130
    Staying in Boconó 131
    Guaramacal National Park 132
    The San Lázaro Road 134
IV - 3. State of Mérida 137
    Introduction 137
    On Getting There 137
        Overnighting Barinas/Altamira 138
        Birding around Altamira 139
    The Barinas - Santo Domingo Road 139
        The río Barragán 139
        The La Soledad Road 142
        The San Isidro Tunnel Road 143
        The Bridge over the Santo Domingo River 146
        On Staying in Santo Domingo 146
        Gustavo's Trail 148
        Trail on the National Park Border 148
        Laguna de Mucubají 149
        The Condor Center at Mifafí 150
        Birding around Mifafí 152
        Birding Spots around "Eagle" Pass 153
    Inexpensive Exploring: the mucuposadas 154
    The City of Mérida 156

La Mucuy and the Humboldt Trail 156
Chiguará 158
Estanques 158
La Mesa de Bolívar & Santa Cruz de Mora 160
The San Felipe Road 160
El Morro 160
On Staying around the city of Mérida 161
La Mucuy Alta 161
La Mucuy Baja 161
Near Tabay 161
In the City of Mérida 162
In the Area of El Valle de la Culata 163
Mérida Tourism 164
The Mérida Airport 164
The Western Side 165
La Azulita 166
La Carbonera, Río Frío and places west of La Azulita 168
IV - 4. State of Táchira 170
Introduction 170
On Getting to Táchira 170
Rubio 173
Tamá National Park 174
The Road to Betania 175
Río Frío / Río Negro - La Palmacera 176
La Petrolia 177
Chorro del Indio National Park 178
On Staying in San Cristobal 179
Caminos Verdes 180
Zumbador 181
Where to Stay near Zumbador 181
The Queniquea Road 182
On Staying in La Grita 183
Road to Mérida 184
Alternative route North from Táchira 184
Birding Around Northern Táchira 185
Birds of the Area of San Juan de Colon / La Fria 185
Section V. The Llanos 187
V - 1. Introduction 188
A Young Land 189
Economy for a Frail Balance 190
The People 191
The Words 191
Dangers 192
V - 2. Wildlife of the Llanos 194
Mammals Most Commonly Seen 194
Reptiles Most Commonly Seen 195
Amphibians Most Commonly Seen 195
Capybara 195
A General Bird List for the Llanos 196

One important birding tip 198
A Year in the Llanos 198
V - 3. Birding the Llanos 200
V - 4. The Hatos 200
   State of Guarico 200
      Hato La Fe 200
   State of Cojedes 201
      Hato Piñero 201
   Something New Has Been Added 202
   State of Apure 204
      Hato El Cedral 204
      Birds seen at El Cedral (not on General List above) 205
      How to Reach El Cedral 206
      Campamento Turístico Mata E' Totumo 207
      Hato El Frío 208
      The Cinaruco-Capanaparo National Park 209
      Options for Lodging in the Park 210
      Another Option for visiting the Park 211
   Barinas State 211
      Hato La Madera 211
      Agropecuario La Bota/Finca Santa María 212
      Hato El Cristero 213
      Centro Turístico El Gabán 213
      Hato Garza 214
      Rio Bumbum 214
V - 5. The Birding Roads 215
   The Calabozo-San Fernando Road 215
   The San Silvestre Road 215
   Dolores to La Ye 216
V - 6. Wintering Dickcissels 217
V - 7. Hotels in the Llanos 218
   In San Fernando de Apure, capital of the State of Apure 218
   In Calabozo, State of Guarico 218
   In Barinas, capital of the State of Barinas 218
Section VI. The Eastern States 221
VI - 1. State of Anzoategui 223
   Introduction 223
   Piritu and Unare 223
   Lagunas de José 225
VI - 2. State of Sucre 228
   Introduction 228
   Cumaná 228
   Paria and Eastern Sucre 229
      Lodging in Carúpano 229
      Lodging in Rio Caribe & Neighboring Areas 229
   The Paria National Park 230
   Places to Stay /Bird in Southern Sucre 234
VI - 3. State of Monagas 238
   Introduction 238

The Oilbird Cave 238
Where to stay in Caripe 241
Birding around Caripe 241
Puertas de Miraflores o del Guarapiche 243
General Bird List for Caripe 244
Maturin 245
Staying in Maturin 245
Caño Colorado 246
Agropecuaria La Ceiba 249
Morichal Largo 251
Going South to Bolivar 252
VI - 4. Delta Amacuro 253
Introduction 253
Birding around Tucupita 253
Coporito 254
Los Güires 255
Indian Crafts 256
Camps and Lodges 256
Birding in the Southern Delta 257
From the Delta south to Bolivar State 259
Section VII. Southern Venezuela 261
VII - 1. Eastern Bolivar State 264
Introduction 264
Rio Grande and the Imataca Forest Reserve 266
The Road South 269
Anacoco / San Martín de Turumbán Road (by Chris Sharpe) 270
Getting there 270
Birding 270
Staying in Tumeremo 271
Birds of the Anacoco / San Martín de Turumbán Road 271
Continuing South 272
The Barquilla de Fresa (The Strawberry Ice Cream Cone) 273
Alternative Lodgings 274
Fascinating birding sites. Read on! 275
The Guyana Trail 275
The Capuchinbird Road 277
Cuyuni River Trip 278
Canaima National Park and World Heritage Site 279
The Escalera 280
The Gran Sabana 285
Santa Elena de Uairen 289
The El Paují Road 289
El Paují 289
Where to Stay in El Paují 291
Birds of the road from Santa Elena to El Paují 291
Canaima - The Western Side of the Park 293
Closing Thoughts 295
VII - 2. Western Bolivar State 296
Introduction 296

Driving from Puerto Ordaz to the Caura 296
The Caura River 297
   Campamento Caurama 298
   Campamento Caura 299
   General Checklist for the Lower Caura 299
VII - 3. State of Amazonas 304
   Introduction 304
   Puerto Ayacucho 305
   Where to stay in Puerto Ayacucho 306
   Refugio Yagrumo-Cataniapo 307
   Babilla de Pinta'o 308
   Junglaven 309
   Checklist for Junglaven (by Dave Sargeant) 310

Section VIII. To wind up...closing notes 315
VIII - 1. The Endemics 316
VIII - 2. A Teaspoon of Economy and Politics 319
VIII - 3. About You in Venezuela 321
   Code of Ethics for Tourists 321
VIII - 4. Clemencia's Advice: What to Bring 323
VIII - 5. Useful Information 325
   Venezuelan Public Holidays 325
   National Holidays 325
   Religious Holidays 325
   Changing Money 325
   Venezuelan Currency 326
   Credit Cards 326
   Dialing Telephone Numbers 326
   National Airlines Directory 327
   International Airlines Directory 327
   Visas 328
   Inparques (National Parks Institute) 328
   Local Offices by State 328
VIII - 6. The Venezuela Audubon Society 331
VIII - 7. A Souvenir... 332

Section I

TO BEGIN WITH...
A BIRD'S EYE VIEW

Hoatzin

I - 1. How to Use this Book

In the previous editions of *Birding,* we followed the nomenclature and taxonomy used in Phelps & Meyer de Schauensee's 1978 **Guide to the Birds of Venezuela,** as these were the names commonly used by both birders and scientists in our country. Now, however, we expect that the new Guide to the Birds of Venezuela by Steve Hilty will be published soon, as well as a new, heavily annotated Checklist of Birds of Venezuela by Clemencia Rodner and Chris Sharpe, so we are using the nomenclature of Clements while we wait for the changes those two books will undoubtedly bring. Hopefully, we will manage someday to get used to the many changes that have taken place in the years since the ground-breaking Phelps & Meyer de Schauensee book came out. For the convenience of those who do not have easy access to the changes in names, I am attaching a list at the end of this section.

Aside from this book, the SCAV has been publishing a series of **Checklists of the National Parks of Venezuela.** To this date, eleven titles have come out, which include some of the parks most frequently visited by birders: Henri Pittier, Canaima, Guatopo, Tamá, Yacambú, Los Roques, Cinaruco-Capanaparo, Paria, the Morrocoy/Cuare/ Represa de Tacarigua complex, the Delta/Mariusa and Macarao. You will find them quite useful when visiting those particular areas.

These checklists have been compiled with utmost care, most under the supervision of Miguel Lentino, drawing not only from his vast field experience, but also from the excellent and quite comprehensive data available in the Phelps Ornithological Collection, where he is Curator, and from the Museum of Rancho Grande Biological Station at El Limón, Maracay.

I would like to take this opportunity to express the great debt of gratitude that the SCAV and all birders in Venezuela have towards William H. Phelps and William H. Phelps Jr., who for 50 years worked enthusiastically to build what is nowadays considered the best ornithological collection of any country in South or Central America and one of the best privately-owned collections in the World. Our sincere thanks also to Francisco Bisbal, Curator of the El Limón Museum, who has always been an invaluable and generous friend to the SCAV, and to all the great people who work with him, especially Ramón Rivero.

Regarding the plan of this book, I have followed again my previous system of a section for each region and chapters for each state. In order to better orient yourself around the book, keep in mind that the regions are organized in somewhat counter clock fashion: Beginning with Caracas and environs, we amble across the northern states towards the west; then down to the Andes; then the Llanos, which in a way form a belt across the middle of the country; then to the eastern states and the Delta; then south to the states of Bolívar and Amazonas.

In addition to the chapters on each region, which make up the meaty part of the book, there are a number of chapters on topics which either I or my nit-picking editor thought were necessary. In these, we have tried to include every possible piece of information on the country, its customs and quirks, its possibilities and limitations, that emerged from adding together a veritable kaleidoscope of our own experiences and that of birders and friends.

This book will make a lot more sense **if you keep a road map at hand.** Unfortunately, it is sometimes difficult to secure an adequate road map in Venezuela. Your best bet would be to contact World Wide Books and Maps, 736A Granville St. Vancouver, B.C., Canada V6Z 1G3, Ph: (604) 687-3320, Fax: (604) 687-5925. These are the best road maps to be had of Venezuela, and if you get a map in advance, it will help you become familiarized with the geography and the roads. Also, check out: http://www.a-venezuela.com/mapas/.

Caveat: All road maps of Venezuela are currently based on the original maps made by the Venezuelan government in the 1970s, and consequently are not always as accurate as they should be. For instance, the maps show a variety of roads going south from Coro, the capital of the State of Falcon, to Churuguara. In reality, there is only one.

On the subject of where to stay, in the years since the third and fourth editions of this book came out, two ecotourism hotel guides have come off the press: Miro Popic's *Ecotourist Guide to Venezuela*, and Elizabeth Kline's *Guide to the Camps, Posadas & Cabins in Venezuela*. Miro includes in his book a description of the National Parks and Monuments, as well as a calendar of natural events by regions, prepared by the Venezuelan Audubon. Elizabeth's guide has been an invaluable tool for me during my travels as she does not hesitate to tell it as she sees it. If an inn or camp is run-down, gives poor service, etc., she is blunt in her description. Furthermore, she updates her book every year. Both of these books can be obtained in almost any bookstore in Caracas.

Regarding tourism guides, I would suggest *Guide to Venezuela* by Hilary Dunsterville Branch published in England. You can order the third edition (1999) from Brandt Publications, 41 Nortoft Road, Chalfont St Peter, Bucks SL9 0LA, UK. In the U. S., the book can be ordered from The Globe Pequot Press, Inc., 6 Business Park Road, P.O. Box 833, Old Saybrook, Connecticut 06475-0833. Hilary has excellent maps of trails in the Andes, those of the Avila National Park above Caracas, San Esteban National Park in Carabobo State, etc. She also has good maps of several of the larger cities. Try also the latest edition of the *Lonely Planet* book on Venezuela. Both are chock-full with information, historic data, anecdotes, curiosities, etc. Both include places where you can stay, from lap-of-luxury hotels to bone-bare essentials *posadas* (inns), tips and guiding for land, water and air transportation. Finally, there is the 2001 edition of the *Travel Planner for Venezuela* by John Benus. This is chock-a-block full of necessary information such as bus schedules to the interior, where to call in the event you lose your credit card, where to exchange your dollars throughout Venezuela, visiting remote islands by sailboat, scuba diving and snorkeling, ultralight flights, taxis, touring and transportation tips, telephone numbers of all airlines and hotels. I do not know how he gathered so much information, but it is a most useful book. This can be purchased through Travel Book Stores, www.leeme.com and www.amazon.com. In Caracas it can be obtained at the gift shops of almost all major hotels.

If you have never been to the tropics, I suggest you read two superb books: *Tropical Nature* by Adrian Forsyth and Ken Miyata (Charles Scribner's Sons, 1984), and *A Neotropical Companion* by John C. Kricher (Princeton University Press, 1997). There is also Steve Hilty´s wonderful book *Birds of Tropical America* published by Chapters Publishing Ltd., 2031 Shelburne Road, Shelburne, Vermont 05482. If you can find a copy of David Snow's masterpiece *The Web of Adaptation,* be sure to read it, as well as the book on tropical forests by John Terborgh Each and everyone of these books will open for you windows of understanding into different aspects of the magical, complex and subtle world of tropical ecosystems. If you read all four, your trip to Venezuela will surely be the richest experience of your life! We also recommend *In Trouble Again - A Journey Between the Orinoco and the Amazon* by Redmond O'Hanlon. It is informative and hilarious - but DON'T read it before coming to Venezuela.

Finally, for a more visual idea of the country, I suggest you check out our own web page: **www.audubondevenezuela.org**

A great page put together by Dr. Carlos Rivero Blanco a Venezuelan scientist is: **www.venezuelatuya.com**
On "Venezuela Tuya" or Venezuela Yours, be sure to check out the sections on Tourism, Geography and Nature. For a general idea of the Amazonas area take a look at **www.amazonasvenezuela.com**

The following is a list of differences of common English names between "A Guide to the Birds of Venezuela" by Phelps and Meyer de Schauensee and *A Checklist of the Birds of the World* by James F. Clements:

Phelps	Clements
Olivaceous Cormorant	Neotropic Cormorant
Brazilian Duck	Brazilian Teal
Common Pintail	Northern Pintail
American Flamingo	Greater Flamingo
White-necked Heron	Cocoi Heron
Chestnut-bellied Heron	Agami Heron
American Wood Ibis	Wood Stork
Sharp-shinned Hawk	Plain-breasted Hawk
Gray Hawk	Gray-lined Hawk
Gray-bellied Hawk	Gray-bellied Goshawk
Lesser Razor-billed Currasow	Crestless Currasow
Common Gallinule	Common Moorhen
Common Dowitcher	Short-billed Dowitcher
Thick-billed Plover	Wilson's Plover
Lesser Golden Plover	American Golden Plover
Common Stilt	Black-necked Stilt
Maroon-faced Parakeet	White-eared Parakeet
Blood-eared Parakeet	Red-eared Parakeet
White-capped Parrot	Speckle-faced Parrot
Yellow-headed Parrot	Yellow-crowned Parrot
Vermiculated Screech-Owl	Variable Screech-Owl
White-winged Potoo	Andean Potoo
Semi-collared Night-Hawk	Short-tailed Night-Hawk
Crowned Woodnymph	Violet-crowned Woodnymph
Pygmy Kingfisher	American Pygmy Kingfisher
Scale-breasted Woodpecker	Scaly-breasted Woodpecker
Yellow-throated Spinetail	Yellow-chinned Spinetail
Plain Thornbird	Common Thornbird
Leaf scrapers	Leaftossers
Bar-crested Antbird	Bar-crested Antshrike
Slaty Antshrike	Eastern Slaty Antshrike
Plumbeous Antshrike	White-streaked Antvireo
Banded Antbird	Banded Antwren
Rufous-tailed Antthrush	Scalloped Antthrush
Brown-breasted Antpitta	Tepui Antpitta
White-ruffed Manakin	White-bibbed Manakin
Yellow-crowned Manakin	Yellow-crested Manakin
Thrush-like Manakin	Thrush-like Schiffornis*
Greater Manakin	Greater Schiffornis*

Cinnamon Manakin	Cinnamon Tyrant*
Cinnamon-crested Spadebill	Yellow-throated Spadebill
White-ringed Flycatcher	Yellow-throated Flycatcher
Greater Pewee	Smoke-colored Pewee
Trail's Flycatcher	Willow Flycatcher
Paltry Tyrannulet	Venezuelan Tyrannulet
Yellow-bellied Bristle Tyrant	Rufous-lored Tyrannulet
Scrub Flycatcher	Northern Scrub-Flycatcher
Collared Jay	Black-collared Jay
Short-billed Marsh-Wren	Sedge Wren
Nightingale Wren	Southern Nightingale Wren
Rough-winged Swallow	Southern Rough-winged Swallow
Warbling Vireo	Brown-capped Vireo
Olive Oropendola	Amazonian Oropendola
American Parula	Northern Parula
Myrtle Warbler	Yellow-rumped Warbler
Brown-capped Redstart	Tepui Redstart
River Warbler	Neotropical River Warbler
Coal-black Flower-piercer	Merida Flower-piercer
Gray-hooded Hemispingus	Gray-hooded Bush-Tanager
Rose-breasted Thrush-Tanager	Rosy Thrush-Tanager
Golden-bellied Euphonia	White-lored Euphonia
Yellow Grosbeak	Golden-bellied Grosbeak
Greater Large-billed Seed-Finch	Great-billed Seed-Finch
Dull-colored Seedeater	Dull-colored Grassquit

I - 2. The Birding Experience in Venezuela

To the birding enthusiast, Venezuela offers just about everything anyone could desire. The country is relatively small for South America - its 352,144 square miles (916,445 square kilometers[1]) make it about the size of Texas and Oklahoma combined, or a little larger than the Iberian Peninsula. Yet, it offers an astonishing variety of habitats and ecosystems: From the Llanos, endless savannas that are both its lowland and its heartland, to snow-capped peaks on the Sierra Nevada de Mérida, in the Venezuelan Andes; from rain-washed lands of the Gran Sabana, the Delta of the Orinoco, the Coastal Mountain Range or the Amazonian region, to sun-baked xerophitic areas along the coast.

Although so-called development has been gnawing away at many of our forests, there are still broad extensions of country that remain quite uninhabited and unspoiled; vast expanses of habitat for many species of birds that are still untouched. In fact, four birding areas in Venezuela can be considered **world-class**:

* **The Escalera** leading to the legendary Gran Sabana, as well as the preceding area surrounding the Barquilla de Fresa in Bolivar State.
* **The forests of the Ventuari River**, such as those found around Junglaven in Amazonas State.
* **The Llanos,** and especially the low Llanos in Apure State such as the savannas of Hato El Cedral and also the high Llanos such as the pastures and woods of Hato Piñero.
* **The cloud forest of the Coastal Mountain Range**, such as those on the ridges of Henri Pittier N.P. and the Palmichal Watershed Reserve.

As for birds, a total of **I,399 species** has been recorded[2] which is only exceeded by the number of species to be found in Peru, Colombia, Ecuador and Brazil. Forty seven species of parrots fly their gay colors in Venezuela and we can also boast of 105 species of hummingbirds, 91 species of antbirds and 137 species of flycatchers.

There is a fairly good system of paved roads and a variety of habitats within a relatively small territory. The ease of accessibility offers both birder and general nature lover an unequaled opportunity to increase their knowledge of neotropical flora and fauna with a minimum of discomfort.

The climate is benign year-round, and seldom does it rain the whole day long, except in the south during the rainy season. The region of Guayana, that part of Venezuela which lies south of the Orinoco River and comprises the states of Bolivar and Amazonas, has the highest annual rainfall. People joke about the difference between the dry and the rainy seasons in Guayana: during the first one it rains every day; during the second, it rains *all* day. I have camped many times in the south (although only twice in the rainy season), and never found the rain to disturb my birding or the general fun of the trip.

Throughout the country, the rainy season runs, generally, from late April or early May to early November. Along the dry areas of the northwestern coast, however,

---

[1] Until the 1960s, the surface area of Venezuela was always quoted as being 912,050 square kilometers. In the late 1970, maps and measurements made using satellites, helped determine the true borders with Brazil, which are defined by the watershed divider of the Orinoco and Amazon basins. These new measurements added 4,395 square kilometers to the Venezuelan territory.
[2] Species count according to the "Checklist of the Birds of Northern South America" (Rodner, Lentino & Restall 2000).

there tend to be two rainy seasons: October to December and then May to July. The rainy season is the time of the year when all the birds seem to outdo each other in song. I've had birders who visited us during the rainy season comment that the rains were never an obstacle to their Birding Experience. Too much to see and hear. In the Llanos, rainy seasons are hot, wet, muddy and buggy, but many of our birds nest during this time, and the land is beautiful with a hundred shades of green. In the Andes, you may find light snowfalls on the páramos in August and September. In the Guayanan rain forests of the south, in Bolívar, Amazonas and the Delta, it may rain any day of the year, but mostly in May and November.

In reality it seems to me that October is the rainiest month, but even that brings a bonus. I visited an hato in the Llanos very recently during a rainy October day and found that the Hoatzins, Greater Anis, Maguari Storks, and practically everything else were all sitting on their nests.

The dry season, on the other hand, is considered by many to be the best time of the year to come visit, especially during the months of January to April, when the vast areas of flood plains in the Llanos dry up and the birds congregate in the remaining water holes. For me though, the last months of the dry season are very sad - after the yearly ritual of the *quemas* (burnings) that Venezuelan peasants traditionally use to clear the land for the next planting, one finds the land parched and burnt. In the past governments fought this terrible practice for years with educational campaigns, but the results so far have been nil. That is why I am grateful when National Parks and, in one notable case, a petrochemical company, protect the watersheds.

You will find rural **people** to be generally friendly and eager to help. Remember, however, that Spanish is our national language and that outside of the main metropolitan areas, English is rarely understood. A little phrase book will come in handy, although you will not find many occasions for phrases such as «I need ink for my fountain pen.» or «Where is the nearest post office?» (many of our little towns have no post office at all). More likely it will be: "*Había una cucaracha enorme en mi ducha.*" «There was a huge cockroach in my shower!». Oh well, tropical nature, you know!

Venezuela is a beautiful country not only for its varied scenery, but also, like so many other nations, for the variety of **cultures** it offers. Food, music, looks, crafts, even accents change as you travel from one part of the country to another. I would like to invite you to get acquainted with the diversity amid the people of the different regions.

Venezuelan **food** is not terribly spicy nor hot; you will classify it as milder than Mexican food. It comes from Spanish tradition, with a heavy dose of Italian, French and Amerindian influence - an appetizing mix indeed! The national dish is called *pabellón,* a reference to the National Colors. If you order it, you will be presented with a platter of neatly arranged rice, black beans, shredded meat (fried with tomatoes and onions) and fried plantains. A four-star pabellón would also have a fried egg on top. A delicious, filling and inexpensive meal!

Amerindian influence can be found in interesting items such as *casabe, hallaquitas* and *cachapas*. These are, in turn, a sort of crumbly pita bread made of taro root; an enchilada-like concoction, made of cornmeal; a pancake made of yellow cornmeal and served hot, filled with cheese. Spanish, French and Italian influence can be found in a variety of vegetable, pasta and rice dishes, and also in desserts, such as *quesillo* (a rich custard) and the cream cakes and patisseries offered in many restaurants.

One thing that remains constant throughout are the convenient and omnipresent *panaderías* (bakeries), where you can find excellent coffee, good Venezuelan bread and the ever-popular *cachitos* (ham rolls) and *pastelitos* (cheese or ham pastries). For an excellent Venezuelan imitation of French bread, order a *canilla* pronounced can ee ya. Recently our "enlightened" President decreed that our bread must be made with rice flour. I suspect that this particular decree will be as successful as it was when issued previously by yet another President. If the Venezuelans do not approve of a law, they have the good sense to just blithely ignore it. After all, they know that their governments are incapable of enforcing the laws and, also, that the politicians are the first to circumvent them.

Try doing as a Venezuelan, and stop for coffee at any of the little road-side soda fountains or bakeries. You will find that the famous Gaggia machines from Italy are ubiquitous, so that most places serve expresso coffee, which is considered the true form for Venezuelan coffee. Venezuelans have turned expresso into a sort of folklore, for they ask for it in a variety of styles, the most popular being *con leche,* (half milk and half coffee), *marrón* (more coffee than milk), *cortado* (just a touch of milk), *guayoyo* (mild black, more like American coffee) or *tinto* (very strong black).

In reviewing the paragraph above, Pamela (one of my hard-working reviewers) told me what I have heard countless times before - that to her, Venezuelan coffee is the best in the world. And it is true. Our coffee is fantastic. Its lack of international fame is due to the fact that we drink it all. Virtually nothing is exported.

Another Venezuelan item that Pamela, that intrepid traveler[1] thinks fantastic, is chocolate. She nagged me to recommend you try buying a bar of El Rey Chocolate at any of the better grocery stores. And then there is Venezuelan beer. Pamela recommends you try Polar, or Solera, or Regional[2].

The most popular breakfast among Venezuelans is an *arepa* - an English muffin-shaped bun made of white corn flour. One may put just about anything inside a breakfast arepa - from black beans to shredded meat, various kinds of cheese, etc. My favorite filling is *queso guayanés*, a creamy white cheese from Guayana. Another remarkably good Venezuelan cheese is the famous *queso de mano,* or "hand" cheese, and a popular variation called *queso telita* or "Rag" cheese.

At many of the soda fountains you will also note that they advertise *batidos,* which are fresh-fruit-and-ice shakes. These you have to try! For a memorable flavor and as a refreshing drink, nothing beats a batido. Try both the tropical fruits, such as *lechosa* (papaya), *parchita* (passion fruit), *guayaba* (guava), *guanábana* (sour sop), *riñón* (custard apple, in season from September to October), *níspero* (sapodilla), *parcha* and *zapote;* as well as the more generally-known flavors, including cantaloupe, banana, orange, strawberry and the delicious mango, which is in season from May to September. Given a chance, stop and ask for those tropical fruits at a local market in any town in the interior, for they are also worth trying *as is,* in other words, not in a shake or a fruit salad. We often buy fresh fruits from roadside venders and eat them right off.

Speaking of salads, Venezuela is one of the few Latin American countries where it is safe to eat salads, including lettuce and tomatoes.

You will be wondering why I make such a fuss about food in a chapter purportedly about the birding experience. What is a vacation abroad - I ask you - without some adventurous meals along the way? I am convinced that beautiful scenery, varied habitats, pleasant climate, good roads, short distances, friendly people and delicious food will help make your birding experience in Venezuela enjoyable, but I know that, most definitely, what will make it unforgettable is the birds. Who are they, where and when to find them, is what this book is all about.

---

[1] Editor's Note: Anyone willing to travel with Mary Lou authomatically qualifies for the title of "Intrepid". Other titles automatically acquired include "Inquisitive" and "Peripatetic".

[2] Editor's Note: Hmm....I wonder. Can Pamela and Mary Lou be trusted on their own?

I - 3. A Birding Calendar

When is the best time to come? - is one of the questions we are most often asked. The proper answer is - It depends! Just read on...

If **hummingbirds** are your bag, then come to Venezuela in the month of September or October, when the Inga trees *(Mimosaceas)* are in flower in the coffee plantations. Best areas are the mountains above the town of Caripe, in the State of Monagas, the states of Mérida and Táchira, or the National Park of the Sierra de San Luis (State of Falcon). The white, feathery flowers of the Inga, called *Guamo* in Venezuela, are a magnet to all the hummingbirds in the area. This is the time of year when it is easy to spot the **White-tailed Sabrewing** in the coffee haciendas that abound around Caripe. In the humid lowlands the deep red, feathery flowers of the Malay-apple trees *(Pomagás)* are full of hummers. As these trees bloom twice a year, you are almost guaranteed to see either hummers at the flowers or tanangers at the fruit. Try visiting Guatopo National Park near Caracas either in October for flowers or January for fruit.

For the **Bearded Helmetcrest Hummingbird**, come to our Andes from July to September, when the populations of insects are at a peak and the birds are displaying. During October and November, the Páramo is covered with the bright yellow blossoms of the "Frailejones", *Espeletia* spp.

Towards the end of September, the birds of the mountains begin to form feeding flocks, and they will be doing so until February, for in March, the breeding season begins and everyone is busy with courtship and nests and that sort of thing. The ambling bands are composed mostly of forest tanagers, with representatives from other families thrown in to amuse us birders. You will find that at the heart of these flocks is the **Common Bush Tanager**, nicknamed the Good News Tanager. Be on the look-out for that particular species. I should point out that September birding can be very daunting as the birds are at their quietest. But, suddenly you may hear the call of the Common Bush Tanager and find yourself surrounded by woodcreepers, Streaked Tufted-cheek and several foliage gleaners, as well as some flycatchers and all the tanangers of the region. Then life is really worth living!

If you want to see the **White-tipped Quetzal** in Palmichal or the Henri Pittier National Park, or the **Andean Cock-of-the-Rock** in Mérida, it is best to come between December and February, at the beginning of their nesting season.

The **Swallow Tanagers** come north to breed in the Andes and the Coastal Cordillera about mid February. In Rancho Grande, they nest in holes of the very walls of the Biological Research Station, and can easily be seen through April.

In the State of Bolívar, to see the **White Bell Bird** along the Escalera, or the **Capuchinbird** near the gold-mining wastelands of Las Claritas, plan your trip in March/April. During these months, the Bellbird will be ringing out his good news from the top of the highest, most visible tree. At other times, you may well hear his call, but it is almost impossible to catch sight of him.

If you aim to add the **Tocuyo Sparrow** to your life list, then go to Yacambu National Park (see the chapter on the State of Lara). I have seen them in December and have had reports for January, February and March, but I suspect they are there all year-round, and it is not so much a question of less birds, but of less birders at other times.

From January through February, the Melastone bushes, *Melastomatacea* spp., have ripe clumps of their plump, small fruit. This is probably the best time to see frugivorous birds in the mountains - especially around Colonia Tovar (Aragua State). They ripen later on the Escalera in southern Bolivar State. These berries lure

House Wren

cotingas, manakins, some flycatchers, euphonias, tanagers and others. Another group of species going to fruit during these last/first months of the year are the *Clusias*, some of which, like the *insipida,* are magnets for birds.

February and March are the months when the Mountain Immortelles *(Erythrina poeppigiana)* are showing off in flame-colored blossoms. The Immortelle flowers attract a bevy of hummers, honey creepers, euphonias, tanagers, etc. Look for these flowering trees in the lower flanks of the mountains, from 400 meters above sea level up to approximately 1,500 m.a.s.l. In the lowlands, it is the Swamp Immortelle *(Erythrina glauca)* that blooms with peach-colored blossoms, and is also sought out by nectar feeding birds and insects. Please note, however that the Mountain Immortelles bloom later in the Andes and around the coffee plantations of Caripe (see chapter on Monagas). For these areas come in April.

During those same months many of our **Manakins** are nesting and singing. Listen for the **Winged Barred** in the mountains and the **Lance-tailed** in the lowlands.

The **Thick-billed** and **Blue-hooded Euphonias** nest in February and March along the Coastal Range, as well as in the Andes. But in the gardens of the Barquilla de Fresa, our favorite lodge in Bolívar, the Euphonias nest in November.

Late afternoon, March to April, is the time of day and year to look for **Purple-breasted** and **Pompadour Cotingas** displaying on the tree-tops, in areas south of the Orinoco. Other birds singing and displaying in the same months and same areas are the **Black Nunbirds** and **White-bearded Manakins**.

To record the full song of the **Vermilion Cardinal**, visit the xerophitic regions surrounding the city of Coro, capital of the state of Falcon, during the months of April and May. This is the same area to look for the **Short-tailed Tody Flycatcher**. See chapter on the State of Falcon. The Cardinals are also common near San Pablo in the state of Lara along the old road from Barquisimeto to Carora. I have also seen them along the xerophitic coast of the State of Anzoategui east of Caracas.

From March through April, the large flocks of **Fork-tailed Flycatchers**, as well as **Small-billed Elaenias** and **Streaked Flycatchers,** are arriving from the austral regions of South America. We believe that these southern migrants push some resident species towards the north, as is the case with the southern Streaked Flycatchers.

To see a full show of **Oilbirds** flying out at dusk from the huge cave where they roost during the day in the Guacharo National Park (*Guacharo* is their Spanish name), come in March when the nesting season begins. See the chapter on the State of Monagas in eastern Venezuela.

August is great for birding along the foothills of the Andes and south of Lake Maracaibo.

As you can see, every season and every month has its attractions. Aside from warning you off of the Easter, Carnival and Christmas holiday pandemoniums (see chapter on Caveats), and from pointing out that perhaps the least interesting month is September, my advice is to come when you can: that should be the best time to visit.

I - 4. A National Parks Manual

At the present time, Venezuela's "National Parks System" comprises an astonishing 88 protected areas, including 43 National Parks and 45 Natural Monuments[1]. These protected areas cover a mind-boggling total of 14,104,386 hectares or 34,837,833 acres. To give you a mental picture, the Netherlands territorial surface is 4,116,000 hectares, so the park lands of Venezuela are 3.4 times the size of the Netherlands.

The national parks protect more than 15 distinct types of ecosystems, which provide the avid birder ample options for birding. Sad to say, however, most of them exist only on paper. Our Presidents and governments have been creating them right and left for the past 30 some years, with no thought on how to provide for their proper protection and management or on how to compensate the farmers and ranchers for the restrictions imposed on their lands.

Few parks are completely uninhabited (only the most remote, inaccessible ones in the south). Land owners within are allowed to continue farming or ranching, but they may not expand their holdings, which has made for a lot of local enemies for the National Parks. Also, many areas contain rich mineral deposits of various kinds, that are coveted by both national and international mining interests. To top it all, many areas are looked upon with hungry eyes by developers, loggers and landless peasants.

The main point though, is that these areas do exist, and that even if many are threatened by problems both outside and inside their borders, their legal status has afforded them much better protection than if nothing had been done. They offer superb birding possibilities. In fact, sometimes I fear that if it were not for the national parks (and for some private and semi-private areas such as the hydrological reserve maintained by a petrochemical company), Venezuela would become as denuded as Haiti within 50 years.

As I stated in earlier editions, Inparques, our National Parks Institute, has long had the possibility of charging an entrance fee. At long last, it is now beginning to do so: **supposedly entrance fees are now required from all tourists visiting national parks.** Few of the parks, however, give the public anything in return by way of services or facilities. That is why we have always been anxious for Inparques to get its act together and start charging all visitors: we will be in complete agreement with the procedure **as long as the fees go towards protecting the park in question and developing the necessary infrastructure.**

It would make me utterly happy to be able to convey the news that this payment is a simple, direct operation, but, alas, no such luck! Inparques has yet to devise a system which is not Kafkian and extremely convoluted. The fees and where they may be paid are the subject of constant changes. At a few parks, you may pay at the entrance; in others, you first have to find the local Inparques office; for yet others, you have to pay at the main Inparques offices in Caracas. Wherever and however you pay, request a receipt and check the amount written thereon. Maybe some day in the far distant future they will hit upon a system that solves all of their various problems

---

[1] Another type of protection area, not included in the National Parks System, are the Wildlife Refuges or Sanctuaries, two of which are very important habitats for aquatic birds: Cuare in the State of Falcon, and the Ciénaga de Los Olivitos on the Eastern shore of the Bay of El Tablazo, directly north of Lake Maracaibo.

and is, at the same time, convenient to visitors. In the mean time, my recommendation is that you get in touch with the Venezuelan Audubon and have them get you the permits for the parks you want to visit. In assisting you to obtain park permits, the Audubon office in Caracas[1] must have your passport number and advice as to where they can deliver the permit to you.

Furthermore, the latest of INPARQUES, is that now **for a tourist to take photographs within a National Park, you must have a special permit.** In all my travels around the globe, the requirement for a permit to take photographs in a National Park just about tops what I would call petty bureaucracy and fifth-world thinking. Of course, it would be impossible for Inparques to apply this rule in Canaima National Park or other very large parks, but you can bet your camera on the fact that in a small park, you will be ticked off for photographing a waterfall or a special flower.

Naturally and understandably, to camp in the parks, you definitely must secure prior permission, either from Caracas or from the nearest Inparques office. The Caracas office is located at Avenida Romulo Gallegos, near the Parque del Este Metro Station. For the purposes of requesting permits, they are open week days, from 2 to 4:30 p.m. only unless they change once again. In Venezuela each incoming government changes all the rules and regulations of the previous one. In the chapter on Useful Information, you will find a list of the addresses of Inparques offices in the different states.

Sometimes, even the permit from the Caracas office is not good enough and you may encounter a Park Guard way off in, say, Tamá National Park, in southwest Venezuela, who, in following local instructions to the letter, will advise you that your permit from Caracas is "only a permit to request another permit", that you must go to the local office in San Cristobal, thereby causing you to lose a whole day of your vacation!

For the most part, as I mentioned above, there are no public service areas with restrooms and/or toilets in our national parks, nor do we have nature trails or visitors' centers. The only parks with facilities are Rancho Grande in Henri Pittier, Sierra Nevada, The Avila, Yacambu, Guatopo and Guácharo National Parks. Even then, you have to have your own toilet paper if you are going to use the restrooms. In Rancho Grande, the trails and toilets are barely maintained by the Research Station, which belongs to the Universidad Central de Venezuela, although it is the National Parks Institute who collects the entrance fee. I should point out, however, that the biological station at Rancho Grande is now charging approximately Bs. 1,000 per person to visit the station.

Aside from visitor services, all Parks are in dire need of management and vigilance. For the most part, our politicians are extremely ignorant in matters of natural resources, ecology and conservation, and their ignorance is reflected in government policies and attitudes. Since most have no clue as to the value of these natural areas, they think that preserving them is a "waste" of funds and an impediment to development.

In these matters, recent administrations have had and continue to have what can be rated as the worst track record of all: they have concentrated not in doing, but in undoing what had been previously achieved. Inparques authorities have been changed every 6 months, while biologists and other technical personnel with long experience have been replaced by political appointees. The maneuvers have convinced conservationists that there is a tacit goal of weakening the National Parks Institute in order to advance a number of nefarious economic or political projects.

---

[1] E-mail audubon@audubondevenezuela.org or Fax: (58-212) 991-0716.

A prime source of concern is Canaima National Park, our largest park. Sir Arthur Conan Doyle took the mysteriously magic scenery of Canaima as a backdrop for his novel "Lost World". Both the most recent and the present government promoted the construction of a huge electric power line across the Park with the aim of selling electricity to northern Brazil. If governmental neglect and mismanagement continue, we fear that this unequaled area will be a world lost.

While the national tourist agency, Corpoturismo, is desperately trying to promote ecotourism, the Ministries of Energy & Mines and of Environment (!!) are pushing for mining in the national parks. Obviously, there is no coherence in these Government's plans. Or is it that they do not understand that ecotourists visit our parks?

Enough of a tirade! While all of the above is true, or can be at some point or other, ON THE OTHER HAND, many of our national parks and wilderness regions are wild, rugged and unspoiled. One can hike long distances and camp without encountering anyone else. You can bathe undisturbed in clear mountain streams and drink water flowing from them. Unlike parks in the developed world, and except in some places during Carnival and Easter week, there are no long lines of cars, overcrowded campsites, Macdonald's, or t-shirts and souvenir stands. If you want to, you can be out there on your own - just you and the rainforest, you and the savanna, you and the mountains, you and the stars.

THE NATURAL MONUMENTS

The following table lists all our National Parks with their location, surface area and year of establishment. But the National Parks System also includes the Natural Monuments. The main objective of Natural Monuments is to preserve scenery and/or geological features that have extraordinary qualities.

According to the Presidential decrees that grant them their legal status, there are 21 of them in the country, but in reality 45 separate areas are included, since the Tepuy Natural Monuments complex includes all 25 separate Tepuis, the table mountains found in southern Venezuela that comprise the mountain range known as the Guayana Shield.

These protected areas are generally much smaller than national parks. The total area occupied by Natural Monuments is 1,123,874 hectares; of these, 1,069,820 correspond to the Tepuy Natural Monuments complex.

NATIONAL PARKS OF VENEZUELA

NAME	STATE	YEAR CREATED	AREA (hectares)
Henri Pittier	Aragua	1937	107,800
Sierra Nevada	Mérida	1952	276,446
Guatopo	Miranda	1958	122,464
El Avila	Federal District	1958	81,800
Yurubí	Yaracuy	1960	23,670
Canaima	Bolivar	1962	3,000,000
Yacambu	Lara	1962	14,580
Cueva Quebrada del Toro	Falcón	1969	4,885
Archipelago Los Roques	Federal Dependencies	1972	221,120
Macarao	Federal District	1973	15,000
Mochima	Sucre	1973	94,935
La Restinga	Nueva Esparta	1974	18,862
Médanos de Coro	Falcon	1974	91,280
Laguna Tacarigua	Miranda	1974	39,100
Cerro Copey	Amazonas	1974	7,130
Aguaro-Guariquito	Guarico	1974	585,750
Morrocoy	Falcon	1974	32,090
El Guácharo	Monagas	1975	62,700
Terepaima	Lara/Portuguesa	1976	18,650
Sarisariñama	Bolívar	1978	330,000
La Neblina	Amazonas	1978	1,360,000
Yapacana	Amazonas	1978	320,000
Duida-Marahuaka	Amazonas	1978	210,000
Peninsula de Paria	Sucre	1978	37,500
Perijá	Zulia	1978	295,288
El Tamá	Táchira	1978	109,000
San Esteban	Carabobo	1987	43,500
Sierra de San Luis	Falcón	1987	20,000
Cinaruco-Capanaparo	Apure	1988	584,368
Guaramacal	Trujillo	1988	21,000
Dinira	Lara/Trujillo	1988	42,000
Páramos Batallón y La Negra	Mérida/Táchira	1989	95,200
Chorro El Indio	Táchira	1989	17,000
Sierra La Culata	Mérida/Trujillo	1989	200,400
Cerro Saroche	Lara	1989	32,294
Turuépano	Sucre/Monagas	1991	70,000
Mariusa	Delta Amacuro	1991	331,000
Ciénaga del Catatumbo	Zulia	1991	250,000
Parima-Tapirapecó	Amazona	1991	3,420,000
Rio Viejo	Apure	1992	68,200
Tirgua	Cojedes	1992	91,000
El Guache	Lara	1992	16,700
Tapo-Caparo	Táchira	1993	205,000

- Total Area in National Parks = 12,980,512 hectares = 14.16% of National Territory.
- Total Area National Territory = 91,644,500 hectares = 916,445 square kilometers.
  (One hectare = 2.47 acres.)

I - 5. *Dos and Don'ts*

ON HEALTH

What precautions should you take prior to and during your visit to the hinterlands of Venezuela? What endemic illnesses exist here? In trying to ensure that you have a pleasant, uneventful visit, I'll endeavor to list here all necessary precautions I can think of, as well as things that may be health hazards in this country.

Common sense and prevention are very important, because in the field, medical help is almost non-existent. In the larger cities, you can find excellent medical doctors and private hospitals, with standards comparable to U.S. or Europe. In all private clinics and hospitals, you are requested to make a deposit (cash or credit card) as soon as you enter, therefore, I recommend that you buy foreign medical coverage from your local insurance company.

The first thing, of course, when traveling to any tropical region in the World, is that you should have your Yellow Fever and Tetanus vaccines in order. Then, there is Malaria, which is definitely becoming more prevalent worldwide, since the *Plasmodiums* are getting smarter and more impervious to traditional medications. Venezuela is and has always been a Malaria country. The areas to be most careful about in this respect are south of the Orinoco River (where Riverine Malaria occurs) and the far eastern regions (eastern Sucre and Monagas). You should buy your preventive medicine before coming, for it is a damned nuisance to secure anti-malarial pills here, and take it strictly according to directions before, during and after your trip[1].

Hepatitis A, sometimes called Travel Hepatitis, is common all through the Tropics, but now there is a new vaccine, which protects you for 10 years. Ask your physician.

Bilharzia is avoided by not swimming in contaminated rivers - especially near populated areas. In the deep interior if you are sleeping under thatched roofs be sure to use a mosquito net, thus avoiding Chagas disease.

For Leichmaniasis, which is a sand fly-transmitted illness, the best prevention is long pants, long-sleeved shirts and repellent. The sand flies that carry this disease belong to the genus *Phlebotomus*. They are crepuscular, tend to fly near the ground, and are found mainly in sandy areas and near the bases of big, buttress-rooted trees. The few cases of this illness that I have heard of proceed from Amazonas and Bolívar, although there are some pockets of endemism along the central coast. As the insect flies near the ground, shorts are not always the wisest of apparel.

Tropical insects can be exotic, gaudy, bizarre, enormous, tiny... They are also abundant, ubiquitous and incredibly varied. Some that look mean are harmless and some that look harmless are... Whew! There are multicolored hairy caterpillars that can cause severe, painful rashes (one fuzzy, beautiful pale yellow species causes such unbelievable level of pain that people have to be hospitalized). An enormous species of ant, found south of the Orinoco, is popularly called "Twenty Four Hours",

---

[1] Editor's Note: I consulted an expert in Malaria from the US Army Center for Health Promotion and Preventive Medicine (Fort McPherson, GA), on this particular point. His advice is - if you are coming for up to two weeks, perhaps it is better not to take the preventive pills. Any more time than that, take the pills!

because the walloping bite it gives takes almost exactly that long to heal. So the best strategy is look where you put your hand, try not to sit on the ground and don't touch! You probably will not see any snakes at all, but just in case, look where you step! It is a healthy practice not to trample on a snake inadvertently. Don't amble around if you are looking through your binoculars, either. That way you will avoid not only stepping on snakes, but also, stepping on cow cakes, falling into ditches, walking into thorny bushes...

In southern Venezuela we have an extremely rare arboreal pit viper - should you find yourself there, check above and around you. Regarding Bush Masters *(Lachesis muta,* popular name *Cuaima Piña),* some crazy scientist in Costa Rica actually put radios on these sweeties to discover where they hang out. He found that they may stay as long as a month by a fruiting palm tree, since they love the spiny rats and other rodents that come to eat ripe palm fruit. The moral of the story: Stay away from fruiting palms.

For those of you who like to hike up mountain streams, be warned that Fers de Lance *(Bothrops* sp., popular name *Mapanare)* are also particularly fond of humid ravines. They like to lie along the banks or on the rocks in the middle of the streams, and they are most active during the early rainy season (May, June). So be careful when hiking around the streams of Henri Pittier, Guatopo, Paria...

In case of a snake bite, the best *immediate* action you can take is to use a venom extractor. With snake venom, as with most venoms, the amount in question is always a crucial factor. If used immediately, the venom extractor helps get rid of a significant portion of the venom, thus increasing survival probabilities until the victim can reach the nearest medical facility. These extractors only cost about $10. My suggestion is to carry one at all times in your rucksack and learn how to use it prior to leaving home[1]. Actually, the worst and most infamous scourge of our wilderness is chiggers. In case you have never encountered them (lucky fellow!), chiggers are not insects but the larval stage of mites, which are small arachnids, members of the Acari family, and thus in the same zoological class as spiders. They are also known as harvest mites or red bugs. Chiggers do not burrow under your skin nor drink your blood. The itch from their bite is caused by an allergic reaction to a tiny tube they form with a secretion from their mouth, which they use to suck up the inner liquids of skin cells. The little darlings!

There are two weapons against chiggers. The first is insect repellents, ranging from the common ones found in any supermarket, to the very specialized Permethrin for your clothes, which is not available in Venezuela. (Can be purchased through Campmor in the U. S.) Another product, Duranon Tick Repellent, is sold by the American Birding Association. Of the common insect repellents available here, my personal favorite is the brand "Avispa", which comes in spray cans, creams or small plastic squirt bottles. In the tropics the spray evaporates quickly and damages the environment so please stick tot he creams or squirts. Avon sells a product called Skin So Soft which you can buy from any Avon representative, that for some mysterios reason, acts as an effective insect repellent while moisturizing your skin!

The second weapon against chiggers is very effective and very inexpensive (we learned it from Robert Clements). Purchase some powdered sulfur from the pharmacy (called *azufre en polvo* in Spanish), put it in an old sock and tie the sock, then store this contraption in a zip-lock bag. Every time you go out in trail or bush, dust yourself around waist and ankles with the sulfur (and don't worry: it does not stain!).

---

[1] Although snakes are no joke, I can say in all sincerity that I have encountered only a handful of them in the more-years-than-I-care-to-say that I've been in the field in Venezuela. Someone told me that only 15% of our snakes are poisonous, compared to, for example, 85% in Australia.

Since the bites itch like mad, everyone has a favorite method of calming down chigger bites. Someone told me recently that taking a garlic capsule a day will keep them away. (As well as other people!) Others use Vitamin B1 (Thiamin) to the same effect... Who knows? My friend Voni Strasser, of the N.E. Pennsylvania Audubon, gave me a tip on what to do with chigger bites - put a drop of green surgical soap on each bite. According to Voni, it works wonders to calm the itching. Another dear friend, Dr. Bill Oberman, of Washington, DC, swears by nail polish remover for the same purpose. I have now taken to buying a liquid soap at any Venezuelan pharmacy called **Betadine**. The bottle says that it is a *Germicida, Bactericida* and *Microbicida*. All I know is that it does calm the itching so I can sleep at night, and best of all - - it is inexpensive!

Aside from those speculative remedies, there are the common-sense precautions: wear long-sleeved shirts and a hat; tuck your pant legs inside your socks or boots; dust with sulfur or spray liberally with repellent (please use pump sprays) around ankles, wrists and waist. Upon returning to your hotel, shower immediately using lots of soap, and when you have been in chigger-infested areas, never wear the same clothes twice without washing them in strong soap and preferably with hot water (if you can get it). Fortunately, we **do not** have Lyme disease in Venezuela.

If you gather from the above that I am paranoid where chiggers are concerned, you are absolutely correct!

One last insect caveat, especially for south of the Orinoco, is to avoid going around barefoot in the field or on the banks of rivers. You may get jigger fleas *(Dermatophilus penetrans)*, here known as *niguas,* embedded under your skin. They are no fun.

I believe I don't need to warn you about drinking water. So much has been written on this subject, that my advice is redundant. Venezuela, though, is not particularly bad in that respect - I would say our bottled water is generally quite safe, and you find it everywhere. The rainy season tends to increase the chances of getting stomach trouble. In one thing Venezuela is the exception, being about the only country in Latin America where it is safe to eat fresh raw vegetables and fruits, and that includes lettuce and tomatoes!

As for swimming in rivers, the rule of thumb is that mountain streams and the rivers and creeks of the Gran Sabana (Canaima National Park) are safe in terms of dangerous fish. The rivers of the Llanos, tempting as they may be in the heat of day, have piranhas, sting rays and electric eels. In Amazonas, people warn about the danger of Candirú, and since it is easily avoided with a stretch swimming suit, never mind whether it is fact or fiction.

One other suggestion - bring those wonderful wax ear plugs for sale at any drug store in more developed countries. There are times, when you are staying at a hotel, that the night you are there is just the night the locals will pick to have a rip-roaring and extremely loud party that lasts until 5:00 a.m., at which time you have to get up! Also, if you are planning to travel by bus around Venezuela, these ear plugs are invaluable aids against the loud salsa music that the drivers love to play at extremely high decibel levels.

One last, and very real, health hazard I wish to emphasize is the sun, specially if this is your first trip to the Tropics. The possibility of sun-stroke should never be taken lightly in Venezuela, particularly in areas of high temperatures and/or scattered vegetation. Wearing a hat, taking drinks often and putting on sun block make a lot of sense.

ON PERSONAL SAFETY

Naturally, when it comes to safety, the same rules apply in Venezuela as elsewhere in the world: never walk on empty or seedy streets of larger cities at night, do not count your money in public and do not leave cash or valuables in your hotel room. Try not to make unnecessary display of objects of value like camera equipment, expensive watches, radios, etc. Aside from these common-sense precautions, you will probably have fewer problems in the interior of Venezuela than you ever would walking in, say, South Beach, Miami. One rule of thumb that I practice when I am alone is to bird where there are houses or people. I would also suggest that you stay on the main roads along the coast and especially in the State of Sucre, unless, of course, you are accompanied by a guide or a local inhabitant.

Since Venezuelan law requires every adult to carry identity papers, never go out without your passport or at least a photocopy of it, otherwise you might end up having a very unpleasant night in a Venezuelan jail, as the local authorities somehow cannot distinguish between illegal aliens and bona fide bird-watching tourists.

Do not leave your car unlocked or your valuables on the seat. If you have an open-type vehicle such as a jeep, do not leave the car parked with your luggage inside in full view. Three British birders lost all their suitcases that way when they went birding inside the University Forest in Mérida, leaving their car behind.

In southern Bolívar do not leave your valuables even in the trunk of the car when you go off for walks. There are many miners and other disreputable characters in that area, who know how to open a trunk in a jiffy, and also know that tourists lock their valuables in it. If you plan to go to the Gran Sabana, make it a point of never stopping where there are miners unless someone stays with the vehicle all the time.

Of late, the U.S. State Department has warned American tourists regarding their personal safety in Venezuela. I do not argue with that position. Yes, Caracas is a dangerous city and so are, to a certain extent, Maracaibo, Puerto Ordaz and Barquisimeto, and so are, as well, all the big cities in the world today, whether it be Miami (where I was robbed), New York, Oklahoma City, Madrid, Tokyo or Paris. One needs to be extra prudent in big cities.

However, I have yet to find a birder who is scared off by warnings regarding the dangers of cities. We don't go to cities, our destination is the field. And it is easy to skip Caracas: plan either to fly, directly upon arrival, to a destination in the interior, or spend your first night in Caracas (or on the coast at Macuto or Caraballeda if and when the hotels reopen after the floods of December, 1999) and fly out to the hinterlands the next day. If you come up to the capital city, see the chapter on Caracas.

One of the cities often unavoidable to birders is Maracay, since the Henri Pittier National Park is a favorite destination. I advise people to be cautious around this particular town. Many areas of Maracay have become a red zone, and there have been muggings of tourists, even near the "fancy" Hotel Maracay before it was closed down, so I don't recommend that birders walk these hotel grounds. However, I have just been advised that the Hotel Maracay is being repaired and will be privatized, in which case I presume that the new owners will have guards.

To bird Henri Pittier, one walks either of the two national roads that cross it. Of course, a stay at the Biological Station to bird the grounds of Rancho Grande is safe and great fun, but if you really want to bird *the park,* you still have to walk the road to Ocumare or the one to Choroni. I am afraid that one of these days a birdwatcher will be robbed while walking those Park roads. In the text on Henri Pittier, I've given several options of places where you can get many of the same birds as in Henri Pittier, including the Cortada de Maya road above Colonia Tovar (see chapter on the State of Aragua), Macarao National Park (see chapter on Caracas) and the Palmichal Hydraulic Reserve, near Bejuma (see chapter on the State of Carabobo).

Car theft is extremely prevalent in Venezuela, and I rather suspect that the various governments have lacked the political will to do something about it. (There is a wonderful Spanish phrase to the effect that if you think badly of something or someone, you will hit the nail on the head - *piensas mal y acertarás*.) In any event, NEVER leave your car unattended and unlocked - not even for 3 minutes.

ON CLOTHES

Regarding clothes, let's start with blue jeans - I find them to be either too hot and heavy for the lowlands or not warm enough for the Andes. Besides, they take forever to dry. Better to buy those marvelous new wash and wear shirts and pants of ExOficio or Columbia. I find them easy to wash in the shower with liquid dish soap, available at any grocery store.

All you shall need for Venezuela are casual clothes, preferably cotton, a sweater or sweatshirt, a water repellent jacket, a swimming suit, a hat and good walking shoes or hiking boots. A pair of sandals (flip-flops or the Teva type) may prove very useful. For the Andes you will need warmer clothes, including a woolen sweater as well as rain gear. A warm sweater also applies for Rancho Grande, the Escalera and the Gran Sabana.

You can buy rubber boots at almost any hardware store outside Caracas, at a reasonable price. If you wear two pairs of socks with rubber boots you protect yourself from chafing, from chiggers and from snake bites (a study made in Cost Rica showed that rubber boots were more effective against snake bites than leather boots). However, I admit that rubber boots are very hot in the lowlands.

As for dress code, the best bet is to aim for conservative (simple slacks, simple shirts) and low profile (leave your Conan-style jewelry, your Schwartzenegger camouflage vest and your baseball cap with the felt moose antlers at home).

ON ARRIVING IN VENEZUELA

A few years ago, the airport in the city of Valencia began to operate internationally with direct flights from Miami. These, and other international flights that service nowadays various airports in Venezuela (Maracaibo, Barcelona, etc.) are a good way of avoiding the frequently chaotic Simón Bolívar International Airport, or Airport of Maiquetía, which serves Caracas (only the public officials use Maiquetía's official name).

When coming to Venezuela from Miami or even New York, be at the airline desk at least two hours ahead of flight time. You will soon see why -- as a rule, every returning Venezuelan must bring back some 3 to 6 large suitcases and boxes containing computers, microwave ovens, baby carriages, even satellite dishes!

▷ When meeting someone at Maiquetía, a good place to agree to meet is the TURISOL booth. You'll find it easily, across the hall as you come out of customs, next to one of the five street entrances.

As I stated above, Maiquetía can be quite anarchic, partly because many a returning resident will be met by at least four or five members of his immediate family, and partly because you often find four or five international flights arriving almost simultaneously. On Sundays, the ride up to Caracas was previously hindered by a million or so Caraqueños clogging up the highway as they returned from the beach. Unfortunately, since the floods of December, 1999, the cities of La Guaira, Catia La Mar, Macuto, etc. along the central coast are practically in the same condition as shortly after the floods. The Central Government has done little or nothing to improve the infrastructure. As of this writing, May, 2001, there are only two hotels open along the coast, and Venezuela Audubon has been arranging for their tourists to be met at the airport and brought to Caracas for overnighting. One important point, do **NOT** under any circumstances speak to anyone who may address you as you are looking for your driver. The Audubon usually requests their drivers to carry a copy of the Phelps book *Guide to the Birds of Venezuela* or some written identification on their letterhead paper.. These are identifying marks that the crooks find very difficult to duplicate. Should you so desire, the Audubon will arrange to have their free-lance driver pick you up at the airport and take you to your destination. He will also take you back to the airport for your flight to the interior.

Another important warning is to hold on to your documents, and keep them in your hands. Never put them down on a counter and turn your attention away form them.

ON TAXIS AND BUSES

I take this opportunity to recommend my favorite free-lance driver Maximino Pozo (otherwise known affectionately as Mino). He is Chilean, is completely responsible and in spite of the fact that he does not speak English, I have known him to solve incredible problems for tourists who did not speak Spanish. I do not know how he does it, but Mino has my complete confidence and faith in his ability. He can arrange to pick you up at the airport or take you there, and better yet, take you to Rancho Grande, to Palmichal or wherever. Ask the Audubon to have him meet you. Telephones: (0) 212-963-2848, (0) 414-325-2595; Fax: (0) 212-963-5884.

If you are not being met, at the present time there is now a desk inside the Terminal where you pay the indicated price for your trip and are then ushered by a uniformed employee to your taxi. How long this excellent innovation will be in force is the $ 64 question. Otherwise, go straight out to the street to look for an official taxi with a yellow, as opposed to a white, license plate, but first agree on the price before even allowing them to put your suitcase in the trunk. You pay at the end of the ride, and **you are not expected to tip taxi drivers.**

Taxis at Maiquetía can be quite a problem. Far from being fair dealers, a good many of them could easily classify in the shark category. So, in the event the new system is no longer in effect, before taking a cab at the airport, you might inquire at the tourist desk in the hope that the sweet, young things there have a clue as to the reasonable cost of a taxi to your destination, and then, be sure to agree on the price before getting yourself or your suitcases in. The average charge would be about $22.

If you plan to go anywhere by taxi from your hotel, your best bet is to ask the desk attendants not only to hire one but to tell you the price in advance. This will give you a price range for the next rides you hire.

Also at Maiquetía, the bus service to Caracas is quite good. However, the blue and white striped public buses only leave when they are full, so check to see how many seats are left. The bus will take you at least 40 minutes and only cost about $ 3. With a good tip ($ 5 per bag), you can easily arrange for porters to take your bags to the bus stop, which is just a short walk away towards the left as you exit from the bottom level of the International Terminal. At the Caracas end, the bus terminal is near the complex of buildings known as Parque Central (very close to the Hilton Hotel), where you can always find taxis to take you to your local hotel. This will be a slower but far cheaper means of transport.

One line of buses which may prove convenient to birders is the excellent and rather luxurious **Aeroexpresos Ejecutivos**, www.aeroexpresos.com.ve, which runs a service between Caracas and Maracay, Valencia, Barquisimeto, and Puerto La Cruz. These are luxury buses, which you may use to get to any of these cities and take your rental car from there. Their office and bus station is located on Avenida Principal de Bello Campo, Quinta Marluz, next to the Foro Romano Restaurant. It is a good idea to purchase tickets in advance. Phone: (0) 212-266-2321, fax: (0) 212-266-9011, info@aeroexpresos.com.ve. Be sure to take a sweater for these buses as the air conditioning is set at the highest level.

There are also the **Expresos del Llano** buses that cover practically the whole country. If you are traveling to eastern Venezuela, these leave from the corresponding terminal in eastern Caracas. For the Llanos and western Venezuela, they leave from the Terminal de la Bandera. (Confusing, isn't it?)

In recent years, some adventurous young (and not so young) birders have come to bird Venezuela, using the inter-city system of buses as their single means of transportation. Other than knowing that it is quite extensive and reaches almost every corner of the country, I have very little experience with the bus network. I advise anyone planning such a trip to buy the most recent edition of the excellent South American Handbook, or the Lonely Planet's "Travel Survival Kit" for Venezuela. I do suggest, however, that you bring the aforementioned ear plugs with you, because rare indeed is the bus that does not have music blaring out. Also bring a warm sweater as it seems a rule of the road that the air-conditioning must be at a level equivalent to my deep freezer. One of the most irksome quirks of the Expreso and Ejecutivo buses is the fact that you cannot see out of the windows since you are not allowed to open the curtains - it might disturb those who are watching the video!

For more information on buses and their schedules, see **Travel Planner for Venezuela** by John Benus. This can be purchased from the Audubon store or from Amazon.com.

With regard to public transportation, I quote from a rather in-depth report by Dr. John van der Woude, of The Netherlands, http://home.woldonline.nl/~jvanderw:

«Looking back on the way we traveled, I think that public transport is a realistic option for a birding trip in Venezuela. Venezuelans travel a lot, but many of them don't have a car. Hence the richness of means of public transport as stated in the beginning of this report. Of course a rental car has the advantage of flexibility. This applies mainly to roadside birding, and only so on a road of reasonable quality. When you leave the car somewhere in the wilderness in order to make a walk in the forest or the fields, you may be bothered about the car all the time. And, if a road to a birding destination becomes too hard to drive on with your rental car (non 4WD of course), you would be better off with public transport of the 4WD kind.

In general minibuses etceteras start early enough in the morning for the birding. Where this is not the case, a private taxi was our alternative, like in Caripe. In several cases you would not need to order the taxi for the way back too, as there will often be porpuesto minibuses or trucks. BTW, a taxi ride in Venezuela is not always fun, as the driver's driving style may differ markedly from your own.

Even when using taxis where needed, public transport will always be cheaper than a rental car, which costs about 80 dollars a day. Well, if you are not bothered about these prices, not bothered about the safety of the car when parked somewhere, then a rental car will be a better option than public transport. But even then, for a superb birding road like in Guaramacal N.P. you will probably need local 4WD public transport anyway. On the other hand, when birding a long and hot road in the Llanos, a car with airco is a valuable thing.

I should not forget one thing that is needed when traveling by public transport in all these different ways, and that is the need for a basic knowledge of Spanish. However, as argued before on BirdChat, this needs be very basic only. For more complicated things like making an appointment with a taxi driver for the next morning, your Spanish vocabulary should be a bit larger than just 20 words of course.»

I have only one comment and that is the fact that in the many, many years I have worked in ecotourism, I have never heard of a rental car being stolen. They may be broken into, especially if you leave any valuables in sight, but not stolen.

ON CAR RENTALS

All the major car rental agencies have franchises in Venezuela and booths at our international airports (Maiquetía, Valencia, Maracaibo, Margarita, etc.). At the airports of the state capitals and major cities in the interior, Budget is the only rental agency that has offices in almost all of them at present time, the exception being Puerto Ayacucho, the capital of Amazonas State. In some areas, such as Mérida, there may be a small local car rental company we trust. In the Puerto Ordaz airport there is Margarita Car Rentals, which works quite well.

During the holiday seasons such as Christmas, Carnival and Easter and during summer vacations (July, August to early September), you may not always be able to get the exact vehicle you wish.

The wisest move is to make the reservation for the car you want from the U.S. or Europe. A new rule of the car rental agencies in Venezuela is that to reserve a vehicle, one must give them a credit card number. Now there is no way that Audubon wants you to send them your credit car number, so make your reservation abroad, and then send the Audubon the reservation number, type of car and amount they are charging you, so Audubon may reconfirm, reconfirm and reconfirm. Hopefully, this will assure you that the exact vehicle you requested will be waiting at the desired place on the specified date and at the agreed price.

Even if Audubon does reconfirm ten times, you may find that upon arrival, the vehicle requested is not available, and they will try to stick you with a more expensive model or not give you the mileage free rate promised you. They are obliged to give you another car for the same price as originally quoted.

Once they give you the car, check that the tires, radiator belts, brakes, clutch, carburetor and hoses are in good condition before you accept it. Make sure the spare tire and jack are in. Not only are the vehicles often in poor condition, but worse yet, even if the price of rental cars in Venezuela verges on the outrageous, the service these companies give is often deplorable. I have a collection of hair-raising tales about rental cars in Venezuela, all with cars from Hertz, Avis, Budget, etc. In a way, I blame the mother companies in the U.S., because they should take better care that their good name is not polluted by the piss-poor performances of their representatives abroad. Actually, it is my personal belief that until something is done about the ridiculous prices charged for rental cars, Venezuela cannot really expect to increase the tourism sector of its economy.

One last cautionary tale about cars for those of you who plan to come for a lengthy trip. A couple of birders from California decided to buy a second-hand car rather than pay the high rental costs. They spent more time in various repair shops than on the road. At the time, exchange controls had been instated in Venezuela, and to add insult to injury, at the end they had a horrendous time, when they sold the car and tried to change the check in bolivars for a check in dollars. Luckily, they did not get saddled with a stolen vehicle, which is a real danger here if you buy a used car off the street.

ON DRIVING

Drive defensively - that's the first rule. Venezuelan drivers do not always obey traffic signals or move in the predictable fashion[1]. Try to remain calm when other drivers are discourteous. Drive with your doors locked, windows closed, air condition on, and don't pick up hitch hikers. **Don't ever drive at night on Venezuelan roads.** Use lots of common sense.

Some signals are cryptic. A driver's arm hanging out the window perhaps means "I'm going to do something", so be careful. An arm waving out of the passenger window on the right may mean the driver is going to move to the right. If someone honks his horn behind you, don't be intimidated. Many Venezuelans, specially taxi drivers, keep a trigger finger on the horn, so they can blow it if they sniff any weakness or hesitation from the guy in front. Pamela (my good traveling pal) claims that Venezuela is the only country she has visited where drivers even honk at police cars if they don't move fast enough!

For driving in Caracas, previous experience as a taxi driver in Calcutta may prove useful. The fact that many streets are sign-less does not help, but when trying to find your way around, always remember that the high mountains are to the north. Many tourists find the Caracas traffic so horrendous that they prefer to take taxis in the city and then fly to their destination in the interior, renting a car in one or another of the state capitals.

When driving up the mountain from the airport towards Caracas, please be very careful. The highway, especially the last segment entering the city, has become an extremely slippery surface due to a serious hazard called the "Black Stain", a fitting name, for it looks exactly like a long oil slick. This is caused by all the old cars, buses and trucks leaking oil onto the roads. With the worsening economic situation, this problem has become far more prevalent, and not only in Caracas.

Some roads in the interior (as well as in Caracas and other cities) are pocked with huge car-swallowing holes that have gone without repair for eons. Notable cases are the road from Camatagua south to El Sombrero in Guárico, the El Baul road, near Hato Piñero in the State of Cojedes and the road from Mantecal to Barinas.

When buying gasoline, get out of the car and watch the meter. Make sure the pump starts at zero, that they put the cap back on, and that you are not overcharged. Now you will be amazed and delighted at the cost of gasoline in Venezuela. I have a Toyota Land Cruiser with a 90 liter tank. It costs me $ 7 to fill the tank! Regarding road maps see the chapter on Useful Information.

After re-reading the above, I wonder why anyone would ever drive in Venezuela. Yet, I have driven here for over 53 years and never had a problem - touch wood!

ON ASKING FOR DIRECTIONS

You will find that most people in the countryside are delighted to be of help in giving directions.

After so many years in Venezuela, I rather suspect that directional dyslexia is an epidemic condition here. When someone tells you to go left, check to see with which

---

[1] Editor's Note: I could not believe my eyes when I read this! Such moderation, such understatement! This is not the Mrs. Goodwin I know. Drivers in this country NEVER obey traffic signals - they are Traffic-signal Blind - and as for moving in the "predictable fashion"... Mary Lou must have had sunstroke when she wrote this. Venezuelan drivers are totally insane. I know - I am one of them.

hand he is pointing, and almost invariably you will find it is the right and vice versa. Follow the direction of the hand.

To the Llaneros, Venezuelan folklore owes two wonderful phrases: the first one is *aquí mismito* (right near here). Whenever they tell you that in the Llanos, you will find the place you were looking for to be a really long way off. From this habit of the Llaneros, comes the second one: *una cuadra llanera* (a llanero block), meaning a grossly underestimated distance. When they tell you some place is only a short ways away, better make sure you have enough gas in the car!

ON ACCIDENTS

In the hopefully remote case that you have an *accidente,* accident, or *choque,* car crash:
1. Keep calm. Don't get the other driver riled up.
2. If at all possible, call the traffic police - *Inspectoría de Tránsito.* It may take them hours to arrive, but if you think there is even a remote chance they will come, do not move your car until they do, even if it is blocking traffic, everyone is honking, and the other driver moves his car. Many of the insurance companies will give you a very difficult time if you do not have a report from the *inspector de tránsito,* traffic cop.
3. Note the license plate number and ask the other driver for his ID card (cédula) number.
4. Call your car rental agency.
5. The police may give you a ticket or citation. They are allowed to examine your license and passport, but are not authorized to keep them. If someone is injured in the accident, even if it is a minor injury, all parties may be detained. Your car may be impounded.
6. Aside from the actual damage to property or persons, collisions with motorcycles are compounded by the fact that most motorcyclists in this country are *mensajeros,* messengers, a breed apart, who feel they have to cluster around their colleague, even if it was he who caused the accident. It is very unnerving to find oneself surrounded by these characters, so keep your cool.

If you have a breakdown, you will find that within minutes everyone in the neighborhood will be looking under the hood with you, giving you gratuitous advice as to what is wrong. In many cases, you know what they say about free advice...

ON NATIONAL GUARDS

This branch of our Armed Forces is in charge, among other things, of guarding our roads, our borders and border crossings, our National Parks and our wildlife. That is the theory. Unfortunately, they are often abusive of their authority and sometimes, quite corrupt.

I have known foreign tourists to be hassled at **Alcabalas.** Alcabalas are permanent check-points, located along the highways at crucial crossroads or near certain towns, and manned by the Guardia Nacional. In most cases, you slow down, they give you a cursory glance and you are waved on. When waved through, I suggest that you limit yourself to nodding or waving in your best Queen Elizabeth imitation. But there is always a possibility that they will stop you. Usually, it is some lower echelon member of the National Guard. If they stop you, show your papers or allow them to check the car without comment. There is no need to be aggressive, surly or servile. Just be serious and realize that the last thing in the world that the soldier wants is for you to demand to see his commanding officer. I have learned not to look them in the eye. As you know, when two animals look each other in the eye, it is almost invariably a threat, so draw your own conclusions.

If you are unreasonably hassled by the National Guard, PLEASE, upon your return home, write a blistering letter to the President, Corporación Venezolana de Turismo, Torre Oeste, Parque Central, Caracas. Ask him how the devil Venezuela expects to develop foreign tourism if the National Guard does not know how to treat tourists courteously (and please again, send Audubon a blind copy so we can pass it on to the newspapers. That is the most effective way to get action, but we would need full details, including date, exact location and, if possible, name of officer involved).

ON HOTELS AND HOTEL RESERVATIONS

There are only several inns in Venezuela to which I'd give 5 stars from the point of view of birders. I do not include Barquilla de Fresa in Bolivar State in this category, because, as one birder put it, Barquilla is not an inn - it is HOME! There is also La Arboleda, a small, friendly inn near the dump of Tucacas in Falcon State. How is it possible to be so close to Tucacas and yet be next to a birding paradise. Casa Maria, near Bejuma in the State of Carabobo, is also excellent. They cater to birders and know what you want. Gradually, other inns are appearing who want to attract birders, and eventually we hope to have a long list to offer tourists.

You will note that I often give hotels or inns anywhere from two to five stars. Now please do not consider that a five star in Venezuela will be the equivalent of the Ritz or similar establishments in more developed countries, but a five star here will be the top shelf of what Venezuela offers.

Several other places are touted as first rate ecotourism destinations. In the text, we have tried to indicate our reasons for not considering them so great for birders.

One of the hitches of a country where nature tourism began to develop only a few years ago, is that an inn which may be excellent this month may suddenly deteriorate badly due to change in management. Also, it has been my experience that as a general rule, inns that are operated by their owners give far better service and food than those operated by employees.

Hotels and inns in Venezuela definitely have their idiosyncrasies. For example, most hotels in lowland areas (the coast, the Llanos) do not have hot water, but you would never miss it: when the mean temperature outside is in the eighties or nineties, you are happy to come inside to a shower at room temperature. Everywhere, the towels they give are no larger than a napkin, so we always take our own. In her book "Guide to Camps, Posadas & Cabins", Elizabeth Kline recommends you also carry an extension cord. I have never found the need for one, but I do carry a flashlight, my own alarm clock and personal soap, usually a small bottle of liquid soap. Venezuelan inns and hotels do not as a rule supply face cloths. Bring your own.

Yet another idiosyncrasy of Venezuelan hotels is that often the hot water is on the right and the cold on the left. If you see the letter "C" that means caliente or hot. "F" means frio or cold, but they are not always so marked.

Then, there is that "curiouser and curiouser" peculiarity of toilets in hotels, restaurants and public rest rooms in Venezuela, especially those outside Caracas, that, for reasons only Ripley knows, the sewage pipes tend to be too narrow. I was recently advised that these places in the interior have septic tanks which are what clog up, and there is no service company that cleans these tanks as in the U. S. Therefore, in order to avoid clogging them up, one should always deposit toilet paper in the waste basket. The majority of public rest rooms throughout Venezuela do not supply toilet paper, so always carry your own little wad in your pocket or rucksack.

There is yet another strange custom in the interior of the country. In Caracas, it seems that everyone goes out to dinner on Sundays and there are hundreds of restaurants open. Just the contrary is the norm in the interior, and for the life of me I cannot understand why. But trying to find a place to dine on a Sunday evening, say in Ciudad Bolivar, is an extremely frustrating experience.

With regard to securing hotel reservations in the interior, things can be a bit complicated. Not only is it necessary to pay in advance, but to do so, one must deposit the payment into the hotel's bank account and then call them or fax them the number of the deposit slip so that they can acknowledge your reservation. (All commercial banks in Venezuela have branch offices in Caracas).

For private lodges such as El Cedral, Piñero, La Arboleda, Barquilla de Fresa, Casa María, Junglaven, Palmichal etc. all arrangements must be made with their representatives in Caracas and with adequate advance notice. You will find their telephone numbers mentioned in the text, or the Audubon can make arrangements for you.

For very small hotels in places such as El Palmar or other out-of-the-way destinations that only birders would visit, a phone call to make the reservation should suffice except during holiday season, but getting that phone call through can be something of an ordeal.

More often than not, hotels and inns require payment when registering.

You are birders and will undoubtedly want to leave the hotel or inn about 5:30 a.m. Always advise the desk clerk or owner of the inn of your departure time the night before and find out who will have the key to let you out at that ungodly hour.

If you have not paid in advance, many inns and hotels in Venezuela charge anywhere from 5% to 15% for the privilege of honoring your credit card, in spite of the fact that it is illegal to do so. The small hotels in remote little towns will only accept cash. However, I do not recommend that you go tramping all over the country with a load of cash. Consequently, whenever possible, it is better to secure your reservations through the Venezuelan Audubon.

The Society has a license to operate as a Travel & Tourism Agency, and have an ecotourism department, specializing in birders, that was granted the only non-profit status ever given to a tourist agency by the Venezuelan IRS. The funds raised by this department go towards supporting their research and activism projects, aimed at preserving the very habitats you are visiting.

The Society needs funds to carry on efforts to save coastal wetlands and rain forests, protect the national parks, etc. Please be assured that the Venezuelan Audubon is most willing to help the free and individual traveler - especially if he or she is a bird watcher. Should you request their help in paying reservations, PLEASE try to give them ample advance notice.

USING ATMS IN VENEZUELA

I am greatly in debt to Mr. Stauffer Miller of Massachusetts for this invaluable information. Get a **CIRRUS** card from your bank, and use it in Venezuela to withdraw cash from your checking account back home. That way you will not need to carry so much cash on you at any one time. It is quite easy to use the ATMs in the Venezuelan airports, and probably the best place to do so for any number of reasons.

ON SLEEPING IN HAMMOCKS

Many (I would say most) birding tourists are totally discouraged of staying at places if the only mode of sleeping accommodation is hammocks. This is a self-imposed limitation that should be overcome, because you may miss some of the most breathtakingly beautiful scenery, places and birds. I would like to take a moment than, to explain to my readers about hammocks.

I personally believe that a hammock is the greatest invention since fire, and there is nothing in this world as delicious as lying in a hammock all cocooned in the mosquito net, and gently drifting off to sleep looking up at the stars and listening to nightjars nearby and owls in the distance. Hammock are also cooler and you are better protected from mosquitoes and other bugs... Especially bedbugs, although that is something I have never come across in Venezuela!

Many people who try for the first time to sleep in a hammock find the experience rather daunting and pass a sleepless night. I am convinced that those first-timers are subconsciously afraid of falling and consequently tighten up their muscles, thus making it impossible for them to relax into a deep sleep. To rest in a hammock, you should adhere to the following rules:

- Always lie diagonally, that is, at an angle of more or less 45° to the line from hang post to hang post.
- Relax, you have as much chance of falling from it in your sleep as you have of falling from a bed.
- You can lie on your back or on your side. I even know of some lunatics (Clemencia Rodner, my editor, for example) who sleep on their tummies!
- If you use a pillow, by all means, bring one! I always use a small one.
- No matter where you are in Venezuela, there is always a significant drop in temperature in the early hours before daybreak. That is the biggest *real* problem of a hammock. I solve it by placing my light-weight sleeping bag inside the hammock, but the traditional manner is to *wrap* yourself in a sheet or blanket.

Most Venezuelan campers will take hammocks and mosquito nets with them, even if they take a tent, and will wear a t-shirt and gym pants as pajamas.

ON REQUESTING THE HELP OF THE VENEZUELAN AUDUBON

Please indicate what level of accommodations you wish - first class, average or as inexpensive as possible. Even if they are first class, your accommodations may not be up to the standard you are accustomed to in Europe or North America. But you are not coming to Venezuela to spend your time in hotels and our birds and natural areas do not take second place behind those of any other country - they are all first class, five stars, premium. Just wait and see!

It would also be of great help if you were to advise the Audubon's Ecotourism Department what kind of a birder you are - hard-core or just a general bird lover. If they know your level of obsession with birding time, they will be able to make better suggestions for your itinerary. And if you are after any particular species, please say so. The Venezuelan Audubon cannot guarantee anything, but they will certainly give you their best directions!

In many of the areas, such as Mérida, Henri Pittier N.P., Maracaibo, the Gran Sabana, the Audubon can assist you in securing local birding guides, some of whom speak English.

Venezuela is in a terrible inflationary spiral. Therefore, prices mentioned will probably have changed when you come to visit us. The problem we are finding is that, due to inflation, the hotels in Venezuela will not honor their original quote. If they make reservations for you in July for your visit in December, you should count on an increase by the time you arrive.

Another recent development is the 14.5% so-called "luxury tax" on all goods and services (including hotels and meals) which is nothing but a sales tax with another name, because you get slapped with it even when buying postal stamps. We never used to have any form of sales tax, mostly because oil revenues made it unnecessary. But our governments have been disastrous administrators! I have still to figure out what we are getting in return for this tax.

Nevertheless, with the exception of the international class five-star hotels, I believe that you will find Venezuela to be cheaper than many other countries you may have visited.

ON PHONE CALLS

Since the privatization of the telephone company in 1992, both national and international telephone communications have become more expensive in Venezuela. The service however, has improved, although not with the speed that we all would wish. At the Audubon, they try to communicate by e-mail whenever possible, or send letters up to be posted in the U.S. with anyone going north. Whenever you wish to communicate with them, though, I recommend that, if at all possible, you fax or e-mail, because the Venezuelan mail service is very much of a disaster, particularly with incoming mail. There is the story of a sweet young newcomer who asked "How is the mail service in Venezuela?" The response form the local expert was "There isn't any!"

If you need information in a hurry and wish Audubon to respond by fax, please cover the cost of the fax they send you, or give them a telephone number where they may call collect. They try very hard to give service to all those requesting help and information, but just cannot afford to make overseas calls. They do have email, so you can communicate with them at: **audubon@audubondevenezuela.org**

Once in Venezuela, if you need to make a telephone call, the quickest and cheapest would be to buy a magnetic telephone card, *Tarjeta Telefónica,* which are sold at most pharmacies, at airport shops, and often by street peddlers who announce them *"Telefonicas!!... Telefonicas!!..."* Look for the CANTV sign on the front of pharmacies and shops. These come in amounts varying from Bs. 3,000 to Bs. 5,000. You can then use them to make phone calls from the public telephones found on the streets or at many of the hotels. Furthermore, it is now possible to use AMEXCO for your overseas calls, and CANTV, the National Telephone Company has finally started issuing magnetic cards for international calls.

Never make a telephone call from your hotel room if you can avoid it, because the hotel will charge ten times the cost of the call. We had an English tourist who made a 9 minute call through his hotel to London and it cost him £ 60!

☞ And remember that when calling long distance, for in-country calls, you dial 0 and the area code; for international calls, you dial 00 and the country code. All calls to mobile phones (codes 0414, 0412 & 0416) are long distance, except from a mobile phone of the same code.

ON CREDIT CARD FRAUD

It is a sad reality everywhere that credit card fraud is on the increase. Venezuela has not escaped the trend. I particularly want to warn you about using credit cards at the fancy hotels in the big cities. Just recently a friend of mine used her Visa card to pay her bill at the Paseo Las Mercedes Hotel in Caracas (a 4-star hotel). Upon her return to the U.S., Visa called to ask if she had charged $2,000 for Avensa airline tickets to her card during her stay in Venezuela! As she only used her card once, it was obvious what happened. Watch the person making out the credit voucher to be sure he or she makes only one voucher, and be sure that you tear up all the carbons. I would be greatly surprised if you were to have this kind of a problem at any of the little inns in the interior of the country.

ON EASTER AND CARNIVAL (AND MAYBE CHRISTMAS)

With a climate that is as close to perfect as you can find anywhere on the planet, Venezuelans don't ever suffer from spring fever. But twice a year, they catch an ailment that must be a close relative of that well-known good-weather madness. There is an unwritten law here that everyone must leave home between Palm Sunday and Easter Sunday to go to the beach, the Gran Sabana, the Llanos, the mountains - any place, but just go! It is a veritable stampede.

As a result, all hotels are booked, it is impossible to secure airline reservations; no cars are available to rent and so on. You can't even find a dentist if you happen to have a toothache! In short - it is better to come either before or after, but not during Easter Week or the Carnival holidays. To a lesser degreee, this situation has now also spread to the week after Christmas and the first week of the year. With sufficient advance notice, the best alternative at those times is to stay at the lodges and camps.

SUMMING IT ALL UP

In his book the "Travel Planner for Venezuela" John Benus has given some excellent pointers, which I quote below:

ALWAYS:
- Settle on the price of a taxi or boat ride before getting in and always pay at your destination.
- Slow down and stop until signaled to proceed by the National Guard at check points or border crossings where you see the sign saying "Alcabala. "
- Take your passport and tourist card when traveling throughout the country.
- Observe what the locals are wearing; for instance, it is not customary for men to wear shorts in Caracas.
- Ask permission before taking photos of people or their children.

NEVER:
- Assume that a restaurant, store or hotel accepts dollars, travelers checks or credit cards. It is best to ask before you order or use their services.
- Carry more money than you need for that day or evening.
- Take more than 2 hours of direct sun and not between 11 a.m. to 2 p.m. & always use sun screen
- Tip a taxi driver. It is not customary in Venezuela

LAST CAUTIONS

Finally - for heaven sakes - **do not lose your Tourist Card**, the little piece of white cardboard which was stamped by Immigration when you arrived. You must return it upon departure.

Be sure to carry 2 or 3 photo copies of your passport, drivers license and credit card, and note down the numbers of your traveler's checks.

In the complaints we receive from tourists, the two topics mentioned most often are car rental agencies and the garbage strewn all over, especially in national parks. You cannot help us with the second problem, for it is a matter of environmental education, which our politicians have never considered a priority. But you certainly are in a position to put pressure on the international car rental companies, so they in turn put pressure on their local agencies. If you receive poor service from Hertz, or

Avis, or Budget, or any of the franchised car rental companies, write to complain! (And send us a copy!)

In the event you have not previously traveled in the third world, please do not expect things to be the same here as at home. You will find that our telephone system is not as efficient as yours. Our mail is delivered by tortoises, if ever it reaches us. Road signs are almost nonexistent and drivers are all reckless. Garbage is simply ignored. But when you begin to summarize the positive points, the scale quickly tips toward the positive side - it is a beautiful country, the birds are magnificent, the scenery wondrous, the people in the interior just great. Come with an open mind and an open heart, and you will have a ball!

Handsome Fruiteater

Section II

CENTRAL VENEZUELA: THE COASTAL RANGE

Country and Regional Endemics:

Band-tailed Guan
Northern Helmeted Curassow
Venezuelan Wood-Quail
Plain-flanked Rail
Red-eared Parakeet
Green-tailed Emerald
Buffy Hummingbird
Copper-rumped Hummingbird
Violet-chested Hummingbird
White-tipped Quetzale
Groove-billed Toucanet
Black-throated Spinetail[1]
Crested Spinetail
Guttulated Foliage-gleaner
Great Antpitta
Scallop-breasted Antpitta
Scalloped Antthrush[2]
Caracas Tapaculo*
Golden-breasted Fruiteater
Handsome Fruiteater
Venezuelan Flycatcher
Venezuelan Bristle-Tyrant
Venezuelan Tyrannulet[3]
Orange-crowned Oriole
Rufous-cheeked Tanager
Fulvous-headed Tanager
Trinidad Euphonia
Black-faced Grassquit
Red Siskin

---

* Recent splits
[1] Previously called Rufous Spinetail.
[2] Previously called Rufous-tailed Antthrush
[3] Previously called Paltry Tyrannulet.

II - 1. Caracas & its Outskirts

GENERAL DIRECTIONS

Flying into the Caracas Airport

Nowadays, international airports in Venezuela include not only the Caracas Airport (generally known as Maiquetía, but officially called Simón Bolívar), but also the airports of Valencia, Maracaibo, Porlamar (on Margarita Island) and a few others.

By and far, the majority of tourists arrive at the Caracas Airport, which is situated on the coast, some 20 km over the mountains down from the city itself. From there, depending on your schedule and your plans, and hopefully when the hotels open up again along the central coast, you may choose to overnight by the sea, in the general area the "Caraqueños" call "el Litoral" (the shore), or to climb the mountain and come to town. If you are taking a flight out to the interior the next day, the first option is obviously the better, but as of this writing, July, 2001, only two hotels have reopened along the central coast after the floods of December, 1999, one is located in a dangerous area and the other charges an arm and a leg. At present it is better to come up to Caracas.

On getting to Caracas from the Airport

If you decide to do so, after picking up your rental car, take the road indicating Caracas and/or La Guaira. When the road exiting from the airport joins with another road coming from behind you, get in the right lane. Two very poorly marked right turns will be coming up. For Caracas, take the **first** one, which is a ramp that takes you on an about-face, leading up onto the westward lane of the highway. The toll is presently Bs. 100, but that may change any day. Prior to reaching Caracas, you will go through two rather long tunnels. When you get to the top of the mountain (it is obvious you are entering the city), you will see that the highway divides - a ramp climbs up to a tunnel straight ahead and a lane goes off to a lower lane on the right that leads to El Valle/Maracay. You will want the lower lane if you are going on to the interior, as this will lead you to the highway to Maracay, the Llanos or points west. If you are coming to Caracas, take the ramp going up through the tunnel. You will then take the turn-off to the "Centro/Petare". Please also see the section "On Arriving in Venezuela" in the chapter on Dos and Don'ts.

On getting out of Caracas

To get out of the city in Caracas, you invariably have to get on the "Autopista del Este". Its official name is **Avenida Francisco Fajardo**, but no one calls it anything but Autopista (freeway). If your goal, after leaving the Maiquetía Airport, is to pass through Caracas as fast as possible, you are in luck, because upon reaching the city, the lower road (mentioned above) flows right into the highway leading out of Caracas. The Autopista is the main east-west thoroughfare in the city, famous for its rush-hour traffic jams, but also a place where you may find yourself as if struck by lightning when a pair of Blue & Yellow Macaws glide majestically in front of you over the bumper-to-bumper line of cars.

To reach the Autopista from any of the hotels in town, ask directions at the desk. Once on it, if you are going to Maracay, follow the signs saying "Coche - El Valle - Maracay". If you are heading for Turgua, follow the signs reading "Prados del Este" and "La Trinidad".

Hotels in Caracas (Area Code 0212)

Caracas is a large, modern metropolis, so there is ample choice of hotels. To this date, though, we have no Bed & Breakfasts, motels or the variety of alternatives in places to stay that are common in other cities. Here are a few telephones. (If calling from abroad, remember to omit the 0 in the area code). (Ratings as per the Venezuelan Tourist Corporation, commentaries as per that ornery person, Mrs. Goodwin.)

Tamanaco International	★★★★★	909-71 11 Reserv.: 909-70 00	Outrageous prices and poor service.
Caracas Hilton	★★★★★	503-50 00	Your run-of-the-mill Hilton. Main art museums of Caracas at short walking distance.
Eurobuilding	★★★★★	902-11 11 902-21 87	Pool great for watching parrots go to feed at 6:00 a.m. and to roost at 6:00 p.m.
Best Western CCT	★★★★	959-06 11	Pool great for watching parrots go to feed at 6:00 a.m. and to roost at 6:00 p.m. Part of a nice shopping mall.
Centro Lido	★★★★★	952-50 40	Very good business hotel near Centro Lido shopping mall and nice restaurants.
Avila	★★★★	551-51 55 553-30 00	VENT groups stay here. Nice birding on the grounds.
Lincoln Suits	★★★★	762-85 75	Near Sabana Grande shopping area. Good for looking for a good restaurant.
Continental Altamira	★★★★	261-00 04 261-60 19	Near many nice restaurants.
El Paseo Las Mercedes	★★★★	993-66 44	Nice mall, nice pizza place and the Audubon office nearby.
Tampa	★★★★	762-88 31	Efficient. Nice area for walking and shopping. Fifteen-minute walk to Phelps Ornithological Collection.
La Floresta	★★★	263-19 55	Close to Metro station.
Campo Alegre	★★★	265-59 46 265-28 44	Simple and comfy. near good restaurants & eateries
Crillon	★★★	761-44 11	Wonderful Swiss Restaurant on ground floor. Bad area for taking a stroll at night.
Caracas Cumberland	★★★★	762-99 61 762-99 69	Near Sabana Grande shopping area. Very good.
Mont Park	★★★	951-04 95	Not too bad area. Fifteen-minute walk to Phelps Ornithological Collection.
Montserrat	★★★	263-35 33	Large, studio-like rooms with kitchenettes.
Las Américas	★★★	951-73 87	Not too bad an area.
Coliseo	★★★	762-79 16	Has a very good Italian restaurant & is near a nice shopping center. Five-minute walk to Phelps Ornithological Collection.
Savoy	★★★	762-19 71	Good area.

The Hotel Campo Alegre

I have been recommending this not-too-big, not-too-fancy hotel to bird watchers for years, because it is serviceable, has a decent restaurant, and is conveniently located in a relatively safe area of town. It sits on the very edge of the residential neighborhood of the same name, Campo Alegre (the Cheerful Field), and in the borough of Chacao, a bustling area of small shops and working-class condominiums.

To reach the Hotel Campo Alegre from the airport, take the highway to Caracas. Upon reaching the outskirts of the city, branch off towards "Centro - Plaza Venezuela." You will be traveling east to about half way across the valley of Caracas and will eventually pass, on your left, a complex of buildings which includes a pair of extremely tall twin towers. Further ahead, in front of you and also to the left of the highway, you will see three buildings sporting the signs "Pepsi" "Polar", "Phillips" and "El Mundo" on top of them, as well as a nearby pyramidal building with a huge digital clock. On your right is the Botanical Garden. Move into the right lane by the Botanical Garden. You will come to an exit on the right, which has 2 lanes divided by a small concrete hump. Take the left lane, following the sign for Plaza Venezuela. You will immediately come to a stop light. Turn left and angle into the right lane, always following the sign for Plaza Venezuela, which is a large traffic circle around a huge fountain. Keep in the far right lane, going half way around the plaza, in order to turn up the street between the Polar Building and the building with the Phillips sign. You will pass in front of a movie theater on your left. Go up one block and you will come to the Avenida Libertador, where you are obliged to turn right. Immediately angle into the left lane in order to go down the ramp to the sunken section of the avenue. Stay on the right lane and watch for the exit to Campo Alegre. Go up the short ramp and turn left, then take the first street on the right and go down some 4 blocks, straight to the end of the street, where you will see the hotel in front of you. Should you get lost, ask for the Clínica San Atrix in Campo Alegre, which is two blocks west from the Hotel. The entrance to the Hotel's parking garage is in the back, so I suggest that you park right in front of the Hotel, lock the car, register, and then ask them to guide you in order to park the car.

While the Campo Alegre has a fairly good restaurant, just across the street from the Clínica San Atrix there are two good restaurants, one being Greek with the best food I have had since Athens but quite expensive, and the other, immediately adjacent, is an Andean Restaurant with good, hearty Andean food.

For a true taste treat while staying at the Campo Alegre, go around to the back side of the hotel (the same street with their garage) and turn left up the street or towards the mountains. Go two blocks to the end of the street. The last business on the right is the bakery/delicatessen Danubio. This is a Viennese coffee and pastry center and jut the place to have breakfast or a snack. Hopefully, they will have Janczi Rigo when you are there - the most sinfully delicious pastry ever to come out of Hungary. Highly, highly recommended but throw your diet out the window.

To reach the Autopista from the Campo Alegre Hotel, when you drive out of the garage you will have to turn right as it is a one-way street. Go down this street, (Calle Guaicaipuro) turn left at the stop light on the first main avenue (called Francisco de Miranda). Go one short block to the next stop light. Turn right and then turn left at the first opportunity (one block). This is Avenida Libertador. Move diagonally across the traffic in order to turn right at the very next corner.

You are now on the street leading to the Autopista and from here you can go towards the south and the Audubon office in Las Mercedes or Turgua via Prados del Este and Baruta, towards the west to Maracay and towards the east, to the states of Anzoátegui, Sucre, Monagas or Bolívar.

Birding in and around Caracas

The tourist who can afford to take only a few hours for birding from an otherwise busy schedule will be pleasantly surprised to discover that a city with a population of more than 5 million, and with the most convoluted, incessant traffic anywhere, can offer a variety of opportunities for seeing birds, both in its midst and in its immediate vicinity.

A visit to the **Parque del Este** is a good introduction to the birds of Venezuela, and there is a Metro station practically at the northern gate of the park. Even in the parking lot you are likely to see Scaled Dove, Red-crowned Woodpecker, Stripe-backed Wren, Oriole Blackbird, Yellow Oriole, Grayish Saltator, the ubiquitous Blue-gray Tanagers, Yellow-hooded Marshbird, several species of herons - even Scarlet Ibis! - can all easily be seen during a stroll through the park. The most common hummingbird in the Park is the endemic Copper Rumped. The Ferruginous Pygmy-Owl is fairly easy to see as well.

The park is open from 5:00 a.m. to 6:30 p.m. Tuesday through Friday. From 5:00 a.m. to 4:30 p.m. weekends and holidays. On Monday it is open only from 5:00 a.m. to 8:30 a.m. to accommodate the crazy early Monday morning joggers (and birders). I would suggest that you take a taxi. I was there a few weeks ago and was amazed to see some 25 pairs of Chestnut-fronted Macaws as well as Orange-winged and Yellow-crowned Parrots, all screaming their heads off. It is definitely worth getting up for.

Another park that might offer a variety of birds is the **Botanical Garden** right next to the Central University by the Plaza Venezuela. The gardens open at 8:00 a.m. At the entrance, you may be requested to pay a small fee (sometimes they charge, sometimes they don't). During the Northern Hemisphere's winter months, you may find some migrant warblers here. Try to stay in the more open and obviously used areas. I have heard it to be a somewhat unsafe place at times. In any event do not go beyond the installations of the herbarium, and do NOT take any of the trails that go up into the hillside.

Caracas lies in a valley, separated from the sea by the northern branch of the coastal mountain range. Fortunately for all of us, in 1958 the government declared 85,192 hectares of this mountain range a national park. It is known as the **Avila National Park**, and provides us inhabitants of the city with a long network of beautiful trails "right outside our door", so to speak. There are birding possibilities, as well as breathtaking views of the cement jungle below.

If you want to walk into the Park, the safest and easiest way is the Sabas Nieves Trail, which begins at the Décima (10th) Transversal street in the neighborhood called Altamira. Tell the taxi driver to take you to the very old and well-known restaurant Tarzilandia. The entrance to the trail is just a few yards west of the restaurant. This trail is used by hundreds of Caraqueños who hike it every day to keep fit, but even with this mob scene hiking up and down all the time, the birds keep going happily about their business. We took some birding friends there and they counted over 30 species in 3 hours, including Long-tailed Sylph, Green Jay and Rufous-collared Sparrow. If you are fit, this could be a whole-day trip for the 3,000 foot climb up towards "No Te Apures" (a sharply climbing stretch of the trail where you "do not hurry"), La Silla or Pico Occidental during which you could pick up Black-throated Spinetail, Golden-breasted Fruiteater, Caracas Tapaculo as well as some nice cloud forest species.

For a shorter and less strenuous hike, take the low altitude trail which branches off to the right across the stream signposted to Quebrada Quintero. On this trail you might see Band-tailed Guan, Red-eared Parakeet, Copper-rumped Hummingbird, Groove-billed Toucanet, Crested Spinetail and Fulvous-headed Tanager. With luck you may also find Bat Falcon, Long-tailed Antbird, and White-winged Tanager. This is semi-deciduous forest. Rufous Nightjar is here in the evening as well as Mottled and Tropical Screech Owls at night, but personally I would rather you not hang around to see those[1][2].

In the near future, if they are able to secure the funds, the Audubon hopes to be able to publish the checklist of the birds of the Avila as compiled by that very hard-working Yorkshire man, Chris Sharpie.

Turgua

Various birders have asked me where to go birding around Caracas on a week-end. The problem is that on Sundays and all public holidays, during Carnival and Easter Week, every place is packed. The highway to Colonia Tovar is like "forget it!". There are long lines of hikers climbing the trails of the Avila National Park, and the Parque del Este is full of picnickers. I was hard put to think of a place to suggest until I remembered Turgua. I should mention that not even many Caraqueños know where Turgua is, for which I am duly grateful.

The first requisite to go to Turgua is to rent a car. Then go to a panadería and buy yourself some bread, ham and cheese *(pan, jamón y queso)*, some sodas and knick-knacks for a picnic lunch, and off you go.

From the Autopista (the main highway that runs East/West through the city, as mentioned above), take the Prados del Este and Baruta turnoff. After the tunnel near Baruta turn right by the gas station. Count the gas station as 0 km At the next stop light you will actually see a sign indicating "El Placer" and "Los Guayabitos". You continue straight on. At the second stop light veer towards the left in order to go up a narrow, winding road which can have some very slow traffic. Continue to climb and eventually, at 4.1 km after the gas station, on the right you will see the entrance to El Placer and immediately after, take the left turn to Los Guayabitos. Should you pass the Universidad Simón Bolívar on your right, you have gone too far. (There is another way to get to this point and that is to take the Autopista as if you were going west to Maracay and take the ramp off to the right at the top of a very long hill, where there is a sign indicating "Baruta". In that case, you would pass the University on your left and take the next right turn to Los Guayabitos). From here on there is relatively little traffic!

At 5.8 km after you are on the Guayabitos road go right to "El Gavilán" (the word for Hawk in Spanish), down a long winding road, passing the Bodega Bella Vista (a *Bodega* is a small general store). Keep left here. At 8 km go left, and at 10.8 km you come to the road leading to Turgua on your right. Turn right. At 12.3 km I suggest you stop in the driveway on your left to bird the area. At 12.75 km there is an entrance on your right. Try stopping and walking down the dirt road for a bit. This has always been

---

[1] Juanita's Comment: Pamela may be a second-rate birder but she's a first-rate hiker and has hiked a good number of Avila's trails.

[2] And of course, a Comment from Pamela: Juanita's being generous. However, if you are staying in Caracas for even a short time, a trek up the Avila is really worth your while. The Sabas Nieves trail is interesting more for people watching than for birding or as a nature hike. For those, take the other trails. They range from fairly easy to difficult if you intend to reach the top. The trails are terrific, great exercise, there are lots of birds as well as remarkable plants and animals, and you get the sense of being far away from a city of approximately 5 million. On clear days, from the top you can see Caracas on one side and the Caribbean on the other. And, I have never had any safety/security problems. Audubon has a number of guides who know the mountain well and can lead you up there.

a productive area for Collared Trogon and Golden-breasted Fruiteater. At 25.3 by yet another store there is a fork leading to the town of Turgua. Ignore same and go straight until you reach 26.2 km where there is a choice of two dirt roads. Take the one on the extreme left and now your real birding begins, for this dirt road provides the best birding in the whole area. It is passable in a regular car for a few km, and then you can walk further on. Be on the look-out for sloths. If, just out of curiosity, you should take the middle road, you will pass "La Huerta de Doña Jean" and then the entrances to the homes of several American/English families who have settled in that area. Up in there you should see higher-elevation birds such as Swallow-tailed Kite (in June), Black Hawk-Eagle, Scaled Piculet, Olivaceous Woodcreeper, Slate-throated Redstart, Swallow-Tanager (from March to September), Guira Tanager, Hepatic Tanager, Fulvous-headed Tanager (always in a family group) and the Ochre-breasted Brush-Finch.

For birding near Caracas, Turgua makes a wonderful place, where you should be able to spot at least 60 species in a day's birding and, depending on the time of day or year, you may see or hear:

Little Tinamou	Groove-billed Toucanet	Southern Rough-winged
Red-legged Tinamou	Scaled Piculet	Swallow
Black Vulture	Golden-olive Woodpecker	Green Jay
Turkey Vulture	Red-crowned Woodpecker	Rufous-breasted Wren
Swallow-tailed Kite	Smoky-brown Woodpecker	House Wren
Roadside Hawk	Red-rumped Woodpecker	Tropical Mockingbird
Black Hawk-Eagle	Olivaceous Woodcreeper	Orange-billed Nightingale
Solitary Eagle	Buff-throated Woodcreeper	Thrush
Yellow-headed Caracara	Streak-headed Woodcreeper	Yellow-legged Thrush
Bat Falcon	Red-billed Scythebill	Black-hooded Thrush
Rufous-vented Chachalaca	Pale-breasted Spinetail	Pale-breasted Thrush
Pale-vented Pigeon	Stripe-breasted Spinetail	Bare-eyed Thrush
Common Ground-Dove	Crested Spinetail	Long-billed Gnatwren
Ruddy Ground-Dove	Plain Xenops	Rufous-browed Peppershrike
Blue Ground Dove	Great Antshrike	Red-eyed Vireo
White-tipped Dove	Barred Antshrike	Scrub Greenlet
Scarlet-fronted Parakeet	Plain Antvireo	Shiny Cowbird
Brown-throated Parakeet	Long-tailed Antbird	Yellow-rumped Cacique
Green-rumped Parrotlet	White-bellied Antbird	Yellow-backed Oriole
Lilac-tailed Parrotlet	Short-tailed Antthrush	Crested Oropendola
Squirrel Cuckoo	Golden-breasted Fruiteater	Carib Grackle
Striped Cuckoo	Chestnut-crowned Becard	Black-and-white Warbler
Pavonine Cuckoo	White-winged Becard	Tennessee Warbler
Smooth-billed Ani	Lance-tailed Manakin	Tropical Parula
Common Potoo	Tropical Kingbird	Blackburnian Warbler
White-collared Swift	Boat-billed Flycatcher	American Redstart
Lesser Swallow-tailed Swift	Streaked Flycatcher	Slate-throated Redstart
Sooty-capped Hermit	Social Flycatcher	Three-striped Warbler
Little Hermit	Great Kiskadee	Golden-crowned Warbler
Blue-tailed Emerald	Brown-crested Flycatcher	Bananaquit
Copper Rumped Hummingbird	Bran-colored Flycatcher	Swallow-Tanager
White-vented Plumeleteer	Yellow-bellied Elaenia	Blue Dacnis
Collared Trogon	Forest Elaenia	Speckled Tanager
Rufous-tailed Jacamar	Blue-and-white Swallow	Black-headed Tanager

Bay-headed Tanager	Hepatic Tanager	Grayish Saltator
Fawn-breasted Tanager	White-winged Tanager	Streaked Saltator
Blue-hooded Euphonia	White-lined Tanager	Ochre-breasted Brush-Finch
Orange-bellied Euphonia	Rose-breasted Thrush Tanager	Black-striped Sparrow
Blue-gray Tanager	Guira Tanager	Ruddy-breasted Seedeater
Palm Tanager	Fulvous-headed Tanager	Yellow-bellied Seedeater
Silver-beaked Tanager	Common Bush Tanager	Lesser Goldfinch

For birding both the Avila and Turgua, I would like to suggest that you request the Audubon to get you a guide. The time you save by having a knowledgeable Caraqueño showing you the way is well worth his fee. Furthermore, I would personally be happier if you do not go alone to Turgua as it is not as safe as years ago when I first discovered it. In any event there is always safety in numbers. Especially on a Saturday there is also the possibility of going with the group of Venezuelan birders. See below.

A small group of Venezuelan members of the Audubon who are gung-ho birders, who speak English for the most part, try to get out in the field every week-end. Knowing them, I suspect that they would be delighted to have you tag along. Try contacting:

- Guillermo Mendez: gamendezc@hotmail.com
  Phones: (0) 212-235-1314 & 232-6625.
- Marieta Hernandez: mariher@telcel.net.ve
  Phones: (0) 414-923-4478; (0) 212-730-1579 & 730-3889.
- Mary Lou Goodwin: igoodwin@cantv.net
  Phones: (0) 212-412-1270
- Gregory & Marie Luz Urruela: mluzcaille@usa.net .

The Universidad Simón Bolívar
Follow the instructions above where I have mentioned the University. We have found that birding the trails way at the far end of the University can be most rewarding. Also, the area is far safer than many others.

The "Litoral" - Vargas State
The Caraqueños call "Litoral Central" (central shore) the stretch of coast that faces the Caribbean just north of Caracas. Along it, there are several spots that would make an ideal beginning or (even better) finishing chapter to your birding vacation in Venezuela. Places to relax, to see many of our more common birds, to build a memory of the exuberant tropics. Therefore, if you find yourself at loose ends at either the beginning or the end of your trip, I highly recommend you drive due east along the coast. It is wise not to go on week-ends, because you'll find crowds in many places.

Unfortunately, the central coast has not completely recovered from the disastrous floods of December, 1999. Nevertheless, we recently rechecked the whole area, to see if it could be recommended and found that there is no reason you cannot enjoy this beautiful area at least during the dry season.

Universidad Simón Bolívar – Central Coastal Branch
That extremely personable Yorkshireman, Chris Sharpe, has recommended a visit to the USB - "*Nucleo del Litoral Central*" in Naiguatá. Drive east from Maiquetía airport, passing the coastal port of La Guaira, passing as well the previous resort towns of

Macuto and Caraballeda. Look for the entrance on the right side of the road. Go in and park in the car park. To quote from Chris's instructions: "From there, walk behind the buildings and bird the area between the buildings and the mountain. there are abundant trails in all kinds of habitats, from cactus scrub to streamside, to secondary growth. It is a good place." Chris has sent me the following list of the birds he saw in three very short visits, semi endemics are asterisked:

Magnificent Frigatebird	Straight-billed Woodcreeper	Tropical Gnatcatcher
Black Vulture	Pale-breasted Spinetail	Golden-fronted Greenlet
Turkey Vulture	Common Thornbird	Crested Oropendola
Gray-lined Hawk	Barred Antshrike	Yellow-rumped Cacique
Osprey	White-fringed Antwren	Carib Grackle
*Rufous-vented Chachalaca	Lance-tailed Manakin	Oriole Blackbird
Common Ground-Dove	Tropical Kingbird	Tropical Parula
Scaled Dove	Boat-billed Flycatcher	Northern Waterthrush
White-tipped Dove	Rusty-margined Flycatcher	Bananaquit
*Military Macaw	Great Kiskadee	Purple Honeycreeper
Green-rumped Parrotlet	Bran-colored Flycatcher	Blue-naped Chlorophonia - low
Squirrel Cuckoo	Common Tody-Flycatcher	altitude record.
Smooth-billed Ani	Yellow-bellied Elaenia	*Trinidad Euphonia
*Pale-bellied Hermit	Mouse-colored Tyrannulet	Thick-billed Euphonia
Blue-chinned Sapphire	Slaty-capped Flycatcher - low	Blue-gray Tanager
Blue-tailed Emerald	altitude record!	*Glaucous Tanager
Golden-tailed Sapphire	Ochre-bellied Flycatcher	Palm Tanager
*Buffy Hummingbird	Gray-breasted Martin	Silver-beaked Tanager
White-vented Plumeleteer	Southern Rough-winged	White-lined Tanager
Green Kingfisher	Swallow	Blue-black Grosbeak
Rufous-tailed Jacamar	Rufous-breasted Wren	Grayish Saltator
*Russet-throated Puffbird	House-Wren	Sooty Grassquit
Lineated Woodpecker	White-necked Thrush	Black-faced Grassquit

I recently traveled the road from La Guaira (the main port of Venezuela) all the way east to the resort town of Higuerote. Although the road was not paved after Los Caracas, it is in good condition as far as **Caruao** and even as far as the junction with the road to **Chuspa**. If you have a few days at the beginning or end of your trip, do not miss the opportunity to travel this spectacular road and enjoy the area. Rent your car at the airport of Maiquetia and head east, passing La Guaira, Macuto, Caraballeda, Naiguatá, **Los Caracas**. It is a bit difficult to wend your way through Los Caracas, which was originally built as a beach resort for the lower middle classes during the 50s by the dictator, Perez Jimenez, but completely abandoned by recent governments. Don´t fret. Just shout "Osma" to any of the passerbys, and they will point you on your way. As you go up the hill and reach the dryer areas, start birding for Rufous-vented Chachalaca, Military Macaw, White-fringed Antwren, Pearly-vented Tody-Tyrant, Yellow-Olive Flycatcher, Northern Scrub-Flycatcher, Long-billed Gnatcatcher, Golden-fronted Greenlet, Scrub Greenlet, Lance-tailed Manakin, Yellow-breasted Flycatcher, Common Tody-Flycatcher, etc. Gradually, you will be reaching more verdant areas such as **Osma, Todasana, La Sabana** and finally **Caruao**. To pass the town of Osma and continue on the road, turn right by the Posada de Max, because the road here almost folds unto itself.

There is an inexpensive, modest but decent hotel/inn at Todasana called **Hotel Egua**. For reservations call Sr. Baena at (0) 414-245-3118; E-mail: nereika_o@hotmail.com.

This is also an excellent birding area as there are trails up into the hills/mountains for you to follow.

From Los Caracas it is approximately 37 km to La Sabana and yet another 4 km to Caruao. Drive through this last town and further for yet another 4 km to find the Posada (inn) **Agua Miel**, where I recommend you stay for a day or two. It is a most pleasant spot with good food and service, not to mention the birding opportunities. When requesting your reservations mention that you are bird watchers. The owner, Carlos Avendaño, also has property up in the mountain and would probably be willing to have a guide take you there to see all the birds on his farm or "finca."

One of the places I also suggest you bird is on the road to **Guayabal**, a distance of 2 km east from the inn. All told, in this general area, look for:

Least Grebe	Green Kingfisher	House Wren
Magnificent Frigatebird	Rufous-tailed Jacamar	Tropical Mockingbird
Neotropic Cormorant	Red-crowned Woodpecker	Bare-eyed Thrush
Brown Pelican	Crimson-crested Woodpecker	Tropical Gnatcatcher
Black Vulture	Straight-billed Woodcreeper	Rufous-browed Peppershrike
Turkey Vulture	Crested Spinetail	Golden-fronted Greenlet
King Vulture	Common Thornbird	Crested Oropendola
Osprey	Great Antshrike	Yellow-rumped Cacique
Gray-lined Hawk	Black-crested Antshrike	Yellow Oriole
Crested Caracara	Barred Antshrike	Orange-crowned Oriole
Yellow-headed Caracara	Lance-tailed Manakin	Giant Cowbird
Wattled Jacana	Ochre-bellied Flycatcher	Tropical Parula
Solitary Sandpiper	Common Tody-Flycatcher	Northern Waterthrush
Spotted Sandpiper	Pale-eyed Pigmy-Tyrant	American Redstart
Ruddy Pigeon	Yellow-bellied Elaenia	Bananaquit
Scaled Dove	Lesser Elaenia	White-lined Tanager
Ruddy Ground-Dove	Black Phoebe	Guira Tanager
White-tipped Dove	Tropical Kingbird	Silver-beaked Tanager
Brown-throated Parakeet	Streaked Flycatcher	Blue-gray Tanager
Green-rumped Parrotlet	Rusty-Margined Flycatcher	Palm Tanager
White-eared Parakeet	Social Flycatcher	Thick-billed Euphonia
Squirrel Cuckoo	Great Kiskadee	Grayish Saltator
Little Hermit	Yellow-Olive Flycatcher	Black-striped Sparrow
White-chested Emerald	Southern Rough-winged	Lesson's Seedeater
White-vented Plumeleteer	Swallow	Dull-colored Grassquit
White-tailed Trogon	Stripe-backed Wren	Blue-black Grassquit
Amazon Kingfisher	Rufous-breasted Wren	Lesser Goldfinch

Should you happen to have a recording of the Ferruginous Pygmy-Owl, it will work miracles in this general area.

For reservations at Agua Miel, call (0) 212-247-2027 or 934-0349 or contact the Venezuelan Audubon. Reservations are a must for week-ends, but again I recommend that you come during the week. Remind the Audubon to tell Sr. Avendaño that you are bird watchers.

The beaches along this coast are famous swimming places, so be sure to take your bathing suit with you. Following the road, they come in the following sequence: Osma, Oritapo, Todasana, La Sabana, Caruao, Chuspa. If you want to try them, I suggest you carry on to La Sabana, celebrated for the shade of its palms and trees. Caruao has the most famous beach of all, because its river/lagoon and sea are wonderful places to bathe, especially if they have opened the mouth of the river - which they do every few days. Riding the river flow down to the sea is great fun - you will find all the kids in town playing there - but be very careful when you hit the waves. There is a strong undertow. The only problem with the beach at Caruao is the lack of shade trees. The people at Agua Miel can also direct you to other bathing areas, including the "Pozo del Cura" where you would have the possibility of bathing in hot springs along the river. And why not go swimming in the early afternoon? After all, tropical birds take siestas! I have only one caveat for you while swimming; Do not leave personal effects unattended!

The Junquito-Carayaca Road[1]

Considering that some bird watchers travel to Venezuela on a trip not related to bird watching, I have added the following sites for those of you who do not have much time, but are still interested in **the birds of higher altitudes** along our Coastal Cordillera for those interesting endemics, fabulous tanagers, etc.

If you find that you can take a Saturday off to go see some birds - I suggest you grab that free Saturday[2] and your binoculars, and head for an area which is on the way to Colonia Tovar[3], but conveniently closer to Caracas.

Try the following: After by-passing the town of El Junquito, which is about half-way to Colonia Tovar, you will see the **Police School** on the left. From here it is 8.4 km to the junction for **Carayaca**, on the right. Take this road, and 13 km after the junction you will see a small store (previously a general country store but now possibly a tire repair shop) on your left. Although you may not notice it at first, there is also a road coming down from the left. Take a sharp left and go up this road. After 1 kilometer you must veer right. After yet another kilometer there is a dirt road coming in from the right. You stay left and continue on, passing a chicken farm called **Avifertiles**.

Ruddy Pigeon	Plain-backed Antpitta	Brown-capped Vireo
Ruddy Ground-Dove	Rusty-breasted Antpitta	Shiny Cowbird
Blue Ground-Dove	Golden-headed Manakin	Yellow-backed Oriole
White-eared Parakeet	Chestnut-crowned Becard	Black-and-white Warbler
Green-rumped Parrotlet	Black-and-white Becard	Tropical Parula
Squirrel Cuckoo	Tropical Kingbird	Slate-throated Redstart
White-collared Swift	Boat-billed Flycatcher	Three-striped Warbler
Chestnut-collared Swift	Streaked Flycatcher	Bananaquit
Chaetura sp.	Golden-crowned Flycatcher	Rusty Flower-Piercer
Sooty-capped Hermit	Dusky-capped Flycatcher	Speckled Tanager
Green Violetear	Cinnamon Flycatcher	Golden Tanager
Sparkling Violetear	Olivaceous Flatbill	Bay-headed Tanager
Violet-headed Hummingbird	Rufous-lored Tyrannulet	Beryl-spangled Tanager
Golden-tailed Sapphire	Mountain Elaenia	Black-headed Tanager
Copper-rumped Hummingbird	Caracas Tyrannulet	Blue-naped Chlorophonia

---

[1] **This is the same road that goes to Colonia Tovar, El Limón** and **Puerto Maya.** For those sites, see Chapter on the State of Aragua in this Section.

[2] Avoid doing this on Sundays - the heavy traffic on this road going to and coming from Colonial Tovar is obnoxious.

[3] In the State of Aragua Chapter, in the segment on Colonia Tovar, you will find detailed instructions on how to get from Caracas onto the road to Colonia Tovar.

Collared Trogon
Groove-billed Toucanet
Scaled Piculet
Golden-olive Woodpecker
Smoky-brown Woodpecker
Olivaceous Woodcreeper
Strong-billed Woodcreeper
Buff-throated Woodcreeper
Red-billed Scythebill
Pale-breasted Spinetail
Stripe-breasted Spinetail
Crested Spinetail
Foliage Gleaner
Scalloped Antthrush
Black-faced Antthrush

Slaty-capped Flycatcher
Blue-and-white Swallow
Green Jay
Whiskered Wren
House Wren
Gray-breasted Wood-Wren
Orange-billed Nightingale
Thrush
Yellow-legged Thrush
Glossy-black Thrush
Black-hooded Thrush
Pale-breasted Thrush
White-necked Thrush
Long-billed Gnatwren
Rufous-browed Peppershrike

Blue-hooded Euphonia
Orange-bellied Euphonia
Blue-winged Mountain Tanager
Blue-gray Tanager
Palm Tanager
Blue-capped Tanager
White-lined Tanager
Fulvous-headed Tanager
Common Bush-Tanager
Grayish Saltator
Streaked Saltator
Ochre-breasted Brush-Finch
Rufous-collared Sparrow
Lesser Goldfinch

Albeit this is a dirt road, it is in good enough condition that you can bird it in a normal car, at least in the dry season. In the rainy season, you may have to leave your car about half-way down the mountain and bird the rest on foot. I birded it again in mid June 2000, after some 5 or 6 years of absence. There has been some intervention by small farmers, but there are still many tree ferns and large trees. Even after the heavy rains of May the road was passable. Actually, the worst part of the road is from the turn off after the main highway until you pass Avifertiles. And the delight of birding here was that in the approximately 5 hours we spent walking the road, only 4 cars passed us. And this was on a Saturday! What a relief compared to the traffic on the Rancho Grande road in Henri Pittier National Park! Of course, we were lucky in that the day was overcast and being the start of the nesting season, everyone and his uncle were singing, nest building, setting up territories. We started birding at 4.6 km after turning off the main road even before the main forest. During our walk along this road we saw:

Black Vulture
Turkey Vulture
Sharp-shinned Hawk
White-tailed Hawk
Broad-winged Hawk
Black-and-white Hawk Eagle
Black Hawk-Eagle
Yellow-headed Caracara
Rufous-vented Chachalaca
Band-tailed Pigeon
Ruddy Pigeon
White-tipped Dove
Smooth-billed Ani
White-collared Swift
Chestnut-collared Swift
Vaux's Swift
Brown Violetear
Green Violetear
Sparkling Violetear
Green-tailed Emerald

Speckled Hummingbird
Bronzy Inca
Long-tailed Sylph
Collared Trogon
Groove-billed Toucanet
Scaled Piculet
Golden-olive Woodpecker
Red-crowned Woodpecker
Smoky-brown Woodpecker
Olivaceous Woodcreeper
Red-billed Scythebill
Pale-breasted Spinetail
Stripe-breasted Spinetail
Black-throated Spinetail
Crested Spinetail Montane
Foliage-Gleaner
Spotted Barbtail
Streaked Xenops
Slate-crowned Antpitta
Chestnut-crowned Antpitta

Caracas Tapaculo
Golden-breasted Fruiteater
Rufous-tailed Tyrant
Tropical Kingbird
Variegated Flycatcher
Golden-crowned Flycatcher
Social Flycatcher
Great Kiskadee
Pale-edged Flycatcher
Yellow-bellied Elaenia
Mountain Elaenia
Caracas Tyrannulet
Brown-chested Martin
Blue-and-white Swallow
Green Jay
Sedge Wren
Mustached Wren
Gray-breasted Wood-Wren
Andean Solitaire
Orange-billed Nightingale Thrush

Yellow-legged Thrush
Glossy-black Thrush
Black-hooded Thrush
Pale-breasted Thrush
Rufous-browed Peppershrike
Brown-capped Vireo
Shiny Cowbird
Yellow-backed Oriole
Eastern Meadowlark
Blackburnian Warbler
American Redstart
Slate-throated Redstart
Black-crested Warbler
Three-striped Warbler

Bluish Flower-Piercer
Masked Flower-Piercer
White-sided Flower-Piercer
Rusty Flower-Piercer
Speckled Tanager
Bay-headed Tanager
Beryl-spangled Tanager
Black-capped Tanager
Black-headed Tanager
Blue-naped Euphonia
Orange-bellied Euphonia
Blue-winged Mountain-Tanager
Blue-gray Tanager
Blue-capped Tanager

Fulvous-headed Tanager
Oleaginous Hemispingus
Common Bush-Tanager
Black-faced Tanager
Plush-capped Finch
Buff-throated Saltator
Streaked Saltator
Golden-bellied Grosbeak
Ochre-breasted Brush-Finch
Yellow-bellied Seedeater
Slaty Finch
Wedge-tailed Grass-Finch
Rufous-collared Sparrow
Lesser Goldfinch

Macarao National Park

Gustavo Rodriguez, one of our most competent and valued biologists and bird guides, has been investigating this Park for a number of years, and thanks to his work, the Audubon has now been able to publish the checklist of the birds of Macarao National Park.

If you are planning to visit Colonia Tovar, going there from Caracas, it is very easy to find the Park. At 8.5 km after passing the Police School on the western end of Junquito mentioned above, you pass the crossroads to Carayaca, and continue straight on towards Colonia Tovar. Going along the crest of the mountain, at 4.8 km after the Carayaca junction, you will pass the Hotel Campesino. Next, at 7.6 km after the Hotel you will see a road on your left leading to **El Jarillo**. Turn here, and head towards this sprawling "village", which has grown fast in recent years from the agricultural overspill of Colonia Tovar.

The road is paved and is a perfectly good, all weather road. I suggest you stop occasionally to bird along the higher slopes for such birds as the Black-throated Spinetail, Caracas Tapaculo, thrushes, flower-piercers etc. If you are fortunate you may see flying Rhinoceros Beetles, which are harmless, very abundant here and a real sight. Actually, one of the principal birding areas is found along the first 10 km. from the main highway. This upper part of Macarao National Park (El Jarillo road) is excellent for higher mountain birds:

There are many species in the Park. Here are some of my sightings: Relatively close to the main road (approximately 1 to 2 km. in) I have seen the Spotted Barbtail. One very early December morning at 4.5 km from the main road, I saw a family of Plush-capped Finches that immediately responded to play back. I rather suspect that this species must nest in September/October. At Km. 5.4 a Masked Flower Piercer was singing in mid May. There is a small shrine at Km. 6.3. Also on the same early December morning I recorded here not only the White-sided Flower Piercer singing his head off but also the Slate-crowned Antpitta. While the latter responded to play-back, he would not come out. Across the road from the shrine and a bit closer to the main highway, there is a trail with a gate (easily passed through). Here we saw and heard a pair of Green-and-Black Fruiteaters in mid May. 2001. Here also were the Black-throated Spinetail, Bluish Flower Piercer and Streaked Tufted Cheek. The Caracas Tapaculo was making a racket and after a while did come out to our play-back.

The other main birding sites of the Park are located approximately 20 to 30 minutes further on from the upper area. At approximately 10 km from the entrance road you will come down a steep hill. Take a sharp right at the sign for Restaurant Gran Jarillo. at 12.8 km turn left and continue on for yet another 9.5 km where you will come to the house of the Park Guard. (The current guard is called Yoni.) Look for the Inparques flag. Drive a few yards further on in order to make a U-turn and go up the dirt road to the side of the house. You will have to show your Parks permit to the Guard (see chapter on National Parks) and request him to lower the chain. Continue along this dirt road for 2 km. where you will see the "Casa Nazareth", a convent retreat far from the maddening world up here in the mountain. Park before the Retreat and start walking. Should any of the Nuns reproach you for being there, show her your Parks permit and explain that you are bird watchers. At first you will be going along a wood with excellent birding, but then you come out onto a burnt area by the signs "Boca de Visita", "Toma 19", "Puente 9". Just a few steps further along from these signs look for Sedge Wren and Rufous-tailed Tyrant. If you continue walking along these grassy slopes, you may find Wedge-tailed Grass-Finch and Stripe-tailed Yellow-Finch, and should you walk far enough, you will come into yet another tract of woods. But if you find that the road is dry when you get to the signs, you go back to pick up your car and drive to the end of the road or what looks like the end. On the right is an old fence. Park to one side of the fence, squeeze through and past all the burnt-over area until you reach a beautiful, mature forest, where it is easy to spend a few hours birding along this forested road.

After birding the road from Casa Nazareth, go back to the Inparques station and continue along the main mountain road. There is a junction at 2.6 km after the Park Guard's house. Go left. After this left turn, drive on 1.8 km until you see a house on the right and a chain across a dirt road to the left. This road leads to yet another area of the Park, called **El Barniz.** You may have to show your permit to the guard who lives in the house and then continue along this beautiful road.

At 1.2 km after the chain you will see a wide swath on your left with a road going into the forest. However, I suggest you drive on a few yards in order to turn around and thus take the grass road head on. The best place to park is at 1.3 km from the dirt road although the road does continue on for about another half kilometer.

I have been here twice and unfortunately, both times were at mid-day, but nevertheless there was plenty to see and hear. I would love to camp here in order to catch the early morning explosion of songs.

You will probably want a few hours to bird this lower section of the Park, and you won't see a soul - just birds and Howler Monkeys.

If you have the misfortune of having to go back to Caracas, upon retracing your steps to the house on the main road, you can turn left and continue down the mountain. At the Pozo de Rosas junction, go left and continue, eventually passing the town of San Pedro and ending up on the Panamerican Highway, which will take you all the way down to the Autopista into Caracas. Even on a Sunday you will see no one else in the Park, but you would have to leave Caracas very early in the morning to avoid the traffic, and the same goes for your return to Caracas, when you should leave the Park around 2:00 and no later than 3:00 p.m.

If you are staying in Colonia Tovar and want to visit Macarao, drive back some 7 km towards Caracas, until you reach the Arch and the gas station. From here it is another two km, going towards Junquito, to reach the road leading to El Jarillo, which will now be on your right.

In order to visit the park very early in the a.m. - at least by 6:00 a.m., I would suggest that you stay the night before in Colonia Tovar, which is just 9 km from the start of the El Jarillo road. For recommendations as to inns and hotels in the area of Colonia Tovar, see the chapter on the state of Aragua.

You will find that there are many more species in the Park than those listed above. The only hitch about visiting Macarao is that you should have a permit from the

National Parks Institute, but the Audubon can help you obtain it. Just send them your passport number, and advise where they should deliver the permit.

The absolutely last comment regarding the areas for birding around the Federal District. We are fortunate in having quite a few competent bird guides living in Caracas, and some of whose fees are relatively moderate. Therefore, should you wish to bird in rather out-of-the-way places such as Turgua, I would feel much happier if you would contact the Audubon for a guide. After all, this is where they live, and they know where the birds are.

Bird Guides living in Caracas

There are several excellent guides we can recommend, all bilinguals:

- **Chris Sharpe**, Phone number: (0) 212-730-9701
  <rodsha@telcel.net.ve>
- **Guillermo Mendez**, Phones: (0) 212-235-1314 & 232-66-25
  <gamendezc@hotmail.com>
- **Rogelio Vasquez**, Phone: (0) 212-265-5687
  <yarianacoral@cantv.net>

Barred Antshrike

II - 2. State of Miranda

INTRODUCTION

Roughly half of the urban area of Caracas sits within the State of Miranda, but no Caraqueño would ever call himself "Mirandino". Although the town of Petare has been engulfed by the urban sprawl of the capital city, and Guarenas and Guatire have become commuter towns for city workers, most of the state is quite rural. In its midst rises a mountainous area where the sources of several important streams are found. Since most of the water for the city of Caracas comes from these thickly-forested mountains, the area was declared a National Park in 1958. This Park is a most wonderful birding area, easily accessible from Caracas, and I recommend it as a first or last stop in Venezuela.

GUATOPO NATIONAL PARK

Such beautiful birds as King Vulture, Swallow-tailed Kite, Solitary Eagle, Crested Guan, White-eared Parakeet, Little Hermit, White-tailed Trogon, Jet Antbird, Golden-headed Manakin, Masked Tityra, Tropical Parula, Green Honeycreeper, Fawn-breasted Tanager, Crested Oropendola and many others may be seen at Guatopo National Park.

⬆️ Venezuelan Audubon has published the **Checklist of the Birds of Guatopo National Park**, which you can secure from the American Birding Association or directly from the Audubon.

The area is about three hours by car from Caracas: You take the western expressway (Autopista Caracas-Valencia) towards Maracay and after the Caracas toll gate at Tazón, leave the highway at the **second** exit, which will take you to the town of **Charallave.** After the toll gate comes a round-about, where you head **east** towards the town of **Santa Teresa.** Go straight through Santa Teresa, cross the bridge and continue on the road towards **Altagracia de Orituco.** After the junction at Los Alpes, where you go **right**, you will soon enter the rain forests of the Park. From Los Alpes it is 9.3 km to the Visitors or Information Center.

There is yet another way to reach the Park from Caracas, and when the freeway or autopista to the Oriente (eastern Venezuela) and the beltway around the towns of Guarenas and Guatire are finally finished, it will be far faster than going through Santa Teresa. See the first page on the state of Anzoategui (Chapter VI) for detailed instructions on how to reach the two towns just mentioned. When you reach the area of Caucagua, turn right to go through this town and on up the hill to reach Los Alpes and the Park.

I suggest that you stop at the **Information Center** as the park guard often puts out fruit to attract the birds. He pays for the fruit out of his own pocket, so a small tip would be greatly appreciated. On the other hand, you could also bring a bunch of bananas yourself to attract the birds. Here you should see Green Honeycreeper, Golden Tanager and Orange-bellied Euphonia. Across the street from the center is a trail that formerly was much used for long hikes by various groups. Unfortunately, it is no longer maintained and has consequently been closed. In the past it has, at times, been worth walking for a short distance, and hopefully will be so again. In February there is a good chance of seeing Golden-headed Manakin at the start of the trail. There are several picnic areas in Guatopo that are very pleasant both for resting and birding. From the Visitors Center to **Agua Blanca** it is 12.4 km Walk the trails back from the parking area at Agua Blanca as well as in the main area on the opposite side of the highway. If there are trees and flowers in bloom, these can be an excellent spots for hummingbirds and tanagers. In June and again during October when the *Pomagás* trees *(Syzigium malaccense,* or Malay Apple) are in flower, they are full of White-necked Jacobins, White-vented Plumeleteers, Violet-headed Hummingbirds, Golden-tailed Sapphires and Purple Honeycreepers, as well as Guira and Gray-headed Tanagers. In the same area look for Marble-faced Bristle-Tyrant. The Pomagás trees are so wonderfully generous to the birds and bird watchers that when they are in fruit in January, there is a surfeit of food for a vast variety of birds and an even greater feast for the bird watchers[1]. I would also recommend the trail around the lagoon at **Santa Crucita**, which is about l.4 kilometer south of Agua Blanca. Here I have often seen White-eared Parakeets, Collared and White-tailed Trogons, Rufous-browed Peppershrikes, Orange-bellied Euphonias and Blue-black Grosbeaks. In July and August look for Lesson's Seedeaters in the open areas.

From the heliport located between Sta. Crucita and the southern exit from the Park, I have watched Military Macaws flying to their roosts between 5 and 6 p.m. You may also see them at the Park Guard Station at the far southern end of the Park.

From Agua Blanca to the Administrative Center it is 6.8 kilometers. Be sure to stop here - especially in January when the guava trees are in fruit. I have had the pleasure of watching a flock of White-eared Parakeets make absolute gluttons of themselves.

I would like to suggest that you stop at the Park Guard Station known as La Colonia at the southern entrance to the Park. The Guard, Habi Veroes, will make you very welcome. In fact, arrangements can be made for you to stay there by calling ahead to him at (0) 414-946-6946. He also advised me that the trail leading down below from his house is super birding early in the mornings.

Rather than return to Caracas, you might wish to continue towards the little Llanero town of **Altagracia de Orituco**[2] in order to spend the late afternoon in the park. There is a reasonable but rather basic hotel in Altagracia called **El Amazor**[3] some 23 kilometers from the Park Guard Station. The food in the past has always been excellent. I can also recommend Hotel Diamante, but the food at the Amazor is better. To find the hotel, at 21.5 kilometers after La Colonia, turn down what looks to be a very steep road, and certainly not the main entrance to the town. At the bottom of the hill turn left and continue straight until you see the two-storied hotel.

For residents of Venezuela fortunate enough to have a 4 X 4, and who opt to stay at Altagracia, I suggest that the next day they visit the **Hacienda La Elvira**, in the south eastern portion of Guatopo National Park. From Altagracia take Highway 11 heading east towards Paso Real. The main road out of Altagracia has a cement divider. Where the divider ends it is 6.7 kilometers to the road leading to La Elvira and the "Morros" (craggy hills) of Macaira. While the road to the interesting village of San Francisco is quite acceptable, the turn-off into the beautiful Hacienda, at 13.6 kms

---

[1] Pamela's Comment: Pomagás is not only for the birds. Try it. It's a delicious tropical fruit.

[2] The southern part of Guatopo spills over the state border into the State of Guárico, where this town is located.

[3] Phone numbers: (0) 238-334-1577, 334-1174 & 334-8764. Address: Calles Pellón & Palacio No. 16.

from the main highway, leaves a bit to be desired (bumpy and rutty). Actually, this is a dry-season trip, but La Elvira is an exceptionally lovely place, and very worthy in terms of birds. At the Hacienda, there still stands the main house and building of the old coffee plantation, dating from the I700s. The enormous courtyard was used for spreading coffee beans to dry in the sun. In the middle of the grassy area of the courtyard there is a large tree where we have seen Lineated Woodpeckers nesting.

You might consider visiting Guatopo either at the end or the beginning of your birding trip to Venezuela, as it is centrally located from all corners of the country. In this event, I suggest that you plan to spend the night at Altagracia de Orituco in order to have ample time for birding in the Park. Allow yourself at the very least four hours or more in either direction between the International Airport at Maiquetia and the **northern** end of the Park at Los Altos.

Caveat: The Park Guard has recommended that visits to the Park should be limited to week days and not to week-ends when noisy and rowdy crowds come from all corners of the area to have their barbecues, etc.

Black - Throated Spinetail

II - 3. State of Aragua

INTRODUCTION

In surface area, Aragua is one of our smallest states, but it supports one of the highest population densities and is the seat, together with Carabobo, of most of the secondary industry in the country. It also shares the Lake of Valencia with Carabobo State[1]. The famous Valleys of Aragua, which you will traverse as you cross the state on the highway, are dotted with historical buildings and sites, and have some of the most fertile soils in Venezuela, where sugar cane and fruit groves have been cultivated since colonial times. The sugar cane is the base for some of our finest rums. The State Capital city of **Maracay** lies just two hours south west of Caracas, and upon arrival in Venezuela many birders head straight for Maracay. What makes this town so desirable to birders? Read on!

GETTING TO MARACAY AND HENRI PITTIER N.P.

To reach Maracay from Maiquetía International Airport, follow the directions given in "On getting to Caracas from Maiquetía", one of the items in Chapter II-One. Once you have taken the lower lane to the right that leads to El Valle/Maracay, you will see a tunnel in front of you. Actually, there are two sets of twin tunnels going through this hill - the ones above which you saw from a distance leads to Caracas, and this lower one that you now find ahead of you, together with its opposite-direction mate will take you to Maracay. After the tunnel, follow signs to Maracay. Many signs are so badly placed that you only see them after passing the exit. This is National Highway 1, only no Venezuelan outside the Ministry of Transport knows it as such. You will skirt the main part of Caracas (which is no small blessing), cross two more tunnels, and eventually realize that you are leaving town. When you reach the toll booth (known as Tazón) at the end of a long hill, take note of your mileage or set your odometer at 0.

The trip to Maracay should take you about 2 hours or slightly more. If you are hungry or thirsty, you might very well enjoy a break at about the half way point, at a roadside eatery called "Oh Campo", some 34.5 km after the toll booth. I can recommend their arepas and coffee. In February, when the Mountain Immortelles on the slope behind Oh Campo are in their full flame-colored glory, while leisurely eating your arepa, you will have a good chance of seeing Slate-headed Tody-Flycatcher, Pale-eyed Pygmy-Tyrant, Thick-billed Euphonia and Guira Tanager, as well as Pearl Kite and Ornate Hawk Eagle sailing overhead.

If you are going straight to the Biological Station of Rancho Grande, leave the Autopista at the **Tapa-Tapa exit**, which is the second one servicing the city of Maracay. A short, straight distance after paying the toll, you come to the end of the street where you must turn. Take the right onto Avenida Bolívar, always following the signs for **El Limón/Ocumare**. Continue along this avenue until you see the dark blue buil-

---

[1] The Lake of Valencia forms an enclosed watershed, the only one in the country, since all other rivers drain to the Orinoco, to Lake Maracaibo, or directly to the sea.

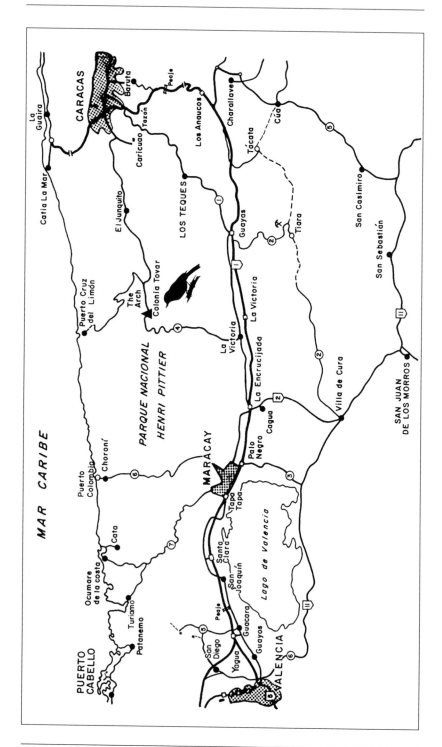

ding of the newspaper "El Siglo" on your left. Angle over into the left lane and turn left at the next stoplight by the Corpoven gas station. From here you go straight until the road ends at a four-lane highway with a stoplight. Turn left. You are now on the Autopista del Limón, officially called State Highway 7, that leads to Ocumare de la Costa (as well as Henri Pittier National Park and Rancho Grande, although the signs never mention this). Within a relatively short distance, you will come to a roundabout. Go half-way around and continue up the four-lane street, which is the main avenue through an area of small shops. This is El Limón proper, where you can purchase supplies for your picnic or overnight stay at the biological station from one of the many grocery and bakery shops.

On the other hand, if you plan to go first to one of the hotels in Maracay, leave the autopista at the first exit called **Palo Negro**, This is 95.3 km from the Caracas toll booth. Your next toll booth is Tapa Tapa at 96.2 km Go around the traffic circle and take the road marked for Avenida Aragua and Avenida Bolívar. Go straight until you arrive at another roundabout and take the road to Las Delicias (passing the Kellogs building). Continue straight always following the signs for Las Delicias. You will have to go around a curve that leads into a wide avenue below. Then continue straight again, always following the signs for Las Delicias/ Choroni. Now you will have to be clever, because some inept government official (I have yet to meet one that is not) started putting up the signs for "Las Delicias/Choroni" several blocks before you should actually turn. Ignore the first signs and continue straight until you see a wide street, Avenida Las Delicias, with a tree-lined divider and a **McDonald's** on the corner. Here you turn right. Actually, you turn right onto Avenida Las Delicias at the third stop light after paying your toll. If you are heading for **Hotel Italo**, turn left at the first corner on Avenida Las Delicias. It is a large blue and white building. Phone: (0) 243-232-2565.

✐ Please note that it is also possible to reach Maracay from the German village of Colonia Tovar. You will find directions for this further down.

To reach Rancho Grande from the Hotel Italo, go back down Avenida Las Delicias until you reach the main street you came in on, which is Avenida Bolívar. Turn right. (Actually, unless it has fallen down or is now covered by a tree, as so often happens here, there is a sign that says "El Limón".) The next main street and stoplight is Avenida Casanova Godoy. You will come upon the wide avenue I mention above, called State Highway 7 or Autopista del Limón. Turn right once more and go all the way along, always following the signs for Ocumare.

It is also possible to travel by bus to Rancho Grande. From the airport at Maiquetía, take a bus to Caracas which will leave you near Parque Central. From there I recommend that you take a taxi to **Aeroexpresos Ejecutivos**, in the area of town called Bello Campo, where you can board one of their buses to Maracay[1]. These buses leave for Maracay at 7:00 a.m., 10:45 a.m., 3:00 p.m. and 6:30 p.m. Then, from the bus terminal in Maracay, take a bus to Ocumare, getting off at Rancho Grande. The buses to Ocumare de la Costa leave quite frequently. However, please take note that the gates to Rancho Grande may well be closed after 6:00 p.m.

---

[1] For information on these bus lines, see "On Taxis and Buses" in the "Dos & Don'ts" chapter in Section I.

HENRI PITTIER NATIONAL PARK (RANCHO GRANDE)

An expanse of 107,800 hectares of Coastal Mountain Range, just north of Maracay, is world-famous among ornithologists for the 578 species of birds found in its various life zones. The Park straddles both slopes of the range, going up from the 400 meter-above-the-sea level on the southern side, over the ridges and down to the sea on the northern side. It is crossed by two national roads, and on one of them (the Ocumare and Cata road), sits the famous **Rancho Grande** Biological Research Station, where William Beebe wrote his celebrated *High Jungle*. Because of that book, because of its birds, its trees and the magnificent half-ruined building, people tend to give the name of this spot to the entire Park.

Since Maracay is about two hours from Caracas and three from the International Airport at Maiquetía, you would be wise to plan to stay the night in the town, in order to be able to bird the park as early as possible in the morning.

If you aim to reach Rancho Grande in the early morning, you may wish to breakfast at the bakery *(panadería)* towards the end of the main street of El Limón. There are actually three bakeries on this long stretch of shops after the round-about, but I usually choose the one on the left called *Panadería El Progreso,* because it opens at 6:30 a.m.

Unfortunately, with the exception of the grounds and trails around the Rancho Grande building, the park can only be birded from one of those two roads that cross it in a north-south direction.

As I mentioned before, the Biological Research Station is situated on the road which leads to **Ocumare de la Costa** and the beautiful bay of **Cata**. The other road goes to the quaint cocoa-plantation town of **Choroni**. Due to the heavy traffic to and from Maracay and Valencia, I would definitely recommend that you **do not bird either road on a weekend or during any public holiday.**

Coming up the Ocumare road to Rancho Grande, just after the checkpoint (Alca-bala) at the park entrance, there is a road to the left. This road leads to the offices of the Venezuelan equivalent of Fish and Wildlife. They have no objection to birders parking and birding in the area. It is a good spot for dry forest birds, but the gate at the entrance is only open during working hours (9:00 a.m. to 4:00 p.m.) on week days.

As you go up the mountain, you will first pass through deciduous and transition forest, and then come into cloud forest near the ridge of the mountain chain. Rancho Grande sits almost on the ridge, amid this cloud forest, at the height where you may

Helmeted Curassow

expect to find some of the endemics, such as Handsome Fruiteater and Rufous-cheeked Tanager.

Visitors can stay at the station, but are expected to pay a small fee per night per person and must first secure permission from the "Instituto de Zoología Agrícola" at the University in Maracay When you arrive at Rancho Grande, the caretakers will ask for the receipt from the Universidad. On the other hand, if your group is using the services of Ernesto and Fenix Fernandez for catering, etc. they will take care of this onerous requirement, and, believe me, that is no small service!

Supposedly the main gate should be open before 8:00 a.m., but if it is not, just shout, so the Park Guard will come to open it (hopefully, that is, if he is in a good mood). He will collect an entrance fee, but do not ask me what service they give in return. Be sure he gives you a receipt, and check the amount that he puts on the receipt. There are caretakers at the biological station who do try to be of help to bird watchers, but these are employed by the University.

You will have to supply your own food, but the station has stoves, refrigerators, pots, pans, etc. I recommend that you also take a towel as well as a sleeping bag if you brought one with you. The accommodations are very rustic, with four large dormitory-type rooms with several bunk beds in each. No hot water, and that water is really cold! If you are with a group, and want catering service, call Dr. Ernesto Fernandez at his mobile phone: (0) 416-447-1182, or at his home after 9:30 or 10 p.m., and until say 11:00 or 11:30 p.m.; phone: (0) 243-245-3470. Ernesto and his wife, Fenix, will take care of all the arrangements at a reasonable cost per meal, and the food is very good.

The building began to be constructed under directions from dictator Juan Vicente Gomez. It was to be a hotel. When Gomez died in 1935, construction was halted and the building abandoned. Eventually, it was converted into a biological research station, and it was here that William Beebe and Paul Schwartz worked. Unfortunately, it was abandoned again for ten years (until 1989) except for the section used by the Maracay branch of the Central University of Venezuela.

Perhaps I should mention here that there have been rumors going around to the effect that the Rancho Grande building is haunted by many ghosts, including those of Gomez, of one of the old park guards, of the great botanist Henri Pittier and the young English Biologist Andy Field, who spent two years studying the ecology of the great "Niños" *(Gyranthera caribensis)* and died when he fell from the platform he had built on one of the giant trees. I personally have had no encounter with any of them. But, then again, they weren't birders.

After those exultant words, I deeply regret the necessity of adding a **caveat** here with regard to Rancho Grande. I have had complaints from birders who maintain that the park guards overcharged on the entrance fee without giving a receipt and helped themselves to belongings entrusted to them while the birders were hiking the trails. Also, these same guards have access to the sleeping quarters of the Biological Station, and considering the unfortunate experience of one of the birders, I suggest you do not leave any valuables, such as cash, in your rooms when out birding. We cannot put our finger on any one in particular, and we most sincerely regret having to warn our readers about one or two of the guards at Rancho Grande, especially considering how absolutely wonderful park guards tend to be at all other National Parks where we have worked. One of our guides wrote in a report:

«*In their defense, the Park Guards have advanced the theory that the ghosts of Andy Field and Henri Pittier are in league and have been knocking off birders' belongings with regularity over the last two years. I have to say that if this is the case, I am appalled at their taste in half-broken Casio Watches!*»

Rancho Grande at dawn is, without doubt, one of the rarest, most exquisite experiences a birder can have anywhere in the world. Veiled in mist, the rain forest emerges from the darkness and the silence at night's end into joyful bird songs and crystal clear light if it is a sunny morning, or flurried activity if it is a rainy day. The early mornings are usually clear during almost 9 months of the year, but you can expect clouds to form about 11:00 a.m. and rain in the afternoon.

There are two trails behind the building that make for good birding in the early morning and late afternoon. Around the main grounds (and from the terrace) you should see Red-eared Parakeet and White-tipped Swifts nest under the balconies. From late February through July, Swallow Tanagers nest in holes in the walls. In the early months of the year, the Russet-backed Oropendolas nest in the trees in front, so you will have them at eye level from the terrace. And at all times of the year, Groove-billed Toucanets may be around. When you tire of watching the birds around the garden area, you may climb the stairs on the far side of the building, which lead to the trails.

As you go up the trail, you will come upon the memorial to Andy Field, the young British botanist whom I mentioned before. There is a trail leading off to the right of this plaque, known as the Guacamaya trail. With luck you should see White-tipped Quetzal here, although in the mating season of February/April it is easier to see them from the terrace of the Station. After the mating season the Quetzals move back down the mountain and are difficult to see around Rancho Grande. In the early morning you stand a good chance of hearing Helmeted Curassow and Venezuelan Wood-Quail calling.

Going out on the main road and slightly farther along towards the sea, there is a wire mesh fence and a door on the left. This is the entrance to the famous trail and Pass of Portachuelo. You may have to request the people of the Station to lend you the key to the gate. The Pass is the lowest spot of the ridge along this central segment of the range. Many northern migrants use it on their annual flight to South America, and local species use it also in a variety of patterns. Flocks of Lilac-tailed Parrotlets, for example, fly across from about the middle of July to November. At other times, they seem to stay at lower altitudes.

Should you visit Henri Pittier during the spring migration of April or the arrival of the northern migrants in October, it is probable that you will stumble upon the volunteers from the Venezuelan Audubon at the banding station in Portachuelo. The banding station was started by our senior ornithologist, Miguel Lentino, many years ago, not only for banding migratory species from the North and the South (yes, we get them too), but also to determine the use of the Pass by local species.

The station is only open during the migration periods. Previously, the station was open for three days a month for years on end. It was the kind of long-term project which slowly adds to our information about neotropical birds. After a couple of years of data, Miguel soon began to notice patterns of use by our own birds on yearly, seasonal and even daily basis. For instance, one November day we suddenly were netting dozens of Golden-tailed Sapphires flying from north to south. Miguel later determined that during November a plant with red flowers blooms along the south side of the mountain. Then there was the occasional Ruby-topaz Hummingbird migrating from the islands off the coast down to the Llanos. An interesting point for our ornithologists has been the gradual accumulation of information on the Sooty Grassquits which periodically appear (from where?) in Henri Pittier to make their nest of bamboo leaves near the bamboo groves. Five species of swifts are banded in Portachuelo - Collared, Gray-rumped, Vaux's, White-tipped and Chapman's, the first four regularly, the last one only occasionally. The data gathered after all these years conforms one of the largest data bases on swifts in the world.

I find it strange that although we may net up to 100 birds a day at the Pass, one does not see that many on the trail, whereas along the trails behind the Biological Station, one seldom nets a bird but you can see many more. Can someone please explain this to me?

Before I finish the section on Rancho Grande, I should perhaps, mention that the trails of Henri Pittier, and especially that behind the building, are excellent areas to collect chiggers! Strangely enough, I have never had chigger problem on the Portachuelo trail.

A few other birds you might see in the park are: Plain-breasted Hawk, Short-tailed Hawk, Ornate Hawk-Eagle, Solitary Eagle, Sooty-capped Hermit, White-tipped Quetzal, Collared Trogon, White-necked Puffbird, Strong-billed, Black-banded and Spot-crowned Woodcreepers, Crested Spinetail, Guttulated Foliage-gleaner, Black-faced Antthrush, Venezuelan Bristle-Tyrant, Southern Nightingale Wren.

Having said all of the above, I now must give you a very serious **Caveat:** Although Audubon has not received information of robberies in the Henri Pittier Park itself, there are many robberies around the Maracay area. For instance, Chris Sharpe told me of an unpleasant experience he had when he was leading a group. "One early morning leaving Maracay for Cumboto, a van passed us and a guy got out with a shotgun -- fortunately too slow for our driver, Miguel, who shot off at full speed." Due to this situation, we are now suggesting Bejuma/Palmichal as an alternative. See the Chapter on Carabobo State. The city of Maracay has definitely become a red zone due to frequent robberies, and I fear that eventually our birders may be held-up while walking the roads in the Park.

As if the above were not enough, the situation at Rancho Grande itself has changed drastically over the last year or so, to the point that it is no longer a Mecca for birders. All told, there are three different organizations in charge or controlling the building - the National Parks Institute, the University at Maracay and the very worthy group known as the Friends of Henri Pittier National Park. Unfortunately, there is no coordination between them, and one never knows how many people will be visiting Rancho Grande at any one time. Not long ago an entomologist friend of ours visited Rancho Grande only to find approximately 100 people there - teenagers with their boom boxes, children running around screaming, etc. As you can imagine, there were no birds to be seen. One of our birders stayed there recently and had the same problem with some 43 teenagers. Therefore, if you want to visit Rancho Grande to climb the trail behind the building at dawn, I suggest you plan on only one night to find those species difficult to find at Palmichal. (See chapter on Carabobo.) Furthermore, the attitude of the University regarding nature tourists is enough to put a finis to the endeavor. For instance, Ernesto Fernandez in the past had a series of bird feeders that he constantly supplied with fruit to attract the birds for the delight of the tourists. However, some petty, small-minded bureaucrat has now given him orders that he is only allowed to have one feeder on the whole terrace. That is just one example but taking into the account the lack of maintenance by both the University and the National Parks Institute, the future of this marvelous destination for bird watchers is of deep concern to me. In Venezuela a "rancho" is a shack or shanty, and I fear that with the mentality of the *petits fonctionnaires* in control of the building, Rancho Grande will never be anything but "un rancho grande."

The experience of Dr. Richard Byrne in August, 2000, unfortunately coincides with my opinion:

«Up to Rancho Grande, where our impressions pretty much agree with yours (especially when 42 very noisy teenagers arrived for the second night), except

that the rooms are now lockable and seemed fairly secure. It seems that Ernesto doesn't cook for small groups, but he did get a pile of shopping for us, and only charged us cost, which was very kind. The research people evidently resent his bringing tourists there, which is understandable... except that they seem relaxed about the awful school parties! Odd. And we found the visitor pressure on the loop trail, the only one that is kept in decent condition, so heavy that one can forget Helmeted Currassows and Venezuelan Wood Quail; luckily, other birds simply get used to people, and as I mentioned, we did well for lurking forest species. I think the compromise of two nights there, and much more time at Palmichal, was a good one.»

⊜ The **Checklist of the Birds of Henri Pittier N.P.** is on sale by the Audubon Society or you can secure it from the American Birding Association.

THE NORTHERN SIDE

Going down towards the sea, the road on the northern side of the range can provide excellent birding. As you descend the mountain, the forest changes, and the bird species change accordingly.

In the area by Restaurant La Curva, below the village of La Trilla, look for Fasciated Tiger-Heron. When you come down to sea level, you will have a choice of turning right towards Ocumare de la Costa or going straight towards **Turiamo**. The Bay of Turiamo is a major Naval Base, so the last stretch of road has been closed to traffic, but if you have the time, bird it until you come up against the guarded gate. There you may turn left in order to bird the short road to **Cumboto**. Here, too, you might see Fasciated Tiger-Heron as well as Streak-headed Woodcreeper, Plain Xenops, Black-backed Antshrike, Wire-tailed and Lance-tailed Manakins, Forest Elaenia, Venezuelan Flycatcher, Flavescent Warbler, White-eared Conebill and Rosy Thrush-Tanager. Dick Ryan actually had "a Rufous-necked Wood Rail run across the stream by the Turiamo Naval Base giving us a great though brief look." As far as I know, this is the first report of that species in the area. If you are diligent and lucky, you should be able to see over 40 species along this road to Turiamo/ Cumboto.

For the general area of Ocumare, where he spent several days during August, 2000, Dr. Richard Byrne of St. Andrews University, Scotland, sent me the following list:

Brown Booby - 1 adult , over sea.
Brown Pelican - c.20, flew in over sea.
Magnificent Frigatebird - c.30, over cliffs.
Hook-billed Kite - 1, black phase.
Laughing Falcon - 1
Grey-necked Wood-rail - 1
Spotted Sandpiper - 1 adult summer
Military Macaw - 12, superb views, including 4 perched on open top of tree socializing and preening, and much flying around by parties; generally moving towards coast, presumably to a roost.
Brown-throated Parakeet - 2
Blue-headed Parrot - c.15

Squirrel Cuckoo - 2
Rufous-breasted Hermit - 1
Lazuline Sabrewing - 1 male, surely most unusual at near-sea level?
Glittering-throated Emerald - 3
Ringed Kingfisher - 1
Green Kingfisher - 1
Rufous-tailed Jacamar - 1
Russet-throated Puffbird - 5, including 2 in the town itself.
Olivaceous Woodcreeper - 1
Streak-headed Woodcreeper - 1
Plain Xenops - 1
Black-crested Antshrike - 2 female, male, brief views.

Black-backed Antshrike - 2, good views of dramatic male after tape playback, also briefer visit by female. (Base of Cumboto road.)
Barred Antshrike - 2 female, male
Lance-tailed Manakin - 1 female
Common Tody-flycatcher - 2
Forest Elaenia - 1
Venezuelan Flycatcher - 2
Rusty-margined Flycatcher - c.5
Grey-breasted Martin - c.800, in two dense groups on telegraph wires in town.
Flavescent Warbler - 1, frequently approached in response to Rosy Thrush-Tanager tape.
White-eared Conebill - 1 male, excellent close views. (Ocumare tip.)
Rosy Thrush-Tanager - 2, both singing in response to tape, but elusive, giving only brief views; male finally seen very well (on third visit to site!), singing on open branch. (Ocumare tip.)
Silver-beaked Tanager - c.10
Blue-grey Tanager - c.10
Crested Oropendola - c.30
Oriole Blackbird - 1

Oh, yes! Ocumare is worth a day or so

In the event you do not wish to return to Maracay in the dark, I can recommend the **Posada Maria Luisa** in **Ocumare de la Costa**. Phone: (0) 243-993-1184, fax: (0) 243-993-1073 or call the Audubon. However, the posada is certain to be booked up during weekends and school holidays. As you drive into the town keep your eyes open for the Farmacia (pharmacy) on your right. There, turn right to reach the Posada.

If you opt to stay at the Posada Maria Luisa, I highly recommend that **early** next morning you go back to the roundabout by the gas station where the various roads fork to Ocumare, Cata and Maracay. Take the road to **Cata**. Within about 15 minutes you will look down on a gorgeous bay, very much disfigured by two Miami Beach-style skyscrapers. (Frank Lloyd Wright would have had a heart attack). At the bottom of the incline turn right to take the road to **Cuyagua**. My only regret for this area is that there is no place to stay at Cuyagua because this road provides extremely good birding. You climb from sea level to 600 meters, giving you the possibility of various habitats. I only had an hour and a half to investigate the whole road but saw or heard the following:

Little Tinamou	White-bellied Antbird	Silver-beaked Tanager
Bat Falcon	Short-tailed Antthrush	Hepatic Tanager
Rufous-vented Chachalaca	Black-faced Antthrush	White-lined Tanager
Pale-vented Pigeon	White-winged Becard	Rosy Thrush-Tanager
White-tipped Dove	Streaked Flycatcher	Black-faced Tanager
Squirrel Cuckoo	Rufous-breasted Wren	Blue-black Grosbeak
Pauraque	Long-billed Gnatwren	Grayish Saltator
Copper Rumped Hummingbird	Scrub Greenlet	Black-faced Grassquit
Rufous-tailed Jacamar	Tropical Parula	Gray Seedeater
Barred Antshrike	Speckled Tanager	

Truly, the Cuyagua road deserves at least four hours of intensive birding, if not more[1].

A tip from Dick Ryan:
«As one leaves Ocumare, heading towards Bahia de Cata (and Cuyagua), there is a dirt road heading to the right from the main road. It is only a couple

---

[1] But **never** on a week-end or a public holiday!

of kms out of town. It is the garbage dump road. However, it is also excellent dry forest birding. I have twice had Yellow-knobbed Curassow along it and several birds usually associated with wetter areas as well. It is also good for North American migrants and on April 22 I had a Hooded Warbler, the first I've seen in South America. Probably the best bird I have gotten there was a Pheasant Cuckoo last year. The dirt road is traversable by ordinary car in the dry season, four-wheel only in wet.»

THE CHORONÍ ROAD

The other main road through Henri Pittier National Park is State Highway 6 that leads to **Choroní**. From the Maracay side, it is a continuation of Avenida Las Delicias that runs past Hotel Byblos, followed almost immediately by a roundabout and the Zoo. Set your odometer at 0 again by the round-about and Zoo, and continue following the signs for Choroni and El Castaño. The Hotel Pipo will be on your left at 2.3 km from the Zoo. The entrance to the National Park is at 5 km. Now you will begin to climb, and climb until you reach the top (1,500 m above sea level) at 16.9 km. I would suggest that you overnight in Maracay, leaving at 5:00 a.m. in order to see the high-altitude birds. At this highest point on the road, where you pass the ridge, there is place where one can park and walk down in both directions, with very good chances of seeing Bronzy Inca, White-tipped Quetzal, Collared Trogon, Black-throated Spinetail, Rufous-cheeked Tanager, Plush-capped Finch (in the *Chusquea* bamboo), Ochre-breasted Brush-Finch and, between the months of August and March, some mind-boggling feeding flocks. Try to be here at dawn in order to see the Guans and Curassows. During February and March you will have a pretty good chance of sighting White-tipped Quetzal along here. Try walking down the road towards Choroni. Some 300 meters from the top you might just see the Streak-capped Treehunter. As a matter of fact, keep on walking for a few kilometers early in the morning. You will be well rewarded.

The road to Choroni is famous for its extremely narrow, hair-pin curves with hardly any place to pull off to bird. Actually, this road, with the exception of the ridge, offers very few places to bird as I will point out below. Although it is probably the most beautiful road I have ever traveled in Venezuela, it is more for the general nature lover or beach lover than for the hard-core birder. Nevertheless, for those who wish to know Venezuelan nature at its most exuberant, I am giving below full details of the road and my personal recommendations for inns.

As you go down the mountain (and look out for the blooming buses) you will first come to a stream that crosses the road itself. On your left is a shallow area to bathe, but if you were to walk up the stream, you would come to a pool known here as the *Nevera* or refrigerator. Guess why. Continuing down, at 35.8 km from the Zoo there is an entrance on the right that leads to small dam or dike and the Casa Cultural, both built by the dictator Gomez. You can only drive in for less than a kilometer where you should park on the right as close as possible to the bank. To your left is a stairway that leads to the dike. Just below the torrent of water coming from the dike is a lovely pool where you can cool off.

At 21.3 km or 2.4 kms below the turn off for the dike you will see a small white house on the left. You can park in the entrance way to the house in order not to leave your car on this very narrow road. The owner, Sr. Raul, sells fresh fruits and natural fruit juices, and, of course, you should pay him for the privilege of leaving your car there where it will be guarded. Across the street from his house is the start of a trail with what is left of a sign stating "*peligro*" or danger. This is due to the fact that part of the trail leading to the river is very rocky - just the place where fer de lances like to hang out. So, keep your eyes open. However, the pool that this trail leads to is absolutely fantastic - deep enough to swim and complete with a "*tobogán*" or watery shoot above. This pool is called El Lajao and is very famous among the younger generation of Maracay, Valencia and Caracas. Warning: Never on a Sunday.

At 40 km there is yet another entrance on the right leading to "*La Planta*" or what was once the "*Museo de Electricidad.*" Just below the museum building is a stream. Cross the stream on the log bridge and continue up on the left trail past the old colonial house of the Hacienda La Sabaneta. Above the house, you will come to another trail. Turn left and start looking for both Lance-tailed and Wire-tailed Manakins. There are leks of both of these species along this trail. The Hacienda La Sabaneta is a privately-owned cocoa plantation. It is beautiful and it well deserves an hour of birding. If you meet the owner, be polite and explain that you are only birding.

On the left of the main road in front of the turn off for La Planta is the **Gran Posada** inn. It is not pretentious - probably 2 ★★ - has 8 simple but spic' n span single and double rooms with private baths (cold water only). Their charges are very moderate and include breakfast. The service is extremely friendly and excellent. The best part is that they have a bird feeder and around the inn we saw or heard Thick-billed Euphonia, Rosy Thrush- Tanager, Glaucous Tanager, Buff-throated Saltator and others. We were also advised that there is a trail leading up to the forest above the building. Phone: (0) 414-445-8664 & 414-589-1438.

Hacienda La Aljorra, phones: (0) 212-242-8626 & (0) 414-496-4656. Located 3 km below La Gran Posada or 2 km before the town of Choroni. The main point of this posada is that they have a total of 155 hectares with tropical forest and a nearby river. There surely must be good birding here although I have not been able to check it out. Apparently, this is a 18th century cacao plantation where the guest area has been restored. They have 9 large rooms with private baths and hot water. Breakfast is included in the price and there is a restaurant as well.

Continuing your trip you will come to the precious, colonial town of Choroni. Get out your cameras.

The next town after Choroni is Puerto Colombia on the beach. It cannot compare in any way to the attraction of Choroni, but your inns are coming up. After Choroni you will see a sign on the left for Portete and **La Casa de las Garcia**. Both are 5 stars, but I highly recommend the latter for birders. La Casa de las Garcia is a 300-year old colonial mansion exquisitely decorated and with a very large garden and quite a few birds. Phones: (0) 243-991-1056 & 991-1257, fax for reservations: (0) 212-662-2858. E-mail: llerandi@telcel.net.ve. Web page: www.posada-garcia.rec.ve. The only thing I objected to at this inn was the fact that they had a parrot and a macaw in cages.

In the town of Choroni itself is the very inexpensive and more rustic **Posada/ Restaurant Los Churuni**, located a short distance after the church and next to the bakery Panadería Pan y Dulce. They offer 4 simple rooms but only 3 have private baths. Cold water.

As you approach closer to Puerto Colombia, you will see the gas station on your left. Across the road is a dirt track with a stone arch. This road leads to **Estancia Akelarre Choroni**. It only has 4 guest rooms, but I would say that it rates even 6 stars. If you are well-heeled and can afford it, this inn is something special. By reservation only. Phones: (0) 212-944-1684, (0) 243-991-1202 & 991-1234 or (0) 414-316-7765.

When I was in the area during October, 2000, I stayed at **La Parchita Inn** (★★★). I liked it because of the location away from the main part of town next to the river whose tranquil song lulled me to sleep. This inn also has only 4 simple clean rooms with private baths, and a most pleasant atmosphere. An excellent breakfast is included in the price. To find this place, upon entering the main part of Puerto Colombia, pass the National Guard post, at the next corner where all the buses from Maracay park, turn left. At the following corner turn again to the left and go straight to the river. There is enclosed parking right next to the inn. Phone: (0) 243-991-1259 or (0) 416-832-2790 & 819-8557.

There are two other very outstanding inns to be found in Puerto Colombia. In fact there are many inns, but I would suggest:

Posada Mesón Xuchytlan (★★★★★). How can I describe this inn except that it is like visiting a Mexican hacienda and the home of the owner. It is delightful. What I liked most about the place was the friendly atmosphere with which we were received. They insisted that we see every single corner and would not allow us to leave until we had partaken of their very special alcoholic preparation. It was delicious, but I would not dare to imbibe more than one. Phones: (0) 243-991-1234 or (0) 414-928-0952 & 255-5657. E-mail: xbteado@hotmal.com .

Finally there is the **Posada Casa Grande** (★★★★★). This inn is larger, with 17 rooms with A.C., hot water, swimming pool, TV parlor, All, of course, decorated with very good taste. Phones: (0) 243-991-1251 or (0) 416-624-6002.

Chuao & Cepe

Puerto Colombia has a beautiful beach called Playa Grande, but it is also known to have dangerous undertows. For swimming and privacy you would be better off to take a *peñero* (launch) from the wharf to either **Chuao** or **Cepe**. Chuao, the first beach/settlement, is known world-wide for the excellent cacao produced there and shipped to the main chocolate-producing countries of the world. Cepe has also been recommended to me by a friend for the **Puerto Escondido** inn. This is a colonial-style building just 150 meters from the beach. The 7 rooms all have private bath, hot water and fan. The owner, César Fischer, is a PADI instructor and marine biologist. Freddy Fisher is a dive master with decades of experience in these waters. For those who wish to fish-watch, they rent equipment for diving and snorkeling as well as inland excursions in the national park. Phones: (0) 243-241-4645 & 241-3614. For bird watchers, please note that there is a lovely path up through the cacao plantation that eventually leads to Colonial Tovar - if you are young, vigorous, and back packing. Where there is cacao, there are birds, and I have made myself a promise to go there as soon as I finish this blasted new edition!

ON STAYING IN MARACAY

We have been recommending the **Hotel Italo**, and to date our birders have been satisfied. See above for the directions to the hotel. Phone: (0) 243-232-1576. Also see their web page: www.hotelitalo.com.ve .

Hotel Caroní has been highly recommended to us as a less expensive but perfectly adequate place to stay. The address is Avenida Ayacucho between Avenidas Bolívar and Santos Michelena. Phone: (0) 243-554-1817. To reach the hotel, as you come down from Rancho Grande, continue along the Autopista del Limón, passing the University on your left. At the stop light where you will see a large sign for "Casa del Pollo" (Chicken House) turn right, passing both the market and "La Ternera" steak house. Continue for two blocks. The hotel is a four-story building with parking facilities. If you are going straight to the hotel from the airport, you should still leave the autopista at Tapa Tapa, turning right at the end of the street after you pass the toll booth. You are now on Avenida Bolívar. Pass the blue "El Siglo" building, the Corpoven gas station, and continue straight until you come to the crossing with Avenida Ayacucho, where you turn left. It is a white and green building half way up the street. The Caroni is a perfectly adequate hotel, but, unfortunately, it is in the midst of the epitome of a Venezuelan city neighborhood with broken sidewalks and garbage everywhere. This contributes to the impact of culture shock for those who have not previously been in the third world.

Hotel Círculo Militar: Yes, this is actually in the military installation and it is the best bargain to be found in Maracay. Phone: (0) 243-242-4118. Go straight up Avenida Las Delicias, keeping your eye open for the hotel on the left side of the road. You can turn directly into the installation from the right side of the road. The quality of the rooms is about the same as the Hotel Caroni, but it is more modestly priced. Naturally, no English spoken nor is there a restaurant on the premises but there are so many places to eat along Avenida Las Delicias that you have a multitude of choices.

Hotel Pipo: Phone: (0) 243-241-3111. Located on the Urbanization El Castaño at the beginning of the road to Choroni. Go straight up Avenida Las Delicias, passing the Hotel Byblos (not recommended) on your right and continue on until you see the hotel on your left.

Posada Entrepajaros B & B: This is a five-star option, European level, with all the comforts including a lovely pool. To reach the inn, go straight up Avenida Las Delicias as if you were heading for Choroni. After passing the Hotel Byblos on your right, continue up the road. Just before you reach the Hotel Pipo, there is a road to your right. Turn. Once you pass the guardhouse count three corners to your left, a small sign on the house right at the corner will tell you that you have arrived. If you can afford it, this is THE place to stay in Maracay. Even at the prices they charge, the inn is less expensive than the Pipo and with far more comfort. Phones: 243-242-5497 or (0) 416-845-9373.

Posada El Limon (also called Caribbean EcoTours). Located in the urbanization of El Limon on the road to Rancho Grande and Ocumare de la Costa. When you come to the cross roads to either Ocumare and/or the main part of the Urbanization El Limon, continue straight ahead, heading for Ocumare. Pass the main commercial area (including the Panadería El Progreso recommended for breakfasts) and continue on until the divider in the middle of the road ends. You will see a bridge ahead and the Abastos Gran Parada in front of you on the right. Turn right and go straight to the end of the road. Turn right again. After one block and almost immediately you will see a sign on your right indicating "Silenciadores El Piñal," but the problem is that the sign faces the other way. On your left is the Calle (street) El Piñal where you should turn. Actually there is a sign indicating the inn on the corner fence of El Piñal, but again the sign faces the other way. After you turn left continue straight up the road for one kilometer until you reach No. 64 on your left. The inn has a large garden with many trees, and since it is so close to the Park, you will find many of the more common birds even in the garden. Both lodging and meals are reasonably priced, and we have been assured that there is no problem of insecurity in the area of El Limon. This is a very good option for a mid-price inn near Rancho Grande. Reservations must be paid for in advance. Phones: (0) 243-283-4925 or (0) 414-444-1915.

ON EATING IN MARACAY

While it is possible to arrange meals for groups at Rancho Grande through Dr. Ernesto Fernandez, some of you may wish to try a typical Venezuelan restaurant. I would suggest "La Ternera" (The Calf). This is a typical steak house where they sell cuts of beef by the kilo. Try the *punta trasera* (rump steak) or the *lomito* (terderloin). Ask also for *yuca frita* (fried taro root), and/or *bollos* and unless you like really hot food, do not ask for anything *picante* - guasacaca is a good alternative. Their mixed salads are very good too. To reach the restaurant, upon coming down from Rancho Grande, at the junction of Autopista del Limón and Avenida Casanova Godoy, go straight. At the first large intersection (divided street with a stop light) turn right. The restaurant is on a corner near the main market.

"El Portón de la Abuela", on Avenida Las Delicias has been highly recommended to us by our guides. Actually, there are practically no end of eateries along Avenida Las Delicias from the excellent food at El Portón de la Abuela near the end of the Avenida before the roundabout to El Castaño, to that scourge of American cuisine, McDonalds, at the beginning of the Avenida.

Hotels in Maracay, Area Code (0) 243		
Posada Entrepajaros	★★★★★	242-5497
Hotel Italo	★★★★	232-1576 / 2565
Hotel Pipo	★★★★	241-3111 / 2722
Hotel Caroní	★★★	254-1817
Hotel Círculo Militar	★★★	242-4118
Posada El Limón	★★★	283-4925

COLONIA TOVAR

How to Get There

The little German village of Colonia Tovar lies nestled in the mountains just two hours by car from Caracas and one hour from the town of La Victoria, State of Aragua. It has a variety of good restaurants, inns and hotels. However, it is definitely a no-no to visit Colonia Tovar on week-ends, as the traffic is unbelievable and all the hotels are full.

Some birders prefer to stay at Hotel El Campesino[1], on the Caracas-Colonia Tovar road, 13.3 kms from the police school at the far end of the town of El Junquito, just to avoid the crowds on the highway and to be in a less developed area.

To reach Colonia Tovar from Caracas, arm yourself with patience and take the "Autopista", the main east--west highway [2] in the westward direction. Follow the signs indicating "Araña" or "Caricuao". Eventually, you will see a sign indicating "El Junquito." Now is when the fun begins. You will get off the autopista by the Social Security Hospital, go straight up a one-block hill and turn right. Watch carefully for on-coming traffic on your left, which is partially hidden by a wall. Once you have braved that corner, try to maneuver into the left lane because at the very first opportunity, you have to make a U-turn to the left in order to get on the upper level of the street. After that life is simpler. Follow that road to the very first large junction and stop-light. Turn right and then follow the heavy traffic up the narrow, winding road, which at the beginning passes through some very poor areas, until some 25 kms up the mountain, you reach the wild-west town of El Junquito. From there on to Colonia Tovar, it is clear sailing for the next 35 kms of State Highway 4.

As you approach the Colonia, you will pass under a large arch welcoming you, but it is yet another 7 kms to the town proper. This arch is a well-known landmark.

---

[1] For reservations Tel. (0) 212-461-7151. Ask for Julio Sánchez.
[2] See "On getting out of Caracas", in Chapter II-One.

Where to Stay

The clearly-marked entrance to a German butcher shop, **Charcutería Tovar**, is 3.6 kms after the arch. Here they make excellent German sausages *(salchichas)*, and also sell delicious coffee and cakes, should you wish to take time out. **Posada Don Elicio** is not far from here, on the left side of the road as you drive towards town. It is probably the best inn of the area, and may also be the most expensive. But their charges include delicious breakfasts and dinners. For reservaqtions, call these phones in Caracas: (0) 212-284-5310, fax 286-2429.

Go straight through the town by all the shops until the street you came on comes to a sort of dead end next to a gas station. Here, you have to take either a left, going sharply down and swinging back into town, or a sort of right, climbing up. Take the latter one and then turn sharply right again, up the hill, for **Hotel Bergland** - my personal favorite (0.4 km from the gas station or 8.1 km from the arch). This road also leads to La Victoria. Phone: (0) 244-355-1994, fax 355-1224, bergland@cantv.net.

Opposite from the Bergland you will find **Cabañas Breidenbach**, which one birder recommended as having nice rooms and being quite a bit cheaper than the Bergland. Phone/Fax: (0) 244-355-1211.

Hotel Edelweiss is slightly above the Bergland.

Hotel Freiburg on Calle E Don Keller, has been recommended as being reasonable and most acceptable. This is somewhat difficult to find at first. Just drive straight through the village until you reach the end by the gas station. Then go left down the hill and continue all the way down until you reach a corner where you must legally turn right for one block. Continue past El Molino restaurant (highly recommended), following the signs indicating the route to the left to the hotel, which take you on a short and relatively flat drive across a narrow valley which separates this sector from the main part of town. (Instructions as per Elizabeth Kline's excellent book). I thought you should turn right after El Molino??

Hotels in Colonia Tovar, Area Code (0) 244		
Posada Don Elicio	★★★★	355-1254 & 355-1073
Hotel Bergland	★★★	355-1994, Fax: 355-1229
Hotel Selva Negra	★★★	355-1415, Fax 355-1338
Hotel Edelweiss	★★★	355-1260
Hotel Freiburg	★★★	355-1313, Fax: 355-1983
Posada Breidenbach	★★	355-1211

Where to Bird

Taking the road from Colonia Tovar towards La Victoria, you will see two roads on the right. The first, which is barely discernible and goes to **Buenos Aires**, is 6.9 kms from Hotel Bergland. This road is almost completely undriveable, but you could drive up a bit and hide your car before striking out on foot. Slightly further on, at 7.9 kms from Hotel Bergland, there is yet another road on the right that goes to **Cortada de Maya**. There is no sign but there is a bus stop at the entrance to this road. Although it is somewhat more traveled, I prefer this second road, for it is partially paved. It can produce some excellent birds. In fact, the further you go on this particular road, the better it gets. From October through February it is an especially good area for feeding flocks. At 2 kms from the start of the road and on the left as you go up, there is a large fig tree *(Ficus insipida)* called *Higuerote* in Spanish. When the large orange-like fruits are ripe in December and January, this tree is full of birds. The Groove-billed Toucanets eat the fruit whole; the thrushes and tanagers take bites; the flower-piercers punch holes in the bottom from which both they and the hummingbirds sip the juice. During the rest of the year the road seems to be very quiet. However, walking these roads slowly can be most rewarding for high mountain birds of the coastal range such as:

Black Vulture	Streaked Tuftedcheek	Yellow-billed Cacique
Broad-winged Hawk	Chestnut-crowned Antpitta	Black-crested Warbler
Black-Hawk-Eagle	Rusty-breasted Antpitta	Bluish Flower-piercer
Band-tailed Pigeon	Caracas Tapaculo	White-sided Flower-piercer
Bronzy Inca	Green-and-black Fruiteater	Golden Tanager
Tyrian Metaltail	Handsome Fruiteater	Beryl-spangled Tanager
Long-tailed Sylph	White-throated Tyrannulet	Blue-winged Mountain-Tanager
White-tipped Quetzal	Blue-and-white Swallow	Blue-capped Tanager
Groove-billed Toucanet	Pale-eyed Thrush	Plush-capped Finch
Smoky-brown Woodpecker	Glossy-black Thrush	Ochre-breasted Brush-Finch
Black-chinned Spinetail		

From Colonia Tovar, there is a road that connects to the town of La Victoria, and from there, to the city of Maracay. It is a road that should not be driven at night, firstly, because the scenery is beautiful, and secondly, because it is a very steep, curving road, and one has to be careful not to burn out the brakes. Going down the mountain, it is better to just stay in second gear until one gets to the lowlands near La Victoria.

TO COLONIA TOVAR VIA LA VICTORIA

From the autopista, take the exit marked "La Victoria". After the toll booth, continue straight until you find yourself forced to take a turn. Turn left. Continue straight for a short distance and you will come to a Maraven gas station. Here you keep to the right. Almost immediately, you come to a Corpoven gas station, which you will pass on your left (as you take the street on the right).

From there you will continue for quite a number of short blocks on this same street, which is busy, narrow, with shops, pedestrians wandering all over the place, and parked cars on both sides. Look out for "Funeraria La Milagrosa" (the Miraculous Funeral Parlor)[1]. On your right, immediately after La Milagrosa, you will find the corner of "Calle Anselmo Cerro". The sign is on the wall facing you on the right hand corner. Here you turn right. Go to the end of the street, where you will find a large green sign pointing your way to Colonia Tovar. Follow the sign by turning left. Shortly after, you will find the "Bodega El Luchador" in front of you, where you take the street on the right side. Next, you find a small village square (although it is not a square but a triangle) with a low brick wall around it. Here, put your odometer at 0, and take the street on the left side.

From there, just follow the main road. It will quickly leave town, pass fields of corn and sugar cane along the bottom of a long, narrow valley and start climbing the mountain.

It is 26.2 Kms from the plaza or triangle at the outskirts of La Victoria to the entrance to the Cortada de Maya road, and then another 7.9 Kms to Hotel Bergland. The road enters Colonia Tovar from above and the Hotel Bergland is on your left just before you come down into the town.

---

[1] Note from the Editor: Rumor has it that they bring clients back from the other world. (Cash on delivery.)

For yet another spot recommended by Dick Ryan near Colonia Tovar, on the road to La Victoria, at approximately 3.7 km from the Bergland take the road going to the left to Capachal.

«It is only paved for a kilometer or so, but there is some good forest along it. It is usually rather quiet, but I have yet to fail to see Southern Yellow-bellied Grosbeak along this road. When you get to the end of the paving, stop and walk the rest, for if the dirt part gets at all wet, it becomes spectacularly slippery.»

Although Dick, who is a superb birder suggested this road, another birder, who sent me a two page e-mail of complaints, stated *«This was a very de-forested area, and not a pleasant drive.»* You decide.

TO MARACAY, FROM COLONIA TOVAR, VIA LA VICTORIA

From the gas station mentioned above, at the end of the main street full of shops in Colonia Tovar, it is 31.8 kms to La Victoria. As you come down into town, you will see a large white building on your right (a school) and the little plaza on the left. (Just next to the school is an excellent bakery for a cup of coffee, and you will need it after coming down that mountain.) From that point:

Turn right at the first corner. At the second corner veer right, passing the government office of SAS (Sanidad or Public Health). At the next corner turn right again, passing the Lagoven gas station. Look left for on-coming traffic and then go straight on to the end of the street and turn right.

You are now on Avenida Loreto, the main, busy street with a multitude of stoplights, pedestrians jay walking and buses stopping at every corner. You will be wise to stay in the left lane.

The first large street or opening on your right leads to the industrial area. Continue on for yet another half kilometer until you come to the next large opening on your right which leads to the Caracas-Valencia Autopista. This is approximately 2.5 kms from the school and small plaza.

Once on the Autopista, to go to Henri Pittier National Park follow the sign for Maracay and Valencia.

EL LIMÓN

Not far from Colonia Tovar, on the northern side of the Coastal Cordillera is an area, generally known as El Limón, that is excellent for birding. Originally it was a large coffee plantation with huge Mountain Immortelle trees (*Erythrina,* called *Bucares* in Venezuela) giving shade to the coffee bushes.

Unfortunately, in just the past few years there has been a great deal of deforestation, especially along the top of the mountains as well as in the coffee plantations, in order to plant strawberries. As a matter of fact, it was a government agency, the National Agrarian Institute, that lent the tractors to help deforest the high area. The result has been erosion and undermining of the road. Nevertheless, although no longer the dream area of yore, it is still good, and really spectacular in the months of September to February, when the feeding flocks are about, and in February and March, when the remaining Immortelle trees are in flower.

To reach El Limón and the sea at Puerto Cruz, from Caracas, just after the gas station and before the large arch welcoming visitors to Colonia Tovar, take the right fork that winds down the mountain. From Colonia Tovar you would take the road towards

Caracas and turn left after passing under the arch. By the by, right next to the above-mentioned gas station is the "Lunchería Breisach," where you can buy a very large and complete Polish sausage sandwich (similar to those served by Subway but far less expensive). The sandwich plus a coffee will keep you going for the remaining of the day.

The road first climbs a bit, goes over the ridge, and then down. As you travel it, stop frequently to check the ever-changing habitats for different species. High in the mountains Beryl-spangled, Blue-capped and Blue-winged Mountain-Tanagers are easily spotted, as well as the beautiful hummingbirds of the higher elevations such as Tyrian Metaltail, Lazuline Sabrewing, Bronzy Inca and Booted Racket-tail.

Shortly after you reach the crest of the road and pass the side road on your right that leads to the coastal village of Chichiriviche[1] you will see a dirt road on your left. You are now at approximately I,400 meters. This is an excellent road to walk and bird in the early morning. (Leave your car locked) During the months from March to June you should hear (and perhaps see) Plain-backed Antpitta and Black-faced and Scalloped Antthrushes. In February, Wing-barred Manakin call in this area. In September, when the main breeding season is over, many of the tanagers and other birds such as Slate-throated Redstart start to form feeding flocks, and you will be hard-put to keep up with the individual species. Also found here are Groove-billed Toucanet, Montane, Guttulated and Buff-fronted Foliage-gleaners, Gray-breasted Wood-wren, Blue-naped Chlorophonia, Blue-winged Mountain-tanager, Crested Oropendola and Yellow-backed Oriole, plus many others.

Some 18.5 kms from the fork to Colonia Tovar you will come to a deep curve to the right going on down to the hamlet of El Limón itself. On the left, take a dirt road that crosses a stream, go up the short hill and turn left. After crossing the second stream, park your car and continue walking uphill through the banana plantation. Hummingbirds love banana flowers, and it is possible here to see White-vented Plumeleteer, Violet-chested and Wedge-billed Hummingbirds, Violet-fronted Brilliant, Lazuline Sabrewing, Black-throated Mango, and Golden-tailed Sapphire. It is a long walk to the top (from an altitude of 900 meters to I,360 meters), but it can be very rewarding, especially during February when the tanagers, hummers and honeycreepers are feasting on the flame-colored blossoms of the Mountain Immortelles.

The main road leads down to the sea and, of course, birding it all the way takes a lot of time, but I have always enjoyed the changes in bird species according to the altitude. I rather doubt that the road through the valley of El Limón is as rich in avifauna as previously, but some of the professional guides have advised me that they are now spending more time with their clients along the road to El Limon than in Henri Pittier. Over the years my list of the birds from the top of the mountain down to the sea at Puerto Cruz includes the following:

Little Tinamou	Bicolored Hawk	Rufous-vented Chachalaca
Red-legged Tinamou	Broad-winged Hawk	Band-tailed Guan
Brown Pelican	Roadside Hawk	Solitary Sandpiper
Magnificent Frigatebird	Short-tailed Hawk	Greater Yellowlegs
Black Vulture	Gray-lined Hawk	Spotted Sandpiper
Pearl Kite	White Hawk	Venezuelan Wood-Quail
Swallow-tailed Kite	Ornate Hawk-Eagle	Band-tailed Pigeon
Hook-billed Kite	Black Hawk-Eagle	Common Ground-Dove

[1] Warning from the Editor: Don't get befuddled, please. There are two Chichiriviches – this one and the one in Falcón.

Ruddy Ground-Dove
Blue Ground-Dove
White-tipped Dove
Ruddy Quail-Dove
Lined Quail-Dove
Brown-throated Parakeet
Red-eared Parakeet
Green-rumped Parrotlet
Red-billed Parrot
Yellow-billed Cuckoo
Squirrel Cuckoo
Smooth-billed Ani
Groove-billed Ani
Striped Cuckoo
Pavonine Cuckoo
Vermiculated Screech-Owl
Tropical Screech-Owl
Ferruginous Pygmy Owl
Mottled Owl
Semicollared Nighthawk
Band-winged Nightjar
White-collared Swift
Lesser Swallow-tailed Swift
Rufous-breasted Hermit
Sooty-capped Hermit
Little Hermit
Lazuline Sabrewing
White-necked Jacobin
Green Violetear
Black-throated Mango
Violet-headed Hummingbird
Blue-tailed Emerald
Blue-chinned Sapphire
Golden-tailed Sapphire
Copper-rumped Hummingbird
White-vented Plumeleteer
Speckled Hummingbird
Violet-fronted Brilliant
Violet-chested Hummingbird
Bronzy Inca
Booted Racketail
Tyrian Metaltail
Long-tailed Sylph
Rufous-shafted Woodstar
White-tipped Quetzal
Collared Trogon
Green Kingfisher
Rufous-tailed Jacamar
Russet-throated Puffbird
Moustached Puffbird
Groove-billed Toucanet

Scaled Piculet
Golden-olive Woodpecker
Red-crowned Woodpecker
Red-rumped Woodpecker
Plain-brown Woodcreeper
Olivaceous Woodcreeper
Strong-billed Woodcreeper
Black-banded Woodcreeper
Barred Woodcreeper
Buff-throated Woodcreeper
Olive-backed Woodcreeper
Streaked-headed Woodcreeper
Spot-crowned Woodcreeper
Red-billed Scythebill
Pale-breasted Spinetail
Stripe-breasted Spinetail
Black-throated Spinetail
Crested Spinetail
Spotted Barbtail
Streaked Tuftedcheek
Guttulated Foliage-gleaner
Montane Foliage-gleaner
Buff-fronted Foliage-gleaner
Streaked Xenops
Plain Xenops
Sharp-tailed Streamcreeper
Great Antshrike
Barred Antshrike
Plain Antvireo
White-streaked Antvireo
Slaty Antwren
White-fringed Antwren
Long-tailed Antbird
White -bellied Antbird
Short-tailed Antthrush
Scalloped Antthrush
Black-faced Antthrush
Plain-backed Antpitta
Chestnut-crowned Antpitta
Rusty-breasted Antpitta
Slate-crowned Antpitta
Caracas Tapaculo
Green-and-black Fruiteater
Golden-breasted Fruiteater
Handsome Fruiteater
Cinereous Becard
Chestnut-crowned Becard
White-winged Becard
Black-tailed Tityra
Masked Tityra
Bearded Bellbird

Golden-headed Manakin
Wire-tailed Manakin
Lance-tailed Manakin
Wing-barred Manakin
Black Phoebe
Tropical Kingbird
Variegated Flycatcher
Boat-billed Flycatcher
Streaked Flycatcher
Golden-crowned Flycatcher
Rusty-margined Flycatcher
Social Flycatcher
Great Kiskadee
Short-crested Flycatcher
Pale-edged Flycatcher
Brown-crested Flycatcher
Dusky-capped Flycatcher
Olive-sided Flycatcher
Tropical Pewee
Smoke-colored Pewee
Cinnamon Flycatcher
Flavescent Flycatcher
Bran-colored Flycatcher
White-throated Spadebill
Yellow-olive Flycatcher
Yellow-breasted Flycatcher
Common Tody-Flycatcher
Helmeted Pygmy-Tyrant
Pale-eyed Pygmy-Tyrant
Marbled-faced Bristle-Tyrant
White-throated Tyrannulet
Yellow-bellied Elaenia
Lesser Elaenia
Mountain Elaenia
Northern Scrub -Flycatcher
Caracas (Paltry) Tyrannulet
Slaty-capped Flycatcher
Olive-striped Flycatcher
Southern Rough-winged Swallow
Green Jay
Whiskered Wren
Rufous-breasted Wren
Rufous-and-white Wren
House Wren
Gray-breasted Wood-Wren
Southern Nightingale Wren
Tropical Mockingbird
Andean Solitaire
Veery
Gray-cheeked Thrush
Yellow-legged Thrush

Glossy-black Thrush
Black-hooded Thrush
Pale-breasted Thrush
Cocoa Thrush
Bare-eyed Thrush
Long-billed Gnatwren
Tropical Gnatcatcher
Rufous-browed Peppershrike
Red-eyed Vireo
Brown-capped Vireo
Golden-fronted Greenlet
Shiny Cowbird
Giant Cowbird
Crested Oropendola
Russet-backed Oropendola
Yellow-rumped Cacique
Yellow-billed Cacique
Orange-crowned Oriole
Yellow-backed Oriole
Black-and-White Warbler
Golden-winged Warbler
Tennessee Warbler
Tropical Parula
Cerulean Warbler
Blackburnian Warbler
Blackpoll Warbler
Northern Waterthrush
American Redstart

Slate-throated Redstart
Black-crested Warbler
Flavescent Warbler
Three-striped Warbler
Golden-crowned Warbler
White-eared Conebill
Bananaquit
Bluish Flower-Piercer
White-sided Flower-Piercer
Purple Honeycreeper
Red-legged Honeycreeper
Speckled Tanager
Golden Tanager
Rufous-cheeked Tanager
Bay-headed Tanager
Beryl-spangled Tanager
Black-capped Tanager
Black-headed Tanager
Fawn-breasted Tanager
Blue-naped Chlorophonia
Blue-hooded Euphonia
Orange-bellied Euphonia
Thick-billed Euphonia
Blue-winged Mountain Tanager
Blue-gray Tanager
Palm Tanager
Blue-capped Tanager

Silver-beaked Tanager
Hepatic Tanager
Summer Tanager
White-winged Tanager
White-lined Tanager
Gray-headed Tanager
Rosy Thrush Tanager
Guira Tanager
Fulvous-headed Tanager
Oleaginous Hemispingus
Common Bush-Tanager
Black-faced Tanager
Blue-black Grosbeak
Buff-throated Saltator
Streaked Saltator
Rose-breasted Grosbeak
Chestnut-capped Brush-Finch
Ochre-breasted Brush-Finch
Black-striped Sparrow
Black-faced Grassquit
Gray Seedeater
Yellow-bellied Seedeater
Ruddy-breasted Seedeater
Blue-black Grassquit
Rufous-collared Sparrow
Yellow-bellied Siskin
Lesser Goldfinch

The best part of El Limon is a secret I have only recently discovered. Some 24 km from the arch you will see the buildings of Hacienda El Limon on your left across the road from a small general store on the right. This is an active coffee plantation but it is also an inn called **Posada Los Conotos** (Oropendola Inn). By staying there, you can bird the whole day coming down the mountain, and not have to go back up immediately. The building itself dates back to 1902. They have just 4 rooms, only one of which has a private bath. The other three share two bathrooms. This may not be a luxurious inn. Perhaps it could rate 2 stars, but as far as I am concerned it is a delightful place for bird watchers, and the welcome you receive is five star. The dining room opens out to the garden where a very cold stream gives you a chance to cool off should you wish. As I was having a cup of coffee I could see Sooty-capped Hermit, Olivaceous Woodcreeper, Black Phoebe, Silver-beaked Tanagers and others I could not identify without binoculars (I was there on serious business – no time for fooling around). They even have an area for campers as well as trails for birders to follow. Lodging with meals is very reasonable, and I do not think you can beat their prices any place -- not with birds thrown in as well! For reservations call the very friendly owner, Moraima Maldonado de Borjas at (0) 416-710-2137. Highly recommended.

PUERTO CRUZ / PUERTO MAYA

After birding all the way down the mountain from the junction with Colonia Tovar and having passed the hamlet of El Limón, you will be approaching a beach area known as Puerto Cruz. (I cannot recommend it for swimming, for the beach is filthy, there is an undertow and sharks in the water.)

Just before the beach there is a dirt road going up the mountain off to your left. The road looks much worse than it actually is, and I believe that an ordinary car could drive it quite easily during the dry season, as long as you do not have too low a clearance. The road leads to the coastal village of Puerto Maya some 14 kms west of Puerto Cruz. This settlement is composed almost entirely of shacks on the beach belonging to the descendants of the original black slaves of the area. I found the people to be helpful and friendly, and the small hotel or inn called **Posada Maya-K-Noa** (formerly Gua-K-Maya), may be nothing to write home about, but it is clean and the employees are pleasant. It is a place to go **during** the week to get away from the world. For reservations, call these Caracas phone numbers: (0) 212-264-6466 & 264-4566.

The road to Puerto Maya runs along the mountains bordering the sea, and although you would not expect to see much in this area, I found the following species:

Brown Pelican	Red-rumped Woodpecker	Pale-breasted Thrush
Magnificent Frigatebird	Black-banded Woodcreeper	Tropical Gnatcatcher
Roadside Hawk	Straight-billed Woodcreeper	Rufous-browed Peppershrike
Yellow-headed Caracara	Crested Spinetail	Red-eyed Vireo
Laughing Falcon	Barred Antshrike	Golden-fronted Greenlet
Ruddy Ground-Dove	White-fringed Antwren	Red-legged Honeycreeper
Scaled Dove	White-bellied Antbird	Trinidad Euphonia
White-tipped Dove	Lance-tailed Manakin	Thick-billed Euphonia
Brown-throated Parakeet	Tropical Kingbird	Blue-Gray Tanager
Green-rumped Parrotlet	Boat-billed Flycatcher	Hepatic Tanager
Blue-headed Parrot	Social Flycatcher	Ultramarine Grosbeak
Squirrel Cuckoo	Great Kiskadee	Streaked Saltator
Ferruginous Pygmy-Owl	Brown-crested Flycatcher	Black-striped Sparrow
Ringed Kingfisher	Pearly-vented Tody-Tyrant	Black-faced Grassquit
Scaled Piculet	Rufous-breasted Wren	

PARQUE NACIONAL MACARAO

I have given full details of this Park in the chapter on Caracas. However, I mention it here once more due to the fact that, if you are going back to Caracas, one of the main entrances to the Park is located on your right after you pass the welcoming arch for Colonia Tovar If you are coming up from Caracas, that main entrance is located just 2 km before the Colonia Tovar arch[1]. This is one of Macarao's best birding areas. While in Colonia Tovar, give it a try!

---

[1] Editor's Note: we go again! This is Mary Lou at her most exquisite – the land mark comes AFTER the place she wishes you to turn into. Never-you-mind: just drive to 2 km the Colonia Tovar arch and then DOUBLE BACK two km to find your entrance. After all what are 2 km more when you are having fun? Gee whizzz!

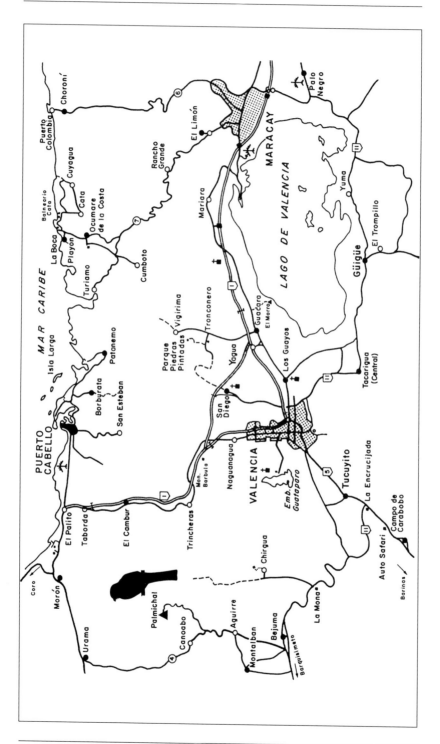

II - 4. State of Carabobo

INTRODUCTION

Carabobo is one of Venezuela's wealthiest states, seat to most of our secondary industry. A vast majority of the small and mid-size factories and industries in the country is located in the industrial areas that surround the state capital of Valencia. Since what are perhaps the best agricultural soils in the country are also found here, the state is also known for its dairy industry and its large extensions of orchards. And yet, it is one of our smallest states, so it is amazing to me that two of the inns that give world-class service to birders in Venezuela are also "concentrated" in this wee small state of Carabobo.

CASA MARÍA

I never thought to find an inn like this one in Venezuela, and I still cannot believe our luck. It is located approximately 3 hours from Caracas via Valencia and then southward to the reach the road going west towards Barquisimeto. As you reach the industrial city of Valencia, you will find that the Autopista ends in an overpass, which is one of the exits towards the north coast from the Autopista. However, you should keep in the far right lane, staying on the lower part of the road, going under the overpass, and then veer immediately to the right to curve down and join the highway coming up from the coast going south.

You are now headed south towards the Andes and high Llanos as well as the city of Barquisimeto and Yacambú National Park (See chapter for the State of Lara). After 17.7 kilometers you turn right, following the signs for Barquisimeto (National Highway 11). From here it is some 31 kilometers to the town of **Bejuma**. Actually, you skirt the town by driving on to the most *western* entrance. You will see a sign for Montalban, Aguirre and/or Canoabo, just across from a large gas station. Turn right off the main highway and head north towards Montalban and **Canoabo** on State Highway 4. At the fork indicating Montalban, keep right. From the turn off on the highway leading to Barquisimeto, it is approximately 16.8 kilometers to a very steep, paved road going off to your right, indicating **Palmichal.**

Casa María is the first house on the right, some 700 meters up this road behind a high white wall. Picture to yourself a large, rambling Californian-style house set in a beautifully lush tropical garden, complete with a swimming pool at an altitude of 730 meters above sea level.

The inn is owned and run by Norbert and Gaby Flauger, two Germans from Berlin, who speak English. They have 6 rooms, all with private baths. Gaby is in charge of the food, and it is superb - from German cookies to delicious tropical fruit deserts and refreshments. Norbert is an entomologist and is raising local butterflies as well as Harlequin and Rhinoceros beetles to study their biology. He will offer to show you not only his collection, but the various stages of development of the insects. One evening after dinner he will give you a slide show. Grab the opportunity. Once you have put on colored spectacles, the next thing you know you will see a huge, gorgeous caterpillar coming out of the screen straight towards you. Not only does Norbert take 3-D slides, he also uses a macro lens for his insects!

For reservations call: Ing. Norbert Flauger. Phone: (0) 249-941-1020, fax: (0) 249-808-1001, nflauger@hotmail.com. There is no doubt that this is a five-star inn. They prefer to have small groups.

Being an entomologist, Norbert leaves a mercury lamp on all night, and in the morning you can observe the birds having their breakfast before you have yours. When walking Norbert's paths in the forest area across the street from the house, my suggestion would be to imitate the Ferruginous Pygmy-Owl's call. Everything present will pop out to see where the owl is. Both around the house and across the street look for the following species:

Little Tinamou	Scaled Piculet	Southern Rough-winged
Red-legged Tinamou	Lineated Woodpecker	Swallow
Black Vulture	Red-crowned Woodpecker	Rufous-breasted Wren
Turkey Vulture	Plain-brown Woodcreeper	Rufous-and-white Wren
Swallow-tailed Kite	Buff-throated Woodcreeper	House Wren
Roadside Hawk	Streaked-headed Woodcreeper	Tropical Mockingbird
Rufous-vented Chachalaca	Pale-breasted Spinetail	Pale-breasted Thrush
Laughing Falcon	Crested Spinetail	Bare-eyed Thrush
Pale-vented Pigeon	Barred Antshrike	White-necked Thrush
Ruddy Ground-Dove	Common Thornbird	Long-billed Gnatwren
Blue Ground-Dove	White-bellied Antbird	Rufous-browed Peppershrike
White-tipped Dove	Chestnut-crowned Becard	Red-eyed Vireo
Scarlet-fronted Parakeet	White-winged Becard	Golden-fronted Greenlet
Brown-throated Parakeet	Black-tailed Tityra	Shiny Cowbird
White-eared Parakeet	Tropical Kingbird	Giant Cowbird
Green-rumped Parrotlet	Variegated Flycatcher	Crested Oropendola
Blue-headed Parrot	Boat-billed Flycatcher	Russet-backed Oropendola
Orange-winged Parrot	Streaked Flycatcher	Tropical Parula
Striped Cuckoo	Black Phoebe	Golden-crowned Warbler
Tropical Screech-Owl	Rusty-margined Flycatcher	Bananaquit
Mottled Owl	Social Flycatcher	Bay-headed Tanager
Great Potoo	Great Kiskadee	Trinidad Euphonia
Common Pauraque	Common Tody-Flycatcher	Blue-gray Tanager
Band-winged Nightjar	Slate-headed Tody-Flycatcher	Palm Tanager
White-chinned Sapphire	Yellow-bellied Elaenia	Silver-beaked Tanager
Glittering-throated Emerald	Small-billed Elaenia	White-lined Tanager
Copper-rumped	Forest Elaenia	Streaked Saltator
Hummingbird	Slaty-capped Flycatcher	Yellow-bellied Seedeater
Rufous-tailed Jacamar	Blue-and-white Swallow	Lesser Goldfinch

PALMICHAL

Where to do the best birding of all? That is the question! On my list one of the first-class sites for birding in Venezuela is the Watershed Preservation Area of **Palmichal,** 6.3 km above Casa María. This is 11,000 hectares of forest managed by Pequiven, a government-owned petrochemical company.

The company obtained the area to recuperate the forest and thus protect the headwaters of the Morón River. There is an 11 kilometer-long dirt road for you to walk that goes from cloud forest at 1,000 meters down to 300 meters above sea level. My first reaction was "Rancho Grande without traffic." The Venezuelan Audubon had permission from Pequiven to make a year-long census of the birds at Palmichal, ending up with some 300 species.

To date we have the following list for **Palmichal**:

Gray Tinamou
Little Tinamou
Black Vulture
Turkey Vulture
King Vulture
White-tailed Kite
Swallow-tailed Kite
Double-toothed Kite
Plumbeous Kite
Bicolored Hawk
Gray-bellied Goshawk
Broad-winged Hawk
Roadside Hawk
White Hawk
Great Black Hawk
Solitary Eagle
Ornate Hawk-Eagle
Black-and-white Hawk Eagle
Black Hawk-Eagle
Osprey
Bat Falcon
Rufous-vented Chachalaca
Band-tailed Guan
Crested Guan
Venezuelan Wood - Quail
Gray-necked Wood-Rail
Yellow-breasted Crake
Ruddy Pigeon
Ruddy Ground-Dove
Blue Ground-Dove
White-tipped Dove
Ruddy Quail-Dove
Lined Quail-Dove
Scarlet-fronted Parakeet
White-eared Parakeet
Green-rumped Parrotlet
Lilac-tailed Parrotlet
Blue-headed Parrot
Red-billed Parrot
Orange-winged Parrot
Squirrel Cuckoo
Greater Ani
Smooth-billed Ani
Striped Cuckoo
Tropical Screech Owl
Spectacled Owl
Ferruginous Pygmy - Owl
Black and White Owl
Mottled Owl

Short-tailed Nighthawk
Pauraque
Band-winged Nightjar
White-collared Swift
Vaux's Swift
Gray-rumped Swift
Rufous-breasted Hermit
Pale-bellied Hermit
Sooty-capped Hermit
Little Hermit
Lazuline Sabrewing
White-necked Jacobin
Violet-headed Hummingbird
Blue-tailed Emerald
Green-tailed Emerald
Fork-tailed Woodnymph
Glittering-throated Emerald
Copper-rumped Hummingbird
Speckled Hummingbird
Violet-fronted Brilliant
Violet-chested Hummingbird
Bronzy Inca
Booted Racket-tail
White-vented Plumeleteer
Long-tailed Sylph
White-tipped Quetzal
Collared Trogon
Ringed Kingfisher
Blue-crowned Motmot
Rufous-tailed Jacamar
Moustached Puffbird
Groove-billed Toucanet
Scaled Piculet
Golden-olive Woodpecker
Lineated Woodpecker
Red-crowned Woodpecker
Smoky-brown Woodcreeper
Crimson-crested Woodpecker
Plain-brown Woodcreeper
Olivaceous Woodcreeper
Strong-billed Woodcreeper
Black-banded Woodcreeper
Buff-throated Woodcreeper
Olive-backed Woodcreeper
Streaked-headed Woodcreeper
Red-billed Scythebill
Pale-breasted Spinetail
Stripe-breasted Spinetail
Crested Spinetail

Common Thornbird
Guttulated Foliage Gleaner
Montane Foliage Gleaner
Streaked Tuftedcheek
Buff-fronted Foliage Gleaner
Streaked Xenops
Plain Xenops
Gray-throated Leaftosser
Great Antshrike
Black-crested Antshrike
Barred Antshrike
Plain Antvireo
White-streaked Antvireo
Slaty Antwren
Rufous-winged Antwren
Jet Antbird
White-bellied Antbird
Short-tailed Antthrush
Black-faced Antthrush
Plain-backed Antpitta
Handsome Fruiteater
Chestnut-crowned Becard
White-winged Becard
Black-capped Becard
Black-and-white Becard
Black-tailed Tityra
Masked Tityra
Bearded Bellbird
Golden-headed Manakin
Lance-tailed Manakin
Wing-barred Manakin
Thrush-like Schiffornis
Black Phoebe
Tropical Kingbird
Variegated Flycatcher
Piratic Flycatcher
Boat-billed Flycatcher
Streaked Flycatcher
Golden-crowned Flycatcher
Rusty-margined Flycatcher
Social Flycatcher
Great Kiskadee
Bright-rumped Attila
Brown-crested Flycatcher
Dusky-capped Flycatcher
Olive-sided Flycatcher
Tropical Pewee
Smoke-colored Pewee
Euler's Flycatcher

Cinnamon Flycatcher
Flavescent Flycatcher
Bran-colored Flycatcher
White-throated Spadebill
Yellow-olive Flycatcher
Common Tody - Flycatcher
Marble-faced Bristle - Tyrant
Venezuelan Bristle - Tyrant
Rufous-lord Tyrannulet
Scale-crested Pygmy - Tyrant
Yellow-bellied Elaenia
Forest Elaenia
Northern Scrub -Flycatcher
Sooty-headed Tyrannulet
Venezuelan Tyrannulet
Slaty-capped Flycatcher
Olive-striped Flycatcher
Tropical Pewee
Southern Rough - winged Swallow
Barn Swallow
Green Jay
Whiskered Wren
Rufous-breasted Wren
Rufous-and-white Wren
Buff-breasted Wren
House Wren
Gray-breasted Wood-wren
Southern Nightingale Wren
Gray-cheeked Thrush
Black-hooded Thrush
Pale-breasted Thrush

Bare-eyed Thrush
White-necked Thrush
Long-billed Gnatwren
Rufous-browed Peppershrike
Red-eyed Vireo
Brown-capped Vireo
Golden-fronted Greenlet
Crested Oropendola
Russet-backed Oropendola
Yellow-rumped Cacique
Orange-crowned Oriole
Yellow-Oriole
Yellow-backed Oriole
Tennessee Warbler
Cerulean Warbler
Blackburnian Warbler
Blackpoll Warbler
Louisiana Waterthrush
Northern Waterthrush
Tropical Parula
Masked Yellowthroat
American Redstart
Slate-throated Redstart
Flavescent Warbler
Three-striped Warbler
Golden-crowned Warbler
Bananaquit
Purple Honeycreeper
Green Honeycreeper
Speckled Tanager
Golden Tanager

Rufous-cheeked Tanager
Blue-necked Tanager
Bay-headed Tanager
Beryl-spangled Tanager
Black-capped Tanager
Black-headed Tanager
Orange-bellied Euphonia
Thick-billed Euphonia
Blue-winged Mountain Tanager
Blue-gray Tanager
Palm Tanager
Silver-beaked Tanager
Summer Tanager
White-winged Tanager
White-lined Tanager
Gray-headed Tanager
Guira Tanager
Fulvous-headed Tanager
Common Bush Tanager
Blue-black Grosbeak
Buff-throated Saltator
Grayish Saltator
Streaked Saltator
Chestnut-capped Brush-Finch
Black-striped Sparrow
Black-faced Grassquit
Lesser Seed-Finch
Gray Seedeater
Yellow-bellied Seedeater
Blue-black Grassquit
Lesser Goldfinch

As you will note from the above list, it is possible to see practically the same birds at Palmichal as at Rancho Grande with the exception of certain cloud forest species that can also be seen in the Andes.

To give you an idea as to what Palmichal is like, I quote once again from a letter received from Dr. Richard Byrne;

«*Palmichal was lovely. We were thoroughly spoilt, everything was done for us by very nice staff, great lunches and dinners, Stuff left for our DIY breakfasts, and we were the only people there. Perhaps 5 full days was slightly generous (though I only saw the Venezuelan Wood Quail on the last morning), but we thoroughly enjoyed it. The owls were amazing. A nightly treat. And, one night we saw an obliging Mottled Owl as well. The forest trail was very good for tyrannulets and other mixed flock species, plus the soaring raptors (B & W, Black Hawk Eagles, Solitary Eagle). The tour to the marsh and reservoir was also enjoyable. Saw our only White-bellied Antbird of the trip, and the Screamers were incredible!*»

One of the most important points to be remembered about Palmichal is the absolute personal security to be found there, as well as the warm welcome from the staff. You will find that Palmichal is more like a biological station than an inn, and you will have the run of the station.

To overnight at Palmichal either contact the Venezuelan Audubon as they are the representatives or contact (0) 414-946-2807, e-mail lvillalo@cantv.net. The rooms, while not luxurious, are perfectly acceptable with private bath and hot water. The food is excellent, and you will be completely pampered by the personnel of the station. You can also visit the station on a day basis, paying Bs. 1,000 entrance fee.

The best trick in Palmichal is to be up on the roof of the building at 7:00 a.m. to watch all the birds eating the insects that have accumulated during the night. This is an exhausting experience and may well require several hours of intense birding. Especially during the rainy season if you are up on the roof before it begins to get light, you will see several high-powered lamps which hang from the perimeter of the roof. Thousands of moths are fluttering in the light beams and chasing after them, are Short-tailed Nighthawks.

To bird the road, try to be there by 6:00 a.m. to walk down as far as possible. Remember that as far as you go down, you will have to come UP, so, to go way down, you should be in fairly good physical shape! Take water with you because it can become quite warm later in the day. At mid-day, when the birding has calmed down a bit, try going up on the roof of the station again to look for raptors. Hopefully, you will have a scope with you. Chris Sharpe sighted four raptors from the roof - a pair of Ornate Hawk-Eagles, Black Hawk-Eagle, Black-and-white Hawk-Eagle, Solitary Eagle and one unidentified hawk - all within less than an hour. Another day while we were taking our afternoon coffee on the roof, we discovered a White-tipped Quetzal on a branch immediately over our heads! See what you can do!

If you do go on your own and wish to visit Palmichal, you must stop at the administration office and request permission *from them* to bird the road.

THE CANOABO DAM

After a couple of days walking the road of Palmichal, you should go down the hill to the **Canoabo Dam** to look for dry-area birds. The most important advice I can give you for this excursion is that you should leave Palmichal or Casa Maria very early in the morning - approximately by 6:00 a.m. -- as it can be exceedingly warm. Or, go late in the afternoon, but the birding is always better in the morning. If you are on your own, from Palmichal drive back to the first cross-roads, some 7 km, turn right to Canoabo. After another 5 km, you will see a gas station on your right at the entrance to the town of Canoabo. This is a very nice little town, where you can buy groceries, beer, visit the quaint church and the pretty university, AND there is an excellent garage and mechanics should something go amiss with your car. In order to reach the dam, be sure to turn left at the very next corner after the gas station, going past the university and continue for 3.5 km where you will come to the cross-roads for **Urama.** Turn right, crossing the bridge. At 10 km from the gas station there is a barely discernible dirt road angling in from the left. Although the road is very rough, I believe that with a normal car you can drive down a short way, park in a secluded place and walk down to the lake. Be sure to lock the car and leave nothing in sight.

It is amazing the birds one can find in this dry scrub including - for starters:

Little Tinamou	Cocoi Heron	Black-crowned Night-Heron
Pied-billed Grebe	Great Egret	Wood Stork
Neotropic Cormorant	Cattle Egret	Masked Duck
Anhinga	Striated Heron	King Vulture

Turkey Vulture	Red-crowned Woodpecker	Southern Beardless Tyrannulet
Snail Kite	Buff-throated Woodcreeper	Yellow-bellied Tyrannulet
Roadside Hawk	Streak-headed Woodcreeper	White-winged Swallow
Osprey	Pale-breasted Spinetail	Brown-chested Martin
Yellow-headed Caracara	Common Thornbird	Barn Swallow
Crested Caracara	Great Antshrike	Buff-breasted Wren
Rufous-vented Chachalaca	Barred Antshrike	House Wren
Gray-necked Wood - Rail	White-bellied Antbird	Tropical Mockingbird
Common Moorhen	White-fringed Antwren	Rufous-browed Peppershrike
American Purple Gallinule	Cinnamon Becard	Red-eyed Vireo
Wattled Jacana	Lance-tailed Manakin	Golden-fronted Greenlet
Black-necked Stilt	Pied Water Tyrant	Scrub Greenlet
Large-billed Tern	Fork-tailed Flycatcher	Shiny Cowbird
Pale-vented Pigeon	Tropical Kingbird	Giant Cowbird
Eared Dove	Boat-billed Flycatcher	Yellow Oriole
Common Ground Dove	Social Flycatcher	White-eared Conebill
White-tipped Dove	Great Kiskadee	Bananaquit
Ruddy Ground-Dove	Lesser Kiskadee	Silver-beaked Tanager
Blue Ground-Dove	Tropical Pewee	White-lined Tanager
Scaled Dove	Fuscous Flycatcher	Ultramarine Grosbeak
Green rumped Parrotlet	Bran-colored Flycatcher	Grayish Saltator
Orange-winged Parrot	Common Tody - Flycatcher	Streaked Saltator
Smooth billed Ani	Slate-headed Tody - Flycatcher	Black-striped Sparrow
Striped Cuckoo	Yellow-breasted Flycatcher	Gray Seedeater
Glittering-throated Emerald	Yellow Tyrannulet	Lesson's Seedeater
Fork-tailed Palm-Swift	Tawny-crowned Pygmy-Tyrant	Yellow-bellied Seedeater
Ringed Kingfisher	Yellow-bellied Elaenia	Ruddy-breasted Seedeater
Rufous-tailed Jacamar	Small-billed Elaenia	Blue-black Grassquit
Russet-throated Puffbird	Northern Scrub- Flycatcher	Saffron Finch
Scaled Piculet	Mouse-colored Tyrannulet	Red Siskin

THE MARSHES OF SAN PABLO

You have birded the forest and the dry scrub area, so it is now time to bird a wetland. However, there is a very sad caveat. Before venturing out to San Pablo, check with either Norbert Flauger or the people of the Palmichal Station. I do hope that it will not come about, but there are plans in the making to dry out the marsh. Ignorant politicians of the current government are talking of turning these lands to agriculture. They have no concept of the value of a marsh or the wildlife to be found there, and worse yet, they have not done studies about peak flow in the river. The marsh exists because the river *needs* the extra space. Nevertheless, hope springs eternally in the breast of conservationists, we will do our best to save the marsh.

To reach the Yaracuy River or the marshes of San Pablo, continue down the main road, passing the Canoabo Dam. At 13.6 km after the entrance you took to bird the area on the dam, or some 36 km from Palmichal, you will come to a main highway. Turn left, go over the bridge (just one block) and immediately turn right. At 42 km from Palmichal, you will come into the village of San Pablo. Continue straight after the Plaza Bolívar. Count the streets on your left. At the 6th corner turn left. Go 1.3 kilometers and turn left. Then go straight. Should you get lost, just ask anyone for the Rio Yaracuy, and they will point you on your way. When you come to the bridge, park and start birding.

Look for Striated Heron, Horned Screamer, Black-bellied Whistling Duck, Swallow-tailed Kite, Plumbeous Kite, Roadside Hawk, Bat Falcon, Rusty-flanked Crake, Wattled Jacana, White-headed Marsh-Tyrant, Stripe-backed Wren, Black-capped Donacobius, White-eared Conebill, Hooded Tanager, Yellow Oriole, etc.

This is a beautiful area and a wonderful place to bird in the afternoon. As it is a total of 48 kilometers from Palmichal to the marsh, and will take you a good hour to drive it, I suggest you leave the Station before 3:00 p.m. or earlier. Arrangements can be made with the people of Palmichal to take you as well.

THE ROAD TO THE CAPITA RIVER

This can be another area for xerophitic birds, at least for the first few kilometers as you go up the hill. I just discovered this road in September, 2000 and have not had the opportunity to bird it as I should like. However, I believe that it is well worth a day of hard work. It all started when one of the workmen at Palmichal mentioned to me that there were hot springs that emptied into a lovely river only 11 km from Canoabo. What he did not say at first was that it would take us a good hour and a half or two hours to drive to the river due to the state of the road - and I have a Toyota Land Cruiser! Nevertheless, let's go! The road was awful, but it went through a fantastic area. Even at high noon in the month of September, when usually nothing is going on, there were birds zipping back and forth across the road like crazy! To reach this road, follow the instructions above to the gas station in Canoabo, continue on as if you were going to bird the dam area, but do not go over the bridge. Continue straight until the end of the road where you will see a dirt road on your left. This is 19.3 km from Palmichal. You undoubtedly will not have the benefit of a 4 X 4, so drive up a little way, trying to pass the garbage area. Park and lock your car and start walking. The higher you go, the better it gets. Be sure to take water with you as it can be hot. Your other option would be to arrange with the people at Palmichal for one of their drivers to take you some 4 or 5 km up the road in one of their vehicles and to come pick you up later in the day. Naturally, they will charge for this service, but it might be the more convenient and a less stressing way of birding the road to the Capita River - not that I expect you to walk all the way to the river!

After a few days in the area of Palmichal/Canoabo, you can either go back to the main Valencia/Barquisimeto highway, turning right on National Highway 11 for Barquisimeto, Quibor, Sanare and Yacambú National Park (see chapter on the State of Lara), or you can go through Canoabo to **Urama** on State Highway 4, turning right at Urama onto National Highway 1 to Morón, where you would join National Highway 3 towards Coro in order to reach the Tucacas/Chichiriviche area (see chapter on the State of Falcon).

After finishing their careful proof reading, both Pamela and Juanita had the same commentary: *"Reading this chapter made me want to go back to Palmichal."* What better accolade?

Yellow - Rumped Cacique

Section III

NORTHWESTERN VENEZUELA

Country and Regional Endemics:

Northern Screamer
Yellow-knobbed Curassow
Black-fronted Wood-Quail
Plain-flanked Rail
Rusty-flanked Crake
Bare-eyed Pigeon
Yellow-shouldered Parrot
Dwarf Cuckoo
Pygmy Swift
Coppery Emerald
Green-tailed Emerald
Shinning-green Hummingbird
Buffy Hummingbird
Copper-rumped Hummingbird
Perijá Metaltail
Russet-throated Puffbird
Groove-billed Toucanet
White-whiskered Spinetail
Crested Spinetail
Perijá Thistletail
Great Antpitta
Handsome Fruiteater
Venezuelan Flycatcher
Short-tailed Tody-Flycatcher
Slender-billed Tyrannulet
Orinocan Saltator
Vermilion Cardinal
Tocuyo Sparrow
Red Siskin

III - 1. State of Falcón

INTRODUCTION

Would you like to see Fulvous and White-faced Whistling Ducks, American Wood Stork, Scarlet Ibis, large flocks of Greater Flamingos, Horned Screamer, Hooked-billed Kite, Plumbeous Kite, White-tailed Hawk, Zone-tailed Hawk, Roadside Hawk, Savanna Hawk, Gray-lined Hawk, White Hawk, Common Black Hawk, Great Black Hawk, Crane Hawk, Rufous-vented Chachalaca, Plain-flanked Rail, Rusty-flanked Crake, Wattled Jacana, Southern Lapwing, Double-striped Thick-knee, Bare-eyed Pigeon, Scaled Dove, Red-and-Green and Chestnut-fronted Macaws, Brown-throated Parakeet, Green-rumped Parrotlet, Yellow-shouldered and Yellow-crowned Parrots, Greater Ani, Sooty-capped Hermit, Black-throated Mango, Ruby-topaz Hummingbird, Glittering-throated Emerald, Ringed Kingfisher, Russet-throated Puffbird, Scaled Piculet, Pale-legged Hornero along with his incredible mud nest, Black-crested and Black-backed Antshrikes, Cinnamon and Cinereous Becards, Lance-tailed Manakin, Cattle Tyrant, Rusty-margined and Fuscous Flycatchers, Brown-chested Martin, Striped-backed Wren sounding like a furious Donald Duck, Black-capped Donacobius, Scrub Greenlet, Crested Oropendola, White-eared and Bicolored Conebills, Burnished-buff and Glaucous Tanagers, Grayish Saltator, etc. etc. and etc.? Then, come to Falcon!

To people who have only a few days to bird in Venezuela and don't want to waste too much time in airports and/or long drives, I am tempted to recommend the State of Falcón as the best all-around Venezuelan birding spot. If you have anything from four to seven days, here you will be able to see bird species of the Llanos, of the Coastal Cordillera, of far western Venezuela and of the xerophitic and coastal areas. Except for the species from south of the Orinoco, and high Andean regions, in Falcon you may get a good sampling of everything. For a short vacation, what more can one ask? And, should you include Palmichal (see chapter on Carabobo State), you will also have rain forest birds.

For those interested in shore and wading birds, there is the Morrocoy National Park, near the town of Tucacas, and adjacent Cuare Wildlife Refuge, near Chichiriviche. This area is well-served by excellent inns, many of which I can recommend. There are what I consider to be five-star inns for birders, as well as less expensive accommodations.

As you will also find in this chapter, Falcon offers the mountainous area of the Sierra de San Luis National Park, as well as a variety of xerophitic areas near the state capital of Coro, along the coast and in the Paraguaná Peninsula.

ON GETTING TO FALCON

It is approximately 300 km by car from Caracas to Chichiriviche, via Maracay and Valencia, on the Autopista Caracas-Valencia or National Highway 1. Coming from Caracas, when you approach the city of Valencia, turn right off the Autopista Caracas-Valencia by the sign indicating Yagua. Should you miss this particular turn, you still have an option. Just before reaching the city of Valencia, but close to it, another highway, the Autopista Valencia-Puerto Cabello, branches off north to El Palito and Morón. Go up this viaduct if you missed the Yagua turn off.

When you come down the mountain from Valencia, you reach the coast at El Palito, past a line of shacks selling all kinds of food. Immediately after, the road swings under an overpass eastwards towards Puerto Cabello. Just after this overpass take the first turnoff to the right which will take you westward along the coast past a refinery and a thermoelectric plant. A bit further on, the road branches with an overpass continuing to Moron while you should keep to your left, go under the overpass and head for Tucacas and the main road to Coro, the capital of the State.

One way to avoid Caracas completely (and I would not blame you) is to arrive in Venezuela at the small international airport in Valencia (State of Carabobo). In this event you would hire your car in Valencia. From the Valencia Airport, which is located in a suburb east of the city, it is only a short hour's drive to the northern coast and the road to Falcón (State Highway 3), or one hour to Casa Maria in Bejuma or Palmichal (see chapter on the State of Carabobo). To get from the Airport to the Autopista Valencia-Puerto Cabello, you drive on as if you were going downtown and as you enter Valencia, take the ramp going up towards Puerto Cabello / El Palito / Moron.

EASTERN FALCÓN

From the turn-off at El Palito, it is only 45 minutes northwest to crossroads at the junction of the El Palito/Tucacas/Coro National Highway 3 with the State highway No. 3 leading to San Juan de los Cayos (and also to Chichiriviche, which sits at the end of a branch-off of this road).

The area around this Y junction is known as Sanare, and here you will see a "MARAVEN" gas station[1]. Please note that I am using the gas station at this junction as your point of reference for many distances and directions in this general area.

Prior to arriving at the San Juan de los Cayos/Coro crossroads, there is another gas station on your left that is also called Sanare. Don't be confused: make sure the gas station you are referring to is a Maraven station on your right as you drive northwest and just a few meters east of the aforementioned junction or crossroads.

WHERE TO STAY

There is certainly no dearth of excellent places to choose from in this area of Falcon as you can see by the following:

As you drive northwest from El Palito, the first largely built- up area that you will come to is that hell hole of Tucacas. This is 47 km from El Palito at the bottom of the hill from Valencia. As you reach the Tucacas area, you will first see the cemetery and then further on a gas station on your left. About 100 meters before the station is a paved road, also on your left, with a sign indicating the airport. Turn left here and take note of your odometer. You are headed towards the small village of **Las Lapas**.

Finca El Siete or El 7 (The Seven) (★★★)
I originally thought that it was so named due to the fact that it was 7 km from the Tucacas highway, but this is Venezuela and nothing is logical. At approximately 4 km

---

[1] Note from the Editor: We very much regret to inform you of the following: the Venezuelan oil company Maraven has been defunct for several years now.

However, news must travel slowly around those parts, because as of the sending of this book to the publishers, the gas station continued to hold its «Maraven» designation. Don't be surprised, though, to find that it has become a BP, or PDV, or Shell, or any-other-oil-co, gas station, by the time you get there.

from Tucacas you will see a dirt road on your left and a sign on the right for Finca Cata. Turn left and within a few meters you will see a gate on your left with the sign "7". The guest area is some distance back from the entrance. There is a large lagoon below the house offering superb birding as well as the area around the house. The price includes lodging and all meals. English spoken. For reservations call either the Venezuelan Audubon or the very attentive and pleasant owner, Alfredo Suarez, at (0) 212-986-1235, (0) 414-920-3644, fax: (0) 212-985-1205, alfredosuarez79@hotmail.com. There are two draw-backs to this inn. The first is due to the fact that Alfredo is an architect, and actually lives in Caracas. Therefore, reservations must be made in advance to give him the opportunity to provide food and to be at the finca. Also, this is chigger land. So be prepared. However, the birding is excellent. Our birding group visited the Finca and counted 64 species in the first hour. The total bird list to date is as follows:

Great Egret;	Greater Ani	Great Kiskadee.
Snowy Egret	Pauraque	Lesser Kiskadee
Striated Heron	White-tailed Nightjar	Brown-crested Flycatcher
Cattle Egret	Glittering-throated Emerald	Yellow-breasted Flycatcher
Rufescent Tiger-Heron	Green Kingfisher	Common Toddy-Flycatcher
Green Ibis	Rufous-tailed Jacamar.	Pale-eyed Pygmy-Tyrant
Whispering Ibis	Russet-throated Puffbird	Yellow-bellied Elaenia
Horned Screamer	Scaled Piculet	Northern Scrub-Flycatcher
Black-bellied Whistling Duck	Spot-breasted Woodpecker	Mouse-colored Tyrannulet
Turkey Vulture	Lineated Woodpecker	Tawny-crowned Pygmy-Tyrant
Black Vulture	Red-crowned Woodpecker	Brown-chested Martin
Snail Kite	Crimson-crested Woodpecker	Stripe-backed Wren
Zone-tailed Hawk	Straight-billed Woodcreeper	Southern House Wren
Laughing Falcon	Pale-legged Hornero	Black-capped Donacobius
Yellow-headed Caracara	Pale-breasted Spinetail	Tropical Gnatcatcher
Crested Caracara	Common Thornbird	Scrub Greenlet
Gray-necked Wood-Rail	Black-crested Antshrike	Yellow-hooded Blackbird
Rusty-flanked Crake.	Barred Antshrike	Yellow Oriole.
Purple Gallinule	White-fringed Antwren.	Oriole Blackbird
Wattled Jacana.	Cinereous Becard	Bananaquit
Ruddy Ground-Dove.	Vermilion flycatcher	Trinidad Euphonia
Scaled Dove	Pied Water-Tyrant	Blue-Gray Tanager.
White-tipped Dove	Cattle Tyrant	Glaucous Tanager
Red-and-Green Macaw	Fork-tailed Flycatcher.	Silver-beaked Tanager
Chestnut-fronted Macaw	Tropical Kingbird	Hooded Tanager
Brown-throated Parakeet	Boat-billed Flycatcher	Grayish Saltator
Green-rumped Parrotlet	Streaked Flycatcher	Gray Seedeater
Yellow-headed Parrot	Rusty-margined Flycatcher	Saffron Finch
Groove-billed Ani.	Social Flycatcher	Ruddy-breasted Seedeater

How is that for birding right off your front porch? Actually, Finca El 7 is probably the best place along the coast to see Rufous-sided Crakes, but if you are not staying at the inn, I most certainly suggest that you pay some $3 to $5 for the privilege of birding the grounds.

La Arboleda Inn (★★★)
To reach this inn, continue south on the road to Las Lapas for a total of 12 km from Tucacas, where you will see a sign that not only indicates "Km. 12", but also a dirt

road on your right. Turn and after only 50 meters there is the entrance on the right to a working cattle ranch and the inn of La Arboleda, owned by Tony Stuyk and his very attentive partner, Edith. (I understand that Tony is planning to open a direct entrance from the paved road.) I have stayed often at La Arboleda and found it to be very home-like, with good food. English spoken. The price includes breakfast and dinner. Dr. Richard Byrne commented on this inn:

«Tony and Edith were just wonderful. It is truly the most delightful place to stay, and the food was the best of the trip; If staying at Barquilla de Fresa were not something so very special, I'd be putting La Arboleda as No. 1. Tony basically ferried us everywhere. I think you might consider sending people to La Arboleda without a guide, if Tony would be prepared to take them to the right places. He was 100% reliable and efficient. If he said 5:30 a.m., he'd be ready by 5:29 a.m.»

One of the big attractions of La Arboleda for me is the fact that it is on the road to birding heaven - Rio Agualinda. (See below.) For reservations call the Venezuelan Audubon or (0) 259-881-5027 or (0) 414-484-1660 & 414-484-5252.

In Tucacas
Before the gas station in Tucacas, a right turn leads to **Morrocoy N.P.** (the entrance is over a hump-backed bridge, and leads through mangroves to a beach). This road is the main shopping street of Tucacas, and on the left, a new **delicatessen**, full of exotic foods and wonderfully air-conditioned, is not to be missed!

Posada Balijú (★★★★)
This is the only inn I would recommend for bird watchers in that most unpleasant town. A very accurate description is given by Elizabeth Kline in her excellent book, "Guide to Camps, Posadas and Cabins." By reservations only. Located on Calle Libertad. Pretty seaside setting in private compound (hence the reason I am recommending it). 12 very pleasant rooms with private bath, hot water, AC. Huge terrace at edge of sea with open caney/bar with tables, hammocks. Price includes – lodging, breakfast, picnic lunch, dinner and excursion to the keys. Phone numbers: (0) 259-812-1580, (0) 412-262-3596.

By the by, do not even think of staying in Tucacas or Chichiriviche on a week-end or holidays (Christmas, Easter, Carnival). The other inns mentioned in this chapter would not be so crowded as they are off the beaten track.

Near Parque Nacional Morrocoy
Villa Mangrovia (★★★★★)
To find this jewel, right after you have passed Tucacas you will see the Hotel Coral Reef on your right. (They called it Coral Reef after they destroyed a huge mangrove area to build it!) From that hotel it is 8.3 kilometers to the entrance of Morrocoy National Park, also on your right. This is not only the entrance to the Park but also the access to the marinas, the National Guard and Park Guard Posts. After 2 km you will pass the actual entrance to the Park and then the National Guard post after an additional 5 km. Carry on until you see a long white wall on your right with a small plaque saying "Mangrovia" by the gate. The inn is set in a beautiful garden on a ridge overlooking the clear waters of the Park. It has 3 tastefully decorated double rooms, two in the main house with private baths as well as a private cabin a few feet from the main house. All have ceiling fans, but no hot water. (Who needs it in that climate?) Superb food. Package includes lodging and three meals, trips to the

islands with snorkeling equipment, towels, etc. The owner, Irina Jackson speaks English, German, Russian and Serbo-Croat. Reservations must be made in advance. Contact the Venezuelan Audubon.

Posada El Paraiso Azul (★★★★)

Follow the road to Villa Mangrovia. Take the second dirt road on your left after the National Guard station. Part of the road has concrete tracks just wheel width. When you reach the top, I suggest you park immediately in the area to your right. The inn has a spectacular view of the Park and its many islands from the dining terrace. There are a total of 15 rooms with AC, thick towels, shampoo, etc. Their package includes lodging, all meals, trips to the islands, etc. For reservations call the Audubon or (0) 212-952-1490 & 953-4901 in Caracas. The telephone for the inn itself is (0) 259-812-0929.

In Sanare

Continuing east along the main highway, there are two other inns which we can certainly recommend:

El Solar de la Luna (★★★★★)

From the infamous Coral Reef Hotel (I am obviously furious with them for destroying the mangrove!) it is approximately 11.7 km to a road on your left to a village called Buena Vista. To help you locate this road, it is just before the gas station also on your left. Turn up the road. After 2.3 km you will pass through the settlement of Buena Vista. Follow the curve of the ascending road to the right. After approximately another 2 km take the next right. Continue yet another block or some 20 meters further, where you will see a very rough road also on your right. At the top of this little hill you come upon the inn - as is usual - on your right. By reservations only. The inn has a panoramic view of the coast from the keys of Morrocoy National Park all the way east to Puerto Cabello. Top quality guest rooms and service with excellent food. For reservations, contact the Venezuelan Audubon or the owner, Berta-Paula Garcia at (0) 259-881-8800 & 881-1222 or (0) 416-644-0915.

Posada-Bar-Restaurant La Pradera (★★★)

This was a find! At 1.4 km after the entrance to Buena Vista, or 12.8 km from the Coral Reef there is a two-story, buff-colored building on your left. There is a well-hidden sign indicating it to be a restaurant. Well, it is a restaurant and quite a good one at that, and it also now has 9 attractive rooms with private baths, hot water, A/C, and direct TV (birders do not need the latter as they will be dreaming in Technicolor of all the birds they have seen.) The very reasonable price includes breakfast and dinner. One of the attractions of this inn is that it is practically in the middle of all of the birding areas. For one thing it is only about 100 meters from the crossroads to Chichiriviche/Coro. Phones: (0) 259-881-1222 or (0) 416-642-0581 & 412-702-0891.

Chichiriviche

Chichiriviche is some 63 km northwest of El Palito or 14 km from Tucacas, going first on National Highway 3, branching off at the Maraven Gas Station into State Highway 3 towards San Juan de los Cayos, and then turning right onto the causeway into town (there is a sign indicating Chichiriviche at the junction).

The only description I can give of the town itself is that it is a big mess. In fact, Clemencia, my editor, more aptly calls it the "ultimate exercise in ugliness." On the other hand, Pamela, my peripatetic traveling companion, states that she "doesn't think Chichiriviche is SO bad. In fact, for North Americans and Europeans who've never seen anything like it, it's quite interesting!" I'll say! My comment to that remark is unprintable. And yet, would you believe that our friend Nigel Redman[1], editor nonpareil, agrees with Pamela? He claims he has seen much worse! I give up.

If you are traveling on a shoe string and would prefer a cheaper place to stay, I would suggest **Hotel Nautico** in Chichiriviche. The Nautico is small, unpretentious and clean, and likes to cater to foreigners and birders. However, breakfast is served too late for most birders unless you go out very early and return for a 9:00 a.m. breakfast. Their fee usually covers breakfast, dinner and transportation to and from one of the keys around the Morrocoy N.P. Birding trips by boat to the canals in the Cuare Wildlife Refuge would be extra. We recently had a complaint from a bird watcher regarding their prices. Since he had gone directly to them, I suspect that they included the cost of excursions in his fee. Bargain with them that you only want a room and dinner.

The problem is finding this hotel. Upon entering the town, turn right between Hotel La Garza and the gas station. This is the very first street you will encounter upon entering the town, and is called Vía Fábrica de Cemento. (At one time there was a cement factory at the end of the road.) Continue straight for 1.2 km until you see a large house on the left with an orange fence. (That is if they have not painted it.) Turn left, go one block, turn right again for one block and then turn left. The hotel is on a mere wisp of beach, practically in the sea. Phone: (0) 259-812-2685 or (0) 212-944-3718, or contact the Audubon.

In her book, Elizabeth Kline has also given several other less expensive places to stay in Chichiriviche which might be satisfactory for bird watchers.

Residencias Kalamar

Phone numbers (0) 259-815-0828 & 818-6262 or (0) 212-235-3339. A sign, "Vía Fábrica de Cemento", indicates the turn to the right on a side street 1/2 block before Hotel Coral Suites (?? I am quoting Elizabeth here!). "This consistently well-maintained lodging, at the end of a quiet street and within a walled compound, has enjoyed a recently-completed remodeling, making what was already one of the best options in town even better. Six normal rooms all with private bath, cold water, central AC, TV, small refrigerator."

Posada Alemania - Casa Mi Lucero

Phone/Fax: (0) 259-818-0912, (0) 416-84-6412. Vía Fábrica de Cemento, on the left side of this street, with the name on the exterior wall. Six comfortable, clean double rooms, most have private bath, cold water. Breakfast or dinner by prior arrangement. German and Italian spoken, but little Spanish. The new owner, Alois Lukas, lives on the premises and personally attends guests. Cash only (including dollars, French francs, German marks).

No matter where you stay, be sure to advise the people of your time of departure the next morning or you may find yourself locked in. Birders' hours are not the same as those kept by normal people.

---

[1] I am very grateful to Nigel for a number of corrections he made to the directions I give in this chapter.

WHERE TO BIRD

(Whew, sit down because you have lots to read!!!)

☞ Venezuelan Audubon has published the **Checklist of the Birds of Morrocoy National Park / Cuare Wildlife Refuge**, which can be obtained from them or from the American Birding Association.

The Road to Rio Agualinda

This, without a doubt, is one of my favorites. Go back to the directions for finding La Arboleda Inn. The dirt road that runs past the inn, just 12 km south of Tucacas, also leads to a tributary of the Agualinda River. Driving without stopping, you could reach the river in an hour, but don't you dare! Take the whole day! In the dry season, I do not believe you would have too much trouble with a normal car. The rainy season is something else again, but arrangements can be made with Tony Stuyk, the owner of La Arboleda, to take you in his 4 X 4. As a matter of fact, Tony is trying to make arrangements to organize trips for bird watchers not only to Agualinda but also beyond to a forest reserve and eventually to Cerro Misión. That would be a marathon of birding.

After passing La Arboleda, you will be going through savannas with the appropriate birds, but after a while you will find a fantastic forest. To date, we have approximately 154 species along this road as follows:

Little Tinamou	Great Black Hawk	Blue-headed Parrot
Great Egret	Crane Hawk	Yellow-crowned Parrot
Snowy Egret	Laughing Falcon	Orange-winged Parrot
Little Blue Heron	Collared Forest Falcon	Dwarf Cuckoo
Cattle Egret	Yellow-headed Caracara	Squirrel Cuckoo
Capped Heron	Crested Caracara	Little Cuckoo
Black-crowned Night-Heron	Aplomado Falcon	Smooth-billed Ani
Rufescent Tiger-Heron	American Kestrel	Groove-billed Ani
Striated Heron	Gray-necked Wood-rail	Striped Cuckoo
Wood Stork	Rusty-flanked Crake	Lesser Nighthawk
Bare-faced Ibis	Common Moorhen	Ringed Kingfisher
Glossy Ibis	Purple Gallinule	Amazon Kingfisher
Horned Screamer	Wattled Jacana	Green Kingfisher
Black-bellied Whistling-Duck	Southern Lapwing	Rufous-tailed Jacamar
King Vulture	Solitary Sandpiper	Russet-throated Puffbird
Black Vulture	Greater Yellowlegs	Rufous-breasted Hermit
Turkey Vulture	Spotted Sandpiper	Black-throated Mango
Pearl Kite	Ruddy Pigeon	Glittering-throated Emerald
Hooked-billed Kite	Eared Dove	Collared Araçari
Plumbeous Kite	Ruddy Ground-Dove	Scaled Piculet
White-tailed Hawk	Scaled Dove	Spot-breasted Woodpecker
Zone-tailed Hawk	White-tipped Dove	Red-crowned Woodpecker
Roadside Hawk	Red and Green Macaw	Lineated Woodpecker
Gray-lined Hawk	Chestnut-fronted Macaw	Red-rumped Woodpecker
White Hawk	Brown-throated Parakeet	Crimson-crested Woodpecker
Savanna Hawk	Green-rumped Parrotlet	Straight-billed Woodcreeper
Common Black Hawk	Orange-chinned Parakeet	Streak-headed Woodcreeper

Pale-legged Hornero	Lesser Kiskadee	Yellow-hooded Blackbird
Pale-breasted Spinetail	Olivaceous Flatbill	Orange-crowned Oriole
Crested Spinetail	Tropical Pewee	Troupial
Common Thornbird	Common Tody Flycatcher	Yellow Oriole
Great Antshrike	Yellow-bellied Elaenia	Oriole Blackbird
Black-crested Antshrike	Mouse-colored Tyrannulet	Red-breasted Blackbird
Barred Antshrike	Southern Beardless Tyrannulet	Eastern Meadowlark
White-fringed Antwren	Brown-chested Martin	Yellow Warbler
White-bellied Antbird	Rough-winged Swallow	White-eared Conebill
Cinereous Becard	Barn Swallow	Bananaquit
Black-tailed Tityra	Black-chested Jay	Trinidad Euphonia
Black-crowned Tityra	Stripe-backed Wren	Thick-billed Euphonia
Lance-tailed Manakin	House Wren	Blue-Gray Tanager
Pied-water Tyrant	Rufous-breasted Wren	Palm Tanager
Vermilion Flycatcher	Buff-breasted Wren	Silver-beaked Tanager
Cattle Tyrant	Black-capped Donacobius	White-lined Tanager
Fork-tailed Flycatcher	Tropical Mockingbird	Hooded Tanager
Tropical Kingbird	Bare-eyed Thrush	Grayish Saltator
Gray Kingbird	Tropical Gnatcatcher	Large-billed Seed-Finch
Variegated Flycatcher	Rufous-browed Peppershrike	Lesser Seed Finch
Boat-billed Flycatcher	Red-eyed Vireo	Gray Seedeater
Streaked Flycatcher	Shiny Cowbird	Lessons Seedeater
Rusty-margined Flycatcher	Crested Oropendola	Ruddy-breasted Seedeater
Social Flycatcher	Yellow-rumped Cacique	Blue-black Grassquit
Great Kiskadee	Carib Grackle	Saffron Finch

Isla de Pájaros
During the months of December and January it is worth making a detour at Tucacas to rent a boat to go past the Isla de Pájaros (Bird Island), where Magnificent Frigatebirds nest, but do not even think of going to this area on a weekend or a public holiday. Naturally, you are not allowed to disembark.

The Cerro Chichiriviche
About 8.6 km north/west of the entrance to Tucacas or 57.7 km from El Palito, there is a road on the right that leads off National Highway 3 to Morrocoy National Park itself. (See instructions for Villa Mangovia.) Follow this road for 3.7 km, until you see another road on the left (there is a sign for Los Claveles), which leads up the hill called Cerro Chichiriviche, to a group of radio towers at the very top. It is good birding and the view from the top is spectacular. When you reach the top, park on your right just across from the towers. Then, facing the buildings and towers, take the path on your right. Look for:

Red-legged Tinamou	Smooth-billed Ani	White-fringed Antwren
Black Vulture	Blue-tailed Emerald	Cinereous Becard
Turkey Vulture	Sooty-capped Hermit	White-winged Becard
Gray-headed Kite	Little Hermit	Golden-headed Manakin
Ruddy Ground-Dove	Rufous-tailed Jacamar	Lance-tailed Manakin
Scaled Dove	Russet-throated Puffbird	Vermilion Flycatcher
Ruddy Quail-Dove	Straight-billed Woodcreeper	Cattle Tyrant
White-tipped Dove	Common Thornbird	Tropical Kingbird
Yellow-crowned Parrot	Black-crested Antshrike	Gray Kingbird
Squirrel Cuckoo	Black-backed Antshrike	Boat-billed Flycatcher

Brown-crested Flycatcher	Yellow-bellied Tyrannulet	Carib Grackle
Bran-colored Flycatcher	Rough-winged Swallow	Oriole Blackbird
Yellow-breasted Flycatcher	Buff-breasted Wren	American Redstart
Rusty-margined Flycatcher	Rufous-and-white Wren	Bananaquit
Great Kiskadee	Southern House Wren	Trinidad Euphonia
Fuscous Flycatcher	Tropical Mockingbird	Thick-billed Euphonia
Common Tody Flycatcher	Long-billed Gnatwren	Blue-Gray Tanager
Slate-headed Tody-Flycatcher	Tropical Gnatcatcher	Palm Tanager
Pale-eyed Pygmy-Tyrant	Rufous-browed	Silver-beaked Tanager
Pale-tipped Tyrannulet	Peppershrike	White-lined Tanager
Yellow-bellied Elaenia	Red-eyed Vireo	Streaked Saltator
Mouse-colored Tyrannulet	Golden-fronted Greenlet	Black-striped Sparrow
Southern-beardless	Scrub Greenlet	Gray Seedeater
Tyrannulet	Crested Oropendola	Saffron Finch

Buena Vista

From the infamous Coral Reef Hotel on the western outskirts of Tucacas, it is approximately 11.7 km to a road on your left to a village called Buena Vista. To help you locate this road, it is just before the gas station also on your left. Immediately to the east of this station there is a road leading to a village called (Guess what) Sanare! Drive up the road as far as possible, passing the plaza (which is only a short distance). Park and lock your car. Continue up the road on foot. You will soon see a large water tank on your left. A path takes off from this water tank towards a most-promising forest. I only had 15 minutes to investigate the forest but suspect that it could be absolutely fabulous for birds, so don't miss it and do please write me what you see. Incidentally, this is the same road that goes to the inn Solar y Luna.

Cuare Wildlife Refuge

The long causeway leading into Chichiriviche from State Highway 3 (the road to San Juan de los Cayos) has long been of interest to birders as Greater Flamingo, Scarlet Ibis, Roseate Spoonbill, herons, ducks, etc. are easily spotted feeding in the shallow waters of the Cuare Wildlife Refuge. This general area is especially attractive at dusk, when Yellow-crowned Parrot, Scarlet Ibis, flamingos, and egrets come in to roost in the mangroves, and during the dry season it is possible to walk into the then-dry swamp from the main highway. Try to be there between 5:30 and 6:30 p.m. One of the main attractions of Cuare is the huge flocks of flamingos, but these come mostly during and towards the end of the rainy season. Some years the lagoons dry up completely by the end of the dry season and nothing is to be seen. The best months for this area are from November to early March.

Nevertheless, on July 30, 2000, Dr. Richard Byrne recorded seeing the following in the mangroves of Cuare:

Brown Pelican c. 50	Common Black Hawk 1
Great Egret c. 20	Snowy Plover 2
Snowy Egret c. 10	Willet 1
Little Blue Heron 3, 1 blue, 2 piebald	Least Sandpiper c. 15
Reddish Egret 1	Semipalmated Sandpiper c. 30
Tricolored Heron c. 15	Short-billed Dowitcher 2, one summer,
Scarlet Ibis c.50	one winter
Roseate Spoonbill c. 311	Black-necked Stilt c. 150
Greater Flamingo c. 500	Large-billed Tern 1

Black Skimmer c. 100
Bare-eyed Pigeon c. 30

Yellow-shouldered Parrot 2
Bicolored Conebill 2

The Dams of Játira and Tacarigua

These man-made wetlands have long been a favorite feeding area for wading birds, and consequently for birders[1].

Ten km north from the junction of the causeway to Chichiriviche with State Highway 3 (taking the road to San Juan de los Cayos), you will cross over the Tocuyo River. Immediately after crossing the bridge you will notice a dirt road on the left. Turn left and follow this road. Hopefully the road will have been repaired and you will have no problem following it! You will be driving through coconut plantations. After passing the last coconut grove you will see two ponds with sedges on your left. (This is just before the Somosagua Ranch.) Look carefully around those ponds for Striped-backed Bittern.

Further along at a total of 7.6 km after your turn-off from the main road, you will come to a spot where the road rises slightly and begins to curve to the right. On the left, you will see another dirt road. This leads to the dike of the Játira Dam, which begins at 0.9 km from that point.

Where the dike begins, you will see that there is road running along the top, and another one running below on the left side. I suggest that you slowly drive all the way to the end on the top road, some 5 km.

At the far end, just before the end of the dike, you will see a path going off to your right. Walk this path for about 200 meters to look for Crested Doradito among the rushes. (It may or may not be here, for it is nomadic.)

When returning to the main dirt road, try taking the lower road beneath the Játira dam.

The above instructions are dependent upon repairs to the Játira dam after the floods of December, 1999, when the walls of the dam were broached. We have been told that repairs are underway, and we certainly hope so. These are just some of the birds of the dam as seen by Dr. Richard Byrne of St. Andrews, Scotland on August 1, 2000:

Striated Heron c.30
Black-crowned Night Heron c.10
American Wood Stork 1
Bare-faced Ibis c.5
Greater Flamingo c.500
Black bellied Whistling Duck c.300
American Kestrel 1
Aplomado Falcon 1
Common Moorhen c.300
Limpkin c.20

Wattled Jacana c.50
Black-necked Stilt c.20
Double-striped Thick-knee 2
Southern Lapwing c.5
Black Skimmer c.30
Scaled Dove c.5
Rufous-tailed Jacamar 1
Straight-billed Woodcreeper 1
Pale Breasted Spinetail c.5
Pale-tipped Tyrannulet 1

After checking out the dam, go back to the dirt road that you came in on and turn left. You will soon come to a small bridge. Stop here and bird the trails on both sides of the road. The number of species to be found in this dry scrub is remarkable, including Ruby-topaz Hummingbird, White-fringed Antwren, Pied Water-tyrant, Lesser Kiskadee and Black-capped Donacobius.

---

[1] Note from the Editor: A favorite feeding area for birders? Birders are welcome to bring their lunches and feed here, she means? While watching birds, she means? Or do you think she is suggesting *we* go there to feed *the birds*? Oh, the heck with it!

The Tacarigua Dam sits on the right side of the main dirt prior to the turn off for Játira. It is deeper than Játira, and not so good for birds. There is a channel, passing under the road, that joins the two. After investigating the areas around the dams, go back to State Highway 3, and turn left.

📖 The Checklist of the Birds of Morrocoy National Park / Cuare Wildlife Refuge, which I mentioned above, includes the birds for the **Játira** and **Tacarigua** dams.

San Juan de los Cayos

From the Río Tocuyo bridge continue north to the little resort town of San Juan de los Cayos, which is unusually clean as towns go in this area. From State Highway 3, you have to turn right in order to cross all the way through the town and get past it to the spit of land on the seaside. Look for a corner house on your right with a blue fence called Quinta Yamel. Turn right there and wind your way east and northward along the coast until you reach a very large lagoon. During the months of April and May this is an excellent area for nesting Cayenne Terns as well as many migratory waders about to take off for northern latitudes. Here you may also find Tricolored Heron feeding, next to both color phases of the Reddish Egret. Keep an eye out for Aplomado Falcons. Please take note that it is impossible to reach this site during the wet season, and I am not too confident as to what has happened to the area as a result of the floods of December, 1999. Furthermore, I have heard a rumor that a consortium is planning to build an airport and a large tourist complex at San Juan de los Cayos.

The Tucurere River Marshes

After leaving San Juan de los Cayos, heading northwest on State Highway 3 towards Capadare and Mirimire, you will soon go past what was previously a National Guard Post on your right. One kilometer further you will see a very large lagoon or the end of a small river on the left. This wetland is part of the marshlands formed by a tributary of the Tucurere River on its last leg to the sea.

You may have past it, but just before the lagoon there is a rough track leading through the bushes and down to the water. During the dry season you can probably drive down to the sandy track below even with a regular vehicle. This is a delightful place to bird, following the course of the river, bordered with red and black mangroves.

Here you are sure to see Common, Snowy and Reddish Egrets (in both color phases), Little Blue and Tricolored Herons, Bare-faced, White and Scarlet Ibis, Roseate Spoonbills, Flamingos, Wattled Jacana, Southern Lapwing, Black-necked Stilt, Double-striped Thick-knee, Black Skimmer, Eared, Common, Plain-breasted and Ruddy Ground-Doves, Green-rumped Parrotlet, White-whiskered Spinetail, Red-breasted Blackbird and many small birds typical of xerophitic areas.

Now here comes a BIG secret. The river (one of the many channels, really) can be navigated by dug-out canoe. The canoe is not very comfortable, so take a pillow, but the waterway will more than compensate the stiff back and sore bones. I did this in February, 2000, and we quietly passed through approximately 4000 Flamingos who had absolutely no fear due to the fact that even the boatman was sitting down to pole. To make this trip the water must be a meter to a meter and a half deep, so it is not something you can do during the dry season. This unforgettable experience can be arranged by contacting either the Venezuelan Audubon or Sr. Henry by calling Sra. Goya Lopez (his mother) at (0) 259-932-5061 or Manuel Faria at (0) 259-932-5393 with sufficient advance notice. We saw:

Olivaceous Cormorant
Anhinga
Great Egret
Snowy Egret
Little Blue Heron
Tricolored Heron
Striated Heron
Cattle Egret
Black-crowned Night-Heron
Scarlet Ibis
Glossy Ibis
Greater Flamingo
Blue-winged Teal
Black-bellied Whistling-Duck
Turkey Vulture
Roadside Hawk
Short-tailed Hawk

Common Black Hawk
Osprey
Yellow-headed Caracara
Crested Caracara
Peregrine Falcon
Aplomado Falcon
Limpkin
Common Moorhen
Purple Gallinule
Southern Lapwing
Snowy Plover
Lesser Yellowlegs
Spotted Sandpiper
Bare-eyed Dove
Eared Dove
Scaled Dove
Greater Ani

Amazon Kingfisher
Rufous-tailed Jacamar
Pale-breasted Spinetail
White-bellied Antbird
Pied Water-Tyrant
Vermilion Flycatcher
Gray Kingbird
Great Kiskadee
Brown-crested Flycatcher
White-winged Swallow
Tropical Mockingbird
Tropical Gnatcatcher
Rufous-browed Peppershrike
Yellow Oriole
Oriole Blackbird
Yellow-hooded Blackbird

THE HIGHWAY SANARE TO CORO

Hato La Corianera

Going northwest some 5.3 km on National Highway No. 3 towards Coro from the Maraven gas station at Sanare, you will see a sign on a wall to your right that says Haras Altamira where they raise thoroughbred horses. Exactly one kilometer past that gate there is an entrance again on your right to a not very fancy house. This is Hato La Corianera. Drive in, park, and ask for permission to bird (observar los pájaros). They will tell you to go half way around the paddock on your right and then go straight. This is one famous, excellent, fantastic place to bird, but be there in the very early morning and take drinking water. If you arrive during the rainy season, be sure to have high rubber boots on. A few of the birds you may see:

Cocoi Heron
Great Egret
Little Blue Heron
Striated Heron
Cattle Egret
Rufescent Tiger-Heron
American Wood Stork
Bare-faced Ibis
White Ibis
Scarlet Ibis
Glossy Ibis
Horned Screamer
Black-bellied Whistling Duck
Black Vulture
Turkey Vulture
White-tailed Kite
Gray-headed Kite
Snail Kite
Slender-billed Kite
Roadside Hawk

Black-collared Hawk
Savanna Hawk
Crane Hawk
Laughing Falcon
Aplomado Falcon
Yellow-headed Caracara
Crested Caracara
Rufous-vented Chachalaca
Limpkin
Gray-necked Wood-Rail
Purple Gallinule
Wattled Jacana
Southern Lapwing
Solitary Sandpiper
Common Ground-Dove
Ruddy Ground-Dove
Blue Ground-Dove
Scaled Dove
Red-and-Green Macaw
Chestnut-fronted Macaws

Brown-throated Parakeet
Green-rumped Parrotlet
Yellow-crowned Parrot
Squirrel Cuckoo
Smooth-billed Ani
Short-tailed Swift
Black-throated Mango
Green Kingfisher
Rufous-tailed Jacamar
Lineated Woodpecker
Straight-billed Woodcreeper
Pale-breasted Spinetail
Pale-legged Hornero
Common Thornbird
Black-crested Antshrike
White-fringed Antwren
Cinnamon Becard
Pied Water Tyrant
Vermilion Flycatcher
Cattle Tyrant

Tropical Kingbird	Barn Swallow	Yellow Warbler
Gray Kingbird	Buff-breasted Wren	Bananaquit
Rusty-margined Flycatcher	Southern House Wren	Trinidad Euphonia
Social Flycatcher	Black-capped Donacobius	Blue-gray Tanager
Great Kiskadee	Topical Mockingbird	Glaucous Tanager
Lesser Kiskadee	Tropical Gnatcatcher	White-lined Tanager
Venezuelan Flycatcher	Rufous-browed Peppershrike	Grayish Saltator
Yellow-breasted Flycatcher	Carib Grackle	Gray Seedeater
Common Tody-Flycatcher	Troupial	Ruddy-breasted Seedeater
Yellow-bellied Elaenia	Yellow Oriole	Saffron Finch
Mouse-colored Flycatcher	Oriole Blackbird	

Cerro La Misión

As above, from the Maraven Gas Station at Sanare, go northwest on National Highway 3 for some 11 km, where you will see an excellent, wide dirt road on the left (if you cross over a medium-sized bridge, you have gone about a couple of km too far). This road leads up into the limestone hills of the Cerro La Misión, but without a four-wheel drive you cannot hope to climb far up the mountain, and when I went there a fortnight ago I couldn't get to the top even with a 4 X 4! However the lower part is absolutely superb for birding in the very early mornings. Just before the road starts to climb the mountain, you will see a path on your left, passing a shack. I recommend you follow this path. If you are young and/or vigorous, a hike up the mountain will also produce some interesting species. Around this area you should look for:

Little Tinamou	Rufous-breasted Hermit	Bran-colored Flycatcher
Red-legged Tinamou	Pale-bellied Hermit	Yellow-breasted Flycatcher
Least Grebe	White-necked Jacobin	Yellow-olive Flycatcher
King Vulture	Fork-tailed Woodnymph	Common Tody-Flycatcher
White-tailed Hawk	White-vented Plumeleteer	Yellow-bellied Elaenia
Black-collared Hawk	Rufous-tailed Jacamar	Slaty-capped Flycatcher
Gray-lined Hawk	Collared Araçari	Gray-breasted Martin
Common Black Hawk	Red-crowned Woodpecker	Southern Rough-winged
Great Black Hawk	Pale-legged Hornero	Swallow
Black Hawk-Eagle	Streak-headed Woodcreeper	Rufous-and-white Wren
Laughing Falcon	Pale-breasted Spinetail	Buff-breasted Wren
Yellow-knobbed Curassow	Crested Spinetail	House Wren
Rusty-flanked Crake	Great Antshrike	Southern Nightingale Wren
Common Snipe	Rufous-winged Antwren	Black-capped Donacobius
White-tipped Dove	White-bellied Antbird	Tropical Mockingbird
Red-and-green Macaw	Black-faced Antthrush	Tropical Gnatcatcher
Green-rumped Parrotlet	Chestnut-crowned Becard	Rufous-browed Peppershrike
Orange-chinned Parakeet	Cinereous Becard	Golden-fronted Greenlet
Lilac-tailed Parrotlet	White-winged Becard	Giant Cowbird
Blue-headed Parrot	Black-tailed Tityra	Yellow-rumped Cacique
Yellow-crowned Parrot	Black-crowned Tityra	Orange-crowned Oriole
Orange-winged Parrot	Lance-tailed Manakin	Tropical Parula
Little Cuckoo	Cattle Tyrant	American Redstart
Smooth-billed Ani	Tropical Kingbird	Bananaquit
Striped Cuckoo	Boat-billed Flycatcher	Red-legged Honeycreeper
Great Potoo	Social Flycatcher	Thick-billed Euphonia
Vaux's Swift	Lesser Kiskadee	Blue-gray Tanager

Palm Tanager	Black-striped Sparrow	Yellow-bellied Seedeater
Silver-beaked Tanager	Sooty Grassquit	Blue-black Grassquit
White-lined Tanager	Gray Seedeater	Saffron Finch
Guira Tanager	Lesson´s Seedeater	Orange-fronted Yellow-Finch
Grayish Saltator	Ruddy-breasted Seedeater	Saffron Finch

Campeche Marsh

Drive northwest some 13.1 km heading for Coro from our well-known Maraven Gas Station to find a road on the right going towards Campeche. During the wet season you will not be able to drive too far in an ordinary car, but no matter. Immediately after you turn into this road you should see a marsh on your right. In November three of us found four Rusty-flanked Crakes feeding here, but I would recommend you try your luck in the late afternoon.

Riecito

Again take the main road to Coro. In the next town, Yaracal, some 25 km from the gas station look for the road across from the Lagoven gas station. This leads to Riecito. When you approach the hamlet you will see a sign on your right : "Panorama del Pueblo." Shortly after, there is a dirt road on your left. Turn and continue down a good dirt road and start birding as soon as you leave the inhabited areas.

Your visit to Falcón has still much more to offer. From the Chichiriviche area, your next destination should be Coro, the state capital, which is two and a half hours northwest from the Maraven Gas Station on National Highway 3 (if you don't stop to bird in the following two places along the way, that is!).

The Tacarigua Marsh

Going towards Coro on National Highway 3, at 74.7 km from the famous Maraven Gas Station, you will see the sign on the left side of the road for "Agropecuaria La Boquita." Next to the entrance to the Agropecuaria there is a dirt road giving easy access into the huge marsh known as Ciénaga de Tacarigua, or Tacarigua Marsh. During the months of March and April, the wild orchids that grow on every tree around the marsh are blooming, and you can find a large variety of birds, including Pale-legged Hornero. Do not try to visit the area during the rainy season, for it is totally flooded. This marsh is so large and so much fun to explore that it is very easy to get lost, so be careful.

Sauca Lagoon

Approximately 75.7 km from the too-often mentioned Maraven Gas Station, you will come to the road on the right leading to the town of San José de la Costa and Sauca Lagoon. The road is frankly in very bad condition, but if you have the time and want an adventure, turn right and follow your nose for approximately 28 km When you finally reach a fork, go left for the Lagoon. The right fork would take you to the town of San José de la Costa. Follow this road, passing a small built-up settlement complete with a little church. Continue down a steep hill. You will see a dirt road at the bottom of the hill just before a small causeway. Park, lock you car and bird along this sandy road. Give yourself ample time for this jaunt to look for American Kestrel, White-whiskered Spinetail and many other xerophilous birds, as well as waders, including Greater Flamingos, Scarlet Ibis, Egrets, Herons, etc. This is the only place I have ever seen the Scarlet Tanager in Venezuela. Next, in your car follow the road along between the lagoon and the sea until you reach a spot where the road starts to go up a hill. From there on I believe the road deteriorates even more.

CORO

The city of Coro was founded in 1527. The center makes an extremely interesting visit, better done on foot. Many beautiful colonial houses and buildings still stand, including the House of the Bishop and those of the Arcaya, Senior and Garcés families; the Cathedral, built from 1583 to 1636 and sacked by British pirates several times; and the Treasury House, a lovely, 18th century building houses a colonial art collection - the Museo Diocesano - painstakingly put together by Monsignor Iturriza, who was Bishop of Coro from 1941 to 1985.

With all its colonial splendor, when it comes to hotels, Coro is not well-endowed, and the situation can be tragic when we talk about good restaurants. Nevertheless, I suggest that you plan to spend a night or two in Coro, for the city has a number of fascinating xerophitic areas nearby, including some on the Paraguaná Peninsula and a wonderful one directly south of the city.

Hotels in Coro, Area Code (0) 268		
Hotel Miranda Cumberland	★★★★	252-2211, 252-3022 & 251-3096
Hotel Federal	★★★	251-1321
Hotel Inter Caribe	★★★	251-1811 & 251-1434

The Miranda Cumberland, located directly in front of the airport and just two blocks away from the colonial area, is without a doubt the best hotel in Coro, but also the most expensive. Their restaurant is the only decent place to eat I have found in Coro. Warning: Ask for a room on the front side of the hotel. They often have very loud parties in the patio on the back side with dancing, live music, etc., lasting until the wee hours of the morning. Bring your ear plugs. Fax: (0) 268-251-3096.

Hotel Inter Caribe (formerly Hotel Venecia), located on Avenida Manaure, seems to be the most popular hotel, but the service, in the past at least, left much to be desired, the restaurant is to be avoided. Fax: (0) 268-251-1434. The **Federal** is more modest, but still adequate.

If you approach Coro from the east on National Highway 3, you will enter the city on Avenida Independencia. At the cross roads with Avenida Los Médanos, turn right and continue for 3 blocks to a stoplight. Turn left. You are now on Avenida Josefa Camejo, which leads to the airport and Hotel Miranda Cumberland. Six blocks after you turn on to Avenida Josefa Camejo from Avenida Los Médanos is a stoplight at the junction with Avenida Manaure. You would turn left on to Avenida Manaure for Hotel Inter Caribe. To reach the Paraguaná Peninsula you should drive due north on Avenida Los Médanos on National Highway 4.

THE PARAGUANÁ PENINSULA

Apart from the architectural beauty of colonial Coro, one of the main reasons for visiting northern Falcón lies just north of the city - the Peninsula of Paraguaná.

Driving north on Avenida Los Médanos, you will suddenly find yourself confronted with huge sand dunes slowly covering the divided highway. The sand dunes and our Ministry of Transport and Communications wage an on-going war over possession of this highway. As you drive across this Saharan scenery, you are now in the **Parque Nacional Médanos de Coro**, or Coro Sand Dunes National Park.

It seems strange to suddenly come upon these huge sand dunes. The explanation for this geological wonder can be found in Dr. Carlos Rivero-Blanco's web site *Vene-*

zuela Ecológica. As he explains, trade winds transport sand from the Caribbean sea bottom adjacent to the isthmus, and this particular area of the Caribbean receives sand from many rivers including the Tocuyo whose headwaters lie in the foothills of the Andean state of Lara, some 400 kilometers to the south. Sand may travel by river, sea and air to the isthmus and once there it crawls above ground, finally moving across the isthmus to the Gulf on the western side.

There is a Guardia Nacional checkpoint as you enter the Peninsula. My friends the Pierces were pulled over, stopped and asked for their "papers." To quote Pamela: "The guy was obviously disappointed that everything was in order so we couldn't offer him a 'donation' to let us by. We followed your advice - as we always try to do with these guys - of neither looking too pissed off nor too obsequious. It works."

Continue north along the causeway, which is approximately 36 km. At the junction for El Cayude, you will turn right, leaving the main highway and heading for Moruy and finally Pueblo Nuevo. Your goal is the **Montecano Forest Reserve**, managed by Infalcosta, a local environmental NGO, and the University in Coro. The reserve is open to visitors from 8:00 a.m. till noon.

The entrance to Montecano is only some 15 minutes from Pueblo Nuevo. To find the entrance, as you come into Pueblo Nuevo, passing the P.D.V. gas station on your right, turn left at the next corner. You will now pass a famous "Dulce de Leche" shop on your right and soon come to a Y in the road. Go left. At 2.4 km from where you first turned left by the Dulce de Leche shop, you are now in an area called El Recreo. You will see on your right a white rectangular house on the top of a hill approached by a short, steep dirt road. This is the house of a famous wood carver named Oloniel Salas. He is particularly known for his incredible and beautiful walking sticks. On your left is a white wall with blue trim by a curve in the road. Following along the road, you will see a crossroads with sign that says "Flia. Salas El Recreo". Here you turn right. The Reserve is 5 km from Pueblo Nuevo. Perhaps an even easier way to find the Reserve would be as follows: As you approach Pueblo Nuevo, you will see a sign at a corner on your left indicating the "Comando de Operaciones de la Guardia Nacional". Turn left here and head for San Jose de Cocorite and Jadacaquiva. This road passes right by the Reserve.

Upon arriving at the Reserve you should sign in and ask for permission to "observar las aves." There are two elderly caretakers, who are most accommodating, Esteban Cuaiero and José Tomás Lugo. There are trails to follow in the Montecano Reserve, and it may well be that Esteban will accompany you to prevent your getting lost. It is amazing that in this extremely xerophitic area you will find Spanish moss in the Montecano Reserve, but the mist coming in off the sea supplies enough moisture to allow the growth of epiphytes. You should see Red-billed Emerald, White-whiskered Spinetail, Barred and Black-crested Antshrike, White-fringed Antwren, Tropical Gnatcatcher, Troupial, Yellow Oriole, etc. Also, you will find it relatively easy to see the Vermilion Cardinal at Montecano. Other abundant wildlife includes tarantulas and a brightly-colored, huge species of locust or cricket.

I would like to suggest that you make friends with these two dear, old, long-time guardians of Montecano. The Reserve and its fauna are the center of their lives. With luck, Esteban will invite you to his house a short distance away, where he puts out food for the birds in his backyard. There you can comfortably photograph White-tipped Dove, Turpials, Yellow Orioles, Vermilion Cardinal and others of the region. Be sure to give them a tip for their efforts because they barely earn a pittance.

Pueblo Nuevo is the "dulce de leche de cabra" (goat's milk sweet) capital of Venezuela. This delicious confection is sold from several private homes in town. It keeps for months and makes a very nice gift to take home. Don't miss it!

Other reasons for visiting the Paraguaná Peninsula are its many beautiful colonial houses and churches. You will see several along the way that date back to the 1600s and 1700s. One very special one is the "Casa de las Virtudes", 6 km north of Moruy on the road to Buena Vista. (The house is a bit set back from the road.) The Peninsula is crisscrossed with roads in every direction, and it is quite easy to get lost, but actually you are never far away from a populated center. A site I personally found interesting were the ruins of the home of Juan Cristófono Falcon at El Vínculo, north from Pueblo Nuevo.

Another point of interest is the "Gustavo Rivera" Zoo at Cardón, near the city of Punto Fijo. I was amazed at the quality of this zoo, from the point of view of the care of the animals and also for the educational aspects the staff tries to emphasize.

All along the semi-circle of the northern coast of Paraguaná runs a dirt road which makes a very interesting drive. During Spring and Fall migrations, one may find waders in the many little coves and stretches of beach one passes. I have also found American Oystercatchers and this would be a place to look for the Reddish Egret. Some stretches of road are difficult and there are no gas stations, so it is better not to take this road unless on a reliable 4WD. Although it may be that by the time you come, the road may have been paved. (We can at least dream!) Along the western part of the road, you'll come upon a immense roving dune, which has been inching its way across the peninsula for decades, leaving a wake of wasteland some hundred meters long. Starting off from Adícora, you will soon pass the salt pans of Las Cumaraguas, glimmering shocking pink under the sun.

Should you wish to spend more time in Paraguaná (and explore a bit more all the trails and side roads of this intriguing area), considering that Pueblo Nuevo is an hour's drive from Coro, you might like to stay in Punto Fijo. There is also a most exceptional inn called Hacienda La Pancha which receives guests only on weekends unless special arrangements are previously made. To find this rare and interesting inn follow the road west from Adícora indicated for El Hato-Pueblo Nuevo. La Pancha is only a few kilometers from Adícora on the left. A handsome colonial-style house set atop a small hill, surrounded by gardens with xerophitic plants. The house is decorated with precious antiques. Exceptionally good food. Reservations must be made and paid for in advance. Contact the Venezuelan Audubon or telephone (0) 414-968-2649 or (0) 212-987-0081.

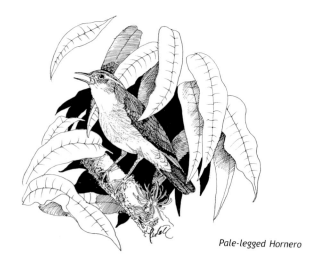

Pale-legged Hornero

THE ROAD TO ACURIGUA: A SHORT OUTING FROM CORO

If you have very little time allotted for Coro, instead of visiting the Paraguaná Peninsula, I suggest you spend one afternoon in the xerophitic area just south of Coro, to find, among other great birds, the Vermilion Cardinal.

Drive due south on Avenida Manaure, crossing the main highway to Maracaibo. Soon you will come to a check point. Five km south of the Alcabala, there is a large bridge and one km. after the bridge you will see a road on your left. Look for a high aluminum water tank. Turn left here, continue on, passing a small village and then a road on your right that leads to La Chapa and Curimagua. Do not turn, but continue straight.

If you look at the map, you will see that this road borders the dam of El Isiro on the south. The dam itself is not very visible from the road, and I have not found it of interest from the point of view of birding, but when Venezuelan Audubon's ornithologist Miguel Lentino did the study of Flamingo populations in Venezuela in the mid eighties, he found this dam to be one of the wetlands that the birds used regularly.

I have never driven all the way to Acurigua, for at 8.3 km after the left turn from the north-south highway, I have found a small pond or marshy area on the right which is quite a good birding spot during the rainy season of September and October. Listen here for the tsk-tsk call of the Common Tody Flycatcher. If you can imitate or record it, out will pop not the Common but the Short-tailed Tody Flycatcher in response to its call. Try playing the Ferruginous Pygmy-Owl tape, and you really will have fun!

If you reach this area in the very early morning or late afternoon, you might be fortunate enough to see Yellow-shouldered Parrots flying out or in from all directions. There is a roost of these very endangered birds around here (perhaps on some of the many palm trees), but we have not found where exactly.

Walk around along the goat trails and look for:

Lesser Yellow-headed Vulture	Ruby-topaz Hummingbird	Tawny-crowned Pygmy-Tyrant
White-tailed Hawk	Buffy Hummingbird	Slender-billed Tyrannulet
Lesser Yellowlegs	Russet-throated Puffbird	Northern Scrub-Flycatcher
Greater Yellowlegs	Straight-billed Woodpecker	Mouse-colored Tyrannulet
Willet	White-whiskered Spinetail	Troupial
Bare-eyed Pigeon	Black-crested Antshrike	Yellow Oriole
Eared Dove	Vermilion Flycatcher	Yellow Warbler
Yellow-shouldered Parrot	Brown-crested Flycatcher	Glaucous Tanager
Lesser Nighthawk	Common Tody-Tyrant	Orinocan Saltator
Pauraque	Short-tailed Tody-Tyrant	Vermilion Cardinal
White-tailed Nightjar		

Actually, this whole road is very good for xerophitic birding, and you may even decide to follow it all the way along. On the other hand, other birding areas await you.

THE SIERRA DE SAN LUIS

At the heart of the State of Falcon, directly south from Coro, lies a mountain range called Sierra de San Luis, a land that begins with thorny trees and spiny bushes in the lower elevations, climbs through dry and secondary forests, through coffee plantations, to mountain tops cloaked in the misty veils of more humid forests. There are many curious settlements here, tiny villages and wee little towns, and there is a national park, predictably called Sierra de San Luis N.P.

You will see in the road map that from Coro, there are two ways to go up the hills and reach this general area. One goes straight to the minuscule hamlet of La Tabla and the other goes via La Chapa, mentioned above. At the present time the road via La Chapa is by far the better one to take and offers interesting areas to bird as you go along.

However, you may wish to investigate the birding along the first part of the road to La Tabla because in the past I have found it to be extremely worth while, and perhaps more so now that it has less traffic. Drive out of Coro due south on Avenida Manaure, passing the alcabala and bridge mentioned above. Keep straight on until you come to a gas station (if it is still operating). In the general area of this station I have had exceptionally good luck with Orinoco Saltator, far north from its Orinoco River neighborhood. Look also for Pearly-vented Tody-Tyrant, White-whiskered Spinetail and Vermilion Cardinal. After you have had a good opportunity to bird this area go back towards Coro to pick up the road to La Chapa. In any case, FILL YOUR TANK at a gas station just before you start up the hills, as there is no gas available around your destination, although it is possible to buy 20 liters or so from private individuals in the town. Go down into the town of Curimagua itself and ask at the bodega (general store) for the direction of the woman who sells gasolina. This perhaps will be a new experience for you.

From Coro it is approximately 40 winding km to your destination of the town of Curimagua in the mountains via La Chapa. There is an inn at a private home or coffee plantation called **Finca El Monte** between the turn off from La Chapa and Curimagua. (8 km past the sign announcing the Park, watch for another, small sign on the right with a stylized mountain announcing the finca.) As you come down the hill from the highest point on the road you will see a church on the left. It is 3.1 km from here to the inn. The Swiss owners offer modest but comfortable and clean rooms with private baths and hot water. Meals can be served by previous arrangements. Swiss German, English and Spanish spoken. I greatly enjoyed my stay here and can recommend it as being informal, comfortable and home-like. Contact Ursula and Ernesto Iseli Suter at (0) 268-416-0622, or send them an e-mail at fincaelmonte@yahoo.com .

SIERRA DE SAN LUIS NATIONAL PARK

The main reason for going to Curimagua is to bird the Sierra de San Luis National Park. (I should advise you that, officially, the name is "Juan Crisóstomo Falcón", but no matter how grand a soldier of the Federation War the General was, no one ever calls the park by his name, not even the park guards[1]) The park extends over 20,000 hectares, and the ones listed below are three of the easily accessible areas to visit and bird. Early in the morning, from the inn, drive towards the town.

At 5.4 km you will see the small church on your left across from the entrance to Los Falcones defunct inn. Here also is the first entrance to the town.
At ± 6 km is the second entrance to the town.
At 1.5 km from Los Falcones is the road leading to El Haiton.
At 6.1 km from Los Falcones there is a road on your right leading up to the antennas and Cerro Galicia.

---

[1] Note from the Editor: *Sic transit gloria mundi.*

Cerro Galicia

This is the highest point in the Park.

There are two areas to bird at Cerro Galicia - one on your left and the other on your right, passing an unfinished building (which was to have been a hotel). This second path soon turns into an overgrown cement road that eventually leads to a helicopter pad. From the point just before you start going down the cement road towards the helicopter pad, there is a spectacular view of Coro and the Paraguaná Peninsula.

The Cerro Galicia is buffeted incessantly by strong winds coming up from the sea, a situation that birds do not like, so you will find few birds in the open, but in the woods the further down you go, the better the birding. Keep in mind that you will have to walk back up again, and it can be very warm!

The path on the left goes through intervened forest, and eventually leads back to the road where you parked the car.

El Haiton

The area around Curimagua is well-known for its many sink-holes and caves, carved into the limestone formation by the frequent rains. El Haiton is perhaps the largest of the known sink-holes, 320 meters deep. The area around it is forested and truly excellent for early morning or late afternoon birding. To reach it, again go 1.5 km from the entrance to Los Falcones towards Cerro Galicia, and turn left down a steep dirt road that would eventually lead to San Luis, the prettiest little town in these parts. The road at first is in deplorable state, but it improves noticeably after a distance. At the present time they are working on the road. When you come to a V, take the lower road on the left. It is 10.2 km from Los Falcones to the Inparques station (now abandoned) at El Haiton. The path leading down to the sink hole (Haiton) can be very good birding and hopefully the Bearded Bell Bird will be shouting as usual. I found a lek of Little Hermits along this trail one morning in early April. The sink hole is interesting in itself, but do not get too near. It is 300+ meters deep and has no barrier or rails. Also, from the road on top, look for Handsome Fruiteater and Bearded Bellbird. After visiting El Haiton, continue walking down the road towards San Luis. You can easily spend a full morning or more on this road.

Flamingoes

La Uria

From Finca El Monte, go back as if returning to Coro, via La Chapa. Take time to bird along the way. If you are very, very lucky, there might be a small flock of Red Siskins milling around. You will eventually see a large rusted gate on your right. Usually, the gate is not locked, so open, but do close it behind you. (Though it forms part of the National Park, I believe this is private land, so if the gate is padlocked, just bird along the road.) This is very nice area to bird in the early morning.

The following is a list of the birds we have recorded for the general area of the **Sierra de San Luis**:

Little Tinamou
Brown Tinamou
King Vulture
Pearl Kite
Swallow-tailed Kite
Hook-billed Kite
Zone-tailed Hawk
Short-tailed Hawk
Gray-lined Hawk
Bay-winged Hawk
Black Hawk-Eagle
Laughing Falcon
Bat Falcon
American Kestrel
Rufous-vented Chachalaca
Crested Bobwhite
Marbled Wood-Quail
Gray-necked Wood-Rail
White-tipped Dove
Scarlet Macaw
Chestnut-fronted Macaw
Brown-throated Parakeet
Green-rumped Parrotlet
Red-billed Parrot
Bronze-winged Parrot
Orange-winged Parrot
Squirrel Cuckoo
Striped Cuckoo
Rufous Nightjar
Lesser Swallow-tailed Swift
Rufous-breasted Hermit
Long-tailed Sylph
Sooty-capped Hermit
Gray-chinned Hermit
Little Hermit
Sparkling Violetear
Ruby-topaz Hummingbird
Golden-tailed Sapphire
Copper-rumped
  Hummingbird

Speckled Hummingbird
Violet-chested Hummingbird
Booted Racket-tail
Collard Trogon
Masked Trogon
Groove-billed Toucanet
Scaled Piculet
Plain-brown Woodcreeper
Crimson-crested Woodpecker
Barred Woodcreeper
Stripe-breasted Spinetail
Rufous Spinetail
Crested Spinetail
Guttulated Foliage-gleaner
Buff-throated Foliage -gleaner
Plain Xenops
Gray-throated Leaftosser
Great Antshrike
Barred Antshrike
Plain Antvireo
Slaty Antwren
Long-tailed Antbird
White-bellied Antbird
Black-faced Antthrush
Rusty-breasted Antpitta
Brown-rumped Tapaculo
Golden-breasted Fruiteater
Handsome Fruiteater
Chestnut-crowned Becard
Bearded Bellbird
Lance-tailed Manakin
Streaked Flycatcher
Rusty-margined Flycatcher
Social Flycatcher
Lesser Kiskadee
Bright-rumped Attila
Olive-sided Flycatcher
Bran-colored Flycatcher
White-throated Spadebill
Scale-crested Pygmy-Tyrant

Marbled-faced Bristle-Tyrant
Mountain Elaenia
Slaty-capped Flycatcher
Olive-striped Flycatcher
Black-chested Jay
Green Jay
Gray-breasted Woodwren
Southern Nightingale Wren
Andean Solitaire
Orange-billed Nightingale
Thrush
Yellow-legged Thrush
Glossy-black Thrush
Black-hooded Thrush
Pale-breasted Thrush
Bare-eyed Thrush
Long-billed Gnatwren
Rufous-browed Peppershrike
Brown-capped Vireo
Scrub Greenlet
Golden-fronted Greenlet
Crested Oropendola
Orange-crowned Oriole
Yellow-backed Oriole
Black-and-white Warbler
Tennessee Warbler
Tropical Parula
Cerulean Warbler
Blackburnian Warbler
Slate-throated Redstart
Flavescent Warbler
Golden-crowned Warbler
Purple Honeycreeper
Golden Tanager
Bay-headed Tanager
Black-headed Tanager
Blue-naped Chlorophonia
Orange-bellied Euphonia
Thick-billed Euphonia
Silver-beaked Tanager

Summer Tanager	Blue-black Grosbeak	Ochre-breasted Brush-finch
White-winged Tanager	Buff-throated Saltator	Black-striped Sparrow
Rosy Thrush-Tanager	Grayish Saltator	Lesser Seed-Finch
Guira Tanager	Rose-breasted Grosbeak	Red Siskin
Common Bush Tanager	Chestnut-capped Brush-Finch	Dark-backed Goldfinch
Black-faced Tanager		

The Spanish Trail

There is one excursion I urge you to take during your stay in Curimagua and that is to climb the cobblestoned Spanish Trail that goes from Curimagua down to the town of Cabure. It will take you about 3 hours although I did it in 5 as I was birding and recording. Since I started this excursion almost at high noon, there were not too many birds at that hour but I did record a pair of Solitary Eagles courting over my head. It can easily be arranged for Ernesto, of Finca El Monte, to take you to the start of the trail in Curimagua and then pick you up again by the inn of El Duende at the end of the trail in Cabure. By the way, I found excellent birding in the coffee groves behind El Duende but I do not recommend that you stay at this particular inn as I believe they overcharge by a good bit for what they offer. You can always have a refreshing beer there as you wait for to come and pick you up, but the meals are also quite expensive.

III - 2. State of Zulia

INTRODUCTION

It is a funny thing, but Zulia, in a way, is like the Venezuelan version of Texas. The main industry in the state is oil, the second industry is oil, and the third industry is oil. Then, there is also cattle. And cattle ranchers, who are big and bold and very macho. Zulians love to brag - everything in Zulia is better and bigger... And the state has had a long history of trying to be "the Independent Republic of Zulia". Sounds familiar? Well, one characteristic Zulia does not share with Texas is the huge groves of bananas and plantains, specially the latter, which form part of the daily meals of every Venezuelan family. Maracaibo, the State Capital, is the second largest city in the country, after Caracas, but there is nothing there that could be of interest to birders, it is just a big, modern city, and hot - very, very, very hot.

The wilderness areas of Zulia are quite another matter - since it is the only State that lies west of the Andes, there are many species, both resident and migrant, which can only be found here, and the semi-isolated mountain chain of Perijá, or Sierra de Perijá, has many endemics. However, most of the Zulian wilderness is VERBOTEN (and this is a very big verboten). Forget about the Perijá endemics, they are "protected" by Colombian guerrillas and Colombian drug mercenaries. The segment of the State west of Lake Maracaibo and the south-western plains are perhaps the most dangerous areas in all of Venezuela, where kidnappings (for ransom), car thefts at gun-point and hold-ups are every-day affairs.

I know that many birders (especially British) have been entering Zulia from the Mérida side, in order to look for Northern Screamers along the road that goes from Sta. Bárbara (or San Carlos del Zulia) to Encontrados and further on to Gallinazo. For the present, at least, I ask you please NOT to do so. That road is quite a risk, for Colombian guerrillas continually incursion into Venezuelan territory through that area. Therefore, I would tell you, with great sadness, that you should stay away from Zulia, except that I found one option, which seems to me quite safe.

CAÑO CONCHA AND THE MARSHES OF JUAN MANUEL

If you look at a map of Zulia, you will see, at the south-western corner of the Lake of Maracaibo, a huge area covered with the little dots, stripes and crescents of dashes that indicate a marsh. This enormous wetland is formed by the Catatumbo River, which flows into Lake Maracaibo from across the Colombian border, and two other large rivers - the Santa Ana and the Escalante. The marsh has a name that I would be willing to bet is the longest name of any marsh in the World - Ciénaga de Juan Manuel de Aguas Claras y Aguas Negras[1]. Most of the marshland (250,000 hectares,

---

[1] Marsh of Juan Manuel of Clear Waters and Black Waters. The name comes from the fact that in some areas of the marsh, the water is part of the Catatumbo flow, which is loaded with silt due to deforestation on the Colombian side of the watershed. This water is the color of pale mud, while in other areas, the high contents of tannins gives it the black, highly reflective appearance typical of non-stagnant marshes.

to be exact) is a national park, officially named Ciénagas del Catatumbo National Park. Adjacent to it, there is also a wild-life reserve, approximately one third of the size of the park.

If you were to make prior arrangements with Maria Rosa Cuesta in Mérida (see chapter on that state), she could probably organize a boat trip from Puerto Concha, a fishing village at the end of a long natural channel called the Caño Concha, to various areas on the coast of the southern part of the Lake of Maracaibo, including the Ciénagas del Catatumbo N.P. to view the wildlife.

There is an area just an hour away from Puerto Concha where you can see both Horned and Northern Screamers, as well as Lesser Yellow-headed Vultures, Common Black Hawk, Jacanas, Yellow-hooded Blackbirds, etc. To go out on the lake, be sure to wear a hat and long sleeves as the sun is usually merciless. Also, on one of my trips, some of my traveling companions had their bathing suits under the clothes, and jumped in for a swim at a lagoon we visited. I would suggest that a half day trip would be adequate.

The first 30 minutes of the trip, the boat takes you through Caño Concha, and I think its name should be changed to Caño Osprey, because we sighted a good half dozen of them critters in August, 1995. It may be, of course, that they had just arrived from the north and were resting before continuing south. The matter on the Osprey nests along Caño Concha was settled by Dick Ryan, for which I am most grateful...

In regard to the nesting Ospreys, most first year birds. and a few second year birds also, stay in the tropics. Second year birds often build what are called 'practice' nests. These nests rarely have eggs and much more rarely hatch any. I know of no successful fledglings from these pairs. This may be the source of the Osprey nest by the Lake. If so, it would be interesting to see results in future years. If the pair stays together into maturity, they are often successful in subsequent years.

By the way, on several trips, Dick has found many Rufous-sided Crakes in the marshes near Puerto Concha.

As it is extremely difficult to penetrate the marsh from the west, we do not worry about the Colombian guerilleros on the lake. On the other hand, by land, the closer you are to the Colombian border, the less safe. If you wish to request the assistance of Maria Rosa Cuesta in organizing a trip for you, contact her by telephone at night (0) 274-416-0005 or through the Venezuelan Audubon. She would need several days' notice to make arrangements with a boatman. On the other hand, I have also been advised by one of our guides that it is possible to go to Puerto Concha on your own and bargain with the boatmen to take you out (if you speak Spanish that is). If they request payment in dollars, tell them you only have Bolívares as their rate of exchange would be outrageous. Also, be sure to leave your car in the house of the owner of the boat for safe keeping.

Enough said. The following birds are listed for the Ciénagas de Juan Manuel:

Great Tinamou	Green Heron	Maguari Stork
Little Tinamou	Striated Heron	Jabiru
Brown Pelican	Cattle Egret	Green Ibis
Neotropic Cormorant	Capped Heron	Scarlet Ibis
Anhinga	Black-crowned Night-Heron	Roseate Spoonbill
Magnificent Frigatebird	Yellow-crowned Night-Heron	Horned Screamer
Great Blue Heron	Rufescent Tiger-Heron	Northern Screamer
Cocoi Heron	Stripe-backed Bittern	Fulvous Whistling-Duck
Great Egret	Boat-billed Heron	White-faced Whistling-Duck
Snowy Egret	Wood Stork	Black-bellied Whistling-Duck

Muscovy Duck
King Vulture
Black Vulture
Turkey Vulture
Lesser Yellow-headed Vulture
Pearl Kite
Gray-headed Kite
Snail Kite
Roadside Hawk
Gray-lined Hawk
Black-collared Hawk
Savanna Hawk
Common Black-Hawk
Great Black-Hawk
Ornate Hawk-Eagle
Crane Hawk
Osprey
Laughing Falcon
Black Caracara
Red-throated Caracara
Yellow-headed Caracara
Crested Caracara
Bat Falcon
Aplomado Falcon
American Kestrel
Rufous-vented Chachalaca
Crested Guan
Yellow-knobbed Curassow
Limpkin
Blackish Rail
Gray-necked Wood-Rail
Sora
Purple Gallinule
Sungrebe
Wattled Jacana
Southern Lapwing
Solitary Sandpiper
Spotted Sandpiper
Common Snipe
Laughing Gull
Common Tern
Caspian Tern
Sandwich Tern
Black Skimmer
Scaled Pigeon
Pale-vented Pigeon
Plumbeous Pigeon
Ruddy Ground-Dove
Blue Ground-Dove
White-tipped Dove
Gray-fronted Dove

Ruddy Quail-Dove
Red-and-Green Macaw
Chestnut-fronted Macaw
Brown-throated Parakeet
Green-rumped Parrotlet
Orange-chinned Parakeet
Saffron-headed Parrot
Red-lored Parrot
Yellow-crowned Parrot
Orange-winged Parrot
Mealy Parrot
Squirrel Cuckoo
Little Cuckoo
Greater Ani
Smooth-billed Ani
Groove-billed Ani
Striped Cuckoo
Crested Owl
Mottled Owl
Common Potoo
Pauraque
Little Nightjar
White-collared Swift
Short-tailed Swift
Rufous-breasted Hermit
Band-tailed Barbthroat
Pale-bellied Hermit
Black-throated Mango
Shining-green Hummingbird
White-chinned Sapphire
White-tailed Goldenthroat
Violaceous Trogon
Ringed Kingfisher
Amazon Kingfisher
Green-and-Rufous Kingfisher
American Pygmy Kingfisher
Blue-crowned Motmot
Rufous-tailed Jacamar
White-necked Puffbird
Russet-throated Puffbird
Collared Aracari
Channel-billed Toucan
Citron-throated Toucan
Chestnut Piculet
Scaled Piculet
Spot-breasted Woodpecker
Golden-green Woodpecker
Lineated Woodpecker
Red-crowned Woodpecker
Red-rumped Woodpecker
Crimson-crested Woodpecker

Plain-brown Woodcreeper
Wedge-billed Woodcreeper
Barred Woodcreeper
Straight-billed Woodcreeper
Buff-throated Woodcreeper
Streak-headed Woodcreeper
Pale-breasted Spinetail
Yellow-chinned Spinetail
Crested Spinetail
Black-crested Antshrike
Barred Antshrike
Eastern Slaty Antshrike
White-flanked Antwren
White-fringed Antwren
Black-faced Antthrush
White-winged Becard
Black-tailed Tityra
Golden-headed Manakin
Wire-tailed Manakin
White-bearded Manakin
Thrush-like Schiffornis
Pied Water-Tyrant
White-headed Marsh-Tyrant
Vermilion Flycatcher
Cattle Tyrant
Fork-tailed Flycatcher
Tropical Kingbird
Gray Kingbird
Piratic Flycatcher
Streaked Flycatcher
Rusty-margined Flycatcher
Social Flycatcher
Great Kiskadee
Lesser Kiskadee
Panama Flycatcher
Euler's Flycatcher
Yellow-olive Flycatcher
Olivaceous Flatbill
Common Tody-Flycatcher
Slate-headed Tody-Flycatcher
Yellow Tyrannulet
Pale-tipped Tyrannulet
Yellow-bellied Elaenia
Forest Elaenia
Scrub Flycatcher
Sooty-headed Tyrannulet
Yellow-bellied Tyrannulet
Ochre-bellied Flycatcher
White-winged Swallow
Gray-breasted Martin
Brown-chested Martin

Bank Swallow
Barn Swallow
Black-chested Jay
Bicolored Wren
Rufous-breasted Wren
Buff-breasted Wren
House Wren
Black-capped Donacobius
Tropical Mockingbird
Cocoa Thrush
Tropical Gnatwren
Shiny Cowbird
Giant Cowbird

Crested Oropendola
Yellow-rumped Cacique
Yellow-hooded Blackbird
Orange-crowned Oriole
Troupial
Yellow Oriole
Oriole Blackbird
Red-breasted Blackbird
Northern Waterthrush
Masked Yellowthroat
Bananaquit
Blue Dacnis
Blue-hooded Euphonia

Thick-billed Euphonia
Blue-gray Tanager
Palm Tanager
Crimson-backed Tanager
Hooded Tanager
Lesser Seed-Finch
Large-billed Seed-Finch
Gray Seedeater
Ruddy-breasted Seedeater
Blue-black Grassquit
Wedge-tailed Grass-Finch

Northern Screamer

GOING TO PUERTO CONCHA FROM THE STATE OF MÉRIDA

It will take you approximately three hours to reach Puerto Concha from either La Azulita or from the city of Mérida.

When driving from Mérida, you enter the town of El Vigía on the main street. Continue straight through the town and then on State Highway 2, towards Sta. Barbara (San Carlos del Zulia), passing by El Moralito. Some 47 km after El Vigía, there is a road to the right which you should take for 12 km, and then turn left for approximately another 15 km to Puerto Concha.

If you are coming from La Azulita, upon reaching National Highway 1, running north/south, turn left (south) towards El Vigía. Just prior to El Vigía you will come to a large National Guard post. Turn right here, and head for Puerto Chama and passing that, Puerto Concha.

Both roads leading to Puerto Concha pass through an area of extensive cattle pastures that it is very good birding for Llano species, as well as wetland birds along the marshy areas. In fact, I know of one birder who actually saw the Northern Screamer in these marshes. Among others, look for:

Anhinga	Aplomado Falcon	Pied Water-Tyrant
Cocoi Heron	American Kestrel	White-headed Marsh-Tyrant
Great Egret	Limpkin	Vermilion Flycatcher
Snowy Egret	Common Moorhen	Cattle Tyrant
Cattle Egret	Purple Gallinule	Fork-tailed Flycatcher
Whistling Heron	Wattled Jacana	Tropical Kingbird
Capped Heron	Southern Lapwing	Gray Kingbird
Black-crowned Night-Heron	Solitary Sandpiper	Boat-billed Flycatcher
Maguari Stork	Greater Yellowlegs	Rusty-margined Flycatcher
Jabiru	Pale-vented Pigeon	Social Flycatcher
Bare-faced Ibis	Ruddy Ground-Dove	Great Kiskadee
White Ibis	Chestnut-fronted Macaw	Lesser Kiskadee
Glossy Ibis	Green-rumped Parrotlet	Yellow-bellied Elaenia
Black-bellied Whistling-Duck	Orange-chinned Parakeet	Common Tody-Flycatcher
Black Vulture	Yellow-crowned Parrot	Gray-breasted Martin
Turkey Vulture	Orange-winged Parrot	Barn Swallow
Lesser Yellow-headed Vulture	Yellow-billed Cuckoo	Tropical Mockingbird
White-tailed Kite	Greater Ani	Red-breasted Blackbird
Pearl Kite	Smooth-billed Ani	Yellow Warbler
Roadside Hawk	White-collared Swift	Bananaquit
Gray-lined Hawk	Pygmy Swift	Blue-gray Tanager
Black-collared Hawk	Ringed Kingfisher	Crimson-backed Tanager
Savanna Hawk	Russet-throated Puffbird	Hooded Tanager
Crane Hawk	Spot-breasted Woodpecker	Grayish Saltator
Laughing Falcon	Red-crowned Woodpecker	Ruddy-breasted Seedeater
Yellow-headed Caracara	Pale-breasted Spinetail	Blue-black Grassquit
Crested Caracara	Yellow-chinned Spinetail	Saffron Finch
Bat Falcon	Common Thornbird	

Should you wish to spend a night at El Vigía, some of our tourists have stayed at Hotel La Suiza in front of the bus terminal on Avenida 15, but I have no personal experience with this hotel. Phones: (0) 275-881-2147 & 881-4082.

Section IV

THE ANDES

Country and Regional Endemics:

Band-tailed Guan
Helmeted Curassow
Venezuelan Wood-Quail
Rose-headed Parakeet
Dwarf Cuckoo
Pygmy Swift
Narrow-tailed Emerald
Green-tailed Emerald
Short-tailed Emerald
Shinning-green Hummingbird
Táchira Emerald
Violet-chested Hummingbird
Golden-bellied Starfrontlet
Blue-throated Starfrontlet
Orange-throated Sunangel
Mérida Sunangel
Coppery-bellied Puffleg
Bronze-tailed Thornbill
Bearded Helmetcrest
Rufous-shafted Woodstar
Russet-throated Puffbird
Crested Spinetail
Ochre-browed Thistletail
Great Antpitta
Táchira Antpitta
Gray-naped Antpitta
Golden-breasted Fruiteater
Páramo Wren
Orange-crowned Oriole
Rufous-cheeked Tanager
White-fronted Redstart
Gray-capped Hemispingus
Slaty-backed Hemispingus

The same curious phenomenon occurs in every other nation along the Andes - the Andean region is like a country within a country.

Everything about it is different from the rest - the land, the people, the villages and houses, the cultivated fields and wooded slopes, the farm animals behind the stone walls, the white snow on the mountains and the white water in the streams...

Come to the Andes, and you come to a land where pastures and thick forests climb to an invisible barrier - on the other side, the scenery suddenly changes to fields of rocky outcrops and woolly bushes.

You come to towns sitting daintily below the severe gaze of white-browed peaks; to paths through montane woods where every branch on every tree is blooming in orchids, mosses, ferns, bromeliads; to Elfin forests, their very name conjuring up visions of fabulous birds.

You come to the páramos, austere lands above the tree line that turn soft with wild flowers during the rainy season; to the steely reflections of clouds on hauntingly remote mountain lakes; to a village fair, children in gay woolens and lustrous eyes, and the local saint parading along the main street on his flowery platform.

Yes, this Andes is a different kind of Venezuela.

The *Andinos,* solemn, hard working and courteous, are also ambitious and can be quite ruthless - most of our dictators have been Andinos. You can tell an Andino even by his distinct accent and more formal manners! Perhaps it is the cold climate that makes the difference.

Politically, the Venezuelan Andes are divided into four neat, self-contained little states. Perhaps I should say three and a half, since some xerophytic areas of Falcón, to the north, and savannas of the High Llanos to the southeast, spill onto the State of Lara, making it a mixture of regions.

Lacing through these states, on its way to Cúcuta, Colombia, is the Pan American road, not an inch wider or less winding than when political prisoners built it *"en tiempo de Gomez"*[1].

In the following chapters, you will find the avian wealth and beautiful birding places of each individual state, and will be very hard put to decide which to choose.

---

[1] Juan Vicente Gomez, the longest-lived of our Andino dictators, ruled Venezuela from 1908 to 1935. He jailed his political opposition and then sent it in chain gangs to do road work.

IV - 1. State of Lara

INTRODUCTION

As I mentioned in previous editions, my Venezuelan friends look askance at me when I include Lara as an Andean state, since we usually think of this region as xerophitic (if not actually desert) lowland. This is quite a misconception, deriving from the fact that what most Caraqueños know about Lara is the environs of Barquisimeto and Carora, which are indeed low and dry.

Most of the State is hilly if not mountainous, with a spur of the Andes reaching across the southwestern part. As a matter of fact, my friend Gordon Young, who was an authority in these matters, said that these mountains are the same age as the latest orogeny of the Andes.

These last ripples of Andes make it possible to find many Andean birds within a seven-hour drive from Caracas, instead of the nine that would take to Trujillo or the twelve hours to Mérida.

YACAMBÚ NATIONAL PARK

For birdwatchers, there is one main reason to come to Lara. It is called Parque Nacional Yacambú. Yacambú has long been one of my favorite parks, a beautiful mountain forest with an intriguing mixture of Andean and Coastal Cordillera birds. We have visited and camped many times in the Park, and netted some breathtaking species when we worked here to compile the checklist for Venezuelan Audubon.

On Getting There

To reach Lara, and the **National Park of Yacambú** from Caracas, take the autopista to Maracay and Valencia. As you drive west towards the industrial city of Valencia, you will find that the Autopista ends in an overpass, which is one of the exits towards the north coast from the Autopista. However, you should keep in the far right lane, staying on the lower part of the road, going under the overpass, and then veer immediately to the right to curve down and join the highway coming up from the coast. You are now headed south towards the Andes and high Llanos as well as the city of Barquisimeto and Yacambú National Park. After 17.7 kilometers you turn right, following the signs for Barquisimeto (National Highway 11).

From there, your goal is the small town of **Sanare,** to the east of Barquisimeto and south of **Quibor.** However, it will probably take you at the very least a half hour to drive through the city of Barquisimeto, which is the State capital; very bustling, populous and sprawling; and will seem endless.

As you enter the city, you will be driving east along Avenida Venezuela. At either Avenida Vargas or upon reaching the busy crossing with Avenida Romulo Gallegos (where Ave. Venezuela dead-ends), turn right and drive approximately 6 blocks to Avenida Libertador (also called Carretera Panamericana). On this, turn left and keep straight on, following the signs for Quibor as you get out of town.

Fortunately, you by-pass Quibor, as the left turn to the road up the mountain towards Sanare is just before Quibor and well-marked. From here it is 19 km to the entrance of Sanare.

On Where to Stay

Sanare is one of those long, narrow towns with a single main street and a maze of side roads, that resemble the rib-cage of a snake. For reasons both obscure and mystical, in this kind of town, you always have to drive all the way through in order to reach the hotel. So, just drive straight through the town until you reach the far end of the Plaza. Here you should turn left and continue straight for two blocks. Turn right. At the end where there is a sign for Posada El Encanto, you turn left. When you come to the T, you would go right for Yacambu or left for the **Posada Turística El Cerrito**. The inn is on the left. This is a modest, but perfectly adequate inn. Phone number (0) 253-449-0016.

As El Cerrito is quite small, you may not be able to secure reservations during holidays. In that case you should stay at the **Hostería Valle de Quibor**, located in the quaint town of Quibor, nestled in a large valley[1]. As you enter the town from the east, take the first street to the left past the Banco de Lara. The Hostería is two blocks down on Avenida 5 at Calle 7. Phone numbers (0) 253-491-0601 & 491-0603.

Dick Ryan found an interesting dirt road about 12 km from the turnoff at Quibor towards Sanare. *«It is on the left and one can park out of sight of the road and walk quite aways. There is a gully on the left with Orinoco Saltators, Black-backed Grosbeaks and many other dry country species.»* Unfortunately, when I was there in January, 2001, there was a well-locked gate that prevented my going down even on foot, but I mention this because in Venezuela things change from one month to the next.

The Park

To reach the Park, turn right out of the car park of Posada El Cerrito. At the end of the street, turn left, going up the hill, out of town[2].

There are two roads going right prior to the entrance to the Park, but at each of these forks, keep left! However, those right-turning roads lead eventually to farms down in the valley, and I have found both of them to be excellent for higher elevation birding. Incidentally, the highest point in the Park is 1,750 meters or 5,600 feet.

From the Park building on the left at the entrance (where the second road to the right forks off the main road), it is 2.5 km to where I have often seen pairs of Masked Trogons; and 5.5 km to a stream where you may see Bronzy Inca, Pearled Treerunner, Flavescent and Cinnamon Flycatchers and Russet-backed Oropendola. In February, 1994, Bob Yukich, an excellent Canadian birder, also saw an Orange-eared Tanager with a feeding flock near the shrine here.

At 7.5 km there is a deep curve going to the right. Try to park on the left. This has often been a most rewarding area. In July and September, I have seen Red-headed Barbets along with feeding flocks of tanagers, including the Saffron-crowned, which is not easy to find. Around 10 a.m. look for Sharp-shinned Hawks circling overhead.

The Park Administration is on the left at 8.2 km. One December, I found a pair of Barbets feeding just across the road from the entrance and a Brown Violetear singing in the trees by the gate. After you enter the Administration area, there is a road to the left to another open area. You can either park up here or leave your car below and walk up to the buildings where you will find an excellent trail leading off behind them.

---

[1] Note from the Editor: Do you think she can be trusted with these complicated directions? I mean, if she had not told me, it would be quite puzzled as to where the Hostería Valle de Quibor is located.

[2] I wish to thank my friend Nigel Redman for the excellent job that he did in correcting the directions I give in this chapter, especially for Sanare and Yacambú NP. Nigel took a draft of the chapter with him when he and his wife visited, and returned it to Clemencia full of red ink!

When we were doing the checklist for the park, we netted a Red-ruffed Fruitcrow along this path. On weekends, you may find a lot of people using the trail, but mid week it is very quiet and birdy.

At 9.2 km, at an elevation of 1,350 meters, a right fork leads to the Laguna El Blanquito, where there should be Least Grebe, Common Moorhen, Caribbean Coot, Wattled Jacana, and possibly the Masked Duck, as well as a great many non-aquatic birds of interest, including Blue-necked Tanager. There are also Rusty-flanked Crakes lurking in the rushes at the edge of the lagoon. In fact, this is an ideal picnic place. In some of my visits, I have found the area with lots of garbage around and looking like maintenance has been forgotten. Still, other times it has been clean and wonderful, so try your luck. It might be an idea to lunch here and plan to spend a few hours walking the trails, including the path behind the lagoon that winds down to the old houses. (One word of warning: this is chigger territory!)

Two fantastic new sightings have recently been reported for Yacambu. Dick Ryan observed a pair of Scaled Fruiteaters (*Pipreola tschudii*) on July 12, 1999 by the road near the highest point through Yacambu at an altitude of 5,600 feet. The birds were about 7 meters up in a tree within two meters of the road sitting on an open limb.

As if the Scaled Fruiteaters were not enough, Chris Sharpe has reported Barred Becard (*Pachyramphus versicolor*) in December, 2000 near the little *capilla* at 5.5 km from the entrance to the Park at 1.700 meters altitude (very low for this species). Chris also sighted the White-sided Flower-piercer (*Diglossa albilatera*). I am hoping that some of you will not only see these species but others to augment our checklist.

Dick Ryan has also recommended driving not only all the way through the Park but to continue down below to about 2,000 meters altitude where he found Magpie Tanager and Rosy Thrush-Tanager.

I would also like to suggest that you try the back way from Sanare that goes towards El Tocuyo. As you pull out of the inn, turn right. At the next corner turn right again and to the end of the street. Then turn left going down the road with signs for El Tocuyo and for Posada El Encanto, that I mentioned above. Put your odometer at 0 and follow this road down the mountain, passing the long series of little houses. At approximately 15 km from El Cerrito you will come to an area of scrub that offers excellent birding: Look for:

??
(Whoops, I lost my list, but I do remember a few!)[1]

Crested Bobwhite	White-fringed Antwren	Glaucous Tanager
Scaled Dove	Tawny-crowned Pygmy-Tyrant	Rosy Thrush-Tanager
White-tipped Dove	Yellow-belied Elaenia	Ultramarine Grosbeak
Brown-throated Parakeet	Mouse-colored Tyrannulet	Grayish Saltator
Rufous-tailed Jacamar	Tropical Mockingbird	Streaked Saltator
Pale-breasted Spinetail	Yellow Oriole	Tocuyo Sparrow

I also remember that it was an exceptionally good area for dry-country birds. (Bring your Ferruginous Pygmy-Owl recording.)

If you plan to return to Caracas after birding this xerophitic area, go back via Sanare as it is some 25 km shorter and by far faster than if you were to go via El Tocuyo. However, unless you leave Sanare at dawn, arm yourself with patience as

---

[1] Note from the Editor: AAAAHHRRRRGGGG!!!

you'll have to go through 28 (that's right, I said TWENTY-EIGHT) stoplights in Barquisimeto before you reach the highway to Caracas!

If you plan to go to the Andes or the Llanos after birding Sanare and the above-mentioned xerophitic area, continue down the same road towards El Tocuyo but turn left when you reach the bridge over the River Tocuyo at the bottom of the hill. You will now be passing Guarico, Anzoátegui and finally Paraiso de Chabasquén[1]. Upon reaching the fork at the bottom of the hills, go right to Biscucuy, Boconó and Guaramacal National Park in the State of Trujillo. Go left for Guanare in the state of Portuguesa and on to Barinas for the low Llanos or Mérida for the high Andes. Take time out to do some birding as you go through the coffee groves down the mountain. The coffee groves start a short ways after the El Tocuyo River.

⊕➔ The Venezuelan Audubon has published the checklist of the birds of Yacambu National Park, which you can obtain either from them or from the American Birding Association.

THE CRAFTS OF TINTORERO AND GUADALUPE

Pardon me if I give you just a bit of typical tourist information. This one is for a place where shopping is great fun.

At more or less half-way along the short stretch of road between the traffic circle for Quibor or Carora and the town of Quibor proper, you will see a sign indicating **Tintorero** on your right.

Tintorero is the weavers capital of Venezuela. Also, you may find here lovely wood carvings, but these come from the town of Guadalupe, slightly to the north. The hammocks, blankets, table mats and wood carvings make excellent gifts to take home. There are many small, family-owned weaving places in the town as well as a center for handicrafts.

Shortly after you enter the settlement of Tintorero (about two minutes from the main highway) you will see a dirt road to your right. Turn right and then right again to reach the handicraft center. After making your purchases, be sure you backtrack the same way you entered the village.

Wood Carvers of Guadalupe

I mentioned the settlement of Guadalupe above, and this is also a wonderful place for a shopping spree to buy a unique present for someone back home. As you come down from Sanare, rather than turning right for Barquisimeto, go straight across the main highway in order to enter the town of Quibor. Continue straight until you reach a V in front of you. Take the right side. Soon you will start to see signs for Guadalupe. Follow these signs, passing through Quibor. When the street dead ends, go right and then left. Guadalupe is 15 km from Quibor, and you will be passing through dry scrub if not actual desert. You will also see the hundreds of match-box dwellings built by the present government in this xerophitic area for the refugees from the floods along the coast. When you enter the hamlet of Guadelupe, stop by the church or plaza to enter the front gate of the large house on the corner next to the school. This is called Tallas de Madera y Cerámica María Chica. It merits a visit.

---

[1] Paraiso de Chabasquén is the only place in Venezuela where I have seen a series of most attractive Potemkin false fronts with the ranchitos behind. It is worth a picture.

Should you by chance be approaching Quibor and Yacambu from the west[1] then you could reach Guadalupe from the north and have yourself a bit of an adventure. From the fork at Agua Viva it is approximately 124 km to the town of Arenales. Some km after Arenales there is the dam of Atarigua (which you may or may not be able to see from the highway). Start looking for a large gas station on your left. Then you will eventually see a large handicraft store also on the left called "Folklore." (How original!) One km east after Folklore there is a dirt road on your right. Turn here and then take the left road. At the next two Ts go right, then left through a gully to approach Guadalupe. This is an interesting farming area with roads leading off in all directions, and it is also interesting birding.

XEROPHITIC BIRDING IN LARA

Vermilion Cardinal
If you are anxious to include the Vermilion Cardinal in your life list, then try the following. I have it on the very best authority that **the** place to find Cardinals in Venezuela is between Barquisimeto and San Pablo on the old road to Carora. To reach this road, you would practically follow the same route as indicated above for Quibor; from the very long Avenida Venezuela at either Avenida Vargas or upon reaching the busy crossing with Avenida Romulo Gallegos (where Ave. Venezuela dead-ends), turn right and drive approximately 5 blocks to Avenida Libertador (also called Carretera Panamericana). On this, turn left. Now I must explain that the most important landmark in Barquisimeto is **El Obelisco**. It is near this monument where the road splits. Just prior to the Obelisco, a road goes right or due north to the Industrial Zone. (Ignore it). After that there is the split in the road with one branch heading due west and the autopista. The other branch is the old road going to San Pablo. You go right!

PAVIA

I really want to emphasize and promote this area as a birding destination in the xerophitic zone. This is due to the fact that the Maryknoll group from the U. S. has been working with the local inhabitants promoting, among other things, ecological education of the young and old alike. Their representative, Phil Brady, asked us to visit their area, and one of our Venezuelan bird watchers went and had a most wonderful and revealing experience. At the same time, due to his enthusiasm, he promoted bird watching among the local people. Isn't that wonderful?

To reach the hamlet of Pavia, I quote from a letter received from Phil Brady:

«*Pavia is not listed on most maps because is was a small settlement until 15 years ago when it started absorbing growth both from the city of Barquisimeto and from the outlying fields. Pavia is located at kilometer 10 on the highway to Bobare, northwest of Barquisimeto. Some maps indicate Las Veras and Padre Diego. Pavia is closer to Barquisimeto than Las Veras.*
From the Obelisco: Take the Avenida Industrial all the way to the end where it passes under the Circunvalación. Continue straight on the same highway

---

[1] Probably the fastest way to reach Caracas from the Andean States of Mérida and Táchira is via the city of El Vigía on the western side of the mountains and then north on National Highway 1 to the fork at Agua Viva, where you would take the right fork towards Barquisimeto.

past the gas stations and the Vertedero Municipal[1]. One kilometer past the vertedero is Pavia Abajo where we will rent horses and burros for guided tours in the protective zone (Valle Yabalitos) starting in 2002. Continue one kilometer past Pavia Abajo to Pavia Arriba. Inquire at the police module or Fe y Alegría school for detailed directions to the Valle Yabalitos.

From Quibor: Go toward Barquisimeto on the Via Barquisimeto - Quibor. Immediately past the restaurant with the large aluminum fish on the roof turn left onto the Circumvalación Norte. Continue on the Circumvalación Norte past El Retoño 3 kilometers up to the first freeway bridge. Immediately past the first freeway bridge, exit the Circumvalación to the right and loop around under the bridge (semi-cloverleaf). Go straight on the highway past the gas stations and the Vertedero Municipal. Follow the instructions above to Pavia Abajo and Pavia Arriba.

The Hotel Obelisco is very comfortable, provides perfect access to Pavia and is close to the airport. But it is also rather expensive.»

Actually, with the experience accumulated in my extensive travels in Venezuela, I would classify the **Hotel Obelisco** in Barquisimeto [phone numbers: (0) 251-441-0311 or 442-2011 & 442-2233, fax: 442-2133] as a rather moderately priced hotel. Moderate, that is, compared to the **Barquisimeto Hilton** or **Hotel Gran Barquisimeto** [phone numbers: (0) 251-256-4103 and (0) 251-442-0511, respectively]. The Obelisco is clean, comfortable and very centrally located on the south side of the Obelisco. From there it should not take you more than 15 or 20 minutes to reach Pavia.

Naturally, staying at the Hosteria Valle de Quibor, would be less expensive, but it will take you longer - possibly 30 to 45 minutes to reach Pavia.

Tocuyo Sparrow

---

[1] Note from MLG: I believe this is the municipal garbage dump.

The following is the list of birds seen by Guillermo Mendez, of the Venezuelan Audubon, during a very short week-end:

Neotropic Cormorant	Groove-billed Ani	Pale-eyed Pygmy -Tyrant
Black Vulture	Ferruginous Pygmy-Owl	Northern Scrub Flycatcher
Turkey Vulture	Lesser Nighthawk	Mouse-colored Tyrannulet
White tailed Hawk	Pauraque	Southern Beardless Tyrannulet
Bay-winged Hawk	Buffy Hummingbird	Bicolored Wren
Yellow-headed Caracara	Blue-tailed Emerald	House Wren
Crested Caracara	Red crowned	Tropical Mockingbird
American Kestrel	Woodpecker	Tropical Gnatcatcher
Bare-eyed Pigeon	Pale-breasted Spinetail	Carib Grackle
Pale vented Pigeon	Black-crested Antshrike	Troupial
Eared Dove	White-fringed Antwren	Yellow Oriole
Plain-Breasted Ground-Dove	White-bellied Antbird	Trinidad Euphonia
Ruddy Ground-Dove	Vermilion Flycatcher	Orinocan Saltator
Scaled Dove	Fork-tailed Flycatcher	Grayish Saltator
White-tipped Dove	Tropical Kingbird	Black-faced Grassquit
Brown-throated Parakeet	Great Kiskadee	Lesser Goldfinch
Green-rumped Parrotlet	Brown-crested Flycatcher	

Have fun in Lara, folks!

IV - 2. State of Trujillo

INTRODUCTION

For the most part, birders tend to by-pass Trujillo. It seems that the collective belief is that there is nothing there for them. How woefully wrong! Trujillo offers beauty and birds by the crate, though it certainly is somewhat off the oft-trodden birding route. Prepare yourself for surprises when you visit here! In August of 95, I took my friend Steve Hilty for his first visit to Trujillo. He liked it so much, especially the Guaramacal National Park, that he remonstrated with me for not making a big ado about it in the previous books. Steve said (and I don't think out of courtesy) that Guaramacal is one of the finest montane forests in S.A. and quite the best in Venezuela. And you know how it goes - with the forest, come the resident birds!

ON GETTING TO TRUJILLO

Depending on where you are coming from, there are several ways to reach the State of Trujillo. I'll go step by step, because this is the most complicated issue about this particular State. Please notice that the Capital City for the State of Trujillo is also called Trujillo - the *city* of Trujillo, that is. In the following directions, **the Trujillo I shall be mentioning is the city.**

From Falcón, drive south to Barquisimeto and then west on National Highway 17 as if to Carora, but turning south on Highway 1 near the settlement of Puente Torres, some 20 km before reaching Carora. From there head towards Monay and Trujillo. After Monay, you will run into traffic going through Tabor, Flor de Patria and Pampan. Your goal is the Hotel Trujillo, where you should overnight in order to bird the road to San Lázaro the next day (see below). To reach it, pass the village of La Plazuela, and continue straight up the hill. To reach Boconó from Trujillo (some 2 hours on the new road), go back to La Plazuela.

From Lara and the Yacambú N.P., drive from Sanare to Guarico, Anzoátegui, **Biscucuy** and **El Paraiso de Chabasquén**[1] and then to **Boconó**. The road is quite good until you reach the State of Portuguesa, shortly after the village of Anzoátegui. There the road lacks culverts, and the runs-off of the rainy seasons have made quite a mess. However, it is a pleasant back-road, away from the main highways and with very good birding along the coffee plantations. It will take you approximately three hours to reach Biscucuy.

From the Llanos, whether heading southwest towards Barinas or heading northeast towards Acarigua / Barquisimeto / Valencia, you have to aim for the city of Guanare. On the southern side of Guanare, you'll find the turn north-west towards Biscucuy, Campo Elías and Batatal. All told, from Guanare to Boconó it will take you some two hours (it is 102 km).

From Mérida, you must aim for the city of Valera. One way is the old route, via Mucuchies and Timotes. North of Timotes, you may go, on almost parallel tracks, via La Puerta, or via La Mesa de Esnujaque.

---

[1] As indicated in the chapter on Lara, Paraiso de Chabasquén is the only place in Venezuela where I have seen a long series of most attractive Potemkin false fronts with the ranchitos or shacks behind. It is worth a picture.

That route winds a lot, going past quaint Andean villages and heavily cultivated areas, so I prefer a "newer" route. To get out of Mérida via La Azulita, take the road along the northern side of the mountain range, past Capazón, Gavilanes and Río Perdido, on to Caja Seca and all the way to Sabana Grande, where you turn right (east) towards Betijoque and Valera. In this general area, there are two roads that should be avoided or taken with great caution: the one going to Boconó via Jajó/Tuñame/Niquitao, and the one to Trujillo via Montero/La Quebrada/Santiago/San Lázaro. Both look good on the map, but real life is, alas!, far different - they are in terrible shape. From Valera to Trujillo on the other hand, the road passing La Cejita and Pampanito is in very good condition.

From Caracas, drive west to Valencia and then south to San Carlos, Acarigua and Guanare. Please note that it is 13.9 km from the beginning of the city of Guanare to the far end where you turn right or north towards Boconó for another 2 hours or 102 km. Should you wish to do the trip from Caracas in two days, as it is a 7 or 8-hour drive from Caracas, I would recommend that you stay at the **Motel Payara** (a real motel in the North American sense of the word), located at the western end of the city of Acarigua/Araure[1]. Phones: (0) 255-621-0975; 621-4747 & 621-4979. To reach the motel, the simplest way would be to take the autopista that goes from the eastern end of Acarigua towards Guanare. Leave the freeway at the exit for Píritu and back-track to Acarigua, thus avoiding the horrible traffic in the city. The restaurant at the Payara is quite good.

Finally, you can also fly to Valera, pick up a rental car and drive that very good highway from Valera to Trujillo, or on to Boconó.

STAYING IN BOCONÓ

Entering Boconó from the south, you will quickly notice that, like so many Andean towns, this neat little city is shaped like a very long sausage. (Steve Hilty described it as "three blocks wide and one hundred blocks long".) The hotel in town that I can recommend is **Hotel La Vega del Rio**. Phone number: (0) 272-652-2992. Fax: (0) 272-652-2493.

Go straight down through town and when you finally reach the bottom, turn right by the sign for the city of Trujillo. You will shortly see the sign on your right for the hotel. Their restaurant is also quite good.

The **Posada Turística Jardín Boconés** has also been highly recommended to me. While the hotel is not at all expensive compared to others in Venezuela, this inn is even less expensive! It is located near the Plaza Venezuela and has a lush central garden within the premises with many bird feeders. The actual address is Calle 1 (Giradot) No. 3-5. It is a new posada in a restored vintage house with 5 handsomely decorated rooms, private baths and hot water. All meals available by prior arrangement. Phone number: (0) 272-652-0171. Cash only.

On the persnickety subject of where to eat in Boconó, Chris Sharpe[2], one of our best bird guides, has advised:

«*For me, the most interesting culinary (and cultural) experience in Boconó is a meal at the* **Museo de Boconó**. *The food is good quality, honest, typical*

---

[1]   The town of Araure sits adjacent to Acarigua, and is nowadays part of its urban area. It has a lot of history, and its church is a lovely example of Colonial archiquecture.

[2]   You will find Chris mentioned often in this book, along with Gustavo Rodriguez. Both are extraordinary bird guides who can expertly lead birdwatchers in Venezuela. Chris is British, graduated in Ornithology from Cambridge University, married to a lovely Venezuelan. E-mail for Chris rodsha@telcel.net.ve.

Andean food, ($5 to $10 per person), and you consume it within the Museum, surrounded by antique telephones, cash registers, plowshares and bicycles, plus photos of notable ("long-lamented") dictators.»

John van der Woude has recommended the restaurant La Casa Vieja, which also has a large collection of things from the past.

GUARAMACAL NATIONAL PARK

Guaramacal National Park is the main reason for visiting Trujillo. In terms of avifauna, it stands second to none among the Andean parks. It is, in fact, much better in many ways, because there is very little traffic going through the Park. (Once you have traveled this road, you will understand why.)

To find the unmarked road to Guaramacal takes both ingenuity and patience. From the hotel in Boconó, retrace your steps somewhat and follow the signs for Biscucuy, going straight up the one-way Calle 5 (also known as Calle Bolívar) until you come to the end where you will have to veer to the right and stop for the traffic entering and leaving Boconó on the main street. Immediately in front of you is a gas station. Turn left again, following the signs for Biscucuy.

At 3.1 km from the gas station, welcoming you to the town, there is a fairly wide entrance on your right with a sign from "Hielo Boconó", as well as the office of the MTC (Ministry of Transport). Opposite there is the "Abastos El Obrero". Turn right. Go one block and turn right again. You are now on the road to Guaramacal.

Three km up the mountain from the "Hielo" sign you will come to a day park known as Laguna de los Cedros. The altitude here is 1,700 meters above sea level (look for Torrent Tyrannulet). However, the birding starts even before this day park.

I must be honest and admit that the road to Guaramacal is not the best road in Venezuela (it is possibly the very worst[1]). However, my Venezuelan friends who have a 4x4s make it quite easily[2].

For our foreign visitors, there is still a way to reach Guaramacal quite painlessly. Contact Oneides Ortegano at Aventuras Andinas, (0) 416-872-4835 or ask the waiter at Hotel La Vega del Río (!). Oneides Ortegano has a 4x4 and has often taken bird watchers to Guaramacal.

There you have it. I would recommend that you bird slowly all the way from the Laguna de los Cedros up to an area known as El Campamento, obviously due to the fact that it is a wide, open area where many people camp. From there up to the top, the road deteriorates so badly that it is far better to walk. Venezuelan birders who know the Park well maintain that the birding is so good on the Boconó side of the mountain, that it is not necessary to go down the other side. It is truly a pity that the governments - both national and state - have not maintained this road. Previously, the farmers at La Vega de Guaramacal transported their produce down to Boconó. Now they have to truck down to the Llanos, which is much farther[3].

One of the most interesting things about the paramo of Guaramacal (approximately 2,900 meters above sea level) is how distinct it is from those of Mérida or Táchira to the south. The *Espeletia* (the woolly plants we call "Frailejon") that grow here are

---

[1] Pamela's Comment: Nah, we've been on worse roads. (She must be thinking of the road to Cerro Humo in Sucre State, because I can think of none other that might possibly be worse.)
[2] Editor's Note: We looove bad roads. But Mary Lou gets the beejeevees at the first sign of ruts or any pebbles larger than fine gravel.

completely different species from those of other National Parks. Considering that there are at least 10 varieties of *Espeletia* in Venezuela, perhaps this is not surprising. The list for Guaramacal has some 300 species. It is a good place for playing a recording of the Andean Pygmy Owl. I've heard of cases when more than a dozen species reacted to the call! And I should point out that Guaramacal is the easiest place in Venezuela to see the Green-and-black Fruiteater. They seem to be all over the place.

As yet, the Venezuelan Audubon has not published a checklist for the birds of Guaramacal. However, you may look for:

Least Grebe	Green Kingfisher	Black-capped Tyrannulet
Roadside Hawk	Emerald Toucanet	Tawny-rumped Tyrannulet
White-rumped Hawk	Black-billed Mountain-Toucan	Venezuelan Tyrannulet
Black-and-Chestnut Eagle	Crimson-mantled Woodpecker	Golden-faced Tyrannulet
Barred Forest-Falcon	Golden-olive Woodpecker	Olive-striped Flycatcher
Band-tailed Guan	Smoky-brown Woodpecker	Blue-and-white Swallow
Andean Guan	Strong-billed Woodcreeper	Southern Rough-winged
Spotted Sandpiper	Olive-backed Woodcreeper	Swallow
Snipe sp.	Spot-crowned Woodcreeper	Pale-footed Swallow
Band-tailed Pigeon	Pale-breasted Spinetail	Collared Jay
Ruddy Pigeon	Rufous Spinetail	Green Jay
Lined Quail-Dove	White-browed Spinetail	White-capped Dipper
Rose-headed Parakeet	Crested Spinetail	Páramo Wren
Speckle-faced Parrot	Pearled Treerunner	Mountain Wren
Squirrel Cuckoo	Streaked Tuftedcheek	Gray-breasted Wood-Wren
Rufous-banded Owl	Montane Foliage-gleaner	Nightingale Wren
Band-winged Nightjar	Slaty Antwren	Andean Solitaire
White-collared Swift	Chestnut-crowned Antpitta	Slaty-backed
Chestnut-collared Swift	Andean Tapaculo	Nightingale-Thrush
Lazuline Sabrewing	Unicolored Tapaculo	Swainson´s Thrush
Green Violetear	Green-and-black Fruiteater	Yellow-legged Thrush
Sparkling Violetear	Black-and-white Becard	Great Thrush
Steely-vented Hummingbird	Golden-winged Manakin	Glossy-black Thrush
Speckled Hummingbird	Smoky Bush-Tyrant	Black-hooded Thrush
Violet-fronted Brilliant	Yellow-bellied Chat-Tyrant	Bare-eyed Thrush
Violet-chested Hummingbird	Black Phoebe	Rufous-browed Peppershrike
Mountain Velvetbreast	Tropical Kingbird	Brown-capped Vireo
Bronzy Inca	Golden-crowned Flycatcher	Tennessee Warbler
Collared Inca	Social Flycatcher	Blackburnian Warbler
Golden-bellied Starfrontlet	Great Kiskadee	Louisiana Waterthrush
Orange-throated Sunangel	Greater Pewee	Slate-throated Redstart
Tyrian Metaltail	Flavescent Flycatcher	White-fronted Redstart
Long-tailed Sylph	Rufous-crowned Tody-Tyrant	Black-crested Warbler
Woodstar sp.	Torrent Tyrannulet	Three-striped Warbler
Golden-headed Quetzal	White-throated Tyrannulet	Russet-crowned Warbler
Masked Trogon	Mountain Elaenia	Blue-backed Conebill

---

[3] Pamela's Comment: On the other hand, one benefit of governmental neglect of the Guaramacal road is that it is now a wonderful hike through the Park. It's beautiful, no one else is on the road, and it's rugged enough to provide good exercise.

Bananaquit	Beryl-spangled Tanager	White-shouldered Tanager
Bluish Flower-Piercer	Black-headed Tanager	Gray-capped Hemispingus
Masked Flower-Piercer	Blue-and-black Tanager	Superciliaried Hemispingus
Glossy Flower-Piercer	Fawn-breasted Tanager	Oleaginous Hemispingus
White-sided Flower-Piercer	Blue-naped Chlorophonia	Common Bush Tanager
Rusty Flower-Piercer	Blue-hooded Euphonia	Chestnut-capped Brush-Finch
Speckled Tanager	Lachrymose Mountain-Tanager	Ochre-breasted Brush-Finch
Golden Tanager	Buff-breasted Mountain-Tanager	Slaty Brush-Finch
Saffron-crowned Tanager	Blue-gray Tanager	Rufous-collared Sparrow
Blue-necked Tanager	Blue-capped Tanager	Yellow-bellied Seedeater
Burnished-buff Tanager	Summer Tanager	

If you come in the dry season and have good weather, you might be interested in staying at a farm next to the Park itself. The **Finca Aguas Claras** is located at «2,000 m.a.s.l. on a hilltop with a marvelous view overlooking the city and valley of Boconó and surrounded by forest-blanketed hills.» Although accessible only on 4x4s, the owners, Marisa and Eduardo Parra-Ganteaume, provide transfers. English spoken. The cozy, rustic-style country house they rent has 3 bedrooms, equipped kitchen and 2 baths with hot water. Caretakers live in an adjacent house so there is always someone nearby to attend to any need including a hearty breakfast with prior arrangement. Excursions or transfers are offered to the Park. My suggestion would be to have them drop you off by El Campamento at dawn to allow you the opportunity to walk back down. The charges are extremely reasonable.

I have very recently heard that the owners are planning to move to the finca and build cabins to receive guests - preferably bird watchers. Olga Gonzalez, one of our Venezuelan bird watchers, reports:

«From the finca one can make excursions to the Laguna de los Cedros (30-minute hike), the Páramo, etc. I found a boy (an expert bird hunter with his slingshot) and asked him how to find the birds. I think I even converted him! At least with regard to hummingbirds. One day we hiked up to the Laguna de Los Cedros through a patch of forest with an incredible number of hummers. Sun Angels, Collared Incas and Long-tailed Sylphs were there in unbelievable numbers along with Sparkling and Green Violetears.»

Hey, let's go!

⟐ A note for those who do not mind carting packages back home: Boconó is famous also for its handicrafts (*artesanía*) and especially, for its beautiful stone pottery. At 6.8 km from Hielo Boconó as you come down from Guaramacal you will see the Calle Tendalito on the right. There is a store on the corner called Artesanía Briceño (usually closed). On the left side of the street is a Serteca car workshop. Turn right here and ask for the house of Sr. Briceño or his daughter. She will take you back to the store. You will be amazed not only by the beauty of this black earthenware, but even more at the low prices.

THE SAN LÁZARO ROAD

Actually, it was Keith Guthrie who put me on to this road out of the city of Trujillo, and I quote below from his letter:

«*Near the city of Trujillo, I found the road leading south to the attractive villages of San Lázaro and Santiago, an excellent place for birds. For most of the route to San Lázaro, the road follows a mountain ridge. It is narrow, but the paved surface is in good condition and there are lots of turnoffs to facilitate parking. The best stretch begins one kilometer south of Sabaneta (specifically, a store called Abastos Sabaneta) where the road crosses from the east to the west slope of the ridge. The steep slopes make treetop observation easy; and the views are magnificent. Further along in the coffee growing areas, there are a number of side tracks and trails that can be explored.*

Approaching San Lázaro, the road switch-backs steeply down to hotter, more arid country, then continues through a rather open valley to Santiago. A second excellent spot is at the very entrance to Santiago where the road curves across a stream, then climbs the canyon wall to the town. Flowering Immortelle trees here were full of birds. In addition, the townspeople have built a concrete walkway up the canyon from the road crossing, and there are many birds to be found along this route.»

For my part, I found many birds even before Sabaneta. A great deal of the habitat is coffee plantation shaded with Inga trees. There are some patches of semi-undisturbed forest along creeks and on the steepest slopes. And remember that the Mountain Immortelle trees bloom in February and March.

As I said above, to bird San Lázaro, you would be wise to spend the night in Trujillo, but, unfortunately, this city is practically devoid of a nice place to stay. There is the Hotel Trujillo, built in the 1950s by the "long-lamented" dictator Pérez Jimenez, and which I believe has now been privatized. I frankly know of no other.

Let us get back to birding: To get to the San Lázaro road, coming out of the hotel, go straight up the hill through an attractive residential area. When you come to a small plaza at the top, go all the way to your right and down the other side of the ridge. You are now on your way for an excellent day of birding.

As for a list of birds on the San Lázaro road, I have seen, heard, received reports of and would greatly appreciate additions to the following:

Black Vulture	Rufous-tailed Jacamar	Rusty-margined Flycatcher
Turkey Vulture	Scaled Piculet	Great Kiskadee
Rufous-vented Chachalaca	Golden-olive Woodpecker	Dusky-capped Flycatcher
Ruddy Ground-Dove	Red-crowned Woodpecker	Common Tody-Flycatcher
White-tipped Dove	Buff-throated Woodcreeper	Yellow-bellied Elaenia
Ruddy Quail-Dove	Streak-headed Woodcreeper	Sooty-headed Tyrannulet
Scarlet-fronted Parakeet	Pale-breasted Spinetail	Golden-faced Tyrannulet
Green-rumped Parrotlet	Stripe-breasted Spinetail	Slaty-capped Tyrannulet
Orange-chinned Parakeet	Streaked Xenops	Olive-striped Flycatcher
Squirrel Cuckoo	Barred Antshrike	Blue-and-white Swallow
Smooth-billed Ani	Black-faced Antthrush	Southern Rough-winged Swallow
Striped Cuckoo	Scaled Antpitta	Green Jay
White-collared Swift	Rusty-breasted Antpitta	Bicolored Wren
Sooty-capped Hermit	Cinnamon Becard	Whiskered Wren
Black-throated Mango	Black-and-white Becard	Rufous-breasted Wren
Golden-tailed Sapphire	Tropical Kingbird	Rufous-and-white Wren
Steely-vented Hummingbird	Piratic Flycatcher	House Wren
Copper-rumped Hummingbird	Boat-billed Flycatcher	Gray-breasted Wood-Wren
Rufous-tailed Hummingbird	Streaked Flycatcher	Tropical Mockingbird

Swainson's Thrush	American Redstart	Palm Tanager
Yellow-legged Thrush	Slate-throated Redstart	Crimson-backed Tanager
Glossy-black Thrush	Golden-crowned Warbler	White-lined Tanager
Pale-breasted Thrush	Bananaquit	Common Bush Tanager
Bare-Eyed Thrush	Swallow Tanager	Black-faced Tanager
Rufous-browed Peppershrike	Rusty Flower-Piercer	Buff-throated Saltator
Red-eyed Vireo	Speckled Tanager	Streaked Saltator
Brown-capped Vireo	Blue-necked Tanager	Rose-breasted Grosbeak
Golden-fronted Greenlet	Bay-headed Tanager	Chestnut-capped Brush-Finch
Crested Oropendola	Burnished-buff Tanager	Ochre-breasted Brush-Finch
Yellow-rumped Cacique	Black-capped Tanager	Black-striped Sparrow
Yellow-backed Oriole	Black-headed Tanager	Gray Seedeater
Black-and-white Warbler	Fawn-breasted Tanager	Blue-black Grassquit
Tennessee Warbler	Blue-naped Chlorophonia	Yellow-bellied Seedeater
Tropical Parula	Thick-billed Euphonia	Rufous-collared Sparrow
Blackburnian Warbler	Blue-gray Tanager	Lesser Goldfinch

As a final note, I would like to add that San Lázaro is one of the most precious towns I have ever found all over the Venezuelan Andes. I would recommend this area not only for bird watchers but for any tourist who loves nature in general.

From Miro Popic's Ecotourism Guide, we discovered that San Lázaro has a small, basic inn on Calle Urdaneta called (what else?) **Posada San Lázaro.** The inn offers four rooms with private bath (cold water) and modest charges for a double[1].

Barred Fruiteater

---

[1] The phone number at Posada de San Lazaro (for reservations, ask for Sra. Emilia Rojo) is (0) 271-82044, but that number will probably change to a seven-digit one in the near future.

IV - 3. State of Mérida

INTRODUCTION

The State of Mérida is extremely popular as a tourist destination. From entire families on holiday, to trekking university students, to troops of Boy Scouts and flocks of bird watchers, to mountain climbers, balloonists and hang-gliders, for everyone there is, in Mérida, a sight, a place, a trail they want to reach.

One feature that lures many a visitor (including some of my perennially voracious friends) is the food. Andean cooking is hearty, varied and delicious. You absolutely must try a "Pisca Andina", a wonderful milk potato, egg and cilantro soup; the Andean *arepas,* which are made with wheat flour instead of corn; the unusual fruit juices, such as *mora, lulo, tomate de árbol, durazno, fresa;* the *dulces abrillantados* and *bocadillos* (sweets); the hot chocolate. And do not, I repeat, do not, miss the 600 varieties of ice creams of the *heladería* Coromoto (in the midst of downtown, City of Mérida).

There are many attractions for the general tourist, and you shall pass by some as you travel in the State, but of those, I will only mention a few places where there's something wonderful to eat or handicrafts are available, for I am positive no one who reads this book is interested in amusement parks and related genera.

There are motels, neat little hotels and cozy posadas (inns) everywhere. Many are family-run, which usually means cleanliness and better service and food. And I think I can safely say that in general, everywhere you go the staff is amiable and accommodating.

For lovers of nature and the great outdoors, Mérida is a paradise. The best known features are, of course, the great peaks of the Sierra Nevada, which are, from east to west, Humboldt (4,942 mts.), Bonpland (4,883 mts.), La Concha (4,920 mts.), Bolívar (5,007 mts.), Espejo (4,765 mts.), El Toro (4,755 mts.), and El León (4,740 mts.). From the city of Mérida, one sees only five, since Humboldt and Bonpland appear as one, called La Corona, and the same happens with Bolívar and Espejo, which are jointly called La Columna. Thus, they are often referred to by their well-known poetic name - the Five White Eagles. These, as well as the famous Humboldt Trail, are a magnet for trekers and climbers from all over the world. There are also many places where one can go camping, hiking or horseback riding, as well as small tourism outfits that supply the necessary guides, animals and gear one may need.

And then, there is the stuff for us birders, the stuff that dreams are made of... Let's see - there are Torrent Ducks, Black-chested Buzzard-Eagles, Mérida Sunangels, Bearded Helmetcrests, Crimson-mantled Woodpeckers, Pearled Treerunner, Golden-winged Manakins, Red-ruffed Fruitcrows, Andean Cocks of the Rock, Páramo Wrens, Páramo Seedeaters... No wonder we all go bananas when we get to Mérida!

ON GETTING THERE

From Caracas, most people reach Mérida by driving to Valencia, and then straight across the upper Llanos, on National Highway 5, via San Carlos, Acarigua, Guanare and finally, to the city of **Barinas** at the foot of the Andes, where they take the road up the mountains (State Highway 1).

Be warned: the segment from San Carlos to Acarigua is so accident prone that people call it the "Guillotine." Built in 1941, it has never been widened. There are a few dozen long and narrow bridges and also a few hundred heavy trucks trying to pass one another (especially on the bridges). The traffic is a nightmare. After Acarigua for unknown reasons the traffic is not quite so bad. Should you wish to take a break in the 7 or 8-hour journey to Barinas, you might try overnighting in the city of **Acarigua,** 365 km or 5 hours from Caracas. Just before you enter Acarigua, you will find the beginning of a freeway – it runs only 50 km. I suggest that you take this super highway and leave it again **after** you pass the city, taking the Píritu (that name again!) exit. Then you will backtrack to Acarigua on a normal road in order to stay at the **Motel Payara** located at the western end of the city, thus avoiding heavy traffic in a city that does not believe in road signs. The Payara resembles an American motel, is comfortable, clean and has a good restaurant. Phone numbers: (0) 255-621-4611 & 621-4970. This way, you can take advantage of the full 50 km of freeway that exist between Acarigua and Guanare. For this freeway, construction began with great enthusiasm, but the Ministry of Transportation and Communications[1] must have miscalculated the cost, or something - of the 83 km between the two cities.

On a visit to the Andes in May, 2001, I discovered that the autopista between **Guanare** and Barinas had been partially constructed. A few kilometers after Guanare, you come to the *Santuario de la Virgen de Coromoto*, the patron saint of Venezuela. Turn left here for a couple of km and then right to access the new highway. Perhaps by the time you come the autopista will be finished all the way to Guanare, but don't count on it. You will reach the outskirts of the city of Barinas, between Barinitas and the round-about at the entrance of Barinas itself. **Take note of your odometer at this round-about, for I will be indicating places along the road according to kilometer readings.**

Overnighting Barinas/Altamira

You may wish to spend the night in Barinas at any of the hotels suggested. (See the chapter on the Llanos.) However, my suggestion would be for you to continue up the mountain for some 35 km from the round-about or slightly less if you have just exited the autopista. At km 35 you will see the sign for the adorable Andean town of **Altamira,** which is some 20 minutes from the main highway. For 7 km, the road weaves through coffee plantations. Birding the coffee groves carefully, all the way down to an iron bridge over the Santo Domingo river, you should see a variety of species. For a charming first impression of what an Andean town is like, continue some 15 minutes beyond the river. Upon arriving at the Plaza Bolívar turn right at the far end in order to reach the unmarked **Posada Cáceres** on the corner and just next to the church. Prior reservations must be made and paid for. Phone numbers: (0) 212-977-1234 & 977-2798 or (0) 414-222-0385; fax: 212-977-0110. E-mail: lodge@cacaotravel.com, or contact the Venezuelan Audubon. The inn is rather expensive, but worth it - a vintage house meticulously restored with 4 huge rooms, private baths, hot water. Exceptionally good taste throughout. Price includes breakfast. There is a telephone to contact them at the corner general store facing the Plaza and just before you turn towards the church. The gentleman who owns the store is extremely helpful, serves excellent coffee and sells lots of interesting what-nots.

---

[1] Note from the Editor: Better known as Ministry of Tricks and Complications.

Birding around Altamira

As to where you should bird in this area, I recommend that you leave the inn very, very early the next morning. Drive straight up the street as if you were going to the town of Calderas (but don't!). At the very first corner, turn right by the large white building with blue trim. Go to the end of this street, walk down a long series of steps and start birding among the coffee groves. We only had an hour, but you should take 3 or 4 hours to bird this beautiful area and look for among others:

Turkey Vulture	Plain-brown Woodcreeper	Green Honeycreeper
Laughing Hawk	Short-tailed Antthrush	Blue-necked Tanager
Rufous-vented Chachalaca	Golden-winged Manakin	Blue-gray Tanager
Rose-headed Parakeet	Rufous-and-white Wren	Silver-beaked Tanager
Copper-rumped Hummingbird	Yellow-legged Thrush	Gray-headed Tanager
Moustached Puffbird	Yellow-backed Oriole	Buff-throated Saltator
Red-rumped Woodpecker		

I personally would very much have liked to spend two nights at the Cáceres in order to investigate and enjoy this area further.

THE BARINAS - SANTO DOMINGO ROAD

To an ordinary tourist, reaching the town of Santo Domingo almost on the Páramo[1] from Barinas takes two hours. We birders take a full day, because there is some jolly good birding to do along the way.

The río Barragán

The first stop, even before Altamira, is by the bridge at 28.3 km from the traffic circle of Barinas, to look for Wire-tailed Manakins. The bridge spans the small Barragán river. You might try walking down the litter-strewn tail to the stream. Early morning or late afternoon birding may be rewarding but the whole area is quiet at midday. In this general area look for Dwarf Cuckoo, Sepia-capped Flycatcher, White-necked Thrush, Mourning Warbler, Red-crowned Ant-Tanager and Pectoral Sparrow. If the stream has dried up to just a few, scattered ponds, the birds may come down to bathe in the late afternoon. I always told people to bird for some distance on the paved side-road going up from right next to the bridge. But, (there always is a but), there has been a lot of deforestation of late. However, Chris Sharpe advises:

«I still like the Río Barragán and have had no problems to date. One advantage is that bird activity goes on virtually all day. A good place for Gray-headed Kite, Pale-headed Jacamar, Yellow-tufted Woodpecker, Ochre-bellied Flycatcher, Lance-tailed Manakin and Collared Jay.»

Maria Rosa Cuesta, the specialist of Andean birds, found the Drab Water-Tyrant along the Barragán. Its usual distribution is not included in this area. She advised:

«Continue along this side road that leads off the main highway for quite a ways. When you come to a big curve to the left, you will then be going along the Rio Santo Domingo and not the Barragán.»

---

[1] The páramos are the lands of the humid Andean mountains that are found above the tree line. On the arid Andes, the lands above the tree line are called puna.

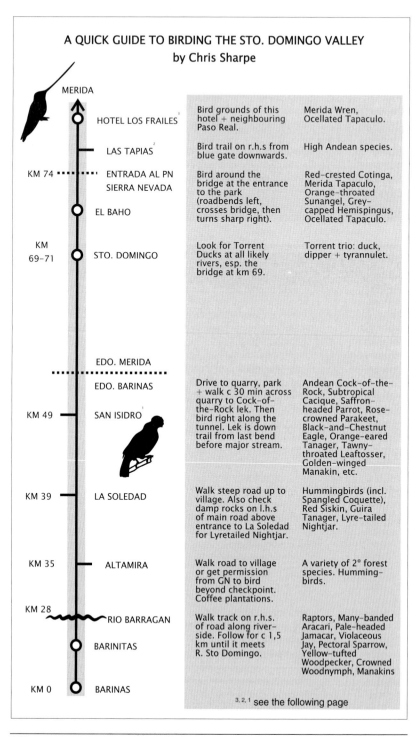

A QUICK GUIDE TO BIRDING THE STO. DOMINGO VALLEY
by Chris Sharpe

Location	Notes	Species
MERIDA		
HOTEL LOS FRAILES[3]	Bird grounds of this hotel + neighbouring Paso Real.	Merida Wren, Ocellated Tapaculo.
LAS TAPIAS[2]	Bird trail on r.h.s from blue gate downwards.	High Andean species.
KM 74 — ENTRADA AL PN SIERRA NEVADA	Bird around the bridge at the entrance to the park (roadbends left, crosses bridge, then turns sharp right).	Red-crested Cotinga, Merida Tapaculo, Orange-throated Sunangel, Grey-capped Hemispingus, Ocellated Tapaculo.
EL BAHO		
KM 69-71 — STO. DOMINGO	Look for Torrent Ducks at all likely rivers, esp. the bridge at km 69.	Torrent trio: duck, dipper + tyrannulet.
EDO. MERIDA		
EDO. BARINAS		
KM 49 — SAN ISIDRO[1]	Drive to quarry, park + walk c 30 min across quarry to Cock-of-the-Rock lek. Then bird right along the tunnel. Lek is down trail from last bend before major stream.	Andean Cock-of-the-Rock, Subtropical Cacique, Saffron-headed Parrot, Rose-crowned Parakeet, Black-and-Chestnut Eagle, Orange-eared Tanager, Tawny-throated Leaftosser, Golden-winged Manakin, etc.
KM 39 — LA SOLEDAD	Walk steep road up to village. Also check damp rocks on l.h.s of main road above entrance to La Soledad for Lyretailed Nightjar.	Hummingbirds (incl. Spangled Coquette), Red Siskin, Guira Tanager, Lyre-tailed Nightjar.
KM 35 — ALTAMIRA	Walk road to village or get permission from GN to bird beyond checkpoint. Coffee plantations.	A variety of 2° forest species. Humming-birds.
KM 28 — RIO BARRAGAN	Walk track on r.h.s. of road along river-side. Follow for c 1,5 km until it meets R. Sto Domingo.	Raptors, Many-banded Aracari, Pale-headed Jamacar, Violaceous Jay, Pectoral Sparrow, Yellow-tufted Woodpecker, Crowned Woodnymph, Manakins
BARINITAS		
KM 0 — BARINAS		

3, 2, 1 see the following page

3. HOTEL LOS FRAILES • PASO REAL

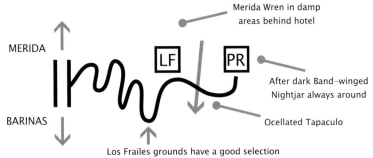

MERIDA

BARINAS

LF **PR**

Merida Wren in damp
areas behind hotel

After dark Band-winged
Nightjar always around

Ocellated Tapaculo

Los Frailes grounds have a good selection
of High Andean stuff-Flowerpiercers, Hummingbirds
(incl. Ocasional sword-billed)

2. LAS TAPIAS

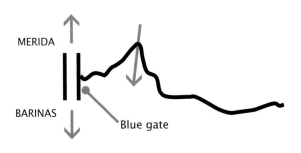

MERIDA

BARINAS

Blue gate

1. SAN ISIDRO TUNNEL

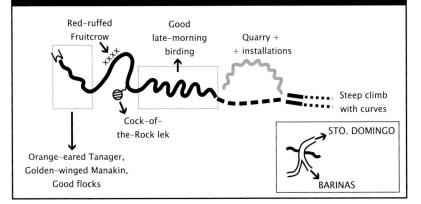

Red-ruffed
Fruitcrow

Good
late-morning
birding

Quarry +
+ installations

Steep climb
with curves

Cock-of-
the-Rock lek

Orange-eared Tanager,
Golden-winged Manakin,
Good flocks

STO. DOMINGO

BARINAS

She found this species at the confluence of the Barragán with the Sto. Domingo River, along the edge of the water near the wild sugar cane and before one starts to climb up the mountain.

The La Soledad Road

Back to the main road, your next stop is the side-road to **La Soledad**, some 5.1 km above the one to Altamira. It is the very **first** paved road on your **left** after leaving Barinitas. There is a small restaurant that serves excellent Andean soups on the right side of the road. Park here if possible. Otherwise, drive less than another kilometer up the road where you can possibly park near a stream. Lock your car and **leave nothing in sight inside**.

Before going up the road, check the wall which supports the embankment between La Soledad road and the stream. The wall is all overgrown with vegetation and it was here that a male Lyre-tailed Nightjar was found some years ago. Unfortunately, the cat of the owner of the cafe proceeded to kill it. The tail of the Nightjar is now displayed in a jar on the owner's bar, but fortunately said cat met his come-uppance with a car. Apparently, there are others to be found around here, well-camouflaged among the dried twigs, some two or three meters above the ground. So check the wall carefully, as well as the bushes on the side of the road as you go up. Maria Rosa Cuesta advised that the owner of the restaurant also owns the land across the road where the trail goes up the mountains, and he has taken due note of bird watcher's interest in this area and advised her that he is thinking of making more trails. However, please take note of the rumor that he offers to show the guides where the birds are to be seen in exchange for $$$. It would be far wiser to patronize his restaurant, and enjoy his soups as an incentive for him to collaborate with birders. A tip would not be out of line, but do not overdo it. A plus for having lunch at his restaurant would be the possibility of seeing both the Red-legged and Purple Honeycreepers across the road as you eat.

It is almost impossible to drive up this road, which is why I suggest "climbing" it. While you do so, look for:

Little Tinamou	Brown Violetear	Crested Spinetail
Black Vulture	Green Violetear	Stripe-breasted Spinetail
Turkey Vulture	Black-throated Mango	Montane Foliage-gleaner
Swallow-tailed Kite	Fork-tailed Woodnymph	Streak-capped Treehunter
Roadside Hawk	Speckled Hummingbird	Streaked Xenops
White-rumped Hawk	Violet-fronted Brilliant	Plain Antvireo
Black-and-chestnut Eagle	Violet-chested Hummingbird	Slaty Antwren
Barred Forest-Falcon	Booted Racket-tail	Rufous-rumped Antwren
Band-tailed Guan	Long-tailed Sylph	Immaculate Antbird
Band-tailed Pigeon	Crested Quetzal	Black-faced Antthrush
Ruddy Pigeon	Masked Trogon	Undulated Antpitta
White-tipped Dove	Red-headed Barbet	Chestnut-crowned Antpitta
Lined Quail-dove	Yellow-billed Toucanet	Rusty-breasted Antpitta
Rose-headed Parakeet	Emerald Toucanet	Rufous-vented Tapaculo
Barred Parakeet	Black-billed Mountain-Toucan	Golden-breasted Fruiteater
Pavonine Cuckoo	Golden-olive Woodpecker	Black-and-white Becard
Rufescent Screech-Owl	Red-crowned Woodpecker	Masked Tityra
Common Potoo	Smoky-brown Woodpecker	Tropical Kingbird
White-collared Swift	Plain-brown Woodcreeper	Variegated Flycatcher
Lesser Swallow-tailed Swift	Wedge-billed Woodcreeper	Lemon-browed Flycatcher
Little Hermit	Spot-crowned Woodcreeper	Golden-crowned Flycatcher

Rusty-margined Flycatcher
Social Flycatcher
Dusky-capped Flycatcher
Olive-sided Flycatcher
Greater Pewee
Cinnamon Flycatcher
Flavescent Flycatcher
Scale-crested Pygmy-tyrant
Variegated Bristle-tyrant
Small-billed Elaenia
Mountain Elaenia
Slaty-capped Flycatcher
Olive-striped Flycatcher
Blue-and-white Swallow
Green Jay
Whiskered Wren
Gray-breasted Wood-Wren
Southern Nightingale Wren
Andean Solitaire
Slaty-backed
Nightingale-Thrush
Spotted Nightingale-Thrush
Swainson's Thrush
Yellow-legged Thrush
Pale-eyed Thrush

Black-hooded Thrush
Chestnut-bellied Thrush
Bare-eyed Thrush
Rufous-browed Peppershrike
Brown-capped Vireo
Giant Cowbird
Crested Oropendola
Russet-backed Oropendola
Yellow-backed Oriole
Golden-winged Warbler
Tennessee Warbler
Tropical Parula
Cerulean Warbler
Blackburnian Warbler
American Redstart
Slate-throated Redstart
Three-striped Warbler
Golden-crowned Warbler
Green Honeycreeper
Speckled Tanager
Golden Tanager
Saffron-crowned Tanager
Blue-necked Tanager
Bay-headed Tanager

Burnished-buff Tanager
Beryl-spangled Tanager
Black-capped Tanager
Blue-and-black Tanager
Blue-naped Chlorophonia
Orange-bellied Euphonia
Blue-gray Tanager
Palm Tanager
Silver-beaked Tanager
Summer Tanager
White-winged Tanager
Oleaginous Hemispingus
Common Bush-Tanager
Magpie Tanager
Black-faced Tanager
Blue-black Grosbeak
Buff-throated Saltator
Rose-breasted Grosbeak
Chestnut-capped Brush-Finch
Yellow-bellied Seedeater
Dull-colored Seedeater
Rufous-collared Sparrow
Lesser Goldfinch
Red Siskin

Chris Sharpe advises that about one km up the Soledad Road, there is an area of the slopes covered in wire netting. Scan it carefully, for Red Siskins have been seen there. On the other hand, the expert from this area (Maria Rosa who else?) commented that every time she walks this trail, she sees the Red Siskin in the trees on the left as you go up and just within 20 meters from the start of the trail. If you come to a curve going right, you have passed the Red Siskin area. To celebrate this earth-shaking event, I suggest you then have a coffee at the restaurant and tell the owner what a wonderful piece of geography he owns and he should not do anything to change it!

Finally, if your guide is unable to show you all of the above species, please do not complain or blame him. They are not always there when you want to see them!

The San Isidro Tunnel Road

After that work-out on La Soledad road, drive some more up the mountain. At some 49.7 km from the round-about of Barinas, you will see a **second** paved road on your **left**. This entrance leads to a kaolin mine and past that, to a service road for the **San Isidro Tunnel**, which I understand is an overflow outlet for the Santo Domingo dam.

A word of caution - The mine is in operation every work day from 7:00 a.m. to around 4:00 p.m., so big trucks often go up or down the road during those hours. Add to that the fact that the road is dirt, very narrow and winding, with huge drops-off on one side and very few lay-bys. To avoid risk, try to time your visit so you go up the road before opening or after closing time, or on a week-end. Once up, there are several places where you can safely park and bird.

Do NOT under any circumstance attempt to drive past the mine or even allow your guide to do so. This is extremely dangerous and tourists have been severely wounded, if not killed, by doing so. Park near the mine where your car will be guarded, and a tip for the watchman would be appreciated. The mine workers always leave a trail for birders to walk, and we are completely accepted as being subnormal beings that need to be protected.

You will have to park near the mine office, which is 2 km in from the main road. Scan the mine's cliffs by the office for Cliff Flycatchers. Past the mine, the really serious birding begins, so you will have to hike in another 2 km, part of these over all the broken-up mountain side that the mining has left. Our friend Richard Ryan recently advised that «*one has to scramble over about 150 feet of loose rock and sand at a steep angle to get through.*»

Once on the other side, walk on to where the forest begins. Down from the road, on this steep mountain side, there is a lek of Andean Cocks-of-the-Rock. The best way to find the barely marked and extremely steep trail leading down to it, would be to walk all the way to the stream and then back track approximately one city block until you see a bare, grassy area.

If you visit between December and February, the birds are quite conspicuous, often foraging about near the waterfalls. You will save yourself having to brave the trail. If you have the good luck of seeing a female, take note of her beautiful blue eyes! I cannot emphasize enough a caution about disturbing the lek's denizens. Please remember that this is their display area - do not disturb the birds with play-backs, noise, etc.

This lek, and the surrounding forest, have been a constant concern of the Venezuelan Audubon since it was found circa 1986[3]. We have had to fight for it tooth and claw several times - in 1988, in 1992, and most recently, in March of 1997. As is the case in most environmental battles, wins are temporary, but the loses would be permanent.

Bearded Helmetcrest

---

[1] Note from the Editor: The original finding has to be credited to Paul Schwartz, who came upon it while exploring the area in the 1960s. He advised the people at the Phelps Ornithological Collection in Caracas. Both Paul and the POC staff kept the information very restricted, fearing, correctly, that it might become known by trappers, feather or egg collectors and other unsavory characters. The latest caper we heard was that an agent for some zoo in Texas got away with *several* pairs of "Gallitos".

Past the trail to the lek, continue walking and birding all along the main trail, until you reach the end, where the entrance to the tunnel is found. To pass the stream, you may have to get your feet wet. Chris Sharpe advises to spend an hour overlooking the gorge from the stream, for quetzals, Red-ruffed Fruitcrow and Cock-of-the Rock. During the dry season you should get frequent feeding flocks all the way to the end of the trail, which may include Golden-winged Manakins and Orange-eared Tanagers. From about 10:00 a.m. onwards, scan the skies for distant views of Black-and-Chestnut Eagle.

Bob Clements has found that the best way to avoid the trucks on the narrow road, is to spend the entire day birding the area, taking a lunch. He is right! There is a lot to see along the San Isidro Tunnel road, but I must warn you - be prepared for chiggers! Look for:

Black Vulture	Golden-headed Quetzal	Slaty-capped Flycatcher
Turkey Vulture	Masked Trogon	Olive-striped Flycatcher
Swallow-tailed Kite	Red-headed Barbet	Blue-and-white Swallow
Sharp-shinned Hawk	Yellow-billed Toucanet	Green Jay
Broad-winged Hawk	Black-billed Mountain Toucan	White-capped Dipper
Roadside Hawk	Scaled Piculet	Whiskered Wren
White-rumped Hawk	Golden-olive Woodpecker	Mountain Wren
Black-and-chestnut Eagle	Smoky-brown Woodpecker	Gray-breasted Wood-Wren
Band-tailed Guan	Wedge-billed Woodcreeper	Andean Solitaire
Venezuelan Wood-Quail	Olive-backed Woodcreeper	Yellow-legged Thrush
Band-tailed Pigeon	Azara's Spinetail	Great Thrush
Ruddy Pigeon	Stripe-breasted Spinetail	Black-hooded Thrush
White-tipped Dove	Spotted Barbtail	Chestnut-bellied Thrush
Ruddy Quail-Dove	Montane Foliage-gleaner	Rufous-browed Peppershrike
Lined Quail-Dove	Streak-capped Treehunter	Red-eyed Vireo
Rose-headed Parakeet	Tawny-throated Leaftosser	Brown-capped Vireo
Saffron-headed Parrot	Slaty Antwren	Russet-backed Oropendola
Speckle-faced Parrot	Immaculate Antbird	Scarlet-rumped Cacique
Squirrel Cuckoo	Chestnut-crowned Antpitta	Yellow Oriole
Band-winged Nightjar	Green-and-black Fruiteater	Black-and-white Warbler
Lyre-tailed Nightjar	Barred Fruiteater	Tennessee Warbler
White-collared Swift	Red-ruffed Fruitcrow	Blackburnian Warbler
Pale-bellied Hermit	Andean Cock-of-the-Rock	Louisiana Waterthrush
Lazuline Sabrewing	Golden-winged Manakin	American Redstart
Brown Violetear	Slaty-backed Chat-Tyrant	Slate-throated Redstart
Green Violetear	Black Phoebe	Three-striped Warbler
Spangled Coquette	Rufous-tailed Tyrant	Bananaquit
Golden-tailed Sapphire	Lemon-browed Flycatcher	Swallow Tanager
Steely-vented Hummingbird	Golden-crowned Flycatcher	White-sided Flower-piercer
Speckled Hummingbird	Dusky-capped Flycatcher	Rusty Flower-piercer
Violet-fronted Brilliant	Greater Pewee	Speckled Tanager
Bronzy Inca	Cinnamon Flycatcher	Golden Tanager
Collared Inca	Cliff Flycatcher	Saffron-crowned Tanager
Golden-bellied Starfrontlet	Yellow-olive Flycatcher	Blue-necked Tanager
Orange-throated Sunangel	Variegated Bristle-Tyrant	Bay-headed Tanager
Booted Racket-tail	Torrent Tyrannulet	Burnished-buff Tanager
Long-tailed Sylph	White-throated Tyrannulet	Beryl-spangled Tanager
Wedge-billed Hummingbird	Mountain Elaenia	Black-capped Tanager
Crested Quetzal	Golden-faced Tyrannulet	Blue-and-Black Tanager

Orange-eared Tanager	Silver-beaked Tanager	Common Bush-Tanager
Blue-naped Chlorophonia	Hepatic Tanager	Black-faced Tanager
Orange-bellied Euphonia	Summer Tanager	Rose-breasted Grosbeak
Thick-billed Euphonia	White-winged Tanager	Chestnut-capped Brush-Finch
Blue-gray Tanager	White-lined Tanager	Rufous-collared Sparrow
Blue-capped Tanager	Gray-capped Hemispingus	Lesser Goldfinch

The Bridge over the Santo Domingo River

Back on the main highway and continuing 1 km up the mountains, you will cross the state border between Barinas and Mérida. At 13.3 km above the entrance to the San Isidro road, you'll find the **Alcabala** of the village of **Mitisús.** Shortly after that you will again see the Santo Domingo River along the right side of the road. At 8 km from the Alcabala, you will go over a bridge where the road crosses over the Santo Domingo. Stop, park, and look for Torrent Ducks and White-capped Dippers on both sides of this bridge, as well as up and down along the river. Maria Rosa has recommended that you walk or drive the equivalent of another block and a half to the bridge that goes to Las Piedras. As this bridge has far less traffic, it is safer and easier to park and walk. Generally, the ducks are here in plain sight, but as from October when the females are incubating, it is more difficult to see them, but you more than likely will find them by walking down towards the main road. There is also an area for parking by a kiosk called El Limoncito on the main highway before reaching either bridge where she saw 7 Torrent Ducks from her car in February, 2001.

On Staying in Santo Domingo

It is approximately 67.5 kilometers from the round-about of Barinas to the first houses of the town of **Santo Domingo**. I would suggest that you plan to spend at least two days at Santo Domingo to bird the various areas. There is a plethora of hotels in and around this quaint Andean town. Of the many, I would recommend...

Hotel Moruco

Phone number: (0) 274-898-8070 & 898-8525. Drive through Santo Domingo. You will find a large, rambling building plus cabins on your right, about 10 or 15 minutes, or 1.2 km, after the Maraven gas station at the end of the town. Their restaurant is excellent and the service very good. Situated at 1,846 mts. or 6,000 feet, this is the place to stay if you want to avoid the high altitude of the other hotels, but it is not as near to the birding areas as...

Finca Agroturística Páramo Maraisa

Phone: (0) 414-741-2990 located 4 km. after Hotel Moruco. 2 rustic cabins with heat and equipped kitchen. Very inexpensive, but also has a good restaurant. Across the street from the inn is a path going up the mountain to Salto Milagroso, the tallest waterfall in Mérida and just a ten-minute walk from the road.

Posada Turística Las Tapias

Phone numbers: (0) 414-747-0961 & (0) 274-244-9849. Located 9 km after Hotel Moruco on your right as you go up the mountain. You will first notice the sign for the Restaurante Las Tapias, as well as a store selling local crafts. Check in at the store. This for me was a find. Extremely comfortable and inexpensive, with 6 recently constructed rooms located down the hill behind the restaurant. Private baths with hot water and heating in the rooms (a must up here). There is a covered balcony-corridor running the length of the building with a beautiful view of the páramo and river below. They also offer a 2-bedroom cabin in the field below with fully equipped kitchen, bath with hot water. Manager, Maura de Meza. Cash only. It is my favorite place to stay, but I was not particularly impressed by the food at their restaurant. So, for a good dinner, go to:

Hotel Los Frailes

Phone numbers: (0) 212-976-0530 & 976-1883. E-mail:hoturvensa@infoline.wffe.com. Located on the Páramo, at 2,850 meters (9,262 feet), this hotel has a singular charm and is truly picturesque, built in the manner of an old monastery from the 1600s. One of our birders, Bonnie Cresap, of Portland, Oregon, aptly described its atmosphere:

> «Los Frailes is the most enchanting place I've ever been, with its stream let through the courtyard flowing to the rushing brook right below the front door, and both hummingbirds and soft Gregorian chants floating in the air at sunset.
> That it had flowers everywhere and hot chocolate and a crackling fire awaiting in the restaurant - it must have been real, because it is beyond my power to fantasize all that in one same place.»

Los Frailes is approximately 12.4 km from the Maraven gas station at the end of the town of Santo Domingo or 83.2 kilometers from the now tiresome traffic circle in Barinas. The food at Los Frailes is excellent.

In the garden of Hotel Los Frailes, look for :

Birds of Hotel Los Frailes

Torrent Duck (up river)	Streaked-throated Bush-Tyrant	Bluish Flower-piercer
Black-chested Buzzard-Eagle	Black Phoebe	Mérida Flower-piercer
Band-tailed Pigeon	Torrent Tyrannulet	Masked Flower-piercer
Band-winged Nightjar	White-throated Tyrannulet	Chestnut-breasted Chlorophonia
White-collared Swift	Brown-bellied Swallow	Blue-and-black Tanager
Sparkling Violetear	Collared Jay	Lachrymose Mountain Tanager
Sword Billed Hummingbird	White-capped Dipper	Blue-capped Tanager
White-vented Plumleteer	Great Thrush	Plain-colored Seedeater
Tyrian Metaltail	Eastern Meadowlark	Slaty Brush-Finch
Brown-backed Chat-Tyrant	White-fronted Redstart	Rufous-collared Sparrow
Slaty-backed Chat-Tyrant	Black-crested Warbler	Andean Siskin

Maria Rosa has advised me that the Sword-billed Hummingbird can be seen every day at Los Frailes. It seems that the waiter puts out hummingbird feeders at the back of the hotel on a daily basis ever since a Brazilian investigator had requested his help in a study the Brazilian was making of these hummers. When the biologist departed, he left the feeders with his previous helper who now delights in feeding the birds. Maria Rosa has requested that if you plan to go to Los Frailes, please bring from the U.S. the special humming bird food as the waiter can only provide sugar and water. Thus both the birds and the waiter would be delighted by your gift.

Hotel Paso Real

Located immediately above Los Frailes and while it is not as outstanding in its architecture, it is perfectly nice. The rooms are very cozy. While at the Hotel Paso Real, just at dusk, a walk around the grounds will lead you to hear and see the Band-winged Nightjar. It is always there!

Hotel Sierra Nevada

Phone number (0) 274-888-0075. This is the place to try, if you are looking for something less expensive but I am of two minds as to whether or not to recommend it. Three of our birders were very unhappy about the treatment they received here, so you might be far better off at Las Tapias. It is located immediately in front of the entrance to the Laguna de Mucubají, on the main road, some 8.5 km above Hotel Los Frailes, at an altitude of 3,350 mts. (that is 10,887 feet!) Elizabeth Kline in her guide to "Camps, Posadas and Cabins" gives this description:

«*Though called a hotel, this has all the characteristics of a died-in-the-wool inn. Owned, built and run by the same family (who live there) for 28 years, it is definitely their baby, and they treat guests like members of the clan. Seven plain but comfortable rooms with hot water, heat (along with thick, hand-loomed woolen blankets), restaurant. Cash only.*»

However, you pay extra for heating in the room and you have to ask for the heater.

Gustavo's Trail

Thus called because it was discovered by our good friend and excellent bird guide, Gustavo Rodriguez, it is one of the outstanding birding spots of this area. To find it, go to the small **Las Tapias** restaurant. Park in front and then walk down a half kilometer until you see the **second** dirt road after Las Tapias, the one with a blue gate. The gate is set slightly down the mountain slope from the highway and is not readily visible when driving down or up the mountain. If you are coming up the mountain from Santo Domingo, the trail is approximately 8.3 km after the entrance to Hotel Moruco. Walking it early in the morning might produce:

Black-chested Buzzard-Eagle	Streak-throated Bush-Tyrant	Black-crested Warbler
Broad-winged Hawk	Smoky Bush-Tyrant	Blue-backed Conebill
Plain-breasted Hawk	Brown-backed Chat-Tyrant	Bluish Flower-Piercer
Mountain Velvetbreast	Smoke-colored Pewee	Mérida Flower-Piercer
Sparkling Violetear	Torrent Tyrannulet	Blue-and-black Tanager
Sword-billed Hummingbird	White-throated Tyrannulet	Chestnut-bellied Clorophonia
Orange-throated Sunangel	Brown-bellied Swallow	Lachrymose Mountain Tanager
Tyrian Metaltail	Collared Jay	Buff-breasted Mountain Tanager
Crimson-mantled Woodpecker	White-capped Dipper	Supercilliaried Hemispingus
Pearled Treerunner	Mountain Wren	Slaty Brush-Finch
Chestnut-crowned Antpitta	Great Thrush	Andean Siskin
Andean Tapaculo	White-fronted Redstart	Rufous-collared Sparrow
Red-crested Cotinga		

Look also for a narrow dirt track some 100 meters down hill from the entrance to Hotel Moruco that descends down to the Santo Domingo River. With luck you may find Bush-Tyrants. You might be able to cross the river here and scamper up the other side where Purple-backed Thornbills have been seen in the past. I understand that they often make a distinctive, dull, scratchy buzz while in flight.

Trail on the National Park Border

Going up towards Los Frailes past Hotel Moruco and before reaching Gustavo's trail, the road crosses a stream. The Sierra Nevada de Mérida National Park begins right here, and there is a Park notice-board some 5 mts. beyond the bridge. Stop to check the bushes near the road around here, as well as the small trail leading down from the uphill side of the bridge, on the left. This trail produces many of the same birds found on Gustavo's Trail plus a nice bonus: the Red-crested Cotinga is often sighted here.

Laguna de Mucubají

The alpine zone of the area from southern Ecuador down through Peru to Bolivia is composed of the dry grassy plain of the Puna. In Venezuela the equivalent is the Páramo, a cold, humid, tundra-like ecosystem of mountains, moors and lagoons originally formed during the ice age. Mucubají is the best-known of all the Mérida National Park mountain tarns. This lagoon of icy, steel-gray waters lies just off the road and only a few meters down from the ridge of the mountain range. From the entrance to Los Frailes continue up the mountain for 8.5 km, where you will find the entrance, well-posted, between the gift shops on the left. Inparques charges a modest entrance fee of Bs. 400 per vehicle. It is extremely difficult to find birds on the Páramo, but the following species have been racked up by Maria Rosa Cuesta, THE ornithological expert of the Andes:

Least Grebe	Spotted Sandpiper	Black Phoebe
Pied-billed Grebe	Least Sandpiper	Cattle Tyrant
Neotropical Cormorant	Upland Sandpiper	White-throated Tyrannulet
Great Egret	Common Snipe	Purple Martin
Cattle Egret	Andean Snipe	Brown-bellied Swallow
Bare-faced Ibis	Large-billed Tern	Blue-and-white Swallow
White-faced Whistling-Duck	Band-tailed Pigeon	White-capped Dipper
Speckled Teal	Eared Dove	Mountain Wren
Blue-winged Teal	Yellow-billed Cuckoo	Páramo Wren
Torrent Duck	Barn Owl	Great Thrush
Lesser Scaup	Andean Pygmy-Owl	Tropical Mockingbird
Condor	Rufous-banded Owl	Páramo Pipit
Black Vulture	Band-winged Nightjar	Red-eyed Vireo
Turkey Vulture	Green Violetear	Eastern Meadowlark
Yellow-headed Vulture	Sparkling Violetear	Black-and-white Warbler
White-tailed Kite	Collared Inca	Tennessee Warbler
Pearl Kite	Mérida Sunangel	Blackpoll Warbler
Sharp-shinned Hawk	Coppery-bellied Puffleg	Blackburnian Warbler
Black-chested Buzzard-Eagle	Speckled Hummingbird	Northern Waterthrush
Broad-winged Hawk	Tyrian Metaltail	American Redstart
Gray-lined Hawk	Bearded Helmetcrest	Blue-backed Conebill
Black-and-chestnut Eagle	Crimson-mantled Woodpecker	Mérida Flower-piercer
Osprey	Bar-winged Cinclodes	Rose-breasted Grosbeak
Peregrine Falcon	Andean Tit-Spinetail	Slaty Brush-Finch
Merlin	Ochre-browed Thistletail	Plain-colored Seedeater
American Kestrel	Streak-backed Canastero	Páramo Seedeater
Caribbean Coot	Pearled Treerunner	Rufous-collared Sparrow
Solitary Sandpiper	Andean Tapaculo	Plumbeous Sierra Finch
Lesser Yellowlegs	Streak-throated Bush-Tyrant	Andean Siskin
Greater Yellowlegs	Brown-backed Chat-Tyrant	Lesser Goldfinch

Obviously many of the above species are transitory or migratory, but at Mucubají you may see many of the local species as well. The Speckled Teal are usually along the shoreline of the lake. Check the bushy hillside area between the lake and the highway for Andean Siskin and Plain-colored Seedeater. The seedeaters will probably be along the ground and the siskins among the frailejones. By following the stream downhill from the lake you might find Streak-backed Canastero, Bar-winged Cinclodes and Plumbeous Sierra Finch. The grassy area along the southern edge of the lake may produce Páramo Pipits and along the areas of Frailejon listen for Páramo Wrens. One of the best areas to find Bearded Helmetcrest and Páramo Wren is the slope and trail in the area known as "Las Cascadas." (ask the local guides or workers for directions). Plumbeous Sierra-Finches and Streak-backed Canasteros are found among the mosses and matted plants where there are few Frailejones. Note that the Streak-backed Canastero has a long, thin bill and has rufous in both wings and tail, whereas the larger Sierra-Finch sports a conical, finch-like bill with a rusty-brown back. The Plain-colored Seedeater has a small, swollen bill with no rust on its back.

I recommend that you also walk from Mucubají to the Laguna Negra, another tarn that lies further up the mountain. You may think that there is not much to see on the Páramo, but somewhere between the two tarns or around the Laguna Negra itself, you should see Bearded Helmetcrest, Ochre-browed Thistletail and Andean Tit-Spinetail. As a note of interest, a group with Richard Ryan of Neotropic Bird Tours sighted a Grasshopper Sparrow near this lagoon in late October, 1992! Also during October you might sight large flocks of Bank and Cliff Swallows flying over the lagoon, and Gustavo Rodriguez actually found a Palm Warbler here.

In her *Checklist of the Birds of Mucubají* Maria Rosa Cuesta, who knows these mountains so well, gives a word of wisdom:

«Remember that in the tropical highlands, everyday is summer and every night is winter, so take with you a hat, suntan lotion, a warm wind-breaker jacket and waterproof boots, for when it starts cooling down.»

To avoid the *soroche,* altitude sickness or *mal de páramo,* as it is called here, caused by the low levels of oxygen in the air, she advises to walk slowly and take sweets for the walk, but my personal favorite, in terms of advice for soroche, is the way they put it in Bolivia: *"Caminar despacito, comer poquito y dormir solito",* which translates "walk slowly, eat little and sleep alone." I might add that you should only walk to the Laguna Negra in the early morning before the fog rolls in about noon. Especially in the rainy season, the clouds come down forming a thick fog in the late mornings, so be cautious and stay on the trails. If you are not accustomed to the high altitude, you may react with headache, dizziness and insomnia. Be careful not to overexert yourself.

Previously, there was a splendid nature center at Mucubají, designed and directed by Dr. Carlos Rivero Blanco. However and unfortunately, the small-minded bureaucrats of INPARQUES made life so impossible for Dr. River, that he just abandoned one of the very best nature centers we had in Venezuela. I understand that now they do open the center but only during the high season and even then with anything but good grace. Until the day comes when government petite fonctionnaires finally realize that the private sector can in many instances do a far better job than party hacks, I see no hope for centers such as this was.

The Condor Center at Mifafí

After you have thoroughly birded Mucubají, turn left when you are back on the main road and continue down the mountain for 3 km where you will meet the cross-roads:

left and south to the capital city of Mérida, or right and north to the town of Timotes. Turn right and go up the mountain for 4.9 km, where you will see a small sign on your left indicating the Condor Center of Mifafí.

Unless you have a 4WD vehicle, you will only be able to drive a short distance up this very bad road. Park and walk up the mountain for 0.8 km until you reach the Center. If the Director, Maria Rosa Cuesta, is there, she will be able to answer your questions in English and you may also approach the huge cage to play with Combatiente, a very tame young Condor. Be warned that he has a passion for shoe laces and sweatshirts! As to altitude, the center is at 3,550 mts, or 11,538 feet.

Background of the Condor Center

The program to reintroduce the Condor along the Venezuelan Andean chain was initiated in 1991 with the help of Dr. Alan Lieberman from the San Diego Wild Animal Park and Dr. Mike Wallace from the Los Angeles Zoo. Maria Rosa Cuesta has been in charge of the reintroduction process, monitoring and of the Center from the beginning of the project. In May 1992 Mifafí in the Sierra de la Culata N. P. was chosen as the release area due to its isolation from large towns, high, open, predator-free land, wind-swept valleys with flight corridors and potential nesting sites. A biological station was built, which is now the Visitor Center. Some 8 km further, deep within the Mifafí valley, a refuge or quarantine and flying platform facility was built.

In February 1993 the first five Condors were received from the Los Angeles and San Diego zoos. In 1995 five additional Condors arrived from the San Francisco and San Diego Zoos., including three females. The birds took between 47 to 68 days to find their own carrion and become independent. On January 25, 1994 an adult male showed up probably from Colombia and flew around with the introduced birds for some eight months. Then on January 15, 1995 a strange adult female arrived to join the others. By 1995 the Condors were flying over an estimated area of 5,250 square kilometers of La Culata N. P.

Andean Condor

Threats to the Condors

47% or 531,100 hectares (1,311,818 acres) of the State of Mérida is covered by National Parks including the Sierra Nevada N.P. created in 1952, as well as Juan Pablo Peñaloza (1989), La Culata (1989), Tapo Caparo (1993). These parks are extremely diverse and, more important, supply drinking water and electricity to the area's major cities and towns, as well as water for irrigation. However, what is considered an important objective from a conservation point of view has little or no meaning to other groups. With an ever-expanding population, particularly of the lower social classes, there has been tremendous pressure on our National Parks, and unscrupulous politicians have not been slow to take advantage of this social pressure to promote their image among their constituents. In 1996 the mayor of the small city of Mucuchies started a campaign against the National Parks Institute among the local population in order to have the Parks turned over to the regional and local governments, thus giving them control over the lands within the National Parks. Unfortunately, the Condors were taken as the symbol of the Parks with the result that four of the birds were shot. Aided and abetted by politicians, including the Governor of the State, the local populace even attempted to take over the Condor Center. Maria Rosa Cuesta fought like a lioness protecting her young to preserve the Center.

As if the above were not enough, a financial crises resulted in the closure of the local bank that had financed the project from the beginning. Left without financial support, as well as no logistical support from governmental agencies, in 1997 the program came close to closing activities. By a miracle Cleveland Metropark's Zoo came to the rescue with funds to cover the basic needs of the project for the next five years. The educational campaign in the schools was reinstated and juvenile condors born in captivity are once again being brought to Venezuela for release. The staff and one of the tame condors visited more than 2,000 schools in the region to give talks. The result has been that gradually the local people once again are taking the condor as their emblem.

The Condors Themselves

The condors are the largest flying birds in the world with a wingspan of 3.3 meters or 10.8 feet. On an average the females weigh 8 kilos or almost 18 pounds and the males may weigh in at 11 kilos or 24 pounds. Due to its large size and long wings the condor is limited to open areas. It is almost impossible for a condor to take off within a heavily forested setting or even find carrion under a forest canopy.

The condors are monogamous upon reaching reproductive maturity at 8 years of age. Unfortunately, they have an extremely low reproductive rate, laying a single egg every other year. Both parents incubate the egg for 56 days and feed the chick for over a year until it becomes independent. Condors do not build nests but utilize caves or rocky edges for nesting. They may live from 50 to 65 years.

One interesting note that was discovered during the project was that the females are the pioneers. They are the ones that open up new territories and stay away from the group longer. One of the released females actually picked the other Condors up and lead them away to new areas she had just discovered. (Well, good for us gals!)

Birding around Mifafí

Across the road from the Center, there are fields of garlic. During the months from late August to October, Bearded Helmetcrests nests along this area, and when the garlic is in bloom, they feast on its flowers.

From the Condor Center, the road goes on a long way, crossing a series of páramo valleys which are part of the National Park, bearing the name of this mountain ridge - Sierra de La Culata. It is a superb place to find high Andean birds, including Dippers in the stream that runs alongside the road as well as Andean Tit-Spinetail, Bar-winged Cinclodes, Streak-backed Canastero and Ochre-browed Thistletail hiding among the frailejones and rocks.

Birding Spots around "Eagle" Pass

Some 7 km up the mountain from Mifafí, at 3,800 meters or 12,350 feet, lies a mountain pass known as the **Paso del Aguila**, Pass of the Eagle, only the large statue of a bird on a pedestal placed at the very top of the pass many years ago, is not of any eagle, but a Condor. The monument commemorates Bolivar's heroic crossing of the Andes in 1813 to liberate Venezuela, after having freed Colombia, Ecuador, Peru and Bolivia from Spanish rule. An effort is being made to have the name changed back to the original *Paso del Condor.*

Right on the pass, behind the monument, there is a small hotel and restaurant. Just prior to reaching the restaurant, you will see a paved road, leading to the town of **Piñango.** Drive along this road some 200 meters past the high antennas where you should search on the right either in the early morning or late afternoon, for some excellent birding. At 3,900 mts. or 12,675 feet, it is such a cold place, that there are no flies, but I found that I had trouble even turning the focus on my binoculars. Here also you are inside the Sierra de la Culata National Park, so in the late afternoons and on a clear day you have a pretty good chance along this road of sighting the Condors flying overhead. Also in this area, you will find a rare species of *Espeletia* that can grow taller than a person. Every year, a crown of leaves dies and a new one grows on top, so the plant gets a tiny bit taller. A 6-foot plant may be a hundred years old. It is certainly worth a drive along this spectacular road in the late afternoon, if for nothing more than the scenery.

Back to the little restaurant by the statue of the Condor, continue approximately 2.5 km on the main road towards Valera, looking for a lagoon on your right. If you continue on over a low rise to the south, you will come to yet another lagoon. Pull off, park and circle either lagoon on foot, checking the shrubs as you go. Andean and Common Snipe were often sighted here until a few years ago, but so many regular tourists nose around nowadays, that recent visits by bird watchers have been fruitless. You will only find the snipes if you flush them - hence the reason for circling the lagoons on foot.

There are other areas to explore going down this road from the statue and paths that may provide good birding.

Coming down the road from the Pass towards Mifafí less than one km, or, if you are going up, at 6.1 km above Mifafí, there starts a **foot path** down the barren mountain side, which is basically a short cut to the lower stretch of the same road. It looks deserted and hopeless, but you will be surprised - walking down this path in the very early morning, you should see just about every special bird of the high Andes! It yields Bearded Helmetcrest, Streak-backed Canastero, Ochre-browed Thistletail, Andean Tit-Spinetail, Páramo Wren, Páramo and Plain-colored Seedeaters, Plumbeus Sierra-Finch and more. The only problem is walking up again, so if any in your group is willing or *very* fit, maybe you can convince him to take the car down and wait for you at the other end.

As you can see from the above, these deceivingly desolate Páramo lands rate a good two days to bird the various areas. However, I should mention that driving can be hazardous during the rainy season, from May to October, when it can be miserable around here, but this is also the time when all the Andean wild flowers are in bloom, and when you can see so many hummers.

During October and November, the Frailejon *(Espeletia sp.)*, covers the páramo with its bright yellow bloom, and the Bearded Helmetcrest clings to the flowers as it probes for insects.

INEXPENSIVE EXPLORING: THE MUCUPOSADAS

Very often young bird watchers come to Venezuela and, understandably, look for inexpensive but unusual places to stay. For them I am dedicating this section and recommend that they try the Mucuposadas. It was Elizabeth Kline who drew my attention to this new development along the Páramos of Mérida, and I want to share her experience and recommendations with the young'uns. If you wonder about how you will reach these places, Elizabeth does it in her little Fiat! I quote below quite liberally from Elizabeth's fantastically helpful guide:

Mucuposadas Programa Andes Tropicales

Phone numbers: (0) 274-263-8633 & 263.6884 or (0) 416-674-1267. Address: Avda. 2 con Calle 4, El Encanto, Quinta Irma, Apdo. 676, Mérida 5101. E-mail: patven@telcel.net.ve, www.andestropicales.org.ve.

«By reservation only. An unique experience worth giving a try if you are at all adventuresome. Visitors will penetrate the impressive and enchanting environment of the páramo (the high moors of this region), following ancient routes of the posadas of the colonial era. You will cross numerous valleys carved out by glaciers which likewise formed the multitude of streams and lagoons which are now the principal sources of water for the lower zones. Sierra La Culata National Park and the centenary agricultural communities therein will be the scenes of these excursions. Lodging on these routes is in 'Mucuposadas', small family posadas simple but clean and with good services, installed in traditional vintage houses which have been reconditioned by their owners (who also serve as your hosts) with the support of the Programa Andes Tropicales. Through the project for rural tourism, visitors are given the opportunity to immerse themselves in the life and setting of the residents of the páramo, penetrating the haunting landscapes by ancestral trails, for a very enriching and renewing experience. The same time, the use of these community tourist services represents a significant collaboration with the efforts of conservation and sustained development of the Andean region. More than a dozen such posadas are being developed. Currently available are the following (along with the more luxurious Mesa Redonda)

Mucuposada El Trigal *is located in the heart of the páramo in the community of Mitibobó at more or less 3,400 m.a.s.l. Three rooms (total cap. 6) bath with hot water, simple but delicious Andean cooking and plenty of home-style warmth served up by the owner, Irene her husband Venancio and their 3 kids. From here they offer excursions on horseback or on foot in the surrounding area with expert local guides (their sons are excellent, well prepared, informative and very friendly guides).*

Mucuposada El Nidal de Gavilán *owned by Juan Carlos Balza is some ten minutes from Mucuchíes, between frailejones and fog, in the area known as Misintá. It has 3 cozy rooms (total cap. 10) 2 external bathrooms, hot water typical Andean meals. In addition, you will enjoy crossing the valley of El Banco and one can arrange for excursions and horseback riding in both locations, guests also receive a gift of handicrafts created by the locals* *(something which is a great stimulus to additional sources of income for the humble residents of the zone).»*

Mucuchíes//Páramo de Gavidia

This is an experience that **all** of you should have, even those who do not plan to overnight up on the Páramo, as well as those who wish to stay at still another Mucuposada. Again I quote from Elizabeth's book because she tells it far better than I can:

«A must is to drive from the town of Mucuchíes to the Páramo de Gavidia very early in the morning. You go through a narrow pass following a river and bordered by steep stone walls which apparently have springs above that keep a certain amount of water flowing over the surface. During cold nights the water freezes, but when the sun hits it in the morning, not only does it glisten like a beautiful wall of crystals, but the ice loudly explodes off of the surface, crashing down to the river below - an incredible show!

Upon arriving at Mucuchíes, you will be a stone's throw from the route you want, but because of the system of one-way streets from the very beginning of the town, you will have to continue to the south until the first opportunity to turn left enables you to reach Calle Independencia, the main one-way street going north. Once on that street, after passing behind the Castillo San Ignacio (it's official name is Castillo, but I have a much more apropos word for it, but do not dare to put it in print) just before the union with the 2-way highway take the well-marked exit for Gavidia. The picturesque drive of more or less 40 minutes takes you through a mountain pass en route to the Páramo.

Mucuposada Muchicaba: *By reservation only. The inn is after the school at the end of the road of the populated area. This modest but clean lodging offer consists of just a single dorm-style room with 2 bunk beds (with good mattresses and stacks of soft hand-woven woolen blankets) and private bath with hot water in the traditional vintage home of the owners and hosts, Rómulo and Rosalía Rangel. The house is unheated, but filled with the personal warmth of this couple. Price of the lodging includes a hearty breakfast. Lunch and dinner are available optionally. The main focus of the stay in these posadas is the excursions offered on horse back with experienced local guides to savor the beautiful natural attractions of the Páramo such as the Laguna El Santo Cristo, the largest of the glacial lakes in Mérida. As in all the Mucuposadas, cash only.»*

The basic cost at these Mucuposadas is approximately $ 11 a night including breakfast. The other meals and excursions are additional, but not out of line in price.

For those of you who are older or wish a more luxurious and consequently more expensive inn, but still want to have the experience of staying on the Páramo, you might like to try:

Refugio Ecológico Mesa Redonda

Telf. the same as the above Mucuposada, Also by reservation only. This lodge is located just outside the southern limits of the Páramo de Piedras Blancas Biological Reserve

«in a fabulous setting for nature lovers. The guest house is a jewel. It has typical center courtyard, red tile roof and stone walls constructed without cement. Modern conveniences such as very nice bathroom fixtures and solar power. First-class service. Two handsome rooms each with double bed and

bunks, private bath, hot water, thick towels, etc. Plus, a dorm with 7 sets of bunks and bath for groups such as researchers. Price includes transfer between Mérida and the posada in 4-wheel drive vehicle, lodging, all meals, (gourmet food), nearby excursions. Arrangements can be made for excursions with very well prepared and friendly guides on horseback or foot.»

Needless to say that at all of these Mucuposadas you will see the same birds along the Páramo as at Mucubají, etc.

THE CITY OF MÉRIDA

From the páramos, it will take you two hours to reach the capital of the state, the charming, cliff-side city of Mérida, spread over a *mesa* - a shelf attached to the mountains on one side and cut on the other by the gorge of the Chama river. There are various areas to bird, using the city as your base, starting with...

La Mucuy and the Humboldt Trail

To reach this area of the Sierra Nevada National Park, drive some 11 km northeast from Mérida until you come to the town of Tabay. By necessity you will have to turn right as you enter the town from the south and then follow the road to the left. Go one block to the Plaza Bolívar and immediately turn right, down a steep street to cross the bridge over the Chama River. After you climb out of the gorge, it is only about 6 km to the end of the road. The National Park begins at the second stream crossing.

At the Park entrance, there is an attractive picnic area where I have often seen Long-tailed Sylph and Masked Trogons, as well as White-capped Dipper along the stream. It may not be possible to drive to the end of the road itself, but during the week there is usually no problem in driving at least to the Forestry School building or, better yet, up to the dormitories. Before going up, walk down to the stream to look for Slaty-backed Chat-Tyrant. From the Forestry School the road winds on up to some of the park buildings.

Bird the bushes for Crested Quetzal, Mérida and Orange-throated Sunangels, Collared Inca, Collared Jay, Azara's Spinetail, Streak-throated Bush-Tyrant, Mountain Elaenia, White-fronted Redstart, Gray-throated Warbler, Beryl-spangled, Blue-and-black and Blue-capped Tanagers and Moustached Brush-Finch as well as North American migrants.

Above the Park dormitories, you will find the start of the **Humboldt Trail** at approximately 2,300 meters. It climbs for about 4 km through humid montane forest and *Chusquea* bamboo thickets before dropping down to a river and then climbing up to the tarn called **Laguna Coromoto,** where you will come upon the elfin woodland. If you keep hiking up, you will eventually reach the Frailejon-dotted páramo slightly below the glacier of Pico Humboldt at 4,800 meters. Of course, if you really want to go all out, and you are well equipped and have a competent guide, you could go all the way up the Pico Humboldt trail to the col between Picos Humboldt and Bonpland, across the backbone of the Andes at 5,007 meter Pico Bolívar to Pico Espejo and then go down via the teleférico trail to Mérida. Frankly, I think you would be a glutton for punishment to do so.

The first part of the trail is good for Andean Guan, Band-tailed Pigeon, Rose-headed Parakeet, Rusty-faced and Speckle-faced Parrot, Rufous-banded Owl, Crested and Golden-headed Quetzal, Crimson-mantled Woodpecker, White-browed Spinetail, Ochre-browed Thistletail, Pearled Treerunner, Flammulated Treehunter, Torrent Tyrannulet, Yellow-billed Cacique, White-fronted Redstart, Blue-backed

Conebill, Chestnut-breasted Chlorophonia, Gray-capped and Slaty-backed Hemispingus. Listen for Andean Tapaculo in the *Chusquea* thickets. Just after dawn, antpittas (Undulated, Chestnut-crowned, Gray-naped and Slate-crowned) can be seen out on the paths in full view. Near the Coromoto Lagoon, look for the Slaty-backed Hemispingus in the bamboo areas.

Maria Rosa Cuesta has published the list of birds for both Mucubají and La Mucuy, but as it is most difficult to come by, I give below the list of birds for the area of La Mucuy or Humboldt Trail:

White-faced Whistling Duck	Mountain Velvetbreast	Slaty-backed Chat-Tyrant
Speckled Teal	Bronzy Inca	Yellow-bellied Chat-Tyrant
Torrent Duck	Collared Inca	Black Phoebe
Turkey Vulture	Golden-bellied Starfrontlet	Cattle Tyrant
Black Vulture	Sword-billed Hummingbird	Tropical Kingbird
Hook-billed Kite	Buff-tailed Coronet	Golden-crowned Flycatcher
Plain-breasted Hawk	Mérida Sunangel	Wood Pewee
Black-chested Buzzard-Eagle	Booted Racquet-tail	Smoked-colored Pewee
Broad-winged Hawk	Tyrian Metaltail	Flavescent Flycatcher
White-rumped Hawk	Bearded Helmetcrest	Variegated Bristle-Tyrant
Short-tailed Hawk	Long-tailed Sylph	Torrent Tyrannulet
Gray-lined Hawk	Rufous-shafted Woodstar	White-throated Tyrannulet
Black-and-chestnut Eagle	Golden-headed Quetzal	White-banded Tyrannulet
Barred Forest Falcon	Masked Trogon	Mountain Elaenia
Yellow-headed Caracara	Emerald Toucanet	Black-capped Tyrannulet
American Kestrel	Crimson-mantled Woodpecker	Venezuelan Tyrannulet
Band-tailed Guan	Smoky-brown Woodpecker	Olive-striped Flycatcher
Andean Guan	Strong-billed Woodcreeper	Green Jay
Andean Snipe	Black-banded Woodcreeper	Collared Jay
Band-tailed Pigeon	Olive-backed Woodcreeper	White-capped Dipper
Ruddy Pigeon	Spot crowned Woodcreeper	Páramo Wren
White-tipped Dove	Azara's Spinetail	Mountain Wren
Lined Quail-Dove	Rufous Spinetail	Tropical Mockingbird
Rose-headed Parakeet	White-browed Spinetail	Andean Solitaire
Rusty-faced Parrot	Ochre-browed Spinetail	Slaty-backed Nightingale-Thrush
Speckle-faced Parrot	Pearled Treerunner	Swainson's Thrush
Scaly-naped Parrot	Streaked Tuftedcheek	Veery
Yellow-billed Cuckoo	Spotted Barbtail	Yellow-legged Thrush
Squirrel Cuckoo	Streaked Xenops	Great Thrush
Tropical Screech-Owl	Undulated Antpitta	Glossy-black Thrush
White-throated Screech-Owl	Chestnut-crowned Antpitta	Chestnut-bellied Thrush
Andean Pygmy-Owl	Slate-crowned Antpitta	Páramo Pipit
Rufous-banded Owl	Unicolored Tapaculo	Yellow-throated Vireo
Band-winged Nightjar	Andean Tapaculo	Red-eyed Vireo
Lyre-tailed Nightjar	Red-crested Cotinga	Brown-capped Vireo
White-collared Swift	Green-and-black Fruiteater	Black-and-white Warbler
Chestnut-collared Swift	Golden-breasted Fruiteater	Golden-winged Warbler
White-tipped Swift	Barred Fruiteater	Tennessee Warbler
Green Violetear	Barred Becard	Tropical Parula
Sparkling Violetear	Streak-throated Bush-Tyrant	Blackburnian Warbler
Spangled Coquette	Smoky Bush-Tyrant	Blackpoll Warbler
Speckled Hummingbird	Brown-backed Chat-Tyrant	Canada Warbler

American Redstart
Slate-throated Redstart
White-fronted Redstart
Black-crested Warbler
Citrine Warbler
Three-striped Warbler
Russet-crowned Warbler
Blue-backed Conebill
Bananaquit
Swallow Tanager
Rusty Flower-piercer
White-sided Flower-piercer
Bluish Flower-piercer

Mérida Flower-piercer
Glossy Flower-piercer
Speckled Tanager
Saffron-crowned Tanager
Rufous-cheeked Tanager
Blue-necked Tanager
Burnished-buff Tanager
Beryl-spangled Tanager
Black-capped Tanager
Black-headed Tanager
Blue-and-black Tanager
Fawn-breasted Tanager
Chestnut-breasted Chlorophonia

Lachrymose Mountain Tanager
Buff-breasted Mountain Tanager
Blue-gray Tanager
Blue-capped Tanager
Gray-capped Hemispingus
Oleaginous Hemispingus
Slaty-backed Hemispingus
Common Bush-Tanager
Plush-capped Finch
Streaked Saltator
Rose-breasted Grosbeak

La Mucuy is very popular during Christmas, New Year's and Easter vacations as well as on the week-ends. At any other time you may be the only one on the trail.[1]

Chiguará

After reading a first rough draft of the previous edition that I sent him, Dick Ryan kindly ticked me off for having excluded Chiguará. I had not been there in years, but after revisiting it anew, have to agree with him. So Dick, following your advice, here goes:

After the outing to La Mucuy, for your next excursion from Mérida, both Dick and I recommend that you drive south on Avenida Andres Bello, heading towards Ejido, Lagunillas, etc. South of Mérida you suddenly enter a dramatically grandiose landscape - xerophitic and pebble-strewn. The dryness and erosion in this area is created by the rain shadow effect of the high mountains. It extends from Ejido to Estanquez, and includes the towns of Lagunillas and Chiguará. The turn-off to Chiguará is 15 km to the south of Lagunillas. Follow Dick Ryan's suggestions:

«I have taken almost every one of my groups there and all have been pleased. Despite its hot, sunny location, the birding has been good even in the early afternoon. The secret is to bear left around the little traffic circle and head downhill. In a couple of blocks, one comes to a chain across the road. Either park there and walk down or see if the gentleman who lives in the house to the left will open the chain for you (a tip is in order if he does). If you drive beyond the chain, drive very slowly as the road is in terrible condition. Within the first 2-to-300 meters there are trees to the right where we have at times found the Black-backed Grosbeak. Bird downhill as far as you wish, it is all pretty good. Pay special attention to the area around the abandoned farm to the right as you go down.»

Estanques

Continuing south from Chiguará, you will come to the next birding spot in this general area - a road going to the hamlet of **Estanques.** Coming from Mérida, it would take you approximately one hour to reach the entrance to Estanques, which is on the left of the main road (the Mérida - Ejido -Tovar - La Grita road). Turn left to go into the

---

[1] Pamela's Comment: This is true. I was amazed at being the only one on the trail in May - amazed and delighted.

settlement, pass the church and turn right at the very first road shortly after the church. This is the road you want, so start counting your kilometers from here. Although in good shape, this road does not mess around - for 9.9 km, from the start near Estanques to where you finally find a lay-by at 1,200 mts., it goes straight up, switch back after switch back.

From that lay-by at 9.9 km, look for the birds of the foothills all the way to a Cecropia grove at 14.7 km:

Bronzy Inca	Glossy-black Thrush	Black-capped Tanager
Yellow-billed Toucanet	Black-and-white Warbler	Black-headed Tanager
Golden-olive Woodpecker	Blackburnian Warbler	Blue-naped Chlorophonia
Long-tailed Antbird	Blackpoll Warbler	Blue-hooded Euphonia
Masked Tityra	Slate-throated Redstart	Orange-bellied Euphonia
Scale-crested Pygmy-Tyrant	Three-striped Warbler	Blue-gray Tanager
Golden-faced Tyrannulet	Golden-crowned Warbler	Blue-hooded Tanager
Green Jay	Rusty Flower-piercer	Summer Tanager
Whiskered Wren	Golden Tanager	Common Bush Tanager
Gray-breasted Woodwren	Saffron-crowned Tanager	Buff-throated Saltator
Slaty-backed Nightingale-Thrush	Bay-headed Tanager	Lesser Goldfinch

Going up the mountain, at 17.7 km from the bottom of the road you will see the entrance to a farm on your right. Slightly further up on the left there is a trail that merits a stop. In addition to the previous birds, here you should see Brown Violetear, Long-tailed Sylph, Venezuelan Tyrannulet and Beryl-spangled Tanager.

At 19 km you will come out from the forest into a very arid area and at 26 km, at an altitude of 2,200 mts. or 7,150 feet, the Páramo vegetation begins. Look for White-sided Flower-piercer. At 29.3 km (2,350 mts.), stop by the curve to look for Rufous Spinetail (this species has been split from the one found along the Coastal Range, as it has no black chin), Pearled Treerunner, White-throated Tyrannulet, White-fronted Redstart and Black-crested Warbler. During my exploration of this road, I had to turn back at 36.6 km (2,350 mts.) due to a thick fog, but there you can find the Band-tailed Pigeon, Black-billed Mountain Toucan and Chestnut-crowned Antpitta.

The road above Estanques merits a full day of birding, especially during the dry season when, hopefully, you will not have fog. For dry area birds, when you turn into the settlement of Estanques from the main highway, rather than going up the hill, continue straight on, veering slightly towards your left. This road eventually gives out, but at about 2 km from the main highway, there are areas to park and to look for:

Striped Cuckoo	Common Tody-Flycatcher	Tropical Mockingbird
Shining-green Hummingbird	Pearly-vented Tody-Tyrant	Yellow-backed Oriole
Rufous-tailed Hummingbird	Pale-eyed Pygmy-tyrant	Bananaquit
Russet-throated Puffbird	Tawny-crowned Pygmy-Tyrant	Thick-billed Euphonia
Red-crowned Woodpecker	Yellow-bellied Elaenia	Blue-gray Tanager
Pale-breasted Spinetail	Mouse-colored Tyrannulet	Black-striped Sparrow
Barred Antshrike	Southern Beardless Tyrannulet	Black-faced Grassquit
Cattle Tyrant	Southern Rough-winged Swallow	Gray Seedeater
Tropical Kingbird	House Wren	

Somewhat north and before reaching the turn-off to Estanques is the new auto-pista to El Vigia through the tunnel. If you are in a hurry to return to Caracas, take this spectacular, beautiful road. They have left so-called windows in the tunnel to allow you to view the fantastic canyon you are passing through. From El Vigia you would turn north for Barquisimeto and Caracas.

The old road to El Vigia is slightly south of Estanques by a National Guard post. Turning right or west here you will immediately come to the ***Museo de Cafe e Imigración***[1] The Coffee and Immigration Museum located in an old colonial building with the huge patio in the middle. Don't miss it. Many of the posters explaining the coffee process are in English, and have yourself a cup of their excellent coffee at the shop.

La Mesa de Bolívar & Santa Cruz de Mora

Continuing up the old road towards El Vigia, you will be going through coffee plantations for approximately 10 to 15 km when you will see the turn on your left for La Mesa de Bolívar. A wee town whose main event of the year is the festival for the Virgen de Candelaria from January 31 to February 2. On the first of February residents set out thousands of candles to line the streets which are all lit simultaneously with a cut-off of electricity between 8 and 8.15 p.m. This is followed by a huge fireworks display. The next day is the dance of the Vasallow de Candelaria, a tradition which has taken place here for more than a century. If you are in Mérida during these dates, you might enjoy seeing this festival[2]. Otherwise, when you reach the town, turn right in order to go by the church and keep going. You want the back-road that leads to Santa Cruz de Mora. This road is not even on the map, but it is good birding. A few kilometers out of La Mesa there is a house on the right where every morning they stick bananas all along the top of the fence. I assure you that every Tanager in the area can be seen here.

The San Felipe Road

If you continue south from Estanques, you will again find yourself in a more narrow, curvy road. When you come to the area where there are stands selling fruit on both sides of the road, look for a road on your left with a sign indicating San Felipe. This road leads through mature coffee haciendas.

Look for hummingbirds, toucanets and parrots, including the Rose-headed Parakeet, and also many of the Andean flycatchers and thrushes and other birds. I haven't had the opportunity of birding this road myself, but it was recommended by Maria Rosa Cuesta and she knows a good birding area when she finds it!

El Morro

This is another place where one may find the Black-backed Grosbeak. To reach it, you must drive east from Mérida, but the road out of Mérida is extremely difficult to find. I would suggest that you contact one of the bird guides mentioned below for Mérida to guide you there. Dick Ryan has recommended El Morro...

«for birders that may have trouble walking uphill at higher altitudes, as they can bird that road much more easily than the Humboldt Trail and some other

---

[1] Pamela's Comment: We all found this to be quite remarkable - a combination coffee and immigration museum.

[2] Note from the Editor: If you are there at night you may see the show of amazing flashes of lightning that appear over Lake of Maracaibo. It is known as "The Lightning of the Catatumbo", because the bolts occur over this river, that flows into the lake from the western side. I have heard the explanation for this strange electrical phenomenon, many times, but don't ask me to repeat it!

spots. The remaining wooded parts are generally not on steep slopes, all birding has to be from the road, parking is easy, and most of the birds of Humboldt Trail or Estanques are available. Of special interest were Wattled Guan and Streaked Treehunter, the latter a northward range extension from what is described in the Venezuelan guide book. I have found the Treehunter off and on in the first significant wooded area on the way up. Despite the problems of finding it, El Morro is still worth the effort.»

ON STAYING AROUND THE CITY OF MÉRIDA

La Mucuy Alta
Posada Mucumajó
(0) 414-974-5617, in La Mucuy Alto at just 0.6 km. from the entrance to the Sierra Nevada National Park. Rather rustic. This might be a good option if you have no vehicle. Arrangements could be made for a taxi to take you to the inn from the city and return you to the airport or bus station. Their prices for the rooms are reasonable, but I understand that their charges for meals are quite high, but up here what option do you have?

La Mucuy Baja
Cabañas Turísticas Xinia & Peter (★★★★★)
Phone numbers: (0) 274-283-0214 or (0) 416-874-7698. E-mail: xiniaypeter@hotmail.com. One km past Tabay and just before the restaurant "Juan Chocolate" there is a sign on the road indicating a left turn to Mucunután. Shortly after leaving the highway, the road splits with the route for Mucunután to the right. You go straight, ascending the road via la Mucuy Baja. After approximately 400 meters you will see a huge colonial house on the right. A small wooden sign here indicates to turn right for these cabins which are 300 meters up the road again on the right. Elizabeth Kline has given these cabins a "Highly Recommended" stating that these are the most gorgeous cabins she has encountered in all of Venezuela, (but expensive) complete with kitchens that made my mouth water. Arrangements can also be made for superb meals to be prepared.

Near Tabay
La Casona de Tabay
To be avoided at all cost

Posada Doña Rosa
Phone: (0) 274-252-8355 or (0) 414-717-3178. This is my favorite. Although not exactly *in* Mérida, but rather in the outskirts near Tabay in an area called El Arenal vía San Jacinto, this inn, housed in a delightful, 140-year old hacienda house and surrounded by woods and fields, is a very pleasant place for birders. Also, the food is quite good, and the attention excellent[1].

To find the inn, if you are coming from the north, at 6 km after the town of Tabay, you will see a sign on the right indicating the turn-off to La Joya, which is on your left. If you

---

[1] Pamela's Comment: Where else can you find a clean, comfortable room with private bath, hot water, a good breakfast and dinner, nice people attending you for only slightly more than $20 a day per person? Yes, in deed. And mind you, you get your own room for that twenty bucks. It's a bargain!

are coming from the city of Mérida, the turn off from the main road is 5 km from the end of the city and, obviously, on your right. Turn down this narrow road, cross the bridge at 0.5 km from the main road. At the first crossroads (0.75 km) turn right in front of the police station. Continue straight on to 1.9 km. Go left after the little bridge. At 2.25 km. by the sign for the Posada go left for 2 more kilometers. From the main highway, it is a little over 4 km to the inn, and the road at the very end is not one of the best, but just hang in there - unless, of course, you should stop to bird. Look for Azara's Spinetail and Moustached Brush-Finch. Speaking of birding, listen at night for Tropical Screech Owl and Rufous Nightjar, on the up-hill side of the Posada. For reservations contact the Audubon.

In the City of Mérida
Hotel Belensate (★★★)
Telf. (0) 274-266-3722 or 266-2963, fax: (0274)-266-1255. Located in the pleasant residential area of La Hacienda. To reach it coming **from the south**, you will be driving along Avenida Andrés Bello. Turn left at the stop light when you see the signs for Avenida Los Próceres and Avenida Las Américas. Then turn left at the very first street. Go straight down through the La Hacienda area until you see the hotel on your left. If you are coming **from the north**, upon entering the city continue straight until you reach the first main cross roads with a stop light. Turn right. This street eventually becomes Avenida Los Próceres. Turn left at the next main cross roads by a stop light. This will put you on Avenida Las Américas. Continue to the very end where you will again turn left. Go one block and turn right and continue straight until you see the hotel. The food at the restaurant is nothing spectacular but it is OK.

Hosteria La Sevillana (★★★★★)
Telf: (0) 274-266-3227 or (0) 414-741-5969. E-mail: sevillana@telcel.net.ve. This is a most attractive inn located at 2,000 mts. above the city of Mérida. To reach the inn, take Avenida Los Próceres south until you see the signs indicating La Pedregoza and the hotel of the same name at almost the end of the avenue. Turn right and follow this road, taking the right fork when you reach the T. Continue to the end of the paved road for approximately 5 km. Twelve beautifully appointed and heated rooms, private bathrooms of course with thick towels and lots of hot water. Prices include full American breakfast. Other meals by previous arrangement. The food is excellent. La Sevillana has the added attraction that should you be accompanied by a non-birder wife, the inn is also a spa[1]. The property extends 1.500 meters up the hill to the páramo, providing walks in the woods to enjoy the flora and abundant avifauna. Elizabeth Kline gave this inn a "Highly recommended."

Posada La Montaña
Phone: (0) 274-252-5977, fax: 252-7055. E-mail: posadalamontana@telcel.net.ve. Located on Calle 24 between Avenidas 6 and 7. A more modest but perfectly acceptable inn. 17 rooms with private bath, hot water, tile floors. They do have a restaurant that serves all meals from Tuesdays through Sundays. On Mondays they only serve dinner. Pleasant and professional personnel. The one drawback is that due to the design of the building, the rooms can be noisy. Bring your earplugs. Unfortunately, they do not have a parking area although there is one a block away, but be sure you settle on the price before leaving your car.

---

[1] Pamela's Comment: Pretty sexist here. Men take spas these days too!

By chance I have just received the following report on Posada La Montaña from Rodney Fuentes, one of our bird guides:

«*I stayed one night in Mérida in a such a gorgeous Posada called La Montaña. Let me explain: It has small rooms, very clean and decorated with very good taste. It has towels, cable TV, and a closet. Very cozy!!! The Posada has loads of plants inside and a very nice corridor. They also arrange tours. There is also a restaurant and the food is simply delicious. We had such a good meal there!!! And the salads are out of this world!!!!! Best of all it is extremely inexpensive.*»

Posada Los Bucares de Mé

Phone/Fax: (0) 274-252-2841. Located on Avenida 4 at the corner of Calle 15. Cozy and tranquil with very pleasant service. A vintage house with open central patio surrounded by 10 comfortable rooms plus 6 new rooms in the back. All have private bath and hot water, good mattresses. This is one of the few inns to be found in the city that has enclosed parking on the premises. The inn also has a handicrafts shop, a beauty shop and a snack bar with service for light meals. The personable owners, Americo and Olga Sánchez live on the premises and some of the well-trained staff speak a bit of English. Prices are very reasonable and about the same as at La Montaña.

In the Area of El Valle de la Culata

In her book Elizabeth Kline mentions that nearly every day in the late afternoon thick fog engulfs this valley, creating a chilly and damp atmosphere and also making driving dangerous on the steep road full of sharp curves. I personally found it to be superb birding on the morning I was there and the scenery was gorgeous. At least **for birding, I recommend it highly**. To find the valley, just as you actually enter the city you will see a police station on your right. Go straight. Then go around the very first traffic circle in order to double back but on the other side of the road and go on up following the signs for El Valle/La Culata.

Hospedaje La Florida

Phone: (0) 416-877-4170, fax: (0) 274-244-2624, e-mail: hospedajelaflorida@yahoo.com. I personally have not been to this inn, but it was recommended by Elizabeth Kline. Sector Playón Alto on the right, 5 km from the start of the road. Four ample, pretty rooms, 2 with double beds and private bath, 1 double and one for four. Full breakfast included. Dinner is available by reservation, with the menu presented in the morning for à la carte selection for that night. Parking within the compound. The prices quoted by Elizabeth seem to me to be very reasonable.

Hotel Valle Grande (★★★)

Phones: (0) 274-244-3153 & 244-3011. E-mail: vallegrande@cantv.net. Although this is a very large and spread-out hotel, I am including it as Dick Ryan always stays there and has found some excellent birding in the area. I do not have the km from the bottom of the road to the hotel, but it is a goodly ways. Again, to quote Dick Ryan:

«*Go uphill from the Hotel Valle Grande a few km till you see a large stone structure on the left near a stream. There is parking near the gate to the structure (you may be questioned as it is a water supply facility). The woods right there and for a half kilometer up hill are excellent birding. Beside the Black-chested Mountain Tanager, we have also seen Blue-winged and Buff-*

breasted Mountain Tanagers as well as Mountain Wren, six species of Flower-piercers, Sword-billed Hummingbird and both species of Sunangels.»

The sightings of the Black-chested Mountain Tanager extend the distribution of this species, as it was previously considered to barely reach Venezuela at the Páramo de Tamá on the Colombian border.

Even if you do stay some place other than El Valle, be sure to spend at the very least a morning birding along the upper part of this road. Try to arrive early in the a.m.

Mérida Tourism

There are a number of fun things to do around Mérida aside from bird watching, and since they really add dimension to your trip and have never disappointed any birder I know, I recommend them with enthusiasm.

First there is the **Teleférico or Cable Car** up the mountain to Pico Espejo. The last part takes you up to where you can almost touch the snow-capped Pico Bolívar, highest in Venezuela. In order to have a clear view, make certain you take the first car up in the morning. The clouds come in early on the high Andes. It may not be an outstanding birding experience (although there is a chance of being eye-ball to eye-ball with a Black-and-chestnut Buzzard Eagle, as he soars near your car), but it is an absolutely spectacular trip, being the longest and highest cable car in the World, necessitating several stations and changes of cars. Please note that it is possible to hike back down the trails from the stations. The trail down form the first station would lead you to the Posada Doña Rosa. Be sure to take warm clothes and your camera.

Another wonderfully amusing and delicious thing to do in the city of Mérida is to visit an ice-cream parlor which boasts nothing less than... 600 flavors! Called **Heladería Coromoto**, it is located at No. 28, Ave. 3 Independencia, in front of the Plaza El Llano (El Llano Square). I can recommend almost all of the flavors including pumpkin, whole wheat, ginger, soy, etc., but forget the garlic ice cream! Now I have to laugh, because I gave Chris Sharpe a draft of this chapter, and *his comment on my comment* on garlic ice cream was as follows:

«NO! This is a must for all garlic lovers, and for me it is the best of the 600. However, eat it only on a solo birding trip as the after effects can be devastating.»

Last but not least, be sure to visit Mérida's **Main Market** on Avenida Las Americas. The first floor is given over to our many wonderful tropical fruits, vegetables and herbs, as well as natural remedies (much cheaper than in the U.S.). Ask for a map of Mérida at the Tourist Desk by the stairway. On the second floor you will see all kinds of shops selling handicrafts and souvenirs. The third floor is where you eat the cheapest lunch in Mérida. Be sure to try the Andean soup called Pisca. It is made with milk, potatoes, cilantro, and at the last minute they beak an egg into the boiling milk. The third floor also has many gift shops and even a gallery selling handicrafts and souvenirs. As a matter of fact, I believe that the better class of souvenirs are to be found on the third floor, so before making your purchase on the 2nd floor, check the one above. Between the two floors you will find an excellent gallery to buy gifts for home.

Caveat: Before I forget, **drink only bottled water** while you are in Mérida.

The Mérida Airport

It sits smack in the middle of town, a source of noise, urban design distortions, traffic and danger for the whole city. It also sits on a slant, one end of the landing strip higher than the other. But there it is, an absurd airport.

Due to the altitude, modern carriers have a hard time taking off, so there is a strict rule that they leave with only a percentage of the seats occupied.

Still, it is an alternative way of getting to or from Mérida, but be warned - if you have reservations, get there earlier than told by the travel agency or airline, with plenty of time to be among the first in the line. People often loose their reservations. For your information at the present time only Santa Barbara and Avior airlines fly to the Mérida airport. Aeropostal flies to El Vigia and from there one goes by bus to the capital of the State.

English-speaking Bird Guides in Mérida (Area Code 0274)	
Maria Rosa Cuesta naurepa@cantv.net	Home: 416-0005 (call nights) Office: 262-2969
Roger Manrique	Home: (0) 274-266-7788 Mobile: (0) 416-474-7933
Evaldo Sandoval evaldosandoval@hotmail.com	(0) 414-741-8429
Allan Highton allenheiton@yahoo.com	224.2748 home call nights
Alvaro Araujo andes@telcel.net.ve	Home: 221-2883 (call nights) Office: 266-2867
Gustavo Villoria gustavovilloria1966@yahoo.es	Home: 271-3217 (0) 414-974-6819
Joe Klaiber (Geman & English) VenezuelaJoe@excite.com	Home: 416-0540 (0) 414-741-3145

Mérida is extremely fortunate in having many qualified bi-lingual bird guides - even more than in Caracas and certainly more than in the state of Táchira, where we have found none.

THE WESTERN SIDE

All the birding you have done so far, the outings near the city of Mérida, took you around the northeastern part of the Mérida Andes, so now let us try the western side of the mountains. I propose that you do this by establishing the town of La Azulita as your base of operations.

From the city of Mérida take Avenida Los Próceres towards Jají, where you may wish to visit the *Museo de los Pájaros* (Museum of the Birds), a little tiny gallery, where a local sculptor shows his work - wood carvings of birds painted in full color. The carvings are quite good but the colors... A bit too garish for my taste.

Apart for a visit to the Museum, there is no reason for bird watchers to actually go to Jají itself. So, if you wish to get on with your birding destination, at the fork to Jaji or La Azulita, take the road on your right. When the road forks again after 1 km take the left-hand road. At the highest spot on the road, there is a three-way fork, but the way to La Azulita is well-marked. there is only one problem on this road, and I cannot tell you exactly where it is. There is one spot where it looks as though the road should go straight although there is also a road to the left. Be sure to go LEFT. The other road goes around a small hill and drops off into nothing. For the most part when you reach the upper regions, you will think you are in Switzerland with rolling hills and Holstein cattle. Without a doubt it is a beautiful road. But, (here we go again) when you approach La Azulita, the road at times narrows down to just one lane, with curves around rocky outcrops. Drive carefully. Coming from Mérida, this spectacular descent into the Lake Maracaibo basin begins with a series of switch backs. The road is not very good, and in the rainy season it is even worse, but this enchanting 5-mile stretch of winding road is one of the first-class birding experiences in Venezuela. At any time of the year, it is best to bird it in the early morning, before the afternoon fog rolls up from the Lake of Maracaibo. More about this birding area below.

La Azulita

This peaceful town is nestled in a valley at an altitude of 1,200 mts. (3,900 feet), and approximately two hours away from Mérida. When it comes to special attractions, the town itself has not much to offer, with the exception of a most pleasant inn, the **"Centro Ecológico El Tao"**, located in its outskirts at 1,300 meters above sea level.

The people who own and manage the Center, Magaly and Orlando, are Taoists, with the result that the place gives an all pervasive feeling of peace and calm and serenity. Orlando knows his neighborhood well, and you can ask him how to reach areas high above La Azulita, to look for curassows, guans, macaws, parakeets, etc. For reservations call (0) 414-960-5888 or contact the Venezuelan Audubon.

To find the Center, upon approaching the town from the city of Mérida, you will see a large white cross on the left. Two km further is a Maraven gas station and shortly after, you will see a low, white wall with large green sign that reads *La Tala - Camino de Dificil Retorno* (Tree-cutting - a Road of No Return.) Turn sharply left up here, and go 3.4 km further to a somewhat road, where you will see a sign on the right pointing down. The main gate is 0.2 km down this narrow street. If the door is shut, ring the bell. Someone will come down to open the gate. Enter and park to your left. Walk across the little bridge and go up to the main house.

If you are approaching La Azulita from the lowlands to the west, as you enter the town, turn right in front of the huge church. At the next corner turn left and then left again, to go half way around the Plaza Bolívar. Continue straight ahead, but at the third street turn right and then right again. At the next corner go left until you see a bridge with a green sign. Go up the hill.

The Center sprawls over 12 hectares, so there are many birds to see just walking the grounds. Many in the following list may also be found walking the road down from the Chapel of San Benito mentioned below - many in that list are found here, but together the two lists should give you a pretty good idea of the birds of this area:

Hook-billed Kite	Sooty-capped Hermit	Booted Racket-tail
Broad-winged Hawk	Gray-chinned Hermit	Long-tailed Sylph
Roadside Hawk	Little Hermit	Scaled Piculet
Rufous-vented Chachalaca	Lazuline Sabrewing	Olivaceous Piculet
Ruddy Pigeon	Green Violetear	Golden-olive Woodpecker
White-tipped Dove	Black-throated Mango	Lineated Woodpecker
Rose-headed Parakeet	Blue-tailed Emerald	Red-crowned Woodpecker
Green-rumped Parrotlet	Fork-tailed Woodnymph	Streak-headed Woodcreeper
Orange-chinned Parakeet	Shining-green Hummingbird	Stripe-breasted Spinetail
Squirrel Cuckoo	Golden-tailed Sapphire	Crested Spinetail
Smooth-billed Ani	Rufous-tailed Hummingbird	Plain Antvireo
Striped Cuckoo	Violet-fronted Brilliant	Cinereous Becard
Green Hermit	Violet-chested Hummingbird	Cinnamon Becard

Black-and-white Becard
Cattle Tyrant
Tropical Kingbird
Piratic Flycatcher
Boat-billed Flycatcher
Streaked Flycatcher
Rusty-margined Flycatcher
Social Flycatcher
Great Kiskadee
Dusky-capped Flycatcher
Tropical Pewee
Bran-colored Flycatcher
Yellow-olive Flycatcher
Common Tody-Flycatcher
Pale-eyed Pygmy Tyrant
Variegated Bristle-Tyrant
Yellow-bellied Elaenia
Mountain Elaenia
Forest Elaenia
Golden-faced Tyrannulet
Rough-winged Swallow
Green Jay
Rufous-breasted Wren
House Wren
Tropical Mockingbird

Swainson's Thrush
Yellow-legged Thrush
Black-hooded Thrush
Black-billed Thrush
Bare-eyed Thrush
Rufous-browed Peppershrike
Yellow-throated Vireo
Red-eyed Vireo
Shiny Cowbird
Giant Cowbird
Crested Oropendola
Northern Oriole
Yellow-backed Oriole
Black-and-white Warbler
Tennessee Warbler
Cerulean Warbler
Blackburnian Warbler
Blackpoll Warbler
Northern Waterthrush
Mourning Warbler
Canada Warbler
American Redstart
Slate-throated Redstart
Flavescent Warbler

Gray-throated Warbler
Bananaquit
Speckled Tanager
Blue-necked Tanager
Bay-headed Tanager
Burnished Buff Tanager
Black-headed Tanager
Blue-hooded Euphonia
Orange-bellied Euphonia
Thick-billed Euphonia
Blue-gray Tanager
Palm Tanager
Crimson-backed Tanager
Summer Tanager
White-lined Tanager
Fulvous-headed Tanager
Magpie Tanager
Grayish Saltator
Gray Seedeater
Yellow-bellied Seedeater
Ruddy-breasted Seedeater
Blue-black Grassquit
Rufous-collared Sparrow
Lesser Goldfinch

For excellent birding you should go back on the road towards Mérida until you see the chapel of San Benito on your left as you go down. It has a stone base and is presently painted red and white. Continue on the main road from the *capilla* or chapel down to the University Forest of La Carbonera. With luck, you should see the following:

Swallow-tailed Kite
Sharp-shinned Hawk
Broad-winged Hawk
White-rumped Hawk
White-throated Hawk
Short-tailed Hawk
Crested Eagle
Black-and-chestnut Eagle
Black Hawk-Eagle
Bat Falcon
American Kestrel
Band-tailed Guan
Andean Guan
Wattled Guan
Band-tailed Pigeon
Plumbeous Pigeon
White-tipped Dove
Lined Quail-Dove
Scarlet-fronted Parakeet
Rose-headed Parakeet

Barred Parakeet
Speckle-faced Parrot
Bronze-winged Parrot
Rufous-banded Owl
Chestnut-collared Swift
Gray-rumped Swift
White-tipped Swift
Long-tailed Hermit
Green-fronted Lancebill
Lazuline Sabrewing
Green Violetear
Short-tailed Emerald
Speckled Hummingbird
Mountain Velvetbreast
Bronzy Inca
Collared Inca
Golden-bellied Starfrontlet
Buff-tailed Coronet
Orange-throated Sunangel
Mérida Sunangel

Booted Racket-tail
Purple-backed Thornbill
Long-tailed Sylph
Rufous-shafted Woodstar
Crested Quetzal
Golden-headed Quetzal
Masked Trogon
Yellow-billed Toucanet
Emerald Toucanet
Black-mandibled Toucan
Smoky-brown Woodpecker
Crimson-crested Woodpecker
Strong-billed Woodcreeper
Black-banded Woodcreeper
Spot-crowned Woodcreeper
Azara's Spinetail
Rufous Spinetail
Pearled Treerunner
Streaked Tuftedcheek
Montane Foliage-gleaner

Streaked Xenops
Chestnut-crowned Antpitta
Andean Tapaculo
Green-and-black Fruiteater
Golden-breasted Fruiteater
Barred Becard
Cinnamon Becard
Red-ruffed Fruitcrow
Yellow-bellied Chat-Tyrant
Black Phoebe
Tropical Kingbird
Golden-crowned Flycatcher
Smoke-colored Pewee
Flavescent Flycatcher
Variegated Bristle-tyrant
White-throated Tyrannulet
Lesser Elaenia
Mountain Elaenia
Black-capped Tyrannulet
Paltry Tyrannulet
Golden-faced Tyrannulet
Olive-striped Flycatcher
Barn Swallow
Collared Jay
Green Jay
Whiskered Wren

Mountain Wren
Gray-breasted Wood-Wren
Andean Solitaire
Swainson's Thrush
Spotted Nightingale-Thrush
Yellow-legged Thrush
Glossy-black Thrush
Chestnut-bellied Thrush
White-necked Thrush
Brown-capped Vireo
Golden-winged Warbler
Tennessee Warbler
Cerulean Warbler
Blackburnian Warbler
Bay-breasted Warbler
Canadian Warbler
American Redstart
Slate-throated Redstart
White-fronted Redstart
Black-crested Warbler
Three-striped Warbler
Russet-crowned Warbler
Swallow-Tanager
Bluish Flower-piercer
Masked Flower-piercer

White-sided Flower-piercer
Red-legged Honeycreeper
Golden Tanager
Saffron-crowned Tanager
Beryl-spangled Tanager
Blue-and-black Tanager
Fawn-breasted Tanager
Blue-naped Chlorophonia
Buff-breasted
Mountain-Tanager
Blue-capped Tanager
Crimson-backed Tanager
White-winged Tanager
Gray-capped Hemispingus
Superciliaried Hemispingus
Oleaginous Hemispingus
Common Bush-Tanager
Plush-capped Finch
Rose-breasted Grosbeak
Chestnut-capped Brush-Finch
Slaty Brush-Finch
Moustached Brush-Finch
Black-and-white Seedeater
Rufous-collared Sparrow
Yellow-bellied Siskin

Yet another tip for around La Azulita, and this one from Maria Rosa Cuesta - Go all the way through the town of La Azulita. To do this is not easy but after you pass the bridge turn right at the first corner and then left down a very steep street. Just before the street ends, turn left until you reach the plaza and church. Here you should turn right and you are now on your way out of town. Before too long you will pass a National Guard post. Just one half kilometer from the alcabala you will see a dirt road going right. Turn down here. This is THE place to be at 5 in the afternoon to watch the macaws and parrots coming to roost, including the Bronze-winged, Orange-winged, Yellow-crowned Parrots and Blue-crowned, White-eyed, Scarlet-fronted and Rose-headed Parakeets plus Military and chestnut-fronted Macaws. I am not saying that other times of day - in the morning for instance - it would not be good birding. Wind your way down through the coffee groves to look for tanagers, flycatchers, etc.

If you were to continue down the road, you would soon come to a paved road on a curve on your left that leads to the village of **Olinda**. However, coming from La Azulita, it is very difficult to make this turn. You should continue down until you can safely make a 180 degree turn and then approach this secondary road with an easier and safer right-hand turn. According to Maria Rosa, both the scenery and birding along this road to Olinda are beautiful.

La Carbonera, Río Frío and places west of La Azulita
From El Tao or La Azulita, drive west down the main road for 18 km, to reach State Highway 1 at Caño Zancudo. There, turn north or right and drive for another 19.5 km, where you will see a small restaurant/hotel called Hotel Rosamar.

This might rate as much as one star, but it is both clean and decent and a convenient option in order to be up at dawn or stay late in the evening birding this area.

Immediately next to and behind the hotel is a paved road that runs approximately 4 km up into the mountains along the **Río Frío**. This is an area that should be birded especially either very early in the morning or late in the afternoon, or both. Aside from the usual stuff such as Crimson-backed Tanagers, look for Swallow-tailed Kites, Chestnut-fronted Macaws, Rose-headed Parakeets, Collared Araçaris, Saffron-headed Parrots and Yellow-tailed Oriole. The road merits time and concentration.

Unfortunately, to date, I've had only one opportunity to explore it, and we only had time for a quick look-see while eating a sandwich and then had to continue north. I would certainly appreciate any trip report on this region.

Yet another area along State Highway 1 is found some 7 km further north from the Hotel Rosamar. Here the road on your right leads east again for some 10 km to the town of **El Charal**. I have not been able to bird it myself, but even Miguel Lentino, our Senior Audubon Ornithologist and Curator of the Phelps Ornithological Collection, has recommended it, so give it a try.

Rufous-Collared Sparrow

IV - 4. State of Táchira

INTRODUCTION

Welcome to my most favorite state!! We have finally arrived!! For me, this far southwestern corner is one of the most beautiful areas of Venezuela. Then there are the people of Táchira, so very friendly, courteous and helpful. There are clean, quaint towns and forests with BIRDS!

Few parks can surpass the Tamá National Park, where one can find high Andean species from Colombia, not seen in any other part of Venezuela, as well as some lowland species more typical of the areas south of the Orinoco River.

The reason for this distinct species mix on the Páramo de Tamá is the Táchira Depression, a valley that extends across the mountains in a northeast-southwest direction, and effectively breaks the long chain into an Eastern Colombian segment and a Venezuelan Mérida segment. The Depression divides the highland faunas of these segments and has served as a barrier to the dispersal of many Andean birds.

The many coffee haciendas also contribute to the wealth of avian fauna. Unlike Costa Rica, Venezuela has very little sun coffee. The vast majority of our coffee is shade grown.

After a visit to Táchira, I am certain you will agree with me that as there are so many places to go birding in this state, it could easily merit more than a week's vacation.

Since almost the entire State is mountainous, the roads are, for the most part, narrow and winding, and some have very heavy car and truck traffic. Taking this into consideration, I always plan to stay near the town of **Rubio** in order to bird the various sites of southern Táchira with a minimum of driving. Then, I continue north to the state of Mérida via the high mountain passes that offer so much in scenery and birds.

ON GETTING TO TÁCHIRA

There are two basic ways to drive to Táchira. You can reach it by traveling southwest across the Llanos on National Highway 5 and what is known as the "Carretera de los Llanos", or you can take the old route, the so-called "Carretera Trasandina" (or National Highway 7), and drive south from Mérida. With the first option, you pass through the city of Barinas, in the state of the same name. With the second, you probably passed through it on your way to Mérida.

If you are driving straight through from Caracas, follow the route directions I give in the chapter on the State of Mérida, breaking the trip to rest the night at Barinas (see chapter on the Llanos), or the inn at Altamira (see the chapter on Mérida) as the Caracas-Barinas leg will take you a minimum of seven hours. From Barinas, Highway No. 5 takes you 316 km (approximately 5-6 hours) south and west to San Cristobal or to Rubio, where as I said above, it will be convenient to establish your center of operations for the birding areas of the southwestern part of Táchira.

If you opt for Highway 5 south, some 48 km after Barinas you will come to the crossroads to **Ciudad Bolivia**. Continue straight on towards the south west and **Socopó** at 86 km from Barinas This is the entrance to a good birding area along the **Bumbum River.** (I am not joking. That is really the name!) This information was sent to us by Andrew Nield, a butterfly expert from the UK who specializes in Venezuelan butterflies. Andrew is right - if there are butterflies, there will also be birds. For more direct information on this and on his excellent butterfly books, his e-mail is a.neild@ndirect.co.uk and www.ndirect.co.uk/~a.neild.

On the right side of the road (west) in front of a large white cross there is a dirt road leading up to the valley of the Bumbum. The road probably is passable with a normal car in the dry season. After some 4 km, you will enter a forest, not exactly primary but still very good. The road climbs through the forest for some 250 to 300 meters. In this area Andrew not only found many butterflies but also saw and heard a goodly quantity of birds. Along the road you will come to a Y junction. The left branch first traverses about 500 meters of cultivated fields and then comes to a hanging foot bridge followed by a path through a beautiful forest along the river. This path eventually leads to the city of Mérida (and I do mean eventually - like two days! It must be an unbelievable hike). The right fork continues through the forest before reaching some pastures. If you have the time, I believe this area would be well worth investigating.

One of the big birding areas reached from Highway 5 is called (of all weird things) **Siberia**. Weirder yet, the name Siberia is not shown on any map, but it is the operations center of a large complex of three dams, the Uribante/Caparo, La Honda and Borde Seco reservoirs. The national electric company, CADAFE, has a huge installation there, complete with apartments, cabins, restaurant, etc. You will ask how an electric complex of this size can be of interest to birders. Just look at the following list of species:

Little Tinamou	Squirrel Cuckoo	Many-banded Araçari
Neotropical Cormorant	Smooth-billed Ani	Black-Mandibled Toucan
Great Egret	Groove-billed Ani	Red-billed Toucan
Snowy Egret	Striped Cuckoo	Scaled Piculet
King Vulture	Tropical Screech-Owl	Spot-breasted Woodpecker
Black Vulture	Spectacled Owl	Golden-olive Woodpecker
Turkey Vulture	Ferruginous Pygmy-Owl	Yellow-tufted Woodpecker
White-tailed Kite	Mottled Owl	Red-crowned Woodpecker
Swallow-tailed Kite	Pauraque	Lineated Woodpecker
Gray-headed Kite	Rufous Nightjar	Crimson-crested Woodpecker
Plumbeous Kite	White-collared Swift	Olivaceous Woodcreeper
Roadside Hawk	Chestnut-collared Swift	Wedge-billed Woodcreeper
White Hawk	Sooty-capped Hermit	Streak-headed Woodcreeper
Black Hawk-Eagle	Little Hermit	Pale-breasted Spinetail
Laughing Hawk	Lazuline Sabrewing	Stripe-breasted Spinetail
Yellow-headed Caracara	Green Violetear	Crested Spinetail
Crested Caracara	Sparkling Violetear	Common Thornbird
Bat Falcon	Black-throated Mango	Chestnut-crowned
American Kestrel	Spangled Coquette	Foliage-Gleaner
Band-tailed Guan	Fork-tailed Woodnymph	Plain Xenops
Spotted Sandpiper	Golden-tailed Sapphire	Great Antshrike
Scaled Pigeon	Glittering-throated Emerald	Barred Antshrike
Ruddy Pigeon	Copper-rumped Hummingbird	Slaty Antwren
Common Ground-Dove	Green-bellied Hummingbird	White-fringed Antwren
Ruddy Ground-Dove	Violet-fronted Brilliant	Dusky Antbird
White-tipped Dove	Masked Trogon	White-browed Antbird
Chestnut-fronted Macaw	Ringed Kingfisher	White-bellied Antbird
Brown-throated Parakeet	Rufous-tailed Jacamar	Black-faced Antthrush
Green-rumped Parrotlet	Moustached Puffbird	Bearded Bellbird
Saffron-headed Parrot	Red-headed Barbet	Andean Cock-of-the-Rock
Mealy Parrot	Yellow-billed Toucanet	Golden-headed Manakin

White-bearded Manakin
Striped Manakin
Black Phoebe
Tropical Kingbird
Piratic Flycatcher
Boat-billed Flycatcher
Streaked Flycatcher
Rusty-margined Flycatcher
Social Flycatcher
Great Kiskadee
Dusky-capped Flycatcher
Smoke-colored Pewee
Cliff Flycatcher
Yellow-breasted Flycatcher
Common Tody-Flycatcher
Slate-headed Tody-Flycatcher
Scale-crested Pygmy-Tyrant
Yellow-bellied Elaenia
Mountain Elaenia
Golden-faced Tyrannulet
Slaty-capped Flycatcher
Olive-striped Flycatcher
Ochre-bellied Flycatcher
White-winged Swallow
Gray-breasted Martin
Brown-chested Martin
Blue-and-white Swallow
Southern Rough-
  winged Swallow
Green Jay
Whiskered Wren
Rufous-breasted Wren
Rufous-and-white Wren
Southern Nightingale Wren

Tropical Mockingbird
Orange-billed
  Nightingale-Thrush
Yellow-legged Thrush
Glossy-black Thrush
Black-hooded Thrush
Pale-breasted Thrush
White-necked Thrush
Long-billed Gnatwren
Rufous-browed Peppershrike
Brown-capped Vireo
Golden-fronted Greenlet
Shiny Cowbird
Crested Oropendola
Russet-backed Oropendola
Yellow-rumped Cacique
Carib Grackle
Yellow-backed Oriole
Oriole Blackbird
Eastern Meadowlark
Black-and-white Warbler
Tropical Parula
Blackburnian Warbler
Blackpoll Warbler
Mourning Warbler
American Redstart
Slate-throated Redstart
Golden-crowned Warbler
Bananaquit
Swallow Tanager
Purple Honeycreeper
Green Honeycreeper
Blue Dacnis
Speckled Tanager

Golden Tanager
Blue-necked Tanager
Bay-headed Tanager
Burnished-buff Tanager
Black-headed Tanager
Blue-hooded Euphonia
Orange-bellied Euphonia
Thick-billed Euphonia
Blue-gray Tanager
Palm Tanager
Silver-beaked Tanager
White-lined Tanager
White-shouldered Tanager
Gray-headed Tanager
Guira Tanager
Magpie Tanager
Black-faced Tanager
Blue-black Grosbeak
Buff-throated Saltator
Grayish Saltator
Streaked Saltator
Rose-breasted Grosbeak
Chestnut-capped Brush-Finch
Black-striped Sparrow
Yellow-faced Grassquit
Gray Seedeater
Yellow-bellied Seedeater
Blue-black Grassquit
Saffron Finch
Yellow-browed Sparrow
Rufous-collared Sparrow
Yellow-bellied Siskin
Lesser Goldfinch

It was racked up by birders from Venezuela Audubon, who have gone twice to this area. To date, one hundred and ninety one species! Not bad for a couple of days' birding. The area is quite peculiar, so I am certain there is a lot there still to be discovered. It will not surprise me if you do better than the 190. You will notice it is a strange mixture of tropical and subtropical species. Let me explain the geography - Siberia sits at only 900 meters, and weather wise it really does not live up to its name, but from there you can either go up the mountains or down. Hence the strange mixture of species.

Presumably you will be driving from Barinas on Highway 5. It is approximately 191 km from the city of Barinas to the Caparo River and the town of **Pta. Piedras** where you enter the State of Táchira. Now you start driving west for another 77 km more or less, to reach the cross roads at a place called **Chururú**. Here you turn right and start going up.

You still have another 68 km to go, but take your time because soon you will start birding. The first large town you will pass through is **La Fundación**, but there are others with the most far-out names ever invented - The Reverend, The Idea, St. Good, The Deforestation... I remember a curve that we called "The Miracle" because it was a hot spot for birding, but I guess we were lucky and caught a large feeding flock. When you come up to Siberia, you will see a fancy road on your right with a watchman and a gate. Here you will have to stop and show your reservation. To make a reservation you should send a fax to the Ing. Blanca Tascón, Directora Gerente, CADAFE, Siberia, Táchira, (0) 276-344-2102 or 276-347-8653. You should state the dates and number of days you wish to stay as well as the number of people in your party. The only hitch here is that you have to write in Spanish, so maybe you had better request the help of the Venezuelan Audubon.

You will be shown your cabin and from there on it is up to you, but I would most heartedly suggest that you contact the Ecological Department (*Departamento de Ecología*) to request permission to drive down the 9 km road to the **Presa Las Cuevas**. That dam has not been built as yet, (thank heavens) but the road down to the river has a gate and yet another watchman, to whom you need to show a permit. This is the road where we had the best luck. We spent a whole day driving and walking down the road all the way to the river and did not see another car or human. Just Saffron-headed Parrots, Many-banded Araçari, Yellow-billed Toucanet, leks of both the Golden-headed and White-bearded Manakins, Yellow-faced Grassquit and many other etceteras.

Upon leaving Siberia to return to Caracas, we took the more easterly road down the mountain towards **San Joaquin de Navay**. Not too long after leaving Siberia, we sighted Mealy Parrots, Yellow-ridged and Red-billed Toucans. When we reached the lowlands even before Highway 5, we started birding again and had a marvelous look at Pale-headed Jacamar.

As indicated above, upon entering Táchira, Highway 5 starts heading west. You will pass by the airport of Santo Domingo; eventually, the headquarters for the "Batallón de Ingenieros de Combate" on your right, and then, the Fuerte Murachi. From this last fort it is approximately 15 km to the turn-off to the town of **El Corozo**, passing first the bridge over the Uribante River and finally, a sign indicating a left turn to El Corozo. Considering all the traffic, I can promise you will think it is endless and will be so very relieved when you can leave this blasted[1] highway for the back roads toward Rubio.

The town of Corozo comes immediately after taking this left turn down from the main road. It is 33 km from there to the entrance to Rubio. If you get lost, ask the way to **Santa Ana**. After a while you will see a bridge on your left leading to Santa Ana. Do not turn into it, but continue on the same road until you come to an intersection and a day-park called **La Petrolia** (more about it later). At this intersection, veer right and continue. The main road from Colombia into Venezuela goes through a couple of towns, now curiously called **Independencia** and **Libertad** (Independence and Freedom), to San Cristobal and then on to the Llanos. As it is in terrible shape, many heavily laden trucks take a detour via Rubio, so be very cautious during the day and do not take this road after dark. Hopefully, the main road will be repaired in the near future.

RUBIO

When you dead-end into Rubio, turn right on to the main street, Avenida Principal, also called Avenida 7, until you see the sign on your right for the Banco de Venezuela on Calle 15. Turn right. Immediately next to the bank you will find **Hotel Marqués**.

---

[1] Note from the Editor: Don't you believe this sweet-li'l-ole-me speech, dear reader. The adjectives most frequently used by Mrs. Goodwin tend to be a wee bit less wholesome, a tad less exultant than these. Just a tad!

This is a small, friendly, family-run hotel with only one significant drawback - they do not have a parking lot. There is a perfectly safe place to leave your car though, and the people of El Marques will go with you to show you how to get there: go back to Avenida Principal, turn left for two blocks, turn right, find a huge gate. El Marques does not have a restaurant either, but for dining, **El Caldero** is at walking distance and has a great onion soup! In fact, it would be hard to find a better restaurant even in Caracas! For a breakfast of coffee and pastry, or to purchase stuff for lunch, there is a nice bakery around the block from the Hotel. Ask the way to both places at the desk. Then there is a wonderful soda fountain/coffee shop on the main street of town called La Petite Poupee. To find it, drive down Avenida 7 to the first stoplight. Turn right and continue until you see the panadería/pastelería/coffee shop/ soda fountain all rolled up into one on the right side of the road at the corner of Calle 15 and Avenida 4.

The owners of the hotel also have an inn called the **Posada del Marqués**, which is some 6 km west of Rubio. Although there is a cellular telephone at the inn itself (0) 414-976-2860, it is necessary to make reservations through the hotel in town, phone (0) 276-762-3714. Upon arriving in Rubio, you should go first to the hotel to check in as it were. To find the inn go back up Avenida 7 (the way you just came into town) for two blocks and turn left. Go straight. You will shortly come to a bridge after which you come to a T in the road with a cross on the right (the Tachirenses are very religious people). Go left. You are now on the road to San Antonio de Táchira and Cucutá, Colombia. Some 6 km from the bridge you have crossed you will be driving over two speed bumps, locally known as "sleeping policemen." On your right will be a small restaurant or eatery specializing in chicken or "pollo." At the next corner turn right and then left. From there on just follow the signs for the Posada. The inn has 14 rooms, private baths with hot water, guarded and enclosed parking area, swimming pool and the best of all -- the inn is set in the middle of coffee haciendas with lots of birds. Meals can be served with prior arrangements, but, bluntly speaking, the food is neither that good nor is it inexpensive. You would be better off eating in Rubio, but this is a wonderful place to stay. If you look down into the valley from the inn, you will see a small white church way below at a hamlet called Coquí. That leads to yet another story to be told below.

Posada Turistica Santa Barbara
Is another inn suggested by Elizabeth Kline for Rubio. It is locataed on Avenida Los Leones (previously called Calle 16), No. 25. This is one block from the Hidrosuroeste water plant. It has nine simple but comfortable rooms, with plans to build 4 more. All rooms have cable TV, private bath, hot water and fans, and there are 3 with air con. They also have laundry service and fenced parking for 10 cars in the back. A restaurant and soda fountain are being added. The friendly owners – Miguel Credes Romero and his wife, Maritza, personally attend to the guests (now that I like !). Phone: (0) 276-762-3386; fax: (0) 276-762-1906.

TAMÁ NATIONAL PARK

The Tama N.P is 139.000 hectares in size, and it has a "sister" park on the Colombian side. Elevations go up to 3,330 m on the Páramo de Tamá and 3,365 m on the Páramo del Cobre.

☞ The Venezuelan Audubon has published the **Checklist of the Birds of Tamá National Park,** which you can buy either from us or from the American Birding Association.

Now for the serious business of where to bird, let me explain that three interesting sites provide access to and thus, make birding possible, within the Park. These sites are:

The Road to Betania

To "do" this area properly, I suggest you take a full day, leaving very early. (Before dawn that is.) **Betania** is a tiny town on the Colombian border, some 3 hours south from Rubio. To get on the way, exit Rubio by driving straight up the Avenida Principal. Pass the town of **Bramón**. Since there are no signs and for those who lack Marco Polo instincts, go through it by going straight up the street as you enter town, and where it dead ends, turn right. Beyond Bramón there is a National Guard Post (Alcabala) where you may be stopped and requested to show your identification. At the far end of the town of **El Diamante** is a gas station. Fill your tank.

At 5.5 km after the Alcabala, you will see a side road on your right leading to an area known as **Matamula** and then **Alto Frio**. This high road can be excellent birding in the very early morning, though you may wish to leave it for another day considering the distance ahead of you to get to Betania. When and if you do come here, look for Booted Racket-tail, Swainson's Thrush, Canada Warbler, Saffron-crowned Tanager and Rusty-winged Barbtail. High mountain birding will be chilly and demand a bit of work, so the names of this area are very apt - Mule-killer and Cold Heights. From the very top of Alto Frio (Cold Heights) you have a great view of a town in Colombia called Ragumbalia. Unfortunately, a number of TV and radio antennas have been built recently on Matamula, and I really do not know what the impact has been on the birds.

After the road to Matamula, you will shortly come down into the town of **Las Delicias**, which again requires an exercise in ingenuity - go all the way down the hill, past the church, until the very end of the street where you will turn left for **Villa Páez**. (Ask for directions if you get lost.) Once you are on the road to Villa Páez, it is pretty clear sailing with beautiful vistas of the Río Táchira gorge and Colombia on the other side. Across the gorge you can see the Colombian town of Herrán. When you reach Villa Páez, you will have to make the loop around the Plaza Bolívar, and you are on your last leg to Betania. At Villa Páez, look for Brown-bellied Swallows behind or on the church steeple.

As you pull into Betania, you will see the Venezuelan flag over an official building. Continue straight up the hill for 0.3 km after the flag. Take a right to Pico de Vela. You will probably have to park down below unless you have a 4x4 vehicle. Walk up the hill to the small remnant stand of forest. Again, in the very early morning, this is superb birding. Look for:

Bronzy Inca	Whiskered Wren	Saffron-crowned Tanager
Collared Inca	Mountain Wren	Blue-necked Tanager
Blue-throated Starfrontlet	Golden-winged Warbler	Blue-and-black Tanager
Gorgeted Woodstar	Blackburnian Warbler	Golden-crowned Tanager
Smoky-brown Woodpecker	Hooded Warbler	Buff-breasted Mountain-Tanager
Pearled Treerunner	Golden-faced Redstart	Black-eared Hemispingus
Streaked Tuftedcheek	Bluish Flower-piercer	Black-capped Hemispingus
Smoke-colored Pewee	Masked Flower-piercer	Slaty Brush-Finch
Rufous-crowned Tody-Tyrant,	Glossy Flower-piercer	Pale-naped Brush-Finch
White-throated Tyrannulet,	Black Flower-piercer	Rufous-collared Sparrow
Venezuelan Tyrannulet		

On the meadow above the forest you might see Short-tailed Night-Hawk and Pale-footed Swallow (I know it is not in the Venezuelan Guide, but Miguel Lentino netted it here!), and in the bamboo areas surrounding the meadow, look for Mountain Wren and Plush-capped Finch.

Next, go to the end of the main road. The last house on the road is that of Don Pedro Asa, a farmer who is quite accustomed to birders tramping through his cow pasture above the house. From here there is a very muddy 4 km path through temperate zone forest, bamboo and brush woodland, and finally the paramo at 3,300 m.a.s.l. Not too far from the house, after skirting the mud and cow paddies, you will once more come to an open pasture. Again you should check the edges. At this upper part of the pasture you may find Amethyst-throated Sunangel, Blue-fronted Starfrontlet, Collared Inca, Tyrian Metaltail, Black-billed Mountain-Toucan, Rufous Wren, Citrine Warbler and mixed species flocks of Golden-fronted Redstart, Capped Conebill, Bluish Flower-piercer, Black-capped and Black-eared Hemispinguses as well as Yellow-bellied Chat-Tyrant, which are all just a few of the beautiful birds of the páramo region of Táchira. Above the bamboo woodland, there is good possibility of finding Golden-crowned and White-capped Tanagers, Glowing Puffleg, Crimson-mantled Woodpecker and Great Thrush. (With this last species I bet you will become blasé - Oh, it is just another one of those!)

About 3 km above Don Pedro's house there is the possibility of finding Bronze-tailed Thornbill, White-chinned Thistletail, Páramo Pipit, Plumbeous Sierra-Finch and the white-eyebrowed form of the Brown-backed Chat-Tyrant.

A word to the wise. This is a very wet region, but January and February are the clearest months and the best time to come. In April and May expect heavy rains, mist and fog. My recommendation is high rubber boots at any time of the year and warm clothes.

Unfortunately, with the possible exception of the Park Guard's house, there is no place to stay at Betania, so this requires a very early start from Rubio. However, I have learned that it might be possible to "camp out" at the community house in the village. You should inquire around for Sr. Oscar Calderón, he being the person who has the key and could give the necessary permission. Also, they have told me that there is a hotel in Las Delicias, but for that matter you might as well stay in Rubio[1]. There are also buses that go from San Cristobal to Betania should you not have a car.

After some 5 years, I returned to this area in May, 2001 and was shocked at the amount of intervention considering that most of the area is a part of the National Park. Unfortunately, there has been tremendous social pressure on the Park due in great part to the population explosion, but the blame actually lies with the politicians. Neither local nor national governments have had any interest in protecting our natural resources or National Parks, and worse yet, environmental education is non existent.

Río Frío / Río Negro - La Palmacera

Here is another example of incredible neglect on the part of the local governments. Previously, another great but exhausting full-day of birding was the road all along the Río Frío/Río Negro which flows through the Tamá National Park. It was necessary to go back to El Corozo and Highway 5. Turn right or east. Some 16 km east of the entrance to El Corozo and 2 km east of the Batallón de los Ingenieros de Combate is a turn off on the right to the "Balneario Río Negro". The road is dirt, but previously a regular car could make it. In May, 2001 I was frightened driving my 4x4 [2].

---

[1] Pamela's Comment: The road from Las Delicias is not much for birding but has fantastic views that sure are worth seeing.

[2] Note from the Editor: As they say in Paris, *sa va sans dire*, it goes without saying. Put 10 pebbles in front of Mary Lou´s truck and she is in conniptions – bad road, bad road!!

This was and still is one no-nonsense birding road, especially in the dry season, when one should get mixed species flocks. This is the only area in Venezuela where I've seen the Green Shrike Vireo, and there are two sight records from top rate birders of the elusive Tachira Emerald[1].

After approximately 6 km on this road there was a track on the right that lead, 2 km straight up, to the Park Station of **La Palmacera**. It was possible to stay at the Station if you had a permit from the Park´s office in Caracas or San Cristobal. We netted 64 species of birds on just two sections of this 2 kilometer stretch, including Golden-headed, White-crowned, Wire-tailed, White-bearded and Striped Manakins. Just walking the trail and the road alongside the river we found some 260 species. The whole area is unbelievably bio-diverse. Now it is completely abandoned by both the local government and INPARQUES. At one time there was also an area for the local people to bathe in the river, and this has also been abandoned.

Back down to the main road we continued birding as the road looped all the way around to the town of Santa Ana - it was along this road that my friend Bill Oberman, of Washington, DC, ran across the largest feeding flock he has ever seen - dozens of birds flitted through for half an hour! Darrell Hutchinson, a Canadian birder, wrote me about this road long ago as follows:

«*In or around that same area I encountered a foraging flock of mostly residents (not migrants), which turned out to be the mother of all foraging flocks. There were hundreds and hundreds of individuals with over 40 species. Many were new to me and there was no time to check the guide. So as one wave would pass, I'd log 4 or 6 species in my head. As the flock subsided, I would madly scratch down some field notes. Then I'd run up or down the road and catch the next wave. This lasted for over 2 hours! It was some of the most deliciously exhausting birding, I'd ever done.*»

When we were there in May, 2001, we had the good fortune of meeting an extremely helpful Park Guard, who warned us not to try to drive on to Santa Ana. He could do so, because he had a motorcycle.

I am telling you all of the above with the illusion that some day Venezuela will have intelligent, incorruptible, enlightened and educated politicians who have the aim of protecting their land and educating their people. In the meantime young, vigorous birders should aim to go on foot, seeking the same experience that Darrel Hutchinson had. I shall envy them.

La Petrolia

You'll remember that I mentioned this day-park above, for one goes by it on the way to Rubio. It is the site where the first oil well was drilled in Venezuela, thus the name "La Petrolia", and also "La Alquitrana", as the locals sometimes call it. The park is included as part of Tamá National Park. It is a well-kept little area, where we have counted some 48 species in an hour or so of birding. It is curious mixture of species, for there are here some very local ones, as well as some that are found mostly south of the Orinoco, or even Perijá.

---

[1] Some silly ornithologists have claimed that the Tachira Emerald is a hybrid. Since none of them have done any field work in this area, and indeed, no serious ornithological survey has been undertaken by anybody else since the team from the Phelps Collection, we will continue to consider our beautiful bird a bona-fide species.

While here, you might as well explore around to find an old hanging bridge spanning the Quinimarí River, below and across the road from the park and from the so-called "Gran Restaurante La Petrolia". People from the neighborhood often come to swim in this spot. A dirt road leads to the bridge and a trail follows from it, which is a remnant of the ancient Spanish road from Bogotá to Caracas. Locals have told me that from here the trail goes all the way to the town of Santa Ana, following along the river.

Hereabouts also is **Río Chiquito**, often mentioned in the Guide to the Birds of Venezuela and a mystery place to birders for a long time, as it does not appear on any map. I found out, also from the locals and much to my surprise, that it is a place and not a river! Can this be true? So, I checked it out on my last visit and was overwhelmed. Not only is it a delightful Andean village, but the road from La Petrolia to Rio Chiquito requires a whole day of walking and birding . As if that were not enough, the road goes on to **San Vicente de la Revancha**. To find this particular road is easy. It goes right past the lower side of La Petrolia. In fact you cross it to see the hanging bridge over the Quinimarí. Do me a favor. Take a day off and bird this road and then send me your list, because I did not have the time to do so. Had to move on to Mérida.

Between the turn-off to Santa Ana and just above La Petrolia, the road is bordered by coffee plantations. One can happily spend also a whole day along that length of road, to be rewarded with such prizes as Black Hawk-Eagle, Rufous-tailed and Green-bellied Hummingbirds, Yellow-vented and Yellow-tufted Woodpeckers, Fasciated Antshrike, Cinnamon Becard, Golden-faced Tyrannulet, Swallow Tanager, Blue Dacnis, Thick-billed Euphonia, Purple and Red-legged Honeycreepers; Summer, Guira, Blue-necked and Burnished-buff Tanagers.

On this list are some of the special birds of La Petrolia. We marked with an asterisk (*) those species found mostly south of the Orinoco.

Black Hawk-Eagle	Streaked Flycatcher	Purple Honeycreeper
Laughing Falcon	Mountain Elaenia	Red-legged Honeycreeper
Black-throated Mango	Golden-faced Tyrannulet	Blue Dacnis
Green-bellied Hummingbird *	Rufous-and-white Wren	Speckled Tanager
Rufous-tailed Hummingbird	Yellow-legged Thrush	Blue-necked Tanager
White-vented Plumeleteer	Black-billed Thrush *	Burnished-buff Tanager
Spot-breasted Woodpecker	Baltimore Oriole	Blue-hooded Euphonia
Yellow-tufted Woodpecker *	Yellow-backed Oriole	Thick-billed Euphonia
Yellow-vented Woodpecker	Tropical Parula	Summer Tanager
Red-billed Scythebill	Masked Yellow-throat	Guira Tanager
Fasciated Antshrike *	Swallow Tanager	Gray Seedeater
Cinnamon Becard		

CHORRO DEL INDIO NATIONAL PARK

Here is another national park in Táchira, located above the city of San Cristobal. I regret to confess that I have never taken the time to bird this park thoroughly - I just never seem to have enough time in Táchira. However, from the pictures I've seen of the Park and its páramo, I suspect that it must be worth a lengthy visit, using San Cristobal as a center of operations. So here is one where you can do some pioneering explorations and then tell us all what you found!

My only brief contact with Chorro del Indio was to bird one of the many entrances to the Park from San Cristobal. To reach this entrance, go all the way to the top of Avenida 19 de Abril in San Cristobal. (This is also the way to Parque Metropolitano and the Inparques Regional Office in Táchira.) Go half way around the traffic circle, and you will see an inconspicuous road leading up the hill with a dilapidated sign reading "Chorro del Indio". This road can take you all the way to Potosí and La Florida, but you can bird any place along the way and take as long as you wish. In a short time early one morning I saw:

Roadside Hawk	Rufous-and-white Wren	Bay-headed Tanager
Black Hawk-Eagle	Swainson´s Thrush	Thick-billed Euphonia
Eared Dove	Yellow-legged Thrush	Summer Tanager
Gray-fronted Dove	Glossy-black Thrush	White-lined Tanager
White-collared Swift	Black-hooded Thrush	Common Bush-Tanager
Olivaceous Piculet	Black-and-white Warbler	Black-faced Tanager
Slaty-capped Flycatcher	Blackburnian Warbler	Ochre-breasted Brush-Finch
Rough-winged Swallow	Slate-throated Redstart	Yellow-bellied Seedeater
Whiskered Wren	Golden-crowned Warbler	

After writing the above, I had the opportunity of speaking to Norberto Rebolledo, a biologist who has lived and worked in Táchira. He advised that to find the good birding areas of Chorro del Indio Park, you should enter as indicated above, but it is a long way to the good birding area where there are no cafes, swimming areas, etc. Still and all, if you have the time, why not try it?

ON STAYING IN SAN CRISTOBAL

San Cristobal is the State Capital, a city of traditions, a reputation for gracious living and lots of young people, as it has three or four colleges and universities. For the tourist, it is a pleasing town with many hotels, good restaurants and a memorable ice-cream parlor.

Hotels in San Cristobal, Area Code (0) 276		
Tamá	★★★★	356-1870
Los Pirineos	★★★★	356-7390
Las Lomas	★★	343-5733
Dinastía	★★★	344-4527
Residencia Palermo		343-7743

As I invariably stay near Rubio, I am not so familiar with the big city of San Cristobal, but that indefatigable Elizabeth Kline knows where to find inns all over the country. She has recommended **Posada Turística Los Pirineos**, phones: (0) 276-356-7390 & 355-8368, fax: 276-355-6528. Quinta El Cerrito, No. 16-38, Urbanización Pirineos. Whether you approach San Cristobal from the north on Avenida Libertador or from the south on Avenida Marginal Torbes, you will connect with a redoma that turns into Avenida Carabobo. You want to go up this last-named street. "One block before the end (a T with a stoplight), turn right, then right again on the second street which is Av. Francisco Cárdenas. The inn is on the left, more or less 2 blocks down. Sixteen large, nicely decorated rooms in a sprawling private home, all with cable TV, small refrigerator, private bath with hot water, AC, phone." The rates are very reasonable and certainly less than the above-named hotels.

A word of warning: In San Cristobal, the annual fair honoring San Sebastián at the end of January is THE big event of the year, with all posadas and hotels adjusting rates for 'high season' and demanding a week's reservation.

One of the best places to eat in town is the **Posada del Leñador**, located in the Pasaje El Aqueducto. There is also an excellent steak restaurant called La Vaquera. Follow Avenida Libertador north to the area called Las Lomas. I like their "Parrilla de Lomito" and the mixed salad.

An absolute must in San Cristobal is the ice-cream parlor **Heladería El Che-Lito**, open from 4:00 in the afternoon until quite late. It is a heaven for ice cream addicts (most of my birding friends), situated on Carrera 16 between Calles 20 and 21.

After birding southern Táchira, it is time to head north for more spectacular birds and scenery. (Having said that, I remember how my editor ticks me off for excessive use of adjectives - words such as "spectacular", "beautiful", "fantastic", etc[1]. On the other hand, Beverly Anderson, a biologist from Florida who once accompanied me to Táchira and Mérida, remarked it would be impossible to write about the Andes and not use superlatives.) In any event, many birding sites in Táchira can only be described with superlatives - one of them is Tama National Park. The others follow.

CAMINOS VERDES

In Venezuela back roads are often called *caminos verdes*. The words have also come to designate the roads that illegal immigrants take to cross the frontiers into Venezuela. To make matters confusing, in Táchira these roads are often called a *camellón*, a word that in the Llanos is applied to roads built atop long mounds of dirt so they can be passable during the rainy season, when the savannas flood. I am going to keep it simple - we shall use the term as per its first meaning[2].

I mentioned the wee church in the valley below the inn Posada del Marques. And from Rubio, there is a road that reaches the hamlet of **Coquí**. Drive down past the church and Plaza Bolívar of Rubio. (You cannot miss the church because it is huge for the size of the town.) Go down two blocks to the bridge. Go left and then right towards an area called La Palmita where you cross another bridge, and go left to the cemetery and on to Coquí. There are also "por puestos" or small buses that go from Rubio to Coquí.

From what I could see, Coquí itself consists of one spotlessly-clean cobblestone street, a lovely, small church, a school, general store and a bar, but just before you reach this area there is a road going off to what would be your right towards **La Mulera** (no sign, naturally!). That should be your target, and it is quite a ways to go. At first the road passes through cattle farms but then it goes up into the hills. At times woods are on only one side of the road and the valleys on the other. Often though there are woods on both sides. From the vegetation I would say it reaches approximately 2,000 m.a.s.l. We were in a hurry because we had a very long way to go that day (excuses, excuses!), but from what I could see, it must be one good birding road. The road itself is in good condition and during the dry season, I honestly believe that a normal rental car could make it. We did not see another car all the way to La Mulera. I have made a promise to go back and investigate this road thoroughly.

---

[1] Note from the Editor: I tick her off, but I sympathize. It's awfully hard not to use superlatives to describe Venezuela's natural "splendor" (kindly notice that I am quoting here a classic example of Mary Lou's frumpy qualifiers).

[2] Pamela's Comment: "Caminos Verdes" Mary Lou taught me this term, literally Green Roads - back roads. Taught and showed me, so much so, that now if a trip doesn't include Caminos Verdes, I don't want to go. In fact, another title for this book could be "Birding and Driving the Green Roads..."

Actually, La Mulera is nothing but a few houses, but it is famous for being the birth place of General Juan Vicente Gomez, dictator of Venezuela from 1909 to 1935. Gomez was a wily Andean, cruel and primitive, who did accomplish one great thing - he united the country. Until his rule Venezuela was divided, a boiling pot of skirmishes between various small-time caudillos (local war lords), each one bent on increasing his power and the lands he controlled. But all that finished "in the time of Gomez.", for the moustached and medal-decked general won over all and then, diligently, went about the task of "eliminating" them one by one.

When you reach a T junction at La Mulera-El Recreo, you will see Gomez's house on your right - an old blue-and-white house, and on your left, a very small, insignificant police station. The house is surrounded by a fence, which the policeman will immediately open for you - a foreign visitor!! - to see. Here, the terrifying dictator is revered, and the Mulerians have even put up a statue of the town son who is its one claim to fame.

Should you wish to continue on to that horrible city of **Capacho**, also known as **Independencia**, at the T junction in front of Gomez' house go right and follow the signs that may be painted on rocks, trees or an occasional wall, saying **"Ruta"**. Follow this same route if you plan to continue towards the north. Otherwise turn back to Rubio.

A last word about Rubio - should you be there on a Saturday morning, do not miss the weekly farmers market on the main street. It occupies a whole block and is the most interesting open market I have seen in Venezuela. It is aimed only at the local population, with all of the local fruits, vegetables, fish, meat, etc. etc. etc. This is a good place to see how the local people live.

On the map there is yet another *camino verde* from Capacho/Independencia to the small city of Michelena, another goal for intrepid birders. Unfortunately, the last times I've been near there, we were headed in another direction, and I have had no possibility of investigating that particular road. Next trip, but in the meantime I am trying to find out if anyone knows about the birding on said *camino verde*.

ZUMBADOR

There is one area of Táchira that you absolutely must visit and that is the **Páramo del Zumbador**, followed by the **Queniquea/San José de Bolívar/La Grita Road**.

From San Cristobal, head north towards **Táriba** and **El Cobre**. Within approximately an hour from San Cristobal, you will reach Zumbador, where there is only an Alcabala (National Guard Post), and a humble restaurant on the right that serves the best "Pisca Andina" soup I have ever had. Just in front of the Alcabala, there is a "y" intersection - the right hand road leads to Queniquea.

I prefer to reach Zumbador via Michelena and suggest that from Capacho Nuevo or Independencia, you take the side road to **Peribeca** (an interesting colonial town) to **El Topón**. At **Palo Grande** I believe you will have to link up with the main highway coming from Capacho to Michelena and **San Juan de Colon**. Unfortunately, it has been impossible to secure a decent road map of Táchira, and I know there are multiple side roads not shown on the maps of the nation as a whole. The road between Michelena and Zumbador follows the crests of the mountains, offering fabulous views and very little traffic. There are several inns after Michelena in the event you are too tired to continue on to the very best (see below).

Where to Stay near Zumbador

Located approximately 8 km from Michelena, with the name painted on the façade, the **Posada Turística Montaña Alta** offers spectacular views of surrounding mountains, restaurant service, 5 rooms, but only one with private bath. Has 9 hectares above the road and 5 below with many trails and a lagoon. The congenial owners, Rufo Rosales Castro and his wife, Belkis, personally attend to guests. Phones (0) 414-702-1962 & (0) 414-703-6140.

Posada Turística Estancia de Bolívar

Phones (0) 276-341-5004 or (0) 416-877-4809 & 416-477-0123. Located some 13 km from Michelena in the Aldea Los Hornos. Has a "tasca" (restaurant-bar), game room, 7 rooms.

Some Venezuelan birders recently visited another inn along this road, just 15 minutes from Zumbador, where they rented a whole house, completely furnished, and she reported that there is a small forest behind with a trail that eventually leads to a settlement called **Casa del Padre**. "It seemed to be full of birds." Contact Maite or Rodrigo at (0) 414-714196.

When you come to the crossroads of the Páramo, there is actually an inn which is aptly named **Posada de Los Vientos** (inn of the winds). It is on the second floor of the Cafetín Marisela (the building with the brown balcony) with the name on the sign facing the road coming from San Cristóbal. Five simple rooms, private baths with hot water but no shower curtain. This is very basic, but it is very near the birding area for early morning birding.

Finca La Huerfana

Located approximately 5 km north of Zumbador on the road towards El Cobre. This is it! This is my FAVORITE. The only thing wrong with this inn is that they absolutely should change the name. It was named after the stream that runs through the property. *La Huerfana* means the orphan girl, but it should be called **Sunangel Lodge.** The impudent Orange-throated Sunangels even come to your breakfast table to help themselves to the flower decorations - usually Astromelias. They are all over the grounds. Of course, there are others as well - Sparkling Violetears, Collared Incas, White-sided Flower-piercers, Mérida Flower-piercers, Golden-tailed Sapphires, Black Phoebes, White-throated Flycatchers, Brown-bellied Swallows, Great Thrushes, Rufous-collared Sparrows, etc. The inn has only one single room. The rest are cabins, all with private baths, hot water. The cabins are extremely comfortable and decorated with good taste, complete with fireplaces, but no kitchens. Meal service by prior arrangement and the food is good. There are 80 hectares extending up to the Páramo de Las Agrias with numerous trails for hiking and birdwatching. Contact the very friendly owners, Jenny Martinez and Manuel Tallafero or the Venezuelan Audubon. This is a very home-like inn and I am certain that you will like it as much as I do. They even have copies of the Guide to the Birds of Venezuela for you to consult, with the birds found at La Huerfana duly marked. Suggest you plan to stay at least two nights here. Phone numbers: (0) 277-414-9637 or 416-777-9393, e-mail: lahuerfana@hotmail.com, and www.abbacus.net/lahuerfana.

Posada Los Mirtos

Is somewhat closer to Zumbador than La Huerfana and easily identified by its bright yellow façade. Seven rooms with bath. Strategically located for birding the Zumbador road in the event that La Huerfana is full. Phones: (0) 276-357-9626 & (0) 414-979-6385.

THE QUENIQUEA ROAD

The best way I've found to bird this mind-boggling side-road is to be there very, very early in the morning. Actually, the birding area that matters most is the upper part of the Queniquea road - it is superb for high montane birds. After that, the road deteriorates and is frankly dangerous, especially in the rainy season. You need four to five hours to do justice to the Queniquea road. At approximately 2,400 meters look for Slaty-backed Hemispingus within about a meter from the ground in the bamboo areas. Among others, look for:

Swallow-tailed Kite	Pearled Treerunner	Slate-throated Redstart
Roadside Hawk	Streaked Tuftedcheek	White-faced Redstart
Band-tailed Pigeon	Gray-throated Leafscraper	Black-crested Warbler
Rose-headed Parakeet	Chestnut-crowned Antpitta	Citrine Warbler
Speckle-faced Parrot	Red-crested Cotinga	Russet-crowned Warbler
Squirrel Cuckoo	Green-and-black Fruiteater	Blue-backed Conebill
Little Hermit	Barred Fruiteater	Bluish Flower-piercer
Brown Violetear	Black Phoebe	Masked Flower-piercer
Golden-tailed Sapphire	Torrent Tyrannulet	White-sided Flower-piercer
Violet-fronted Brilliant	White-throated Tyrannulet	Saffron-crowned Tanager
Collared Inca	White-banded Tyrannulet	Beryl-spangled Tanager
Golden-bellied Starfrontlet	Mountain Elaenia	Blue-and-black Tanager
Orange-throated Sunangel	Black-capped Tyrannulet	Blue-capped Tanager
Tyrian Metaltail	Pale-footed Swallow	White-shouldered Tanager
Long-tailed Sylph	Collared Jay	Superciliaried Hemispingus
Wedge-billed Hummingbird	Mountain Wren	Slaty-backed Hemispingus
Emerald Toucanet	Gray-breasted Woodwren	Common Bush-Tanager
Crimson-mantled Woodpecker	Andean Solitaire	Stripe-headed Brush-finch
Spot-crowned Woodcreeper	Great Thrush	Slaty Brush-Finch
White-browed Spinetail	Blackburnian Warbler	Black-and-white Seedeater
Rufous Spinetail	American Redstart	Rufous-collared Sparrow

Another birding adventure I would like to suggest is to take the road all the way to Queniquea, birding the different altitudes as you go down into the valley. From Queniquea continue on to San José de Bolívar and then take the gravel road to **La Grita**. This is to be done **only in the dry season**, but it can then be driven with a normal car. This drive will enable you to do some very good high mountain birding with no traffic to bother you. Upon reaching the small city of La Grita, you can either stay there or drive back to La Huerfana. This is a whole day trip.

On Staying in La Grita
From Zumbador direct to the town of La Grita, it is approximately 34 km. Should you wish to over-night at this town, I suggest the **Hostería Los Naranjos**, a most reasonable place to stay. Clean and simple, situated on Calle 2 No. 371. Phone: (0) 277-881-2678, fax: 881-2854. To find it, go straight up the main street entering La Grita until you reach a large turn on your left. (La Grita is the usual sausage-shaped Andean town). Curve around to the left* and then left again to go back all the way down the busy, traffic-filled shopping street. Los Naranjos is on your right after passing the second large church.

⮞ If by chance you need to buy ice, the best and only place is to be found right after your first turn to the left. I mention this because we had one devil of a time finding ice in La Grita. We could not even find a licorería, and that is a first for Venezuela!

ROAD TO MÉRIDA

If you plan to go north towards Mérida after birding the area of Zumbador, my suggestion would be to go via Las Porqueras (the Pig Farms) towards the town of Bailadores not too far (as the crow flies) after the state border. You will be going through dairy farms at first but eventually as you reach the higher areas with corresponding vegetation and no farms, you should start birding. To reach this particular road, go straight up the main street that enters La Grita from the south. When you reach a plaza with a train car in the middle, go left towards the **Páramo del Batallón National Park**. The road from La Grita continues up and up and then goes vertically down, down to Bailadores. Stop frequently all along the upper part to try your luck, looking for the Red-crested Cotinga and the Andean Siskin in the high areas.

My suggestion would be for you to take the whole day to go from La Huerfana to Bailadores. There is the **Hotel Toquisay** in Bailadores, phone number: (0) 275-70136 & 70192[1]. You should have no problem finding it as the road entering the town practically circles it. From personal experience I would recommend you stay the night here rather than continuing on to the city of Mérida, which is a long ways yet to go.

ALTERNATIVE ROUTE NORTH FROM TÁCHIRA

If you would rather not brave the mountains on your trip north, then take the "Autopista" out of San Cristobal or Capacho, heading north towards **San Juan de Colón** and **La Fría**. From La Fría take State Highway 1 towards El Vigía. Before reaching San Juan de Colón, take a little time and a detour to visit the delightful town of **San Pedro del Río**, with its cobbled streets and white houses. It is a tourist place, but an especially nice one.

Powerful Woodpecker

---

[1] Note from the Editor: Since telephone service is changing to seven-digit numbers in Venezuela, these numbers may change in the not too distant future.

BIRDING AROUND NORTHERN TÁCHIRA

Between San Pedro del Rio and San Juan de Colón, as well as in the coffee plantations to the north of San Juan, you may see the Táchira Emerald (just to prove that it was not a figment of someone's imagination), Blue Cotinga, Black-headed Tody-Flycatcher, Purple-throated Euphonia, White-eared Conebill and such migrants as Bay-breasted and Mourning Warblers plus Black-billed and Yellow-legged Thrushes.

Try birding the coffee groves just north of San Juan. Always remember, of course, to ask permission, but usually the owners have no objection to your visiting their lands. Try your luck at some 6 km after San Juan (on the left or west side of the road). Next you will be driving over a bridge high above a river. Try birding around here as well. Some 11 km further you should bird the coffee groves again. All of these instructions are from times way past, and I am not too certain that they are still valid, but the general area should be excellent still.

The road from San Juan de Colón to La Fría is very heavily traveled, but has many side roads (mostly dirt) that can be investigated. I suspect that most of them will offer something of interest. I followed one that was 8.7 km south of the turn-off for La Grita and was rewarded with Black-mandibled and Yellow-ridged Toucans, Crimson-backed Tanager and a Gray-headed Kite.

Olga Garcia, a Venezuelan birder, wrote that 9 km after La Fria she passed two bridges. The first was called Carira II and the second had no name but was probably Carira. After the second bridge she took the first dirt road to the right. This road goes for 6 km through farms (full of birds according to Olga) and then it goes up the mountain to join the road that goes from Caño Hondo to Las Mesas and on to La Grita.

Some 7 to 10 km south of El Vigía there is a dam on the east side. The paved road to the dam cuts off the main road at a very shallow angle just south of a large bridge. The road curves around to the dam and a side road cuts off to the right just before. Dick Ryan drove across the dam with no problem and into the woods beyond, where he found Band-tailed Guan and Black Caracara. He warned about the traffic bumps, recently installed at the beginning of the dam, that are indeed impressive - *If one has an ordinary car, make everyone except the driver get out. Then cross them very, very slowly.*

Just about any dirt road you may take along here will be rewarding.

Birds of the Area of San Juan de Colon / La Fria

Little Tinamou	Yellow-ridged Toucan	Social Flycatcher
Black Vulture	Scaled Piculet	Dusky-capped Flycatcher
Turkey Vulture	Red-crowned Woodpecker	Tropical Pewee
Gray-headed Kite	Red-rumped Woodpecker	Yellow-olive Flycatcher
Swallow-tailed Kite	Pale-breasted Spinetail	Black-headed Tody-Flycatcher
Roadside Hawk	White-fringed Antwren	Common Tody-Flycatcher
Ruddy Ground-Dove	Blue Cotinga	Yellow-bellied Elaenia
White-tipped Dove	Chestnut-crowned Becard	Forest Elaenia
Green-rumped Parrotlet	Cinnamon Becard	Greenish Elaenia
Yellow-billed Cuckoo	Black-tailed Tityra	Golden-faced Tyrannulet
Smooth-billed Ani	Black Phoebe	Southern Rough-
Striped Cuckoo	Tropical Kingbird	winged Swallow
White-necked Jacobin	Piratic Flycatcher	Gray-breasted Wood-Wren
Táchira Emerald (?)	Boat-billed Flycatcher	Nightingale Wren
Rufous-tailed Hummingbird	Streaked Flycatcher	Yellow-legged Thrush
Black-mandibled Toucan	Rusty-margined Flycatcher	Black-billed Thrush

Bare-eyed Thrush	Mourning Warbler	Crimson-backed Tanager
Rufous-browed Peppershrike	Canada Warbler	White-lined Tanager
Red-eyed Vireo	Bananaquit	Guira Tanager
Brown-capped Vireo	White-eared Conebill	Buff-throated Saltator
Golden-fronted Greenlet	Purple-throated Euphonia	Streaked Saltator
Crested Oropendola	Thick-billed Euphonia	Blue-black Grassquit
Yellow-rumped Cacique	Blue-necked Tanager	Gray Seedeater
Tennessee Warbler	Bay-headed Tanager	Yellow-bellied Seedeater
Tropical Parula	Burnished-buff Tanager	Ruddy-breasted Seedeater
Bay-breasted Warbler	Blue-gray Tanager	Black-striped Sparrow
Northern Waterthrush	Palm Tanager	Wedge-tailed Grass-Finch

As to where you might pass a night along here, just after you pass the state line into Mérida, there is a road going right towards **Zea** and **Tovar**. In the town of Zea there is a perfectly acceptable small hotel called Murmuquena. Your best bet then would be to drive on to the city of Tovar the next morning and then on to the charming city of Mérida

On the other hand, if you wish to go all the way to El Vigia, you could then take the new, beautiful tunnel road up the mountain to Mérida.

Section V

THE LLANOS

Country and Regional Endemics:

Yellow-knobbed Curassow
Bare-eyed Pigeon
Dwarf Cuckoo
Copper-rumped Hummingbird
Pale-headed Jacamar
Russet-throated Puffbird
White-bearded Flycatcher
Venezuelan Flycatcher
Orange-crowned Oriole
Orinocan Saltator

V - 1. Introduction

A look at the map of Venezuela will show you how a long line of mountains marches along the coast across northern Venezuela, forming the range called the "Cordillera de la Costa". These mountains are an effective barrier between the Caribbean Sea and a vast expanse of plains that lie at the center of the country. **Those inland prairies, a wide arch of land known as the Llanos**, represent almost one third of Venezuelan territory, bound in the west by the Venezuelan and Colombian Andes, to the north by the Coastal Cordillera and to the southeast by the mighty Orinoco River.

Looking at the lay of the terrain and the landscape, one realizes that there are really two distinct Llanos: the High Llanos - a country of rolling hills and random forest tracts, skirting the mountains all the way from the State of Anzoátegui, across southern Aragua, northern Guarico and Cojedes, to Portuguesa and western Barinas; and the Low Llanos, a land of flood plains, of vast open spaces and endless horizon, sweeping over southern Guárico, eastern Barinas and Apure.

The Low Llanos represent perhaps the ideal of the Llanos every Venezuelan carries in his heart, a scenery aptly described by the Venezuelan writer Rómulo Gallegos in his novel "Doña Bárbara". Gallegos said one could look in any direction to *"más allá del más nunca"* - farther than never more. And it is these immense Low Llanos that will grant to a visiting birder some of the most extraordinary birds and unforgettable images of his entire trip to Venezuela.

Everywhere in the Llanos, the land slopes ever so gradually towards the Orinoco. During the rainy season, from May to November, the great river carries massive outflows from the vast rainforests that lie on the southern parts of its watershed. This increased flow acts like a dike, holding up the flow of the northern rivers. The stoppered water spills over the plains, flooding much of the lower Llanos.

The flooding happens very quickly and remains for some months, until the rains stop, the dry season returns, the waters recede and the savannas gradually turn yellow. This cycle of birth and death, of growth and decay, has been describing its circular path since the end of the Eocene, some 20 million years ago, when the Llanos finally rose from the sea (see below, the segment entitled "A Young Land").

To understand how so much of the Llanos floods, one must realize how flat the land is, a fact that is easy to see if one considers that at its *upper* basin by the Caño Casiquiare, at a point that is 2,000 kms from the sea, the Orinoco is barely 114 meters above sea level! The quantity of water that falls on the Llanos during the rainy season is colossal - from the north and the west, the flooded rivers are draining the entire eastern slope of the Andes and the entire southern side of the Coastal Mountain Range into the Orinoco.

When the rains arrive, travel by land becomes impossible, except on roads built on a *camellón* or a *terraplén* (see below, in the segment on Words). For all living things , it is time for re-birth - fish, frogs, insects, cayman, the palms, the trees, the reeds and grasses, everything springs to reproduction, life and effervescence. Most of the insectivorous birds of the Llanos nest during this beginning of the rainy season, from April or May through June and July.

On the other hand, at the peak of the dry season, when the seasonal wetlands have turned to dusty, empty bowls, great concentrations of birds gather at the remaining streams and water holes. It is a spectacle of nature, a vision from the dawn of time, as beautiful and stunning as few others in the world.

With so much water moving through the seasons, the Llanos are undeniably waterfowl country, but they are also raptor country. A birder can easily spot more than a dozen species in one day as they glide and spy their prey over the endless pastures. Also, there are the birds of the galleries and other scattered patches of forest - many species of flycatchers, Pale-headed and Rufous-tailed Jacamars, Russet-throated Puffbirds, Gray-Necked Wood-Rails, Yellow-knobbed Curassows - and the birds of the grasslands - Burrowing Owls, Southern Lapwings, Thick-knees, wandering bands of seedeaters...

Visitors sensitive to magic will receive from the Llanos another special gift - an indelible memory to take with them - the opening of the starry firmament after nightfall. It does not matter if the constellations of these equatorial skies are not familiar - the Llanos give the viewer a million stars and the beauty of the entire vault of heavens, the entire circle of the horizon, regardless of the direction he looks[1].

If you wish for a wonderful description of the feelings an experience of the Llanos can elicit, I recommend you pick the one written by Steven Hilty in an article published in American Birds[2]. And before I forget, let me recommend also the best time of the year for a bird watcher to visit the Llanos, which is the dry season, when the birds congregate at the water holes.

▣ In addition to the general description which opens this Section, there are a few specific aspects of these lands, such as the geology, the people, economy, local idioms and general wildlife notions that are worthy of a few lines.

A YOUNG LAND

Geologically speaking, the Llanos are the among the newest lands of Venezuela. They formed after the rising of the Andes, which occurred in several stages as a consequence of continued pushing and encroaching by the Caribbean Plate on the Continental Plate of Venezuela.

Once the Andes and the Coastal Cordillera began to rise, a great inland sea was formed, enclosed by the new mountains on the west and north and by the old ones, the highlands of Guayana, on the south, but open to the ocean on the east. The Orinoco did not exist. Instead many of the rivers that we know today, including the Caura and especially the Caroní, poured into this vast bay that extended all the way to Colombia.

As the new mountains took shape, huge amounts of sediments were washed down, and the inland sea began to silt up, receding gradually from the south and west towards the east and north. Erosion was also occurring on the southern mountains. The Caroní was one of the great suppliers of sand - it had a delta, with extensive marshes protected behind sand bars. The Caura and the Aro also had deltas.

By the end of the Eocene period (approximately 20 million years ago) Apure and Barinas were already above water. During the Pliocene period, what we know today as the Llanos was, for the most part, a delta sort of environment.

The Galeras, those curious, craggy low hills that crop up randomly in the Llanos in Guarico, Cojedes and Apure, have a tectonic origin, different from the plains around them.

---

[1] Pamela's Comment: It is a wonderous thing to be able to see both the North Star and the Southern Cross in the night sky at the same time.

[2] Issue of Fall, 1992. Vol. 46: No. 3: 360-368.

ECONOMY FOR A FRAIL BALANCE

The Low Llanos, especially eastern Barinas and the State of Apure, are among the economically poorest regions of Venezuela, neglected and ignored by political parties and governments except at elections times. And yet, there are as many hair-brained development schemes for the Llanos as for the forests south of the Orinoco. Over the years, governments have made plans to drain them completely for agriculture, a disastrous idea because the soil is so poor and acidic; or to dredge and channel the rivers in order to promote east-west movement of goods by river barges. Aside from digging us ever deeper into debt and providing a grab-bag for corrupt politicians, these mirages of riches would terminate the budding ecotourism industry and the traditional extensive cattle ranching.

This latter activity emerged from the delicate balance that nature maintains in these prairies: the natural grasses are low in nutrients, so each head of cattle needs around two hectares to provide it with sufficient food. Planting better pasture species has often proved economically unfeasible. What works are large ranches, where the cattle literally roam free.

Every year, the herds are moved to lower terrain during the "summer" (the dry season) to take advantage of the fresh shoots that grow briefly when the waters recede, and then, to escape the floods, they are moved back to higher ground during the "winter" (the rainy season). The move may involve long treks across many kilometers of savanna and a number of streams. The Llanero ranch hands that escort a *punta de ganado,* as a herd is called, spend the nights under the stars and the days on horse back, whistling melancholy *tonadas* as they go.

Fulvous Whistling Ducks

THE PEOPLE

A description of the scenery and the wildlife of the Llanos tells only half the story. The other half are the *Llaneros,* the people of the Llanos, who are unique in so many ways. I am extremely fond of Llaneros, their music and their ways.

The music, accompanied by three instruments - a small and somewhat primitive version of a harp; the *cuatro,* a four-string guitar, and the *maracas* (rattlers) - is perhaps what would be considered true Venezuelan folk music.

The songs make frequent mention of the wildlife and flora of the Llanos, as do the sayings, which are always witty and often show how well the Llaneros know their animals. Just look at these Llanero bits of wisdom: *Cachicamo llamando a morrocoy conchudo* - armadillo calling the tortoise thick-skinned. *El Cubiro pia cuando hay un extraño* - the Rusty-margined Flycatcher warns when a stranger approaches. *Si canta la Chiricoca es que va a llover* - if the Wood-Rail sings, it is going to rain.

There is no one like a Llanero for nailing you with the exact nick-name - they will describe a self-assured person as singing, whistling and jumping like a *Tordito* (Carib Grackle), and a dull one as sleepier than a *Bobito* (Puffbird).

To the foreigner (and in this case, even a Caraqueño would be a foreigner), one very perplexing trait is that Llaneros will never disagree with you - it would be discourteous! Therefore, conversations with a Llanero tend to run into the surreal:

«Have you seen a tiger (jaguar) in this ranch recently?»
«Oh yes, many times!»
«But they tell me that they were all hunted out many years ago!?»
«Oh yes, they were all wiped out!»
«But you say you saw one recently?»
«Oh yes, he was around and then he went away.»

It would not surprise me to find them agreeing if I said it is snowing, but then, they would turn around to their friends and comment, in their own particular brand of Spanish, that the poor señora *musiu* (foreigner - from the French *Monsieur)* is completely *loca.*

Another confusing trait is a knack for underestimating distances and times. If you ask for directions and they tell you it is *aquí mismito* (right near here), beware! [1]

THE WORDS

Many words and idioms in the Venezuelan vernacular come from the Llanos. Some describe physical features of the land; others, the wildlife; yet others, the tools and items of daily living.

A **Banco** is a slightly elevated area that does not flood during the rainy season. Here is where you will see trees or bushes, and where many of the flycatchers and other birds roost and nest. Where the bancos are high enough, often a miniature jungle has developed over the centuries. These isolated patches are called **Matas**. You see them in the distance in the Low Llanos - large emeralds jutting out amid the sea of yellow grasses.

A **Bajío** is a slightly lower area that floods gradually during the rainy season, but dries out and is exposed in the dry season. As the bajíos dry up, the birds congregate in large numbers to fish in the remaining waters. Turtles nest in the bajíos at the end

---

[1] Pamela's Comment: And if you ask how long it will take to get somewhere, the answer is always, "Veinte minutos" - 20 minutes!

of the dry season, and when the rains come moistening the soil, the young are able to dig out of their nests.

The **Esteros** are the lowest lands of all, the areas which remain flooded throughout the year. They play a fundamental role in the life cycles of fish and other animals. The most famous and largest in all the Llanos is the Estero de Camaguan, which you will pass on the right of the road, if you drive from Calabozo to San Fernando de Apure.

The **Galeras**, as I mention above, are rocky outcrops that rise abruptly from the plains. They originated from volcanic activity. In the State of Cojedes, there are some near the Pao River, and in the state of Apure, some near the Cinaruco. Also, a few others can be seen in Barinas and Guarico.

Morichales are stands of Moriche Palms, *Mauritia flexuosa,* which only grow in boggy or marshy areas. Though often very small in surface, they are very specialized ecosystems, and have a number of species of mammals, birds, reptiles and plants that are associated almost exclusively with them.

A **Camellón** is a long and narrow mound of dirt built to support a dirt trail on top that will be traversable year-around. It is often built also as a dike. A **Terraplen** is the same thing, except wider and longer, usually built to support a frequently-used road

A **Prestamo** is a large, shallow borrowing pit, dug out to "lend" the soil for the construction of a terraplén or camellón. (In Spanish, *préstamo* means loan.) All the roads of the Low Llanos are followed by series of préstamos on one side or the other. These pits fill with water during the rainy season, thus turning into wetlands for all the fauna. If deep and large enough, they turn into permanent bodies of water and provide a watering place during the long months of relentless dry heat.

A **Falso** is a gate. Basically, it is a segment of the ubiquitous barbed-wire fence that can be untied and moved aside to let a car or a herd of cattle (called a **Punta**), go through.

A **Guachiman** is a guard or gatekeeper. The word comes from the English "watch-man", and in the same manner does **Guaya**, a rope or cable, derive from "wire".

A **Fundo** is a small homestead, often a segment of a much larger Hato, or cattle ranch. The huge Hatos, many thousands of acres in surface, are usually managed by subdividing them into fundos, each fundo having its own resident manager.

When something is abundant, for example Ground-Doves or Mastranto (a small, wide-spread, lavender-smelling bush), the Llaneros will say that it is found "**como arroz**", like rice, or sometimes "**como humo**", like smoke.

DANGERS

A visit to these wide open plains requires planning and a certain amount of fortitude. Since I believe it wiser in the long run to warn guests of possible pitfalls, here are the main ones, so you may be prepared and truly enjoy your experience in this magic land.

First, the inconveniences to be encountered: Be prepared for intense heat at midday and avoid heat stress. Never take the sun lightly - it can burn you to a crisp in a matter of minutes! In any event, birds are active early in the morning and late in the afternoon. But be sure you have ample supplies of drinking water or refreshments with you, and wear a hat. During the rainy season count on true tropical rainstorms, mud, heat and insects.

The bane of the Llanos are chiggers and ticks[1], and mosquitoes in the rainy season. Come prepared to combat them with boots and long cotton socks over your trousers.

---

[1] Lyme Disease does not exist in Venezuela. Aside from itching, chigger and tick bites are harmless.

Wear long-sleeved shirts and shower as soon as possible, when you return to your hotel or camp. When you have been in a chigger-infested area (such as tall grasses or a pasture) do not use the same clothes twice without washing them first. One other important advice is never to swim in the rivers of the Llanos. Sting rays and piranhas, (called *rayas* and *caribes* in Venezuela) are always present. By taking these elementary precautions, you should avoid discomfort and have a birding experience to treasure for the rest of your life. Just the visit to the Llanos of Apure is worth a trip to Venezuela.

V - 2. Wildlife of the Llanos

The following lists - **Mammals**, **Reptiles** and **Amphibians** - represent general lists for each group, that is, the species found everywhere in the Llanos, *that there is a likelihood of seen*. For the mammals we thank Professor Omar Linares, of the Simón Bolívar University, and for the reptiles and amphibians, Herpetologist Alfredo Paolillo.

MAMMALS MOST COMMONLY SEEN

English Name	Venezuelan/Spanish Name	Scientific Name
Common Opossum	Rabipelao	*Didelphis marsupialis*
Giant Anteater	Oso Palmero	*Myrmecophaga tridactyla*
Tamandua Anteater	Osito Melero	*Tamandua tetradactyla*
Three-toed Sloth	Pereza	*Bradypus variegatus*
Savanna Armadillo	Cachicamo	*Dasypus savanicola*
Dark Sac-winged Bat	Murcielago de Rayas	*Saccopteryx bilineata*
Fishing Bat	Murcielago Pescador Grande	*Noctilio leporinus*
Weeping Capuchin Monkey	Mono Capuchino	*Cebus olivaceus*
Red Howler Monkey	Araguato	*Alouatta seniculus*
Savanna Fox	Zorro Común	*Cerdocyon thous*
Crab-eating Raccoon	Zorro Lavamanos or Cangrejero	*Procyon cancrivorous*
Striped Hog-nosed Skunk	Mapurite	*Conepatus semistriatus*
Tayra	Zorro Guache	*Eira barbara*
Giant Otter	Perro de Agua	*Pteronura brasiliensis*
Ocelot	Cunaguaro	*Leopardus pardalis*
Jaguarundi	Onza	*Herpailurus yagouaroundi*
Puma	Puma	*Puma concolor*
Jaguar	Tigre	*Panthera onca*
River Dolphin	Tonina de Río	*Innia geoffrensis*
Red Brocket Deer	Locha or Venado Matacan	*Mazama americana*
Gray Brocket Deer	Locha or Venado Matacan	*Mazama guazubira*
White-tailed Deer	Venado Caramerudo	*Odocoileus virginianus*
Red-tailed Squirrel	Ardilla	*Sciurus granatensis*
Capybara	Chigüire	*Hydrochaerus hydrochaerus*
Red Agouti	Picure	*Dasyprocta leporina*
Rabbit	Conejo	*Sylvilagus floridanus*

REPTILES MOST COMMONLY SEEN

English Name	Venezuelan/ Spanish Name	Scientific Name
Spectacled Cayman	Baba	Caiman crocodilus
Green Iguana	Iguana	Iguana iguana
Tegu Lizard	Mato Real	Tupinambis teguixin
	Mato	Ameiva ameiva
	Guaripete	Tropidurus torquatus
Gecko	Tuqueque	Thecadactylus rapicaudus
Llanos Pond Turtle	Galapago Llanero	Podocnemis vogli
Yellow-head Sideneck Turtle	Terecay	Podocnemis unifilis
Red-footed Tortoise	Morrocoy Sabanero	Geochelone carbonaria
Boa	Tragavenados	Boa Constrictor
Anaconda	Anaconda	Eunectes murinus
Rattle Snake	Cascabel	Crotalus durissus
	Verdegallo	Chironius carinatus
Whiptail Lizard	Verdin	Cnemidophorus lemniscatus

AMPHIBIANS MOST COMMONLY SEEN

English Name	Venezuelan/ Spanish Name	Scientific Name
Tree Frog	Rana Platanera	Hyla crepitans
		Ololygon x-squata
Common Frog	Sapito Lipón	Pleurodera brachyops
Whistling Frog	Rana Silbadora	Liptodactilus fuscus
		Physalaemus pustulosos
		Hyla misera
Marine Toad	Sapo Común	Bufo marinus
	Sapito Granuloso	Bufo granulosus
	Rana Lechera	Phrynohyas venulosa
	Rana Piscua	Elachistocleis ovalis

CAPYBARA

Probably the mammal that most captivates first-time visitors to the Llanos is the Capybara, the world's largest rodent, also known as a water rat. They do spend a large part of their time in the water in rather large family groups, and the young especially are adorable. But, aside from the fact that they are herbivorous, their ability to digest grasses and how they do so is anther fascinating facet of this mammal. Since grasses are generally poor in nutrients, herbivorous mammals need to eat large amounts to survive. This is the reason why they forage during most of the day, and often part of the night. Grasses consist mostly of cellulose, a material that does not decompose into nutrients in the digestive system. However, the digestive tract of most herbivores contains symbiotic bacteria which aid in the assimilation of cellulose by biochemically decomposing it. The Capybara, have developed additional nutritional strategies. The bacteria that decompose cellulose are found in their rectum. Therefore, they are not able to decompose it during its first passage through the intestine. So they practice what is technically called *Coprophagy* - they eat their own feces, to assimilate cellulose. That is the reason they seem so inactive during the mornings, when they are simply recycling the grasses they ate the previous afternoon and evening.

The Capybara, is ponderous, barrel-shaped and stand very low to the ground. Therefore, at any threat they take to the water where they spend most of the time they are not foraging on land. They are excellent swimmers and even copulate in the water.

A GENERAL BIRD LIST FOR THE LLANOS

This list is based on the one compiled by Betsy Trent Thomas for the renowned Masaguaral Ranch, in western Guárico, seat of the Smithsonian Research Station. I chose it as the basic list for the Llanos, in part due to Masaguaral's central location in relation to the entire extension of the Venezuelan Llanos, and in part because its compiler had worked with and knew the birds of the Llanos better than anyone else I know. As we go through the various sites, I will give you any additional species recorded for each place.

Red-legged Tinamou	Bare-faced Ibis	Bicolored Hawk
Least Grebe	White Ibis	White-tailed Hawk
Neotropical Cormorant	Scarlet Ibis	Zone-tailed Hawk
Anhinga	Glossy Ibis	Roadside Hawk
Cocoi Heron	Roseate Spoonbill	Gray -lined Hawk
Great Egret	Horned Screamer	Bay-winged (Harris) Hawk
Snowy Egret	Fulvous Whistling-Duck	Black-collared Hawk
Little Blue Heron	White-faced Whistling-Duck	Savanna Hawk
Striated Heron	Black-bellied Whistling-Duck	Great Black Hawk
Cattle Egret	Blue-winged Teal	Crane Hawk
Whistling Heron	Comb Duck	Osprey
Capped Heron	Muscovy Duck	Laughing Falcon
Black-crowned Night Heron	King Vulture	Collared Forest-Falcon
Yellow-crowned Night Heron	Black Vulture	Yellow-headed Caracara
Rufescent Tiger Heron	Turkey Vulture	Crested Caracara
Boat-billed Heron	Lesser Yellow-headed Vulture	Bat Falcon
Wood Stork	White-tailed Kite	Aplomado Falcon
Maguari Stork	Pearl Kite	American Kestrel
Jabiru	Gray-headed Kite	Rufous-vented Chachalaca
Buff-necked Ibis	Hook-billed Kite	Yellow-knobbed Curassow
Sharp-tailed Ibis	Snail Kite	Crested Bobwhite
Green Ibis	Slender-billed Kite	Limpkin

Gray-necked Wood-Rail
Paint-billed Crake
Purple Gallinule
Azure Gallinule
Sunbittern
Wattled Jacana
Southern Lapwing
Solitary Sandpiper
Greater Yellowlegs
Spotted Sandpiper
Least Sandpiper
Common Snipe
Black-necked Stilt
Double-striped Thick-Knee
Black Skimmer
Bare-eyed Pigeon
Pale-vented Pigeon
Eared Dove
Plain-breasted Ground-Dove
Ruddy Ground-Dove
Blue Ground-Dove
Scaled Dove
White-tipped Dove
Scarlet Macaw
Brown-throated Parakeet
Green-rumped Parrotlet
Orange-chinned Parakeet
Yellow-crowned Parrot
Hoatzin
Dwarf Cuckoo
Yellow-billed Cuckoo
Dark-billed Cuckoo
Gray-capped Cuckoo
Squirrel Cuckoo
Greater Ani
Smooth-billed Ani
Groove-billed Ani
Striped Cuckoo
Barn Owl
Great Horned Owl
Spectacled Owl
Ferruginous Pygmy-Owl
Burrowing Owl
Striped Owl
Great Potoo
Common Potoo
Lesser Nighthawk
Nacunda Nighthawk
Pauraque
White-tailed Nightjar
Spot-tailed Nightjar

Fork-tailed Palm-Swift
Black-throated Mango
Ruby-Topaz Hummingbird
Blue-chinned Sapphire
Blue-tailed Emerald
White-tailed Goldenthroat
Glittering-throated Emerald
Copper Rumped Hummingbird
Amethyst Woodstar
Ringed Kingfisher
Amazon Kingfisher
Green Kingfisher
American Pygmy Kingfisher
Pale-headed Jacamar
Rufous-tailed Jacamar
Russet-throated Puffbird
Scaled Piculet
Spot-breasted Woodpecker
Lineated Woodpecker
Red-crowned Woodpecker
Red-rumped Woodpecker
Crimson-crested Woodpecker
Straight-billed Woodcreeper
Streak-headed Woodcreeper
Red-billed Scythebill
Pale-breasted Spinetail
Yellow-chinned Spinetail
Common Thornbird
Streaked Xenops
Black-crested Antshrike
Barred Antshrike
White-fringed Antwren
Cinereous Becard
White-winged Becard
Black-crowned Tityra
Lance-tailed Manakin
Pied Water-tyrant
White-headed Marsh-tyrant
Vermilion Flycatcher
Yellow-browed Tyrant **
Cattle Tyrant
Fork-tailed Flycatcher
Tropical Kingbird
Gray Kingbird
Variegated Flycatcher
Piratic Flycatcher
Boat-billed Flycatcher
Streaked Flycatcher
Rusty-margined Flycatcher
Social Flycatcher
White-bearded Flycatcher

Great Kiskadee
Lesser Kiskadee
Short-crested Flycatcher
Brown-crested Flycatcher
Dusky-capped Flycatcher
Fuscous Flycatcher
Bran-colored Flycatcher
Yellow-breasted Flycatcher
Common Tody-Flycatcher
Slate-headed Tody-Flycatcher
Pale-eyed Pygmy-Tyrant
Yellow Tyrannulet
Pale-tipped Tyrannulet
Yellow-bellied Elaenia
Small-billed Elaenia
Plain-crested Elaenia
Lesser Elaenia
Forest Elaenia
Mouse-colored Tyrannulet
Southern Beardless
  Tyrannulet
White-winged Swallow
Gray-breasted Martin
Blue-and-white Swallow
Southern Rough-winged
  Swallow
Bank Swallow
Barn Swallow
Bicolored Wren
Stripe-backed Wren
Buff-breasted Wren
House Wren
Tropical Mockingbird
Veery
Pale-breasted Thrush
Bare-eyed Thrush
Tropical Gnatcatcher
Rufous-browed Peppershrike
Red-eyed Vireo
Golden-fronted Greenlet
Scrub Greenlet
Shiny Cowbird
Yellow-rumped Cacique
Carib Grackle
Yellow-hooded Blackbird
Orange-crowned Oriole
Troupial
Yellow Oriole
Oriole Blackbird
Red-breasted Blackbird
Eastern Meadowlark

Bobolink	Glaucous Tanager	Blue-black Grassquit
Northern Waterthrush	Palm Tanager	Large-billed Seed-finch
American Redstart	White-lined Tanager	Gray Seedeater
Chestnut-vented Conebill	Hooded Tanager	Lined Seedeater
Bananaquit	Guira Tanager	Lesson´s Seedeater
Tropical Parula	Grayish Saltator	Ruddy-breasted Seedeater
Trinidad Euphonia	Orinocan Saltator	Saffron Finch
Thick-billed Euphonia	Red-capped Cardinal	Pileated Finch
Burnished-buff Tanager	Blue-black Grosbeak	Black-striped Sparrow
Blue-gray Tanager	Dickcissel	Grassland Sparrow

** Although the Yellow-browed Tyrant is indicated in the "Guide to the Birds of Venezuela" as being a migrant from the south, it is, in reality, a scarce permanent resident of the low Llanos of Apure and southern Guarico State.

ONE IMPORTANT BIRDING TIP

If you want to see Whistling Heron or Double-striped Thick-Knee when in the Llanos, look for them out on the savannas or on the *bancos*. They don't hang around the water holes.

Pied Lapwing

A YEAR IN THE LLANOS

A team of hard-working Audubonians, including Nicla Camerin, Clemencia Rodner, Viviana Salas and others, put together a **Calendar of Natural Events in Venezuela.** From that and from my own experience, I have extracted a few items for the Llanos:

January	Sideneck Turtles laying eggs.
	Few mosquitoes and bugs.
February & March	Birds of prey nesting.
	Huge concentrations of wildlife at remaining water bodies.
	Vermilion Flycatchers nesting.
	Lots of vertebrates die due to drought.
	Few mosquitoes and bugs.
April & May	Llanos Sideneck Turtles are born.
	Iguanas are born.
	Savanna Armadillos are born.
June & July	Frogs singing and pairing.
	Egrets & ibises forming huge nesting concentrations.
	Lots of mosquitoes and bugs.
July & August	Many insectivorous birds nesting including Pied Water Tyrant.
	Concentration of egrets & ibises continues in nesting areas.
	Spectacle Caymans on nests.
	Ducks nesting.
	Lots of mosquitoes and bugs.
August & September	Yellow-rumped Caciques nesting.
	Egrets & ibises begin to disperse.
October	American Wood Storks replace egrets & ibises at nesting concentrations.
	Most Capybara are born.
	Most White-tailed Deer are born.
November	Storks & Roseate Spoonbills on nests.
	Young Spectacled Caymans in streams and ponds.
December	Storks and Roseate Spoonbills still at nesting areas.

V - 3. Birding the Llanos

Birding in the Llanos is somewhat different from birding elsewhere, mainly because almost all the areas one would wish to visit are private lands. Therefore, instead of the democratic opportunities we birders find in the national parks and wild lands of other regions of Venezuela, here we have to deal with access to private property.

One thing I want to make sure to warn you about is that these are turbulent times in the Llanos - cattle rustling is extremely common and the farmers and ranch owners are facing severe personal security problems. *Do not trespass anywhere.* You could be mistaken for a bandit of some kind *and shot.*

There are TWO OPTIONS for birding the Llanos, the main differences between the two being comfort and cost.

The first option is a visit to one (or more) of the various private cattle ranches, called **Hatos**, which receive nature tourists. Their prices, as well as their services, vary considerably, but still come out more expensive than the second option. Without exception, for all the Hatos, **you must have a previous, pre-paid reservation.**

The second option is birding from the **roads**, and here, I give you two that in my experience can produce as many species, and as satisfying a birding outing as any *inside* trip in an Hato.

One exception to all this is the **Cinaruco-Capanaparo National Park.**

V - 4. The Hatos

Before going into the detail of the various hatos, I would like to emphasize that if you have the Audubon de Venezuela make your arrangements for you, while there is no additional cost to you, the Audubon does receive a commission from the hatos that otherwise would stay in the pocket of the hatos. The funds raised by the Audubon in this manner go towards their conservation and scientific projects.

STATE OF GUARICO

Hato La Fe
I mention this lodge first due to the fact that it borders onto Hato Masaguaral and, as a guest of La Fe, you are taken there to bird. In fact, this is the only way to obtain entrance to Masaguaral, the world-renowned birding area of Venezuela due to decades of scientific investigations carried out at this hato.

To reach this lodge you should drive due south from Caracas, as if you were heading towards Maracay. Approximately 19.7 km after the Caracas toll booth of Tazón, take the second exit from the autopista, heading towards **Charallave.** Then on towards **Cua, San Sebastián, Camatagua.** Some 14 km after the crossroads to Camatagua and almost immediately after going over a bridge, you come to a split in

---

[1] Pamela's Comment: The potholes were so big when we drove this road in February, 2001, that my husband called them "moon craters."

the road where the right fork will take you towards **El Sombrero** and eventually **Calabozo**. **Caveat**: from the crossroads south, as long as you are in the state of Aragua, the road is quite good, but once you cross over into the state of Guarico, it becomes a nightmare. This is nothing new. The problem has existed for decades and it is not due to the fact that it is heavily traveled by trucks at night. The road will be fixed, and within a short length of time, it is once again full of potholes. [1] I have always maintained that this situation is due to the corruption prevalent in the state of Guárico – bet you they cut corners in the expensive ingredients of paving mix. Fortunately, once you reach the main east/west highway where you turn right or west, the road improves. After a few kilometers, as you approach El Sombrero, you will find several gas stations and eating places and then a bridge. Before crossing the bridge, turn left or south towards Calabozo. As usual, there is no sign indicating this is the road to Calabozo. You still have almost 140 km to travel. You should pass the city of Calabozo on the outskirts and travel due south. At the southern end of the city is a bridge going over what is left of the Guárico River (after the dam of the same name). From here it is 52 km to an area known as **Corozo Pando**, where you will first see a gas station and then a National Guard post on the left. The entrance to the hato is on the right across the road from the National Guard.

I would be tempted to give this lodge 5 stars (as least as far as birding is concerned) were it not for the fact that of the 8 double rooms only 3 have private baths. The remaining 5 rooms share two bathrooms. That is the only nit-picking drawback I have regarding La Fe. The hospitality is extremely warm and outgoing; the food is superlative, and the birding!!!!! They offer options of lodging alone (there is also a small kitchen for the use of guests), lodging with breakfast and dinner or a complete option of three meals and excursions. Their prices are somewhat lower than those at Piñero or El Cedral. Advance reservations required with full payment due at least 72 hours prior to arrival. For reservations either contact the Venezuelan Audubon or Piedras Vivas Turismo: Phone (0) 212-959-7393; fax: (0) 212-959-1718; e-mail: soreliafranco@hotmail.com.

Regarding birding, let me give you a hint. For me the best time to go to La Fe is towards the end of the rainy season; that is the end of November or at least by mid January. Better yet go in mid December. La Fe has a gorgeous, incredibly beautiful wet land or caño, and you must go there while the water is still deep enough to go out at 5:00 a.m. on their boat. I went out at dawn on a clear December morning and watched the sun come up in the east spotlighting the nests of Maguari Storks. Those are the best photographs I have ever taken of the Llanos. We watched the Scarlet Ibis slowly abandoning their rookery along with all the other ibises, egrets and herons. They also advised me at that time that they are in the process of importing an electric engine to avoid the noise of the outboard motor.

STATE OF COJEDES

Hato Piñero

This 80,000 hectare or 197,680 acre hato is located in the High Llanos, near the town of **El Baul,** in the State of **Cojedes**. It is, without a doubt, the best-known of all the "birding" Hatos. It is also the most expensive, but so far, their service to birders has been in accordance with the price.

As a consequence of its location, Piñero offers more varied habitats than the ranches of the Low Llanos, and you will find a lot of undisturbed habitat.

The Government has granted Private Wildlife Sanctuary status to the ranch. The Branger family, who own the ranch, banned hunting on their land almost 50 years ago, with the result that birds and mammals are easily seen and enjoyed.

A friend who visited Piñero some time back was delighted to find that the ease of viewing applied not only to birds but also to mammals, such as Howlers, Capybaras, Deers, Tamanduas and Foxes, which he found everywhere. During the after-dark excursions, one finds not only Owls, Nightjars and Potoos, but also Jaguarundy, Taira and many other resident mammals.

The guest lodge is gorgeous, hand built in the traditional style with bare wood beams, white-washed plastered walls and decorated with exquisite taste; eleven double rooms with private bath, ceiling fan. Open bar (this is an exception in the hatos since most charge).

If you go to Piñero during the month of April, have your camera at the ready. On all the hills the Yellow Puis, *Tabebuia chrysantha,* are flowering, and it is a spectacular, never-to-be forgotten sight. These Araguaneys, as they are called in Venezuela, are our National Tree.

To reach Piñero from the International Airport of Maiquetía, you will have to drive to Caracas, and on through Maracay and Valencia, then south towards San Carlos, capital of the State of Cojedes. A short distance *before* San Carlos, in the town of **Tinaco,** you will take the road south as if heading towards El Sombrero/El Pao. In Tinaco fill your gas tank (there is no gas station inside the ranch). From here on, it will take you some two hours to reach Piñero. At 36 km from Tinaco on this south road, take the turn off to **El Baul**. The entrance to the ranch is located 60 kms from that turn off. As you come down the road, look for a little school on the left and turn into the dirt road next to it. From here to the main house it is still 22 kms, and you will cross four gates.

For the entire trip from Maiquetía, count on some 7 to 8 hours (the total distance from the toll gates of Tazón, where you exit Caracas, to Tinaco is 234 kms), so it makes sense to break the trip in Maracay or Valencia. On the other hand, should you visit Piñero when returning from the Andes, I suggest you spend the previous night in **Barinas** or **Acarigua**. The trip from Barinas will take approximately 6 hours. In any event, the managers insist that tourists arrive after lunch. Arrangements for lunch to be served on the day of arrival would have to be made prior to arrival, but lunch is served on the day of departure.

Breakfast is usually served by 6:00 a.m., early enough to allow a first-hours-of-the-morning excursion. The food is, for the most part, excellent, and unlike the other Hatos, there has always been a complete breakfast, not just the disgusting corn flakes with which many Hatos try to solve both the early breakfast and cold storage problems. However, as I have stated before, the quality of the services always depends upon the current manager, and I must admit that we have received complaints from time to time, regarding service as well as the *quantity* of food provided. Even then, I have never heard of anyone *regretting* his or her visit to Piñero.

For reservations, phone (0) 212-992-4413 & 992-4531, fax (0) 212-991-6668, e-mail: hatopinerovzla@telcel.net.ve , or contact the Venezuelan Audubon. Information regarding the names and numbers of passports or cédulas (the Venezuelan national ID cards) of each person as well as data (make, color, license number) of the vehicle used for transport must be given to their Caracas office 48 hours prior to your arrival at the hato.

Something New Has Been Added:
La Fe to Piñero along the Portuguesa River
You have just got to do this! Somehow, some way don't miss it. The only problem is that it must be done either after the start of the rains, during the rainy season or early in the dry season when the rivers are still deep enough.

ROUTE FROM CARACAS TO THE HATO PIÑERO

DISTANCE FROM TOLL BOOTH, PEAJE, 352 KM

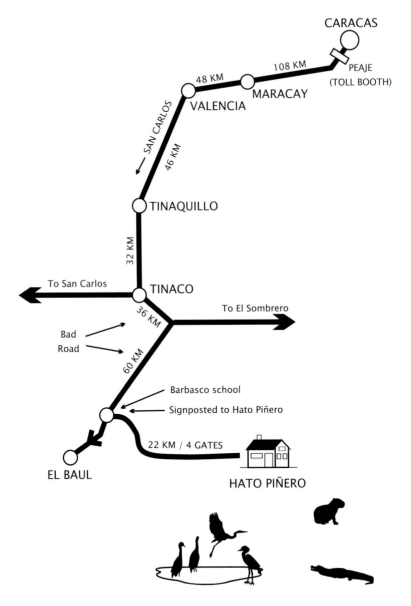

This is a joint excursion and collaboration between Hato La Fe and Hato Piñero. The basis of the excursion is two nights at Hato La Fe, with three excursions, a trip by river from Camaguan (about an hour south of La Fe) up two rivers to Hato Piñero, 2 nights at Piñero with 3 excursions and then back to La Fe by boat. Rather than just give you these dry statistics, I will translate below from a letter I received from Alberto Blanco when he recently made the trip:

«We left La Fe very early in the morning and drove to Camaguan - only about an hour. We embarked from Camaguan on the Portuguesa River at 7:30 a.m. As soon as we left the port, we started to see Fresh Water Dolphins, and continued to see them during the whole trip. After only fifteen minutes along the river there was a three-meter Anaconda! We also saw Red Howler monkeys in the trees all along the river, as well as Spectacled Cayman, turtles, and our boatman said that he often sees Nutrias on the trip. At 8:30 a.m. after 34 Km. we stopped at the town of La Union in the state of Barinas. Here one can buy beer, water, soft drinks, etc. We did not stay long but continued up the river to the village of Guadarrama arriving at 10:40 a.m. After a short stop we continued until we reached the Cojedes River in the state of the same name, some 161 km from Camaguan. It was now 12:35 p.m. As we went up the Cojedes, we were very much on the alert looking for Capybara, Long-tailed Weasels as well as the Orinoco Crocodiles. The Cojedes River has the largest population of Orinoco Crocodiles in Venezuela.

After 5 hours and 177 km we arrived at Arenales, which is within Hato Piñero. There we were picked up by the transport from the Hato and driven for 40 minutes to the guest house. Now we began to see wildlife in earnest: deer, Capybara, Cayman. We were also on the lookout to find the Greater Anteater, which lives along here, as well as Danta, Lynx, etc. etc. Here too we saw hundreds of birds.

As you know, going along rivers one does not see too many birds, and yet we did see Neotropical Cormorants, Anhingas, Egrets and herons including a Green Heron, Rufescent Tiger Heron, Agami Heron, Ducks, hawks and kites, even a Sungrebe, Black Skimmers doing their antics, macaws and parrots, Hoatzins, kingfishers, Fork-tailed Flycatchers, hundreds of Yellow-rumped Caciques.

After lunch the people of Piñero took us on an excursion as well as two more on the next day. We spent two nights at Piñero before taking the boat back to Camaguan, where we were met by the people from La Fe.

What a wonderful, fantastic experience!»

Should you wish to have this ultimate of Llano experience, contact the Venezuelan Audubon or either La Fe or Hato Piñero, as well as wildnatureexp@hotmail.com. For a visual picture of the two hatos see: www.piedravivas.com or www.hatopinero.com

And, remember from La Fe you can continue on to Amazonas to have a truly tropical experience.

STATE OF APURE

Hato El Cedral

This ranch in the Low Llanos of western **Apure** is *the* place to go for waterfowl and wading and water birds. Unlike Piñero, few untouched areas are accessible to bird watchers. As far as I know, there is only one trail into the gallery forest. However, for huge concentrations of wetland birds, nothing can beat El Cedral, and I definitely would recommend it for the general nature lover. Speaking of the general nature lover, I give below the report from Pamela Pierce:

Hato El Cedral

«*This is why I came to South America. You can't move your head fast enough - exotic plants and animals are everywhere. You see anacondas and anteaters, crocodiles and speckled caymans. There are huge iguanas, bats, monkeys, turtles, fox and deer. And the capybaras - big ones, little ones- are everywhere you turn. It is an amazing, incredible spectacle.*

And then there are the birds. This 3-rate birder saw, just for openers: Jabiru Storks, Sunbitterns, Jacanas, Great Potoos, Boat-billed Herons, Scarlet, Barefaced and White Ibises. And I saw the funny Ringed Kingfishers and the remarkable Hoatzins. And an Orinoco Goose family, Anhingas, Capped Herons, Aplomado Falcons and Garzón Silbador [NOTE TO MLG: I don't know what this is in English. She Means Whistling Herons]. And I saw the beautiful national bird of Venezuela, the Turpial.

About the Hato itself: it's a vast, prosperous, exceedingly well-run ranch. (Coming from Texas, she should know a well-run ranch when she sees one - MLG) It accommodates about 50 people in 25 comfortable rooms with air conditioning, private bath, hot water. It isn't cheap - about $120-150 per person per night. This includes two excursions per day, usually one in an open truck and the other on a boat. You get three not bad meals each day, but alcoholic beverages, even beer and wine, are extra.

In the past, I understand, they had their set excursions and their set times, and that was that. But now they honor special requests, especially for Birders. When I was there, a group of Chinese photographers with giant lenses on their cameras spent four days sitting in a boat, in one spot, taking pictures of Scarlet Ibises. That's it, just ibises. If that's what they wanted, that's what they got - complete with a guide.

And the guides are pretty good birders. They have the bible "Birds of Venezuela" (as does everybody), and they're good at spotting them.

They offer another, optional excursion. It's a hike through a gallery forest. And for a change, I followed Mary Lou's advice regarding wearing shorts. This time, I wore long pants and used her sulfur power concoction to combat the chiggers. And it worked! I recommend it highly. A friend of mine recently came back from the Llanos with both her legs covered with those little red chigger bumps - they were driving her crazy.»

If you are going on your own, upon requesting reservations, be sure to emphasize that you are a bird watcher and that furthermore, you expect to have at least one outing in the early morning as well as one in the afternoon. In other words, put your requirements in writing. They have assured us that every effort will be made to satisfy bird watchers and they are as good as their word.

Birds seen at El Cedral (not on General List above)

Pied-billed Grebe	Southern Pochard	Ornate Hawk-Eagle
Green Heron	Brazilian Duck	Long-winged Harrier
Agami Heron	Masked Duck	Peregrine Falcon
Orinoco Goose	Short-tailed Hawk	Spotted Rail

Yellow-breasted Crake	Chestnut-fronted Macaw	Olive-sided Flycatcher
Gray-breasted Crake	Blue-crowned Parakeet	Eastern Wood Pewee
Sungrebe	Spectacled Parakeet	Tropical Wood Pewee
Pied Lapwing	Orange-winged Parrot	Yellow-olive Flycatcher
Black-bellied Plover	Little Cuckoo	Bearded Tachuri
Collared Plover	Tropical Screech-Owl	River Tyrannulet
Wilson's Phalarope*	Short-eared Owl	Northern Scrub Flycatcher
Ruff*	Band-tailed Nighthawk	Greenish Elaenia
Upland Sandpiper*	Little Nightjar	Brown-chested Martin
Giant Snipe*	Ashy-tailed Swift	Black-capped Donacobius
Lesser Yellowlegs	Pale-bellied Hermit	Gray-cheeked Thrush
Ruddy Turnstone	Green-and-rufous Kingfisher	Yellowish Pipit
White-rumped Sandpiper	Cream-colored Woodpecker	Prothonotary Warbler
Pectoral Sandpiper	Plain-brown Woodcreeper	Yellow Warbler
Semipalmated Sandpiper	Striped Woodcreeper	Blackpoll Warbler
Western Sandpiper	Buff-throated Woodcreeper	Masked Yellowthroat
Stilt Sandpiper	Rusty-backed Spinetail	Lesser Seed-Finch
Buff-breasted Sandpiper	Plain Xenops	Yellow-bellied Seedeater
Hudsonian Godwit	White-naped Xenopsaris	Grassland Yellow-Finch
Common Dowitcher	Wire-tailed Manakin	Orange-fronted Yellow-Finch
Paraguayan Snipe	Riverside Tyrant	Wedged-tailed Grass-Finch
Laughing Gull	Amazonian Black-Tyrant	Yellow-browed Sparrow
Large-billed Tern	Eastern Kingbird	Lesser Goldfinch
Yellow-billed Tern	Venezuelan Flycatcher	

* Species reported but not actually checked out.

How to Reach El Cedral

If you are going to El Cedral after visiting the Andes, upon reaching the city of Barinas, you want to take the road to **La Luz,** and **Libertad** in order to continue south to the Apure River. To do so, upon reaching the round-about at the outskirts of the city, go three-quarters of the way around the traffic circle and exit following the signs to "Centro" or "Barinas. " At the very first stoplight after you leave the traffic circle turn right. You are now on Avenida Cuatrocentenria, the by-pass for the main part of the city of Barinas. After about 3 km you will be facing a shopping center and a supermarket with a big CADA sign. Go straight across when you have the green light. This being Venezuela, the name of the street now changes to Avenida Agustín Codazzi. Continue due south on this road. After some 20 km you will notice a road on your right that leads to San Sebastián. You continue straight. At the next junction you should go left towards La Luz and then some 117 km from the city of Barinas you will reach Dolores, where you will join the road coming from Boconito or Puente Páez in the north and going south to **Pta. Nutrias** and **Bruzual** on the Apure River. After Bruzual you should head towards but not to **Mantecal.** Before you reach the town of Mantecal, you will come to the crossroads known as **La Ye** (the Y) where there is a big white cross . From here it is 10 km to reach the gate of El Cedral on the west side of the road going due south. It will take you some 4 hours to reach the Hato from the city of Barinas, so you may wish to overnight in the city before continuing south. See the section on hotels in Barinas.

   From Caracas, there are two ways to reach Hato El Cedral Probably the fastest would be to take the autopista to Maracay, Valencia, San Carlos, Acarigua, Guanare and then continue west to the large National Guard Station known as **Puente Páez**

or **Boconoito**. Here you turn south to **Bruzual** and on towards **Mantecal**. Before reaching Mantecal, you will find the crossroads of **La Ye** , where you take the road going south. See just above.

The second option from Caracas or Maiquetia Airport would be to take the highway towards Maracay, leaving the autopista at the second exit, which you will find 19.7 kms after the Caracas toll booth at Tazón. This is the same route as that for Hato La Fe. You will pass **Charallave, San Casimiro** and **Camatagua**, in the direction to **El Sombrero**. Just before reaching El Sombrero, you will meet an east-west highway, where you turn right (west). After a few kilometers, as you approach El Sombrero, you will find several gas stations and eating places with a bridge straight ahead. Do not cross the bridge but rather turn left or south on the road with no sign that leads to **Calabozo**. Here, it would be wise to spend the night at the **Hotel Tiuna** (see segment on Hotels below), for it will take you five to six hours from the airport at Maiquetía. The next morning, leave early towards the south and **San Fernando de Apure**[1]. As soon as you have crossed the bridge over the Apure River, turn right at the very next corner and continue on for ten kilometers, always bordering the river. When you see the sign for "Avenida Intercomunal," turn left and then go straight for a short distance until you reach the main highway where you should turn right. Follow the signs for **Achaguas**. From Achaguas head due west for **Mantecal**. Fill your tank at the gas station by the entrance to Mantecal. After passing Mantecal, continue until you reach **La Ye**, a Y junction where you turn south. This second leg of the trip should take you approximately 5 hours.

One can also come by air - flying into San Fernando de Apure and/or Barinas, where you can be picked up for the four or five-hour trip to the Hato. (It costs another several hundred dollars though) For reservations at Hato El Cedral either contact the Venezuelan Audubon or direct to hatocedral@cantv.net (www.hatocedral.com) Phone number (0) 212-781-8995; fax 793-6082.

    ▣ El Cedral publishes a checklist of the nearly 300 birds reported for the Hato, which was edited by the Audubon. It can be purchased at the Hato or from the Venezuelan Audubon.

Campamento Turístico Mata E' Totumo
This 32.000-hectare hato belongs to and is operated by the Universidad de los Llanos (UNELLEZ) and is located in one of the *módulos*, a system of dikes designed to control the extremes between the flooding during the rainy season and the extreme aridity of the dry season. This is your opportunity to visit an hato at a very reasonable cost, but I highly recommend that you visit the camp during the dry season from November through April.

To reach the camp, follow the directions to El Cedral above. 57 km southeast of Bruzual (assuming that you are coming from Barinas) there is a Y (not the famous Ye mentioned for El Cedral, and I believe it is slightly north of the Ye) with a large sign indicating a turn to the right. you are now on the main road leading to the famous *módulos de Mantecal*. Continue along this paved road for 39 km where there is another

---

[1] Pamela's Comment: I know MLG doesn't particularly care for San Fernando, but we liked it. As the capital of a huge agricultural region, it is a bustling market town. The people are very friendly - almost innocently so. And in the early morning truckloads of agricultural goods of all sorts - dead and alive - fill the streets. It's fun!

sign telling you to turn right once again. The camp is yet another 8 km. along this side road. You will find a lot of the wildlife on both sides of this last section. The camp offers four simple but adequate private rooms - two with internal baths and fans. The other two also have fans but share an external bath. These are located in a large building with a screened corridor and hammocks. (I'll take the hammocks thank you.) Another building has two dormitories each with more or less 20 bunks. Camping is also permitted. Campers can either prepare their own food or arrange for food with the people at the camp.

They normally offer packages including lodging, meals and excursions all very flexible according to the needs of their guests. The excursions are by boat and/or truck. The camp administrator is Solmina Cerrada.

Reservations should be made either through the Venezuelan Audubon or directly through the travel agency of the UNELLEZ: "Agencia de Viajes Cosebaca", to the attention of Roisbel Figuero. Phone numbers (0) 273-533-3966 & 533-5065; fax: (0) 273-533-4189. E-mail: reunellez@telcel.net.ve.

Hato El Frío

This legendary, 85,000 hectare (209,950 acre) cattle ranch is located also in the Low Llanos of Apure, not far from El Cedral. It was an excellent birding destination and without a doubt, one of my favorite birding areas in Venezuela, one that I would highly recommend for hard-core birders. El Frío was my favorite among the birding hatos of Apure for many years. Of late, a significant reduction of the surveillance and security systems has brought about severe poaching problems, which in turn have caused a noticeable reduction of its wildlife. It is no longer the ecological paradise it was in the past. It is good, but at the moment it cannot compete with El Cedral or Piñero for wildlife. For the sake of one of the most wonderful natural places in Venezuela, we keep hoping for a general improvement of the safety conditions in Apure, that will enable the Hato´s management to give better attention to conservation.

There is a small lodge at El Frío, an independent concession allowed by the owners. Due to the poor service there, the Audubon had stopped sending birders to El Frío, but I understand that now they have new management, which I trust will result in better service. Contact: Jacobo Riera, phone (0) 244-743-5329; fax (0) 247-882-1223. E-mail: elfriolosllanos@cantv.net.

Here is a list of birds found in El Frío, in addition to the General List for the Llanos that appears above:

Chestnut-bellied Heron	Semipalmated Sandpiper	Jet Antbird
Pinnated Bittern	Upland Sandpiper	Riverside Tyrant
Orinoco Goose	Paraguayan Snipe	River Tyrannulet
Brazilian Teal	Large-billed Tern	Yellowish Pipit
Short-tailed Hawk	Yellow-billed Tern	Crested Oropendola
Slate-colored Hawk	Common Ground-Dove	Yellow Warbler
Peregrine Falcon	Chestnut-fronted Macaw	Blackpoll Warbler
Merlin	Blue-crowned Parakeet	Masked Yellowthroat
Sungrebe	Little Cuckoo	Silver-beaked Tanager
Pied Lapwing	Band-tailed Nighthawk	Pileated Finch
Collared Plover	Pale-bellied Hermit	Grassland Yellow-Finch
Lesser Yellowlegs	Green-and-Rufous Kingfisher	Orange-fronted Yellow-Finch
Ruddy Turnstone	White-bellied Piculet	Yellow-browed Sparrow
Pectoral Sandpiper	Rusty-backed Spinetail	

For birding spots in El Frío, begin with the large grove of mangoes found across the road from the Station. From March through April, when the mangoes are in season, the trees are full of Scarlet Macaws, Orioles, Howler Monkeys, etc., etc. At other times of the year the birds are there but not so noisy. Also, there is a good-sized caño just next to the tourist facilities, where you can observe Hoatzins, kingfishers, flycatchers and a host of other gallery forest birds.

To reach El Frío from the Andes, follow the same instructions as for El Cedral, but from at **La Ye**, turn east (left) towards **Mantecal** and then go on east some 40 kms, until you find the arch of the entrance gate to the Hato on your left.

From the Caracas, follow the same instructions as for El Cedral, but after San Fernando, it is approximately three hours to this ranch. There is a gas station on the highway at the entrance to Samán de Apure. Fill up your tank, and from there to the gate of the ranch it is 28 km If the gate is locked, you will have to leave the car by it and walk to the Station, which is approximately 1 km from the gate. To find the latter, pass several buildings on your right and go through two gates you will encounter, until you see yet another gate on your right. Walk to the right a short distance and then left to go over a causeway. The Tourist Lodge is on your left after your pass the stream. Be sure to close all gates after you.

As in the case of El Cedral, it is possible to fly from Maiquetía National Airport to San Fernando de Apure where you can be picked up for the trip to the ranch. Naturally this is an easier way to reach the Hato but also more expensive.

The Cinaruco-Capanaparo National Park

Venezuela has two great National Parks in the Llanos - the Aguaro-Guariquito, in southern Guarico, and this one in southeastern Apure. Its official name is Santos Luzardo, but everyone calls it Cinaruco-Capanaparo for the two rivers that border the Park to the south and north. (Aguaro-Guariquito is not tackled in this book, because it is not interesting as a birding area.)

Cinaruco-Capanaparo, where you may find not only such rarities as Festive Parrot, Crestless and Yellow-knobbed Curassows, Double-striped Thick-knee, Versicolored Emerald and many other Llano birds, but also some species that make their way up from the Amazonian areas, makes an interesting trip out of San Fernando de Apure.

The Park is representative of an unique ecosystem of the Llanos, characterized by vast stretches of tree-less savannas where sand dunes are randomly scattered and *galeras,* the elongated rock hills dating from the Precambrian era, crop up here and there. The wetlands are lagoons and rivers bordered by Moriche Palms, *Mauritia flexuosa,* as well as boggy or marshy areas with large stands of these palms, known as *morichales.*

You must either stay in San Fernando, approximately 120 kms away, or use the few facilities in the Park. No matter which way you visit the camp be sure to have an ample supply of liquid (it can be horribly hot during the day).

Although the road could be improved, it is relatively simple to reach the Park. Approximately 29 kms west of San Fernando there is a junction known as **Biruaca**. Turn south by the gas station towards **San Juan de Payara**, which is 28.3 kms from Biruaca. After going through San Juan de Payara, turn left at the last street and continue on to the gas station.

Fill your tank with gasoline here, as the next gas station is on the southern side of the **Cinaruco River**, 200 kms to the south. (It is sometimes possible to buy gas, for double the usual price, by the ferry landing on the south side of the Capanaparo River.)

Before reaching the Capanaparo, you will pass over the **Arauca** and the **Cunaviche** rivers. Whenever passing the larger rivers, as you travel south, be on the look-out for fresh-water dolphins. There is a famous saying in Venezuela that to really know the Llanos, one has to have traveled *Cunaviche adentro,* meaning further than the Cunaviche - deep into the Llanos.

At 50.4 kms south of Biruaca, veer to the right. At 113 kms, you reach the **Capanaparo River** and after crossing it by *chalana* (ferry), you will be inside the Park. You should have a four-wheel drive vehicle if you plan to get off the main road.

One of my favorite spots is known as **Laguna Brava** (the Fierce Lagoon - filled to the brim with calm, placid waters), but you may need a 4X4 to reach it. After you leave the ferry, drive for about 50 yards and turn right towards the road going south (not paved but in relatively good condition). At 3.6 kms south from this junction you will see a sandy road going west. Turn right (west) and continue on this road for 5.8 kms, when you veer towards the left (south). At 7.3 kms turn left (east). The Lagoon is 8.6 kms from the Capanaparo.

Here I have seen almost all the savanna and water birds listed for the Park, including Scarlet Macaw, Red-bellied Macaw, Blue-crowned Parakeet, and Festive Parrot.

Approximately one km further south from the road to Laguna Brava, there is a *mata* (copse of trees growing on a *banco* of higher, sandy ground). In this small area I counted over 50 species of Llano birds including Festive Parrot, Yellow-crowned Parrot, Gray-headed Kite, Streak-headed Woodcreeper, Rusty-backed Spinetail, White-winged Becard, White-bearded Flycatcher, Short-crested Flycatcher, Mouse-colored Tyrannulet, Yellow-breasted Flycatcher, and if you walk all the way around the *mata,* you may see a resident pair of Swallow-wings.

Continue south, and you will pass over a beautiful *caño* (creek or stream) called **Caño La Pica**. Stop here to look for Giant River Otters, as well as the special birds of Morichales, including Sulphury Flycatcher and Moriche Oriole.

At 35.5 kms south of the Capanaparo River, there is a small stream that has been dammed up to allow for the road construction. Just past the stream on the right side of the road (west), it is possible to make your way along the gallery forest. Look for Yellowish Pipit and Plumbeous Seedeater in the meadow. If you investigate the gallery forest around here, you should see Sunbittern, Crestless Curassow, Jet Antbird and Black-throated Antbird.

At 43.6 kms south of the Capanaparo, the road on the left (east) leads to the **galeras**. It will take you at least 45 minutes to drive to the galeras, as the road is awful, but I recommend that you try do so if you have the time, enough gasoline and a 4WD vehicle. This area is wilder and affords an even greater variety of birds, including Yellow-crowned Manakin. Here you will also find clear streams where it is safe to bathe.

The **Cinaruco River** is approximately 48 kms south of the Capanaparo, and forms the southern boundary of the Park. If you were to continue south, you would come to Puerto Páez, where you can take the ferry across the Orinoco to Puerto Ayacucho, the capital of Amazonas State.

A visit to the Cinaruco-Capanaparo Park is possible only during the dry season, as this *entire* area is under water when the rains come - not to mention the fact that the mosquitoes will eat you alive.

Options for Lodging in the Park

At the present time I can recommend no place to stay in the Park. but there is a possibility that the Hato Santa Luisa between Biruaca and San Juan Payara may open for tourism in the future. If it does, it will be an excellent opportunity as I do not doubt that the accommodations will be first class and the birding excellent. Remember though that San Juan de Payara is still 22 km from the Capanaparo River and the Park itself although the ecology is quite similar. Still it is much closer to the Park than San Fernando and you would be in the country. Should you be interested, check with the Audubon or call (0) 212-959-0267.

Another Option for visiting the Park
Another option would be to take advantage of the services of Henry Jaimes, who can pick you up at San Fernando, take you through the Park, and arrange for you to stay at one of the private hatos. Henry knows the Park, and I believe you would find him to be both reliable and knowledgeable. Contact him at his travel agency in Puerto Ayacucho in Amazonas at (0) 248-521-3964 or through his e-mail wildnatureexp@hotmail.com. As a suggestion, you could even continue on with Henry to Amazonas after visiting the Park.

The total check-list for the Park includes 320 species. The Audubon has published the **Checklist of the Birds of the Cinaruco-Capanaparo National Park**, which can be secured from American Birding Association or the Audubon in Caracas.

BARINAS STATE

Hato La Madera
This is a much less fancy destination, but the lack of comfort is more than made up by the warmth of their hospitality, and the way they put themselves out to show you everything. The hato is located approximately 45 km southeast of the city of Barinas. From Barinas take the same road as indicated above for Hato El Cedral. When you reach the split indicating Torunos and La Luz, be sure to take the left fork to La Luz. From here it is 3.2 km to the entrance on the left. The first thing that will probably impress you are the HUGE trees, even by the entrance. The camp has 8 very rustic rooms, shared bathrooms with cold water, but I can vouch that the food is excellent. There are also hammocks with mosquito nets (my favorite way of sleeping). Apparently their idea is to give visitors the experience of genuine life on a Llanos ranch rather than the atypical citified luxury accommodations[1]. I must admit that I enjoyed the hato very much, but I am accustomed to roughing it.

My first reaction to the ranch was that it was very much like the high Llanos with the same birds as Masaguaral. Due to the beautiful trees and forested areas, it does not seem to be the wide open type of ecosystem as found in the lower Llanos of Apure, They apparently do have a lagoon with a huge roost, but we could not reach the roost as one of the big tree had fallen across the road. So we contented ourselves watching the Great Potoo and a large group of Hoatzins. We were barely 24 hours at the ranch, but without really trying I counted 105 species, including the Bat Falcon, Barn Owl, Tropical Screech Owl, Spectacled Owl, and lots of hawks.

Like Hato Piñero, arrival is normally in the afternoon with dinner that night. The next morning you bird on foot until the heat drives you in to the cool shade of the

---

[1] Pamela's Comment: This is true! One of the many things I liked about this hato is that visitors are not separated from the working part of the ranch, as they are at El Cedral for instance. You are right there, among the Llaneros going about their normal activities. They'll even - and enthusiastically - let you milk their cows.

building. In the afternoon they take you to the roost, but be sure to request that they leave early in order to bird that fabulous road. In fact, I would prefer to spend the morning along the road as well because it is a long way with a lot of interesting areas. The next day is usually a boat tour on the Apure river and tributaries to observe birds and monkeys. A picnic lunch is provided and in the afternoon you return to the hato.

For reservations either contact the Venezuelan Audubon or the kind and thoughtful owner, Rafael Medina, Tel. (0) 273-533-0882, e-mail: rafaelmedina60@hotmail.com. Cash only.

Agropecuario La Bota/Finca Santa María

Tel (0) 273-552-5493, Administrator Raul Jiménez (0) 414-973-1366 or (0) 273-541-1921 (home, call nights).

To find this ranch you should again drive due south on Avenida Agustín Codazzi, passing the airport on your right. From there it is approximately 20 km to the only fork on the right along this highway. Go right and head towards San Silvestre. (I have to tell you that absolutely none of the maps I have consulted for this area are correct! They all show two separate roads going south either to San Sebastián or Luz/Libertad. In reality there is only one with left or right forks to the west or east.) After you pass the bridge at the entrance to San Silvestre, turn right at the very next corner. You still have 9 km to go to reach the gate at the entrance of the ranch. When you see the office of the Andes electric company on your right, go right at the very next corner. You will be passing a church and large plaza also on the right. By the water tower turn right. Continue on until you see (again on your right) a blue and white school. Take the left fork. You will eventually come to the gate and guard house.

They apparently offer both full day tours as well as lodging. For the day tour (and probably also for lodging) reservations must be made at least one week in advance for a minimum of 5 people or with fewer people paying the equivalent of a group of five. This would come to about $100 for the day tour. According to Elizabeth Kline, the lodging is quite elegant with five handsome rooms with private bath, hot water, AC in a two-story house. You could fool me. The day we were there, they did not want to show us the lodging because the woman who cleans had not come to work and the rooms apparently were still not cleaned up after the last guests. Now that seems very strange to me, and, furthermore, if an employee was to have reported for work in the morning but was a no show, that should be sufficient reason to blooming well change employees.

As to the ranch, here you very definitely are in the low Llanos. With 3,500 hectares it is relatively small in comparison with most of the ranches in the Llanos, but it certainly has a tremendous amount of wildlife. They maintain that they have the greatest density of Capybara in Latin America, and I believe them. Capybaras are all over the place. 2,000 hectares of the ranch are irrigated, creating ample wetlands for birds. In fact, they claim that they have every species of birds to be found in the Llanos, and I can believe that too. There is a 145-hectare lagoon, complete with anacondas, Spectacled Cayman, turtles, fish, etc. I did not see any forested areas, but since they also own 7 km along the Pagüey River, it could well be that they do have a gallery forest.

Without a doubt this ranch has tremendous potential for ecotourism, but I believe that neither the staff nor management live up to that potential. Having seen the ranch, it is obvious that there is big money behind all the infrastructure, and it could well be that the owners are not particularly interested in developing ecotourism, or it may also be as I have always maintained......for a well run hato, lodge, inn or what have you, the owners have to take a personal interest.

As an example of what I am talking about, one of our bird guides and independent tour operator e-mailed me recently from Barinas that he was stuck there with some tourists for a few days and did I know of any place they could go that was not too far from the city. I told him to call Finca Santa Maria. He e-mailed me back to the effect that he had contacted the ranch to ask for either a day tour or one night's lodging. The woman told him that **she was too tired to receive them** and they should call back the following week!!!!! That is no way to build tourism or any other kind of business where service is involved. Of course, an employee doesn't care whether or not the establishment losses both income and good will.

Irrespective of the above, I do recommend the Finca, but be certain to make your arrangements well in advance and only with the Administrator, Raúl Jimenez. Spanish only.

Hato El Cristero

Here we have a very well-run, five-star establishment-beautiful grounds, comfortable rooms and superb food all managed by the extremely friendly family of Humberto Concha.

To reach Hato El Cristero, again take Avenida Augustín Codazzi south, and when you come to the fork for San Sebastián go right. From this point it is 8.5 km to El Cristero on the west or right side of the road.

They also offer day tours as well as lodging with meals and excursions along rivers, etc. I have only one criticism of this lodge and that is the fact that they do have parrots, Jabirus, etc. in large, well-cared-for cages. El Cristero would probably be better for the general nature lover than the hard-core birder, but it is also a good option for overnighting in order to make day tours to Finca Santa Maria or Hato Maderera. Also, in the event you plan to break your trip to Hato El Cedral by a lay-over in Barinas, I assure you that you will be much happier for a short stay at El Cristero than in the hotels of Barinas. You will be reluctant to part from the Concha family.

Phones (0) 273-552-2695 or (0) 416-673-1790. The Venezuelan Audubon would also be happy to make reservations for you.

Centro Turístico El Gabán

This is a choice for you if you are exploring the Llanos on your own.

Follow the exact instructions for the route to El Cedral from the city of Barinas, but in this case you are headed towards Dolores, 106 km south of Barinas or only 16 km northwest of Pta. Nutrias on the Apure river. As a matter of fact, the road from Dolores to La Ye in Apure State is very good birding.

This is an attractive, well maintained complex with a central swimming pool surrounded by 24 simple but comfortable rooms with AC, private bath (cold water naturally - what else did you expect?), a restaurant with AC as well and good food. Unfortunately, there is also a tasca, but just avoid the place on a Friday or Saturday night. They also offer excursions to the river for wildlife observation but with a minimum of ten persons. I have been given to understand that the personnel are very friendly, and besides, this is one of the few inns to be found in the Llanos where they do accept credit cards!

El Gabán would be an inexpensive option for birding the lower Llanos. Unfortunately, it is very difficult to reach them by telephone due to the congestion on the few lines of the zone. It is best to call after 10:00 p.m. (remember they are out in the boonies!) Phone/Fax: (0) 273-552-6183

Hato Garza

This, frankly, is for the really well-heeled bird watcher[1]. The Swarovski family were so taken with nature in the Llanos of Venezuela, that they bought the ranch and are now behind this particular tourist destination. Elizabeth Kline has advised me that the facilities being installed are spectacular. Four huge rooms with details such as king-size, 4-poster bed (rustic style with tree trunk posts) and enormous bathrooms, all with first-class fixtures, finishing details, etc. The operation is to open soon and is located in south-east Barinas. Activities contemplated are bird watching, nature travel, photo safari and soft adventure, all with personalized guides. The service will be all inclusive except for alcoholic beverages. (Now that is where they differ with Hato Piñero and La Fe that have open bars.) For further information, for the present contact Leopoldo Garcia at leopoldogarcia@hotmail.com or by fax to (0) 212-284-1551. As of this writing they do not as yet have a definite e-mail address for reservations, but expect it to be: reservaciones@hatogarza.com or you can contact the Venezuelan Audubon Society.

Rio Bumbum

This is definitely not Llanos birding, and I confess to having mentioned it already as a stop on the road to Táchira, but it is in the state of Barinas, so I am repeating myself in the hope that some reader will visit the area.

To reach the river from the city of Barinas you can either take the route indicating "San Cristóbal" by the often-mentioned round-about at the entrance to the city of Barinas or if you are staying in the city itself, from the CADA commercial center go up Avenida 23 de Enero, passing the University on your right. Continue straight until you dead end onto Highway 5, where you will turn left as if you were going to San Cristóbal.

Some 48 km after Barinas you will come to the crossroads to Ciudad Bolivia. Continue straight on towards the south west and Socopó at 86 km from Barinas. This is the entrance to a good birding area along the **River Bumbum**. (I am not joking. That is really the name!) This information was sent to us by Andrew Nield of butterfly reputation, and Andrew is right. If there are butterflies, there will also be birds. For more direct information his address is a.neild@ndirect.co.uk. www.ndirect.co.uk/~a.neild

On the right side of the road (west) in front of a large white cross there is a dirt road leading up to the valley of the Bumbum. In a normal car you can probably do this road in the dry season. After some 4 km, you will enter a forest, not exactly primary but still very good. The road climbs through the forest for some 250 to 300 meters. In this area, Andrew not only found many butterflies but also saw and heard a goodly quantity of birds. Along the road you will come to a Y. The left branch first traverses about 500 meters of cultivated fields and then comes to a hanging foot bridge followed by a path through a beautiful forest along the river. This path eventually leads to the city of Mérida (and I do mean eventually - like two days!). The right fork continues through the forest before reaching some pastures. If you have the time, I believe this area would be well worth investigating.

---

[1] Note from the Editor: Well, some of us poor buggers, the poorly-heeled birders, got invitations to do research at Hato Garza. Since everything that MLG describes above is hearsay, we will inspect at the first opportunity and report our findings.

V - 5. The Birding Roads

If you can afford a visit to one of the lodges, by all means do so. I cannot deny that they offer the ultimate experience of the Llanos. But don't be discouraged please, if their prices are beyond your pocket (as they are beyond mine in most cases). The Llanos can be birded on a shoe string. You just have to work a little harder. Furthermore, I have included above several less expensive options.

If you are doing the Llanos on your own, there are two possibilities, and which one you choose should depend upon where else in the country you plan to visit.

THE CALABOZO-SAN FERNANDO ROAD

For instance, if you are also visiting **central, eastern or southern Venezuela**, my suggestion would be to "do the Llanos" on the nearly 165 kms of the **Calabozo-San Fernando de Apure road**, in the state of **Guárico**.

For this road in the heart of the Llanos, I would make my headquarters at **Calabozo**, some 6 hours south of Caracas. (See instructions above on how to drive to Hato El Cedral.) There you can stay, as I mentioned before, at the **Hotel Tiuna** (see segment on Hotels in this chapter), and spend the next day birding along the road to San Fernando de Apure.

There are plenty of places to pull off the road in order to observe birds. Also, a birder friend told me about State Highway 1, leading out of Calabozo towards the Orituco River, which he found quite good, but I have not investigated the area. In any event, you will occasionally see a side road, which you may wish to check out.

From the city of San Fernando de Apure west to Barinas it is 375 km or almost 10 hours of driving. From San Fernando to Mantecal the road is quite good, but the good birding only starts shortly after El Samán de Apure or approximately the last 75 km to Mantecal. From Mantecal north - some 203 km - the road is pretty bad, but the birding is excellent. Therefore, unless you are heading for the Andes, the trip from San Fernando to Barinas is one long drive. Furthermore, there is no hotel I can recommend between San Fernando and Barinas although there are a couple of camps or inns as mentioned above.

If you are going to or coming from the Andes the following option would be more convenient.

THE SAN SILVESTRE ROAD

If you are visiting the Andes in western Venezuela, I suggest you make the city of Barinas your headquarters. The **road to San Silvestre** goes off to the southeast out of Barinas. See instructions for Hato Cristero.

Richard Ryan wrote that he found between 25 to 30 Chestnut-vented Conebills scattered in every grove of scrubby trees from Barinas to San Silvestre. To go on this road, follow Highway 4, right past the airport in Barinas. Approximately 15 kms after the airport look for a sign saying "Zona Militar" and a bridge of regular size. All the way to San Silvestre the road is good birding, but apparently this bridge area is the best. A couple of hundred meters before the bridge is a road leading left to some low white buildings with a radio tower. These are the military headquarters. Since I know the military mind[1] (following page), I recommend that you go down there to request permission to stop and bird around. In his most recent letter Dick Ryan advises:

*«I have recently been driving to **Canagua**, well beyond San Silvestre. There are quite a few marshy areas and ponds between San Silvestre and Canagua that are worthwhile. There is also a ranch with several buildings right by some power lines - crossing the road at a right angle about midway, I have found Bicolored Wren, Stripe-backed Wren, Troupial and Orinocan Saltator. Near here I have found Rusty-backed Spinetail, which is a northwestward extension of the published range. I would add Sunbittern, Pied Lapwing, Buff-necked Ibis, Green Ibis, Capped Heron and Chestnut-fronted Macaw to the bird list.*

On the way back to Barinas (and some distance after passing San Silvestre) look for a sign listing three ranches pointing to the right. Take this road till it crosses a creek, park and bird the creek and woods. This is a good place for Bat Falcon, Sunbittern, Dwarf Cuckoo and other interesting birds.

When returning to Barinas take a left on a paved road 2 or 3 kms beyond the Zona Militar. This will take you into Barinas a couple of kilometers south of the airport. Just turn left when you reach the 4-lane divided road and you will go back to the airport. This road almost guarantees Crested Bobwhite in the late afternoon. Drive slowly and watch in the grassy shoulders. For lunch along the San Silvestre Road there is a small but clean and inexpensive restaurant on the left about 200 meters beyond the bridge as one enters San Silvestre.

Another spot to include is an almost sure spot for Hoatzin along the San Silvestre road. If you do not get it by the bridge near the military post, watch for a good gravel road leading south about one third of the way from San Silvestre to Canagua. This road will be blocked almost immediately by an iron post gate with concrete gate posts. Pull off to the side and walk to the gate. Look into the marsh and stream side trees on the right of the gate and there will almost always be Hoatzins there. If the owner happens to be there, engage him in conversation. He speaks good English and will usually invite you onto his property to bird. I have found Rusty-backed Spinetail here occasionally.»

Aside from what is on the General List and the above, look for Stripe-backed Bittern, Pinnated Bittern, Short-tailed Hawk, Long-winged Harrier, Spotted Sandpiper, Band-tailed Nighthawk, Violaceous Jay, Yellow Warbler, Grassland Yellow-Finch and Yellow-browed Sparrow.

DOLORES TO LA YE

From Barinas there is also the option of birding from Dolores south to La Ye. The approximately 30 kms between Bruzual and La Ye offer superb birding . When you reach the river check below the bridge as the Sun Grebe has been seen here. If you opt for this alternative, your best bet would be to use the Centro Turístico El Gabán as your headquarters.

On the other hand, from the southern Andes do not even think of using the road from Táchira via Guasdualito, for the area is stomping grounds to Colombian guerrillas and drug traffickers.

---

[1](following page) Note from the Editor: Mary Lou is such a diplomat! What she means is that to a military mind, no one in his sane mind would use his or her time in such a sissy occupation as watching birds. Therefore, since you are bound to be suspected of spying, M.L. is suggesting you go in there and assure them you are just a harmless lunatic.

V - 6. Wintering Dickcissels

If you come to Venezuela during the northern winter, you will have timed your trip to be here with the Dickcissels. The people from mid-western U.S.A. will shrug their shoulders and say - So what?

But I am sure they do not imagine or have ever before seen more than a million Dickcissels gather in one single roost. Nothing prepares you for that - it is one of the most thrilling experiences I ever had since I started to bird. Put aside all preconceived notions about Dickcissels and come see this wonder of nature in the **High Llanos** of the states of **Cojedes** and **Portuguesa.**

Around 5:30 p.m., the birds begin to fly to their roost. If you are near a field where they are feeding, you first see them rise to the sky in huge spirals. If you are far away, you see clouds of "smoke" approaching on the horizon. As they get near, the smoke turns to be flocks of birds - far too many to count. When they hit the roost in a cane field, it sounds like waves hitting the beach.

As for the exact location of a roost, they change every year, and local farmers often burn the roosts at night to kill off the birds, so my suggestion is that you take the road leading out of Acarigua towards **Payara** and **El Palmar**, and begin to scan the skies and follow the clouds.

Should you be interested in seeing this wonder, arrange your itinerary to stay overnight at the city of **Acarigua**, in the State of **Portuguesa**. At the far western end of town, there is the excellent **Motel Payara**. Phones: (0) 255-621-4611; 621-4979 & 621-2775.

Coming from Barinas, leave the 50-kilometer stretch of freeway at the exit for Píritu and go east on the surface road. Coming from the east, when you reach the roundabout at the eastern end of Acarigua, take the upper road marked Guanare. This road goes around Acarigua and will take you to the western end of town, where the Payara is on the left. When ready to go on, if you are continuing west, go left out of the Motel on the surface road and join the autopista near the town of Píritu. This sounds complicated but is far the easiest way.

Dickcissels

V - 7. Hotels in the Llanos

IN SAN FERNANDO DE APURE, CAPITAL OF THE STATE OF APURE

Nuevo Hotel Apure
Located on the left of the street after you cross the bridge over the Apure River and almost in front of the strange fountain that "decorates" the entrance to the city, which my editor, with her gift for discreet commentary, calls the "Remedy for Hiccups." I can't really call it a dump (the hotel, I mean) but it is a long way from a Hilton. However it does have a closed parking lot and is inexpensive. Phone (0) 247-341-4759. By the way, the fountain is worth a photo of all your group to take home. Clemencia says it gives the group portrait a "shock added value".

Gran Hotel Plaza
Located next to the Plaza Bolívar. The name and lobby of this hotel give you the impression that the fanciness will extend to the rest of the hotel, but no, all effort towards deluxe stops as you pass into the corridors, and the rooms or restaurant can in no way compare with the standard set by the Tiuna in Calabozo. Phones (0) 247-342-1255 & 342-1746.

IN CALABOZO, STATE OF GUARICO

Hotel Tiuna
Located towards the southern outskirts of town, on the western or right side of the road coming from El Sombrero and leading to San Fernando. The Tiuna is unpretentious, but it is the best I have ever found in the Llanos, clean and with a good restaurant. (If you like a good piece of beef, order the *lomito* steak. Clemencia says it is to die for.) Phones (0) 246-87-6296 & 871-4506 & 871-6440.

IN BARINAS, CAPITAL OF THE STATE OF BARINAS

Hotel Internacional
Although this hotel combines the worst of the art deco period with a strong modern Italian styling[1], we in the Audubon put all our birders up here. Their friendliness and service are excellent. To reach the hotel (coming from the east, along the upper Llanos, as well as from the Andes and the west) by the large roundabout at the end of the east-west highway, take the road indicating *Centro*. Drive straight for 4.6 km You will see a Maraven gas station and the Plaza on your right. The hotel is on the far side of the Plaza, on Calle Arzobispo Mendez. There is an enclosed parking area around the back. For reservations call or fax: (0) 273-551-1749 & 551-2434, or contact the Audubon. The food at the Internacional is not of the best[2], so I would suggest that you go to Hotel Bristol for your dinners, but I also understand that if you walk from the Internacional towards the Plaza Bolívar, there is a typical steak

---

[1] Note from the Editor: I think she means Mussolinian, but maybe it is only Neo Mausoleum. Hotel builders in the Llanos are quite eclectic!

[2] Note from the Editor: Nor very "international".

restaurant[1]. There is an excellent bakery next to the Hotel Internacional where you can breakfast if you do not leave too early in the morning.

Motel Los Guasimitos
(0) 273-546-1546, located just before you reach the round-about at the very end of the old east-west highway. There is a restaurant next door, which is perfectly satisfactory and inexpensive.

Hotel El Hotel
Conveniently located on the old east-west road shortly before you reach the round-about. Perfectly adequate, probably quieter than Los Guasimitos and quite inexpensive.

Hotel Turístico Varyna
This is the hotel I prefer in Barinas. Actually, it is a motel. From the oft-mentioned round-about at the beginning of the city of Barinas, go three quarters of the way around the traffic circle and exit following the signs to "Centro" or "Barinas." At the very first stop-light after you leave the traffic circle, turn right. You are now on the by-pass for the main part of the town. You will drive for at least 3 kms on this by-pass, until you are facing a shopping center and supermarket with a big CADA sign. Go straight across the road once you have the green light. Go to the next stoplight and turn right, passing the airport on your left. Go all the way to the end of the street, turn right again and continue to the next stoplight on to the main avenue. Once more hang a right, but this time make sure that it is a very sharp, tight right. The reason for approaching the hotel in this ass-backward way is due to the fact that this main street, Avenida 23 de Enero, is not only a divided street -- it is divided into **4** segments! You want the far right segment. The hotel is located about two blocks above the CADA supermarket. This is the best place to stay in the city, but for the time being, at least, we do not recommend their restaurant. Phones: (0) 273-533-3984, 533-5094 & 533-2477.

Hotel Comercio
Dick Ryan recommends this hotel "for its helpful staff and low prices as well as its convenience to the major roads. Only 2 blocks away is an excellent Tasca-type restaurant. The hotel staff will provide directions." To find the Comercio, again as you approach the city of Barinas and reach the round-about at the end of the east/west highway, go three quarters of the way around the traffic circle and exit following the signs to "Centro" or "Barinas", the same as for Hotel Varyna. After 7 kms, when you face the shopping center, turn left. Pass the Hotel Bristol on your left, and after one or two blocks you will see the sign for the Comercio down a side street on your right. Phone: (0) 273-532-1068.

There is a variety of hotels in Barinas including the three star **Hotel Bristol**, which we do not recommend due to their surly service and the fact that they don't always honor reservations, but the best place to eat in Barinas is the restaurant of the Hotel Bristol.

---

[1] Note from the Editor: This Plaza Bolivar is a masterpiece of urban planning - next to the funeral parlor, there is a florist shop, and next to it, a bar called ¡Por Fin! - At last! Therefore, when a Barines dies, he can, at last, R.I.P. No need to worry about mourning friends or relatives - they have all they need at hand.

Posada El Toreño

Is a very small inn, I suggest that you call or e-mail first. To find the inn from the cross roads by the CADA commercial center turn right to go up the Avenida 23 de Enero, passing the University on your right. Turn left by the stoplight just before you see the MacDonalds ahead on your right. The entrance to El Toreño is on the left just past Adagro silos. A very simple and inexpensive option for staying in Barinas. 6 rooms with AC, private bath, hot water and AC. The owner, Astolfo Navas, is extremely pleasant. E-mail elcorral@telcel.net.ve; Phone/Fax (0) 273-533-1670 & 533-0529.

Horned Screamer

Section VI

THE EASTERN STATES

Country and Regional Endemics:

Band-tailed Guan
Yellow-knobbed Curassow
Bare-eyed Pigeon
Tepui Parrotlet
Yellow-shouldered Parrot
Dwarf Cuckoo
White-tailed Sabrewing
White-chested Emerald
Green-tailed Emerald
Scissor-tailed Hummingbird
Buffy Hummingbird
Copper-rumped Hummingbird
White-tipped Quetzal
Russet-throated Puffbird
Groove-billed Toucanet
Black-dotted Piculet
Crested Spinetail
White-throated Barbtail
Guttulated Foliage-gleaner
Handsome Fruiteater
White-bearded Flycatcher
Venezuelan Flycatcher
Orange-crowned Oriole
Yellow-faced Redstart
Gray-headed Warbler
Venezuelan Flower-piercer
Orinocan Saltator
Vermilion Cardinal

Nature in Eastern Venezuela has astonishing variety and disparity. If you were to come in from the Caribbean Sea, the twin peninsulas of Araya and Paria would announce what you can expect from the rest of these lands - they are like night and day. The first one reaches out towards the west all barren and parched, a point of land seldom blessed by the rains; while the second one marches towards Trinidad (almost touches it) dressed in its mantle of lush rain forests. As you drive through Anzoategui, Sucre, Monagas and the State of Delta Amacuro, you will often meet with these sorts of contrasts.

Oilbird

Also with some oddities of nature - in Monagas and particularly in Sucre, there are thermal springs of various kinds everywhere, even one that gushes up from the sea-floor, barely a few feet from the edge of the water. In Monagas, the sandstones that crop up in the mountainous north are as holey as Swiss cheese - riddled with caves, including the Guácharo, which is one of the largest in Venezuela. The Morichal Largo River meanders for kilometers through a breathtakingly beautiful stand of *Mauritia flexuosa* Palms, while a short distance north of it, there is an asphalt lake, Guanoco, largest of its kind in the World and of almost mythical reputation and atmosphere, where the asphalt seeping from below has allowed nearly two centuries of extraction (some three million tons) without any loss in size for the lake.

In Anzoategui, there are vast expanses of grasslands where millions of stunted Curatella trees bear witness to uncounted years of dry-season fires. The Curatellas are the only trees that survive these recurring savanna fires. If you touch their leaves you will find they are the texture of sandpaper, and as such were used by the Indians in making their artifacts. Anzoategui is the second oil state of Venezuela (the first being Zulia) and you will find oil rigs and oil pumps peppering the landscape and oil pipes running along roads and crisscrossing the countryside.

There is the Delta of the Orinoco River, with its profuse vegetation cramming the tortuous channels - palms and mangroves, trees and water grasses, lilies and large-leafed water plants, all reflecting perfectly in the mirror of the darkling waters and then swaying gently in the wake as the boat goes by. The Delta, and also the tangle of coastal channels and waterlands of Monagas, are home to huge flocks of Scarlet Ibises, crowds of Blue and Yellow Macaws, Manatees, Giant River Otters, Caymans, Anacondas and, among a myriad other creatures, to *Anableps anableps,* weird little fish with double eyes (one for under the water and one for above), which pop up their heads at the water's edge. Even to this day, the immense jungles of the Delta remain barely studied, to the point that there are rumors of a species of large nocturnal monkey which still remain to be confirmed or dispelled.

The "Oriente", as Venezuelans call the region, is the source of some of the loveliest national music, as well as some of the most whimsical folklore.

These eastern states offer a variety of birds not found elsewhere in the country, and even better, a good number not found elsewhere in the World. Come and see - you'll surely get some of them!

VI - 1. State of Anzoategui

INTRODUCTION

To reach both eastern Venezuela and the eastern side of the State of Bolivar, you have to drive from Maiquetía International Airport to Caracas, follow the "Autopista" (main highway) all the way across the valley of Caracas and then take the exit (to the right) that leads to the main road to eastern Venezuela. Follow the signs that point you on your way to Barcelona, capital of the State of Anzoátegui, where the road divides on an overpass into two main routes - east to Cumaná, capital city of the State of Sucre or south to Ciudad Bolivar, ditto of the State of (what else?) Bolivar.

After crossing Caracas, you will be traveling through two bedroom communities, Guarenas (approximately 32 km) and Guatire. Not too far after Guatire, you will connect up with the so-called autopista to the east. Unfortunately, it does not last very long, and long before your reach the area of Caucagua (some 40 km from Caracas) you will be back on the two-lane highway as the road gradually descends through the mountains. Caucagua is an area where many people stop for gasoline, coffee, arepas, and what have you. Shortly after Caucagua, be on the alert for a very small sign on your right indicating Barcelona.

The road now passes through an area, explosively fertile and exuberantly tropical, called Barlovento, the Spanish name for "windward". Here you are still in the State of Miranda, passing the area of El Guapo and Cúpira. Cupira is approximately 128 km from Caracas and here you will see stalls on both sides of the road where they sell fruit and casabe. All along the road through Barlovento you will see side roads to your right leading down through cacao plantations. Drive down any of them to have your picnic lunch and bird a bit.

Continuing on the main road, little by little the vegetation will turn dryer and more and more to thorny scrub. You will know you have entered Anzoátegui by Boca de Uchire, for the state is nearly or completely xerophitic over most of its length and width.

Up to recently I have maintained that for the most part, from the point of view of birding, Anzoategui is a pass-through state. I have had to eat my words, because it does have some remarkable birding areas. Unfortunately, to reach many of these places you need a 4x4. The twin coastal lagoons of Píritu and Unare, are two of those birding areas, interesting for water birds and especially for migrant waders.

PIRITU AND UNARE

The town of **Boca de Uchire** sits at the western end of the Laguna de Unare. Turn left or down onto the main street of the town just before the Corporven gas station. Drive past the commercial area to the church. Turn right on the first street after the church. You are now on the causeway or the northern border of the lagoon. This so-called road runs for 26 km between the lagoon and the sea. During the dry season I do not believe you will have any problem, but the rainy season may be something else again. If you find that the road is in such deplorable condition that you are hesitant to drive it, turn back.

If you can handle the road (hopefully it will have been repaired), drive the entire length to the fishing village of El Hatillo, stopping along the way to observe whatever passerines you may find, as well as the gatherings of sea and water birds. This area is especially worthy of a trip during the months of August and September when the waders arrive from the north. Then you will want to spend quite a few hours trying to figure out what the devil you are seeing, because the birds are mostly in their off-season plumage. However I also drove this road in February and found a huge congress of terns - we had a devil of a time figuring out the Sandwich, Caspian, Least, Royal, Cayenne Terns. It was great fun. In fact, we spent so much time birding along this road that we were late arriving at our next destination, so perhaps you should consider staying at one of the inns along this causeway.

Should you wish to dawdle along here, bring your bathing suit! There is a relatively nice inn for overnighting called **Posada Sol, Luna y Estrellas**, Calle 8 in Marylago at 8 km from the church of Boca de Uchire. The inn is the last place on the street immediately before the beach. Prior reservatons are required and the price includes breakfast, lunch and dinner. However, they have now advised us that they are open usually only on week-ends but they would make an exception for 5 or more persons. Phone numbers: (0) 281-751-1152 or 753-7551 and (0) 414-249-5595.

That limits that accommodation for bird watchers, so I would therefore recommend the inn called **Posada Oro Verde**. This is situated at some 12 km from the oft-mentioned church, and is easily located by a very high telephone antenna next to the entrance. They happily accommodated us on short notice in the middle of the week and made our stay most pleasant. During the hot hours of the afternoon when the birding activity dies down, I can recommend a dip in the sea. We were the only people in miles and miles of beach. By the way, in the vacant lot just to the west of the driveway to Oro Verde you may quite easily spot a pair of Burrowing Owls. Phone numbers: (0) 212-979-8957, 979-9086; fax: (0) 212-979-8412; mobile phone: (0) 416-681-7988.

The following is a checklist for the Unare causeway.

Least Grebe	Bay-winged Hawk	Semipalmated Sandpiper
Brown Pelican	Savanna Hawk	Western Sandpiper
Neotropic Cormorant	Common Black Hawk	Sanderling
Magnificent Frigatebird	Yellow-headed Caracara	Stilt Sandpiper
Great Blue Heron	Crested Caracara	Whimbrel
Great Egret	Aplomado Falcon	Common Dowitcher
Snowy Egret	Merlin	Black-necked Stilt
Little Blue Heron	American Kestrel	Laughing Gull
Reddish Egret	Sora	Large-billed Tern
Tricolored Heron	Wattled Jacana	Gull-billed Tern
Striated Heron	Southern Lapwing	Common Tern
Cattle Egret	Black-bellied Plover	Least Tern
Yellow-crowned Night-Heron	Semipalmated Plover	Royal Tern
Scarlet Ibis	Thick-billed Plover	Cayenne Tern
American Flamingo	Lesser Yellowlegs	Sandwich Tern
Fulvous Whistling-Duck	Greater Yellowlegs	Caspian Tern
White-faced Whistling-Duck	Spotted Sandpiper	Black Skimmer
White-cheeked Pintail	Willet	Black-necked Stilt
Blue-winged Teal	Wilson's Phalarope	Ground Dove
Cinnamon Teal	Willet	Scaled Dove
Lesser Scaup	Red Knot	Groove-billed Ani
Turkey Vulture	Least Sandpiper	Fork-tailed Palm-Swift
Pearl Kite	Baird's Sandpiper	Buffy Hummingbird
Gray-lined Hawk	White-rumped Sandpiper	Red-crowned Woodpecker

Pale-breasted Spinetail	Venezuelan Flycatcher	Carib Grackle
Common Thornbird	Brown-crested Flycatcher	Yellow Oriole
Black-crested Antshrike	Pearly-vented Tody-Tyrant	Oriole Blackbird
Barred Antshrike	Southern Beardless Tyrannulet	White-eared Conebill
White-fringed Antwren	White-winged Swallow	Bicolored Conebill
Pied Water-Tyrant	Rough-winged Swallow	Bananaquit
Cattle Tyrant	House Wren	Pileated Finch
Tropical Kingbird	Bi-colored Wren	Black-faced Grassquit
Great Kiskadee	Tropical Gnatcatcher	

At the end of this feast of water birds, one comes to El Hatillo, where the road again turns south towards the main highway and the town of Clarines. Next to the village grow the mangroves of the delta of the Unare River, which divide the two lagoons. The Flamingoes and the waders feed in both, but there is no bridge, so one cannot access the bar of the Píritu Lagoon. The Unare does not have a mouth directly to the sea, but spills into the Píritu Lagoon. The road spans over the connecting spillway after you pass the town of El Hatillo. Once you reach the main road, turn left to continue towards Barcelona.

The towns of Clarines and Píritu are endowed with what are, without a doubt, the two most beautiful colonial churches in Venezuela, and among the most remarkable and old in South America. Of the Clarines Church, one sees only the superb, unusual towers from the road, while the Píritu Church can be seen perfectly well, sitting in splendid isolation on a buff above the town; its austere, elegant lines standing boldly in the sunshine. Perhaps you might like to take a closer look, in which case, for Clarines, detour into the town, and for Píritu go down into town and across it. In either case, it will not be difficult to find your way to the Church.

Following your itinerary, continue east past Píritu, to get to Barcelona and Puerto La Cruz. However, let me warn you (once again) that as you approach Barcelona, you have to go over a bypass, as I mentioned in the first paragraph. Be on the alert. If you take the right turn off, you will be heading south, but (here we go again!) the sign for Ciudad Bolivar is all twisted, turned around and set in concrete so you can probably only see it from a hovering helicopter. Fortunately the sign for Barcelona on the left is in plain view.

Some of our tourists prefer to fly directly to Barcelona upon their arrival in Venezuela, pick up a car there and perhaps even stay overnight prior to going east or south. There is an excellent hotel we can suggest at the western entrance of Barcelona and which has the added advantage of being very close to the airport. This is **Hotel Dorado**, located on the south side of the main highway entering Barcelona and just before the roundabout for the airport. Phone numbers: (0) 281-276-9166 or 276-9245; fax: (0) 281-276-9366.

LAGUNAS DE JOSÉ

Now should you have the time there is another opportunity for you to enjoy some of the birds of Anzoategui. Anthony Pierce, one of our local birders, showed us this well-kept secret for Anzoategui, and I am most grateful to him.

From the roundabout I just mentioned turn WEST as if you were going back to Caracas (heaven forbid)! You will be driving approximately a total of 15.7 km west. After you go through the toll gate, watch your odometer. From there it is 2.3 km to a sign on your right indicting the oil installations of **Jose**. There you will see a gate. Go through, drive straight and go through yet another semi-gate and continue straight again. At 0.7 km after leaving the highway, you will come out into the open area of a xerophitic zone. Turn left and park your car under some trees. There are two lagoons in this area - one to the left (go there first) and another to the right (a bit farther away). If it is not too hot, walk around among the bushes to look for Buffy Hummingbirds and the Vermilion Cardinal. To date these are the birds listed for the **Lagunas of Jose**:

Least Grebe	Yellow-headed Caracara	Yellow-throated Spinetail
Brown Pelican	Crested Caracara	Plain-fronted Thornbird
Neotropic Cormorant	Crested Bobwhite	Barred Antshrike
Magnificent Frigatebird	Common Gallinule	Pied Water-Tyrant
Great Blue Heron	Wattled Jacana	White-headed Marsh-Tyrant
Cocoi Heron	Southern Lapwing	Vermilion Flycatcher
Great Egret	Greater Yellowlegs	Cattle Tyrant
Snowy Egret	White-rumped Sandpiper	Fork-tailed Flycatcher
Little Blue Heron	Common Stilt	Tropical Kingbird
Tri-colored Heron	Double-striped Thicknee	Great Kiskadee
Striated Heron	Black Skimmer	Brown-crested Flycatcher
Cattle Egret	Bare-eyed Pigeon	White-winged Swallow
Black-crowned Night-Heron	Eared Dove	Brown-chested Martin
Yellow-crowned Night-Heron	Common Ground-Dove	Stripe-backed Wren
Rufescent Tiger-Heron	Scaled Dove	Tropical Mockingbird
American Wood Stork	White-tipped Dove	Shiny Cowbird
Scarlet Ibis	Brown-throated Parakeet	Carib Grackle
Roseate Spoonbill	Green-rumped Parrotlet	Yellow-hooded Blackbird
Black Vulture	Smooth-billed Ani	Yellow Oriole
Turkey Vulture	Striped Cuckoo	Oriole Blackbird
White-tailed Kite	Buffy Hummingbird	Grayish Saltator
Snail Kite	Red-crowned Woodpecker	Vermilion Cardinal
Roadside Hawk	Straight-billed Woodcreeper	Red-capped Cardinal
Black-collared Hawk	Pale-breasted Spinetail	Black-faced Grassquit
Great Black Hawk		

To return to Barcelona, go back to the highway and continue driving west until you see the official entrance to the oil installation. Drive through and you will soon see a tunnel allowing access to the other side of the autopista. Unfortunately, you will have to pay the toll once again.

From Barcelona if you are going to Cumaná, you will pass through the city of Puerto La Cruz and soon enter the State of Sucre. However, getting through Barcelona and Puerto La Cruz is something else again. By the airport round about of Barcelona, keep right and take the turn off, following the signs for Puerto La Cruz. The two cities melt into one another, and traffic will probably be bad so count on 30 to 45 minutes to be on the road to Cumaná.

If your destination is Ciudad Bolivar, from the overpass at the western entrance to Barcelona you will drive the entire north-south length of Anzoategui, via the oil fields of the Mesa de Guanipa, past the Llanero town of El Tigre. From here, all the way to the Bridge of Angostura where it crosses the Orinoco, the road is traced straight as an arrow. These are the famous *rectas del Tigre*, (straight stretches of El Tigre), so boringly monotonous that they make drivers very sleepy. Be cautious.

With the exception of the coastal lagoons, the State of Anzoategui wins my prize as the ugliest state in the nation. The fact that the soils are terribly poor is compounded with the local inhabitants' bad habit of every year burning every last vestige of greenery, from the Orinoco River to the Caribbean Sea. The end result is a savanna of Curatella and inedible bunch grasses that covers 90% of the state.

If your goal is Sucre, one other relatively good birding area is found after you drive through Puerto La Cruz and pass the round about to the port area of Guanta. Approximately 7 kilometers after this round about, you will see a paved road on your right with a sign Los Altos de Santa Fe. If you have the time, drive up this road almost to the very top. When you see a red house on the right that actually belongs to the municipality, bird for a while. One of the interesting things to note up here are the huge slabs of limestone.

There are beautiful coffee plantations above Guanta, with many birds of the higher elevations, but here again you need a 4x4.

One intriguing place that is somewhat in Anzoategui is the Cerro Turimiquire. I say "somewhat" because Turimiquire sits on the very corner where the three states - Sucre, Monagas and Anzoategui - meet. And I say "intriguing" because many of the records of endemic birds of the eastern region that are deposited in the Phelps Ornithological Collection come from this area. The sad thing about Turimiquire is that it is fairly inaccessible - there are no roads to it, or those that do approach the Cerro once again require a 4x4. It is also reputed to be deforested up to its mid slopes. However, it is the highest spot in its general area and there remains (rumor has it again) quite a bit of untouched forest at the very top. At least, the Cerro keeps producing most of the water that fills the reservoirs that supply, through a submarine pipeline, the Island of Margarita. I have never been on the Turimiquire, but researchers from the Audubon and avid birders like Josep del Hoyo and Tom Brown have actually been there, and way up, found some good habitat and very interesting species, including the Gray-headed Warbler. I am telling about it with the hope that some fearless young birder decides to venture up there and then writes to me all details (and birds) of his adventure.

Venezuela Troupial

VI - 2. State of Sucre

INTRODUCTION

In terms of birding, Sucre is superb. It more than compensates for the dearth of birding opportunities in Anzoategui, which you have just left behind. I still feel that it is little known, that not too many birders have realized what there is to be found in this state. It offers a wide variety of habitats from dry, xerophitic areas to cloud forests, an unbelievable abundance of wetlands and a beautiful coastline. And if that is not enough, if icing on the cake was necessary, there are *several* endemics *found only* in these parts of the country.

Historically, Sucre was the stage of some of the first Spanish settlements on mainland America, and its capital city, Cumaná, claims to be "the first-born of the Continent". The Criollos[1] of Sucre were gloriously heroic during the Venezuelan Independence Revolution, contributing heavily, not only intellectually and financially, but with their lives - hundreds were killed in the war. The economy of the State, on the other hand, has never been exactly bright, but rather, in spite of the fisheries, in spite of the cocoa and coconut plantations, in spite of its potential for tourism, Sucre has always been one of the poorest states.

To visit Sucre, one usually drives from Caracas, but it is also possible to fly to the cities of **Cumaná** or **Carúpano**. When driving, one arrives first to **Cumaná**, and having spent 6 to 7 hours on the road from Caracas, I suggest that you stay your first night in this capital city. Try not to do the drive from Puerto La Cruz (in Anzoátegui) to Cumaná at night, not only because you'll miss the breathtaking scenery of the Mochima National Park, but also because this mountainous road can be dangerous.

Many tourists, including Venezuelans, have Mochima National Park as their goal in Sucre due to its superb beaches and snorkeling (both reached by boat from the wharf). However, I presume that you are here to bird watch and not fish watch, so will not go into further detail.

CUMANÁ

In Cumaná, I can recommend the **Hotel Minerva**, facing the Gulf of Cariaco on **Avenida Perimetral**. The Perimetral, or perimeter highway, is a beltway around the downtown of the city. (For which you can be duly grateful because the city authorities do not believe in putting up road signs.) To find the Hotel, as you approach the city, you will see some large buildings on your left, near a traffic interchange. Take the turnoff veering to the left. Eventually, you will come to a roundabout with a statue of some idiot holding a large fish. Go half way around the circle and take the road on the left. You are now on the Perimetral or beltway. You will be going past shops and businesses, as well as a sign on your left indicating the Ferry, just before you pass over a bridge. After you go over this bridge, you will see the beautiful Gulf of Cariaco also on your left. Continue on for a few blocks more until you see the Hotel Minerva on your right. This is a three-star

---

[1] The Criollos (Creoles) were the American-born descendants of Spanish settlers. They became the upper classes of the Colonies and were principally responsible for the Revolution of Independence.

hotel, clean, friendly, and quite reasonable. Ask for a room on the fourth floor, in order to have a view over the Gulf instead of staring at a blank wall. Dinner on the balcony of their restaurant means good food and a pleasing view of all the lights on the fishing boats out on the Gulf of Cariaco. Phone numbers: (0) 293-431-4471 & 431-2705.

If you fly to Cumaná, after you have picked up your car and pulled out of the airport, you should turn left (west) onto the main east-west highway. As you enter the city you will be going along a tree-lined, divided street and after about 10 minutes you will notice that most of the cars are veering right in order to reach the Perimetral. Follow them. You still have another five or ten minutes of driving before you see the Minerva on your left.

CAVEAT: The long walkway along the sea front is very enticing in the early morning or late afternoon. BUT do **NOT** walk along this equivalent of a board walk with any of your valuables. Leave everything in your hotel, especially in the early morning. There are more people around in the late afternoon.

PARIA AND EASTERN SUCRE

For me, the real Sucre starts east of Cumaná. To reach eastern Sucre and the **Peninsula of Paria** from Cumaná, take the road east along the Gulf of Cariaco, the expanse of water harbored between the Peninsula of Araya and the mainland. If you stayed the night at the Minerva, upon pulling out of the parking lot of the Hotel, turn right onto the avenue and follow the signs for **Cariaco** and **Carúpano**. Just before reaching Cariaco, take the road to **Casanay** and then on to Carúpano.

Lodging in Carúpano
Should you wish to overnight in Carúpano, you have three options: The first is **El Colibrí** inn. Coming from Cumaná and Casanay, when you reach the traffic circle with Hotel El Yunque on your left, follow the Perimetral avenue towards the right and along the water front. Keep your eye open for a green traffic sign indicating a right turn for Avenida Sur. The inn is the second house on the right on Avenida Sur, kitty-corner from the Arenera Carúpano. Phone number: (0) 294-332-3583.

Also on the Perimetral the **Hotel Euro-Caribe,** a four-star hotel and rather expensive. Phone number: (0) 294-331-3911, Fax: 331-3651.

Finally, and probably the best option is the inn **Posada La Colina.** To find this inn on Calle Boyacá No. 52, continue along the Perimetral passing the old and dilapidated Hotel Victoria (thank heavens we now have other options for this area!). Turn right on the first street after the Victoria, then right again at the next corner. This is Calle Boyacá and will lead you directly to the inn on a hill behind the Victoria and with a view of the sea. The Colina is also a good option for lunch. Phone number (0) 294-331-7297.

To reach the Paria Peninsula and other birding areas of Sucre, you have two options. One is to head for the towns of Pilar and Tunapuy. The other is probably longer, but far more attractive. After Carúpano, follow along the coast to the picturesque fishing town of **Río Caribe**.

Lodging in Rio Caribe & Neighboring Areas
When you come down into the town of Río Caribe, the coastal road dead ends at **Hotel Mar Caribe**, which is right on the shore behind all the colorful fishing boats. It is one of the lodging options you have around here, and it isn't a bad one, but I think you will be better off at the places I mention further down. Phone numbers (0) 414-779-5975 & (0) 294-782-2046. By the way, their restaurant is quite good.

In the town itself there are two inns. First choice is the **Posada Caribana**, a four-star option, extremely comfortable, decorated with excellent taste and with good food.

Located on the left of the second block on the main street or Boulevard Bermudez. You cannot miss Avenida Bermudez even if you tried as it starts from Hotel Mar Caribe and is the only wide avenue divided in the middle by a long stretch of beautiful trees. Phone/Fax: (0) 294-646-1242. In Caracas (0) 212-263-3649

Another good, clean and friendly inn is the **Posada de Arlet,** a bit more difficult to find but less expensive. No. 22, Calle 24 de Julio. Go up Boulevard Bermudez until you see the sign "Autotapiceria." Turn right and go straight until the end of the street. Turn left. The inn is on the corner. only wide avenue divided in the middle by a long stretch of beautiful trees. Phone/Fax: (0) 294-646-1290.

The best restaurant in Rio Caribe is **Paria@Cafe** almost next to the Caribana on Boulevard Bermudez. The woman who owns this small restaurant is a biologist and her husband a journalist. If you tell them you are from the Audubon, they will overwhelm you with hospitality.

Should you overnight in Rio Caribe, try to be on the wharf in the early morning to see the fishing boats come in, clean and sell their catch. The pelicans are the show of the day as they beg for scraps from the fishermen.

Now, while I adore the town of Rio Caribe, I realize that many would prefer to overnight in the countryside. Since your goal is undoubtedly the **Paria National Park**, you will be driving up to the end of Avenida Bermudez until you reach the gas station. Turn left. After two kilometers you will see a long rust-colored wall on your left of the very friendly, inexpensive inn of **Posada Ruta de Cacao**. The clean and pleasant cabins are set in a garden with many hummingbirds darting through the foliage. This is a family type inn and if you are in for something other than mad birding, they also offer horseback rides to secluded beaches. Phone number (0) 414-994-0115.

Paria offers so many delightful inns that it is hard to choose. The road you are now traveling leads to the crossroads of Bohordal, and there are yet two more possibilities. At approximately 5 kilometers from the gas station there is a dirt road on your left. Traveling this road for 8.9 kilometers more will bring you to the inn **Playa de Uva**. The inn is set in exuberant tropical foliage and has its own private beach. Also, the food is superb. However, it has a drawback because to reach the rooms you have to walk down the hill. Also, they do have electricity problems which, in turn, result in no water. Since 50% of Playa de Uva is owned by the people of Caribana, arrangements can be made to use this private beach if you are staying at Caribana. Reservations through Caribana.

At 13 kilometers from the gas station is the 5-star **Hacienda Bucare** set in a beautiful cacao plantation. I do not doubt that there are many avian species to be found in this plantation, but we had no time to investigate, and, unfortunately, they do not have a bird list. They have asked us to make one for them, but when will we have the time? Phone numbers: (0) 294-808-3003 and (0) 414-994-0054; fax: (0) 294-808-2004.

Eastern Sucre can also be reached by flying to Carúpano from the Airport at Maiquetía. All the lodges that I mention above offer their guests pick-up service from the Carúpano Airport. However, as of the present time there are no car rental agencies in Carúpano.

Now as to *where* to bird, there are numerous areas, although most of them are rather distant from Rio Caribe, but that town is your entrance to the birding areas unless you stay at La Vuelta Larga lodge. (see below.)

THE PARIA NATIONAL PARK

The **Peninsula of Paria** has a beautiful, if very neglected, national park that bears its name. The Park is famous for its numerous endemic and near-endemic species of fauna and flora. Among them are birds *endemic to Paria*. These are White-tailed Sabrewing, Scissor-tailed Hummingbird, White-throated Barbtail, Urich's Tyrannulet (a recent split and endemic to this region), Yellow-faced Redstart and Venezuelan Flower-piercer. Other beautiful Venezuelan birds found here are the Handsome Fruiteater, Tepui Parrotlet, Tufted Coquette and Slate-crowned Antpitta. As a matter of fact, this is THE spot in all of Venezuela to see the Handsome Fruiteater.

To see most of the endemics of the Park, you should bird the trail that goes up **Cerro Humo** (Smoke Mountain). The Humo is the tallest mountain in the Paria Range and a visit to this place requires both determination and a four-wheel-drive vehicle.

The "door", so to speak, of the Peninsula proper, is the village of **Las Melenas,** which is 84 km from Rio Caribe. As I indicated above, from Rio Caribe, drive straight up the divided street outside the Hotel Mar Caribe and head southeast. **Bohordal** is 61 km from Rio Caribe. You will be passing through coffee and cocoa plantations, which will surely render some good birding, so stop when you feel like it. When you reach the cross-roads at Bohordal, turn left or east onto the main highway, towards **Irapa** and your goal - **Las Melenas,** the kick off for **Cerro Humo!**

Before you reach Irapa, there is a road on your left to **Río Grande Arriba** and on to **Las Melenas**. There is actually a sign indicating the turn, but this being Venezuela, the sign faces east, so you can't read it! If you come to a gas station, you have passed it! In any event, you need a 4x4 to reach the Park Guard station at Las Melenas from Rio Grande Arriba. But don't give up. In Venezuela there is always a solution. Sr. Amado Viarroel, the father of the Park Guard, has a small truck and during the dry season, arrangements can be made for him to take you up to Las Melenas by calling him in advance at (0) 294-952-9765. I would suggest that you arrange to stay overnight at the **Hotel Mar Yoli** in Irapa, phone numbers (0) 294-989-7315 and 989-7227, and have him pick you up very, very early the next morning. The Maryoli has to struggle to rate two stars, but I believe it is satisfactory. On the other hand, if you are staying at one of the lodges, you may arrange for an excursion to Cerro Humo with them. Also, Daniel Muller of Finca La Vuelta Larga (see below) is a good bird guide, and should you be staying there, he knows Cerro Humo extremely well. My recommendation would be that no matter where you stay, you contact Daniel to take you up to Las Melenas and lead you. His expertise is well worth his fee. **Make sure that the people of the lodges understand that you must leave for Las Melenas at 5:00 a.m.**

From the main road it is 4 km to Rio Grande Arriba. Turn left, passing the overgrown plaza. At the next corner turn right and continue up the hill. When you come to a "Y" take the road on your right. From here it is 8.6 km to where the so-called road dead ends at the house of the Park Guard. I drove it in September, 2000, and white-knuckled it all the way up.

The trail up to the mountain starts just behind the station. You will be required to pay a daily fee of about Bs. 1,500, possibly more. What you get for this fee is utterly beyond me. When I last visited the Park, the main trail was in extremely bad condition, very narrow, rutted, slippery, etc. It is not a trail for the light hearted, and you should be in good physical condition.

[1]Since my last visit, I've learned that it is also possible to follow the trail that leads from the Park Guard house down through a coffee plantation to eventually connect with the higher trail. Since this trail is used constantly by the campesinos, it is easier to hike.

---

[1] Since this is a National Park, it is the responsibility of the National Institute of Parks to maintain the trail, but that comes under the heading of "Mañana". Undoubtedly they will tell you that they have no funds. One can't help wondering what was actually, really achieved and carried out with the loan of $85 million from the World Bank to help out the National Parks, which we now must pay back.

Before I forget, when I was there in September, the ginger plants, Inga trees and Heliconias were all in flower resulting in a plethora of hummingbirds. We practically had to fight them off.
As you walk up the trail, you will be going through some of the most beautiful forest I have seen in Venezuela. **Do stay on the trail, since Paria is famous for its Bush Masters and Fer-de-Lances.** Also, stay away from fruiting Palm trees, which sometimes harbour these snakes at their base, waiting for the small rodents that may be attracted by the fruits.
It is possible to rent a room with two bunk beds, sleeping four, at the house of the Park Guard. If you are able to give advance notice by telephone to Ramón and Raina Subero in Las Melenas it might be possible to stay with them as an alternative and have your meals thrown in. Telephone (0) 414-779-3120. However, I did receive a complaint from a birder that this couple is now overcharging.
Chris Sharpe tells me that many of the local villagers will volunteer to take you up into the forest on Cerro Humo if you are on your own. Ask the Park Guard or the "Comisario" (something akin to a sheriff), but do be careful that the person you go with has been duly recommended by a figure of local authority.
The Venezuelan Audubon has published a check list of the birds of the Park but in the meantime to whet your appetite, here is a partial list :

Gray Tinamou	Laughing Gull	Band-rumped Swift
Brown Pelican	Common Tern	Short-tailed Swift
Brown Booby	Band-tailed Pigeon	Rufous-breasted Hermit
Neotropical Cormorant	Pale-vented Pigeon	Band-tailed Barbthroat
Magnificent Frigatebird	Ruddy Pigeon	Green Hermit
Common Egret	Common Ground Dove	Sooty-capped Hermit
Cattle Egret	Ruddy Ground Dove	Gray-chinned Hermit
Black Vulture	Blue Ground-Dove	Little Hermit
Turkey Vulture	White-tipped Dove	White-tailed Sabrewing
Swallow-tailed Kite	Gray-fronted Dove	White-necked Jacobin
White-tailed Kite	Violaceus Quail-Dove	Brown Violetear
Hook-billed Kite	Lined Quail-Dove	Green Violetear
Plumbeous Kite	Scarlet-fronted Parakeet	Black-throated Mango
Sharp-shinned Hawk	White-eyed Parakeet	Ruby-topaz Hummingbird
White Hawk	White-eared Parakeet	Violet-headed Hummingbird
Black-collared Hawk	Green-rumped Parrotlet	Tufted Coquette
Great Black Hawk	Golden-winged Parakeet	Fork-tailed Woodnymph
Solitary Eagle	Tepui Parrotlet	Golden-tailed Sapphire
Black-and-white	Lilac-tailed Parrotlet	Copper-rumped Hummingbird
Hawk-Eagle	Blue-headed Parrot	Scissor-tailed Hummingbird
Crested Caracara	Squirrel Cuckoo	Long-tailed Sylph
Aplomado Falcon	Smooth-billed Ani	Black-eared Fairy
American Kestrel	Groove-billed Ani	Long-billed Starthroat
Rufous-vented Chachalaca	Ferruginous Pygmy Owl	Rufous-shafted Woodstar
Band-tailed Guan	Vermiculated Screech-Owl	White-tipped Quetzal
Crested Guan	Mottled Owl	Collared Trogon
Yellow-knobbed Curassow	Oilbird	Blue-crowned Motmot
Marbled Wood Quail	White-collared Swift	White-necked Puffbird
Limpkin	Chestnut-collared Swift	Groove-billed Toucanet
Southern Lapwing	Chapman´s Swift	Black-necked Araçari
Semipalmated Sandpiper	Gray-rumped Swift	Channel-billed Toucan

Red-billed Toucan
Scaled Piculet
Golden-olive Woodpecker
Chestnut Woodpecker
Waved Woodpecker
Cream-colored Woodpecker
Lineated Woodpecker
Red-crowned Woodpecker
Red-rumped Woodpecker
Plain-brown Woodcreeper
Olivaceous Woodcreeper
Wedge-billed Woodcreeper
Strong-billed Woodcreeper
Black-banded Woodcreeper
Straight-billed Woodcreeper
Buff-throated Woodcreeper
Streak-headed
  Woodcreeper
Spot-crowned Woodcreeper
Red-billed Scythebill
Pale-breasted Spinetail
Stripe-breasted Spinetail
Common Thornbird
White-throated Barbtail
Guttulated Foliage-Gleaner
Streaked Xenops
Plain Xenops
Gray-throated Leaftosser
Great Antshrike
Barred Antshrike
Slaty Antshrike
Plain Antvireo
Slaty Antwren
Long-tailed Antbird
White-bellied Antbird
Black-faced Antthrush
Plain-backed Antpitta
Slate-crowned Antpitta
Handsome Fruiteater
Chestnut-crowned Becard
Bearded Bellbird
Golden-headed Manakin
Crimson-hooded Manakin
Lance-tailed Manakin
White-bearded Manakin
Wing-barred Manakin
Pied Water-Tyrant
Fork-tailed Flycatcher
Tropical Kingbird
Gray Kingbird
Streaked Flycatcher

Rusty-margined Flycatcher
Social Flycatcher
Great Kiskadee
Lesser Kiskadee
Bright-rumped Attila
Short-crested Flycatcher
Brown-crested Flycatcher
Swainson´s Flycatcher
Dusky-capped Flycatcher
Tropical Pewee
Euler´s Flycatcher
Fuscous Flycatcher
Cinnamon Flycatcher
Bran-colored Flycatcher
Royal Flycatcher
White-throated Spadebill
Olivaceous Flatbill
Common Tody-Flycatcher
Helmeted Pygmy-tyrant
Pale-eyed Pygmy-tyrant
Marble-faced Bristle-Tyrant
Yellow Tyrannulet
Slaty Elaenia
Forest Elaenia
Southern Beardless
  Tyrannulet
Greenish Tyrannulet
Golden-faced Tyrannulet
Yellow-crowned Tyrannulet
Slaty-capped Flycatcher
Olive-striped Flycatcher
Ochre-bellied Flycatcher
Blue-and-white Swallow
Rufous-breasted Wren
Rufous-and-white Wren
Gray-breasted Wood-Wren
Tropical Mockingbird
Yellow-legged Thrush
Bare-eyed Thrush
White-necked Thrush
Pale-breasted Thrush
Long-billed Gnatwren
Rufous-browed
  Peppershrike
Yellow-throated Vireo
Red-eyed Vireo
Brown-capped Vireo
Golden-fronted Greenlet
Crested Oropendola
Yellow-rumped Cacique
Carib Grackle

Yellow-hooded Blackbird
Orange-crowned Oriole
Yellow Oriole
Tennessee Warbler
Tropical Parula
Blackburnian Warbler
Cerulean Warbler
Northern Waterthrush
Canada Warbler
American Redstart
Yellow-faced Redstart
Three-striped Warbler
Golden-crowned Warbler
Bicolored Conebill
Bananaquit
Venezuelan Flower-piercer
Purple Honeycreeper
Red-legged Honeycreeper
Green Honeycreeper
Blue Dacnis
Speckled Tanager
Turquoise Tanager
Bay-headed Tanager
Fawn-breasted Tanager
Blue-naped Chlorophonia
White-vented Euphonia
Trinidad Euphonia
Thick-billed Euphonia
Violaceous Euphonia
Blue-gray Tanager
Palm Tanager
Blue-capped Tanager
Silver-beaked Tanager
Hepatic Tanager
White-winged Tanager
Red-crowned Ant-Tanager
White-lined Tanager
White-shouldered Tanager
Guira Tanager
Fulvous-headed Tanager
Blue-black Grosbeak
Grayish Saltator
Stripe-headed
  Brush-Finch
Black-striped Sparrow
Lesser Seed-finch
Lessons Seedeater
Yellow-bellied Seedeater
Blue-black Grassquit
Wedge-tailed Grass-finch
Yellow-bellied Siskin

From Las Melenas, there is a beautiful hike through the National Park that ends down at the fishing hamlet of Sta. Isabel, on the north coast. It takes some 6 hours if your are not birding, but it is also an excellent birding walk, where all the endemics can be seen. Arrangements should be made through the private camps or lodges. I understand that there is a *Señora* called Cucha, who receives tourists in her house at Sta. Isabel (either a room or hammocks) and also supplies meals. **Do not under any circumstances try this trip on your own.** A couple of our own Audubon members did so and were robbed of all of their belongings. The official guides know whom to trust and where to take their tourists.

PLACES TO STAY /BIRD IN SOUTHERN SUCRE

Río de Agua Camp
Located between **Tunapuy** and **Bohordal** in the midst of a cattle ranch, sits at the edge of a huge marsh. There are five simple, spotless cabins, each with two beds and private bath, with screens on the windows and kerosene lamps. The Camp bears the name of this ranch of 1,000 hectares, where the "cattle" raised is water buffalo. The owners, Mr. & Mrs. Wilfred Merle, place great emphasis on conservation of their natural surroundings. As sources of energy, they have installed solar cells and a biogas plant which uses the buffalo paddies. No pesticides or chemical fertilizers are used. They have also set up a Foundation, named after their late son Thomas, dedicated to environmental education. They are indeed warm and welcoming people.

They offer the complete array of possible day trips for the area - river trips by canoe; a trip across the marsh by amphibious vehicle down to the streams leading to the Delta of the Orinoco, excursions to Cerro Humo and Paria National Park, to the Oilbird Cave (see chapter on Monagas) and down Caño Ajies. I suggest that arrangements be made in advance for any of these excursions.

Their charge includes room and full board, non-alcoholic drinks, and transfer to and from Carúpano should you travel by air. Phone numbers: (0) 294-331-2283 & 331-5241, fax: (0) 294-331-2067.

La Vuelta Larga
Is an inn and also a buffalo ranch, where one can get some of the best birding in Paria. Actually, the inn is a few kilometers north of the ranch. To reach the inn drive west from Irapa to Bohordal and continue on passing the larger town of **Tunapuy**. A few kilometers west of Tunapuy there is a paved road on the left that goes to the village of **Guaraúnos**, but naturally there is no sign! However, there is a bus stop on the right or north side of the road. One kilometer south of the main road you will see a stand of Australian fir trees (*Casuarianas*) as well as large palm-thatched rectangular constructions on your left. This is the entrance to Posada La Vuelta Larga, but again, no sign. If you are coming directly from Carúpano after passing the small city of El Pilar be on the lookout for the road going south. In this case you would be turning right.

This lodge has some nice features - an ecologically-sound architectural design and built bio-efficiently so that neither fans nor AC are necessary. They do have fans, but we did not need them. Claus Muller, the owner, is a transplanted German, and his son, Daniel, is a fairly competent bird guide. Phone (0) 294-69052. They also offer transfer service to and from the Carúpano airport.

The first place Daniel will take you will be to the finca (farm or ranch) very early in the morning and probably before breakfast. Not too long after passing Guaraúnos, you will be going through cocoa plantations and then open marsh land with a variety of side roads leading off on both sides of the main road. Unfortunately, there has been a tremendous amount of deforestation and burning over the last few years, but the finca has been kept intact - thank God. The farm covers 500 hectares of marsh, a fantastic forest, savanna and a large lagoon. These various ecosystems have resulted in a surprising variety of avifauna. Furthermore, due to the proximity of the Gulf of Paria along with the many mangrove-lined streams and rivers that empty into the Gulf, it is possible to find species in this area that are normally listed for the area of the Delta of the Orinoco[1].

The Caño Ajies

Ajies is a paltry, dirty little place indeed, but the Caño [2] is a totally different story. It sometimes happens that way here: a dumpy place is the doorway to a birding heaven.

Caño Ajies now forms part of the Turuepano National Park. I suggest that you request they take you down by dugout canoe with paddles *(canaletes)* instead of using an outboard motor, for you will see and hear the birds better. Three or four hours on the Caño would be sufficient and most enjoyable. Among the possible treats are the Rufous Crab-Hawk, the Great Potoo, the Green-and-rufous Kingfisher and the American Pygmy Kingfisher. If you are staying at one of the lodges, they all take care of the arrangements to go down the Caño. This excursion is included in the over-all charge of La Vuelta Larga.

Guariquen

This is a special excursion offered by La Vuelta Larga to enable you to see a huge rookery (between 500 and 1,000) of Scarlet Ibis. They will drive you south from the lodge for an hour and a half to the settlement of Guariquén, where you will camp for the night and be there when the birds fly in very late in the afternoon. The next day you return to La Vuelta Larga.

During your stay in this general area of southern Paria, hopefully you will see some or many of the following species:

Little Tinamou	Black-bellied Whistling-Duck	Rufous-Crab Hawk
Neotropic Cormorant	Black Vulture	Common Black Hawk
Anhinga	Turkey Vulture	Great Black Hawk
Cocoi Heron	White-tailed Kite	Laughing Falcon
Great Egret	Pearl Kite	Black Caracara
Snowy Egret	Gray-headed Kite	Yellow-headed Caracara
Striated Heron	Slender-billed Kite	Crested Caracara
Cattle Egret	Zone-tailed Hawk	Peregrine Falcon
Black-crowned Night-Heron	Roadside Hawk	Aplomado Falcon
Yellow-crowned Night-Heron	Short-tailed Hawk	Merlin
Wood Stork	Gray-lined Hawk	Rufous-vented Chachalaca
Scarlet Ibis	Long-winged Harrier	Limpkin
Green Ibis	Black-collared Hawk	Gray-necked Wood-Rail
Horned Screamer	Savannah Hawk	Russet-crowned Crake

[1] Pamela's Note: La Vuelta Larga is one of my favorite inns, but while walking in the fantastic forest of the farm I had no opportunity to observe the birds because I was too busy killing all the multitudes of insects that were feeding on my person. Mary Lou will go on and on about the *real* source of the problem not being the overflowing bug population but my *insistence* on wearing shorts in marshy areas. Don't listen to her – the place is buggy indeed!

[2] In Venezuela a "caño" may be a creek, a stream or even a small river.

Azure Gallinule
Sunbittern
Wattled Jacana
Southern Lapwing
Solitary Sandpiper
Lesser Yellowlegs
Spotted Sandpiper
Willet
Bare-eyed Pigeon
Pale-vented Pigeon
Common-Ground Dove
Ruddy Ground-Dove
White-tipped Dove
Red-shouldered Macaw
White-eyed Parakeet
Scarlet-shouldered Parrotlet
Yellow-crowned Parrot
Orange-winged Parrot
Hoatzin
Squirrel Cuckoo
Little Cuckoo
Greater Ani
Smooth-billed Ani
Striped Cuckoo
Striped Owl
Great Potoo
Pauraque
Vaux's Swift
Short-tailed Swift
Fork-tailed Palm-Swift
Rufous-breasted Hermit
Green Hermit
Reddish Hermit
Green-breasted Mango
Black-throated Mango
Ruby Topaz Hummingbird
Tufted Coquette
Blue-chinned Sapphire
Fork-tailed Woodnymph
White-tailed Goldenthroat
Copper-rumped Hummingbird
White-chested Emerald
Glittering-throated Emerald
Ringed Kingfisher
Amazon Kingfisher
Green Kingfisher
American Pygmy Kingfisher
Green-and-rufous Kingfisher
Rufous-tailed Jacamar
Russet-throated Puffbird
Black-necked Araçari

Red-billed Toucan
Scaled Piculet
Black-dotted Piculet
Spot-breasted Woodpecker
Cream-colored Woodpecker
Lineated Woodpecker
Red-crowned Woodpecker
Red-rumped Woodpecker
Crimson-crested Woodpecker
Olivaceous Woodcreeper
Buff-throated Woodcreeper
Streak-headed Woodcreeper
Red-billed Scythebill
Pale-breasted Spinetail
Yellow-chinned Spinetail
Plain Xenops
Great Antshrike
Black-crested Antshrike
White-fringed Antwren
Cinnamon Becard
White-winged Becard
Black-crowned Tityra
Crimson-hooded Manakin
Lance-tailed Manakin
Pied Water-Tyrant
Fork-tailed Flycatcher
White-headed Marsh-Tyrant
Tropical Kingbird
Piratic Flycatcher
Variegated Flycatcher
Boat-billed Flycatcher
Streaked Flycatcher
Rusty-margined Flycatcher
Social Flycatcher
Great Kiskadee
Lesser Kiskadee
Cinnamon Attila
Short-crested Flycatcher
Tropical Pewee
Yellow-breasted Flycatcher
Olivaceous Flatbill
Common Tody-Flycatcher
Spotted Tody-Flycatcher
Helmeted Pygmy-Tyrant
Yellow Tyrannulet
Yellow-bellied Elaenia
Lesser Elaenia
Scrub Flycatcher
Southern Beardless
  Tyrannulet
Ochre-bellied Flycatcher

White-winged Swallow
Gray-breasted Martin
Blue-and-white Swallow
Southern Rough-winged
  Swallow
Stripe-backed Wren
Rufous-breasted Wren
House Wren
Black-capped Donacobius
Tropical Mockingbird
Pale-breasted Thrush
Bare-eyed Thrush
Tropical Gnatcatcher
Rufous-browed Peppershrike
Golden-fronted Greenlet
Scrub Greenlet
Shiny Cowbird
Giant Cowbird
Crested Oropendola
Green Oropendola
Yellow-rumped Cacique
Carib Grackle
Velvet-fronted Grackle
Yellow-hooded Blackbird
Troupial
Yellow Oriole
Oriole Blackbird
Red-breasted Blackbird
Yellow Warbler
Northern Waterthrush
American Redstart
Golden-crowned Warbler
Bananaquit
Turquoise Tanager
Trinidad Euphonia
Violaceous Euphonia
Blue-gray Tanager
Palm Tanager
Silver-beaked Tanager
Red-crowned Ant-tanager
White-lined Tanager
Grayish Saltator
Buff-throated Saltator
Red-capped Cardinal
Lesser Seed-Finch
Large-billed Seed-Finch
Gray Seedeater
Lessons's Seedeater
Ruddy-breasted Seedeater
Blue-black Grassquit

One last note – on a recent visit to La Vuelta Larga, Daniel Muller mentioned that he had found the area of the coastal lagoon of **Chacopata,** on the Araya Peninsula to be very good birding. I have only flown over Chacopata, years ago when we were doing our censuses of Flamingos, but it may well be rewarding. As a matter of fact, I recently had a phone call from a North American birder who did go there from Cumaná, advising me that it was superb birding. He had even seen Yellow-shouldered Parrot. If you are on your own, there are a variety of inns on Araya Peninsula from luxury to rustic.

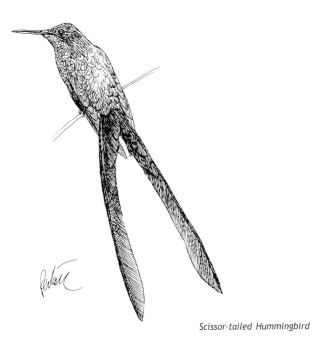

Scissor-tailed Hummingbird

VI - 3. State of Monagas

INTRODUCTION

Aside from its endless, numbing "winter" rains, a long-known fact about Monagas is its wealth in natural resources, both above and below the soggy ground. In the mountains, coffee plantations have been in production since the Corsican immigrants that established them came to settle in the mid XIX Century, and from the same period date the groves of cocoa nestled in the valleys. The wide savannas that fall down gently from the foothills to the Orinoco, are ideal for cattle, while deep under all this verdant scenery lie great reservoirs of oil and natural gas. A labyrinth of rivers, marshes and creeks afford an abundant provision of fish and as already said, it rains copiously, so all kinds of crops can be grown, such as the oil palms and a variety of fruits that have been established in recent years.

All this riches have made Monagas prosperous, but the growth in production had been gradual and the quality of life in the capital city of Maturin, as well as in towns and villages and everywhere, is peaceful and pleasant.

For us birders, Monagas will always offer its fabulous Oilbirds, as well as several great birding places, beautiful scenery, good roads and easy access from both the west and north (Barcelona and Cumaná), and the south (by crossing the Orinoco from the State of Bolivar).

THE OILBIRD CAVE

The Chaima Indians had a ringing name for the Oilbirds – Guácharos. It was quickly adopted by the Spanish settlers and duly registered by Baron Alexander Von Humboldt[1], when in 1799, the Chaimas guided him up a precipitous ravine and through dense forests to see the fabled cave and its magical birds. Elated, Humboldt describes in his dairy the difficult trek and then his astonishment and admiration for this wonder of nature he had witnessed[2].

Modern-day naturalists will find access to the Cueva del Guácharo has greatly improved since Humboldt's visit - the cave's entrance is but a stone's throw from the State Highway leading to Caripe - but the spectacle of the birds spilling out from the cavernous portal into the night sky remains the same fantastic sight as when that first intrepid bird watcher came to get this "lifer" for his Life List.

The best way to visit the cave is to stay in the charming town of **Caripe** (namesake of the Oilbird's scientific name - *Steatornis caripensis*), which is provided with small motels and inns and surrounded by a number of places to go birding. To get there, you have several options:

- Drive from Caracas via Barcelona and Cumaná (a good six hours - see chapters on Anzoátegui and Sucre), overnight in Cumaná, and continue the next day to Caripe.
- Fly from the International Airport of Maiquetía to either Barcelona or Cunamá and rent a car to drive there.

---

[1] Although Humboldt speculated that the name came from an ancient Castillian word.
[2] Alexander Von Humboldt, *Travels to the Equinoctial Regions of the New Continent*.

- Drive from the State of Bolivar by crossing the Orinoco on the chalana (ferry) at Ciudad Guayana, to Los Barrancos and then north via Maturin.

When driving eastward, if you decide to have fun birding the lagoons of Anzoategui, you will probably wish to overnight in Cumaná. In that event, in Cumaná, I can recommend the Hotel Minerva, facing the Gulf of Cariaco on Avenida Perimetral. I will rewrite here exactly what I mention in the chapter on Sucre State. (I personally hate it when an author tells me to refer back to chapter such and such for the necessary information. Then all I do is jump from one chapter to another and forget what I was doing in the first place[1].) The Perimetral, or perimeter highway, is a beltway around the downtown of the city. (For which you can be duly grateful because the city authorities do not believe in putting up road signs.) To find the Hotel, as you approach the city, you will see some large buildings on your left, near a traffic interchange. Take the left road. Eventually, you will come to a round-about with a statue of some idiot holding a large fish. Go half way around the circle and take the road on the left. You are now on the Perimetral. You will be going by quite a few shops and businesses, as well as a sign on your left indicating the Ferry, just before you pass over a bridge. After you go over this bridge, you will see the beautiful Gulf of Cariaco also on your left. Continue on for a few blocks more until you see the Hotel Minerva on your right. This is a three-star hotel, clean, friendly, and quite reasonable. Ask for a room on the fourth floor, in order to have a view over the Gulf instead of staring at a blank wall. Dinner on the balcony of their restaurant means good food and a pleasing view, and you will enjoy watching the lights of the fishing boats out on the Gulf of Cariaco. Phone numbers (0) 293-431-4471 and 431-5209.

On the other hand, if you are a glutton for long grueling drives and want to go straight to Caripe, as you approach Cumaná go straight at the interchange. Thus you will completely miss the city. From Cumaná, in Sucre, take the road that borders the Gulf of Cariaco, past San Antonio del Golfo and heading for Villa Frontina, which you will find at 72 km from the Hotel Minerva in Cumaná. Or, if you are driving straight through Cumaná on the belt-way, it is some 67 km. The junction to Caripe is near Villa Frontina, and I know from experience that it is extremely easy to miss this turn-off. Be on the lookout for a Corpoven gas station on your right. The road to Caripe is immediately before the gas station, but typically there is no sign, so you have to be on the alert. If you pass Cerezal or Terranova, you have missed the turn. From Villa Frontina it is another hour to reach Caripe. You will be climbing through dry scrub up a narrow, winding road, until you reach 800 meters above sea level, where the coffee plantations begin.

Before reaching Caripe the road crosses over the dam of a large reservoir called Embalse Las Clavellinas. Shortly after the dam there is a dirt road on the left which can provide good birding for an hour or so. Look for Black-bellied Cuckoo. By the dam itself you could see:

Little Blue Heron	White-winged Swallow
Osprey	Southern Rough-winged Swallow
Common Ground Dove	Grayish Saltator
Brown-throated Parakeet	Pileated Finch
Barred Antshrike	Gray Seedeater
Gray-breasted Martin	Blue-black Grassquit

---

[1] Note from the Editor: When other mortals (editors, for example), forget what they were doing in the first place, they are referred to (quite uncharitably) as "Apple-sauce Heads".

The Guacharo Cave's Visitors Center is easily found, for you will drive right by it as you approach Caripe. When you arrive at the ivy-covered chapel take the road on the right of the chapel to reach the cave. It is open to visitors from 7 a.m. to 5 p.m., but one must go in with a guide, so there may be a bit of a wait, as all the guides may be busy or they may want to gather a small group. The Visitors Center has a small museum and even smaller cafeteria. If they are open, while you wait, you may look around or have a coffee and watch the Green Jays that come looking for handouts.

Aside from birders and spelunkers, few foreigners have ever even heard of the Oilbirds or their cave. Nevertheless, the visit is well worth the fee charged, because it is extremely interesting. The mouth opens at the base of a beautiful rocky cliff of gray limestone, home to many Scarlet-fronted Parakeets and White-eared Parakeets. The total length is slightly over 10 km, with some 150 side passages and intriguing formations. The general public is allowed to enter only to the first 1.5 km, but to us birders, this does not matter, because the Oilbirds inhabit the main gallery, and only as deep as 700 meters.

As you go in, you will start hearing the clicks they make to navigate in the dark by echo-location, and you will catch sight of shadows that cross the vast darkness above your head. The guides will briefly shine their gas lamps towards one or two of the many ledges, nooks and crannies, to show where the birds perch and nest. During the latter part of the nesting season you will probably see young Oilbirds on the ground as it often happens that the young, when attempting to make their first flight, do not make it and land instead.

To appreciate how many Oilbirds actually roost and nest in the cave, one has to watch them fly out after nightfall, and the best way to do this is to sit quietly to one side of the stone path, by the boulders at the entrance (immediately after the little stone bridge). Then you can see them silhouetted against the sky, as Humboldt saw them. They begin to come out at approximately 7:00 p.m., and you will first hear them as they gather closer to the mouth of the cave, making strange growling noises that sound a bit like a ranting Donald Duck. In my experience, however, it will be around 8:00 when they are really pouring out, hundreds upon hundreds. I am told that the show is even better when the birds return to the cave about 4:00 a.m. - if you are an intrepid birder. In either event, take a sweater because it can be quite cool.

For those of you who have little information or knowledge of these fascinating birds, let me explain that not only do the Oilbirds live in caves, they also have an echo-location devise and feed only at night on the fruits of Laurel trees and various species of palms. While these fruits contain approximately 58% carbohydrates, they have only about 9% protein. The result is that the young of Oilbirds have one of the lowest growth rates among all birds in both temperate and tropical environments. After approximately two months of assiduous feeding by the adults, the young weigh more than their parents. It is then that the adults usually abandon their young , and at this time, also, the Chama Indians previously would take the young for their fat - hence the name Oilbirds. By their third month the young weigh about the same as the adults and start to fly and search for food along with the rest of the birds at night.

The best time to visit is the period when the birds are nesting, from May through August. From September to February, the Oilbirds tend to disperse, and usually there are less birds roosting in the cave than during the nesting period.

Immediately across the street from the Visitors Center, you will find a paved path leading to a waterfall called "La Paila" (the cooking pot). The trail is a little over one km long and passes through what was once a coffee plantation. It is a pleasant walk and in the early morning can produce a few good birds. This hill is the Cerro Negro, now a part of the National Park, and until recently the only known remaining abode of the Gray-headed Warbler.

WHERE TO STAY IN CARIPE

Agriculture is the economic base of Caripe - coffee, citrus fruits, vegetables - but as the second industry in the Caripe area is tourism, there are plenty of good inns. To name a few:

Posada La Cuchilla (★★★)
As you come down from the cave you will soon reach the crossroads Maturin/Caripe. Turn left for approximately 400 meters where you will see a road on your right leading to La Cuchilla. This is almost directly in front of the church of the town of Guácharo. Turn right and follow this beautiful road through all the coffee groves for exactly 3 km. The road itself reminds me very much of the Andes, and I am certain you will agree. At the end of the road go straight ahead through the gate and park near the sign for the reception. There are only four individual rooms but they also have cabins. I personally prefer the cabins as I found the rooms lacking in home-like amenities such as bed-side lamp and a small rug by the bed. (It can be very cool at night). Also, although their prices are very reasonable, I think I would prefer to prepare my own food or go out to dinner along the main street of the town. Be warned: immediately before the road deadends at the gate to the inn, there is a dirt road on your right. Do not even dream of driving down there, but it is a perfect road to walk for birding. More on that later. Phone numbers (0) 292-545-1469 & 545-1331. E-mail: leopardi@cantv.net. Contact: Maryflor Leopardi.

Hotel Pueblo Pequeño (★★★★)
This is more of an upscale lodging complete with tasca, etc. Although it is not in a birding area, I am including it as some may want more comfort or just plain luxury. Unfortunately, I do not have the address but considering that Caripe is a small town, you will have no problem finding it. Phone number (0) 292-545-1256.

Campamento Agroecológico Campo Claro (★★★)
Contact: Francisco and Nery Betancourt. This inn does not have such a spectacular location as La Cuchilla, but the owners are very tuned in to bird watching and nature. Also, it is a 70 hectare plantation with shade coffee, orange groves, etc. They offered to show me the forested area, but unfortunately I had no time to stay. (The usual blight of my life). Their meals are excellent and any passerby may stop for breakfast. Other meals would require prior arrangement. They also sell homemade cakes, cookies and jams as well as their own organically-grown shade-coffee, and I can assure you that it is the best coffee in Venezuela. I would not recommend the inn during Christmas, Easter, school holidays, etc. as they tend to have a lot of children and larger groups. Phone/Fax: (0) 292-545-1013. E-mail: campoclaro@cantv.net .

To reach Campo Claro, drive all the way east through the town of Caripe (some 7 + km from the crossroads below the cave), passing the ice plant at 10 km. You will come to a fork and the blue and white building of the "Bodega La Gran Parada", where you go on the left side of the building to continue on the main road towards Teresén. When you reach the T of the town or village of Teresén turn right and continue to almost 14.5 km from the crossroads below the cave where you will see a bridge. Go left for Campo Claro.

By the by - just because Caripe is a very small town does not mean that it is backward. It even has a **Cybercafe!**

BIRDING AROUND CARIPE

Practically any time of the year is good birding around Caripe. From September to November when the Inga trees that shade the coffee are in full blossom, it is very easy to find the White-tailed Sabrewing, and other hummingbirds as well as tanagers, honeycreepers, etc. in the coffee groves around Caripe. But so also are the months of March and April when the Mountain Immortelles festoon the hills with their flame-colored blossoms, forming a sharp contrast with the brilliant flowers of the Yellow Pui or Araguaney, the national tree of Venezuela.

I mentioned above the possibility of birding in the coffee groves of La Cuchilla. Walk down the dirt road just before the main entrance to the inn and look for:

Forest Falcon sp.	Plain Brown Woodcreeper	Pale-breasted Thrush
Band-tailed Guan	Olive-backed Woodcreeper	Crested Oropendola
Rufous-vented Chachalaca	Streak-headed	Orange-crowned Oriole
White-tipped Dove	Woodcreeper	American Redstart
Scarlet-fronted Parakeet	White-winged Becard	Golden-crowned Warbler
White-eared Parakeet	Boat-billed Flycatcher	Speckled Tanager
Smooth-billed Ani	Great Kiskadee	Bay-headed Tanager
Ferruginous Pygmy Owl	Dusky-capped Flycatcher	Burnished -buff Tanager
White-tailed Sabrewing	Eastern Wood Pewee	Fawn-breasted Tanager
Copper-rumped	Slaty-capped Flycatcher	Blue-naped Chlorophonia
Hummingbird	Ochre-bellied Flycatcher	Trinidad Euphonia
Long-billed Starthroat	Green Jay	Hepatic Tanager
Groove-billed Toucanet	Bi-colored Wren	Summer Tanager
Spot-breasted Woodpecker	House Wren	White-lined Tanager
Lineated Woodpecker	Tropical Mockingbird	Guira Tanager

Another birding area I very much enjoyed during my stay at La Cuchilla was along the trail in the valley past the buildings.

Yet another good birding site are the coffee and orange groves above the town of Teresén, heading towards the hamlet of Santa Ines, some 17 km east of Caripe. To reach this area from Caripe, drive out towards the east on the main street, the same as if you were going to have breakfast at Hacienda Campo Claro, but at the bridge go right. You are now headed for Santa Inés. From there, you have two options - the road to La Margarita and the road to Yacucural. The first one is straight on, winding its way up the mountain. You will cross a large bridge over the Rio Colorado. Stop to bird in this vicinity. Unfortunately, this general area has been built up a great deal since first I visited it ten years ago, but I still believe it is worth birding. You will eventually come to another river only to find that the bridge is out. However, they have made a make-shift bridge which I believe you can drive over in your rental car - at least in the dry season. Upon reaching the other side, park, lock your car and walk. We birded the area just before this second stream and saw:

Swallow-tailed Kite	Ferruginous Pygmy Owl	Rufous-browed Peppershrike
Double-toothed Kite	Black-and-white Becard	Yellow-rumped Cacique
Solitary Eagle	Black-tailed Tityra	Silver-beak Tanager
Green-rumped Parrotlet	Yellow-legged Thrush	Lesser Goldfinch

Here I must make a confession. During my recent visit to this area, I was seized by an uncontrollable urge to explore, so rather than bird (as would have been proper, since that was the original idea), I continued on to the end of the road at the hamlet of La Margarita, some 31.5 km from La Cuchilla. The road left a lot to be desired, but the views were spectacular. There went a role of film. Therefore, I am not ashamed to admit my neglect of the birds.

The second option is a good dirt road that you can investigate by taking a very steep street that you will see on the right as you go through Santa Ines. It climbs very high, winding through beautiful shade coffee plantations towards Yacucural.

Perhaps I should point out that during this last visit we used the recording of the Ferruginous Pygmy Owl with astonishing results, not the least of which was the fact that the Owl itself came out every time and no matter where we were.

Many birders hope to see the Gray-headed Warbler while in Caripe. If this is one of your goals in life, you will need a guide and very good physical condition, for finding the birds requires a no-nonsense hike up Cerro Negro. To get a guide, there are several of the Park Guards/Guides at the cave who know how to reach the heights of Cerro Negro and are your best option, so you should ask around and establish contact with Fernando, Benjamin or Blas at the Visitors Center, requesting help to go up the Cerro Negro by the Sabana de Piedra entrance across the road from the office of the Jefe Civil. Plan to leave before dawn (best about 4:30 a.m.) to climb the hill, and count on approximately an eight-hour round-trip. There is an excellent article by Thomas Brooks on "Finding Gray-headed Warbler on Cerro Negro" in the Autumn 2000 edition of Cotinga (No. 14), the journal of the Neotropical Bird Club.

The Warbler has also been seen recently by Josep del Hoyo in Las Puertas de Miraflores. Josep and his guide, Daniel Muller from La Vuelta Larga in Sucre, discovered it with the aid of Jesús Gonzalez, the Park Guard of Las Puertas de Miraflores. How to reach Miraflores is explained below, but you will need the assistance of the Park Guard to find the general area of the bird. However, during the dry season of 2000/2001 so many fires were set in this region, that I now believe it would be useless to look for the bird around Miraflores, at least for a few years.

Apparently, Park Guard Jesús Gonzalez can often be found at the Cueva del Guacharo, so you might ask around there for him to determine if there is any possibility of finding the bird in his area of Miraflores.

PUERTAS DE MIRAFLORES O DEL GUARAPICHE

Aside from looking for the Warbler, I have one last side trip to suggest before you leave Caripe, although this one is not so much a bird-watching excursion as one of adventure. If you have the time, want to see something truly spectacular and are not decrepit (I did it at the age of 70[1]), then take a day off to go to the Puertas del Guarapiche, (the "gates" of the Guarapiche River, also called Puertas de Miraflores, as the place is above the town of Miraflores).

Before you set out, make sure the day it is not a week-end or public holiday. Be prepared to wet your feet, wear a bathing suit, and leave a change of dry clothes and shoes in the car, as you will be walking in the river, sometimes with water to your waist.

To reach the spot where this fun trek begins, exit Caripe towards the west, past the town of El Guácharo and on to a dam called Embalse El Guamo. There is a park here where you might want to stop to look for water birds - there may be grebes, egrets, Blue-winged Teal, Common Gallinule, Caribbean Coot, Wattled Jacanas, etc. The access road to Parque Recreacional Turístico El Guamo can be found where the main highway veers towards the west on a wide curve. By the road look for Slate-headed Tody-tyrant, Pale-eyed Pygmy-tyrant, and Ochre-bellied Flycatcher.

---

[1] Note from the Editor: It's a bird! It's a turkey! It's a bat! No, wait! It's Super-little-old-lady-in-tennis-shoes!

Next to the dam, there used to be a town called San Francisco but the site was flooded when the dam was completed. The maps, however, still show San Francisco. Here, you turn north, continuing past the town of San Antonio. After the towns of San Antonio, Rincón and Triste, when you reach the hamlet of Campo Alegre, turn right, following the signs for the "Balneario Miraflores." This is 44 km from the many-times aforementioned crossroads of the cave with the road to Maturin.

There is a parking lot where you can leave your car (well locked). Walk past the swimming hole and the various houses, and look for the start of a path on the other side of the river, leading up-stream. It is not hard to find, but if necessary, ask where to cross the river to find el sendero. Once on the other side you will be walking through coffee and orange groves, and will cross the river another four or five times, until suddenly you come upon a very narrow, deep limestone canyon, some 100 meters high by 10 meters wide.

The Guarapiche River has carved out this narrow gorge. During the dry season there is no problem in making your way up the gorge, but I was there in the rainy season, and the force of the water was daunting. At the upper end of the gorge, the canyon opens out into a sylvan place, cool and filled with great old trees. Here the river has formed over the sandstone ledges a natural pool, ideal for swimming. On the banks there are large slabs free of vegetation where one can sit for a picnic. The trek from the Balneario takes about an hour to an hour and a half, depending on the amount of time one takes on the river crossings and the search for the trails on the opposite sides. It is an absolutely wonderful trek!

General Bird List for Caripe

Little Tinamou	Green Violetear	White-winged Becard
Gray-lined Hawk	Black-throated Mango	Black-tailed Tityra
Yellow-headed Caracara	Ruby Topaz	Black Phoebe
Rufous-vented Chachalaca	Blue-tailed Emerald	Tropical Kingbird
Ruddy Pigeon	Green-tailed Emerald	Boat-billed Flycatcher
Ruddy Ground Dove	Fork-tailed Woodnymph	Streaked Flycatcher
White-tipped Dove	Golden-tailed Sapphire	Golden-crowned Flycatcher
Lined Quail-Dove	Copper-rumped Hummingbird	Social Flycatcher
Brown-throated Parakeet	White-vented Plumeleteer	Great Kiskadee
Scarlet-fronted Parakeet	Rufous-shafted Woodstar	Tropical Pewee
White-eared Parakeet	White-tailed Trogon	Cinnamon Flycatcher
Golden-winged Parakeet	Collared Trogon	Bran-colored Flycatcher
Red-billed Parrot	Groove-billed Toucanet	Yellow-olive Flycatcher
Squirrel Cuckoo	Scaled Piculet	Yellow-bellied Elaenia
Smooth-billed An	Golden-olive Woodpecker	Slaty-capped Flycatcher
Groove-billed Ani	Red-crowned Woodpecker	Olive-striped Flycatcher
Tropical Screech Owl	Smoky-brown Woodpecker	Ochre-bellied Flycatcher
Ferruginous Pygmy-owl	Plain-brown Woodcreeper	Blue-and-white Swallow
Oilbird	Olivaceous Woodcreeper	Southern Rough-winged Swallow
White-collared Swift	Buff-throated Woodcreeper	Green Jay
Vaux´s Swift	Streak-headed Woodcreeper	Bi-colored Wren
Gray-rumped Swift	Strong-billed Woodcreeper	Whiskered Wren
White-tipped Swift	Pale-breasted Spinetail	Rufous-breasted Wren
Green Hermit	Crested Spinetail	Tropical Mockingbird
Sooty-capped Hermit	Great Antshrike	Orange-billed
White-tailed Sabrewing	Chestnut-crowned Becard	Nightingale Thrush

Yellow-legged Thrush
Glossy Black Thrush
Pale-breasted Thrush
Bare-eyed Thrush
White-necked Thrush
Rufous-browed Peppershrike
Red-eyed Vireo
Golden-fronted Greenlet
Giant Cowbird
Crested Oropendola
Orange-crowned Oriole
Yellow Oriole
Blackburnian Warbler
Tropical Parula

American Redstart
Slate-throated Redstart
Three-striped Warbler
Golden-crowned Warbler
Bananaquit
Venezuelan Flower-piercer
(seen by Rio Colorado bridge)
Purple Honeycreeper
Red-legged Honeycreeper
Swallow Tanager
Blue-naped Chlorophonia
Speckled Tanager
Bay-headed Tanager
Burnished-buff Tanager

Black-headed Tanager
Blue-gray Tanager
Palm Tanager
White-winged Tanager
White-lined Tanager
Guira Tanager
Fulvous-headed Tanager
Grayish Saltator
Streaked Saltator
Yellow Grosbeak
Blue-black Grassquit
Yellow-bellied Seedeater
Ochre-breasted Brush Finch
Rufous-collared Sparrow

MATURIN

The State Capital is a pleasing city. There are wide streets, large parks and the city is generally clean and well-kept. It is also well-endowed with decent places to eat. Many streets are shaded by Malay Apples and when they blossom, a carpet of bright reddish-purple filaments carpet the sidewalks and a mob of birds are found gorging on the fruits or the flowers, especially hummingbirds, who have a passion for the bright blossoms.

To reach it from Caripe, drive west, passing the town of El Guácharo and continue west to the crossroads at San Francisco, where you will turn south towards Aragua de Maturin, past Guayuto and Chaguaramal. Maturin is only 89 km from Caripe, but due to the road, it will take you about two and a half hours.

Arriving like this, from the north, you will enter town on the divided Avenida Ugarte Pelayo; pass, on your right, the regional headquarters of Lagoven, and then on your left, the fancy Stauffer Hotel. You will find a large traffic interchange just as you come into the city. The best strategy here is to take the far left fork that goes towards the airport. You will now be on the main highway or Avenida Presidente Raul Leoni, that goes south all the way to the Orinoco River. If you are staying at Hotels Colonial or Emperador, you can turn right when you reach Ave. Bolivar. If you are staying at Tobago's Inn, at the round-about, go straight on to Avenida Juncal and turn left at Calle Monagas. Keep your eye peeled for the Banco Mercantil on your left because the hotel is on the very next corner. Turn right on Calle Montserat for the entrance.

From Caracas and the coast, one comes via Barcelona in Anzoátegui. Just west of the outskirts of Barcelona, you will approach an overpass which divides into two ramps over the highway passing underneath (National Highway 16). The left ramp leads to downtown Barcelona (and turning back will take you hours!); the one to your right leads to National Highway 16 and the south. A sign indicating the two destinations was finally installed a few months ago. Make sure you take the right ramp and then head south on Highway 16 for 52 km, until you find the turn east onto State Highway 13, which will lead you to El Tejero, El Furrial and eventually to Maturin.

Staying in Maturin

Maturin is an oil city, and consequently quite expensive, but there are options. There are several good hotels, including the four-star **Stauffer Maturin,** which you pass on your left if you are coming from Caripe, as it is situated slightly north of the city. Phone numbers: (0) 291-643-0622 & 643-1111.

If you are coming from Caracas on Highway 13, you will pass in front of the five-star **Hotel Morichal Largo** on the left. Phone numbers: (0) 291-651-4222 & 6514422. Highway 13 becomes Avenida Bicentenaria once you have entered the city and eventually becomes Avenida Bolivar. Continue on Avenida Bicentenaria, until you reach the first stop light, where you should turn left. You will soon be passing a hospital, on your left, and a block and a half after the stop light you will pass, on the right, the two-star **Hotel Emperador,** which previously was quite acceptable. However, one of our guides just informed me that he had very recently stayed there and found cockroaches everywhere. The restaurant, on the other hand, was very good but quite expensive.

Another hotel recommended to us is the three-star **Hotel Colonial,** located almost in the center of town, on the south side of Avenida Bolívar. Phone: (0) 291-642-1175. My guide-friends say that the food at the Colonial is the best in Maturin, but you may have to ask them several times to lower the music so you can at least hear yourself think.

Finally, there is the **Tobago's Inn** (★★★) mentioned above. Phone: (0) 291-643-8473, fax: (0) 291-643-9142, Calle Monagas with Calle Giradot, 200 meters from the Banco Mercantil. This hotel has recently opened in a renovated building and is quite acceptable, plus the fact that it is just a half block off of Avenida Bolivar, where there are numerous small places to eat.

I would especially like to recommend the small Arab restaurant just around the corner on Avenida Bolivar. There I had the best Shawarma sandwich of my life. Outside the restaurant there is a stand with sheaves of chicken or beef from which they cut slices to make you this special treat complete with vegetables. Inexpensive too.

If you are traveling on to the State of Bolivar, turn right on Presidente Leoni, as this is Highway 10, the road leading south. Be sure to buy gas at the station on the southern end of town because it is a long , long way to the next station.

Should you have a few free hours and wonder where to go birding around Maturín itself, drive south on Avenida Presidente Leoni. Five km after the now defunct Chama Inn, there is a road coming in from the west or right which is a by-pass around the city. The road is in bad shape, but it is good birding, especially in the rainy season.

CAÑO COLORADO

The area of Caño Colorado, and later the route to the lower Guarapiche River, both to the east of Maturin, were first discovered as excellent birding sites by Peter Boesman. After exploring around quite thoroughly, Peter wrote an article on the Caño Colorado for Cotinga[1], the journal of the Neotropical Bird Club. (By the way, if you are interested in Neotropical birds, I recommend you become a member of this club, as the information contained in their publication is excellent.)

To do this area justice you will need two days in Maturin, but don't do as I did when I first went there, and attempt it in the wet season. For one thing, the path to the Caño Colorado goes through varzea forest, which means that it is flooded a good part of the year. According to Peter, during the dry season one can drive almost to the Colorado, but you should have a 4 X 4. For the solution to that problem, see below. In the wet season... Forget it!

To bird the Caño Colorado trail, you should leave Maturin by 5:00 a.m. Drive east on the street that goes to the airport, Carrera 2, passing the entrance to the airport terminal, towards La Pica and then the small village of Vuelta Larga. From the junction

---

[1] Issue No. 3.

of the Avenida Raul Leoni with Carrera 2 (the airport road), to the village of Vuelta Larga, it is 17.8 km. At 23 km, the dirt road starts practically where the plantations of African Oil Palms begin. At 24 km is the first cross roads (more about that later). Drive past yet another cross roads at 26 km, and at 28 km there is a concrete house on the left where one should park, lock up and start walking east. You will have to walk or drive some 4 km before you reach primary forest. I must warn you that until you reach the forest, it is one hot walk (especially on your return trip in the afternoon), so take an ample supply of liquids. Considering the distance and the heat, you would be better off to hire a 4 X 4.

In his Cotinga article, Peter Boesman tells it better than I ever could, so with his kind permission, I will quote here a good deal of what he said:

«*Around 20 years ago the area was mainly forested and was included within the "Reserva Forestal de Guarapiche." Unfortunately, when the cultivation of African Oil-palms made the area economically valuable, deforestation began (a legitimate activity within a "reserva forestal"). At present the first 9 km of dirt road pass through degraded habitat, primarily comprising oil-palm plantations. Further on, the forest becomes increasingly intact. There are many side roads along which other patches of good forest can presumably be reached.*

The whole area is below 20 meters altitude and in the wet season (June to September) the last 8 km of the main road are inaccessible by car. At this time, large areas of forest are flooded (i.e. varzea), whilst terra firma is restricted to raised areas. The varzea is characterized by a relatively open understorey, a low canopy and (especially from the caño onwards) many natural palms. Caño Colorado is probably representative of the large area of intact habitat that still exists behind the mangroves and swamps lining the coasts of Sucre and Delta Amacuro.

A wide variety of species can be seen in the deforested area and along forest borders where observation is easier, but many of the more interesting species occur only in continuous forest. A morning walk down the main track normally produces 90-100 bird species, which is remarkable for a forested area north of the Orinoco with one basic habitat at one altitude.

Several larger forest species are still present despite hunting pressure from the "campesinos." One can walk for hours, however, without seeing anybody, which makes birding a delight. From July 1993 to August 1994, I made some 20 visits to the area, mainly in the dry season, and observed a total of 220 species. Of these, no less that 40 (8%) are not mentioned by Meyer de Schauensee & Phelps for Monagas state, and 16 species are new for north-eastern Venezuela. The area undoubtedly holds many more species as I averaged five new species for the local checklist on each of my last five visits. Birding is best from just before dawn until 10:00, at which time it begins to get too hot. Access is easy from January to April, but during the wet season the area is virtually impenetrable as grass grows to head-height, and water reaches a depth of 30-80 cm in the flooded forest.»

I mentioned above the first dirt road at 24 km from the junction of Avenida Presidente Leoni with the airport road. This led to the other super trail that Peter Boesman ferreted out and eventually reached the Guarpiche River. Here it was necessary or advisable to have rubber boots. Unfortunately, during my recent visit I found that there have been some intrusions in this area by small settlers or squatters, and I was unable to find this very best birding path, but you may have better luck because I did not have my instructions with me! Turn left on this road. Go for 1.75 km passing a small bridge, and upon reaching a small parking area where the road turns to the right, park and walk past the houses, following the trail that leads towards the east. After a while the trail turned into a clearing. At the opposite side, a large fallen tree served as a bridge over the stream that bordered the clearing. The trail leading to the Guarapiche River started at the other side of this stream and follows it, coming eventually onto a very nice forest. The trail goes for several km and finally reaches the river.

Here is a bird list for this general area, Caño Colorado - Guarapiche, and I will appreciate very much your reports on additions you may find:

Little Tinamou	Red-shouldered Macaw	Red-billed Toucan
Red-legged Tinamou	White-eyed Parakeet	Black-dotted Piculet
Cocoi Heron	Painted Parakeet	Chestnut Woodpecker
Great Egret	Green-rumped Parrotlet	Cream-colored Woodpecker
Striated Heron	Golden-winged Parakeet	Ringed Woodpecker
Capped Heron	Lilac-tailed Parrotlet	Red-crowned Woodpecker
Horned Screamer	Scarlet-shouldered Parrotlet	Golden-collared Woodpecker
King Vulture	Black-headed Parrot	Lineated Woodpecker
Black Vulture	Blue-headed Parrot	Red-rumped Woodpecker
Greater Yellow-headed Vulture	Orange-winged Parrot	Crimson-crested Woodpecker
Swallow-tailed Kite	Squirrel Cuckoo	Plain-brown Woodcreeper
Plumbeous Kite	Little Cuckoo	Olivaceous Woodcreeper
Slender-billed Kite	Greater Ani	Striped Woodcreeper
Bicolored Hawk	Smooth-billed Ani	Buff-throated Woodcreeper
Roadside Hawk	Striped Cuckoo	Streaked-headed Woodcreeper
Gray-lined Hawk	Spectacled Owl	Curve-billed Scythebill
Black-collared Hawk	Common Pauraque	Common Thornbird
Savanna Hawk	White-collared Swift	Plain Xenops
Great Black Hawk	Short-tailed Swift	Barred Antshrike
Black Hawk-Eagle	Rufous-breasted Hermit	Eastern Slaty Antshrike
Laughing Falcon	Reddish Hermit	Plain Antvireo
Red-throated Caracara	Little Hermit	White-flanked Antwren
Crested Caracara	White-necked Jacobin	White-fringed Antwren
American Kestrel	Green-throated Mango	Jet Antbird
Blue-throated Piping Guan	Black-throated Mango	Black-chinned Antbird
Limpkin	Blue-chinned Sapphire	Spot-winged Antbird
Gray-winged Trumpeter	Blue-tailed Emerald	Silvered Antbird
Gray-necked Wood-Rail	Fork-tailed Woodnymph	White-bellied Antbird
Purple Gallinule	White-chested Emerald	White-winged Becard
Sunbittern	Plain-bellied Emerald	Black-capped Becard
Wattled Jacana	Long-billed Starthroat	Black-crowned Tityra
Solitary Sandpiper	White-tailed Trogon	Bearded Bellbird
Pale-vented Pigeon	Ringed Kingfisher	Golden-headed Manakin
Ruddy Pigeon	Green Kingfisher	Crimson-hooded Manakin
Common Ground-Dove	Green-and-rufous Kingfisher	White-headed Marsh-tyrant
Ruddy Ground-Dove	Rufous-tailed Jacamar	Drab Water-tyrant
Blue Ground-Dove	Russet-throated Puffbird	Tropical Kingbird
Gray-fronted Dove	Swallow-wing	Variegated Flycatcher
Blue-and-yellow Macaw	Black-necked Araçari	Piratic Flycatcher
Red-and-green Macaw	Channel-billed Toucan	Boat-billed Flycatcher

Streaked Flycatcher	Yellow-crowned Elaenia	Yellow Oriole
Rusty-margined Flycatcher	Ochre-bellied Flycatcher	Oriole Blackbird
Social Flycatcher	White-winged Swallow	Bananaquit
Great Kiskadee	Southern Rough-winged	Purple Honeycreeper
Cinnamon Attila	Swallow	Blue Dacnis
Grayish Mourner	Stripe-backed Wren	Turquoise Tanager
Cinereous Mourner	Rufous-and-white Wren	Violaceous Euphonia
Short-crested Flycatcher	Buff-breasted Wren	Thick-billed Euphonia
Dusky-capped Flycatcher	House Wren	Blue-gray Tanager
Yellow-bellied Flycatcher	White-breasted Wood-wren	Palm Tanager
Rufous-tailed Flatbill	Black-capped Donacobius	Silver-beaked Tanager
Common Tody-flycatcher	Cocoa Thrush	White-lined Tanager
Slate-headed Tody-flycatcher	Long-billed Gnatwren	White-shouldered Tanager
Helmeted Pygmy Tyrant	Rufous-browed Peppershrike	Grayish Saltator
Short-tailed Pygmy-tyrant	Golden-fronted Greenlet	Dickcissel
Yellow Tyrannulet	Giant Cowbird	Lesser Seed-finch
Yellow-bellied Elaenia	Crested Oropendola	Gray Seedeater
Slaty Elaenia	Green Oropendola	Lesson´s Seedeater
Forest Elaenia	Yellow-rumped Cacique	Yellow-bellied Seedeater
Southern Beardless Flycatcher	Velvet-fronted Grackle	Blue-black Grassquit

I would like to take this opportunity to introduce you to my friend Jesús Molinos, who lives in Maturin (when he is not on his farm to the south), speaks English and does have a 4 X 4. I highly recommend that you get in touch with Jesús at (0) 414-772-5288; e-mail: campamentolaceiba@hotmail.com or laceibajm@cantv.net and arrange for him to take you to Caño Colorado.

AGROPECUARIA LA CEIBA

Agropecuaria La Ceiba is Jesús Molinos´ farm. Actually, Jesús has two houses on this stretch of lands of the Savannas of Monagas, both in need of some fixing up, which Jesús keeps threatening to do in order to have guests who are both birders or general nature lovers[1].

Those of us who are residents of Venezuela delight in staying at his ranch/farm and sleeping in hammocks under the thatched roof of an open-sided caney. We have the use of the kitchen and also the bathrooms[2]. If you are intrepid, ask about the possibility of staying at the ranch with *chinchorros* (hammocks) and *mosquiteros* (the mosquito nets are made specially for hammocks and are an absolute must), which you will be able to hang in the very pretty caney.

The farm is located some 57 + km south-east of Maturin, in the midst of the Llanos of Monagas. As you drive out of Maturín, you will pass the defunct Hotel Chaima on your right. Count approximately 40 km south from the Chaima, when you will arrive at the toll booth of El Blanquero. Immediately after the toll, there is a road on the left with a gate and a guard for the oil substation. Just tell him that you are going to the finca of Jesús Molinos. This is a good dirt road leading east and most interesting for

---

[1] Last minute news - Jesus has just called us that the main house is now fixed up and ready to receive guests!!

[2] Jesus has built outdoor showers and johns near the caneys.

birding. You may eventually meet another gate that may be shut, but it is never locked. You should be able to open it and pass through without much ado. At 14 km from the main highway, you will find the main gate to the farm on the right. Now here comes the problem. From this main gate it is 7 km to the house on a very bad road, although Jesús did assure me recently that it would soon be repaired (?) The best thing though, is to arrange to meet with Jesús in Maturin, so he can drive you to his place in his 4WD, for this last leg of road into the farm is a real humdinger.

The local birds in the farm are, for the most part, Llano birds, but with odd, exciting additions such as Black-spotted Piculets, Velvet-fronted Grackles and Crimson-hooded Manakins, so that in our most recent visit, we counted 132 species in one day as well as Giant Otters and Capybaras.

The great thing however, is that Jesús can also takes birders on boat rides along the Tigre River, which borders the farm. The Tigre is not as wide and long as the Morichal Largo to the south, and the vegetation is different - gallery forest with only small, scattered patches of morichal habitat. For the most part I have never had much luck birding from a boat, but the Tigre has been the exception.

Another fascinating trip that Jesús can arrange for you would be to take you first cross country through his various neighbors' holdings (where you will go bonkers seeing all the birds) and then in a launch down the Caño Buja. The Buja eventually empties into the Delta of the Orinoco and runs through gallery, Morichal and mangrove forests[1]. It is a beautiful trip for some 45 minutes to the dwelling of a Warao Indian family. The head of the family took us all round his island, explaining carefully what leaves, what sap, bark etc. they use for sundry illnesses; which palm trees they use for their roofs and which for the sides of their houses and much more. It was a wonderful trip.

By the way, we birders have to push the tourism establishments in all areas of the Delta to learn about bird watchers. We need silence. Therefore, we need canoes and paddles, none of this motorboat business. Jesús has already realized this. He is a most enterprising young man, and I believe that if he goes ahead with his plans to develop tourism for bird watchers in the area, it will turn out to be most interesting bird-wise, since it offers a fascinating mixture of Llano species and birds from the Orinoco Delta. I hope to be able to visit the area some time in the future to check out new sites in all this general area. My problem is that there are just too many places to bird in Venezuela!

A general list of the birds around the farm, including the Caño Buja would include the following:

Neotropical Cormorant	Black Vulture	Great Black Hawk
Cocoi Heron	Turkey Vulture	Long-winged Harrier
Great Egret	Greater Yellow-headed Vulture	Laughing Hawk
Whistling Heron	Roadside Hawk	Yellow-Headed Caracara
Jabiru Stork	Harris Hawk	Crested Caracara
Maguari Stork	Savanna Hawk	Aplomado Falcon
Wood Stork	Black-collared Hawk	American Kestrel
Horned Screamer	Rufous-crab Hawk	Crested Bobwhite

[1] In February, 2001 the national Government declared the "Gran Morichal de Monagas" Wildlife Sanctuary. The area either runs very close to the borders of La Ceiba if it does not actually include the ranch. To date I have not seen a detailed map, but I know it encompasses Morichal Largo and possibly Caño Buja. This is a tremendously good news since it means that the wonderful wildlife of this region is now legally protected.

Purple Gallinule	White-chested Emerald	White-winged Swallow
Wattled Jacana	White-tailed Trogon	Southern Rough-winged
Southern Lapwing	Ringed Kingfisher	Swallow
Pied Lapwing	Rufous-tailed Jacamar	Violaceous Jay
Sandpiper, sp.	Russet-throated Puffbird	Bi-colored Wren
Double-striped Thick-knee	Black-dotted Piculet	Stripe-backed Wren
Pale-vented Pigeon	Cream-colored	Buff-breasted Wren
Scaled Dove	Woodpecker	Scrub Greenlet
White-tipped Dove	Lineated Woodpecker	Velvet-fronted Grackle
Brown-throated Parakeet	Common Thornbird	Yellow-rumped Cacique
Orange-winged Parrot	Black-crested Antshrike	Orange-crowned Oriole
Hoatzin	Crimson-hooded Manakin	Troupial
Squirrel Cuckoo	Pied Water-Tyrant	Yellow Oriole
Smooth-billed Ani	White-headed Marsh-Tyrant	Oriole Blackbird
Greater Ani	Vermilion Flycatcher	Red-breasted Blackbird
Rufescent Pygmy Owl	Fork-tailed Flycatcher	Eastern Meadowlark
Burrowing Owl	Boat-billed Flycatcher	Yellow Warbler
Pauraque	Streaked Flycatcher	Trinidad Euphonia
Reddish Hermit	Great Kiskadee	Thick-billed Euphonia
Green-throated Mango	Brown-crested Flycatcher	Violaceous Euphonia
Ruby -topaz Hummingbird	Dusky-capped Flycatcher	Silver-beaked Tanager
Blue-tailed Emerald	Slate-headed Tody-Flycatcher	Red-capped Cardinal
White-tailed Golden-throat	Pale-eyed Pygmy-Tyrant	Yellow-browed Sparrow
Glittering-throated Emerald	Southern Beardless Tyrannulet	Blue-black Grassquit

Posada Rancho San Andres

If you are heading straight south from Maturin, going to the south Delta or Bolivar State, there is only one place I can recommend to stay en route. This would also be a good alternative to camping at Finca La Ceiba, and still be close enough to go on the various excursions with Jesús Molinos. Because it is a cattle ranch with very few trees, Posada Rancho San Andres is not especially an area for bird watchers. However, it is an extremely comfortable inn complete with swimming pool, good food and attention. They do offer horse-back rides, but I have yet to meet a birder with binoculars on horseback! Some 11 km south of the toll booth of El Blanquero there is a road to the right leading to Aribí. Another point of reference is the Restaurant La Antena at the intersection (there is a huge antenna nearby). Twelve km down this road you will see an entrance with the sign Rancho San Andres. (Do not confuse it with Hacienda San Andres a few km before.) They require a minimum of 72 hours prior reservation. Contact Claud Baillie or Federic Janssen. Phone/fax: (0) 291-641-6278; phones: (0) 291-643-0298 & (0) 414-760-0095. French and English spoken. E-mail: Janssenfred@cantv.net.

MORICHAL LARGO

Even if you do plan to visit the Delta of the Orinoco, but more especially if you are not, and are intent on driving from Maturin straight on south to the Gran Sabana, the Morichal Largo River is worth every minute of time spent on a visit.

Leaving Maturin at 5:00 a.m., it will take you about an hour to reach the river - 82 km south of Maturin, and there are half day and full day tours, but arrangements to have the boat and guide pick you up should be made in advance. All tours depart from a small wharf by the main road's bridge over the River (National Highway 10).

Contact either Quintero Tours in Maturin, Tel. (0) 291-651-2775, or the travel agency Centro del Mundo, Tel. (0) 291-641-3533, both of which do the Morichal Largo tour. Probably, Jesús Molinos or the people at Rancho San Andres can also help you. The young people of Quintero Tours know what birders are looking for and try to accommodate to our crazy mania for spotting birds. I should also mention that the lunches they supply are excellent.

The main idea behind this trip is for you to be able to enjoy a most unique riparian scenery, where the main element is the exquisite Moriche Palm, *Mauritia flexuosa*. There are some birding bonuses too. My batty editor says that the Morichal Largo is the international convention center for the Black-capped Donacobius - there is one holding his own on every two square meters of water hyacinths. It is the easiest place in the entire country to find this species. There are many other birds too, and you get a beautiful sampling of the exuberant flora of the Delta. Look for:

Anhinga	Gray-necked Wood-Rail	Red-billed Toucan
Cocoi Heron	Purple Gallinule	Spot-breasted Woodpecker
Rufescent Tiger-Heron	Pale-vented Pigeon	Lineated Woodpecker
Wood Stork	Red-bellied Macaw	Black-crested Antshrike
Green Ibis	Red-shouldered Macaw	Silvered Antbird
Horned Screamer	Green-rumped Parrotlet	Black-chinned Antbird
Lesser Yellow-headed Vulture	Yellow-crowned Parrot	Pied Water-Tyrant
Greater Yellow-headed Vulture	Orange-winged Parrot	White-headed Marsh-Tyrant
Short-tailed Hawk	Mealy Parrot	Tropical Kingbird
Black-collared Hawk	Hoatzin	Piratic Flycatcher
Savanna Hawk	Little Cuckoo	Rusty-margined Flycatcher
Rufous Crab-Hawk	Greater Ani	Bi-colored Wren
Black-and-white Hawk-Eagle	Fork-tailed Palm-Swift	Black-capped Donacobius
Ornate Hawk-Eagle	White-chested Emerald	Rufous-browed Peppershrike
Osprey	White-tailed Trogon	Red-eyed Vireo
Laughing Falcon	Ringed Kingfisher	Yellow-rumped Cacique
Crested Caracara	Green Kingfisher	Orange-crowned Oriole
Bat Falcon	Amazon Kingfisher	Moriche Oriole
Barred Forest Falcon	Green-and-rufous Kingfisher	Palm Tanager
Rufous-vented Chachalaca	Swallow-wing	Silver-beaked Tanager

After wading through all of the above, I hope that you will agree with me that Monagas is a state too long neglected by bird watchers because it has a tremendous variety of species to offer us.

GOING SOUTH TO BOLIVAR

If your next destination after Monagas is Bolivar and the Gran Sabana, from Maturin or Agropecuaria La Ceiba take National Highway 10 (the main highway going south), past the bridge over the Morichal Largo to the small town of El Rosario, (96 km from Maturin) where Highway 10 forks right to the port of Los Barrancos on the Orinoco River. From El Rosario to Los Barrancos it is yet another 86 km. At Los Barrancos you take the ferry across the Orinoco. Do not confuse Los Barrancos (with an "o") with Barrancas (with an "a"), as they are two quite different places. The ferry leaves approximately every half hour and takes from 20 to 30 minutes to reach the cities of San Félix/Puerto Ordaz on the south side of the river. You will find the trip rather fascinating with hawkers wandering between cars, selling everything from watches to perfumes to sun glasses, soft drinks, etc. and more etcs.

VI - 4. Delta Amacuro

INTRODUCTION

Since both the Federal Territory corresponding to the huge delta of the Orinoco River and the Federal Territory of our Amazonian region have finally been granted State status, school children no longer have to recite, in the usual sing-song, that Venezuela has "twenty States, two Federal Territories, one Federal District and the Dependencias Federales". We now have twenty two states, the same old mess of the Federal District, and, *Gratia Dio!*, the same smattering of beautiful, fairly unspoiled Dependencias Federales, this being the status allotted to our islands in the Caribbean.

For reasons beyond my comprehension, this newly constituted state, rather than being named after the mighty Orinoco, is called Delta Amacuro after the Amacuro River, one of many indistinguishable small rivers that flow from Bolivar State into the southern Delta.

The Delta is truly huge. 16,000 square miles of a vast, intricate labyrinth of some 60 waterways and 40 river carrying the waters of the Orinoco to the Atlantic, complete with swamps, lagoons, mangroves, floating carpets of water hyacinth. Some of the rivers are brown with erosion; others black from tanic acid.

So far, few bird watchers have ventured into this water-bound area, perhaps due to a scarcity of decent accommodations, but more probably because every bird watcher knows that it is extremely difficult to see birds from boats. You hear the birds, you know they are there, yet you are completely frustrated because you cannot see them. You can seldom find a good place on *terra firma* to look for them. Nevertheless, there are a couple of good areas near Tucupita itself which you can visit without the necessity of spending hours on a boat. Also, there is one lodge that is trying to cater to bird watchers by taking them up the narrow waterways, floating with the tides. See Boca de Tigre below.

After four separate visits to the Delta, I consider it to be composed of two distinct segments. The northern side, accessible from the capital city of Tucupita and from southern Monagas, is probably the most frustrating from a birder's point of view, as I described above. It is also more spectacular - thousands of little channels everywhere, choked by tangled bulwarks of leaves and vines, trunks and aerial roots; a living, throbbing, multiform mass of greenery.

It is in this northern sector that we recently had a spat of renewed oil exploration. For the most part, the fields did not yield what the companies were hoping for, and the area reverted to being a quiet back water.

On the southern segment, many of the islands are inhabited - little hamlets here and there - often deforested and turned into pasture lands. You don't find the fantastic vegetation of the northern channels. Bird-wise though, I believe the southern Delta may be more interesting.

BIRDING AROUND TUCUPITA

To reach Tucupita from Maturin, drive due south on National Highways 10 and 15 (see chapter on Monagas). Shortly before reaching the Orinoco, at the turn-off to Barrancas, the road veers northeast towards Tucupita. You will come to a National Guard's Alcabala, and approximately 14.5 km after it, you will find the Hotel Saxxi on your left.

The Saxxi is the only decent hotel[1] in or near Tucupita; phone number (0) 287-721-2112. Since the town has been growing outwards along the road in this direction, from the hotel there are still 7.6 km to down town Tucupita.

As I mentioned above, there are two places I can recommend to bird, using the Saxxi as your base of operations:

COPORITO

Leave the Saxxi at dawn. Here, the old wisdom about birds being more active in the early hours applies with even greater accuracy - this part of the world is extremely hot later in the day and by noon, not even the mosquitoes, not even mad dogs or Englishmen are about under that midday sun.

Drive back 13 km as if exiting town, towards the National Guard checkpoint. Just before the Alcabala (barely a hundred meters from it), there is a road coming in on the south (your left). This leads eventually to Coporito. After a few km, there is a split - take the road going up. At 6.2 km you pass the junction to Macareito. At 8.9 km there is yet another junction where the lower road dead ends at the hamlet of Coporito, but you continue on the upper road. At 13.4 km, stop where there is a water tower, for you will find some good birding around it. After that, the road soon disintegrates badly but with care, you can carry on in a normal car, at least in the dry season. Park at 14.8 km to bird. Look for:

Anhinga	Ruddy Ground-Dove	Yellow-chinned Spinetail
Great Egret	Scaled Dove	Common Thornbird
Striated Heron	White-tipped Dove	Barred Antshrike
Cattle Egret	Brown-throated Parakeet	Black-crested Antshrike
Wood-Stork	Green-rumped Parrotlet	Jet Antbird
Horned Screamer	Orange-winged Parrot	White-winged Becard
Black Vulture	Little Cuckoo	Cinereous Becard
Lesser Yellow-headed Vulture	Greater Ani	Pied Water-Tyrant
Greater Yellow-headed Vulture	Smooth-billed Ani	Cattle Tyrant
White-tailed Kite	Striped Cuckoo	Fork-tailed Flycatcher
Pearl Kite	Pauraque	Tropical Kingbird
Slender-billed Kite	Green-throated Mango	Boat-billed Flycatcher
Roadside Hawk	White-chested Emerald	Rusty-margined Flycatcher
Black-collared Hawk	Ringed Kingfisher	Social Flycatcher
Great Black Hawk	Amazon Kingfisher	Great Kiskadee
Black Hawk-Eagle	American Pygmy Kingfisher	Cinnamon Attila
Laughing Falcon	Rufous-tailed Jacamar	Common Tody-Flycatcher
Yellow-headed Caracara	Russet-throated Puffbird	Slate-headed Tody-Flycatcher
Crested Caracara	White-bellied Piculet	Yellow Tyrannulet
Rufous-vented Chachalaca	Black-dotted Piculet	River Tyrannulet
Limpkin	Spot-breasted Woodpecker	Yellow-bellied Elaenia
Spotted Sandpiper	Lineated Woodpecker	Small-billed Elaenia
Pale-vented Pigeon	Cream-colored Woodpecker	Mouse-colored Tyrannulet
Ruddy Pigeon	Pale-breasted Spinetail	Southern Beardless Tyrannulet

---

[1] Note from the Editor: Decent, yes, but saxxi? Well... In the back, it has a beach on the Caño Manamo with a little island... Does that make it saxxi? Bring a bikini, just in case - you never know.

White-winged Swallow
Bicolored Wren
Striped-backed Wren
House Wren
Tropical Mockingbird
Pale-breasted Thrush
Tropical Gnatcatcher
Rufous-browed Peppershrike
Scrub Greenlet
Crested Oropendola

Yellow-rumped Cacique
Yellow-hooded Blackbird
Carib Grackle
Moriche Oriole
Yellow Oriole
Yellow Warbler
Blue-gray Tanager
Silver-beaked Tanager
Grayish Saltator
Orinoco Saltator

Red-capped Cardinal
Blue-black Grassquit
Greater Large-billed Seedeater
Gray Seedeater
Lesson´s Seedeater
Saffron Finch
Orange-fronted Yellow-Finch
Yellow-browed Sparrow
Grassland Sparrow

You may have noticed that many of the birds listed for Coporito are also typical birds of the Llanos. This is not surprising, since extensive areas of the Delta, including many of the islands, have been cleared for cattle raising.

After a morning of birding at Coporito, I suggest you go back to the Saxxi for lunch and a siesta. The latter is no laughing matter. To the contrary, aside from a sacred tradition, a midday rest is an absolute survival necessity in these parts. And you know what they say: "When in Rome..." At around 3:00 p.m. leave again to go in the opposite direction, to look for what might be called more "exotic" birds, around...

LOS GÜIRES

After your lunch and a siesta drive towards Tucupita, cross over the bridge and drive past the Plaza Bolivar on your left. From the Saxxi to the square, it is 7.9 km. Counting the Plaza as 0 km, continue straight ahead to the end of the street at 0.7 km from the Plaza. Turn left and continue for 1.8 km, when you will see a water tower on your right. Turn right and drive past all the garbage. The next junction, where you again turn left, is 4.7 km from the Plaza. Continue past Las Mulas (9.1 km from the Plaza) and carry on. Start birding at about 10 km after the Plaza, and from there just follow the birds. At 25 km the road forks - one side paved, the other dirt. We have followed the dirt road for a short while and found a huge roost of Orange-winged Parrots. Among the special birds here, we have had Hook-billed Kite, Slender-billed Kite *and* (as if those were not enough) Rufous Crab-Hawk. Also White-bellied and Black-spotted Piculets, and Cinnamon Attila. As Clemencia would say, "they ain't chicken feed!"

Great Egret
Snowy Egret
Striated Heron
Cattle Egret
Wood-Stork
Horned Screamer
Black Vulture
Turkey Vulture
Lesser Yellow-headed Vulture
Hook-billed Kite
Slender-billed Kite
Roadside Hawk
Gray-lined Hawk
Black-collared Hawk
Savanna Hawk
Rufous Crab-Hawk

Black Hawk-Eagle
Laughing Falcon
Crested Caracara
Rufous-vented Chachalaca
Ruddy Ground-Dove
Gray-fronted Dove
Brown-throated Parakeet
Green-rumped Parrotlet
Orange-winged Parrot
Squirrel Cuckoo
Little Cuckoo
Greater Ani
Smooth-billed Ani
Great Potoo
Reddish Hermit
White-necked Jacobin

Green-throated Mango
Rufous-throated Sapphire
White-chested Emerald
American Pygmy Kingfisher
Russet-throated Puffbird
Black-necked Araçari
White-bellied Piculet
Black-spotted Piculet
Chestnut Woodpecker
Cream-colored
Woodpecker
Red-crowned Woodpecker
Little Woodpecker
Crimson-crested Woodpecker
Straight-billed Woodcreeper
Buff-throated Woodcreeper

Pale-breasted Spinetail	Yellow-breasted Flycatcher	Crested Oropendola
Plain-crowned Spinetail	Common Tody-Flycatcher	Yellow-rumped Cacique
Rusty-backed Spinetail	Yellow Tyrannulet	Carib Grackle
Black-crested Antshrike	Yellow-bellied Elaenia	Yellow Warbler
Jet Antbird	Small-billed Elaenia	Bananaquit
Cinereous Becard	Southern-Beardless Tyrannulet	Turquoise Tanager
White-winged Becard	Mouse-colored Tyrannulet	Violaceous Euphonia
Cattle Tyrant	White-winged Swallow	Trinidad Euphonia
Fork-tailed Flycatcher	Brown-chested Martin	Blue-gray Tanager
Tropical Kingbird	Gray-breasted Martin	Palm Tanager
Gray Kingbird	Southern Rough-winged	Silver-beaked Tanager
Boat-billed Flycatcher	Swallow	Hooded Tanager
Rusty-margined Flycatcher	Bi-colored Wren	Grayish Saltator
Social Flycatcher	Stripe-backed Wren	Great-billed Seed-Finch
Great Kiskadee	Buff-breasted Wren	Blue-black Grassquit
Lesser Kiskadee	House Wren	Gray Seedeater
Cinnamon Attila	Tropical Mockingbird	Lesson's Seedeater
Short-crested Flycatcher	Rufous-browed Peppershrike	Saffron Finch
Brown-crested Flycatcher	Golden-fronted Greenlet	Orange-fronted Yellow-Finch
White-throated Spadebill	Scrub Greenlet	Yellow-browed Sparrow

To return to the Saxxi from Los Güires, retrace your way to the water tower and turn left. Go straight but when you see a needle-shaped concrete monument, turn right. You will now pass the Plaza Bolivar on your left. Turn left at the upper corner and continue for two blocks. Turn right, cross the bridge and you are now on your way back to the hotel.

INDIAN CRAFTS

Tucupita is one of the best places to buy Indian crafts in all of Venezuela. The Waraos, the Indigenous People of the Delta, are among the most gifted craftsmen in the New World, their specialty being basketry, which can only be described as exquisite.

To purchase some of their wares, I highly recommend the inconspicuous store called **Artesanía Toucan**, located on the Plaza Bolívar. Coming from the Saxxi, when you reach the Plaza drive along the length of it to the far corner and turn left to park beside its lower side. The store is named Toucan but has no name on the door and is ensconced across the street from the Plaza, practically next door to a bar. Amble into the bar and ask that attendants open the door for you because you wish to buy *artesanía* from Sra. Pepita Fernandez. They have fabulous baskets and other artifacts, and comparatively speaking, the prices are very reasonable.

CAMPS AND LODGES

After a visit to the Delta in February of 2001, I discovered there are several good and comfortable camps for nature lovers to visit in the Delta from Tucupita.

The one most recommended for general nature lovers is the **Orinoco Delta Lodge** of Tucupita Expeditions: Phone (0) 287-721-1953; Phone/Fax (0) 287-721-0801 & (0) 414-789-8384. E-mail: tucexpedelta@cantv.net or anthony@orinocodelta.com. See also www.orinocodelta.com and www.think-venezuela.net. The camp is found on Caño Guamal, some 300 meters off Caño Manamo and one and a half hours by fast boat from Tucupita. They have 31 individual cabins each with 2 or 3 single beds and private bath. I have been given to understand that the food is superb, which is most unusual in this area. Finally, they have acquired a number of "pets" which were baby animals found orphaned, were raised with love and now come and go as they please, hunting for their own food in the jungle and caños but tame around people. These include 3 nutrias, a beautiful ocelot, a giant anteater, etc. An alternative is to combine a stay at the main lodge with several days in their Simonia Camp, more rustic but comfortable in the northern part of the Delta. This means hammocks to sleep in and bathing in the caño, but possibly more wildlife. English, Dutch, Arabic, German spoken.

Campamento Mis Palafitos
Is another recently opened camp, belonging to the owners of Hotel Saxxi in Tucupita. Phones: (0) 278-721-3445 & 721-5166 or (0) 414-878-3586; e-mail: mispalafitos@cantv.net. This camp is located at the mouth of the Morichal Largo River where it empties into the Caño Manamo, requiring a boat ride of approximately an hour and a half. It has 30 attractively decorated palafitos (cabins built on stilts or pilings) for 2 to 4 beds with private bath. Excursions consist of the usual activities: exploring narrow caños in curiara (dugout canoes) including a night outing, a jungle walk, a visit to a Warao community and observation of fauna and flora on boat tours. English-speaking guides are available. I had hoped to visit the camp during my very short stay in Tucupita, but when I was advised that the cost was $75.00 per person for a whole day excursion, I declined. But I do feel that it might be an interesting place for bird watchers to visit.

Boca de Tigre Lodge
A 90-minute drive from the city of Maturin, the capital of the State of Monagas, will take you to the Port of Buja, where you will board an air boat. The airboat is necessary as parts of the channels are completely blocked by floating meadows of water hyacinth. Boca de Tigre is located at the mouth of the Tigre River, and the influence of the salt waters of the Atlantic combined with the waters of the river contribute to an interesting mixture of fauna. The manager of the lodge has scouted out several small waterways where it is possible to see a wide variety of fauna, both avian and mammal, as you float up the stream with the tide. Also, they are located very close to Bird Island where you can watch the arrival of several thousand Blue-headed Parrots and Scarlet Ibis every evening. As if the above were not enough, the Waraos or native inhabitants of the Delta bring their handicrafts to the Lodge to sell them at very low prices to the tourists. Phones: (0) 291-651-4457 & 651-4954; e-mail: deltaor@telcel.net.ve.

BIRDING IN THE SOUTHERN DELTA

There are two reasonably good options for the southern part of the Delta, but they both require a very long boat ride of approximately 5 hours:

Campamento Mares
The camp is located in front of the Warao community of San Francisco de Guayo near the Atlantic Ocean. This camp was opened in 1985 by the Lara family, pioneers in Delta tourism. There are various lodging options from hammocks to private cabins. For the most part they offer excursions more suited to the general tourist - fishing, visiting Warao communities, etc. but they do also offer travel in dugout canoes with Warao guides for bird watching. It is necessary to request reservation and deposit cost 6 days prior to departure. A minimum of five passengers are required to effect a trip on any given date. Phone/Fax: (0) 287-721-0553.

Tobe Lodge

This lodge is also located in the Warao community of San Francisco de Guayo, but departures are from Puerto Ordaz (Club Nautico) in Bolivar State. They also offer excursions in curiaras with Warao guides to explore narrow caños in the jungle, as well as the usual visits to Warao communities to buy handicrafts, fishing trips, visits to the beaches on the Atlantic Ocean, etc. Again a minimum of 5 passengers are required to make the trip. E-mail: tobelodge@yahoo.com or tobelodge@telcel.net.ve. Phone/Fax: (0) 286-952-1842, phone: (0) 414-864-8843.

The city of **Puerto Ordaz** adjoins and has engulfed the town of San Felix. (For hotels, see chapter on the State of Bolivar). Together, the joint cities are now called **Ciudad Guayana**, a name that was coined for the extensive urban area that was planned in the 60s by a team of urban planning experts from Harvard, the University of Chicago, Stanford and the Central University. The common people, however, tend to stick to the old ways, so the names Puerto Ordaz and Ciudad Guayana are used indistinctly nowadays. Taking advantage of the confluence of the mighty Orinoco and the no-less magnificent Caroní, it was meant to be a focus of regional development, and, learning from the lessons of Brasilia, it was wisely planned over an area that already had a settled population and a life of its own.

I had only a few hours to bird in the southern Delta, but here is what I found. Should you go to there, look for (and please add to):

Neotropic Cormorant	Sungrebe	Red-billed Toucan
Anhinga	Sunbittern	White-bellied Piculet
Cocoi Heron	Wattled Jacana	Cream-colored Woodpecker
Great Egret	Southern Lapwing	Spot-breasted Woodpecker
Snowy Egret	Greater Yellowlegs	Lineated Woodpecker
Little Blue Heron	Spotted Sandpiper	Straight-billed Woodcreeper
Striated Heron	Large-billed Tern	Pale-breasted Spinetail
Cattle Egret	Scaled Dove	Yellow-throated Spinetail
Capped Heron	Pale-vented Pigeon	Plain-crowned Spinetail
Black-crowned Night-Heron	Common Ground-Dove	Rusty-backed Spinetail
Rufescent Tiger-Heron	Gray-fronted Dove	Common Thornbird
Zigzag Heron	Blue-and-yellow Macaw	Rufous-tailed Xenops
Wood-Stork	Red-and-green Macaw	Great Antshrike
Green Ibis	Golden-winged Parakeet	Black-crested Antshrike
Horned Screamer	Yellow-crowned Parrot	Streaked Antwren
Black-bellied Whistling-Duck	Orange-winged Parrot	Cinereous Becard
Orinoco Goose	Hoatzin	River Tyrant
Muscovy Duck	Little Cuckoo	Pied-water Tyrant
Black Vulture	Greater Ani	White-headed Marsh-Tyrant
Turkey Vulture	Smooth-billed Ani	Cattle Tyrant
Greater Yellow-headed	Striped Cuckoo	Tropical Kingbird
Vulture	Pauraque	Piratic Flycatcher
Swallow-tailed Kite	Fork-tailed Palm-Swift	Boat-billed Flycatcher
Roadside Hawk	Rufous-breasted Hermit	Rusty-margined Flycatcher
Black-collared Hawk	Reddish Hermit	Social Flycatcher
Osprey	Green-throated Mango	Great Kiskadee
Yellow-headed Caracara	Ringed Kingfisher	Lesser Kiskadee
Crested Caracara	Amazon Kingfisher	Common Tody-Flycatcher
Helmeted Curassow	Green Kingfisher	Spotted Tody-Flycatcher
Gray-necked Wood-Rail	American Pygmy Kingfisher	Helmeted Pygmy-Tyrant

Pale-tipped Tyrannulet
Yellow-bellied Elaenia
White-winged Swallow
Barn Swallow
Strip-backed Wren
Buff-breasted Wren
House Wren
Black-capped Donacobius
Cocoa Thrush

Rufous-browed Peppershrike
Slaty-capped Shrike-Vireo
Shiny Cowbird
Crested Oropendola
Yellow-rumped Cacique
Yellow-hooded Blackbird
Yellow Oriole
Carib Grackle
Red-breasted Blackbird

Bananaquit
Blue-gray Tanager
Silver-beaked Tanager
Grayish Saltator
Orinoco Saltator
Red-capped Cardinal
Ruddy-breasted Seedeater
Orange-fronted Yellow-Finch

My recommendation for you to really visit the Delta of the Orinoco would be to try one of the camps.

FROM THE DELTA SOUTH TO BOLIVAR STATE

To go across the Orinoco to Bolivar, upon departing the Saxxi, drive back to the main National Highway 15. From where the road turns north, it will be 24 km to the first crossroads by Paso Nuevo. Turn south-west here and drive another 71 km to reach the ferry landing at Los Barrancos.

The ferry crosses the Orinoco to the southern landing at San Felix approximately every half hour and the trip takes a half hour. You will find the trip rather fascinating with hawkers wandering between cars, selling everything from watches to perfumes to sun glasses, soft drinks, etc. and more etcs.

Upon reading this chapter, Juanita Tyzska, one of my proofreaders, asked if bird watchers always carry a compass. It would not be a bad idea!

SOUTHERN VENEZUELA

Country and Regional Endemics:

Tepui Tinamou
Gray-legged Tinamou
Barred Tinamou
Fiery-shouldered Parakeet
Tepui Parrotlet
Dwarf Cuckoo
Rufous-winged Ground-Cuckoo
Roraiman Nightjar
Tepui Swift
Rufous-breasted Sabrewing
Buff-breasted Sabrewing
Peacock Coquette
Tepui Goldenthroat
White-chested Emerald
Velvet-browed Brilliant
Black-dotted Piculet
Tepui Spinetail
Orinoco Softtail
Roraiman Barbtail
Neblina Foliage-gleaner
White-throated Foliage-gleaner
Streak-backed Antshrike
Roraiman Antwren
Gray-bellied Antbird

Yapacana Antbird
Caura Antbird
Tepui Antpitta
Red-banded Fruiteater
Rose-collared Piha
Scarlet-horned Manakin
Olive Manakin
White-bearded Flycatcher
Venezuelan Flycatcher
Ruddy Tody-Flycatcher
Chapman's Tyrannulet
Black-fronted Tyrannulet
Great Elaenia
Tepui Greenlet
Golden-tufted Grackle
White-faced Redstart
Brown-capped Redstart
Saffron-breasted Redstart
Greater Flower-piercer
Scaled Flower-piercer
Olive-backed Tanager
Orinocan Saltator
Tepui Brush-Finch
Duida Grass-Finch

White-plumed Antbird

We have now reached the lands of the deep south. This southern-most region of Venezuela is divided politically into two states - Bolivar and Amazonas. The two share many features, but are also different in many ways.

Perhaps the most significant shared feature is the Guayana Shield, a cluster of tabular mountains that date from the Precambrian era and are considered to be some of the oldest geological formations on the planet. It is interesting to note that contrary to the Andes, which were created and shaped by tectonic forces, the mountains of the Shield are the result of erosion - water and wind action in the grandest of scales, through the longest of eons. These table mountains, called **tepuis**, define our southern landscape.

Most of the Shield is located within Venezuela, with some outer fringes extending over to Brazil and Guyana. In Venezuela, there are some 25 tepuis, each a distinct, separate table, each rising like an island above the sea of jungles at its feet, and like an island holding each its own particular flora and fauna. Nowadays, from the level of 300 meters above the sea, the table mountains are protected areas, forming part of what is called the Tepuis Natural Monument.

Another shared feature of Bolivar and Amazonas are the mighty rivers that cross both states, and their portentous waterfalls. Based on the river systems, geographers and scientists in Venezuela talk about an Orinoquia and a Venezuelan Amazonia - an area belonging to the Orinoco basin and an area connected to the basin of the Amazon River by way of the Rio Negro and the Caño Casiquiare, a geographical oddity of a channel that joins the two watersheds.

Both states are home to many different indigenous peoples. To name just a few, there are the Pemones in the Gran Sabana; the Makiritares or Yekwanas in the Caura River, the Piaroas in the northern parts of Amazonas and the Yanomamis in the south, the Panares, the Hotis, the Sanemas. Each people with its own language, it own types of dwellings, it own crafts, culture, legends, lore. Some groups, such as the Hotis, are contained within Venezuelan territory, while the ancestral lands of others, such as the Pemones and Yanomamis, extend across the borders to Guyana and Brazil.

Mineral resources are in astounding abundance, especially gold and diamonds, but this wealth is yet to show that it will bring happiness and not perdition. So far, anywhere where exploitation has taken place, the result has been complete, utter destruction of habitats and biodiversity, and when the "placers" run dry and are abandoned, they lie like festering mortal wounds upon the land.

In both states, vast extensions are uninhabited, isolated, remote; accessible only via the rivers, long treks through unopened country or helicopter. There are literally billions of acres covered by a variety of types of Amazonian rain forests, from dry deciduous ones to varzeas and caatingas. Countless other millions of acres, equally wide and equally varied, are occupied by savannas - sadly, some of these are man-made.

Considering southern Venezuela from a very macro point of view, the landscape and habitats could be divided into two major areas - the low lands and the high lands - with marked ecological and environmental differences, but harboring, between the two, some of the greatest biodiversity that Venezuela has to offer, including a fantastic avifauna.

As you have already guessed from the list of endemics that opens this Section, when visiting the states of Bolivar and Amazonas, prepare yourself for the birding experience of your life.

VII - 1. Eastern Bolivar State

INTRODUCTION

Eastern Bolivar has two doors - Ciudad Bolivar and Puerto Ordaz. You will come into the State through one or the other, depending on where you come from and how you arrive, if by land or flying in.

If you rented a car in Maiquetía and have been birding your way across eastern Venezuela, you may drive south directly from Barcelona[1] and will enter into Ciudad Bolivar, crossing the river over the splendid bridge at Angostura; or you may drive south from Maturin, in which case you will cross the river on the ferry to Puerto Ordaz.

People[2] who decide to fly usually do so into Puerto Ordaz, where a number of car rental companies have counters at the airport, and where they are closer to the usual birding destinations - the Escalera, the Gran Sabana, the Imataca forests, etc.

The drive from Caracas to Ciudad Bolivar takes a good eight to nine hours and is approximately 546 km Should you wish to overnight at Ciudad Bolivar, we recommend the **Hotel Valentina,** located near the airport. Phones: (0) 285-632-2145 & 632-7253. Fax: (0) 285-632-9311. After you cross the bridge, take the auto-pista going towards Puerto Ordaz but exit at the Marhuanta Distributor, which is the last distributor prior to Puerto Ordaz. Do not take the first exit for Ciudad Bolivar after the toll booth or you will end up in a horrendous traffic jam. From the Marhuanta Distributor, continue straight all the way up the street you came in on, Avenida Upata, until you see the sign for the airport. Follow the signs for the airport, and when you can actually see the hangars, angle over to the right-hand lane. You want to turn right at the stop light in front of the main entrance to the airport building on your left. This will put you on Avenida Táchira. Go two blocks and turn right on Avenida Maracay for half a block where you will see the small **Hotel Valentina** (3 stars), probably the best restaurant in town.

If you have purchased a cooler for your trip, you can buy ice very near to the hotel. Go straight down the street in front of the Valentina until you come to a round-about. Go half way around the traffic distributor and then go down a small, narrow, unpretentious street. The ice plant is on the left.

Another plus for the area of the Hotel Valentina is the fact that it is close to one of the best stores - shops- or just plain places to buy native artifacts in all of Venezuela. Handicrafts from all the tribes in Venezuela are there including baskets, wood carvings, weavings, etc. It is only a couple of blocks away from your hotel, but ask there how to reach the home of:

⊜ **Rosalia de Zagala**
Quinta Mea-Lares, diagonal (across the corners) with Hotel Transmontano, phone: (0) 285-632-1580. Ciudad Bolivar

---

[1] Directions to be found in chapter on State of Sucre.
[2] Directions to be found in chapter on the State of Monagas.

Even if you are not in the mood to pick up handicrafts, a visit is most educational to see the different types of work done by the various indigenous peoples of the country. It is like browsing in a museum.

Very recently the Cacao Expeditions group have opened an inn at Ciudad Bolivar. This is the same group that have the inns at Altamira in the Andes, Orinoquía in Amazonas and Caura Cacao in western Bolivar. This inn is called **Posada Angostura**, and although I have not visited it, I have seen pictures, and it appears to be absolutely lovely. To find the inn, after your pass the bridge over the Orinoco and pay your toll, take the first road to the left. Follow this road until you reach the first round-about (this is before the bus terminal). Take the street called Paseo Orinoco by the Texaco gas station. When you see Banco Guayana, go right onto Calle Carabobo. Go up to the end of the street veering towards the left. You are now on the Calle Patrio, which will take you to the Plaza Bolívar and the Casa de los Gobernadores. Immediatley turn left on to Calle Boyacá. Within a half block you will find the inn, painted yellow with a sign indicating the name of the inn.

If you opt for overnighting at Ciudad Bolívar, the next day go back to the autopista the same way as you came in on. Then take the relatively new *autopista* to the east, which will put you, in one hour, into the city of Puerto Ordaz. As I have said before, together, the joint cities of San Felix and Puerto Ordaz are called Ciudad Guayana, a name that was imposed upon the traditional ones in a fit of grandiloquent gesturing, that malignant disease that seems to infect Venezuelan presidents as soon as they take office. The common people, however, wise and forbearing, have stuck to the old ways, so Puerto Ordaz it is for the great majority.

Once you have arrived at Puerto Ordaz, there is one point of interest - the beautiful **Parque Cachamay.** To find this park and its gorgeous waterfall, after you pass the airport in Puerto Ordaz, you will be driving along Avenida Guayana and will pass right in front of it on your right. The parking is ample and there are guards. Take one hour out to visit Cachamay and see the **Caroní River** tumbling down the impressive series of short steps. This will be your first encounter with the black-water rivers of this region, and it really merits a visit.

From Puerto Ordaz head towards **Upata**. The way from Puerto Ordaz to Upata is well marked except for the last, vital turn (isn't that always the way?). Avenida Guayana suddenly seems to end at the crossroads with the Avenida coming up from the docks of San Felix. When you see a T intersection with a stoplight ahead, angle over to the right in order to curve around south. You will be going through a lot of wild traffic for a short distance but after that the road from Puerto Ordaz to Upata is an excellent freeway, but even so, it will take you yet another hour. Should you wish to overnight at Upata, there is the **Hotel Andrea**, located at the southern end of Upata. Phones: (0) 288-221-3656, 221-3618 & 221-3735; fax: (0) 288-221-3736. The Andrea is just in front of the usual round-about. On the far corner of said distributor is a very good, new *panadería* (bakery) offering good coffee and buns for breakfast, but they do not open until 7:00 a.m. Warning, the restaurant of the hotel is definitely not recommended.

Upon returning to Puerto Ordaz from the south, life becomes very tricky indeed. The last time I was in Puerto Ordaz, I found myself driving by the famous seat of my pants. Just try to find and stay on Avenida Guayana. At practically the last minute you will come to a division. The left says **Center** and the right says **Airport**. If you want the airport, go **LEFT!**[1]

---

[1] Pamela's Comment: "Mary Lou, the sign shows the airport going down to the right. Mary Lou's answer: 'Don't you believe it!' As usual, she is right."

RIO GRANDE AND THE IMATACA FOREST RESERVE

While en route to or from the Gran Sabana, many birders make the side trip to the Río Grande area of Imataca Forest Reserve, in order to see the Harpy Eagle. Unfortunately, there has been tremendous deforestation in this so-called "Reserve" during the last few years, but I believe it is still worth a visit. Tragic though it is, the new areas opened by the deforestation make it easier to see the birds[1].

To reach Río Grande, when leaving Upata you will soon pass through a National Guard Alcabala. From there it is 8 km to where you will see a road on the left going to the "Minas de Manganeso". Turn here. (This road does not appear on most maps.) When you come to the crossroads leading to the Minas, you turn right towards **El Palmar**. It is almost a three-hour drive from Puerto Ordaz to El Palmar.

Please note that there are two approaches to Palmar; one from Upata, taking the road to Minas de Manganeso as explained above, and the other approach is much further south at **Villa Lola** This latter one is more convenient for those who are coming from the Gran Sabana. See below.

In the town of El Palmar, the place to stay is the rustic but friendly **Parador Taguapire**. The difficult part is entering El Palmar from the north and looking for the Plaza Bolívar. You want to drive past the church on your right with the Plaza on your left and go for another kilometer until you see the Parador on your left. If you reach the National Guard Alcabala, back track approximately 100 meters. For reservations at the Taguapire, phones: (0) 288-881-1196 & 881-1195; fax (0) 288-881-1196, or contact the Audubon. The inn is basic, but it is clean, and the host, Sr. Stokfim, kind and obliging. Also, the meals are quite good.

To reach the Forest Reserve from the Taguapire, drive east 21 km, for approximately 30 minutes. You will pass through the village of Rio Grande and at the next junction keep right. This road is certainly not very good, but in a normal car you will perhaps be able to drive as far as the bridge. From there, unless you have a 4x4. I suggest you hitch a ride with any of the trucks.

Probably the main reason for going to Imataca is to see the Harpy Eagle. Here is where you will need a guide with a 4x4 . The owner of Taguapire, Levis Stokfim, can arrange for the guide, but the day's trip may cost you up to $70. Also, I believe that to find the Eagle's nest (when it is actively nesting) involves a walk through the forest of about an hour.

The road goes on towards the east for some 17 km after the bridge, and there are many side roads that would make excellent camping areas, but I hesitate to recommend that you camp in the Reserve. This is not so much because of the forestry company staff, who tend to go about their business in a somewhat predictable way, but because there are miners in all this region, and they do appear out of nowhere. With respect to the presence of miners in a Forest Reserve let me tell you that, unbelievable as it seems, there are officially granted mining concessions inside Imataca. Our Government is very definitely insane.

As if that were not enough, I regret to inform you that as of March, 2001, since the government is not earning enough money to cover their expenses from the present high cost of petroleum, the national government has once again granted forestry concessions in Imataca. I have no idea what will be the impact on the Eagle or other birds of the area.

---

[1] Note from the Editor: We fear this will not last long, that there will a slow but relentless decline in the number of species, for that is the process that takes place whenever forest fragmentation occurs.

The Audubon has not published a checklist for the **Imataca Forest** as yet, so I include here one for the Forest Reserve and the El Palmar area in general.

Great Tinamou
Little Tinamou
Variegated Tinamou
Neotropic Cormorant
Anhinga
Cocoi Heron
Great Egret
Snowy Egret
Striated Heron
Agami Heron
Cattle Egret
Capped Heron
Rufescent Tiger-Heron
Green Ibis
White-faced Whistling Duck
Black-bellied Whistling-Duck
Orinoco Goose
King Vulture
Black Vulture
Turkey Vulture
Lesser Yellow-headed
  Vulture
Greater Yellow-headed
  Vulture
White-tailed Kite
Pearl Kite
Swallow-tailed Kite
Hook-billed Kite
Double-toothed Kite
Plumbeous Kite
Snail Kite
Tiny Hawk
White-tailed Hawk
Roadside Hawk
Short-tailed Hawk
Gray-lined Hawk
White Hawk
Black-faced Hawk
Black-collared Hawk
Savanna Hawk
Great Black Hawk
Harpy Eagle
Black-and-white Hawk-Eagle
Black Hawk-Eagle
Crane Hawk
Laughing Falcon
Lined Forest-Falcon
Red-throated Caracara

Yellow-headed Caracara
Crested Caracara
Bat Falcon
American Kestrel
Little Chachalaca
Marail Guan
Black Curassow
Crested Bobwhite
Marbled Wood-Quail
Gray-necked Wood-Rail
Paint-billed Crake
Common Moorhen
Purple Gallinule
Sunbittern
Sungrebe
Wattled Jacana
Southern Lapwing
Solitary Sandpiper
Scaled Pigeon
Pale-vented Pigeon
Ruddy Pigeon
Plumbeous Pigeon
Eared Dove
Common Ground-Dove
Plain-breasted Ground-Dove
Ruddy Ground-Dove
Scaled Dove
White-tipped Dove
Gray-fronted Dove
Ruddy Quail-Dove
Red-and-green Macaw
White-eyed Parakeet
Brown-throated Parakeet
Painted Parakeet
Dusky-billed Parrotlet
Golden-winged Parakeet
Lilac-tailed Parrotlet
Black-headed Parrot
Caica Parrot
Blue-headed Parrot
Dusky Parrot
Yellow-crowned Parrot
Orange-winged Parrot
Mealy Parrot
Red-fan Parrot
Squirrel Cuckoo
Black-bellied Cuckoo
Smooth-billed Ani

Groove-billed Ani
Striped Cuckoo
Rufous-winged Ground-Cuckoo
Tropical Screech-Owl
Tawny-bellied Screech-Owl
Ferruginous Pygmy-Owl
Amazonian Pygmy-Owl
Great Potoo
Long-tailed Potoo
Common Potoo
Short-tailed Nighthawk
Pauraque
White-tailed Nightjar
Blackish Nightjar
White-collared Swift
Band-rumped Swift
Short-tailed Swift
White-tipped Swift
Lesser Swallow-tailed Swift
Rufous-breasted Hermit
Pale-tailed Barbthroat
Long-tailed Hermit
Reddish Hermit
Gray-breasted Sabrewing
White-necked Jacobin
Black-throated Mango
Tufted Coquette
Blue-chinned Sapphire
Blue-tailed Emerald
Fork-tailed Woodnymph
Rufous-throated Sapphire
White-chinned Sapphire
White-chested Emerald
Glittering-throated Emerald
Crimson Topaz
Black-eared Fairy
White-tailed Trogon
Black-throated Trogon
Violaceous Trogon
Ringed Kingfisher
Amazon Kingfisher
Green Kingfisher
American Pygmy Kingfisher
Blue-crowned Motmot
Yellow-billed Jacamar
Green-tailed Jacamar
Paradise Jacamar
Great Jacamar

White-necked Puffbird
Pied Puffbird
Black Nunbird
Swallow-wing
Black-spotted Barbet
Black-necked Araçari
Green Araçari
Channel-billed Toucan
Red-billed Toucan
Golden-spangled Piculet
Yellow-throated Woodpecker
Chestnut Woodpecker
Waved Woodpecker
Lineated Woodpecker
Yellow-tufted Woodpecker
Red-fronted Woodpecker
Red-crowned Woodpecker
Golden-collared Woodpecker
Crimson-crested Woodpecker
Red-necked Woodpecker
Plain-brown Woodcreeper
Long-tailed Woodcreeper
Olivaceous Woodcreeper
Wedge-billed Woodcreeper
Red-billed Woodcreeper
Black-banded Woodcreeper
Barred Woodcreeper
Chestnut-rumped Woodcreeper
Buff-throated Woodcreeper
Streaked-headed Woodcreeper
Curve-billed Scythebill
Pale-breasted Spinetail
Plain-crowned Spinetail
Ruddy Spinetail
Buff-fronted Foliage-Gleaner
Rufous-tailed Foliage-Gleaner
Plain Xenops
Black-tailed Leaftosser
Fasciated Antshrike
Great Antshrike
Barred Antshrike
Mouse-colored Antshrike
Eastern Slaty Antshrike
Dusky-throated Antshrike
Cinereous Antshrike
Pygmy Antwren
Streaked Antwren
Rufous-bellied Antwren
Brown-bellied Antwren
Long-winged Antwren
Gray Antwren

Rufous-winged Antwren
Ash-winged Antwren
Gray Antbird
Dusky Antbird
Ferruginous-backed Antbird
White-plumed Antbird
Rufous-throated Antbird
Scale-backed Antbird
Rufous-capped Antthrush
Thrush-like Antpitta
Purple-breasted Cotinga
Spangled Cotinga
Screaming Piha
Pink-throated Becard
Black-tailed Tityra
Black-crowned Tityra
Purple-throated Fruitcrow
Red-ruffed Fruitcrow
Golden-headed Manakin
White-fronted Manakin
White-crowned Manakin
Blue-backed Manakin
White-throated Manakin
Wing-barred Manakin
Thrush-like Schiffornis
Long-tailed Tyrant
Cattle Tyrant
Fork-tailed Flycatcher
Tropical Kingbird
Variegated Flycatcher
Piratic Flycatcher
Yellow-throated Flycatcher
Boat-billed Flycatcher
Streaked Flycatcher
Rusty-margined Flycatcher
Social Flycatcher
Great Kiskadee
Lesser Kiskadee
Bright-rumped Attila
Cinnamon Attila
Cinereous Mourner
Grayish Mourner
Olive-sided Flycatcher
Short-crested Flycatcher
Dusky-capped Flycatcher
Ruddy-tailed Flycatcher
Sulphur-rumped Flycatcher
Royal Flycatcher
White-crested Spadebill
Golden-crowned Spadebill
Yellow-margined Flycatcher

Gray-crowned Flycatcher
Olivaceous Flatbill
Rufous-tailed Flatbill
Common Tody-Flycatcher
Painted Tody-Flycatcher
Helmeted Pygmy-Tyrant
Short-tailed Pygmy-Tyrant
Yellow-bellied Elaenia
Forest Elaenia
Southern Beardless
   Tyrannulet
Mouse-colored Tyrannulet
Slender-footed Tyrannulet
Yellow-crowned Tyrannulet
White-lored Tyrannulet
Ochre-bellied Flycatcher
McConnell's Flycatcher
Ringed Antpipit
White-winged Swallow
Brown-chested Martin
Gray-breasted Martin
Blue-and-white Swallow
Southern Rough-winged
   Swallow
Barn Swallow
Cayenne Jay
Coraya Wren
Buff-breasted Wren
House Wren
White-breasted Wood-Wren
Wing-banded Wren
Musician Wren
Tropical Mockingbird
Pale-breasted Thrush
Cocoa Thrush
White-necked Thrush
Rufous-browned
Peppershrike
Red-eyed Vireo
Slaty-capped Shrike-Vireo
Buff-cheeked Greenlet
Tawny-crowned Greenlet
Shiny Cowbird
Crested Oropendola
Amazonian Oropendola
Yellow-rumped Cacique
Red-rumped Cacique
Troupial
Yellow Oriole
Eastern Meadowlark
Red-breasted Blackbird

Tropical Parula	Turquoise Tanager	Guira Tanager
Yellow Warbler	Opal-rumped Tanager	Yellow-backed Tanager
Blackburnian Warbler	Bay-headed Tanager	Magpie Tanager
Bay-breasted Warbler	Violaceous Euphonia	Blue-black Grosbeak
Blackpoll Warbler	Rufous-bellied Euphonia	Buff-throated Saltator
Northern Waterthrush	Plumbeous Euphonia	Grayish Saltator
Rose-breasted Chat	Golden-sided Euphonia	Yellow-green Grosbeak
Golden-crowned Warbler	Blue-gray Tanager	Slate-colored Grosbeak
Neotropical River Warbler	Palm Tanager	Pectoral Sparrow
Bananaquit	Silver Beaked Tanager	Lesser Seed-Finch
Swallow Tanager	Fulvous-shrike Tanager	Gray Seedeater
Purple Honeycreeper	White-lined Tanager	Lined Seedeater
Red-legged Honeycreeper	Flame-crested Tanager	Lesson's Seedeater
Green Honeycreeper	Fulvous-crested Tanager	Yellow-bellied Seedeater
Blue Dacnis	Red-shouldered Tanager	Yellow-breasted Seedeater
Spotted Tanager	White-shouldered Tanager	Blue-black Grassquit
Dotted Tanager	Gray-headed Tanager	Lesser Goldfinch

As you can see from the above list, the Río Grande area merits two or three days of birding before you start south or return north.

If you plan to go to the Gran Sabana after El Palmar, or if you have come to El Palmar from the south, either way you should take the road to or from **Villa Lola**. For those coming from the south, Villa Lola is 52 km north of the town of Guasipati. This road not only goes by the only gas station in El Palmar, but it also passes by a marsh, where you can stop to bird for the usual birds of the wetlands. Villa Lola itself (which is nothing but a crossroads) is 26.8 kilometers from the Taguapire inn. The marsh is 23 km from Taguapire or less than 3 km from the main north-south highway. Stop for a while at the marsh to look for:

Neotropical Cormorant	Smooth-billed Ani	Lesser Kiskadee
Anhinga	Ringed Kingfisher	Gray-breasted Martin
Cocoi Heron	Amazon Kingfisher	Brown-chested Martin
Striated Heron	Crimson-crested Woodpecker	Blue-and-white Swallow
Wattled Jacana	Yellow-chinned Spinetail	Yellow-hooded Blackbird
Red-shouldered Macaw	Pied Water-Tyrant	Ruddy-breasted Seedeater

THE ROAD SOUTH

Now we're headed for fabulous fun! Now comes the best in all respects - birds, place to stay, scenery... The road that connects Venezuela with Brazil, crossing the Gran Sabana in Canaima National Park, will allow a birder to reach some of the most fantastic birding spots in the country.

You will drive past **Guasipati**, which is some 52 km south of the crossroads of Villa Lola. After Guasipati come the towns of **El Callao**, which you by-pass, **Tumeremo**, where you must fill your gas tank.

And now comes something new - something I have not even done, but you absolutely must. All of the following information came from my friendly Yorkshireman, **Chris Sharpe**, and I believe this road will soon replace the Guyana Trail further south. Chris spent 8.5 mornings birding along this road when he was involved in the Bird Atlas work, and the following is his report

ANACOCO / SAN MARTÍN DE TURUMBÁN ROAD (BY CHRIS SHARPE)

«*This road offers a rare opportunity to bird a large area of largely primary forest by car along a reasonably good surfaced road, yet without the frustration of continual traffic. During April 2001 (including the entire Easter week) an average of five vehicles passed along the mid-section of the road in a morning. In the dry season at least, the road can be driven in any type of vehicle except a low slung car, although a 4 X4 is preferable. The road provides an opportunity to see many of the birds of the premontane forests of the river Cuyuní basin, which drains into the Essequibo watershed. Thus many of the species to be found along the traditional Guyana Trail are also to be encountered here, (and you do not have to walk so much either - MLG).*

In addition to the main road, there are more than fifteen unsurfaced side roads which lead off to mines and forest parcels and which are reminiscent of the tracks in the Las Claritas area at the base of the Escalera.

Specialties:
4 species of Tinamous
Black Curassow
Gray-winged Trumpeter
20 plus species of raptors including Ornate Hawk Eagle
12 species of Psittacids at least
Todd's Antwren
Red-ruffed Fruitcrow - one of the most common species
White Bellbird
Blue-backed Manakin
Cayenne Jay
Red-rumped Cacique - a couple of good colonies
Puma - we saw one lope across the road»

Getting there
The entrance to the Anacoco /San Martin de Turumbán road is a left fork immediately after the Alcabala (National Guard post) known as Casa Blanca, twenty minutes south of Tumeremo. Casa Blanca is 17.8 km south of the Texaco gas station on the left hand side as one leaves the town of Tumeremo. **Be sure to fill up your gas tank at this point.** The road is approximately 70 km long, as measured from Casa Blanca to the alcabala at San Martín de Turumbán, which is on the Cuyuní River. Set your odometer at zero at Casa Blanca.

Birding
The first stretch of the road traverses chaparral which soon gives way to disturbed secondary vegetation. Between Km 15.6 and Km 22.2 the road climbs through low hills and provides access to blocks of primary forest interspersed with swidden agriculture plots. This area is well worth checking, though it is advisable to press on to the primary forest as early as possible. **Good primary forest is to be found between Km 38.5 and Km 61.** Nevertheless, the secondary forest beyond can also be productive, and it is also worth visiting the Cuyuní River at the end of the road.

Km 29
Black Curassow, Gray-winged Trumpeter, Spectacled Owl, Common Potoo,Otus, sp. Blue-backed Manakin leks all along the road.
Red-ruffed Fruitcrow leks all along the road.

Staying in Tumeremo
Despite outward appearances, Tumeremo is a friendly town and the visitor can feel relatively safe there. The center of the town is, of course, the Plaza Bolivar, which is reached by turning left some blocks after the gas station on the right hand side as you enter town from the north. There are several places to eat. The pizzería on the south side of the Plaza Bolívar prepares excellent pizzas which can be enjoyed in the open air whilst one soaks up the ambiance of the Plaza. It opens at 7:00 p.m. On the opposite side of the Plaza are cafes for cachapas and falafels. Good breakfast provisions (coffee, sandwich ingredients, pasteles, etc.) can be purchased two blocks south of the Plaza on the Avenida Piar.

Hotels
There is an inn at Tumeremo, that I was told about at the last minute: **Hospedaje y Restaurante 'El Secreto de la Crema'**, the secret of the cream[1], phone: (0) 288-771-0270. On the main street going through Tumeremo towards the south, watch for a sign indicating a right turn for this establishment. It is only a short distance from the corner. Fourteen rooms with private bath, cold water, fan. Parking in enclosed compound. Extremely inexpensive.

In **Guasipati** there is a motel, the **Merey de Oro,** the golden cashew[2], **that looks perfectly acceptable, but that is 52 kilometers to the north of Tumeremo, and you would have to leave by 4:00 a.m.**

Chris stayed with friends in Tumeremo. I remember that some twenty years ago I stayed at a hotel in this town, and maybe it still exists. It is up to you to ferret out if the Secret of the Cream is creamy, or if there is another option in town.

Birds of the Anacoco / San Martín de Turumbán Road

Great Tinamou	Great Black Hawk	Russet-crowned Crake
Little Tinamou	Ornate Hawk-Eagle	Purple Gallinule
Variegated Tinamou	Crane Hawk	Sunbittern
Red-legged Tinamou	Collared Forest-Falcon	Wattled Jacana
Capped Heron	Slaty-backed Forest-Falcon	Southern Lapwing
Rufescent Tiger-Heron	Barred Forest-Falcon	Solitary Sandpiper
Green Ibis	Red-throated Caracara	Scaled Pigeon
King Vulture	Yellow-headed Caracara	Pale-vented Pigeon
Black Vulture	Crested Caracara	Ruddy Pigeon
Turkey Vulture	Bat Falcon	Plumbeous Pigeon
Greater Yellow-Headed	American Kestrel	Plain-breasted Ground-Dove
Vulture	Little Chachalaca	Gray-fronted Dove
Swallow-tailed Kite	Spix's Guan	Red-and-Green Macaw
Hook-billed Kite	Black Curassow	Brown-throated Parakeet
Double-toothed Kite	Crested Bobwhite	Painted Parakeet
Plumbeous Kite	Marbled Wood-Quail	Green-rumped Parrotlet
Roadside Hawk	Limpkin	Dusky-billed Parrotlet
White Hawk	Gray-winged Trumpeter	Golden-winged Parakeet
Black-collared Hawk	Gray-necked Wood-Rail	Black-headed Parrot

[1] Editor's Note: You better not ask...
[2] Editor's Note: Nope. Not here either. The less questions the better.

Blue-headed Parrot
Dusky Parrot
Squirrel Cuckoo
Black-bellied Cuckoo
Smooth-billed Ani
Tropical Screech Owl
Spectacled Owl
Ferruginous Pygmy-Owl
Common Potoo
Short-tailed Nighthawk
Pauraque
Band-rumped Swift
Short-tailed Swift
Lesser Swallow-tailed Swift
Fork-tailed Palm-Swift
Long-tailed Hermit
Reddish Hermit
White-necked Jacobin
Blue-chinned Sapphire
Fork-tailed Woodnymph
White-chested Emerald
Black-eared Fairy
Long-billed Starthroat
Black-tailed Trogon
White-tailed Trogon
Black-throated Trogon
Violaceous Trogon
Green Kingfisher
American Pygmy Kingfisher
Blue-crowned Motmot
Green-tailed Jacamar
White-necked Puffbird
Pied Puffbird
Black Nunbird
Swallow-wing
Black-necked Araçari
Green Araçari
Channel-billed Toucan

Red-billed Toucan
Golden-spangled Piculet
Chestnut Woodpecker
Lineated Woodpecker
Yellow-tufted Woodpecker
Red-crowned Woodpecker
Crimson-crested Woodpecker
Red-necked Woodpecker
Wedge-billed Woodcreeper
Buff-throated Woodcreeper
Plain-crowned Spinetail
Fasciated Antshrike
Great Antshrike
Black-crested Antshrike
Mouse-colored Antshrike
Guianan Slaty Antshrike
Pygmy Antwren
White-flanked Antwren
Todd's Antwren
Gray Antbird
Dusky Antbird
White-browed Antbird
White-bellied Antbird
Rufous-capped Antthrush
Black-faced Antthrush
Screaming Piha
Black-tailed Tityra
Black-crowned Tityra
Purple-throated Fruitcrow
White Bellbird
Golden-headed Manakin
Blue-backed Manakin
Wing-barred Piprites
Fork-tailed Flycatcher
Tropical Kingbird
Piratic Flycatcher
Streaked Flycatcher
Rusty-margined Flycatcher

Great Kiskadee
Bright-rumped Attila
Grayish Mourner
Short-crested Flycatcher
Dusky-capped Flycatcher
Yellow-olive Flycatcher
Slate-headed Tody-Flycatcher
Helmeted Pygmy-Tyrant
Forest Elaenia
Southern Beardless Tyrannulet
Sooty-headed Tyrannulet
Yellow-crowned Tyrannulet
White-winged Swallow
Gray-breasted Martin
Barn Swallow
Cayenne Jay
Buff-breasted Wren
Southern House-Wren
Tropical Mockingbird
Long-billed Gnatwren
Tropical Gnatcatcher
Rufous-browed Peppershrike
Red-eyed Vireo
Lemon-chested Greenlet
Buff-cheeked Greenlet
Giant Cowbird
Crested Oropendola
Green Oropendola
Yellow-rumped Cacique
Tropical Parula
Blue Dacnis
Turquoise Tanager
Violaceous Euphonia
Palm Tanager
Silver-beaked Tanager
White-lined Tanager
Lesser Seed-Finch
Blue-black Grassquit

CONTINUING SOUTH

If you plan to go straight towards the south and miss the fun of the Anacoco Road, it will take you six hours from either El Palmar or Puerto Ordaz to reach what will hopefully be the first destination on this "Road South", and a place where you will wish to stay for the next few days.

After Turmeremo you have yet another 60 kilometers to **El Dorado**, which you also by-pass, because the road forks, and instead of taking the right branch, which goes into town, you stay on the eastern road, which is the one going south towards the Gran Sabana.

This junction is the ZERO POINT from which all kilometers on the Gran Sabana road are measured. From here on, going south, everything is located by the kilometer reading, so don't forget to take a reading on your odometer. (Crazy isn't it?)

Shortly after you fork to the left, you will come to the **Cuyuni River**, and to the nice old bridge spanning it. However, a new bridge has recently been built over the river - where the pavement already has holes, unlike the old bridge, (As my husband would say: "They don't make them like that anymore.") You are aiming for a destination located just before Kilometer 85, which is the site of the despicably ugly mining town of Las Claritas.

THE BARQUILLA DE FRESA (THE STRAWBERRY ICE CREAM CONE)

Just before you enter Dante's Inferno in Las Claritas (Km 85), you will see a lovely large lawn on your right and a gate. Ring the bell and Henry Cleve will come to welcome you to what must be the most incongruously named birder's paradise.

From the instant you drive in, you will know that this is a special place. Just imagine sitting in the garden in the afternoon, having a nice cold beer, as you watch the birds from the porch. You can, of course, equally well, enjoy your morning coffee in the same manner.

Considering the pleasures of Henry's garden, you would do well to plan for a few hours of easy birding right there. Henry knows his birds, and he knows what you are looking for. At night, you sometimes hear Crested and Spectacled Owls near the house. Henry also told me that during April, huge flocks of Fork-tailed Flycatchers are to be seen from the garden as they migrate north. That does not surprise me, because I saw the same thing one April down near the Brazilian border -- wave upon wave of Fork-tailed Flycatchers coming up from Brazil and Argentina. That is one of the nice things about Venezuela - during the northern winter, we get the Warblers, etc. from up north, and then, during the southern winter, we get the birds from down south!

There is a tree in Henry's garden that bears red flowers. He could not tell me the name of the tree but apparently, it blooms in April and September, and the flowers and fruit can last up to three months each time. That tree is a magnet for the Crimson Topaz. I saw it one November and was mesmerized. Also, right in front of the porch there is a tree that Henry calls the *Palo Blanco*. This tree also has red fruits in April and apparently attracts the Cotingas. It begins to look like April is *the* time to visit the Cleve family. Here is a list of the special birds seen in or from the garden of Barquilla de Fresa at various times - and what a list!

Gray-headed Kite	Fork-tailed Woodnymph	White-flanked Antwren
Plumbeous Kite	Rufous-tailed Hummingbird	Purple-breasted Cotinga
Black-faced Hawk	Crimson Topaz	Spangled Cotinga
Orange-breasted Falcon	Black-eared Fairy	Pompadour Cotinga
Painted Parakeet	Long-billed Starthroat	Tropical Kingbird
Golden-winged Parakeet	Amethyst Woodstar	Yellow-throated Flycatcher
Dusky-billed Parrotlet	Brown Jacamar	Rusty-margined Flycatcher
Sapphire-rumped Parrotlet	Paradise Jacamar	Black-fronted Tyrannulet
Black-headed Parrot	White-necked Puffbird	Gray-breasted Martin
Dusky Parrot	Pied Puffbird	Cayenne Jay
Blue-cheeked Parrot	Swallow-wing	Crested Oropendola
Red-fan Parrot	Black Nunbird	Moriche Oriole
Mealy Parrot	Black-spotted Barbet	Swallow Tanager
Rufous-breasted Hermit	Green Araçari	Green Honeycreeper
Long-tailed Hermit	Black-necked Araçari	Paradise Tanager
Gray-breasted Sabrewing	Channel-billed Toucan	Violaceous Euphonia
White-necked Jacobin	Golden-collared Woodpecker	Chestnut-bellied Seedeater
Brown Violetear	Cinereous Antshrike	

You will not necessarily see all of the above while you are at the Barquilla de Fresa. In fact, as of April, 2001 very few were to be seen except at the hummingbird feeders, thanks to our current and recently-past governments. For reasons that we environmentalists cannot understand, they have insisted upon the construction of an electric grid from the Guri Dam in northern Bolivar all across the Gran Sabana to Brazil. Venezuela will be selling electricity at a subsidized cost to the nation of Brazil. In fact, we in Caracas will pay more for our electric power than the Brazilians. The construction has caused tremendous environmental damage with the consequent impact on wildlife. Henry himself fought like a David against the Goliath of EDELCA, the national electrical company, trying his best to save his forest behind the garden. He won something of a Pyrrhic victory, forcing them to reduce the swath cut through his forest from a width of 100 to 30 meters, but still the impact on his fauna has been extremely negative. We can only hope that in the future the birds will return. However, in spite or irrespective of EDELCA, you can easily spend a few hours of pure joy observing the hummingbird feeders. You no sooner spot one species, than another pushes it out of the way, each feeding in its own style.

The area in general is very interesting and enticing to bird watchers, and at Barquilla de Fresa, if you want breakfast at 5 or 5:30 a.m. it will be ready and waiting for you, and it will be a "full English." Your picnic lunch will also be ready.

The Cleve family are such a delight, you will feel you are visiting long-known friends. Henry's wife, Magaly, is not only a wonderful cook, but a fantastic, hard-working and sincere help-mate. Then there is their daughter, Selva Roraima, she is a sweetheart. I have never been able to understand how is it possible for Henry to have lived all these years in such close proximity to the dregs of humanity that live in Las Claritas, and has never been touched by their filth.

Unfortunately - or perhaps fortunately - Barquilla de Fresa is small and can take only a limited number of guests. There are six double rooms that are easily converted with bunk beds to sleep four. There are no private bathrooms, but since there are four of them, it is more than adequate - usually you find at least one that is free. The water in the showers may not be hot but it is tepid and the temperature is such that you do not really miss a hot shower. Henry is currently constructing two more double rooms with private baths which should be ready in the near future.

Since the Barquilla is one of the top birding destinations in Venezuela, reservations should be made well in advance. As there are no mail service nor telephones in this part of the world, in the past it has been extremely difficult to make contact with Henry. However, he has just purchased one of those very fancy telephones that cost an arm and a leg to call but that may be used in an emergency: (0) 415-212-5002. The usual contact for reservations is to call or fax Alba Betancourt (0) 212-256-4162, or write barquilladefresa@cantv.net. Naturally, reservations can also be made through the Venezuelan Audubon.

ALTERNATIVE LODGINGS

If, as often happens, Barquilla de Fresa is booked up, you might try one of the following:

La Montañita
At Km 70, on the west side of the highway. Has both cabins with private baths and churuatas for hanging hammocks. Meals would have to be arranged for beforehand. No telephone.

Campamento Anaconda
Right in the middle of Las Claritas. For obvious security reasons, they do close the gates at night, in case you plan to arrive after dark. Has 13 A-frame cabins with private bath. (cold water naturally). Sometimes they have restaurant service and sometimes not. Perhaps the best option, but due to its location it can be terribly noisy. Remember your ear plugs. Phones: (0) 286-923-7966 & (0) 416-787-9151, fax: (0) 286-992-6572.

Campamento Turístico Gran Sabana
Phone/Fax: (0) 289-808-2001, 808-2002. Has 16 plain, but adequate double rooms in cabins with private bath, hot water (whoopee) and fan. Quiet setting and enclosed parking. Slightly south of Anaconda in Las Claritas. Has restaurant for guests only. Elizabeth Kline had some doubts about this option, so check out the cabins prior to making a commitment

Chalet Raymond
Phone: (0) 414-852-1257. On the left side of the road just past Campamento Turístico Gran Sabana. Five double rooms with private bath (hot water showers!) Parking inside the fenced property and private guard service.

Hotel Pilionera
At Km 88. Very, very simple but with the AC on it can be quiet and not too uncomfortable. No phone.

FASCINATING BIRDING SITES. READ ON![1]

The Guyana Trail
The Guyana Trail is a path through the forest which goes all the way across the border to Guyana. The Indigenous people on both sides of these parts have known about it and used it for years. Birders discovered it as a great birding trail in the seventies, thanks to the indefatigable curiosity and birding skills of Chris Parrish and Allan Altman, who lived in Venezuela and were members of the Audubon at the time.

The Trail used to come out onto the road at Km 74, but it now comes out slightly south of Km 66. You should park your car by the houses at San Miguel, at Kilometer 66, and walk south some 100 Mts. until you see it leading off on your left. It can be very hot, so take a good supply of liquid with you, and plan to spend several hours hiking in and back. One important point to remember *before* you leave Barquilla de Fresa to do this hike, is to *take all possible preventive measures against chiggers* - the Guyana Trail is one of the most chiggery places I have ever known!

The path was abandoned for several years, but Henry Cleve recently cleared about 2 km and a fellow birder, James Black of ChupaFlor Tours pitched in as well. When you come, ask Henry as to the condition of the trail.

At first, it doesn't look very promising, as it goes through some very disturbed areas, including places where gold mining has completely destroyed the vegetation. The forest begins after you walk through a long grass area and past two scrapes. Actually, you will have to pass through a lot of small holdings before you reach it.

---

[1] Editor' Note: Honestly, guys, Mary Lou sometimes sounds like my First Grade teacher, Miss Blanca: 'Teach, this word is too long…' 'No it is not, Clemencia, it is just new. Read on!'

About 50 meters into the forest, after the second scrape, a Musician Wren has made his home on the right, and also a Waved Woodpecker. After that, look for:

Great Tinamou
Variegated Tinamou
King Vulture
Black Vulture
Greater Yellow-headed
    Vulture
Plumbeous Kite
Gray-lined Hawk
Great Black Hawk
Black-and-white Hawk-Eagle
Crane Hawk
Laughing Falcon
Collared Forest Falcon
Red-throated Caracara
Little Chachalaca
Gray-winged Trumpeter
Wattled Jacana
Scaled Pigeon
Ruddy Ground-Dove
Blue Ground-Dove
Gray-fronted Dove
Ruddy Quail-Dove
Red-and-green Macaw
Painted Parakeet
Green-rumped Parrotlet
Golden-winged Parakeet
Sapphire-rumped Parrotlet
Black-headed Parrot
Blue-headed Parrot
Dusky Parrot
Orange-winged Parrot
Mealy Parrot
Red-fan Parrot
Squirrel Cuckoo
Black-bellied Cuckoo
Smooth-billed Ani
Ferruginous Pygmy-Owl
White-collared Swift
Gray-rumped Swift
Band-rumped Swift
Short-tailed Swift
Lesser Swallow-tailed Swift
Rufous-breasted Hermit
Long-tailed Hermit
Reddish Hermit
Gray-breasted Sabrewing
White-necked Jacobin
Fork-tailed Woodnymph

White-chinned Sapphire
White-chested Emerald
Crimson Topaz
Black-eared Fairy
Long-billed Starthroat
Black-tailed Trogon
White-tailed Trogon
Black-throated Trogon
Violaceous Trogon
Ringed Kingfisher
Amazon Kingfisher
Green-and-Rufous Kingfisher
Yellow-billed Jacamar
Green-tailed Jacamar
Paradise Jacamar
Great Jacamar
White-necked Puffbird
Pied Puffbird
Collared Puffbird
Black Nunbird
Swallow-wing
Black-spotted Barbet
Green Araçari
Black-necked Araçari
White-throated Toucan
Guianan Toucanet
Channel-billed Toucanet
Red-billed Toucanet
Golden-spangled Piculet
Yellow-throated Woodpecker
Chestnut Woodpecker
Waved Woodpecker
Lineated Woodpecker
Yellow-tufted Woodpecker
Golden-collared Woodpecker
Crimson-crested Woodpecker
Red-necked Woodpecker
Plain-brown Woodcreeper
Wedge-billed Woodcreeper
Black-banded Woodcreeper
Barred Woodcreeper
Chestnut-rumped Woodcreeper
Buff-throated Woodcreeper
Red-billed Scythebill
Curve-billed Scythebill
Pale-breasted Spinetail
Cinnamon-rumped
    Foliage-Gleaner

Buff-throated Foliage-Gleaner
Olive-backed Foliage-Gleaner
Rufous-tailed Xenops
Plain Xenops
Black-throated Antshrike
Mouse-colored Antshrike
Leaftosser sp.
Dusky-throated Antshrike
Cinereous Antshrike
Pygmy Antwren
Rufous-bellied Antwren
Brown-bellied Antwren
White-flanked Antwren
Long-winged Antwren
Gray Antwren
White-fringed Antwren
Gray Antbird
Dusky Antbird
White-browed Antbird
Warbling Antbird
Black-chinned Antbird
Spot-winged Antbird
Black-throated Antbird
White-plumed Antbird
Rufous-throated Antbird
Scale-backed Antbird
Rufous-capped Antthrush
Spangled Cotinga
Pompadour Cotinga
Screaming Piha
Pink-throated Becard
Black-tailed Tityra
Purple-throated Fruitcrow
Capuchinbird
White Bellbird
Bearded Bellbird
Guianan Red-Cotinga
Guianan Cock-of-the-Rock
Golden-headed Manakin
White-crowned Manakin
Blue-backed Manakin
Thrush-like Schiffornis
Long-tailed Tyrant
Tropical Kingbird
Piratic Flycatcher
Yellow-throated Flycatcher
Streaked Flycatcher
Rusty-margined Flycatcher

Social Flycatcher
Bright-rumped Attila
Cinereous Mourner
Dusky-capped Flycatcher
Ruddy-tailed Flycatcher
Sulphur-rumped Flycatcher
Cinnamon-crested Spadebill
Yellow-olive Flycatcher
Olivaceous Flatbill
Common Tody-Flycatcher
Helmeted Pygmy-Tyrant
Ochre-bellied Flycatcher
McConnell's Flycatcher
White-winged Swallow
Gray-breasted Martin
Cayenne Jay
Coraya Wren
Buff-breasted Wren
House Wren

Musician Wren
White-necked Thrush
Long-billed Gnatwren
Red-eyed Vireo
Tawny-crowned Greenlet
Giant Cowbird
Crested Oropendola
Amazonian Oropendola
Red-rumped Cacique
Rose-breasted Chat
Neotropical River Warbler
Bananaquit
Purple Honeycreeper
Red-legged Honeycreeper
Green Honeycreeper
Blue Dacnis
Black-faced Dacnis
Opal-rumped Tanager
Paradise Tanager

Spotted Tanager
Bay-headed Tanager
Violaceous Euphonia
Golden-bellied Euphonia
Blue-gray Tanager
Palm Tanager
Silver-beaked Tanager
Summer Tanager
Flame-crested Tanager
Fulvous-crested Tanager
Yellow-backed Tanager
Magpie Tanager
Buff-throated Saltator
Blue-black Grosbeak
Red-and-Green Grosbeak
Yellow-green Grosbeak
Pectoral Sparrow
Lesser Seed Finch
Blue-black Grassquit

The Capuchinbird Road

Three km south of Barquilla de Fresa, opposite the "Banco de Guayana" office at Kilometer 87 (no longer functioning), there is a dirt road leading west. This is the road we birders have come to call the "Capuchinbird Road", but do not ask for it by this name, since no local will know what you are talking about or be able to direct you to it.

It should be visited first very early in the morning - no later than 6:00 a.m. - and you should follow it all the way to the River. At approximately 5 km from the main highway, there is a junction. The road going to the right leads to a mining company, whereas the main one eventually leads to the river and the ruins of a log bridge built by miners. You want to bird around the junction. Previously, this was an area of garimpeiros, the Brazilian name for independent gold miners. However, since the fall in the price of gold, mining has decreased considerably along with the consequent environmental destruction and use of mercury. (May gold continue to decrease!)

Henry Cleve showed me the hidden trail to the actual lek of the Capuchinbirds. In the morning listen for a distant mooing or growling sound. Some people compare the sounds to that of an outboard motor or a chain-saw. If you have a recorder, it is relatively easy to call them out, but please do not abuse of this practice. Thanks to Henry, I discovered that to actually see the birds at their lek and to get a recording that practically hits the highest decibels the best time is in the late afternoon, say about 4:00 p.m. Just hang around until the birds arrive. From the junction mentioned above, walk straight some 120 meters towards the river until you see a faint path on your left. Follow this path for more or less 5 minutes. Henry claims that the best time to be there is at 5:00 p.m., but I would not want to take a chance on missing the critters. I did find though that the best time of year to hear and see the Capuchinbird is towards the end of the dry season - between February and May.

Aside from the Capuchinbirds, here is a list for the road:

Great Tinamou
Greater Yellow-headed Vulture
Plumbeus Kite

White Hawk
Black-faced Hawk
Limpkin

Ruddy Pigeon
Plumbeous Pigeon
Painted Parakeet

Lilac-tailed Parrotlet	Red-billed Toucan	Yellow-throated Flycatcher
Black-headed Parrot	Golden-spangled Piculet	Rusty-margined Flycatcher
Caica Parrot	Waved Woodpecker	Grayish Mourner
Blue-headed Parrot	Lineated Woodpecker	Helmeted Pygmy Tyrant
Mealy Parrot	Yellow-tufted Woodpecker	Yellow-crowned Tyrannulet
Squirrel Cuckoo	Crimson-crested Woodpecker	Musician Wren
Ferruginous Pygmy-Owl	Red-necked Woodpecker	Crested Oropendola
White-collared Swift	Wedge-billed Woodcreeper	Red-rumped Cacique
Chapman's Swift	Rufous-tailed Foliage-Gleaner	Bananaquit
Long-tailed Hermit	Rufous-tailed Xenops	Red-legged Honeycreeper
Gray-breasted Sabrewing	Pygmy Antwren	Purple Honeycreeper
White-necked Jacobin	Streaked Antwren	Green Honeycreeper
Black-throated Mango	Plain-winged Antwren	Blue Dacnis
Fork-tailed Woodnymph	Gray Antwren	Opal-rumped Tanager
Crimson Topaz	Dusky Antbird	Turquoise Tanager
Black-eared Fairy	Spot-winged Antbird	Bay-headed Tanager
Long-billed Starthroat	Warbling Antbird	Paradise Tanager
White-tailed Trogon	Black-throated Antbird	Blue-gray Tanager
Green Kingfisher	Rufous-throated Antbird	Palm Tanager
Paradise Jacamar	Spangled Cotinga	Red-crowned Ant-tanager
White-necked Puffbird	Pompadour Cotinga	Silver-beaked Tanager
Black Nunbird	Black-tailed Tityra	Red-shouldered Tanager
Swallow-wing	Screaming Piha	Yellow-backed Tanager
Black-spotted Barbet	Capuchinbird	Blue-black Grosbeak
Green Araçari	Golden-headed Manakin	Slate-colored Grosbeak
Black-necked Araçari	White-crowned Manakin	Yellow-green Grosbeak
Channel-billed Toucan		

I suspect that the above is only a small portion of the birds to be seen along the Capuchinbird road. Henry Cleve has seen the Yellow-billed Jacamar by a small marsh on the right as you drive towards the junction, and Chris Sharpe commented that it is an excellent area for all Cotingas, particularly when the Cecropias are fruiting. Give yourself three or four hours to bird the road, and I promise you will enjoy those hours thoroughly.

Cuyuni River Trip

This was a new experience for me and one that I want to share with all of you. You will have to leave your vehicle by the junction as the road from there to the River deteriorates badly. It is only a kilometer which you can easily and enjoyably walk. When you come to the river, ask around for Oswaldo Perez or his brother, El Pavo. You can make arrangements with them to take you out along the tributary of the Cuyuni to the actual Cuyuni itself. Agree on prices and time (at least 7:00 a.m.). Also, Henry Cleve has a boat and is talking about the possibility of buying an electric motor to take his guests out down the river. On our trip we saw:

Striated Heron	Black-tailed Trogon	Black-necked Araçari
Sungrebe	Ringed Kingfisher	Crimson-crested
Scarlet Macaw	Amazon Kingfisher	Woodpeckers
Dusk y Parrot	Green Kingfisher	White-winged Swallow
White-tailed Trogon	Paradise Jacamar	White-banded Swallow

To complete our experience, Oswaldo took us along a beautiful path in the forest that I baptized Green Mansions. The trip was well worth both the time and the small sum it cost us.

CANAIMA NATIONAL PARK AND WORLD HERITAGE SITE

The best description I have read of the Park is that written by Chris Sharpe and his wife Lokiñe Rodríguez in Volume 14, Number 3 of the George Wright Forum, 1997. I am grateful to them for giving me permission to quote from this article:

«*Canaima National Park is located in the southeast of Venezuela in the state of Bolívar, close to the borders with Brazil and Guyana. The Park protects the northwestern section of the Guyana Shield, an ancient geological formation shared with Brazil, Guyana and Colombia. .... Its size was increased to 30,000 sq. km in 1975 to safeguard the watershed functions of its river basins. The total area is equivalent to that of Belgium in Europe or larger than the state of Maryland in the U.S.A.*

The best-known features of Canaima National Park are its characteristic flat-topped mountain formations, known as tepuis from the local indigenous name.

The geological history of the area is only superficially understood. There are three main geological formations. The oldest is an underlying igneous-metamorphic basement formed some 1.2-3.6 billion years ago whilst South America was joined to Africa as the super-continent Gondwanaland. Between 1-1.6 billion years ago, this was overlain with a sedimentary cover. The first of these formations is too deeply buried to be visible within the Park, but the second one (known as the Roraima Group) forms the basis of the area's extraordinary topography. It consists of quartzite and sandstone strata which were probably laid down in shallow seas or large inland lakes during the Pre-Cambrian period. Lastly, during Palaeozoic and Mesozoic times magma repeatedly penetrated the existing sediments forming intrusive rocks, which are typically diabases, and to a lesser extent granites.

The tepui formations, not unlike those found in the deserts of northern Arizona, came into being by a process of erosion of the surrounding lands over millions of years. The tepuis are sandstone massifs, and it is thought that what are today mountains once formed harder or less-faulted strata which were more resistant to erosion.

There is an impressive array of different soil types. The low mineral content of the parent rocks of the Guyana Shield, the high rates of weathering that occur in tropical climates, and the age of the sediments has produced soils which are generally acid and nutrient-poor.

The vegetation of the Canaima National Park is quite strikingly divided between the mainly savanna-forest mosaic of the eastern sector of the park, known as the Gran Sabana, and evergreen forest in the west. It is still not clear what causes this difference and, in particular, how the savanna originated. While some authors are inclined to believe the savanna to be a product of a rainfall shadow caused by the eastern tepuis, others consider the formation to be entirely anthropogenic, being a product of repeated burning by indigenous peoples. The presence of 107 plant species found only in these savannas demonstrates that they have existed at least long enough to allow new species to form.

The savannas are dominated by grasses, and fire-resistant sedges which form a small cushion on which it raises itself above the ground to avoid the worst of the savanna blazes. Stunted shrubs are also found at low densities. The high meadows, on the other hand, are composed of typically Guyanan herbs. The shrublands are usually composed of shrubs and bushes up to two meters tall, most of which are hard-leaved. The evergreen montane forests are often humid and luxuriant.

The tepui tops themselves are sometimes forested, with dwarf forests. In other cases, meadows prevail on the tops. One feature of these extremely nutrient-poor environments is the presence of carnivorous plants, such as pitcher plants and sundews.

An important formation in the lower altitudes closer to the rivers and shallow valley bottoms of the basins are the seasonally flooded palm savannas, or morichales, which are dominated by the Moriche palm.

Some 9,400 species of plants have been recorded from the Venezuelan Guyana, of which 2,320 are registered from the tepuis. This includes more than 700 species of orchids. The flora is highly endemic with two endemic families and 23 unique genera. At the species level, approximately 33% of the tepui species are endemic to the region, with 99 species endemic to Chimantá alone.

The traditional inhabitants of the southeast of Venezuela, including Canaima National Park, are the Pemón indigenous people, part of the Carib linguistic group. Their entire population approaches 20,000, with about three quarters of these people living within the national park.

The date of first occupation of the Gran Sabana is not known, but the Pemón are thought to have immigrated into the region some 200 years ago, although there are archeological remains of human settlements which date back 9,000 years. Perhaps this 'late colonization' of the Gran Sabana is a function of it's poor soils: This is certainly some evidence to suggest that low productivity is responsible for the relatively low population density of its present-day inhabitants in relation to the indigenous inhabitants of, for example, the Amazonian lowlands. Despite this short history of settlement, the Pemón have an intimate relationship with their landscape. The names of rock formations, waterfalls, rapids, lakes and streams all have their origins described in myth. In particular the Pemón relationship with the tepuis is complex and profound. The tepuis are sacred mountains for the Pemón. Only in the last two decades, with the increase in tourism, have some Pemón begun to disregard these traditional beliefs by taking hikers to some of the more accessible tepuis such as Roraima, Kukenám and Auyantepuy.»

THE ESCALERA

You will now head for birding heaven. So that nothing mars your bliss, fill your gas tank at Kilometer 88, that indescribable last stand of "civilization" before the wilds of the Gran Sabana. As you drive south you will see a range of mountains in the distance. This is the **Sierra de Lema**, the northern boundary of the Gran Sabana sector of **Canaima National Park**.

The road climbing the northern cliffs of this range is known as **La Escalera** - The Stairway. It starts at Kilometer 98 by the **Piedra de la Virgen** - the Rock of the Virgin, a huge granite monolith - and it is one of the very best birding roads in the whole country. I suggest you start birding right there very early in the morning. This is what you have come for!

Birding the Escalera is mind boggling, but it is also **very** hard work. You *have to be* on the outlook for fruiting trees, as that is where you will find the birds. Certain spots on the road are known to be better for birding, but everything depends on whether the trees are in fruit. Below are a few suggestions as to where you *might* find the birds. Many of these sightings were given to me by our bird guides or hot-shot birders.

Km 92	Cayenne Jay	Tropical Parula
	Amazonian Oropendola	Spotted Tanager
Km 98	Ruddy Pigeon	Cliff Flycatcher
400 masl[1]	Gray-breasted Sabrewing	White-tipped Swift
	Short-tailed Swift	White-fronted Manakin
		Lesser Seed-Finch
Km 99	Swallow-tailed Kite	White Hawk
	Chestnut Woodpecker	Bat Falcon
	Orange-breasted Falcon	Todd's Antwren
	Sapphire-rumped Parrotlet	Lesser Seed Finch
	Black-eared Fairy	
Km 100	Straight-billed Hermit	White-lored Euphonia
	Roadside Hawk	White-throated Manakin
	Blue Dacnis	White-bearded Manakin
	Bananaquit	Black Manakin
		Channel-billed Toucan
Km 101.8	Red-and-green Macaw	Spotted Tanager
	Tepui Parrotlet	Yellow-green Tanager
	Fork-tailed Woodnymph	White-lined Tanager
	Tufted Coquette	Olive-backed Tanager
	Warbling Antbird	
Km 102	Variegated Tinamou	
Km 103	Marail Guan	Blue-cheeked Parrot
600 masl	Orange-breasted Falcon	Golden-headed Manakin
	Caica Parrot	
Km 106	Black-eared Fairy	Short-billed Honeycreeper
	Slaty Grosbeak	Black-fronted Tyrannulet
Km 108	Racket-tailed Coquette	Fulvous-crested Tanager
700 masl	Golden-spangled Piculet	Hooded Siskin
Km 110	Red-banded Fruiteater	Speckled Tanager
820 masl	Waved Woodpecker	Tepui Swift
	Streaked-backed Antshrike	White Bellbird
	Sharpbill (look high)	Sierran Elaenia

[1] m.a.s.l. = meters above sea level.

Km 111	Long-tailed Hermit Olivaceus Woodcreeper Plain Xenops Roraiman Antwren Warbling Antbird Cliff Flycatcher Gray-crowned Flycatcher Slaty-capped Shrike-Vireo Fulvous Shrike-Tanager Slate-colored Grosbeak	Golden-olive Woodpecker Barred Woodcreeper Gray Antbird Green-backed Becard Black-capped Becard Sharpbill White-necked Thrush Flutist Wren Red-eyed Vireo
Km 111.5	Amazonian Pygmy-Owl Chestnut-vented Toucanet	Guianan Cock-of-the-Rock White Bellbird
Km 112	Tepui Spinetail	Coraya Wren
Km 113	Golden-olive Woodpecker Slate-colored Grosbeak	Yellow-green Grosbeak
Km 115 Flycatcher	Slaty Elaenia Orange-breasted Falcon Golden-tufted Grackle	Yellow-margined Swallow-wing
Km 116	Velvet-browed Brilliant Blue-cheeked Parrot Tepui Swift	Blue-fronted Lancebill Slender-footed Tyrannulet
Km 117	Blue-and-white Swallow	
Km 117.5 1000 masl	Purple-throated Euphonia	
Km 118	Rufous-collared Sparrow	
Km 119 1180 masl	Crested Eagle Rufous-breasted Sabrewing Rose-collared Piha	Olive Manakin White-fronted Manakin

(This is the area of the 'Salto El Danto', the Tapir's Waterfall)

Km 121 1250 masl	Rufous-tailed Tyrant Streak-backed Antshrike Golden-crowned Spadebill	Fiery-shouldered Parakeet Olive-backed Tanager Thrush-like Schiffornis
Km 122	Red-and-Green Macaw Greater Flower Piercer Tepui Parrotlet Rufous-breasted Sabrewing Velvet-browed Brilliant Flutist Wren Olive Manakin	Blue-headed Parrot Amethyst Woodstar Masked Trogon Red-necked Woodpecker Rose-collared Piha Ruddy Tody-Flycatcher Olive-backed Tanager

Km 123
1360 masl

Swallow-tailed Kite
Rose-collared Piha
Olivaceous Woodcreeper
Chestnut-rumped Woodcreeper
Tepui Spinetail
Rufous-collared Sparrow
Tepui Brush-Finch

Back-billed Trush
Golden-tufted Grackle
Two-banded Warbler
Red-shouldered Tanager
Black-fronted Tyrannulet
White-necked Thrush

Km 126

(Look for birds in the meadow)
Rufous-breasted Sabrewing
White Bellbird
Along the forest edge look for
Flutist Wren (singing in July)

Streaked-backed Antshrike

Two-banded Warbler

Km 130

Bat Falcon
Chestnut-tipped Toucanet
Sharp-tailed Streamcreeper
Olive-backed Tanager
Rufous-brown Solitaire

Bearded Bellbird
Red-banded Fruiteater
Rose-collared Piha
Black-fronted Tyrannulet
Speckled Tanager

Km 131

Great Jacamar (What on earth is he doing here?)
Red-banded Fruiteater   Sharpbill

Km 132.5

Least Grebe
Paraguayan Snipe
White-tailed Goldenthroat
Scarlet-horned Manakin – **A LEK!**
Rufous-brown Solitaire

Bay-headed Tanager
Paradise Tanager
Yellow-bellied Tanager

Km 133

Scarlet-shouldered Parakeet
Bearded Bellbird
Streak-backed Antshrike

Brown-capped Redstart
Olive-backed Tanager
Dusky Spinetail

Km 134

Marail Guan
Blue-fronted Lancebill
Blackburnian Warbler
Scarlet-horned Manakin - **A LEK!**
Paradise Tanager
White-fronted Manakin
Olive Manakin
Ruddy Tody-Flycatcher
Black-hooded Thrush
Tepui Brush-Finch

Chestnut-tipped Toucanet
Brown Violetear
Brown-capped Redstart

Speckled Tanager
Yellow-bellied Tanager
Black-headed Tanager
Tepui Greenlet
Golden-tufted Grackle

Km 135

Dusky-capped Flycatcher
Black-billed Thrush
Rufous-crowned Elaenia

Great Elaenia
Black-faced Tanager

At the Statue of the Pioneer Soldier
Lesser Seed-Finch   Bearded Tachuri

In addition to the above, our friend Dr. Richard Byrne, of St. Andrews University in Scotland, found the following from Km 122 to 134 when he was here in July, 2000:

Rufous-thighed Hawk	Long-tailed Hermit	Roraiman Antwren
White Hawk	Peacock Coquette	Smoke-colored Pewee
White-tailed Hawk	Golden-collared Woodpecker	Tepui Redstart
Spix's Guan	Red-necked Woodpecker	Dotted Tanager
Blue-cheeked Parrot		

And at Km 136, at the very edge of the Gran Sabana, Dr. Byrne saw:

Copper-rumped Hummingbird	Tawny-headed Swallow
McConnell's Flycatcher	Black-billed Thrush

If you are just dying to see the Guianan Cock-of-the-Rock, arm yourself with patience and sit quietly between km 111 and 112. Eventually - about noon just as you have about given them up - they will come zooming down the mountain from above.

If you want to bird around the National Guard Alcabala, before ambling about, speak to them first and advise what you are doing. They are extremely suspicious of anything weird, such as birders. Which reminds me - **you should have a permit from Inparques to visit the National Park**. They may not ask you for it, but then, again, if they do, you had better have it or you might be sent back. The last time I was in the area, they did not stop me, but the time before they gave me a very bad time indeed. It all depends upon what they had for breakfast, if they are bored, if their boots are too tight, if their wives are witches, if they are in the mood to hassle tourists... (We can be worth a barrel of laughs, you know!)

At Kilometer 102 there is a pipe coming down the mountain where cistern trucks fill up. Immediately south, next to that spot, there is a trail leading up the hill. It is about a 15 minute hike up to the ridge of the mountain and the edge of a very steep precipice. Here you will have an outstanding view of the northern wall of the massif of the Gran Sabana with miles and miles of tropical forest spreading out before you. If it has been raining, take care as you walk across the ledges of Guianan sandstone. They are often covered by a thin film of algae and can be very slippery. Note the six-foot tall ground bromeliads and look for, but **don't touch**, brightly colored yellow and black frogs. If you hear an unfamiliar bird song, it might be the Silvered Antbird.

Across the road from the Kilometer 121 sign you will find a path leading to a wonderful bathing spot.

✍ The Venezuelan Audubon has published the **Check List of the Birds of Canaima National Park**, which includes all species found in the entire 3 million hectares of the Park. For the Escalera, the above may help to find the various species. Everything depends upon your luck, perseverance and what trees are fruiting. In January and February when the Melastone trees are in fruit, you should be very lucky indeed.

If you should have any doubt about birding the general area of Eastern Bolivar, I quote below from a letter I recently received from James Black of Chupaflor Tours:

«My trip to Venezuela was terrific. The birding was great and the places we stayed were all nice.

Henry's was very quaint and he is a very nice and good host. The Pilionera at Km 88 was very, very simple, but with the A/C on, quiet and comfortable. FORGET the Anaconda! Way too noisy.

The Taguapire was very pleasant and for basically being the only place one can stay in that area, I'd say it was excellent. Mr. and Mrs. Stockfim were very kind and obliging to us. The rooms were clean, quiet, sufficient and very comfortable. The meals Levis prepared for us were delicious and ample. I agree it (Taguapire) was basic and certainly no sight-seer's dream lodge, but if birders can't handle these types of accommodations, then perhaps they should stick to countries like Costa Rica.

I will be perfectly honest with anyone I meet who desires to travel/bird in Venezuela. It is no Costa Rica and not for the yuppy type. Rather, it is a little rough around the edges, but the birds are very unique and come at a delightful rate as one enters each different habitat zone. I describe my trip as a real birder's adventure in which I always felt safe and accepted by most people. The only disappointment was the price of the rental car which was continuously driven up, up and up until finally I said 'enough!'

You need to understand I am completely fluent in Spanish. I could tell as soon as they saw our bright 'white' faces that the price they had on their advertised sign would go up. You know, for this and that. I finally met them half way, and we did better than I thought we would. Anyhow, we had a great car (Fiat Uno) and not a single problem with it.

The Harpy experience was exciting and the Imataca fantastic and warrants at least three days visit.

P.S. Mino was terrific and punctual. Jim»

That says it all!

THE GRAN SABANA

At Km 135, at an altitude of 1,400 meters, you come out of the forest and onto the Gran Sabana.

While the birding will not be exceptional on the Sabana, the sights of this World Heritage Site are breathtaking and the scenery unbelievably beautiful, so it would be a crime to go to the Escalera and not continue on south to see, even if from a distance, the tepuis of the "Lost World". The road is paved all the way to the Brazilian frontier (Km 320).

Make sure you have all your identification with you, including car papers, as you may have to show all, including passports of all members of your party, at the National Guard Alcabala by the village of San Francisco de Yuruani.

At the very beginning of the Sabana, you will find the Monument to the Pioneering Soldier (Km 136). By the entrance, at about 5:30 in the evening, look for the Bearded Tachuri.

If you have the time, take a detour on the road leading west towards Kavanayen, to visit the spectacular **Aponguao-meru Falls**. But, I confess, this road could do with a lot of improvement. The road to Kavanayen turns off to the right at Km 147, after passing the army base at Luepa. After approximately 34 km, there is an even rougher road on your left leading south to a Pemón Indian village. (I suggest you check with the local inhabitants or Henry Cleve as to the condition of these roads before venturing forth.) The Pemón will canoe you across the river for a small fee, and from there you hike across the Savanna for a pleasant hour's walk. On the other hand, you can be

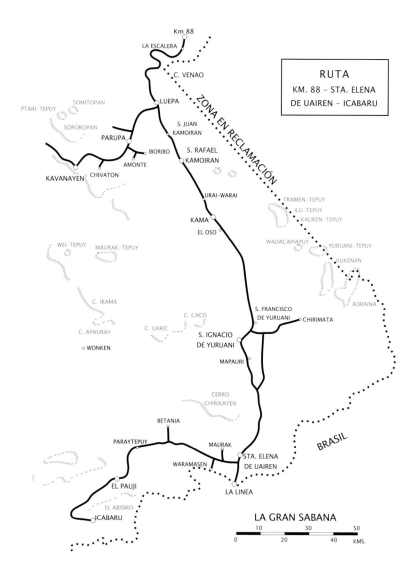

RUTA

KM. 88 – STA. ELENA
DE UAIREN – ICABARU

LA GRAN SABANA

ferried half way to the falls by boat for a fee. A few birds will be around and check the skies for raptors. The waterfall is fantastic - shortly before you reach it, you see the Aponguao River suddenly disappear. When you reach the shore, you will see the water thunder down a 200-foot drop at your feet.

Meru means waterfall in the Pemón dialect. You will see the word everywhere, because there is an incredible number of falls on the Sabana.

At Km 194 there is the entrance on the left or east to the area of Kaui Meru. It is necessary to pay a very small fee to be allowed to walk down the path to view this gorgeous waterfall and the surrounding area of jasper. The falls themselves are only about 15 meters high, but the geological formation is outstanding. Do not miss it.

For some, one of the most spectacular falls (besides Aponguao), is **Kamá-meru** (Km 201,5) and **Arapan-meru**. Below Arapan-meru, take a delightful dip in the bathers' paradise of "**Quebrada de Pacheco**" (Km 238). Also, there is **Arapena-meru**, the wide falls of the **Yuruani River** (Km 247). For these, the best view is from the bridge, so park on the far side and walk back. Above all, do not miss a visit to the **Quebrada del Jaspe** (Jasper Creek), called Kako-paru in Pemón (Km 273.5).

By Kamá Falls, there are little restaurants and a shop where you can buy Pemón handicrafts, especially small carvings in jasper. Please note that the Pemón are in no way backward. You will see churuatas with solar panels here!

As you travel south, you will behold one after another of the remarkable Precambrian tepuis rising up to the east. The largest and most famous is Roraima located immediately to the south of the Kukenám Tepui, where the world's second highest waterfall is located.

Many birders inquire about climbing the tepuis, especially Roraima. In theory, it is legally forbidden to climb the tepuis, but that regulation is very much ignored. If you have five or six extra days and are looking forward to a long hike across the savanna to the base of Roraima and then a day's climb, either contact the Audubon, or Juan Carlos Rodriguez of Akanan Tours in Caracas at akanan@sa.omnes.net , Phones (0) 212-234-2323 or Ana Matilde López, Director of Mount Roraima International Tours in Santa Elena de Uairen. Mobile phone: (0) 414-886-3870, e-mail address: mountroraima@cantv.net. Both groups are very reliable.

Caveat: You should be in excellent physical condition because this is one tough excursion[1].

While we are on the subject of the Gran Sabana, I highly recommend that you try to secure a copy of an excellent guide book in both Spanish and English written by Roberto Marrero and published by Oscar Todtmann Editores in Caracas in 1997. Their telephone in Caracas is (0) 212-763-0881. Fax: (0) 212-762-5244. They are located in Caracas at Centro Comercial El Bosque, Local 4, Avenida Libertador. The book is titled "Guide of the Gran Sabana." It may also be possible to secure the book through the Audubon in Caracas. Besides the excellent maps and beautiful pictures, the book gives detailed information on the paths or even side roads that lead to hidden waterfalls or excellent viewpoints of the various tepuis. This book will very definitely enhance any trip across the Gran Sabana.

---

[1]   Pamela's Comment: I recently did this hike/climb and I consider it the adventure of a lifetime. It isn't easy; in fact it is a hard 5- 6-day trek. But you bathe in pristine rivers, sleep out under the stars, and walk across an absolutely incredible landscape. The climb up Roraima is pretty rigorous, it's steep, and there is a heavy waterfall you have to pass through. But once on top, the scene truly is a Lost World. It is amazing and unlike anything you've ever seen. If you ever have the opportunity to take part in this excursion, grab it. An added plus is that when it's over, you'll be in great physical condition.

At Km 170, by the Rapids of Kamoiran, it is possible to secure lodging in one of the 25 simple but comfortable rooms that have private baths (cold water) as well as electricity from 6 p.m. to midnight. There also is a gas station[1], as well as quite a good restaurant. The inn and restaurant are owned by Emilia Castro de Rodríguez, a Pemón. Cash only. Before I forget to warn you - almost all lodging, eating facilities, etc. run by the Pemón in the Gran Sabana are **closed** on Saturdays (while they attend services of the Evangelist missionaries). One other point to remember, while the temperature is ideal during the day, nights can be quite cool. Bring a sweater. Remember also the saying that in the Gran Sabana during the dry season it rains **every** day. During the rainy season, it rains **all** day. However, I have not found that to be true. I have camped in the Gran Sabana during the rainy season and the rain has not been a hindrance to my birding. When the rains did come, they were torrential so the obvious thing is to take shelter while they last. The driest months are from December to March. July and August are the rainiest and the coolest.

Another point to remember is that by all the rivers, streams, falls there are very fierce no-see-ums (called jejenes or puri puri in Venezuela). My suggestion is wear long pants and use insect repellent.

And one belated explanation: The nearest commercial bank to any of the above-mentioned places is found at Tumeremo, some 144 km to the north from Barquilla de Fresa. This is the reason why almost all establishments will only accept cash.

Take note that at km 244 there is a trail going west for 2 km that leads to one of the best swimming and camping spots. To the east also at Km 244 there is a trail that goes for one km to a superb view of the tepuis and especially Kukenám. To see the Kukenám Falls (the second highest in the world) at Km 247, there is a trail going east that leads to a lookout point of both the falls and the river. This involves about a 25 minute walk.

At Km 250 you will come to the Pemón town of San Francisco de Yuruani. Here is where the trail starts for Roraima, and here, also, you will find various little shops.

The birds on the Sabana are a completely different set from what you find at La Escalera. Look for:

Turkey Vulture	Versicolored Emerald	Bay-breasted Warbler
Greater Yellow-headed Vulture	Dusky Spinetail	Burnished-buff Tanager
Yellow-headed Caracara	Tepui Spinetail	Red-shouldered Tanager
White-tailed Hawk	Sierran Elaenia	Black-faced Tanager
Short-tailed Hawk	Tawny-headed Swallow	Grassland Sparrow
Aplomado Falcon	Sedge-Wren	Plumbeous Seedeater
Bat Falcon	Tropical Mockingbird	Ruddy-breasted Seedeater
White-tipped Swift	Yellowish Pipit	Hooded Siskin
Tepui Goldenthroat	Eastern Meadowlark	Rufous-collared Sparrow

At Km 302 you will see a road going east that leads to an abandoned bridge. This is an excellent place to bird early in the morning or late in the afternoon. Look for:

Little Tinamou	Little Cuckoo	White-bearded Manakin
Red-bellied Macaw	Red-billed Toucan	Paradise Tanager
Plumbeous Pigeon	Streak-headed Woodcreeper	Plumbeous Euphonia
Blue-headed Parrot	Black-crested Antshrike	Rufous-browed Peppershrike
Orange-winged Parrot	Common Tody-Flycatcher	

---

[1] Beware! It is open only until 7:00 p.m., so do go get gas, Gus!

I do not doubt that you will find many more species if you go early in the morning rather than late as I did the one time I was there.

An Unfortunate Blight

As you climb the Escalera and drive across the Gran Sabana, you will be struck by the wanton deforestation and ecological damage caused by the electric grid to Brazil. Perhaps the most irritating for you as a tourist will be the fact that the pylons were often placed between you on the road and the tepuis, making it impossible to take a picture of these glorious table-top mountains. What can I say? We all know that government designers are not known for their intelligence, and certainly the EDELCA engineers are no exception to this rule.

SANTA ELENA DE UAIREN

Your next stop after the abandoned bridge will be **Santa Elena de Uairen**, the border town that acts as the gate between Venezuela and Brazil, and that has been growing at amazing speed since the road was finished in 1990.

There are various places to stay at Santa Elena but I definitely recommend **Campamento Yakoo** above all others. To find it follow the signs for the area of Cielo Azul. You should find a sign for a nature store - turn left here to follow the road to Sampay. The entrance to Yakoo is well marked. Around this area I have seen the White-throated Kingbird.

Yakoo is tops - the rooms are comfortable, the service is excellent and the food is some of the best I have ever had at any hotel or lodge in this country. They even have a natural swimming hole formed by the stream that goes past the lodge. For reservations contact the Audubon or call (0) 289-995-1332 & 995-1742. Naturally, like everything in this life, Yakoo has one drawback, and that is the very steep dirt road leading to the camp. During the dry season a normal car should have no problems, but when the rains come? I asked the people what happens when it rains, and they assured me that they would take charge of getting you up the hill. They will, too.

THE EL PAUJÍ ROAD

Yakoo is an ideal place to stay for a couple of nights and take the opportunity to bird a bit of the southern Gran Sabana. The best road for this purpose is the one that leads to **El Paují** and beyond, to end in the mining town of **Ikabaru**. Take the highway as if to the Brazilian border, but branch off towards the airport. As you leave the outskirts of Santa Elena, you will pass an Alcabala. After the first 42 km, there is a National Guard Post. (This is an outpost for this near-the-border area - it is not an Alcabala.)

EL PAUJÍ

The road to the town of El Paují itself is in excellent condition, and I am informed that it now takes only an hour, rather than the previous four, to drive there from Santa Elena. El Paují was founded a number of years ago by a group of young Caraqueños - mostly professional - who wanted to get away from the materialism of modern civilization. This was the time, of course, of the hippie movement, but for the most part they stayed on and developed a well founded community. There are quite a few places of interest in the area, including the beautiful swimming holes of Catedral and Esmeralda. Above all, for those in reasonably good condition there is the hike up to

El Abismo. From up there one can look across miles and miles of pure Amazonian forest. With luck you will sight King Vultures or other raptors flying below you. The good news I have received is that young Alejandro Scull and his cousin, Manuel (who speaks perfect English) have founded a camping area at the start of the trail to the Abismo complete with shower, toilet, etc. They also arrange excursions down the face of the Abismo on the other side. Now that should be superb birding.

With regard to that most important of all activities, BIRDING, there is an Englishman, Anthony (Tony) Crease and his Swiss wife, Rita, who have recently retired in El Pauji.

Tony is a bird watcher, and knowing him, I am certain that he would be delighted to show any fellow birder his favorite and best birding areas. He did send me a note that to date he has found 192 species between Santa Elena and El Pauji with particular emphasis on El Pauji. This includes 46 species not listed by me in the fourth edition of this book! Tony can be contacted at trcrease@cantv.net or by cellular phone (0) 414-886-1177 (leave a message). There is only one public telephone in El Pauji as yet, but about once a fortnight Tony goes to the web cafe in Santa Elena to pick up his e-mail and messages. I quote below from a letter I recently received from him as I believe his advice worth considering:

«If I were to plan a birding tour in East Bolivar for someone without previous experience of the area, I would perhaps bring them to the Pauji area first for a few days, then go on to the Escalera, Km 88 and Imataca. They could thus become acquainted with a lot of species in ideal climatic and observational conditions during their acclimatization period, and be able to concentrate on the more unusual species in the other areas to be visited subsequently. I say ideal observational conditions because the Pauji road carries hardly any traffic which allows you to stop where you like and bird without any inconvenience from motorists.

Depending on the number of days, one would spend the dawn to 10 am peak birding hours at different locations along the road, Independencia (5 mins), Cinco Ranchos (20 mins), Pilón to Betania (35 mins) etc. Then in the middle of the day one can return to the village for a siesta and/or fairly active birding of the commoner species in the village; or there are lots of beautiful walks mostly along rivers with wonderful swimming pools and sparse birding (including the one which appears to be inhabited by Cocks of the Rocks); or climb the famous Abismo and view the drop off the Sabana to the vast Amazonian jungle extending southwards; or walk north into the nearby jungle and try one's birding skills in the jungle which is very challenging at any time of day in my experience. In the afternoon, bird activity picks up again around 3 p.m., though not to the same pitch as in the morning.

I would also offer an option to visit the low sabanas of Northern Brazil as a side trip, which has plenty of species different from those of the Gran Sabana and jungle areas, It is within an hour of Santa Elena and could be fun especially for those who have never entered Brazil before[1] Ideally one would probably spend the night in Brazil (Boa Vista), spending the prior afternoon and following morning birding. Lots of cheap hotels and good food in the Brazilian style.

---

[1] U.S. citizens must have a visa to visit Brazil which can be obtained at the Consulate in Santa Elena.

As to facilities for birders in the Pují area, I know them pretty well. A significant bonus is that we have an experienced, English speaking, very pleasant and enthusiastic, birding guide with prior professional experience, living just 6 km down the road from here. His name is Iván Tepedino and he is a good friend of Henry Cleve. I think you will remember him too[2]. He is trying to make a go of farming in the Sabana with his wife Mareli and little girl, but it is hard to make ends meet and he was telling me recently that he would really welcome the chance to do some bird guiding again. We visited him yesterday and he confirms he would indeed be interested, for groups based in Pují or Santa Elena. By the way he had just seen an Occelated Crake a few days before. He can be contacted by e-mail at: cafegoldfieber@cantv.net or by Phone/Fax at (0) 289-995-1562.»

Unfortunately, with the new road I am afraid that civilization with all its litter and noise will not long delay in arriving along with buses full of tourists. As a matter of fact, you might also request the good services of Tony to make reservations at his son's small inn.

Where to Stay in El Pují
As to lodging - I would suggest **Hospedaje Las Brisas** (also known as El Pují) of Miguel Angel Robaina. This is located on the eastern outskirts of El Pují on a solitary hill with beautiful views of the surrounding area. Miguel Angel is one super dooper carpenter who designed and made all his furniture. He has seven spacious, comfortable, clean rooms with private baths and expanses of glass offering unequal views. Meals offered. Miguel Angel also happens to be a excellent musician.

You might also try **Hospedaje Chimantá**, phone/fax (0) 289-995-1431, e-mail: chimanta@cantv.net or stop at the handicrafts shop of the owner's wife, Francia Vivas, in Sta. Elena, Calle Roscio, Edif. Orgi-Etorri. The owner, Luis Scott, has a restaurant called La Comarca, at "the" intersection of El Pují in front of the park. (His home-made bread has been highly recommended by Elizabeth Kline.) The inn itself is located some 200 meters east down the street from the restaurant, set back from the road and surrounded by trees. Eight rooms with private bath, hot water and porch.

A third place recommended to me is the **Amaribá** owned by Marlene Murillo. The inn is located next to a forest, which should offer some good birding. There is a large salon with a fabulous view and where artistic performances are often performed.

Birds of the road from Santa Elena to El Pují and surrounding areas

Little Tinamou	Lesser Yellow-headed Vulture	Tiny Hawk
Variegated Tinamou	Greater Yellow-headed Vulture	Gray-bellied Goshawk
Cattle Egret	White-tailed Kite	White-tailed Hawk
Rufescent Tiger-Heron	Pearl Kite	Roadside Hawk
Black-bellied Whistling Duck	Swallow-tailed Kite	Gray-lined Hawk
King Vulture	Gray-headed Kite	White Hawk
Black Vulture	Hook-billed Kite	Short-tailed Hawk
Turkey Vulture	Plumbeous Kite	Savanna Hawk

---

[2] Ivan is not only a guide for the area immediately adjacent to El Pují, but to the entire Gran Sabana area. I suggest you contact him through Tony Pierce but with sufficient advance notice.

Black-and-white Hawk-Eagle
Black Hawk-Eagle
Collared Forest-Falcon
Slaty-backed Forest-Falcon
Red-throated Caracara
Yellow-headed Caracara
Crested Caracara
Orange-breasted Falcon
Bat Falcon
Aplomado Falcon
American Kestrel
Little Chachalaca
Marail Guan
Spix's Guan
Black Curassow
Marbled Wood-Quail
Limpkin
Russet-crowned Crake
Paraguayan Snipe
Scaled Pigeon
Pale-vented Pigeon
Ruddy Pigeon
Plumbeous Pigeon
Common Ground-Dove
Plain-breasted Ground-Dove
Ruddy Ground-Dove
Blue Ground-Dove
White-tipped Dove
Gray-fronted Dove
Ruddy Quail-Dove
Red-and-green Macaw
Red-shouldered Macaw
White-eyed Parakeet
Brown-throated Parakeet
Painted Parakeet
Fiery-shouldered Parakeet
Tepui Parrotlet
Black-headed Parrot
Caica Parrot
Blue-headed Parrot
Orange-winged Parrot
Mealy Parrot
Red-fan Parrot
Squirrel Cuckoo
Dark-billed Cuckoo
Smooth-billed Ani
Groove-billed Ani
Striped Cuckoo
Tawny-bellied Screech-Owl
Ferruginous Pygmy-Owl
Burrowing Owl

Black-banded Owl
Great Potoo
Common Potoo
Short-tailed Nighthawk
Least Nighthawk
Lesser Nighthawk
Pauraque
White-tailed Nightjar
Blackish Nightjar
White-collared Swift
Band-rumped Swift
White-tipped Swift
Lesser Swallow-tailed Swift
Fork-tailed Palm Swift
Sooty-capped Hermit
Reddish Hermit
Gray-breasted Sabrewing
White-necked Jacobin
Brown Violetear
Black-throated Mango
Tufted Coquette
Blue-chinned Sapphire
Blue-tailed Emerald
Fork-tailed Woodnymph
White-chinned Sapphire
Versicolored Emerald
Glittering-throated Emerald
Copper-rumped Hummingbird
Green-bellied Hummingbird
Gould's Jewelfront
Black-eared Fairy
Long-billed Starthroat
Amethyst Woodstar
Black-tailed Trogon
White-tailed Trogon
Violaceous Trogon
Ringed Kingfisher
Green Kingfisher
Green-and-rufous Kingfisher
Blue-crowned Motmot
Brown Jacamar
Paradise Jacamar
Black Nunbird
Swallow-wing Puffbird
Black-spotted Barbet
Black-necked Araçari
Many-banded Araçari
Green Araçari
Guianan Toucanet
Many-banded Araçari
Channel-billed Toucan

Red-billed Toucan
Golden-spangled Piculet
Golden-olive Woodpecker
Yellow-throated Woodpecker
Chestnut Woodpecker
Scaly-breasted Woodpecker
Lineated Woodpecker
Yellow-tufted Woodpecker
Golden-collared Woodpecker
Crimson-crested Woodpecker
Red-necked Woodpecker
Plain-brown Woodcreeper
Olivaceous Woodcreeper
Wedge-billed Woodcreeper
Chestnut-rumped Woodcreeper
Lineated Woodcreeper
Dusky Spinetail
Pale-breasted Spinetail
Speckled Spinetail
Rufous-tailed Foliage-Gleaner
Olive-backed Foliage-Gleaner
Ruddy Foliage-Gleaner
Slender-billed Xenops
Plain Xenops
Fasciated Antshrike
Great Antshrike
Barred Antshrike
Mouse-colored Antshrike
Eastern Slaty Antshrike
Dusky-throated Antshrike
Cinereous Antshrike
Pygmy Antwren
Stipple-throated Antwren
Long-winged Antwren
Roraiman Antwren
Ash-winged Antwren
Gray Antbird
Dusky Antbird
Warbling Antbird
Black-throated Antbird
White-plumed Antbird
Spangled Cotinga
Pompadour Cotinga
Screaming Piha
Black-capped Becard
Pink-throated Becard
Black-tailed Tityra
Black-crowned Tityra
Capuchinbird
White Bellbird
Bearded Bellbird

Guiana Cock-of-the-Rock
Golden-headed Manakin
White-crowned Manakin
Blue-crowned Manakin
White-throated Manakin
White-bearded Manakin
Striped Manakin
Black Manakin
Dwarf Tyrant-Manakin
Thrush-like Schiffornis
Long-tailed Tyrant
Fork-tailed Flycatcher
Tropical Kingbird
White-throated Kingbird
Variegated Flycatcher
Piratic Flycatcher
Yellow-throated Flycatcher
Boat-billed Flycatcher
Streaked Flycatcher
Social Flycatcher
Rusty-margined Flycatcher
Great Kiskadee
Cinereous Mourner
Dusky-capped Flycatcher
Sulphur-rumped Flycatcher
Bran-colored Flycatcher
Cliff Flycatcher
Yellow-olive Flycatcher
Gray-crowned Flycatcher
Royal Flycatcher
Yellow-margined Flycatcher
Common Tody-Flycatcher
Pearly-vented Tody-Tyrant
Helmeted Pygmy-Tyrant
Short-tailed Pygmy-Tyrant
Yellow-bellied Elaenia
Small-billed Elaenia
Plain-crested Elaenia
Lesser Elaenia
Rufous-crested Elaenia
Forest Elaenia
Slender-footed Tyrannulet
Yellow-crowned Tyrannulet

Sepia-capped Flycatcher
McConnell's Flycatcher
Sharpbill
Brown-chested Martin
Gray-breasted Martin
Blue-and-white Swallow
White-thighed Swallow
Tawny-headed Swallow
Southern Rough-winged Swallow
Barn Swallow
Cayenne Jay
Coraya Wren
Wing-banded Wren
House Wren
Tropical Mockingbird
Black-billed Thrush
Lawrence's Thrush
Long-billed Gnatwren
Rufous-browed Peppershrike
Red-eyed Vireo
Buff-chested Greenlet
Tawny-crowned Greenlet
Giant Cowbird
Crested Oropendola
Amazonian Oropendola
Red-rumped Cacique
Moriche Oriole
Red-breasted Blackbird
Eastern Meadowlark
Black-and-white Warbler
Masked Yellowthroat
American Redstart
Neotropical River Warbler
Bananaquit
Swallow Tanager
Short-billed Honeycreeper
Purple Honeycreeper
Red-legged Honeycreeper
Green Honeycreeper
Blue Dacnis
Black-faced Dacnis
Opal-rumped Tanager
Paradise Tanager

Green-and-gold Tanager
Spotted Tanager
Speckled Tanager
Masked Tanager
Turquoise Tanager
Bay-headed Tanager
Burnished-buff Tanager
Blue-hooded Euphonia
White-vented Euphonia
Purple-throated Euphonia
Violaceous Euphonia
Plumbeous Euphonia
Blue-and-gray Tanager
Palm Tanager
Silver-beaked Tanager
Hepatic Tanager
Summer Tanager
White-lined Tanager
Flame-crested Tanager
Fulvous-crested Tanager
Red-shouldered Tanager
White-shouldered Tanager
Guira Tanager
Yellow-backed Tanager
Magpie Tanager
Black-faced Tanager
Blue-black Grosbeak
Buff-throated Saltator
Grayish Saltator
Yellow-green Grosbeak
Pectoral Sparrow
Sooty Grassquit
Lesser Seed-Finch
Plumbeous Seedeater
Lined Seedeater
Yellow-bellied Seedeater
Ruddy-breasted Seedeater
Wedge-tailed Grass-Finch
Blue-black Grassquit
Stripe-tailed Yellow-Finch
Grassland Sparrow
Rufous-collared Sparrow
Hooded Siskin

CANAIMA - THE WESTERN SIDE OF THE PARK

Many people have asked me why, since it is so well known, I do not recommend they go to Canaima. The best answer I can give is to reprint here an article that appeared in the weekly **Magazine** of the **London Times**, in March 1993, entitled "A Trip to Canaima in Venezuela has joys and dangers", written by **Tim Austin**:

«*The ancient Dakota rumbled past the thatched terminal, along the jungle airstrip and lifted off, banking sharply to the left towards the distant hills. Fifteen minutes flying time away was Angel Falls, at 3,200 ft. the world's highest waterfall and, according to the tourist literature, Venezuela's Great Adventure in the Lost World of Bolivar State.*

Apprehension quickly gave way to awe as the DC3, specially converted with wide panoramic windows, hugged the contours of the wooded hills above the Rio Carrao. Ten minutes into the flight and the wing-tips seemed perilously close to the sheer cliffs of the Auyan-Tepui, the dramatic outcrop rising from the savanna that stretches to the Orinoco basin 175 miles to the north. We entered the densely wooded canyon of the Rio Churun into which the Angel Falls plunge and had our first view of the towering cascade, the crashing water creating a cloud of spray at its base. A recalcitrant Frenchman obscuring my view made me forget any apprehension about our proximity to the mountainside, and I practically kneed him to the floor in my eagerness to catch a final glimpse of the cascade as the clouds closed in and we began our return to the airstrip at Canaima.

The realization that the falls are named after the American airman Jimmy Angel, who discovered them in 1937, and not from any ethereal association, offers the first hint of disillusion.

Every day, just after noon, the domestic Venezuelan airline Avensa deposits more than 100 passengers on its DC9 flight from Caracas on to the airstrip at Canaima. They will have paid from 110 pounds sterling a night for a one, two or three-day stay at Camp Canaima, run by Avensa, and practically the only accommodation near the falls, plus the 55 pound return air ticket from Caracas. For 275 pounds you get the flights, the Dakota trip to the falls, plus meals and accommodation for two days and two nights and a delightful but minimal 20-minute boat trip on the lagoon at the edge of the camp.

The meals are plentiful and quite satisfactory, provided you don't mind self-service canteens. Drinks, at 2 pounds for a gin-and-tonic, are certainly not cheap, although to sip them on a terrace overlooking the lagoon mitigates the feeling of being ripped off.

Accommodation is also fairly rudimentary: the white-thatched huts have passable beds but no air-conditioning or overhead fans, which would be appropriate at that price in a tropical environment. When the lavatory does not flush either, there is cause for complaint.

But perhaps the worst feature of Camp Canaima is an attitudinal one. The only member of staff I saw smiling in my 48 hours there was a cheery Guyanese, who tried unsuccessfully to fix a trip to Angel Falls by boat up river - undoubtedly the best way to see them if you are able to do so. Although we were assured the rivers were passable because of recent rainfall, and spent hours negotiating a price, the woman in charge of Canaima Tours finally turned us down without explanation. We had the impression that the company's profit would be not enough. Sad though it is, Canaima Tours left us with the impression that they were willing to provide no more than the basics, while Camp Canaima emerged as an unfortunate cross between Fawlty Towers, Butlin's in the Fifties and the African Queen.

Paradise entirely lost? No, of course not: the Angel Falls fulfill every expectation and remain one of the world's most spectacular natural wonders. But the Venezuelan Tourism Ministry could, and should, do much more to build on the infrastructure at Canaima. International tourists rightly expect value for money. Virtual monopolies are there to be broken. And tourism officials are there, among other things, to smile.»

Having quoted the above, let me add that there are, for reasons I do not quite know, relatively few birds to be seen around the Canaima Lagoon, and you don't see very much either if going up river on a boat with an outboard.

Also, if you wish to see Angel Falls by air, it is possible to do so at much lower prices, on a day trip from Ciudad Bolívar or Puerto Ordaz.

If you do want to stay in the area of Canaima for a couple of days, then by all means go to Camp Ucaima, above Canaima. Although its founder, the renowned Jungle Rudy, passed away some years ago, his daughters now run the Camp, and also run the best trips by boat up-river to the base of the falls. Having been on one of them, I can personally recommend these trips, but none others. Be willing, however, to pay a lot for this unforgettable experience - it is a very costly operation.

The only problem is that Avensa Airlines, that has the concession for the Canaima Camp, and are not always willing to fly in passengers who may be booked for other camps. As Mr. Austin said - this is a monopoly, it stinks and tourists are stuck!

That is one of the reasons I never recommend that people fly in Avensa. The other is that as an airline, they stink!

Closing Thoughts
Having re-read all through the above, as well as the section on Western Bolivar -- It's too much. Bolivar just offers far too much. Perhaps you should plan to spend one full vacation just in Bolivar.

Amazonian Umbrellabird

VII - 2. Western Bolivar State

INTRODUCTION

Birding western Bolivar generally means birding the northernmost reaches of the great forests that cover the **Caura River** basin.
To reach this area:

- One may come from the east, by driving or flying to **Ciudad Bolivar** or **Puerto Ordaz** and then simply driving west in the direction of **Maripa**. Maripa is a town on the fringe - by the Caura, near the forests and on the frontier of "civilization".

- Coming from the west, one drives down from points north, via the terrible **Chaguaramas** road, to the town of **Cabruta** on the northern shore of the **Orinoco**, to cross the mighty river by chalana (ferry) to the town of **Caicara**, almost directly across on the southern shore. This crossing of the Orinoco is quite interesting, often accompanied by Yellow-billed and Large-billed Terns and sudden glimpses of River Dolphins. From Caicara, you just have to drive east on the main road until you reach Maripa.

- Then there is the adventure road for those who have been visiting Amazonas. They drive from Puerto Ayacucho north to Caicara and then east to Maripa.

- No matter which way you are coming from, it is a long, long way there. However, since most people fly into Puerto Ordaz, and pick up rental car, I will give more detailed information on this particular odyssey in the next paragraphs.

DRIVING FROM PUERTO ORDAZ TO THE CAURA

As you pull out of the airport at Puerto Ordaz, you have to turn right or west, which, by some miracle, is exactly the way you want to go. There is an excellent super highway from Puerto Ordaz to Ciudad Bolivar, the capital of the State. In fact, it is such a good road that you will reach C.B. (as we are inclined to call it) in an hour. Considering that Maripa is 223 kilometers away and you still have another three + hours to drive, you might want to overnight in C.B., in which case you should exit at your first opportunity at the Marhuanta Distributor. Continue straight all the way up the street you came in on, Avenida Upata, until you see the sign for the airport. Follow the signs for the airport, and when you can actually see the hangars, angle over to the right-hand lane[1].

You want to turn right at the stop light in front of the main entrance to the airport building on your left. This will put you on Avenida Táchira. Go two blocks and turn right on Avenida Maracay for half a block where you will see the small **Hotel Valentina** (★★★) on your left, good restaurant, telf. (0) 285-632-2145 & 632-7253, fax: (0) 285-632-9311.

Your next problem (and believe me it is a big one), is how to find the road to Maripa. I actually saw a sign that said "Maripa xxx kilometers", so I just carried on and practically ended up crossing the Orinoco. Your best bet would be to buy a map of the city and ask, and ask and ask. There are hundreds of road signs in C.B. It is

---

[1] Pamela's Informative Note: In front of the airport, as a monument, you will find the airplane of the legendary Jimmy Angel. In 1937 he landed on top of the Auyantepui, one of the largest of the flat-top mountains, of the "Lost World". He was looking for gold, but instead, found the highest waterfall in the world, that now bears his name – Angel Falls.

just that none of them mention Maripa! I know that it is at the end of civilization, but it does exist and it is in the state of Bolivar, so why the devil do they not show you how to get there? Anyway, after a thorough search of the area, my suggestion now is that you drive back to the autopista from Puerto Ordaz, exiting, as you came in, on the Marhuanta Distributor and heading for El Tigre to the north. Seven km from the Marhuanta Distributor you will see an inconspicuous crossroads. Turn left. Naturally, there are no signs indicating that this is the road to Maripa. If you miss the turn and end up at the toll booth prior to the bridge, go back another 6 km, and then turn right[1].

If you have purchased a cooler for your trip, you can buy ice very near to the hotel. Go straight down the street in front of the Valentina until you come to a round-about. Go half way around the traffic distributor and then go down a small, narrow, unpretentious street. The ice plant is on the left.

Another plus for the area around Hotel Valentina is the fact that it is close to one of the best stores - shops- or just plain places to buy native crafts in all of Venezuela. Handicrafts and artifacts from all the tribes in Venezuela are there, including baskets, wood carvings, weaving, etc. It is only a couple of blocks away from your hotel, but ask there how to reach the home of:

Rosalia de Zagala
Quinta Mea-Lares
Diagonal from Hotel Transmontano
Ciudad Bolivar

Even if you are not in the mood to pick up handicrafts, a visit is most educational to see the different types of work done by the various indigenous peoples of the country. As my friend Juanita Tyzska said, it is a museum for browsers.

THE CAURA RIVER

After the Caroní, the Caura is the second most important tributary of the Orinoco. Its basin of approximately 45,336 square kilometers, holds and nurtures one of the largest, most pristine tracts of lowland rain forest that still exist in Venezuela, or for that matter, in all of South America. For the most part no roads have been built in the area. The Caura forest is the territory of an Indigenous group with two names - the Makiritares or Ye`kuanas, the boat-builders.

The Makiritares, as they are called by others, are famous for their skills at dugout-building, at basket-weaving and at navigating the great river's rapids. They literally "own" the river, thus the name they call themselves, Ye`kuana, which means "river people". Their dugout building expertise is so legendary that other Indian groups, such as the Pemón and the Piaroa, actually *buy* dugouts from them.

Five million hectares of the Caura forests have been designated a Forest Reserve, and fortunately, no forestry exploitation has been planned so far. (However, we fear for the future.)

The avian fauna of the Caura is as pristine and as wonderful as its forests and there was an excellent road for birding - quite level for most of its length, with many shady spots, and quiet - blissfully, joyfully quiet. Unfortunately, of late a very large group of the Guahibo indigenous people from the savannas of Amazonas and Colombia have invaded the lower section of the forest, destroying some 100 hectares of

---

[1] Editor's Hopeful Note: Don't worry, guys. By the fifty seventh edition, we will finally get it right!

the forest by fire. Therefore, the first 25 to 35 kilometers of this road are of little interest to us. The Ye`kuanas/Makiritares inherited the territory of the watershed of the Caura, but even they can do nothing to stop the deforestation of their lands by the Guahibos as the latter receive protection from the local politicians. At the time of the last elections, the Guahibos were trucked in to vote for the present government.

As this area is so remote, you have to stay at least overnight, and there are two really nice camps available.

Campamento Caurama

This comfortable camp was established a number of years ago. It operated successfully for a long while but its owner needed to attend business matters elsewhere and was forced to close it. Now, he has recently rented the camp to a young couple, who have re-opened it . Access by land is easy, and they also have a private landing strip. To reach the camp, from the gas station at the cross-roads of Maripa, continue straight for 4.2 kilometers where you will see a dirt road on the right. From there it is one kilometer to the main gate. Prior to your visit, you should advise the camp of your approximate arrival time so that the gate will be open. From here it is still 2 kilometers to the camp. At first you will feel that this is just plain Llano or the same old savanna you have been driving through for the past hours with the exception of all the cashew trees. Just wait.

For one thing, Caurama can boast of one of the most beautiful and large "Morichales" that I have ever seen. (The Moriche palm only grows in marshy areas or in stands of low water.) In fact, it is the only Morichal that I have actually penetrated **into** and found an extremely interesting blend of avifauna from Pinnated Bittern to Point-tailed Palmcreeper, parakeets, parrots, etc. This is THE place to be at dawn and it is only 10 minutes by car from the camp. As if that were not enough, the birds around the camp itself do their best to wake you early in the morning and keep you running after them in the late afternoon. The manager, Jean Posner (John to us English-speaking clients) is extremely knowledgeable regarding the local natural history from geology to flora and fauna, including, naturally, the birds.

Since the road to Las Trincheras is in such very bad shape, Jean can arrange to take you there (for heaven sakes leave at or before dawn) to bird all morning or until things have quieted down. He has also advised me of a special place called the Cave of Giant Cockroaches up in the hills of La Leona to observe the Guayana Cock of the Rock. Furthermore, Jean knows where to find the Toucans, Black Nunbird, Black-spotted Barbet, etc. & etc. Yes, he is a very handy man to have around as well as a most interesting conversationalist.

To complete your stay at Caurama, a most enterprising young man from the camp can take you to the various houses of the Ye'kuanas/Makiritares in Maripa to view and perhaps purchase their basketry. Believe me when I say that these baskets are works of art that could be found in any of the world's museums, and the prices are unbelievably low. They are made by the women of these industrious indigenous peoples way to the south in their main settlements. The finished baskets are sent down river to be sold in the large cities.

My main recommendation for this trip would be to come in December or January when it is cooler. I made the trip in March and nigh on to died from the heat.

Contact either Jean or his wife Eva Posner, by fax at (0) 212-284-0443. They do have e-mail: aventuracaura@cantv.net, but at the time I went the computer was down. Therefore, the fax is a sure thing. Or contact the Audubon. English, French, Dutch and Spanish spoken. Caurama is very popular with fishermen from abroad, so you should be certain to reserve in advance. The camp is made up of three principal buildings of simple, rustic design but with modern conveniences including fresh well water and electricity. The rooms are well ventilated and screened with private bath. There is also a small swimming pool to cool off in the afternoon, but I would prefer the bathing spot by one of the many Morichales of crystal clear waters. Here you can not only bathe but also contemplate the rich aquatic life of this ecosystem. It is a natural aquarium of interest to both the amateur and professional.

Campamento Caura

This is a beautiful place to use as a base for birding the Caura Forest Reserve. It is located on the banks of the Caura, next to the settlement of **Las Trincheras**. To reach it from Ciudad Bolívar, you have to drive 3 to 4 hours to the entrance of the town of Maripa, and then backtrack 15 kms east to turn south into the dirt road leading to **Puerto Cabello del Caura**, **Las Trincheras** and **Jabillal**. The reason for doing things in this crazy manner is that you should fill up your gas tank at the only gas station available in all this wilderness.

Caveat: This road is now so bad that you need a 4 X 4. However, for my Venezuelan friends, and as Pamela pointed out, for other resident aliens crazy enough to drive here, I give below the necessary details. For foreign visitors, arrangements have to be made to be picked up at Maripa and driven the last 52 kms. to the Camp by the people from there.

As I indicated above, at first you are driving through the same open, burnt-over savanna you have been traversing all the way from Ciudad Bolivar. Previously, the forest began after some 14 kms. (See above) At one kilometer further south, you go over the bridge on the small Río Urbani, which is no more than a wide creek. **The good birding starts here.**

After another 12 kms you will pass by the road leading to Puerto Cabello del Caura. I have heard from birding friends that this road leads to some excellent birding areas, but I confess I have not birded there. Keep straight ahead for another 11 kms until you reach yet another road coming in from your right. This road leads to **Las Trincheras**, so turn right. From this intersection, it is 5 kms to the camp. As you enter the hamlet, drive straight ahead until you see the largest house on your left. Here you should turn left, but the next few meters are both narrow and rough until you reach the entrance to the camp itself.

One afternoon, no later than 3 p.m., I suggest that you request the people at the camp to take you up river to see birds. Also, perhaps, to an Indian village, to purchase some excellent Indian handicrafts, especially baskets.

The camp offers a variety of options from sleeping in hammocks in a large *churuata* (an Indian building consisting of a thatched roof without walls), to a small house with two double rooms and baths. There is a large dining room as well as a pleasant bar in yet another churuata. To top it off, there is a tree house some three stories above the ground and reached by a very long, built-in ladder. This would be ideal for observing birds. Actually, I believe that this camp is more tuned in to adventure tourism, offering over-night excursions to Para Falls up the Caura River, etc. than to nature tourism, but a group of Venezuelan bird watchers recently made an excursion there and were very pleased with the birding. The fact is that the camp is located next to the forest and thus easily affords very good birding especially at dawn and dusk.

For reservations contact the Venezuelan Audubon or Cacao Expediciones, Fax: (0) 212-977-0110 or cacaotravel@cantv-net

General Checklist for the Lower Caura

I am indebted to Jean Posner and Gerlit Sosa for supplying me with this list.

Great Tinamou
Little Tinamou
Variegated Tinamou
Neotropic Cormorant
Anhinga
Cocoi Heron
Great Egret
Snowy Egret
Striated Heron
Agami Heron
Cattle Egret
Whistling Heron
Capped Heron
Black-crowned Night-Heron
Yellow-crowned Night-Heron
Rufescent Tiger-Heron
Zigzag Heron
Pinnated Bittern
Boat-billed Heron
Wood Stork
Maguari Stork
Jabiru
Buff-necked Ibis
Green Ibis
Bare-faced Ibis
Scarlet Ibis
Roseate Spoonbill
Fulvous Whistling Duck
White-faced Whistling-Duck
Black-bellied Whistling-Duck
Orinoco Goose
Blue-winged Teal
Brazilian Teal
Muscovy Duck
Masked Duck
King Vulture
Black Vulture
Lesser Yellow-headed Vulture
Greater Yellow-headed Vulture
Pearl Kite
Swallow-tailed Kite
Gray-headed Kite
Hooked-billed Kite
Double-toothed Kite
Plumbeous Kite
Snail Kite
Tiny Hawk
White-tailed Hawk
Broad-winged Hawk
Roadside Hawk
Short-tailed Hawk

Gray-lined Hawk
Harris' Hawk
White Hawk
Black-faced Hawk
Black-collared Hawk
Savanna Hawk
Great Black Hawk
Black Hawk-Eagle
Harpy Eagle
Crane Hawk
Osprey
Laughing Hawk
Collared Forest-Falcon
Barred Forest-Falcon
Black Caracara
Red-throated Caracara
Crested Caracara
Bat Falcon
Aplomado Falcon
Orange-breasted Falcon
American Kestrel
Little Chachalaca
Marail Guan
Spix's Guan
Blue-throated Piping-Guan
Crestless Curassow
Black Curassow
Crested Bobwhite
Gray-winged Trumpeter
Gray-necked Wood-Rail
Ash-throated Crake
Ocellated Crake
Sunbittern
Wattled Jacana
Southern Lapwing
Pied Lapwing
Collared Plover
Solitary Sandpiper
Greater Yellowlegs
Spotted Sandpiper
Least Sandpiper
Upland Sandpiper
Whimbrel
Paraguayan Snipe
Black-necked Stilt
Double-striped Thick-knee
Large-billed Tern
Yellow-billed Tern
Black Skimmer
Scaled Pigeon
Pale-vented Pigeon

Ruddy Pigeon
Eared Dove
Common Ground- Dove
Plain-breasted Ground-Dove
Ruddy Ground-Dove
Blue-Ground Dove
Scaled Dove
White-tipped Dove
Gray-fronted Dove
Ruddy Quail-Dove
Blue-and-Yellow Macaw
Military Macaw
Scarlet Macaw
Red-and-green Macaw
Chestnut-fronted Macaw
Red-bellied Macaw
Red-shouldered Macaw
Blue-crowned Parakeet
White-eyed Parakeet
Brown-throated Parakeet
Painted Parakeet
Green-rumped Parrotlet
Dusky-billed Parrotlet
Golden-winged Parakeet
Black-headed Parrot
Caica Parrot
Blue-headed Parrot
Dusky Parrot
Festive Parrot
Yellow- crowned Parrot
Orange-winged Parrot
Mealy Parrot
Red-fan Parrot
Hoatzin
Dwarf Cuckoo
Yellow-billed Cuckoo
Pearly-breasted Cuckoo
Squirrel Cuckoo
Black-billed Cuckoo
Little Cuckoo
Greater Ani
Smooth-billed Ani
Groove-billed Ani
Striped Cuckoo
Rufous-winged Ground-Cuckoo
Barn Owl
Tawny-bellied Screech-Owl
Crested Owl
Great Horned Owl
Spectacled Owl
Ferruginous Pygmy Owl

Burrowing Owl
Black-banded Owl
Great Potoo
Common Potoo
Lesser Nighthawk
Band-tailed Nighthawk
Pauraque
White-tailed Nightjar
Black Nightjar
Ladder-tailed Nightjar
White-collared Swift
Band-rumped Swift
Short-tailed Swift
Fork-tailed Palm-Swift
Rufous-breasted Hermit
Pale-tailed Barbthroat
White-bearded Hermit
Long-tailed Hermit
Sooty-capped Hermit
Reddish Hermit
Gray-breasted Hermit
White-necked Jacobin
Black-throated Mango
Ruby-Topaz Hummingbird
Tufted Coquette
Festive Coquette
Blue-tailed Emerald
Fork-tailed Woodnymph
White-chinned Sapphire
White-chested Emerald
Versicolored Emerald
Glittering-throated Emerald
Plain-bellied Emerald
Copper-rumped Hummingbird
Green-bellied Hummingbird
Black-eared Fairy
Long-billed Starthroat
Black-tailed Trogon
White-tailed Trogon
Violaceous Trogon
Ringed Kingfisher
Amazon Kingfisher
Green Kingfisher
Green-and-Rufous Kingfisher
American Pygmy Kingfisher
Blue-crowned Motmot
Brown Jacamar
Yellow-billed Jacamar
Green-tailed Jacamar
Rufous-tailed Jacamar
Great Jacamar

White-necked Puffbird
Pied Puffbird
Chestnut-capped Puffbird
Collared Puffbird
Russet-throated Puffbird
Black Nunbird
Swallow-wing
Black-spotted Barbet
Chestnut-tipped Toucanet
Black-necked Araçari
Many-banded Araçari
Green Araçari
Ivory-billed Araçari
Tawny-tufted Toucanet
Channel-billed Toucan
Yellow-ridged Toucan
Red-billed Toucan
Cuvier's Toucan
White-bellied Piculet
Scaled Piculet
Golden-spangled Piculet
Spot-breasted Woodpecker
Yellow-throated Woodpecker
Chestnut Woodpecker
Scaly-breasted Woodpecker
Cream-colored Woodpecker
Ringed Woodpecker
Lineated Woodpecker
Yellow-tufted Woodpecker
Red-crowned Woodpecker
Little Woodpecker
Golden-collared Woodpecker
Crimson-crested Woodpecker
Plain-brown Woodcreeper
White-chinned Woodcreeper
Long-tailed Woodcreeper
Olivaceous Woodcreeper
Wedge-billed Woodcreeper
Barred Woodcreeper
Straight-billed Woodcreeper
Striped Woodcreeper
Chestnut-rumped Woodcreeper
Buff-throated Woodcreeper
Red-billed Scythebill
Pale-breasted Spinetail
Plain-crowned Spinetail
Ruddy Spinetail
Yellow-chinned Spinetail
Point-tailed Palmcreeper
Cinnamon-rumped
  Foliage-Gleaner

Buff-fronted
  Foliage-Gleaner
Ruddy Foliage-Gleaner
Buff-throated Foliage-Gleaner
Chestnut-crowned
  Foliage-Gleaner
Plain Xenops
Short-billed Leaftosser
Black-tailed Leaftosser
Sharp-tailed Streamcreeper
Fasciated Antshrike
Black-throated Antshrike
Great Antshrike
Black-crested Antshrike
Barred Antshrike
Blackish-Gray Antshrike
White-shouldered Antshrike
Mouse-colored Antshrike
Eastern Slaty Antshrike
Spot-winged Antshrike
Plain Antvireo
Dusky-throated Antshrike
Cinereous Antshrike
Pygmy Antwren
Streaked Antwren
Rufous-bellied Antwren
White-flanked Antwren
Plain-winged Antwren
Spot-tailed Antwren
Spot-backed Antwren
Rufous-winged Antwren
White-fringed Antwren
Gray Antbird
Dusky Antbird
Jet Antbird
White-browed Antbird
Black-faced Antbird
Black-chinned Antbird
Caura Antbird
Silvered Antbird
White-bellied Antbird
Black-throated Antbird
White-plumed Antbird
Dot-backed Antbird
Scale-backed Antbird
Winged-banded Antpitta
Rufous-capped Antthrush
Scaled Antpitta
Spangled Cotinga
Pompadour Cotinga
Screaming Piha

White-naped Xenopsaris
Cinereous Becard
White-winged Becard
Black-capped Becard
Pink-throated Becard
Black-tailed Tityra
Black-crowned Tityra
Purple-throated Fruitcrow
Bare-necked Fruitcrow
White Bellbird
Guianan Cock-of-the Rock
Golden-headed Manakin
White-crowned Manakin
White-fronted Manakin
White-bearded Manakin
Dwarf Tyrant-Manakin
Wing-barred Manakin
Thrush-like Schiffornis
Long-tailed Tyrant
Riverside Tyrant
Pied Water-tyrant
White-headed Marsh-Tyrant
Vermilion Flycatcher
Drab Water-Tyrant
Yellow-browed Tyrant
Cattle Tyrant
Fork-tailed Tyrant
Tropical Kingbird
Gray Kingbird
Sulphury Flycatcher
Variegated Flycatcher
Piratic Flycatcher
Boat-billed Flycatcher
Streaked Flycatcher
Rusty-margined Flycatcher
Social Flycatcher
Gray-capped Flycatcher
White-bearded Flycatcher
Great Kiskadee
Lesser Kiskadee
Bright-rumped Attila
Cinereous Mourner
Short-crested Flycatcher
Swainson's Flycatcher
Dusky-capped Flycatcher
Wood Pewee
Tropical Pewee
Euler's Flycatcher
Fuscous Flycatcher
Ruddy-tailed Flycatcher
Sulphur-rumped Flycatcher

Black-tailed Flycatcher
Roraiman Flycatcher
Royal Flycatcher
White-crested Spadebill
White-throated Spadebill
Yellow-olive Flycatcher
Yellow-margined Flycatcher
Rufous-tailed Flatbill
Common Tody-Flycatcher
Slate-headed Tody-Flycatcher
Black-chested Tyrant
Helmeted Pygmy-tyrant
Pale-eyed Pygmy-Tyrant
Short-tailed Pygmy-Tyrant
Yellow Tyrannulet
Bearded Tachuri
Pale-tipped Tyrannulet
Yellow-bellied Elaenia
Plain-crested Elaenia
Forest Elaenia
Gray Elaenia
Scrub Flycatcher
Mouse-colored Tyrannulet
Southern Beardless Tyrannulet
Yellow-crowned Tyrannulet
White-lored Tyrannulet
Sepia-crowned Flycatcher
Ochre-bellied Flycatcher
McConnell's Flycatcher
Ringed Antpipit
White-winged Swallow
Brown-chested Martin
Purple Martin
White-banded Swallow
Black-collared Swallow
Southern Rough-winged
  Swallow
Barn Swallow
Violaceous Jay
Cayenne Jay
Bi-colored Wren
Stripe-backed Wren
Coraya Wren
Buff-breasted Wren
Southern House Wren
White-breasted Wood-Wren
Flutist Wren
Wing-banded Wren
Tropical Mockingbird
Black-capped Donacobius
Swainson's Thrush

Black-hooded Thrush
Pale-breasted Thrush
Bare-eyed Thrush
White-necked Thrush
Long-billed Gnatwren
Tropical Gnatwren
Yellowish Pipit
Rufous-browed Peppershrike
Red-eyed Vireo
Lemon-chested Greenlet
Buff-cheeked Greenlet
Scrub Greenlet
Tawny-crowned Greenlet
Shiny Cowbird
Giant Cowbird
Crested Oropendola
Green Oropendola
Amazonian Oropendola
Yellow-rumped Cacique
Red-rumped Cacique
Carib Grackle
Moriche Oriole
Orange-crowned Oriole
Troupial
Yellow Oriole
Northern Oriole
Oriole Blackbird
Red-breasted Blackbird
Eastern Meadowlark
Bobolink
Tropical Parula
Yellow Warbler
Rose-breasted Chat
American Redstart
Bananaquit
Swallow Tanager
Short-billed Honeycreeper
Purple-Honeycreeper
Red-legged Honeycreeper
Green Honeycreeper
Blue Dacnis
Black-faced Dacnis
Yellow-bellied Dacnis
Opal-rumped Tanager
Paradise Tanager
Masked Tanager
Turquoise Tanager
Bay-headed Tanager
Burnished-buff Tanager
White-lored Euphonia
White-vented Euphonia

Trinidad Euphonia	Magpie Tanager	Lesser Seed-Finch
Purple-throated Euphonia	Black-faced Tanager	Large-billed Seed-Finch
Thick-billed Euphonia	Blue-black Grosbeak	Slate-colored Seedeater
Violaceous Euphonia	Buff-throated Saltator	Gray Seedeater
Blue-gray Tanager	Grayish Saltator	Yellow-bellied Seedeater
Palm Tanager	Orinocan Saltator	Ruddy-breasted Seedeater
Silver-beaked Tanager	Slate-colored Grosbeak	Blue-black Grassquit
White-winged Tanager	Yellow-green Grosbeak	Saffron Finch
White-lined Tanager	Dickcissel	Orange-fronted Yellow-Finch
Flame-crested Tanager	Red-capped Cardinal	Striped-tailed Yellow-Finch
White-shouldered Tanager	Pileated Finch	Grassland Sparrow
Yellow-backed Tanager	Black-striped Sparrow	Rufous-collared Sparrow
Orange-headed Tanager	Pectoral Sparrow	Lesser Goldfinch

As you can see from the above, the area of the Caura River offers a variety of species, some in common with the Llanos to some in common with Amazonia, a mixture, in a way, of everything. It gives you ample opportunity to increase your Life List.

However, please remember that you are approximately 6 degrees north of the Equator. Here, at high noon, the birds do not fly. Nor do mad dogs or Englishman walk. Bird watchers should be relaxing in their hammocks!

Black-dotted Piculet

VII - 3. State of Amazonas

INTRODUCTION

The mostly-wild State of Amazonas is becoming increasingly popular with bird watchers, due to the incredible number of species that it is possible to add to one's list during a visit to this region. By and large, the birding one does here is of the most difficult kind - looking for tall-forest species - but the rewards are marvelous.

Amazonas is difficult to reach by land, but it can be done and the scenery for the most part will be awe inspiring. There are only two main roads - the one that goes from **Caicara** (State of Bolivar), to **Puerto Ayacucho** the capital of the State of Amazonas. For this road you would drive to eastern Guarico State to the town of Las Mercedes and continue on to Cabruta where you take the *chalana* (a barge-like ferry) for approximately an hour to reach Caicara del Orinoco in the state of Bolivar. One of the problems of this route is that the ferry across the Orinoco leaves only every two hours, so you may have a long wait. The other road goes from the Llano State of Apure across the Cinaruco Capanaparo National Park.

The fastest way to go by car from Caracas is the latter, and the roads south from the city of Calabozo in Guárico are in good shape, but at the present time it will take a good twelve hours from Caracas due to the fact that you have to take three ferries. My suggestion would be to drive south from Caracas to the city of Calabozo and continue on for approximately 50 km until you see the National Guard post at Corozopando. Almost in front of the National Guards you will see the entrance to an inn I highly recommend called La Fe. (For more details on this inn see the chapter on the Llanos.) Spend the night at La Fe and continue on the next morning. Or, if you really want to see a lot of Llano birds, spend a day or two at La Fe. I guarantee that you will not regret doing so.

Some 58 kilometers to the south of La Fe you will come to the bridge over the Apure River. As soon as you have crossed the bridge, turn right at the very next corner and continue on for ten kilometers, always bordering the river. When you see the sign for "Avenida Intercomunal," turn left and then go straight for a short distance until you reach the main highway when you should turn right. After approximately two more kilometers you will see the PDV (Petroleos de Venezuela) gas station at Biruaca. Turn left and head for San Juan Payara. Be sure to fill your gas tank at the station at the far end of the town of San Juan de Payara as this is the last gas station for many, many kilometers. It is 107 km from Biruaca to the Capanaparo River, where you will take your first of three ferries. Here you will be entering the beautiful Cinaruco Capanaparo National Park. For more details on this Park see the chapter on the Llanos, but as you drive south, notice the sand dunes that characterize this area. From the Capanaparo River it is yet another 53 kilometers to your next ferry on the Cinaruco River and then finally 44 kilometers to the Orinoco and your last ferry. In October, 2000 each ferry charged Bs. 2,000, but that may change any day. Crossing the rivers will take only about ten minutes, but you may have to wait in line to get on board. On the south side of the Orinoco you will come to - believe it or not - a spot called El Burro in Bolivar State.

You are still 80 kilometers away from Puerto Ayacucho, but now for me comes the most incredible part of the journey. North of the Orinoco the land is as flat as a pancake, but just after crossing the Orinoco as you start your drive towards Puerto Ayacucho, you will come upon huge, ancient granite monoliths which form a part of the Guyana shield coming across from the area of the Tepuis of Bolivar State. Get out your camera not only for the geological formations but also for the indigenous communities of the Guahiba people.

You can also visit Amazonas by bus if you are traveling on a shoe string. For the bus, go to the Bandera bus Terminal in Caracas and take one of the Expresos del Llano buses to San Fernando de Apure. Should you wish to stop at Posada La Fe, the bus will stop right in front. Ask the driver to stop at the Alcabala of Corozopando. (An Alcabala is a National Guard post). The first bus for Puerto Ayacucho leaves the terminal at San Fernando at 5:00 a.m. Be sure to take a sweater for this trip because the air conditioning on these buses goes full blast, and do not forget your ear plugs. Pamela Pierce has asked me if the buses have toilets. Well, that depends on the kind and size of the bus, the bus company and a few other things, but they do stop often to allow the passengers to buy coffee or to stand in line for a ferry, etc. etc.

Aside from the above two roads and a short road from Puerto Ayacucho to Samariapo, the rest of Amazonas travel is by boat on the great Orinoco and its many tributaries; or by air, in the many "avionetas", small airplanes flown by bush pilots, that give service to a number of middle-of-the-jungle landing strips. Therefore, expect your visit here to be fairly expensive. On the other hand, if you limit your stay to the general area around Puerto Ayacucho, it is really not that expensive[1].

PUERTO AYACUCHO

The capital city is certainly worth a day or two to bird, do a little bit of sightseeing, and buy native artifacts. As to how you are to get around, you have two options: One is to hire a taxi and driver. To do this, try asking the people in the office of the Air Taxi to help you out. If you are booked in to one of the near-by camps, they will pick you up at the airport and may also take you to your birding destinations. The people from Junglaven have also advised that they can arrange for a car and driver. Your second option would be to hire a car from Cars Rental Amazonas, C.A. on Avenida Aguerrevere No. 64. Telf. (0) 248-521-0762. (Oscar Ortiz is the president of the agency.) Dr. Dennis Paulson did just that, paying some $86 for a small Chevrolet when he was stuck in Puerto Ayacucho for an extra day. He advised that the agency also rents 4x4 vehicles, but I shudder to think how much they would cost!

In her excellent book "Guide to Camps, Posadas & Cabins in Venezuela" Elizabeth Kline gives a warning, which I believe merits quoting:

«*WARNING: There are many free-lance guides who pounce on tourists arriving at the airport, offering bargain tours. Not only are they operating illegally, but putting yourself in the hands of people of unknown qualifications for excursions to remote areas where emergencies can easily arise, can put you in life-threatening situations. Don't take chances just to save a few bucks!*»

There are several good agencies who can provide you with reliable service such as Tobogán Tours run by Pepe Jaime Telf. (0) 248-521-4865 or Henry Jaimes at (0) 248-521-3964. Through Henry you can also secure a guide by the name of Patrick, who speaks English. According to Pamela Pierce, Patrick knows a lot about the river,

---

[1] Editor´s Note: On the first draft of this edition, at this very spot, Pamela wrote in big red letters: "You can't! You'll miss a great adventure!"

something about geology and a great deal about indigenous communities and their cultures, but she does not think he knows that much about birds.

While in Puerto Ayacucho, don't miss the opportunity of visiting the excellent **Ethnological Museum**.

If you wish to buy native handicrafts, take a taxi to **CEPAI**, the indigenous center where they sell all sorts of handicrafts. However, try to ascertain that they are open for business before you go[1]. Your best buy is the exquisite baskets made by the Makiritare/Ye'kwana people. Many of the pieces are fit for any museum in the World.

Where to stay in Puerto Ayacucho

For lodgings, there are 3 or 4 places which we can suggest. First off, there is the **Campamento Genesis/Tucan** near the bus terminal via Avenida Perimetral with a long unpaved driveway with no identification, and, worse yet, there is no sign to the camp. If you have problems finding it (most likely), ask for the house of the González-Herrera family. They have four modules with simple but comfortable rooms, some with air conditioning others with fans, private bath with cold water. (In this climate who needs hot water?) They usually book only packaged tours including excursions and all meals, but during the low season or when space is available, visitors can rent rooms by the night. This is a pleasant alternative to all the other places in town and easily merits three stars. I don't think they are keyed in to bird watchers, but it is a very nice camp. For reservations contact either the Venezuelan Audubon or directly to Tel/Fax: (0) 248-521-1378 or call Adriana at (0) 416-547-5968 or (0) 416-448-5273.

For a rather decent hotel in town itself we could suggest **Hotel Apure** , Telf. (0) 248-521-0516. The front of the hotel is certainly not imposing, but most of our birders who have stayed there have been satisfied. However, we were warned by Dr. Dennis Paulson that the room offered should be checked out first. The first time he stayed at the Apure there was an ants nest in the shower resulting in some 20 to 25 bites. The air conditioning was so loud they could not sleep, but it was too hot to turn it off. When he was stuck in Puerto Ayacucho for another night, they did give him a better room, but remember the saying of *caveat emptor*.

There are several other camps not too far from the city. One of them is **Campamento Orinoquia** some 18 km south of the city via the road to Samariapo. The entrance is clearly marked with signs on the right of the road for Campturama Camp (now closed and not recommended by us anyway since they were dealing in wildlife). The entrance is a dirt road at first until you come to the huge granite rocks, and here you might have a bit of a problem winding your way down to the camp, although I am recommending that they put small colored arrows to point the way. Until they do, the car tracks will guide you.

This camp is located on an exceptionally beautiful site, overlooking the Orinoco. The cabins are comfortable and most original, being built to resemble native *churuatas* (something like a Native American Logan). Private baths but no hot water. My comment above about this still holds. Phone, in Caracas (0) 212-977-1234 & 2798. Fax: (0) 212-977-1001, e-mail: lodge@cacaotravel.com.

As yet, they are really not tuned in for bird watchers but rather for adventure tourism to the fantastic Tepui of Autana, etc., but the owners are interested in enticing

---

[1] Editor's Note: I found them closed when I last passed through Pto. Ayacucho on the way to San Carlos de Rio Negro, but that is another story. It was one of those long weekends – a religious or patriotic festivity of some sort, I forget. Better ask before wasting your time and money in taxis.

bird watchers, and as you can see from the following list of birds, your time would not be wasted. Clemencia stayed there on her way to San Carlos de Rio Negro, but that is another story. She loved it! (Not San carlos de Rio Negro, but the Campamento Orinoquia, I mean.) The place, according to that apple-sauce head editor of mine, is "dreamy". They have now changed management which has resulted in better service than when I was there.

From the parking area and facing the cabins go left, passing several small granite tongues that enter into the forest. You will soon come to a path crossing a small grassy area and then you will enter into the first of two forests. After the first area of trees, you will come to yet another deforested part, but even when you hear the White-bearded Manakin, do not enter into the grass for fear of rattlesnakes. Birding there for two mornings we racked up the following species:

Little Tinamou	Black Nunbird	Helmeted Pygmy-Tyrant
Capped Heron	Swallow-wing	Yellow-bellied Elaenia
White-tailed Kite	Green Aracari	Forest Elaenia
Roadside Hawk	Red-crowned Woodpecker	Yellow-crowned Elaenia
Black-collared Hawk	Crimson-crested Woodpecker	Greenish Elaenia
Savanna Hawk	Olivaceous Woodcreeper	Southern Beardless Tyrannulet
Crane Hawk	Wedge-billed Woodcreeper	Yellow-crowned Tyrannulet
Laughing Falcon	Long-billed Woodcreeper	Rufous-browed Peppershrike
Crested Caracara	Buff-throated Woodcreeper	Red-eyed Vireo
Spix´s Guan	Great Antshrike	Scrub Greenlet
Crested Bobwhite	Black-crested Antshrike	White-winged Swallow
Spotted Sandpiper	Eastern Slaty Antshrike	Black-collared Swallow
Pale-vented Pigeon	Pygmy Antwren	Bank Swallow
Ruddy Pigeon	Streaked Antwren	Barn Swallow
Common Ground-Dove	White-flanked Antwren	Buff-breasted Wren
Ruddy Ground-Dove	Plain-winged Antwren	House Wren
Blue Ground-Dove	White-browed Antbird	Tropical Mockingbird
Scaled Dove	White-bellied Antbird	Pale-breasted Thrush
Brown-throated Parakeet	Amazonian	Long-billed Gnatwren
Blue-headed Parrot	Umbrellabird	Tropical Gnatcatcher
Yellow-crowned Parrot	Guianan Cock-of-the-Rock	Yellow-rumped Cacique
Squirrel Cuckoo	Black-tailed Tityra	Moriche Oriole
Ferruginous Pygmy-Owl	White-bearded Manakin	Yellow Oriole
Fork-tailed Palm Swift	Drab Water-Tyrant	Oriole Blackbird
Long-tailed Hermit	Boat-billed Flycatcher	Bananaquit
Blue-chinned Sapphire	Rusty-margined Flycatcher	Turquoise Tanager
Glittering-throated	Great Kiskadee	Palm Tanager
Emerald	Bright-rumped Attila	Silver-beaked Tanager
White-tailed Trogon	Brown-crested Flycatcher	White-lined Tanager
Ringed Kingfisher	Yellow-breasted Flycatcher	Flame -crested Tanager
Green-tailed Jacamar	Common Tody-Flycatcher	Buff-throated Saltator

Refugio Yagrumo-Cataniapo

This is an extremely basic camp, with hammocks for sleeping in a very large churuata. But, the food offered by the owner, Renny Barrios, beats any place else I have eaten in the area. Then there is the birding! Wow! I visited the camp in October, 2000 and while walking up the trail to the main road early one morning, I had the exceptionally good luck to see and observe a Cinereous Tinamou. Better yet, there is the birding along the main highway, especially between Km. 17 and 21 after turning off the road from Puerto Ayacucho to Samariapo. Take note that by Km 17 there is a rather run-down adobe house belonging to Marcos Silva (otherwise known as *El Brujo* or the witch). Behind his house there is a trail that leads to the nesting area of the Guayana Cock-of-the-Rock where you may also see the Blue-crowned Motmot. If Silva is at home, it is possible to hire him to lead you to the area, some 45- minute walk. Renny offers boat trips in a *curiara* (an Indian dug-out canoe) up the Cataniapo River which flows right by his camp. In the rainy season he will also take you up a small *caño* (a stream) where you will undoubtedly be overwhelmed by the exuberant vegetation.

To reach Renny´s camp, drive south from Puerto Ayacucho until you reach the Cataniapo River and the road to Gavilán. Turn left and drive for 20.5 km where there is a dirt road into his camp. Phone: (0) 416-448-6916.

The following is the bird list we have for both the main road and the area around the camp.

Cinereous Tinamou	Green Aracari	White-crowned Manakin
Greater Yellow-headed Vulture	Ivory-billed Aracari	Dwarf-Tyrant Manakin
Gray-headed Kite	Yellow-ridged Toucan	Grayish Mourner
Double-toothed Kite	Red-billed Toucan	Dusky-capped Flycatcher
Black Hawk-Eagle	Golden-spangled Piculet	White-banded Swallow
Laughing Falcon	Waved Woodpecker	Blackpoll Warbler
Black-headed Parrot	Lineated Woodpecker	Northern Waterthrush
Mealy Parrot	Yellow-tufted Woodpecker	Amazonian Oropendola
Band-rumped Swift	Eastern Slaty Antshrike	Purple Honeycreeper
White-chinned Sapphire	Amazonian Antshrike	Opal-rumped Tanager
White-tailed Trogon	Rufous-winged Antwren	Yellow-backed Tanager
Black Nunbird	Gray Antbird	Blue-black Grosbeak
Black-spotted Barbet	Spangled Cotinga	Buff-throated Saltator
Many-banded Aracari	Golden-headed Manakin	Slate-colored Grosbeak

Babilla de Pinta'o

Another area I was able to bird on a recent trip was the road going past **Pinta'o**. Again take the road south until you see the marker to Pinta'o. Turn left. You will first go through one indigenous community and soon come to another which is Babilla de Pinta'o. Here you must stop to request permission from the local Capitán or Comisario to continue past the village to the forest beyond. No trouble, all they want is the courtesy of a request. After Babilla you will come to remnants of good forest as well as the *conucos* or small holdings of the local population. Keep on walking or driving, leaving the car at open areas to walk some more. You will finally come to really good forest, but the road is good birding all the way. We arrived shortly after dawn and were there until 11:00 a.m., when we reluctantly had to leave. I believe this could be a whole day's excursion. The following is the bird list we had for this road:

Little Tinamou	White-chinned Sapphire	Couvier´s Toucan
Roadside Hawk	Black-eared Fairy	Golden-spangled Piculet
Red-throated Caracara	White-tailed Trogon	Lineated Woodpecker
Laughing Falcon	Green-tailed Jacamar	Crimson-crested Woodpecker
Marbled Wood-Quail	White-necked Puffbird	Ruddy Spinetail
Gray-fronted Dove	Black-spotted Barbet	Great Antshrike
Blue-headed Parrot	Green Aracari	Pygmy Antwren
Ferruginous Pygmy-Owl	Channel-billed Toucan	Gray Antbird

White-browed Antbird	Yellow-breasted Flycatcher	Crested Oropendola
White-bellied Antbird	Painted Tody-Flycatcher	Amazonian Oropendola
Black-faced Antthrush	Red-eyed Vireo	Buff-throated Saltator
Screaming Piha	Buff-breasted Wren	Blue-black Grosbeak
Bright-rumped Attila	Blackpoll Warbler	Slate-colored Grosbeak

I have just been advised of two other birding spots. First there is Provincial Lagoon just 15 minutes north of Puerto Ayacucho going towards El Burro. This spot is more for Llano birds. Then there is one that makes me drool with envy. It is a beautiful stream or caño just south of the entrance to Orinoquia camp called **Caño Paria**. The bridge is just before the indigenous community of Paria. Upon advance request, the people of Orinoquia can arrange to take you along this stream by dugout canoe. Look for Yellow-crested Manakin.

Before I forget, I want to emphasize that the native peoples of Amazonas are called indigenous people. One should never call them Indians.

JUNGLAVEN[1]

With 420 species this is, without a shade of doubt, a world-class birding camp. Unless you navigate up river for five days, it can only be reached by air. From **Puerto Ayacucho**, you should take the morning **Air Taxi** of **Wayumi**, leaving Puerto Ayacucho at 6:30 a.m. flying first to San Juan de Manapiare and then on to the Junglaven landing strip, arriving approximately at 8:00 a.m. It would be wise to check in with Wayumi when you first arrive at Puerto Ayacucho, or at least the day before your departure for Junglaven. (Please note that you are limited to 10 kilos of luggage on these flights.)

Since life is as it is in Venezuela, the flight from Caracas arrives after the Air Taxi leaves, in which case you have the options of staying overnight in Puerto Ayacucho or paying for a chartered flight. Please take note, **the Air Taxi does not fly on Sundays or public holidays**. As an added complication, they will need *a copy* of your passport when requesting reservations.

If you opt for staying the night in Puerto Ayacucho, put up at Campamento Orinoquía, Campamento Toucan, Hotel Apure mentioned above, or we can also recommend the **Hotel Orinoco**, near the river. It is clean, decent and inexpensive, and you can take advantage of your stay to visit the Ethnological Museum.

At the other end of your flight to Junglaven, the plane puts down on a grass landing strip, where the transport from the camp will meet you and take you along a dirt road through 12 km of Amazonian forest. Every day of your stay at the camp, you will want to walk this road very early in the morning, as well as lateish in the afternoon. At midday, it is extremely hot and nothing is to be seen so, by all means, take a siesta! One afternoon the people at the camp will probably take you on a boat trip, which should produce a lot of birds, including - keep you fingers crossed - the Umbrella Bird. When you review the bird list, you will understand why I recommend a minimum of three days at Junglaven. Four or five would be even better.

The accommodations at Junglaven consist of cabins built in the style of indigenous churuatas but with all modern amenities including beds and private bathrooms. The walls go up only halfway and the rest is screened, so it is fairly cool and comfortable at night. Everything is very clean, the food quite nice and what bugs there are do not

---

[1] E-mail: junglaven@hotmail.com

bother you. For reservations, contact the Audubon in Caracas. Please be aware of the fact that Junglaven is flooded during the rainy season and, consequently, is only open during the dry season.

Checklist for Junglaven (by Dave Sargeant)

Great Tinamou
Cinereous Tinamou
Little Tinamou
Undulated Tinamou
Gray-legged Tinamou
Variegated Tinamou
Neotropical Cormorant
Anhinga
Black-bellied Whistling-Duck
Muscovy Duck
Blue-winged Teal
Little Blue Heron
Snowy Egret
Capped Heron
Cocoi Heron
Great Egret
Cattle Egret
Striated Heron
Agami Heron
Black-crowned Night-Heron
Boat-billed Heron
Rufescent Tiger-Heron
Zigzag Heron
Green Ibis
Jabiru Stork
Wood Stork
Black Vulture
Turkey Vulture
Gtr. Yellow-headed Vulture
King Vulture
Osprey
Gray-headed Kite
Hook-billed Kite
Swallow-tailed Kite
Double-toothed Kite
Plumbeous Kite
Crane Hawk
White Hawk
Great Black Hawk
Savanna Hawk
Black-collared Hawk
Roadside Hawk
Harpy Eagle
Black-&-white Hawk-Eagle
Black Hawk-Eagle

Ornate Hawk-Eagle
Black Caracara
Red-throated Caracara
Crested Caracara
Yellow-headed Caracara
Laughing Falcon
Lined Forest-Falcon
Salty-backed Forest-Falcon
Collared Forest-Falcon
Bat Falcon
Little Chachalaca
Spix's Guan
Blue-throated Piping-Guan
Crestless Curassow
Black Curassow
Marbled Wood-Quail
Crake spp.
Gray-necked Wood-Rail
Sungrebe
Sunbittern
Gray-winged Trumpeter
Wattled Jacana
South American Snipe
Giant Snipe
Upland Sandpiper
Lesser Yellowlegs
Solitary Sandpiper
Spotted Sandpiper
White-rumped Sandpiper
American Golden Plover
Collared Plover
Pied Lapwing
Southern Lapwing
Yellow-billed Tern
Large-billed Tern
Black Skimmer
Pale-vented Pigeon
Scaled Pigeon
Ruddy Pigeon
Eared Dove
Plain-breasted Ground-Dove
Blue Ground-Dove
Gray-fronted Dove
White-tipped Dove
Ruddy Quail-Dove

Scarlet Macaw
Red-and-green Macaw
Chestnut-fronted Macaw
Red-bellied Macaw
Red-shouldered Macaw
White-eyed Parakeet
Brown-throated Parakeet
Maroon-tailed Parakeet
Green-rumped Parrotlet
Cobalt-winged Parakeet
Tepui Parrotlet
Scarlet-shouldered Parrotlet
Sapphire-rumped Parrotlet
Black-headed Parrot
Orange-cheeked Parrot
Blue-headed Parrot
Yellow-crowned Parrot
Orange-winged Parrot
Mealy Parrot
Yellow-billed Cuckoo
Squirrel Cuckoo
Black-bellied Cuckoo
Greater Ani
Smooth-billed Ani
Rufous-winged Ground-Cuckoo
Tropical Screech-Owl
Tawny-bellied Screech-Owl
Variable Screech-Owl
Mottled Owl
Black-banded Owl
Crested Owl
Spectacled Owl
Ferruginous Pygmy-Owl
Great Potoo
Long-tailed Potoo
Common Potoo
Short-tailed Nighthawk
Least Nighthawk
Sand-colored Nighthawk
Lesser Nighthawk
Band-tailed Nighthawk
Pauraque
Rufous Nightjar
White-tailed Nightjar
Blackish Nightjar

White-collared Swift
Tepui Swift
Band-rumped Swift
Gray-rumped Swift
Short-tailed Swift
Fork-tailed Palm-Swift
Lesser Swallow-tailed Swift
Long-tailed Hermit
White-bearded Hermit
Dusky-throated Hermit
Reddish Hermit
Gray-breasted Sabrewing
White-necked Jacobin
Black-throated Mango
Ruby-topaz Hummingbird
Festive Coquette
Racquet-tailed Coquette
Blue-chinned Sapphire
Blue-tailed Emerald
Rufous-throated Sapphire
White-chinned Sapphire
White-tailed Goldenthroat
Green-tailed Goldenthroat
White-chested Emerald
Versicolored Emerald
Black-eared Fairy
Long-billed Starthroat
Black-tailed Trogon
White-tailed Trogon
Violaceous Trogon
Ringed Kingfisher
Amazon Kingfisher
Green Kingfisher
Green-and-rufous Kingfisher
American Pygmy-Kingfisher
Blue-crowned Motmot
Brown Jacamar
Yellow-billed Jacamar
Green-tailed Jacamar
Bronzy Jacamar
Paradise Jacamar
Great Jacamar
White-necked Puffbird
Brown-banded Puffbird
Pied Puffbird
Spotted Puffbird
Rusty-breasted Nunlet
Black Nunbird
Swallow-wing
Black-spotted Barbet
Green Aracari

Ivory-billed Aracari
Many-banded Aracari
Tawny-tufted Toucanet
Osculating Toucan
Channel-billed Toucan
Red-billed Toucan
Couvier's Toucan
Golden-spangled Piculet
Yellow-tufted Woodpecker
Golden-collared Woodpecker
Red-stained Woodpecker
Yellow-throated Woodpecker
Golden-green Woodpecker
Scaly-breasted Woodpecker
Chestnut Woodpecker
Cream-colored Woodpecker
Ringed Woodpecker
Lineated Woodpecker
Red-necked Woodpecker
Crimson-crested Woodpecker
Plain-brown Woodcreeper
White-chinned Woodcreeper
Olivaceous Woodcreeper
Wedge-billed Woodcreeper
Long-billed Woodcreeper
Barred Woodcreeper
Black-banded Woodcreeper
Straight-billed Woodcreeper
Striped Woodcreeper
Chestnut-rumped Woodcreeper
Buff-throated Woodcreeper
Streak-headed Woodcreeper
Lineated Woodcreeper
Ruddy Spinetail
Pale-breasted Spinetail
Rusty-backed Spinetail
Orinoco Softtail
Cinnamon-rumped
  Foliage-Gleaner
Orinoco Spinetail
Buff-fronted Foliage-Gleaner
Olive-backed Foliage-Gleaner
Leaftosser spp.
Rufous-tailed Xenops
Slender-billed Xenops
Plain Xenops
Fasciated Antshrike
Black-throated Antshrike
Great Antshrike
Black-crested Antshrike
Blackish-gray Antshrike

White-shouldered Antshrike
Eastern Slaty Antshrike
Amazonian Antshrike
Spot-winged Antshrike
Cinereous Antshrike
Pygmy Antwren
Streaked Antwren
Cherrie's Antwren
Rufous-bellied Antwren
Stipple-throated Antwren
White-flanked Antwren
Gray Antwren
Spot-backed Antwren
Gray Antbird
Dusky Antbird
White-browed Antbird
Warbling Antbird
Black-chinned Antbird
Silvered Antbird
Spot-winged Antbird
White-bellied Antbird
Black-throated Antbird
White-plumed Antbird
Rufous-throated Antbird
Wing-banded Antbird
Spot-backed Antbird
Scale-backed Antbird
Rufous-capped Antthrush
Cinereous Mourner
White-browed Purpletuft
Screaming Piha
Spangled Cotinga
Pompadour Cotinga
Bare-necked Fruitcrow
Amazon Umbrellabird
Golden-headed Manakin
White-crowned Manakin
Wing-banded Manakin
Black-Manakin
Yellow-crested Manakin
Dwarf Tyrant-Manakin
Olive-striped Flycatcher
Ochre-bellied Flycatcher
Slate-headed Tody-Flycatcher
Painted Tody-Flycatcher
Ringed Antpipit
Slender-footed Tyrannulet
White-lored Tyrannulet
Southern Beardless Tyrannulet
Mouse-colored Tyrannulet
Yellow Tyrannulet

Yellow-crowned Tyrannulet
Forest Elaenia
Gray Elaenia
Greenish Elaenia
Small-billed Elaenia
Plain-crested Elaenia
Rufous-crowned Elaenia
Pale-tipped Tyrannulet
Short-tailed Pygmy-Tyrant
Helmeted Pygmy-Tyrant
Rufous-tailed Flatbill
Yellow-olive Flycatcher
Yellow-margined Flycatcher
Gray-crowned Flycatcher
Yellow-breasted Flycatcher
Yellow-throated Spadebill
Golden-crowned Spadebill
White-crested Spadebill
Bran-colored Flycatcher
Ruddy-tailed Flycatcher
Fuscous Flycatcher
Euler's Flycatcher
Olive-sided Flycatcher
Drab Water-Tyrant
Amazonian Black-Tyrant
Pied Water-Tyrant
Cinnamon Attila
Citron-bellied Attila
Bright-rumped Attila
Grayish Mourner
Pale-bellied Mourner
Dusky-capped Flycatcher
Swainson's Flycatcher
Short-crested Flycatcher
Brown-crested Flycatcher
Tropical Kingbird
Gray Kingbird
Fork-tailed Flycatcher
Variegated Flycatcher
Sulphury Flycatcher
Streaked Flycatcher
Rusty-margined Flycatcher
Social Flycatcher
Dusky-chested Flycatcher

Piratic Flycatcher
Lesser Kiskadee
Great Kiskadee
Thrush-like Schiffornis
White-winged Becard
Black-capped Becard
Pink-throated Becard
Black-tailed Tityra
Black-crowned Tityra
Violaceous Jay
Rufous-browed Peppershrike
Red-eyed Vireo
Black-whiskered Vireo
Gray-crested Greenlet
Brown-headed Greenlet
Dusky-capped Greenlet
Tawny-crowned Greenlet
Veery
Gray-cheeked Thrush
Swainson's Thrush
Cocoa Thrush
Tropical Mockingbird
Buff-breasted Wren
House Wren
White-breasted Wood-Wren
Long-billed Gnatwren
Tropical Gnatcatcher
White-winged Swallow
Brown-chested Martin
Purple Martin
Gray-breasted Martin
White-banded Swallow
Black-collared Swallow
Southern Rough-winged
  Swallow
Bank Swallow
Barn Swallow
Yellow Warbler
Blackpoll Warbler
American Redstart
Prothonotary Warbler
Northern Waterthrush
Connecticut Warbler
Rose-breasted Chat

Rufous-collared Sparrow
Grassland Sparrow
Bananaquit
Black-faced Tanager
Yellow-backed Tanager
Flame-crested Tanager
Fulvous-crested Tanager
White-shouldered Tanager
Red-shouldered Tanager
Summer Tanager
Silver-beaked Tanager
Blue-gray Tanager
Palm Tanager
Plumbeous Euphonia
Purple-throated Euphonia
Violaceous Euphonia
White-lored Euphonia
White-vented Euphonia
Rufous-bellied Euphonia
Turquoise Tanager
Paradise Tanager
Burnished-buff Tanager
Opal-rumped Tanager
White-bellied Dacnis
Black-faced Dacnis
Yellow-bellied Dacnis
Blue Dacnis
Green Honeycreeper
Short-billed Honeycreeper
Red-legged Honeycreeper
Swallow Tanager
Orange-fronted Yellow-Finch
Wedge-tailed Grass-Finch
Yellow-bellied Seedeater
Lesser Seed-Finch
Buff-throated Saltator
Blue-black Grosbeak
Amazonian Oropendola
Yellow-rumped Cacique
Moriche Oriole
Yellow-hooded Blackbird
Giant Cowbird
Bobolink

I would like to make one last caveat. Personally, I am inclined to recommend you visit Amazonas towards the end of the rainy season - October, November - or during the dry season. March seems to be the hottest month of the year in Amazonas, but it is not such a humid heat as you will encounter during the rainy season. Also, I must admit that during the rains the mosquitoes are quite formidable[1][2][3][4].

Finally, I might make the suggestion that you take advantage of the fact that you are actually in Amazonas State to make a three or four-day trip by boat to the famous sacred mountain of Autana. It is camping and hammocks, but I can assure you that the experience is uniquely beautiful. Take a peek at: www.amazonasvenezuela.com. Arrangements can easily be made through Henry Jaimes in Puerto Ayacucho, wildnatureexp@hotmail.com, or directly through the Venezuelan Audubon Society.

The same group as the Autana tour also offers a 3-day tour to the beautiful River Cuao. They take you by jeep from the Orinoquia lodge to the port of Samariapo, where you board a *curiara* (dug-out conoe) to travel first on the Orinoco with a stop at Raton Island. From there you would travel up the Sipapo River, stopping to swim and have lunch by a beautiful beach. After lunch the tour continues for two hours up the Cuao River to reach an indigenous village of the Piaroa by the Raudal del Danto or Danta Rapids. Until dinner you have an opportunity to go fishing, swimming or even better bird watching. It's hammocking that night as you observe the stars through your mosquito net.

After breakfast on the second day there is a rather short walk to the upper part of the rapids where you again board your curiara for a 40-minute trip. Then comes a two and a half hour hike through a gorgeous forest. The Piaroa are not only your guides, showing you their medicinal plants and giving explanations of other interesting details of their forest. but they also carry all supplies for your meals, etc. On this walk you will be passing right by a lek of the Guayanan Cock-of-the-Rock, and it is hoped that you will have an excellent opportunity to observe them. The camp is at the base of the "Serranía (hills or mountains) de Cuao." After lunch there will be another walk to a look-out by the Caño (stream or river) Paraíso where you can have a refreshing swim in the slide and pools of the caño. Another night in hammocks.

On the third day you start your return trip. A few of the birds you should see on this tour are:

Anhinga	Capped Heron	Red-throated Caracara
Cocoi Heron	Greater Yellow-headed Vulture	Orange-breasted Falcon
Little Blue Heron	Black Caracara	Spix's Guan

---

[1] Pamela´s Note (with respect to biting critters): In all the places I have been in Venezuela - in the WORLD, I have NEVER encountered as many rapacious, voracious mosquitoes, puripuris or jejenes (no-see-ums) as I did in Amazonas. If people don't bring and use liberally plenty of repellent, they'll be miserable.

[2] Editor´s Note to Pamela´s Note: Mary Lou, with characteristic sweetness, insists (I am quoting now, so you may read this with a sargent major tone of voice), that first off, Pamela went off to Amazonas at the height of the rainy season, and secondly that, in spite of all of Mary Lou´s nagging, scolding and interminable warnings, Pamela insists upon wearing shorts in the wilderness. So, according to Mary Lou, what can she expect? I would have thought that she was expecting to be cool, but Mary Lou´s dictum is the old Venezuelan claim, that the Devil knows more because he is old than because he is a devil.

[3] Pamela´s Two-Cents Note regarding all of the above: I absolutely recommend Amazonas. It is one of my most favorite places in the world – never mind the bites and the itching.

[4] Editor's Comment to all of the above: (And I promise it is the last!) When in those mosquito or puri-puri infected regions, do the following: In the morning, before dressing, COVER yourself in Off, the creamy type. Put clothes on. Once on, spray clothes, shoes, everything you have on with clouds and fogs of Off, the spray-pump type. Then take the sulfur bag and dab sulfur all over your pants and socks. Now you are ready to face the world. Do not forget behind the ears!

Blue-throated Piping Guan	Scarlet Macaw	Many-banded Araçari
Sunbittern	Red-shouldered Macaw	Tawny-tufted Woodpecker
Solitary Sandpiper	White-tailed Trogon	Lineated Woodpecker
Lesser Yellowlegs	Ringed Kingfisher	Streaked Antwren
Spotted Sandpiper	Green-tailed Jacamar	Long-billed Gnatwren
Least Sandpiper	Black Nunbird	Green Honeycreeper
Pectoral Sandpiper	Green Araçari	Short-billed Honeycreeper
Upland Sandpiper		

I am certain that a really good birder like you would be able to add many more species to this list.

It almost looks as though you should spend your whole vacation in Amazonas doesn't it?

When you arrive back home from Amazonas, be sure to read Redmond O'Hanlon's book "In Trouble Again." Then you will understand why I laughed so hard.

Section VIII

TO WIND UP...CLOSING NOTES

White-headed Marsh-Tyrant

VIII - 1. The Endemics

As an opening to each chapter, you have found a list of endemics. Some are "country", meaning species *found only in Venezuela;* some are "regional", meaning species *with relatively small ranges that extend over one or two national borders.*
Many people ask us the crucial question: What are the chances of seeing any of these endemics? Here, to the best of our experience, is an approximation.
We have ranked the species according to the possibility/probability of finding them.
- **1** means that if in the proper location, you should see it. In other words, you will hardly miss it.
- **2** means that if in the proper location, you might see it. In other words, there is good possibility that you will see it.
- **3** means Forget it! In other words, the species is either too scarce or rare, or the proper location inaccessible.

You must remember that these are subjective evaluations - they do not reflect quantitative data on the populations of the different species, since, sad to say, there is almost none available.

Tepui Tinamou	CE	3	S.E. Bolivar, Canaima N.P., tepui slopes.
Gray-legged Tinamou	RE	3	S. Amazonas; open woodland.
Barred Tinamou	RE	3	S, Amazonas, Caño Casiquiare; rainforests.
Northern Screamer	RE	1	Zulia, Lake Maracaibo shores.
Band-tailed Guan	RE	2	Andes & Coastal ranges; montane & cloud forests.
Helmeted Curassow	RE	2	Andes & Coastal ranges; cloud forests.
Yellow-knobbed Curassow	RE	2	Llanos; gallery forests.
Black-fronted Wood-Quail	RE	3	Andes & Perija ranges; cloud forests.
Venezuelan Wood-Quail	CE	2	Andes & Coastal ranges; Henri Pittier NP.
Plain-flanked Rail	CE	3	Falcon; mangroves.
Rusty-flanked Crake	CE	2	Falcon & Lara; Yacambu NP; lagoons & swamps.
Scaly-naped Pigeon	RE	2	Coast & islands; arid woodland.
Bare-eyed Pigeon	RE	1	Coast; deciduous forests, xerophytic brush.
Blood-eared Parakeet	CE	2	Coastal Range; Henri Pittier NP.
Fiery-shouldered Parakeet	RE	1	Forests on slopes of tepuis; Canaima NP.
Rose-headed Parakeet	CE	2	Merida Andes; Sierra Nevada NP; cloud forests.
Tepui Parrotlet	RE	2	Sucre: Paria NP; Bolivar: Canaima NP.
Yellow-shouldered Parrot	RE	2	Falcon coast & Margarita Island; arid woodland.
Dwarf Cuckoo	RE	2	Zulia to Delta, Llanos & lowlands; forests.
Rufous-winged Ground-Cuckoo	RE	3	Amazonas & Bolivar; Tropical Zone rainforests.
Roraiman Nightjar	RE	3	SE Bolivar, tepui slopes.
Tepui Swift	CE	2	Bolivar, Canaima NP; cliff & canyons.
Pygmy Swift	RE	2	Zulia, Merida, Tachira; forests & open fields.
Rufous-breasted Sabrewing	RE	2	Bolivar, Canaima NP; cloud forests & open terrain.
Buff-breasted Sabrewing	RE	2	S Amazonas & SW Bolivar; cloud & open forests.
White-tailed Sabrewing	RE	2	Sucre: Paria NP, Monagas: Guacharo NP; cloud forests.
Peacock Coquette	RE	2	Amazonas & Bolivar; tepui cloud forests.

Coppery Emerald	RE	3	Zulia: Perija Range; upper Tropical Zone.
Narrow-tailed Emerald	RE	2	Andes; cloud forests & low scrub at high altitudes.
Green-tailed Emerald	CE	1	Northern mountains from Lara to Sucre.
Short-tailed Emerald	RE	1	Tachira: Tama NP, Merida; Temp. & Subtrop. Zones.
Shinning-green Hummingbird	RE	2	Zulia, foothills of Perija & W Andes; dry open areas & woods.
Tepui Goldenthroat	RE	2	Amazonas & Bolivar; tepuis: forests & open terrain.
Buffy Hummingbird	RE	1	Coast & islands; xerophytic areas & mangroves.
White-chested Emerald	RE	2	Miranda to Delta, NE Bolivar, N Amazonas; Trop. Zone.
Tachira Emerald	CE	3	Tachira; rainforests.
Copper-rumped Hummingbird	RE	1	Northern mountains & tepuis: slopes & foothills; Llanos.
Velvet-browed Brilliant	RE	2	Amazonas & Bolivar; tepui forests.
Scissor-tailed Hummingbird	CE	1	Sucre: Paria NP; cloud forests.
Violet-chested Hummingbird	CE	1	Andes & Coastal ranges, Henri Pittier NP.
Golden-bellied Starfrontlet	RE	2	Tachira, Tama NP; cloud & dwarf forests.
Blue-throated Starfrontlet	RE	2	Tachira, Tama NP; cloud & dwarf forests.
Orange-throated Sunangel	RE	1	Merida, Trujillo; cloud & dwarf forests.
Merida Sunangel	CE	2	Merida, Sierra Nevada NP; cloud & dwarf forests.
Coppery-bellied Puffleg	RE	2	Merida: Sierra Nevada NP, Tachira: Tama NP; paramos.
Perija Metaltail	RE	3	Zulia, Perija Range; open country.
Bronze-tailed Thornbill	RE	2	Tachira, Tama NP; paramo.
Bearded Helmetcrest	RE	2	Merida, Sierra Nevada NP; paramos.
Rufous-shafted Woodstar	RE	2	Andes & Coastal ranges; cloud forests & edges.
White-tipped Quetzal	RE	1	Coastal Range, Henri Pittier NP; cloud forests.
Pale-headed Jacamar	RE	2	Llanos; semi-arid areas & open woodlands.
Russet-throated Puffbird	RE	1	Llanos; xerophytic areas & open woodlands.
Groove-billed Toucanet	CE	1	Coastal Range, Henri Pittier NP; cloud forests.
Black-dotted Piculet	CE	1	Delta Amacuro; forests & second growth.
Black-throated Spinetail	CE	1	Coastal Range; cloud forests.
White-wiskered Spinetail	RE	2	Zulia, Falcon, Lara: xerophytic areas.
Crested Spinetail	RE	1	N of the Orinoco River, Subtropical Zone; forests.
Tepui Spinetail	RE	2	Amazonas & Bolivar: tepuis forests.
Ochre-browed Thistletail	CE	2	Tachira, Merida, Trujillo; paramos.
Perija Thistlketail	RE	3	Zulia: Perija mountains; paramo.
Orinoco Softtail	CE	3	Amazonas: upper Orinoco River rainforests.
Roraiman Barbtail	RE	2	Bolivar, Canaima NP; tepuis forests.
White-throated Barbtail	CE	2	Sucre: Paria NP; cloud forests.
Guttulated Foliage-gleaner	CE	2	Coastal Range, Henri Pittier NP; cloud forests.
Neblina Foliage-gleaner	RE	3	Amazonas: Cerro (tepui) Neblina.
White-throated Foliage-gleaner	RE	2	Amazonas & Bolivar: tepui cloud forests.
Streak-backed Antshrike	RE	3	Amazonas & Bolivar: tepuis forests.
Roraiman Antwren	RE	3	Amazonas & Bolivar: tepuis forests.
Gray-bellied Antbird	RE	3	Amazonas, Caño Casiquiare forests.
Yapacana Antbird	CE	3	Amazonas: Cerro (tepui) Yapacana.
Caura Antbird	RE	2	Amazonas & Bolivar; rainforests.
Great Antpitta	CE	3	Andes, Perija & Coastal ranges; cloud forests.

Tachira Antpitta	CE	3	Tachira: Tama NP; cloud forests.
Gray-necked Antpitta	CE	3	Tachira & Merida; cloud forests.
Brown-breasted Antpitta	RE	3	Amazonas & Bolivar: tepui cloud forests.
Scallop-breasted Antpitta	CE	2	Coastal Range; cloud forests.
Golden-breasted Fruiteater	RE	2	Andes, Perija & Coastal ranges; cloud forests.
Handsome Fruiteater	CE	2	Coastal Range, Henri Pittier NP; cloud forests.
Red-banded Fruiteater	RE	2	Bolivar, Canaima NP; tepui cloud forests.
Rose-colored Piha	RE	2	S Bolivar; tepui cloud forests.
Scarlet-horned Manakin	RE	1	Amazonas & Bolivar (Canaima NP); tepuis, rainforest.
Olive Manakin	RE	2	Amazonas & S Bolivar; tepuis, rainforest.
White-bearded Flycatcher	CE	1	Llanos, N of the Orinoco River.
Venezuelan Flycatcher	RE	2	General: Tropical Zone rainforests.
Short-tailed Tody-Flycatcher	CE	2	Falcon & Zulia; xerophytic coastal areas.
Ruddy Tody-Flycatcher	RE	2	Bolivar, Canaima NP; tepuis forests.
Venezuela Bristle-Tyrant	CE	2	Coastal Range: Henri Pittier NP; cloud forests.
Chapman's Tyrannulet	CE	2	Bolivar, Canaima NP; tepuis forests.
Black-fronted Tyrannulet	CE	2	Bolivar, Canaima NP; tepuis forests.
Slender-billed Tyrannulet	RE	2	Zulia, Falcon, Lara: xerophytic areas.
Gray Elaenia	CE	2	Bolivar, Canaima NP; tepuis forests.
Caracas Tyrannulet	CE	2	Coastal Range, Temperate Zone.
Paramo Wren	CE	1	Merida, Sierra Nevada NP; paramos.
Tepui Greenlet	RE	2	Amazonas & Bolivar: tepuis, rain/cloud forests.
Golden-tufted Grackle	RE	1	Bolivar, Canaima NP: La Escalera; rainforests.
Orange-crowned Oriole	RE	2	N of Orinoco River; Tropical & Subtropical Zones.
White-fronted Redstart	CE	2	Tachira: Tama NP; cloud forests.
White-faced Redstart	CE	3	NW Amazonas: tepui forests.
Brown-capped (Tepui) Redstart	RE	1	Bolivar, CanaimaNP; tepuis, cloud forests.
Yellow-faced Redstart	CE	1	Sucre: Paria NP; cloud forests.
Saffron-breasted Redstart	CE	3	Bolivar: Cerro (tepui) Guaiquinima cloud forests.
Gray-headed Warbler	CE	2	Monagas: Guacharo NP: Cerro Negro heights.
Greater Flower-piercer	RE	2	Bolivar, Canaima NP; tepuis, cloud forests.
Scaled Flower-piercer	RE	3	Amazonas & SW Bolivar: tepuis, cloud forests.
Venezuelan Flower-piercer	CE	2	Sucre: Paria NP; cloud forests.
Rufous-cheeked Tanager	CE	1	Coastal Range, Henri Pittier NP; cloud forests.
Olive-backed Tanager	RE	2	Bolivar, Canaima NP; tepui forests.
Gray-capped Hemispingus	CE	2	Tama NP & Guaramacal NP; cloud forests.
Slaty-backed Hemispingus	CE	2	Tachira(Paramo Zumbador), Merida; cloud forests.
Orinocan Saltator	RE	2	Llanos: gallery forests; coastal xerophytic areas.
Vermillion Cardinal	RE	2	Coastal xerophytic areas.
Tepuis Brush-Finch	RE	2	Bolivar, Canaima NP; tepui forests.
Tocuyo Sparrow	RE	2	Zulia, Falcon, Lara: xerophytic areas.
Duida Grass-Finch	CE	3	Amazonas: Cerro (tepui) Duida.
Red Siskin	RE	3	Coastal Range & Lara mountains: foothills.

VIII - 2. A Teaspoon of Economy and Politics

In spite of all its oil reserves and highly developed oil industry, Venezuela is a under-developed country, with all the problems and shortcomings inherent to that condition, including, first and foremost, a very uneven distribution of wealth, a high rate of population growth, huge portions of the population living in poverty, a tiny middle class, insufficient and grossly mismanaged public services...

A seemingly endless succession of incompetent and corrupt governments, aided by an extremely faulty (if not actually corrupt) election system, is the principal cause for much of our present critical socioeconomic situation. Many believe that one thing that has helped Venezuela on its road to economic perdition is its perennial good luck. You read correctly: it seems that every time we reach the end of our rope and are about to fall into the abyss, something completely external happens that saves the situation. It may be an oil strike in Mexico or a war in the Gulf or some such incident. But the end result is that instead of learning wisdom from our crises, we have become more and more irresponsible and incompetent.

Perhaps it would not be an exaggeration to say that Venezuela is a democracy only in name, irrespective of all the platitudes that our politicians spout to the contrary. It has been said that it is actually a dictatorship of the party that happens to be in power. Every five years, the ranks of officialdom are swept clean by the newly elected president, who places his own party's people in all key positions, and pays election supporters by giving them governments jobs. There are over 1,900,000 public employees for a population of circa 25.000.000 - about one bureaucrat for every 13 citizens !!!

One very odd fact in this political environment is freedom of the press, which is respected quite widely (in spite of threats to the contrary), and is the only thing that saves us from total despotism.

With regard to the National Assembly, even though the people are increasingly critical of the system, half of our congressmen continue to be elected not by individual name but through political party slates. Consequently these representatives are responsible to their party rather than to the people, and public opinion carries very little weight. The judges are also appointed by the political party in power, which explains why no politician has been sent to jail for corruption over the last 43 years.

For many years, oil revenues were huge enough to pay for over-grown bureaucracies, to invest in inefficient industries and to subsidize public services. One such subsidy is the controlled price of fuel and lubricants, at levels which astonish visitors from abroad. We are very rich and therefore, we do not need to work, or become educated and competitive, or seek order and efficiency.

Our political and trade-union leaders have become increasingly more demagogic and paternalistic, making utopian promises to the people and convincing the great majority that no effort on their part is necessary, that every need will be fulfilled by our omnipresent and oversized government. They have almost managed to erase all capacity for self-reliance and private initiative on the part of the people.

When oil prices cave in, our governments continue to spend recklessly and to accumulate an incredible national debt. The end result has been that although our oil industry still makes us one of the richest nations in Latin America, many of our roads are in deplorable state, our public education system would lose in comparison to that of some of the poorest countries in Africa, our public hospitals are in shambles. The cities all suffer from water shortages because, except for cosmetic repairs, nothing has been done to maintain and up-date the water systems during the last 43 years. Then there is our postal system! The only thing I can say about it is the fact that it may take from *one to three months* for a letter to reach us - if ever!

Soon, the politicians will have to face the hard realities of insurmountable government deficits and fast-growing public discontent. Thanks to our free and investigative press, Venezuelans are probably more aware of what is going on than the citizens of most nations. The present crisis is bringing about many changes, for I see positive signs of the people stirring out of their lethargy and complacency. Perhaps, given a little time, Venezuelans will develop the strength to fulfill their duties and demand their rights.

VIII - 3. About You in Venezuela

It often happens that there is a great distance between the political arenas of a country and the common people one meets along the way. Most Venezuelans I know are completely divorced from the corruption in government I have often mentioned here, valiantly trying to survive a political and economic turmoil not of their making.

My Venezuelans are warm, hard-working, extremely decent, hospitable and fun. Some are quite eccentric, many suffer the national strain of dyslexia and confuse right and left, and a great number are unreliable with regard to time. But then, some are among the wittiest and most cultured people I know.

Venezuelan friendliness and helpfulness is particularly true amongst the people in the interior, in the countryside and the small towns. In 35 years of birding trips to every nook and cranny of this country, I've found myself in trouble scores of times. There is not a single instance where someone did not come along to rescue me and help me on my way. Gaining a Venezuelan's good will is easy - it all depends on your approach - and a smile and soft words are the best calling cards.

Even in Caracas I have had multiple experiences of the kindness of Venezuelans. No matter how crowded the Metro of Caracas may be, I have never had to stand. Someone has invariably given me their seat. Would the same be true in New York?

However, here I feel I should also mention another disease - probably genetic - that I suspect most, if not all, Venezuelans suffer. I personally call this illness "*Yo voy a*" meaning... I am going to....whatever. They are truly sincere at the moment of uttering this phrase, but the complications of life in this country often get in the way, and they never accomplish what they proposed to do originally. The vast majority of Venezuelan politicians suffer from this complaint (to the frustration of their constituents), and, unfortunately for Venezuela, the current President of the nation suffers from a near fatal case of the disease. Therefore, if a Venezuelan says he or she will call you or write to you or do something, do not take them too seriously. That way you can be pleasantly surprised if they do follow through.

Over the years I have received many letters from birders, telling me how much they enjoyed their visit to Venezuela. These letters have given me great pleasure because I deeply love this country, its people, its natural beauties and its birds, and this love I wish to share with all birders.

In the midst of all that positive correspondence, once an extremely negative letter arrived, blasting the country and all its inconveniences. Upon reading it a couple of times, it became quite evident that, even when the mishaps and inconveniences the writer encountered were very real, a lot of his bad experience had been the product of his *attitude*. That letter propelled me to include the following, a free adaptation of the one published not too long ago by the Ecumenical Coalition on Third World Tourism.

CODE OF ETHICS FOR TOURISTS

1. Travel in a sympathetic and humane spirit, with genuine desire to learn about the people of your host country. Be sensitively aware of their feelings - try to prevent what might be offensive behavior on your part (this applies very much to photography). Venezuelans love to have their picture taken, but ask first.
2. Train yourself to the habits of listening and observing rather than merely hearing and seeing. You will grow in knowledge and in understanding if you analyze the experiences you have had each day.

3. Be aware that often, the people in the country you visit have time concepts[1] and thought patterns different from your own. But diversity is the salt of the Earth - be glad of differences, instead of deploring them.
4. If you really want your experience to be a "home away from home," it is foolish to waste money on traveling.
5. Don't go looking for "tropical paradises" - discover the realities of a different way of living and you'll find how enriching it is to see life through other eyes.
6. Acquaint yourself with local customs. What is courteous in one country may be quite the reverse in another - people will be happy to help you.
7. Instead of the western practice of "knowing all the answers," cultivate the habit of asking questions.
8. Remember that you are only one of thousands of tourists visiting this country and do not expect special privileges.
9. Do not make promises to people in your host country, unless you can carry them through.
10. When shopping, remember that the "bargain" you are purchasing is possible only because of the low wages paid to the maker.

Now you have read all the good as well as all the bad I had to say about Venezuela. Have I left you in doubt, dreaming of the wonderful birds and the beautiful scenery, but fearing the shortcomings? I hope not! Birding is always such an adventure! I told you the bad so that you would know what to expect and would have no disappointments. Besides, while all countries have shortcomings, very few can compete with Venezuela in natural beauty and abundance of birds. After all, there has to be a reason for the fact that I came for 2 years but have stayed for 54, especially considering that I came from Oregon, rated to be, without a doubt, the best state in the Union!

As a last note, I would like to make a special request: upon returning home from your birding trip, kindly write the Audubon your reactions to your stay in Venezuela. Criticisms of the lodgings, transports, areas, services, etc. are extremely useful, for they help keep the various lodges and hotels, tour and car-rental companies and others, on their toes.

As you have probably found by now, in every new edition of Birding in Venezuela we have incorporated information provided by visiting birders. Repeat visitors become friends, and we always look forward to seeing them on their next visit. Their letters are always welcome, and so will yours... Don't forget to write! We thank you in advance.

Also, please do not forget to advise of any special finds, particularly birds. Visiting birders should also be aware that as of November, 2000 we have a "Venezuelan Rare Bird Committee" which evaluates unusual records. As well as genuinely rare birds and potential first records, the Committee also reviews unseasonable records (for migrants) and possible range extensions. Observers are encouraged to submit noteworthy records to the Committee through the Venezuelan Audubon Society:

- ecoturismo@audubondevenezuela.org
- audubon@audubondevenezuela.org
- presidencia@audubondevenezuela.org

A list of accepted records is expected to be published annually in a refereed journal.

---

[1] When it comes to time concepts, none worse than those of my procrastinating editor, Clemencia Rodner. I am positive I "earned" some of my gray hair learning to adapt to it!

VIII - 4. *Clemencia's Advice: What to Bring*

(This chapter has been included at the insistence of my obstreperous editor. I am innocent.)

Fellow Birder:

Greetings! You will arrive in Venezuela to spend a few glorious days birding. Surely the last thing you will want to do is waste time shopping for things you could have brought with you. Mary Lou thinks you need no advice - she believes everyone is like her: Wonder-Birder-know-it-all.

On the other hand, I humbly recognize that I always forget something, even elementary things (i.e. socks, toothpaste, my asthma medicine). Perhaps some of you out there are like me. To help fellow bird-brained birders, here is a list with a few things that you might consider stuffing into your suitcase before leaving home.

Medicines: A small bag with all prescription medicines you take regularly or occasionally, as well as something for diarrhea, band-aids, something for headaches, something for colds, eye-drops.

However, you can buy practically all medicines over the counter in Venezuela., including antibiotics (from traditional stuff like Ampicilline and Amoxicilline, to more modern stuff like Azitromicine).

Tea: If this is your brew of choice, bring your own ample supply of tea bags. The stuff they give you here, even in five-star restaurants and hotels, is dreadful. And if you ask for a tea with milk, sometimes you will get *a cup of hot milk with a tea bag swimming inside.* Yuck !!![1]

Trail Food: Such as nuts, raisins and other dried fruits, granola bars, and especially **peanut butter**, the ultimate quick sandwich-maker, which is seldom available in Venezuelan grocery stores. (If you have any left over at the end of the trip, the charitable thing is to contribute it to the welfare of the Audubon's staff.)

Swimming Suit : Especially if you are going to the south of Venezuela, there are many opportunities to go swimming, and yet, outside of the big cities, forget about finding a suit.

Towel: The best are those smallish, thin, cheap ones that are sold in places like K-Mart. Even better are the relatively new shami towels (like the ones used to dry your car). They dry fast and take little space. What most hotels in the interior call towels, you would probably classify as face-cloths.

Old Sneakers: A pair that you can throw away at the end of the trip will be useful when the sand is too hot, or the river bed pebbly, or the showers are not too clean. River shoes are great too.

---

[1] Editor's Note: Pamela Pierce, my co-editor, asks why on earth would you want to drink tea when Venezuela has the world's best coffee. Wisest words were never spoken.

Plastic Poncho: A light-weight, inexpensive one will do. Rain here can be torrential, but the hot weather will seldom allow it to chill your bones, except in the Andes.

Hat: This is the Tropics! Don't ever trust the sun.

Sun Screen: Ditto.

Insect Repellent: I find the cream types to be best in every respect. Insect repellents are easily available even in small local shops in the interior. The most common brands are Off and Avispa, but there are a few others, most of them quite good. Remember to keep them away from your optics.

Chigger Bag: A Zip-Lock bag containing an old sock, filled with ± one cup of powdered sulfur and tied with a rubber band. This you use to powder your clothes with. It is your best bet against ticks and chiggers (it is what the soldiers in Vietnam used).

Benadryl Gel: For when you do get bitten, and a small bottle of BETADINE soap, to keep bites from infections and keep chiggers from clinging to you.

Ear Plugs: You will bless these when you find yourself riding on a bus with a radio blaring salsa music at Chinese torture levels. Also, when the window of your hotel room opens upon the scene of the crowning of the Queen of the Harvest, or Carnival or Syndicate, or Baseball, or whatever (towns in the interior love crowning queens. It is a national mania).

Paperback Book: There will be times when you will have to wait.

Flashlight: You will find yourself in places where the plant is turned off at midnight, or there are frequent break-downs. Don't forget the extra batteries and bulbs!

Swiss Army Knife: That, or a Leatherman Tool. I am extremely fond of my Leatherman, which has proven to be good for everything the ads claim and for a hundred other uses.

Duct Tape: A small roll. This is THE all-purpose fixer.

Photocopy of all papers: Your passport, of course, but it is a wise thing in cases of airline weirdness, to have copies of all your tickets stashed away at the bottom of your backpack. Also, of all your reservations and important telephone numbers, including the ones to notify credit card loss, the Audubon's - (0212)-992-3268 & (0212)-992-2812 - and your Embassy's office in Caracas. (Keep a card with these important telephone numbers in the little hide-away pouch, together with your money.)

VIII - 5. Useful Information

VENEZUELAN PUBLIC HOLIDAYS

National Holidays

New Years	January 1
Declaration of Independence	April 19
Labor Day	May 1
Battle of Carabobo	June 24
Independence Day	July 5
Simón Bolívar's Birthday	July 24
Columbus Day	October 12
Christmas	December 25
Monday of Carnival	Variable
Tuesday of Carnival	Variable
Holy Thursday	Variable
Good Friday	Variable

- Carnival is 6 weeks before Easter week.
- The Carnival holiday starts on the Friday *before* Carnival Monday.
- The Easter holiday lasts from the Friday before Palm Sunday to Easter Sunday.

Religious Holidays

Feast of the Magi	January 6
St. Joseph's Day	March 19
St. Peter's and St. Paul's Day	June 29
Virgin Mary's Assumption	August 15
All Saints Day	November 1
The Immaculate Conception	December 8

- Banks and insurance companies close either the Monday before or after a religious holiday, depending upon whether the holiday falls prior to or after Wednesday. These holidays are not really observed by other commercial offices.
- Many factories, car workshops, etc. shut down for their annual vacations from December 15th to January 7th, thus making a virtue out of a necessity.

CHANGING MONEY

If your plan is to take off for the hinterlands immediately upon arrival, remember to change your travelers' checks or cash at the airport, as it will be quite difficult outside the larger cities. Although this is not a fixed policy, the currency exchange offices at Maiquetía International Airport sometimes limit the exchange to $200 per person. There are offices of Italcambio at the following airports in the interior; Barquisimeto, Maracaibo, Maturin, Mérida, Puerto La Cruz., Valencia

The best exchange rates can be obtained from *Casas de Cambio,* currency exchange houses, in Caracas and the larger cities - Valencia, Maracay, Puerto Ordaz, Ciudad Bolívar, Barquisimeto, Barcelona, Mérida, etc. You will have to show your passport and tourist card. They give no trouble with traveler's checks. Two well-known ones in Caracas are Italcambio (on Plaza Altamira Sur and other locations), and Thomas Cook, located in the offices of the Maso Internacional tourist agency, Edificio Seguros Adriatico, Plaza Altamira Norte.

Banks are seldom willing to change traveler's checks to non-clients, often asking that you show the purchase receipt to prove that they are really yours, or changing only a small amount (one to two hundred $$$).

Some tourists have found that they are able to withdraw bolívares from ATMs of some banks. As explained in the chapter on Dos and Don'ts, it is necessary to have a **CIRRUS** card from your personal bank. I frankly do not know if there is any additional charge to your personal bank account for this transfer of foreign funds.

VENEZUELAN CURRENCY

Coin denominations are: Bs 1; Bs 2; Bs 5; Bs 10; Bs 20; Bs 50 and Bs 100.

Bill denominations are: Bs 5; Bs 10; Bs 20; Bs 50; Bs 100; Bs 500; Bs 1,000; Bs 2,000; Bs 5,000; Bs 10,000 and Bs 20,000 [1]

Please notice that there are both coins and bill worth Bs. 5, Bs. 10, Bs 20, Bs 50 and Bs 100, and that some of the bills (i.e. the Bs 2,000 and the Bs 20,000), look somewhat alike and may be easily confused.

CREDIT CARDS

If lost, call the U.S.:

American Express:	001-910-333-3211
Diners	001-303-799-1504
Master Card	001-314-275-6690
Visa	001-410-581-9994

For information, call in Caracas:

American Express	0212-206-0333
Diners	0212-503-2561
Master Card	0212-507-1379
Visa	0212-265-0900

DIALING TELEPHONE NUMBERS

- Country Code for Venezuela: **+ + 58.**
- All Area Codes in Venezuela begin with zero.
- When calling from abroad, **omit the zero in the Area Code.**
- Area Code for Caracas: **0212.**
- For Long Distance phone calls, the best is to do so through the Long Distance Operator: **122.**
- To dial from a public phone, you need a **Telephone Card**, which can be obtained at the airports or from a variety of shops, including drugstores (farmacias).
- In all main airports and in most towns, there is an office of the telephone company **(Oficina Publica de CANTV)**, where you can go to make long distance phone calls. These are through an operator. You often have to wait a bit, but the system works.

---

[1] We understand thet the government will soon issuing Bs. 50,000 bills - which tells something about our inflation!

NATIONAL AIRLINES DIRECTORY

Aeropostal (National & international flights)
Reservations: (0) 212-800-28466

Aeroejecutivos (Chartered flights)
Reservations: (0) 212-991-7942 / 991-2069 / 991-9286

Aerotuy (National flights only)
Reservations: (0) 212-761-0052 / 0298 / 0842 / 8043

Aserca (National flights only)
Reservations: (0) 212-800-88356
Maiquetía: (0) 212-352-2432 / 352-3334

Lai (National flights only)
Reservations: (0) 212-267-0297/266-6379
Maiquetía: (0) 212-352-4746

Laser (National flights only)
Reservations: (0) 212-235-0062 / 6979 / 1909
Maiquetía: (0) 212-352-3634 / 352-0143

Rutaca (National flights only)
Maiquetía: (0) 212-352-4412

Santa Barbara (National & International flights)
Reservations: (0) 212-800-72682/(0) 212-242-1633

Servivensa (National & International flights)
Reservations: (0) 212-561-3366 / 562-3366 / 563-3366
Maiquetía: (0) 212-352-1555 / 355-1683
(Servivensa and Avensa are the same company.)

Zuliana de Aviacion (National flights only)
Reservations: (0) 212-993-9855 / 2220
Maracaibo: (0) 261-351-4775 / 352-7161

INTERNATIONAL AIRLINES DIRECTORY

Aerolineas Argentinas Reservations: (0) 212-267-8666

Aeroperu Reservations: (0) 212-283-45312 / 284-2797

Air France Reservations: (0) 212-283-5855

Alitalia Reservations: (0) 212-800-66656

AMERICAN Reservations: (0) 212-209-8111 / 212-285-4433
Maiquetía: (0) 212-521410 / 11 / 12

ALM Reservations: (0) 212-953-7086, 953-7168

Avianca Reservations: (0) 212-953-5732, 953-7254

British Airways Reservations: (0) 212-261-8006
Maiquetía: (0) 212-521180 / 81 / 82

BWIA Reservations (0) 212-265-7542 / 261-5062

Iberia Reservations: (0) 212-267-8666

KLM Reservations: (0) 212-285-3333 / 285-0283

LAN Chile Reservations: (0) 212-284-1211
Maiquetía: (0) 212-552775

LACSA Reservations: (0) 212-959-2293 / 959-2302
Maiquetía: (0) 212-352-1041

Lloyd Aereo Boliviano Reservations: (0) 212-762-9857 / 762-0324

Mexicana Reservations: (0) 212-952-7593 / 952-7604

SAETA Reservations: (0) 212-761-6530 / 761-6630

TAP Air Portugal Reservations: (0) 212-951-0511

UNITED Reservations: (0) 800-100-6147
Maiquetía: (0) 212-355-1133 / 34 / 40

VARIG Reservations: (0) 212-237-7311 / 238-2111

VISAS

For most birders, the normal entrance to the country will be by air, and the normal stay, less than 60 days, in which case, all you'll need, a 60-day **Tourist Card**, will be provided by the airline in which you fly in.

If you plan to come any other way, *allowing plenty of time prior to your departure to Venezuela*, request a **multiple-entrance tourist visa** from the nearest Venezuelan Consulate.

INPARQUES (NATIONAL PARKS INSTITUTE)

Local Offices by State

Amazonas
  • Regional Office for Amazonas
    Edif. Funeraria Amazonas, second floor, end of Calle La Guardia, Barrio Unión, Puerto Ayacucho.

Anzoátegui   (See Sucre.)

Apure   Superintendent Cinaruco-Capanaparo N.P.

Edif Pascuali, Oficina #2, Calle Bolivar (in front of Palacio Los Barbaritos), San Fernando de Apure.

Aragua
- Regional Office for Aragua, Carabobo & Cojedes
  Parque Zoológico Las Delicias, Maracay.
- Superintendent Henri Pittier N.P.
  Las Cocuizas Recreational Area, Carretera Maracay-Choroní.

Bolívar
- Regional Office for Bolívar
  Av. Germanía & Calle Andrés Bello, Edificio CVG, 1st. floor, Ciudad Bolívar.
- Superintendent Canaima N.P., Eastern Sector
  El Dorado - Sta. Elena de Uairen road, Campamento Aponwao.
- Superintendent Canaima N.P., Western Sector
  Campamento Edelca, Laguna de Canaima.

Carabobo
- State Coordination Office
  Antigua Estación Alemana, Ave. Paseo Cabriales, Plaza Los Enanitos, Valencia.
- Superintendent San Esteban N.P.
  Qta. Asturias, Calle Principal Tejerías, Pto. Cabello.

Cojedes
- Superintendent Tirgua N.P.
  MARNR Office, in front of IAN, San Carlos.

Delta Amacuro (See Monagas.)

Falcón
- Regional Office for Falcón
  + Superintendent Médanos de Coro N.P.
  Jardín Botánico Xerofítico, Avda. Intercomunal Coro-La Vela, Coro.
- Superintendent Morrocoy N.P.
  Inparques Office, in front of the National Guard office at Tucacas.
- Superintendent Sierra de San Luis N.P. Cabure.
- Superintendent Cueva Quebrada del Toro N.P.
  Santa Cruz de Bucaral.

Federal District
- Regional Office for the Capital
  "Vivero Didactico", Parque del Este, Caracas.
  Tel. 0212-238-3983.
- National Parks Headquarters Office
  Ave. Rómulo Gallegos, near Parque del Este Metro Station, Caracas. Tel. 0212-285-4106 / 4360 / 4859.
- El Avila N.P. Headquarters Los Venados sector (within the Park), on the road to Galipán.
- Superintendent Macarao N.P.
  Kilometer 21 on the road to Colonia Tovar (next to the National Guard on the entrance to the town of El Junquito.)

Guárico
- Regional Office for Guárico & Apure
  + Superintendent Aguaro-Guariquito N.P.

Av. Principal del Centro, Edif. MARNR, Calabozo.
- Superintendent Guatopo N.P.
El Lucero Administrative Center (within the Park),
Santa Teresa-Altagracia de Orituco road.

Lara
- Regional Office for Lara, Yaracuy & Portuguesa
  + Superintendent Dinira N.P.
  + Superintendent Cerro Saroche N.P.
Av. Los Leones, in front of the "Las Trinitarias" shopping center and next to the Army's Third Brigade, Barquisimeto.
- Superintendent Yacambú N.P.
El Blanquito Recreational Area (within the Park.).
- Superintendent Terepaima N.P.
MARNR Office (next to the Coca Cola plant) on the Intercomunal Cabudare - El Carabalí road.

Mérida
- Regional Office for Merida & Trujillo
  + Superintendent Sierra Nevada N.P.
  + Superintendent Sierra La Culata N.P.
N° 5-44, Calle 19 between 5th & 6th Ave., Mérida.

Miranda
(See Federal District.)

Monagas
- Regional Office for Monagas & Delta Amacuro
Parque Andres Eloy Blanco, Carretera Vía Sur, Maturín.
- Superintendent El Guácharo N.P.
Cueva del Guácharo.

Portuguesa
- State Coordination Office
Parque Musiú Carmelo, Av. Páez & Av. Chalet (next to the bus station), Acarigua.

Sucre
- Regional Office for Anzoátegui & Sucre
  + Coordination Office P.N. Mochima
Parque Guaiquerí, Av. Arismendi & Blvd. La Margariteña, Cumaná.
- Superintendent Península de Paria N.P.
Ave. Principal Campo Claro, Irapa.

Táchira
- Regional Office for Táchira + Superintendent Tamá
  + Superintendent Chorro del Indio N.P.
Parque Metropolitano, Av. 19 de Abril (in front of Policlínica de Táchira), San Cristóbal.
- Superintendent Páramos Batallón & La Negra N.P.
Vivero (nursery) of MARNR, Bailadores.
- Superintendent Tapo-Caparo N.P.
Oficina Auxiliar Santa Maria de Caparo, Desurca.

Trujillo
(See Mérida.)

Yaracuy
- State Coordination Office + Superintendent Parque Leonor Bernabo, end of Av. Los Baños (in front of Hotel Yurubi), San Felipe.

Zulia
- Regional Office for Zulia
  MARNR Office, at the entrance to the Bridge over the Lake,
  Punta de Piedra sector, Maracaibo.
- Superintendent Sierra de Perijá N.P.
  + Superintendent Cienagas de Juan Manuel N.P.
  MARNR Office, Machiques-La Fría road, Machiques.

VIII - 6. The Venezuela Audubon Society

The Venezuela Audubon (SCAV) is over 30 years old. And to think that I was one of the founding members... Don't laugh, please! This is one of the oldest chapters outside of the US, and quite proud of the conservation work done all these years.

At present, the SCAV has some thousand members, a staff of 6 as well as some dedicated volunteers. There are also scores of members who participate very enthusiastically in an astonishing variety of activities: excursions, courses and conferences, field research, bird surveys, the Board, the Migration Monitoring Program, our Bulletin, our store...

Present and past conservation work includes field research projects, such as the one on Flamingoes and the Los Roques Project; the Bird Migration Monitoring Program at the Pass of Portachuelo, Rancho Grande, now in it 12th year; publication projects, such as the one on Coastal Wetlands, the Checklists of the National Parks and the work on Forest Conservation and Forest Reserves; activism projects such as the one on Los Olivitos, the one on gold mining, the one on the wild bird trade...

The SCAV is an enthusiastic members of the Audubon - Americas family, as well as the BirdLife International Partner in Venezuela.

I will not tire you with more about achievements. Let it suffice that nowadays, the Venezuelan Audubon is considered one of the most respected conservation voices in the country.

The office, where they also take care of international travelers and where they work on scientific projects, activism, have a small library open to public use, etc., is located on the first floor of Edificio Matisco, Calle Veracruz, Las Mercedes. This is only a block and a half away, due north and east, from the Paseo Las Mercedes. To help you locate the office, when you come along the Calle Veracruz, look for the sign of MRW, our neighbors downstairs, which is more visible than the sign of our building.

OfficeTelephones: (0212) 9923268 & 9922812
Fax from abroad: ++ 58 - 212 - 9910716
from Venezuela: 0212 - 9910716

Postal Address
Apartado 80450
Caracas 1080-A, Venezuela

Email:audubon@audubonvenezuela.org

VIII - 7. A Souvenir...

Since you have finished this book, I assume you are about to leave Venezuela. I fervently hope this was the best birding trip of your life.

Together with all the memories, something of us will go with you. Some "invisible friends" asked us to toast to your happy memories by quoting Mr. Ogden Nash, who said it best:

> «There was a young belle of Old Natchez
> Whose garments were always in patchez
> When comment arose
> On the state of her clothes,
> She replied, When Ah itches, Ah scratchez.»

> (This O. Nash poem presented to you courtesy of the **Chiggers.**)

And as long as we are quoting Mr. Nash, we can't but share with you this old favorite of ours:

> Up from the Egg:
> **Confessions of a Nuthatch Avoider**
>
> Bird watchers top my honors list.
> I aimed to be one, but I missed.
> Since I'm both myopic and astigmatic,
> my aim turned out to be erratic,
> and I, bespectacled and binocular,
> exposed myself to comment jocular.
> We don't need too much bird lore, do we,
> to tell a flamingo from a towhee;
> yet I cannot, and never will,
> unless the silly birds stand still.
> And there is no enlightenment so obscure
> as ornithological literature.
> Is yon strange creature a common chickadee
> or a migrant alouette from Picardy?
> You rush to consult your nature guide
> and inspect the gallery inside,
> but a bird in the open never looks
> like its picture in the birdie books...
> Or if it once did, it has changed its plumage
> and plunges you back into ignorant gloomage.
> That is why I sit here growing old by inches,
> watching the clock instead of finches,
> but sometimes I visualize in my gin
> the Audubon that I audabin.

Cheers!

Mary Lou, Clemencia, Juanita, Pamela & Robin

...able:

, of Spain and Portugal (Andrew Paterson)
...panish Imperial Eagle (Miguel Ferrer)
_...es_ (André Konter)
...sta Comentada de las Aves Argentinas / Annotated Checklist of the Birds of Argentina (Juan Mazar Barnett & Mark Pearman)
• _Annotated Checklist of the Birds of Belize_ (H. Lee Jones & Andrew C. Vallely)
• _A Field Guide to the Birds of Peru_ (James F. Clements & Noam Shany; colour illustrations by Dana Gardner & Eustace Barnes)
• _Guía de las Aves de España_ (Eduardo de Juana & Juan M. Varela)
• _Guía Sonora de las Aves de Europa_ (10 CDs, Jean Roché & Jerôme Chevereau)
• _Catàleg dels ocells dels Països Catalans_ (Jordi Clavell)
• _Guía de los Mamíferos de España_ (Francisco J. Purroy & Juan M. Varela)
• _Mamíferos Carnívoros Ibéricos_ (Javier Rodríguez Piñero)
• _Flora y Fauna de España y del Mediterráneo_ (Paul Sterry)
• _Guía de las Mariposas de España y de Europa_ (Tom Tolman; colour illustrations by Richard Lewington)
• _Guía de las Orquídeas de España y de Europa_ (Pierre Delforge)
• _Arte de Pájaros / Art of Birds_ (Pablo Neruda)
• _Boscos vells / Mature Forests. Artists for Nature in the Catalan Pyrenees_ (Artists for Nature Foundation / Fundació Territori i Paisatge)
• _Parques Nacionales de España. 26 itinerarios para descubrirlos y conocerlos_ (Oriol Alamany & Eulalia Vicens)
• _Threatened Birds of the World_ (BirdLife International)
• _Handbook of the Birds of the World_ (J. del Hoyo, _et al._)
Vol. 1: Ostrich to Ducks
Vol. 2: New World Vultures to Guineafowl
Vol. 3: Hoatzin to Auks
Vol. 4: Sandgrouse to Cuckoos
Vol. 5: Barn-owls to Hummingbirds
Vol. 6: Mousebirds to Hornbills
Vol. 7: Jacamars to Woodpeckers
Vol. 8: Broadbills to Tapaculos

For more information, please visit our website:

www.hbw.com

Lynx Edicions

Montseny, 8, E-08193 - Bellaterra, Barcelona (Spain)
Tel.: (+34) 93 594 77 10
Fax: (+34) 93 592 09 69
E-mail: lynx@hbw.com